CHRISTIANITY AND ETHNICITY IN CANADA

Edited by Paul Bramadat and David Seljak

Over the past decade, scholars and policy makers interested in Canadian multiculturalism have begun to take religion much more seriously, and Christian communities have become increasingly aware of the impact of ethnic diversity on church life. Until very recently, however, almost no systematic academic attention has been paid to the intersection between the ethnic and religious identities of individuals or communities. This gap in both our academic literature and our public discourse is an obstacle to understanding and integrating the large numbers of 'ethnic Christians,' most of whom either join existing Canadian churches or create ethnically specific congregations.

In *Christianity and Ethnicity in Canada*, eleven scholars explore the complex relationships between religious and ethnic identity within nine major Christian traditions in Canada. The contributors discuss the ways in which changes in the ethnic composition of these traditions influence religious practice and identity, as well as how the nine religious traditions influence communal and individual ethnic identities. An introductory chapter by Paul Bramadat and David Seljak provides a thorough discussion of the theoretical, historical, and empirical issues involved in the study of Christianity and ethnicity in Canada. This volume complements *Religion and Ethnicity in Canada*, in which the authors address similar issues within six major non-Christian communities in Canada, and within Canadian health care, education, and politics.

PAUL BRAMADAT is director of the Centre for Studies in Religion and Society and associate professor of History at the University of Victoria.

DAVID SELJAK is associate professor of Religious Studies at St Jerome's University and Chair of the Department of Religious Studies at the University of Waterloo.

Christianity and Ethnicity in Canada

Edited by Paul Bramadat and David Seljak

UNIVERSITY OF TORONTO PRESS
Toronto Buffalo London

© University of Toronto Press Incorporated 2008
Toronto Buffalo London
www.utppublishing.com
Printed in Canada

ISBN 978-0-8020-9875-7 (cloth)
ISBN 978-0-8020-9584-8 (paper)

Printed on acid-free paper

Library and Archives Canada Cataloguing in Publication

Christianity and ethnicity in Canada / edited by Paul Bramadat and
David Seljak.

ISBN 978-0-8020-9875-7 (bound). – ISBN 978-0-8020-9584-8 (pbk.)

1. Christianity – Canada.   2. Ethnicity – Canada.   3. Ethnicity –
Religious aspects – Christianity.   4. Church and minorities – Canada.
5. Religious pluralism – Canada.   6. Religious pluralism – Christianity.
7. Multiculturalism – Canada.   8. Multiculturalism – Religious
aspects – Christianity.   9. Canada – Religion.   I. Bramadat, Paul 1967–
II. Seljak, David, 1958–

BR570.C42 2008   277.1089′00971   C2008-901700-5

University of Toronto Press acknowledges the financial assistance to its
publishing program of the Canada Council for the Arts and the Ontario
Arts Council.

University of Toronto Press acknowledges the financial support for its
publishing activities of the Government of Canada through the Book
Publishing Industry Development Program (BPIDP).

For our children,

Daniel Anton-Philippe, Michaela Anna, and Gregory André de Salaberry Seljak and Max Milan Palmer Bramadat

Contents

List of Tables and Figures

Tables

Figures

Preface

It is not an exaggeration to say that virtually all public discussions about religion in Canada are de facto conversations about religion and ethnicity. After all, most conversations about religion in the public arena tend to revolve around anxieties either about the putative security threat posed by a particular religion, or about the supposedly pervasive process of secularization affecting Canadian society and religion. In both of these discursive themes – security and secularization – ethnicity and religion are two of the most crucial forces at work (alongside political and socio-economic issues, of course). Increasingly, scholars are discovering that it is futile to study religion in isolation. Instead, they study religious identity, belief, practice, forms of community, and institutions as they intersect with other markers of identity and solidarity such as gender, class, race, sexual orientation, and of course ethnicity.

For scholars and students of religion, ethnicity is emerging as one of the most important dimensions of modern religious phenomena – its influence on the broader scene of religion in Canada clearly rivals that of the traditional components of religion: ritual, cosmology, ecclesiology, heresiology, worldview, theology, doctrine, etc. For example, one cannot hope to understand the causes or the aftermath of the events of September 11, 2001 – not to mention the public debates currently raging in Quebec and throughout Europe about religious diversity and multiculturalism – without understanding the ways ethnic, political, and religious forces intersect in the modern era.

This book is the second instalment of a larger project on religion and ethnicity in Canada that we conceived in 2001. The project as a whole operates under the auspices of the Centre for Studies in Religion and Society at the University of Victoria. Both *Religion and Ethnicity in Can-*

ada and *Christianity and Ethnicity in Canada* employ the innovative approach to collaborative interdisciplinary research that characterizes many of the projects housed at the CSRS. This model for producing advanced interdisciplinary research useful to academic specialists, students, and policy makers involves, among other things, face-to-face meetings of all authors, rigorous group editing, as well as the involvement of policy makers (from federal departments interested in the issues being addressed) and community members (from religious and activist communities associated with the topics and issues addressed).

In *Religion and Ethnicity in Canada*, we explored the dialectical relationship between religious and ethnic modes of identity in Canada's six 'major minority' traditions (Buddhism, Hinduism, Sikhism, Judaism, Islam, and Chinese religion); we also examined the three public policy issues (health care, education, and federal policy making) around which revolve the most significant debates about religion and Canadian society. We felt then that the book would serve as an important resource for Canadians wishing to understand the current state of religion in a globalized world. When we began discussing the contents of our earlier book we realized immediately that it would be nearly impossible to address three public policy arenas, the six main minority traditions *and* Christianity in the same book. After all, the Christian communities in Canada are very large (comprising roughly 90 per cent of the country's population until the twentieth century); are spread out over the entire country; include members of almost all ethnic, linguistic, and national sub-communities; and have evolved over more than three hundred years of history. Consequently, we decided to devote an entire book to the interplay between Christianity and ethnicity in Canada.

To be more precise (and verbally awkward) we might perhaps have used 'Christianities' and 'ethnicities' instead of the singular versions of these terms, since we discuss in this book a number of both phenomena that are often profoundly dissimilar. When convenient, we have tried to problematize these terms in order to convey the rich diversity within the categories of, for example, 'Roman Catholic' and 'Italian,' categorical labels that would lead a scholar to inquire into which kind of Roman Catholicism (liberal, liberationist, conservative, ultra-montanist), and which kind of Italian (which regional affiliation, which social class, which dialect, which gender, which generation) we have in mind when we use such terms.

Each of the authors we have selected discusses in depth the ways in which ethnicity and Christianity sometimes work together and sometimes are at odds in the overall project of determining and communicating individual and group identities. Each author is a renowned scholar in his or her field and each brings his or her own disciplinary background (as historian, theologian, or sociologist, for example) to bear on the tradition he or she has been asked to discuss. Although each chapter reflects the perspective and academic background of the author, each author was also asked to address a general template of topics so that a number of common themes are found in all chapters. As such, this book is a hybrid academic product: it is a collection of important and original research by a variety of authors in a number of specialized areas, such as one might expect from an edited volume of articles, but it is meant to avoid the sometimes arbitrary and uneven nature of such collections. Our goal was to produce a collection of scholarly articles that would come as close to a monograph as possible.

As with any edited book, decisions about which topics and traditions to exclude were extremely difficult. All decisions of this nature reflect our editorial evaluation of the overall relevance of a particular ethnic or religious community to the general phenomenon of Christianity in Canada. In order to avoid imposing too great a burden on the reader, not to mention the publisher, we had to make difficult decisions about the content of this book. Since we were not able to justify devoting a full chapter to interesting groups such as the Church of Jesus Christ of Latter Day Saints (the Mormons), the Jehovah's Witnesses, the Salvation Army, the Amish, and many 'Eastern' Christian communities, they are addressed very briefly within other chapters as branches of the main root of a particular tradition. We hope that their omission in the present volume will inspire scholars to pursue those topics.

Readers will note that while many writers discuss the churches' historically fraught relations with Aboriginal peoples, there is no separate chapter on the often highly creative blending of Aboriginal and Christian modes of spirituality that one can witness within contemporary Christian communities. On this issue, we decided to heed the advice we received from leading proponents of the academic study of Aboriginal Christianity and have opted to include such a chapter in a future book devoted exclusively to Aboriginal spirituality in Canada.

We have no doubt that some readers will disagree with our decisions about which communities to exclude; however, we recognize that this disagreement is an inevitable consequence of such a project. In our first chapter, we discuss more fully the range of issues surrounding the communities we have selected and the nominal categories (seven 'denominations' and two 'traditions') we have used throughout the book.

We would like to thank Conrad Brunk, the outgoing director of the Centre for Studies in Religion and Society, for his tireless support throughout the development of *Christianity and Ethnicity in Canada*, as well as Harold Coward, the founding director of the Centre and the overall 'shepherd' and 'grandfather' of the broader project. We are deeply indebted to Leslie Kenny and Susan Karim, the superbly competent administrators at the Centre, who have helped to keep the project as a whole and this book in particular on track. John Biles, director of Partnership and Knowledge Transfer at the Metropolis Project (Citizenship and Immigration Canada), has provided encouraging and insightful advice on the connection between the communities we have addressed and the actual practice of policy making at the federal level. Not only has John offered us his incisive critiques of all of our chapters, but he has found ways to provide crucial financial support throughout the project.

We would also like to thank the authors of the chapters of this volume for their enthusiastic and valuable participation in this unusual endeavour, as well as their patience with our sometimes exacting editorial work. Throughout this and the previous volume, we have appreciated the support of both the University of Winnipeg (for Paul Bramadat) and St Jerome's University (for David Seljak). We would also like to extend our gratitude to Peter Beyer of the University of Ottawa for providing the statistical tables found in the appendix. At the University of Toronto Press, assistant managing editor Richard Ratzlaff and Social Science editor Stephen Kotowych were most helpful in moving our book fairly rapidly through the review and production phases. Ian MacKenzie, the copy editor at Paragraphics, was exceptionally discerning and judicious in his examination of our writing. Retired Professor of English at St. Jerome's University, Dr Douglas Letson also gave a close and careful reading of the galley proofs. Co-editing a book takes an enormous amount of time and energy, and so we would like to thank our families for their tireless support throughout the process.

CHRISTIANITY AND ETHNICITY IN CANADA

1 Charting the New Terrain: Christianity and Ethnicity in Canada

PAUL BRAMADAT AND DAVID SELJAK

Introduction

Surprisingly little has been written on the role of ethnicity in shaping Canada's Christian churches, although our own experience tells us that it is significant. For example, one author of this chapter, David Seljak, grew up in a Slovenian Canadian family. The hub of the Toronto Slovenian community was Marija Pomagaj (Mary, Help of Christians) Roman Catholic Church.[1] There Slovenian Canadians went to Mass, got married, had their children baptized, and paid their last respects to deceased friends and family members. After Mass, they frequently met in the church basement to meet members of their extended family, chat, discuss politics, or play chess or *tarok* (a card game wildly popular in Slovenia and central Europe). On special occasions, they would eat traditional Slovenian stews, sausages, roast meats, and fried potatoes prepared by members of the parish's Catholic Women's League. Before Christmas and Easter, traditional cookies would be on sale as well as the much-loved *potica*, a traditional walnut roll cake. But Sunday was not the only day that the church was busy. Parishioners came to study the Slovenian language, literature, and culture at the Saturday morning *šola* (school), participate in Slovenian sports clubs and Scouts, attend concerts and cultural events, as well as save and borrow money at the two credit unions that operated out of church offices. The back of the church bulletin featured advertisements for realtors, travel agents, plumbers, insurance brokers, and grocers, highlighting the church's role as the centre of business connections among Slovenians. No major event in the community failed to feature the parish priest as honoured guest. Feast days (especially Christmas), national holidays, as well as baptisms, weddings, and funerals all brought the community to Marija Pomagaj. Lest this portrait seem too nostalgic, we should acknowledge that the conservative Catholicism of the Marija Pomagaj Parish also bolstered a paternalistic social hierarchy, conservative gender roles, restrictive sexual ethics, and a latent authoritarianism in the community. These too were part of the community ethos.

Nevertheless, this portrait of the Roman Catholic Church's centrality in this particular ethnic community, and – equally important – the ethnic community's centrality in the life of the church, will be quite common, not only to Canadian Roman Catholics, but to many other Christians. What is puzzling is the fact that this common and intimate relationship between Canadian Christianity and Canada's various ethnic communities has not yet received comprehensive treatment by scholars of Canadian religion or ethnicity. While scholars have conducted many small-scale studies of specific ethnic Christian communities, no one has yet examined the phenomenon in a broader Canadian perspective. Moreover, far too few studies have been conducted on the newer Christian immigrant communities, such as African Presbyterians, Haitian Roman Catholics, Chinese Anglicans, and Asian Mennonites.

While most of us understand that the majority of Canadians from Latin America and Europe identify themselves as Christians, it often surprises people to learn how many of the 'visible minorities' they might see in their cities – including many of the Chinese, some of the South Asian, many of the Arab, most of the West Indian, and most of the African Canadians – are also Christians. It is certain that the overall ethnic diversity of the Canadian population is increasing; it is also the case that the minority religious traditions – especially Islam, Sikhism, Hinduism, Chinese religion, and Buddhism – are growing very rapidly. The spectacular growth rate of these smaller religious traditions – most of which have doubled or nearly doubled in the past ten years – has garnered a great many headlines in recent years.[2] However, the increases in religious and ethnic diversity associated with this relatively new phenomenon have tended to distract observers from the related changes happening within the much larger and still numerically dominant Canadian Christian community. The dramatic changes within the ethnic composition of many Canadian denominations will likely be apparent already to many older urban Christians who have watched their congregations change over the last few decades, but for younger Christians, their communities have always been ethnically diverse.

Of course, the reason that so many visibly different 'ethnic' Canadians arrive in Canada as Christians is that they have come from countries that were more or less thoroughly Christianized in the past by generations of European – and, more recently, North American – missionaries. To meet a first- or second-generation Canadian of African descent who is in fact a third-, fourth-, or twenty-fifth-generation Christian, reminds us of the global reach of Christianity. It also draws our attention to the recent consequences of globalization that have made Canada such a thoroughly multicultural and perhaps even post-colonial state.

Contemporary Christianity in a Post-Colonial Canada

We can say that we live in a post-colonial world in the sense that in the periods following both world wars of the twentieth century, states such as Great Britain, France, Belgium, Germany, Italy, Portugal, and Holland withdrew from countries that had been under their administrative, economic, military, and political control. One might say that from the beginning of the colonial period (roughly from the end of the fifteenth century) until the decades following the Second World War, many Europeans considered their determinative presence in colonized countries to be morally unproblematic. While controlling another country or region was acknowledged to be a complex and challenging logistical and political undertaking, the *moral* right of economically, militarily, and technologically superior countries to involve themselves directly in the rule of other countries was widely recognized as a problem only in the last fifty or sixty years.[3] To put it another way, our parents and grandparents grew up in a period during which formally diminished levels of independence were largely unquestioned matters of fact for the majority of the world's regions, countries, and individuals. The sun has now set on the European imperial period, at least in the classical sense in which a particular country seeks to exert direct and permanent control over another. However compelling might be the evidence for a Leviathan-like American unilateralist imperial entity (especially in the wake of the Cold War and 11 September 2001), it is clear that the nature of empire has changed in our so-called post-colonial period. It is true that the American military and economic interest in many countries very often problematizes the development of indigenous democratic institutions. However, it would probably be incorrect to characterize this as a simple return to empire, along the lines of the kind of empire enjoyed by Britain in the nineteenth century.[4] The Cold War certainly did lead to the political reorganization of most of the world after the end of the Second World War, but it lasted fewer than fifty years, and was much less entrenched than the colonial system and the deeper Weltanschauung with which it was associated. Important for this book's authors is the fact that, during and before the Cold War, we witnessed the de jure independence of many former colonies and the growing effort in many Western democracies such as Canada to come to terms with the shadow side of the much older world-organizing force of colonialism.

The Churches and Colonialism in Canada

To understand the role and status of Christianity in Canada it is important to explore the place of Christianity in our home-grown and imported forms of colonialism. After all, the Christian churches have played an integral role in the colonization of this land and its evolution into a complex society. Until very recently, the European colonization of Canada has always occurred under the sign of the cross; that is, the Europeans who first created Canada imagined it always as a Christian project.[5] This assumption has both benevolent and malevolent implications. Regarding the benevolent implications, it must be said that in the social and personal lives of common settlers, farmers, entrepreneurs, and soldiers of this new country, the tradition and institutions of Christianity provided a relatively stable sense of meaning and purpose in a world that must have been experienced as sometimes threatening, alienating, and unpredictable. It is difficult for us in contemporary Canada to appreciate the existential challenges associated with the transition many people made from Europe to North America. To journey across an ocean to a new continent that existed well beyond the known world of most Europeans, and then to find oneself in the middle of an enormous, 'uncivilized' land characterized in places by astonishingly cold weather, new illnesses, mosquitoes, and other natural challenges, must have been harrowing for many people. Moreover, in frontier societies, as well as in the disarray of early industrial towns and cities, there were no social institutions that could match the churches for providing basic social and community services. The churches' facilitation of these services probably explains the central role they played in addressing the psychological, social, and spiritual needs of immigrants. In these early centuries of settlement, the churches played a crucial role in forming and cultivating communities and in providing individuals with a sense of their role in the grand narrative of European Christian civilization and its expansion to the new world.

As for the less benevolent features of the arrival of Christianity in the New World, we are reminded again and again that many of the settlers, clergy, soldiers, and political leaders who were so attracted to this continent believed that to conquer this land was to bring it under the control of a Christian monarch. To 'civilize' its inhabitants, they presupposed, was to Christianize them. For modern readers, it may be difficult to imagine how naturally and organically these two ideas were enmeshed in the imaginations of Canada's first explorers, conquerors, and settlers. Moreover, it is also difficult to understand how interwoven church and state were. Both in New France and the early years of British North America, the same well-to-do families often provided leaders both in religion and politics; bishops, abbots, and other members of the higher clergy enjoyed the same privileges, lifestyle, wealth, and mindset as members of the political and economic elite. It was assumed that the state would defend the interest of the church (including suppressing its competitors) and that the church would teach people to submit to the lawful authority of their political and social masters.

Not only did the first Europeans in Canada – the French – wish to build a Christian society, they dreamed of recreating the religious conditions of the European metropole (in this case, Paris) in their colony. Political allegiance to a single monarch, they believed, had to be cemented by adherence to a single faith and membership in one church.[6] In France, the Roman Catholic Church, the aristocratic system, and French culture operated as one integrated system. Consequently, when the French established permanent colonies in New France, they imagined and built them as explicitly Christian communities in which the Roman Catholic Church would exercise a religious monopoly. In fact, after 1627, only French-born Roman Catholics were allowed to immigrate to the colony.[7] New France was organized administratively in parishes and the curé or pastor served as the civil administrator alongside a military administrator who handled security and policing. The church monopolized education, ran the hospitals, and provided poor relief. The higher clergy advised the governor.

However, the image of New France as a theocracy is greatly exaggerated. What failed here was the project to create what sociologist Max Weber called a 'church,' that is, a religious community that was coextensive with the whole society, completely at home with the culture of the people, reflective of the hierarchy of the broader society, led by a professional, educated clergy, and composed of a population that was born into it rather than converted to it. A number of factors worked against this project. The colonial population was too dispersed, too independent, and too poorly educated to be controlled by conventional means. Moreover, the church lacked resources. For example, by 1760, there was only one priest for every five parishes.[8] Finally, the goals of the economic and political elites often conflicted with those of the church. Consequently, the project of re-establishing the Roman Catholic Church as the foundation of the colonial society was never completed. In any case, the project of recreating French society on Canadian soil came to an abrupt end in 1763 when the Treaty of Paris transferred the colony to the British four years after the military defeat of the French on the Plains of Abraham outside of Quebec City. It was now the turn of British Protestants to attempt to transplant their version of Christendom in Canadian soil.

Before 1750, there were only very limited and short-lived experiments in bringing British rule and Protestantism to Canada. Now that the province of Quebec was part of the British Empire, the British government and the Church of England, specifically the Society for the Propagation of the Gospel, could dream of recreating British Protestant Christianity in Canada. At first, the Roman Catholic Church was suppressed and the Church of England favoured – a strategy that persisted despite later concessions to the large French population.[9] For example, the Constitution Act of 1791 divided British North America into Lower Canada (the region around the St Lawrence) and Upper Canada (the recently settled lands in what is now Ontario). The act also set aside one seventh of all public land in the two provinces as 'clergy reserves,' that is, property of the Church of England to be used to pay for the maintenance of a 'Protestant clergy,' as well as for the construction of churches and parsonages.

Despite this official government support, the Church of England was to run into the same challenges the French Catholic Church encountered (a dispersed population, lack of resources, and competing interests) as well as much greater religious competition. First, the French inhabitants of the colony, who formed a sizeable majority, remained faithful to their language and religion. The British governors wisely saw that forcing these Roman Catholics to convert to Protestantism would promote rebellion and alliance with the unruly thirteen colonies in the present-day United States, and so gave their Roman Catholic subjects increasing autonomy and protection. Moreover, among the British and non-francophone settlers, religious pluralism, at least *within* the Christian community, obstructed the formal establishment of any one church. The Church of Scotland, for example, lobbied for recognition as a co-established church. Moreover, as several of the authors in this book demonstrate, immigration brought Lutherans, German Reformed Christians, Presbyterians, Methodists, Congregationalists, and Roman Catholics. In the Maritimes, the New Light Baptist movement created a sizeable religious community that refused to submit to the officially established Church of England (Christie 1990). Like the New Light Baptists, the Methodists in Upper Canada provided 'cheap religion' to people on the frontier who could not afford to support the Church of England with its elaborate places of worship and paid clergy (Clark 1962, 134–7). As these Methodists grew in number and power, they would challenge the privileges of the established church. In his famous report after the rebellions of 1837–8 in Upper and Lower Canada, Lord Durham observed that one of the causes of the unrest in Upper Canada was the privileges enjoyed by the Church of England. Consequently, in 1840 the government decided to divide the clergy reserves among a larger number of denominations – although the Church of England and the Church of Scotland still received the lion's share. In 1854, the government liquidated the clergy reserves altogether. The dream of an established church – Protestant or Roman Catholic – in British North America was over.

While the idea of an established church died in 1854, Canada was still imagined – not only by its elite but also by the vast majority of its inhabitants and immigrants – as an essentially Christian project. For example, at the time of Confederation, Sir Samuel Leonard Tilley, a pro-Confederation politician from Fredericton, New Brunswick, recalled the words of Psalm 72, verse 8: 'He shall have Dominion also from sea to sea, and from the river unto the ends of the earth,' a biblical passage (referring to the ancient kingdom of Israel) that would become the motto used in the Canadian coat of arms. The new entity – neither exactly a colony nor an independent nation state – was called the Dominion of Canada, a name that spoke to its unresolved political identity vis-à-vis Great Britain as well as its unquestioned Christian foundations. For both the British and French communities alike, to be Canadian was to be Christian. From that assumption arose the support of Christian public education, the creation of social services institutions for the poor, the legislation of Christian morality (in the cases of sexual

behaviour and alcohol consumption, for example), laws protecting the
Lord's Day, state-sponsored Christian missions to the Aboriginal peo-
ples (including the disastrous residential school system), efforts to
'Christianize' immigrants, and religious discrimination – sometimes
amounting to persecution – against religious non-conformists, be they
Christian or not (Airhart 1990, 101–31; J.W. Grant 1977, 13–16).

From Confederation until the 1960s, the mainstream Protestant
churches[10] (the Anglicans, Presbyterians, and the United Church of
Canada, later joined by 'junior partners' such as the Lutherans, Baptists, and evangelical groups) along with the Roman Catholic Church
formed a 'plural establishment.' In the United States, the problem of
religious pluralism was solved by articulating a theory of individual
rights and erecting a 'wall of separation' between church and state.
Although many Canadians today believe their society is also characterized by this American constitutional innovation, in fact the Canadian
solution was more conservative, and no such de jure separation of
church and state has ever existed here. The government formally recognized a limited number of mainstream denominations and supported
their work. Moreover, the primary Christian churches enjoyed a cultural and social 'establishment' in that the dominant culture and political, economic, and social institutions were clearly defined by Christian
values. Talal Asad has argued that the elite of any society claims the
right to define its official 'personality' (2003, 7–8), for better or worse. In
the case of Canada, Christianity set the foundation of that personality
for the century after Confederation.

The character of nationalism in Canada highlights this connection
between Christianity on the one hand and the dominant English- and
French-language cultures on the other. Broadly speaking, British culture and politics, Protestantism, and a belief in modern political, economic, and scientific 'progress' formed the three pillars of Canadian
nationalism in English Canada. Roman Catholics, other Christians,
and, of course, non-Christians struggled to find a legitimate place in
this society.[11] By contrast, among French Canadians, the French language and culture, the Roman Catholic faith, and the traditional agricultural lifestyle (anchored by the patriarchal family) formed the core
of their national identity (Rioux 1976, 89; see Solange Lefebvre's chapter 3 in this book). Remarkably, even though most French Canadians
had become urban industrial workers by 1931, French Canadian
nationalists still heralded and romanticized the life of the simple, pious,
habitant farmer as the ideal well into the 1950s (Behiels 1985, 98). Both

English and French versions of Canadian nationalism defined non-Christians as 'other.' Members of non-Christian groups, from Hindus and Sikhs to Jews and atheists, experienced marginalization and even persecution.[12]

The marriage between Christianity and Canadian nationalism has done much to determine the shape of Canadian society. Clearly the churches aided the Canadian state as it expanded its control over the country, and, as part of this hegemonic national project, the churches participated in the residential schools system. However, as is often the case in such matters, the overall effect of the churches' intimate relationship with the Canadian state has been ambiguous. As mentioned earlier, the established nature of Christianity in Canada must have been experienced by most Euro-Canadians as a boon to their lives as they sought to make sense of their new and sometimes inhospitable environment. However, beyond the personal or existential benefits reaped by individuals living in a context in which their own religion is viewed as normative, the established or semi-established status of Christianity also had many largely positive social implications that contemporary Canadians continue to enjoy. For example, most of our social welfare agencies are now state-funded, secularized versions of originally Christian initiatives. At the turn of the century, neither political leaders nor the captains of industry saw it as their responsibility to ensure the welfare of the population, especially the neediest. Churches developed offices of poor relief, hospices for the elderly, orphanages, hospitals, and other such agencies (J.W. Grant 1972, 96–9). In English Canada, governments began to take over these agencies after the First World War, a process that was accelerated by the great need during the Depression of the 1930s and the rising expectations of the post-war boom of the 1950s. In Quebec, the churches controlled the social welfare bureaucracy for the entire province until the death of the conservative premier, Maurice Duplessis, in 1959. Even the Quebec school system was controlled by the churches until the government established a Ministry of Education in 1964. Until the 1960s, Christianity touched every element of Canadian public life.

Secularization in Canadian Society

However great the influence of Christianity, it was not the only social force that shaped Canada. From the mid-nineteenth century on, government and business leaders also pursued the political and economic modernization of Canadian society, guided by the ideologies of liberalism and capitalism. In the first two periods of the development of church–state relations in Canada – the attempt at official establishment (1608–1840) and the creation of a 'plural establishment' (1840–1960)[13] – there were clear tensions between the goals, values, practices, and vision of Christian churches and those of the political and economic elites. However, both the leaders of organized religion and their critics operated in a symbolic and social world deeply marked by Christian ideas, beliefs, and values.[14] While we usually think of the secularization of Canada as beginning in the 1960s, in fact it began in the nineteenth century. Immediately after the First World War, there was a period of accelerated political and economic modernization, and the actors in the state and market began to feel restrained by religion. By the 1920s already, the provincial and federal governments started to constrain the powers of the churches and to take over areas of social service. The expansion of powers of the state and the presence of the market after the Second World War further accelerated this secularization. It is important to remember that in the 1950s, for example, it appeared that the churches were booming, and they were, in terms of raw numbers. However, the growth of church membership was a quite predictable by-product of the post-war baby boom and increased immigration. In fact, proportionally – that is to say, in relation to the overall growth in the Canadian population – all the Protestant churches were declining (Bibby 1987, 12–14). It was difficult to see this change while Christians were busy building churches, rectories, and halls in the rapidly expanding suburbs as fast as they could to keep up with the growing population (J.W. Grant 1972, 160).[15] As Reginald Bibby put it, 'Paradoxically, more people than ever before were staying away at precisely the same time as more people than ever before were attending' (1987, 14).

The process of secularization therefore is not an exclusively post-1960s phenomenon. Since the end of the First World War, secularization in Canada was pragmatic, as actors in political and economic society sought to free themselves from the authority of the churches. In the name of liberty and efficiency, Canada's elite – both English and French – began to define a public sphere free of religion.[16] At first, institutions attached to the state and market simply declared their independence from the churches. Factories, mines, and other enterprises, for example, operated on Sundays. However, as both the state and market expanded the fields of their involvement, they soon took over activities that had been the prerogative of the churches. One can see this change dramatically in the case of public education. Already in the 1960s, civil servants in Ontario were uncomfortable with the Christian culture and power of the clergy in most public schools. They sought to curtail the teaching of Christianity and to remove the church officials. At the same time, the Parent Commission in Quebec recommended the creation of a Ministry of Education, a move that signalled the beginning of the end of the churches' control of schools in that province. Finally, the *Canadian Charter of Rights and Freedoms*, along with a growing concern to promote a secular public school system, led to the de-Christianization of public schools across Canada.[17] Through the regulation of existing institutions, governments have also taken control of church-sponsored hospitals and social welfare agencies – even though they may still be officially owned and operated by religious communities.

To use the vocabulary of Talal Asad, the official personality of Canada is now religiously neutral. Nevertheless, it must be said that to the extent that any religion is privileged in Canada, it is mainstream Christianity. For example, important features of Canadian public life, such as the Constitution, the head of state, Parliament, the national anthem, currency, and the national motto retain references to Christianity. Often sessions of legislatures or municipal councils begin with the Lord's Prayer. Christian feast days (e.g., Christmas, Good Friday) are still statutory holidays (Biles and Ibrahim 2005, 167). Other vestiges of Christian privilege remain. For example, the military supports an active chaplaincy that is almost exclusively Christian.[18] As we shall see in the chapters of this book, Christian communities continue to control an extensive variety of public institutions: schools, colleges, universities, hospitals, social service agencies, credit unions, newspapers, cooperatives, and more. Moreover, Christian values and structures form the basis of many of our institutions – a reminder of this tradition's historical privileges.

Nonetheless, the point is that while the process of formally disentangling Christianity from important state institutions is incomplete, its current trajectory is undeniable.[19] The secularization of Canadian society has unfolded in fits and starts and has been expressed unevenly across regions and sectors. It has also met with a great deal of resistance from members of the Christian community who felt and still feel – correctly, we would argue – that the world their parents and grandparents knew is passing away. Many of these Canadians experience the current de-Christianization period as a betrayal of the arrangement upon which Canada had been founded.

The effort in the past several decades to diminish the role of religion (read: Christianity) in official circles was motivated by two convictions. On the one hand, religion as such was considered by some secularists to be a relic of an earlier, less rational time and thus should be encouraged to disappear gracefully. One reason for this assumption among many members of the elite was the tacit acceptance of the idea that the modern state – and, perhaps even more importantly, the free market – needed to operate according to 'rational' principles rather than religious customs and traditions. On the other hand, many people considered religion to be inherently socially divisive and thus inappropriate in the institutions of a truly multicultural society. In other words, the involvement of religion in state affairs, they argued, would only hamper the development of a mature democratic, liberal, and multicultural society. Justice demanded the equal treatment of all Canadians, regardless of their religion, and state recognition of one religion hampered the search for social harmony. While Canada does not boast an official de jure 'separation of church and state,' it has adopted a political culture based on that principle.

Finally, secularization developed as an unintended cultural consequence of the broader project to build a politically and economically modern Canada. Much has been written about the rise of modern individualism. Life in a democratic society of political equals and in a wage labour–consumer economy promoted a loosening of community bonds, including ethnic and religious bonds. Canadians – including many Christians – no longer relate to their religious institutions in the same manner. Sociologists have identified the privatization and subjectification of religion as important trends in Canada. What matters to people today, even to churchgoers, is their personal, subjective experience of the faith, rather than belonging to the right institution. Although Canadians have not become atheists in great numbers, it is true that they simply do not identify with denominations in a traditional way. British sociologist Grace Davie (1994) called this phenomenon 'believing without belonging.' Consequently, in Canada, we have seen dramatic drops in membership and attendance in almost every Christian denomination.[20] This drop represents a crisis for many denominations because smaller numbers means near-empty churches on Sunday, fewer services, and poorer financial resources. Enormous churches, built for thousands of worshippers, are now occupied and supported by a few hundred – or even a few dozen – participants, usually older Canadians. For example, as Wendy Fletcher argues in this volume, the vast structure of the Anglican Church of Canada is supported by the financial contributions of a small handful of mostly older members. Moreover, in Quebec the provincial government has intervened to save some Catholic churches as historical monuments.

While Canadian Christians are staying away from religious institutions in record numbers, they are still attached to their Christian identity. Reginald Bibby (1987, 1993, 2002) reports that, despite low levels of membership and attendance, the majority of Canadian Christians still identify with the religious denominations of their parents. For most Canadians, Bibby argues, Christianity is still an important marker for questions of culture, meaning, and identity. However, others wonder exactly what this identity means, given that Canadians are decreasingly informed about the basics of Christian history, ritual, belief, and ethics. Danièle Hervieu-Léger (2006) uses the term 'belonging without believing' to describe people who claim to be Christian but really have a very diffuse, latent, or implicit connection to the tradition.[21] As well, one sometimes hears the term *cultural Christians* used to describe people who formally identify themselves with Christianity but avoid Christian practices and are not familiar with the Bible, or Christian doctrines or history. So-called cultural Christians, for example, might hold Christian beliefs alongside beliefs in reincarnation, astrology, and Buddhism (Bibby 1987, 73–6).[22]

As editors, we noticed a recurrent theme in our mid-project discussions with the book's authors. In almost all of the churches we have examined, we observed a distinctive rhetoric – or, to use a broader term, discourse – of loss. After all, in several of these chapters, the story being told is one of often rapidly diminishing communities struggling to remain viable religious institutions. More than just dismay at declining attendance and membership, this discourse of loss reflects the fact that the churches can no longer assume that their values and objectives are, in the Weberian sense, co-extensive with the values and objectives of the larger society. This is not to say that the churches no longer provide many of the existential benefits described earlier, but rather that things have changed categorically for them vis-à-vis their role in the broader society.

Secularization and Post-Colonialism in Canada

In recent decades, the structural, long-term pressures towards secularization (Swatos 1999) have been accelerated by cultural trends connected to the broader complex shift in Canadian society from colonialism to post-colonialism. As Canadian governments over the last few decades have sought to make amends for past injustices, the historic role of the churches in the settlement of Canada has come under intense scrutiny, and for many people these institutions have not fared well under this close inspection. This is not the place for a full discussion of the problems these changes have created, but some of them need to be enumerated.

First, and most fundamentally, it has become a fixture of educated public discourse that European Christianity was an integral part of the European colonial project – in Canada as in other countries. Especially among elites, its position has predictably led to some resentment and cynicism toward Christianity for its contribution to colonial arrogance. Christianity might have been welcomed by some indigenous peoples around the world, but in many places it was also a means of colonizing the imaginations of the indigenous people and of preparing them for their servitude to European masters.

Second, and more specifically, the contemporary social, economic, and physical disadvantages of Canadian Aboriginals are linked to the cooperation between the churches and the Canadian state. After all, the churches were instrumental in what many Aboriginals consider to be cultural genocide; residential schools were federal projects, but they were staffed by church members who felt that physically and symbolically tearing children away from their families was the best and most merciful approach to dealing with what the head of the Department of Indian Affairs, Duncan Campbell Scott, called 'the Indian problem.'[23] It must be said that in some of these schools students were treated well by teachers and administrators who were sincere in their efforts to help the children adjust to the new political situation in which they found themselves. However, in the 1980s more and more students who attended these schools began to go on public record about the physical, sexual, psychological, and spiritual abuse they suffered, as well as the ethnocentric arrogance of the entire enterprise. Of course, they complained not just about the government policy on residential schools, but also about the complicity of the churches in their suffering (A. Grant 1996). While relations between residential school survivors on the one hand and the Canadian government and churches on the other hand are far from resolved – as the following ten chapters indicate – major legal and religious initiatives are underway toward this goal.

Third, Canadians, and especially young Canadians, are increasingly alienated by the church leadership's attitude to sexuality. High-profile sexual abuse scandals in a number of denominations and traditions since the 1980s had a damaging effect on Christianity's public image. Roman Catholic and evangelical churches certainly came under the most scrutiny for such abuses during this period, but such episodes certainly occurred in other (Christian and non-Christian) groups. Nonetheless, the sex scandals in a variety of Christian denominations brought into the foreground the deep ambivalence about human sexuality that is at the heart of Christian teaching (see Brown 1988). The sexually saturated popular culture that wields so much power among contemporary youth has widened the gulf between largely conservative churches and largely liberal youth. Moreover, with some notable exceptions (like the United Church and a faction within the Anglican Church), the churches' positions in the widely publicized debates on same-sex marriage seems likely to alienate some youth, since studies have shown that support for expanding the definition of marriage is much higher for Canadians under age thirty-five than it is for those over sixty-five.[24] Finally, in a society in which feminism has made remarkable advances, it is difficult to expect younger women and men to accept the exclusion of women from the upper echelons of church leadership (as is the case in all Roman Catholic, Ukrainian Catholic, Eastern Orthodox, and most conservative Protestant churches). If the churches continue to espouse views on sex and gender equality that younger Christians (and their non-Christian peer group) consider to be anachronistic, the degree of alienation some youth already feel will almost certainly increase. As several chapters in this book illustrate, within larger denominations ethnic minority subgroups (such as, for example, Korean Canadian United Church members and African Canadian Anglicans) often espouse views on women's rights, sexual activity, and same-sex marriage that are more conservative than those of the dominant anglophone or francophone denominational communities. However, such discrepancies may diminish over time as the second generation of immigrants assumes control of the subgroups.

All of these changes are by-products of our post-colonial context. No longer can Christianity assume its role as the companion of the empire as the latter bestows European enlightenment upon the whole world. No longer can the Christian churches assume that their foundational principles with respect to sex and gender will be accepted – or even understood – by contemporary adherents of any ethnic background. No longer will Christians be able to assume that the church has or will ever regain the same officially privileged place in the centre of North American society that it historically enjoyed, even though most individuals in that society are themselves Christians. Moreover, and perhaps most relevant to this book, no longer will Canadian Christians be able to assume that their co-religionists are all of European extraction.

The Religion-Ethnicity-Culture Distinction

It has become commonplace for individuals to make clear distinctions between their religious and ethnic identities; such lines are also drawn for them by others. By now it should be clear that such distinctions are problematic. On the surface, most of us believe we understand what a friend or colleague means when he or she says, 'I am ethnically but not religiously Mennonite,' or 'I was baptized and confirmed in the Roman Catholic Church in Quebec but I would not really consider myself to be religiously Christian,' or 'I am thoroughly Greek, but I'm not Orthodox.'[25] These kinds of earnest and seemingly self-evident comments may be emblematic of our current state of modernity or postmodernity, but it is far from obvious that we are prepared to understand their implications.

According to a common (though disputed) way of understanding history, individuals and communities are now afforded unprecedented latitude in the way they define themselves. Previously – or so the story goes – the different strands in one's identity were more or less ascribed by one's family and community. Thus, for the overwhelming majority of the world's Greeks for over a millennium, to be Greek was to be Greek Orthodox; during this long period, there was little inclination among Greeks to disentangle their Greek-ness from their attachment to the Greek Orthodox form of Christianity. In Canadian society (and also among Greek Canadians), the current disintegration – or at least attenuation – of such integrated modes of ethno-religious identity is a manifestation of the individualism and structural differentiation that have come to characterize our society in the past forty years. In modern societies, religion has not disappeared as predicted by many, but it has been assigned a distinct, more differentiated, and in some cases much more concentrated function, meaning that it has become disembedded from its previously more diffused and integrated role. Thus redefined, it must obey the ground rules set by more powerful spheres, such as the state (especially in its legal and administrative modes) and the marketplace. This repositioning naturally has diminished religion's overall systemic power and has turned it into a kind of object, a commodity, subject therefore to fragmentation and piecemeal adoption by individuals (Berger 1967; Bibby 1987; V. Miller 2004).

So, for example, as a result of the fact that Greeks in Canada travel more, are more aware of the broader world, and are probably less singularly attached to the nation state of Greece than any generation of Greeks in the past thousand years, individual Greeks are now far freer to choose the features of communal Greek identity that suit their individual tastes. In addition, Greek Canadians, living as they do in a multicultural environment, can also choose to embrace features associated with entirely different cultures. The latitude many people have in 'negotiating' distinctive identities – not to mention the relatively small costs one must pay to do so – is quite new and reflects the current shifting terrain in our culture. Imagine, for example, a Greek Canadian who adopts both Buddhism and vegetarianism and who marries an African Canadian atheist; we would speculate that such a person is less likely to be rejected by his friends and family today than ever before.[26]

Many people would applaud such a loosening in the bonds between the social realities into which one is born and one's (increasingly 'chosen' or 'negotiated') identity; the proponents of this change are inclined to see it as a manifestation of the liberating impetus that is at the heart of the Enlightenment tradition that is itself so central to Western societies. However, underlying the claims mentioned above – that one is an ethnic but not religious Mennonite, Quebecer and Roman Catholic but not Christian, Greek but not Greek Orthodox – are some complex and often subconscious presuppositions about religion, ethnicity, and identity that look far more tenuous when they are examined closely. The primary problem in these distinctions is the artificial separation that is made between these modalities of identification.

For example, in the Mennonite case the ethnic and cultural features associated with this tradition are intimately bound up with the religious features. In chapter 9, Roy Loewen explains that the distinctive language of Low German that distinguishes many Mennonites from other Europeans emerged (like Yiddish among Jews) as a result of centuries of explicit religious discrimination against this community by their European neighbours. As well, the long tradition of social activism and pacifism one finds in contemporary Mennonite culture (and also among those Mennonites who say they have no interest in religion) is in fact directly derived from the determinative role that pacifism (even perhaps anti-statism) played throughout the development of the Mennonites as an explicitly religious group.

The difficulty in extracting religion from ethnicity is made very clear in the case of francophone Quebecers – as Solange Lefebvre makes clear in her chapter. In 1970, Roman Catholic priest, sociologist, social activist, and nationalist Jacques Grand'Maison observed that French Canadians in the 1950s did not know if they embraced the religion of their culture or the culture of their religion (1970, 194). Even after Quebec culture became relatively secular after the 1970s, the Catholic Church still enjoyed a special symbolic position. Moreover, French Quebecers today – even though they do not, for the most part, participate in Roman Catholic rituals – do not convert to Protestantism in any significant numbers and continue to describe themselves as Roman Catholic when asked about their religion (Bibby 2004, 38). This ambiguous attitude to Catholicism is now a common feature of French Québécois national identity. This example illustrates that we need to pay attention to the local discursive backdrop against which assertions about religious and ethnic identity are made. That is, we need to see categories such as Mennonite, French Canadian, and Greek Orthodox as the *beginning* of a conversation about identity rather than the climax or conclusion of such a discussion. Since the meanings of all ethnic, national, and religious categories are increasingly fluid, it is important to be able to move beyond these labels and to ask people precisely what they mean when they describe themselves with reference to one of these categories. In other words, we need to avoid the fetishization of increasingly anachronistic notions of authenticity (Bramadat 2005b). For example, when a French Canadian claims to be Catholic but also claims not to attend church, partake in the sacraments, concern herself with the pope's rulings, or even hold traditional beliefs about God, some people would be inclined to conclude that she is therefore not 'really' Catholic. However, it is best to avoid imposing assumptions on this individual about what makes one authentically Catholic, since she may indeed contribute to the emergence of a new form of Roman Catholic identity.

In fact, the issue of identity is complex for almost everyone. A Canadian Christian woman of Nigerian descent, for example, stands at her own unique identity crossroads. She is a woman, an Anglican, a Nigerian citizen (recently and perhaps still), from a particular socio-economic class, educated to a certain level, healthy or unhealthy, married or single, a mother or not, homosexual or bisexual or heterosexual, a member of a particular family and tribe, a member of a specific generation, and so on. When we meet her, of course, we can come to know only a few of these dimensions of her identity. What interests us in this book is the way both her religious and ethnic self-understandings commingle in her own mind and in her interactions with others. In this book we seek a more nuanced understanding of these two particular features of her multidimensional identity because they are, in many – perhaps even most – human communities, two of the most influential forms of both self-identification and ascribed identification.

Often a person will make unequivocal statements about which parts of her identity are religious and which are ethnic. When she is questioned about this distinction, however, she will very often become confused, revealing to what extent identity and all of its strands are dynamic personal *projects* rather than *idées fixes* or things-in-themselves.[27] Recently philosophers have argued that a self (whether it is a Croatian, a Catholic, an atheist, or a Lutheran self) does not exist inviolably as an object of one's own objective description. Rather, the self is to a large degree a wrought object, a fiction brought into being by its insertion at birth into a very specific set of social circumstances (constituted by class, caste, gender, race, religion, economy, nation, etc.). This is not to say that selves are ethereal or illusory; far from it – they are indisputably real, but they are constructed, highly mutable, highly creative, and always socially situated. One of the underlying assumptions of this book is that we cannot understand the Nigerian woman and the communities in which she is embedded unless we pay close attention to the ways religion and ethnicity, as two major components of her identity, interact – or to use more current anthropological language, the ways she 'negotiates' these two interpenetrating strands of her identity.

Racial and Ethnic Diversity in Canada

The key terms used in this book – *race, ethnicity, religion, multiculturalism* – are the subjects of a great deal of debate within the academic disciplines most closely related to them (so sociologists and biologists debate the notion of race, political scientists debate the notion of multiculturalism, anthropologists and philosophers debate the notion of culture, and so forth). Although this is not the place for a full discussion of these debates, some comments on the key matters at stake are warranted.[28]

Take, for example, the issues of race and racism. In Canadian churches, the presence of visible minorities as well as Aboriginal peoples has awakened Christians to ethnic and racial pluralism.[29] A Roman Catholic church filled with Irish, German, Polish, and Italian worshippers is in fact quite diverse, but it does not offer the same *visual evidence* of diversity as one that welcomes Filipino, Haitian, Vietnamese, and West African Catholics along with those of European descent. Given the history of racialized thinking in the West, Canadian churches, like the broader Canadian society, inevitably struggle with the issues of racism. For example, today several denominations are discussing the question of whether or not ethnic, racial, or otherwise 'visible' minorities are sufficiently represented in church leadership positions.

This new sensitivity to ethnic and racial diversity has been fostered by Canada's tradition of multiculturalism, understood both as an important Canadian policy and a widespread social tradition. The policy did not create the tradition; one might argue that some form of multiculturalism existed in Canada for decades before Trudeau created the policy in 1971. Some would point to Canada's history of relative calm with respect to ethnic conflict, its reliance on immigration, and its general pattern of allowing newcomers to govern many aspects of their lives according to their own community's sensibilities, as evidence of the deep roots of this tradition. However, while this proto-multicultural tendency within Canadian history might have foreshadowed our current situation, any consideration of the historical and contemporary plight of First Nations communities – not to mention the officially sanctioned discrimination faced by Black, Chinese, and South Asian newcomers until the middle of the twentieth century – reveals that for most of this country's history, Canadian policies related to race, ethnicity, and culture were solidly colonialist and exclusionary.[30] It has only been in roughly the last thirty-five years that Canadians have committed themselves (and still only incompletely) to the principles of tolerance and equality that were finally enshrined in the 1982 *Charter of Rights and Freedoms*.

Just as the policy did not give birth to the tradition, the tradition did not create the policy in any linear and predictable manner. The formal policy grew out of a combination of daring political insight and shrewd political calculation. It represented, among other things, the Liberal Party's attempt to ensure that ethnic, racial, and religious minority communities could participate more actively in Canadian cultural, social, economic, and political life; this participation, many assumed, would foster loyalty to the Liberal Party within ethnic communities.[31] While the special statuses of Canada's 'two founding nations' on the one hand and First Nations peoples on the other hand are entrenched in foundational Canadian documents, at least in theory multiculturalism quietly undermines the notion that any ethnic or national group (or cluster of groups) can claim supremacy in this country. The tradition espouses a notion of national, ethnic, and personal identity that is rooted in the reality that identities emerge out of ongoing dialogues between cultural groups, and between individuals, groups, and the larger society (Taylor 1994).[32]

Debates on the issue of multiculturalism often stem from conflicts within and between communities over the definition of ethnicity itself. Scholars usually define an ethnic group as a group of people, putatively related through common filiation – that is, through 'blood' or genes – whose members also usually feel a sense of attachment to a particular place, a history, and a culture (including a common language, food, clothing, etc.). To the group, this feeling often seems both innate (or natural) and immutable. However, many readers will be aware that many scholars suggest that ethnic identity, the sense of belonging to a 'peo-. ple,' is constructed or at least heavily influenced by a variety of political, economic, and social forces.[33] Some would argue that an ethnic consciousness emerges among a group of people who, in fact, may not be markedly different – genetically, historically, or culturally – from those of other supposedly distinct ethnic communities. Moreover, an ethnic identity is fluid; its core elements change over time. Since an ethnic group is as much a construction of a particular time and place as it is a primordial social or genetic fact (although the groups usually claim the latter),[34] it is important to remember the powerful role of social and political forces in the creation or definition of putatively biologically linked groups.

In modern societies, the term *ethnicity* also raises another problem. It is often used to describe minority groups, as if the culture of the majority were not also an ethnic culture. The culture of the majority is recast as natural or at least unfettered by irrational ethnic custom and tradition. In the Canadian context, most of the thinking and writing about 'ethnicity' examines only those communities that are assumed to operate at one or two steps removed from the centres of power, wealth, and status of Canadian society. In public and academic discourse, we tend to describe Canadians of Italian, Chinese, Portuguese, Greek, and South Asian descent as 'ethnic,' whereas we rarely use this term to describe Canadians of British or French heritage. This renders the culture and ethnicity of these dominant groups invisible while defining other groups outside of the circle of normality. The point is simply that those we consider 'mainstream' or 'non-ethnic' Canadians (Canadians of British and French descent) should also be considered ethnic Canadians. The ethnic communities associated with the descendents of British and French settlers are, of course, far larger and more heterogeneous than, say, Calgary's Armenians, but nonetheless, one can – and should – still speak of the two 'founding nations' as communities of people bound together by a common historical narrative, genetic heritage, language, culture, food, and, to a·very large extent, religion: that is, as ethnic groups.

The emergence of a 'Canadian ethnicity' is an excellent example of the fluidity of this phenomenon. In the 1991 Census, as the result of a 'Count Me Canadian' campaign, some 750,000 people (mostly from Ontario) wrote in 'Canadian' as their ethnic identity – a choice not offered on the census form. In the subsequent census of 1996, about 8.8 million people chose to identify themselves as Canadian either solely (some 5.3 million) or in combination with another origin (3.5 million). In the 2001 Census, 11,682,680 people (or 39 per cent of the total population) identified their ethnic origin as 'Canadian,' by far the largest single category (Jedwab 2003, 36).[35] Do these choices reflect the emergence of a new 'Canadian ethnicity'? The people who identified their ethnic origins as Canadian were mostly people who spoke English or French as a mother tongue and who had two parents born in Canada (Jedwab 2003, 37). In fact, the choice was most popular in Quebec, where the French term *Canadien* has a slightly different meaning, that is, someone who feels part of a French-language people that is distinct from both France and the rest of the anglophone cultures of Canada and the United States. Moreover, many people felt that pride in being Canadian did not contradict their pride in having Italian, Greek, or Hungarian roots as well. Indeed, Canada's official policy of multiculturalism affirmed the choice to embrace both identities and celebrate both heritages (Jedwab 2003, 38–40).

In Quebec, a parallel development has led to the widespread idea of 'Québécois' as a unique ethnic identity. After the Quiet Revolution of the early 1960s focused the attention of French Canadians on the Quebec state apparatus as the most important means of national self-determination (it was the only government in which they exercised majority control), francophone Quebecers started thinking of themselves as 'Quebecois,' a term previously used only to describe residents of Quebec City. The nationalist movement, and especially the election of the 'independentist' Parti Québécois in 1976, fortified the already strong identity and solidarity that many francophone Quebecers shared.

In dealing with the question of Christianity and ethnicity in Canada, several of the authors of this volume noted that, in their communities, Christians were beginning to view their churches as uniquely Canadian. In the case of Quebec, many francophone Quebecers view the Roman Catholic Church as uniquely Quebecois. Indeed francophone Quebecers simply refer to the Roman Catholic Church in that province as 'l'Église du Québec' or simply 'the church.' This raises the important question of the interaction of Canadian and francophone Quebecer ethnicity and Christianity.

Religion has played a major role in the construction of Canadian 'ethnicity.' As noted above, the English Canadian version of this national identity was generally informed by British and American culture, language, and political institutions, by participation in Anglo-American capitalism, and by an adherence to Protestantism. Just as Protestants, the dominant players in American society, after the Second World War began to accept Roman Catholics and Jews (Herberg 1983) as legitimate citizens, a similar opening up was beginning to occur in Canadian society. Moreover, as Canada became more secular the role of religion became more indirect. Protestant values (such as its individualism, strong sense of moral self-reliance, work ethic, etc.) remained central to a certain 'Canadian' ethnic identity – even as religious tolerance became a core feature of that identity. In turn, the Canadian experience reinforced in people an idea that they were separate from their religious counterparts in other countries. For example, over the course of history Scottish Presbyterians here loosened their connections to Scotland and began to think of themselves as comprising a fundamentally Canadian church. The United Church *of Canada* is the most overt example of a church community (or, in this case, several communities) severing ties with the founding communities in Great Britain and the United States and identifying itself wholeheartedly as Canadian. However, even Canadian Anglicans and Roman Catholics, who maintain strong ties to their international bodies, think of themselves as *Canadian* Anglicans and Catholics.

The connection between Christianity and Canadian or francophone Quebecer identity becomes clearer when we ask when churches ceased to be 'branch plant' operations of a foreign denomination. All of the large historical churches have had to wrestle with this issue. Three criteria may be suggested in an analysis of when a church ceased being a

mission field tied to the mother church and thereafter became a self-sufficient Canadian church. First, when did the church cease to rely on
resources from the 'homeland' and begin to provide its own resources,
especially in terms of clergy? Second, when did the denomination gain
administrative or legal autonomy from its 'home' church in the United
Kingdom, Europe, or the United States?[36] Third, when was the church
recognized by the Canadian government for inclusion in national programs such as health care, education, involvement in Aboriginal residential schools, and provision of chaplains for the armed forces and
prison system? When a church meets these requirements, it can be said
to be a 'Canadian' institution. Participation in such institutions promotes a shared world of meaning for their members (Deutsch 1962).
Such shared horizons help to create in the minds of participants the
notion of a unique Canadian or French Quebecer ethnic identity.[37]

Religion and the Heterogeneity of the Christian Community

The growing consensus in the academy about the socially constructed
nature of ethnicity, race, and culture has made scholars reluctant to create rigid definitions for any of their core topics, including – even, especially – religion. Although the debate about the definition of religion is
ongoing, this book is less concerned about the study of religions in the
abstract than it is about the study of the relationship between Canadian
ethnicities and Canadian Christianity (or, perhaps, Christianities).[38]
This perspective implies two things about how we will approach religion. First, we will have to account for religion in its phenomenological
totality. When not preoccupied with texts, the common definitions of
religion employed in academic and public discourse tended to emphasize either the religious experiences or beliefs of individuals.[39] Religion,
many assumed, was essentially an experience or a set of ideas about
reality. Practices, forms of community, and institutions were thought to
have been derived logically from these experiences and beliefs.
Recently, scholars have questioned these assumptions by looking at
religion as a multidimensional social phenomenon.[40] Almost all religions make theological and cosmological assertions about transcendent
or ultimate reality. However, all religions include practices and rituals,
forms of community, and institutions, all of which are just as important
as – and some might even argue, precede – the beliefs and experiences
of individuals (Bell 1997; Lincoln 2003, 6–8). Consequently, in order to
give a full description of the interaction between Christianity and eth-

nicity in Canada, the authors in this book examine religious beliefs, to be sure, but also religious practices, communities, and institutions, and the broader social context in which these are rooted.

Second, there is a growing consensus that religion should not be thought of simply as a timeless homogeneous 'thing' that we as scholars can easily subject to dispassionate, objective study. The term *Christianity* appears to name a single phenomenon, but is in fact a term somewhat artificially imposed on a wide variety of ideas, values, practices, and institutions about which some insiders and outsiders will contend there is very little consensus. For example, in North America there are evangelical and fundamentalist Protestants who object to the common sociological assertion that the majority of North Americans are Christians. In fact, as Bramadat discovered in his fieldwork (2000), many evangelicals estimate that only roughly 10–15 per cent of Canadians are, in fact, authentic 'Christians' (a figure much lower than the usual census-based estimates of roughly 75–80 per cent). These conservative Protestants prefer to limit the term to those people who claim to have a 'personal relationship with Jesus.' As a matter of course, some evangelicals exclude almost all Roman Catholics from the category of Christian because of the latter's alleged disinterest in this form of personal relationship (Bramadat 2000; Stackhouse 1993).[41] Moreover, there are members of this conservative tradition who adhere to a literalist approach to the Bible and Christ's divinity who are extremely uncomfortable with others – such as some of the more liberal members of the United Church of Canada – who view the Bible as one important book of wisdom among others, and who view Jesus as an exemplary but not necessarily uniquely divine figure.

The tensions between liberal United Church Christians, Roman Catholics, and their fundamentalist Christian neighbours represent just some of the broader cleavages in the Christian tradition; there are, of course, others, including those around religious rituals such as the Eucharist, the religious calendar, as well as the role of women, and, more recently, the morality of same-sex marriage. Nevertheless, although the internal diversity within Christianity is dramatic, and sometimes categorical, there is usually enough overlap in the histories and the sources of these communities that those of us on the outside can consider them to be variants of the same tradition. Still, any thorough analysis of Canadian Christianity, or even of one of its constituent denominations, must wrestle with the coexistence of significant heterogeneity and enduring similarity.

Institutional Completeness

Given that our approach accepts the socially constructed nature of religion, it follows that we would be concerned with the vehicles of this construction, especially institutions. Even the most privatized and personal faith requires an institutional structure.[42] Self-help books, seminars in spirituality, meditation seminars, and the like all require institutions to continue. Publishing houses, retreat facilities, new religious movements, bookstores, and the Internet contribute to a distinct institutional framework for these highly individualistic forms of religiosity. They operate alongside churches, schools, social service agencies, youth clubs, and other more traditional forms of institutionalization. The Canadian sociologist Raymond Breton coined the term *institutional completeness* to describe the degree to which members of a given ethnic or religious community can live their whole lives within the orbit of their own community. For example, the Canadian Jewish communities in Montreal, Toronto, and Winnipeg – all three of which are well-rooted – are usually cited as the classic examples of high levels of institutional completeness (Brym, Shaffir, and Weinfeld 1993; Ravvin 2005). Jews in these three cities can make use of explicitly Jewish schools, recreational facilities, grocery stores, restaurants, social service agencies, theatre companies, museums, dating services, cemeteries, and medical services including (with the exception of Winnipeg) hospitals. Obviously, these social structures protect and promote Jewish identity both at the individual and communal levels. The Cambodian and Vietnamese Buddhist communities, on the other hand, are often cited as ethno-religious communities with very low levels of institutional completeness (Boisvert 2005; Bramadat and Seljak 2005; McLellan 1999); such low levels are fairly assumed to limit the potential for social integration and mobility of members of these communities.[43]

Of course, one can also determine the institutional completeness of not just religious communities as a whole, but also of ethnic communities within the majority Christian population. For example, when an Italian Roman Catholic immigrates to Canada, he can make use of a large number of secular and religious organizations to aid his integration. On the one hand, if he makes the same choice that the vast majority of immigrants make – that is, to live in Montreal, Toronto, or Vancouver – he can involve himself in secular Italian social service agencies, private cafés, sports teams, and political associations, all of which are created by and for Italian Canadians. On the other hand, regardless of how religiously observant he was in Italy, he can very easily become part of a large and institutionally entrenched Italian Roman Catholic community in Canada. Moreover, in many provinces he can enjoy a privilege very few non-Christian immigrants enjoy: he can send his children to state-funded Roman Catholic schools. In other words, he does not need to worry about whether or not his new Italian community is – either in the secular or religious spheres – well established.

While Breton originally coined the term *institutional completeness* to study ethnic and religious minorities, we do not want to ignore Canada's ethno-religious majority groups and how their own identity is embedded in Canadian social institutions. Just as we wish to foreground the ethnicity of the dominant Canadian cultures, we also want to unearth the more subtle networks of power in which Canadian Christianity is embedded. Consequently, it behooves us to observe again the way in which the traditional dominant ethnic communities in Canada – that is, the French and British, but also the members of other well-integrated western European ethnic communities such as the Dutch, Belgians, Germans, and Scandinavians – enjoy what we might describe as government-sponsored institutional completeness. This is evidenced most obviously in the two official languages in Canada, the Eurocentric nature of our school curricula, the combination of French and British roots of our legal systems, the many privileges afforded to the Anglican, Roman Catholic, and certain Protestant churches for many decades, the federal provisions guaranteeing state funding for Roman Catholic separate schools in Ontario, as well as the patchwork of provincial arrangements for state funding of religious education.[44]

To put it in real terms, a British Anglican immigrant does not need to worry that she will find herself in a totally foreign world upon her arrival in Halifax; a Somali Muslim immigrant does. In itself, this is not an indication of discrimination. This reality merely reflects which communities arrived here first, and therefore which communities were able to become institutionally complete first. It is, however, important to note that when the British immigrant seeks to integrate into Halifax, she will find dozens of stately old Anglican churches. She will find government offices, schools, businesses, social clubs, and every variety of institution organized according to cultural principles that she can understand. Moreover, every bureaucrat, real estate agent, school principal, lawyer, banker, grocer, and waiter she meets will speak English (thanks in part to the state-supported pre-eminence of English). In short, she will be able to take advantage of a deeply rooted and publicly funded form of institutional completeness. This is simply because the nation state functions to guarantee the culture of one particular group (Gellner 1983). What immigrants from other cultures must fight for, members of the dominant group take for granted.

The Somali immigrant, on the other hand, faces a large number of obstacles, including a new language, a new set of moral and social customs, and many negative stereotypes. In addition, the institutions she was so familiar with in Somalia are absent here. She must adapt to schools, hospitals, businesses, and government offices that are organized in ways radically different from those with which she is familiar.[45] Because the Italian immigrant mentioned above may not speak English as a first language, he will likely face greater challenges than the British immigrant, but almost certainly less than the Somali immigrant. While he may find many Canadian institutions foreign, others (such as Italian restaurants, stores, businesses, cultural and sports clubs, and, significantly, state-sponsored Roman Catholic schools) will ease his integration and adaptation to Canadian life.[46] The point is that all immigrants must come to terms with – or, in some cases, can enjoy – the existing state-funded institutional completeness that characterizes the descendents of the early European settlers.

Christianity and Ethnicity in Canada

Given these complex questions about the relationship between ethnicity and religion in Canada, it is surprising that no one has addressed the issue in a sustained and systematic way. That is what this book attempts to do. In most co-edited books, chapters are loosely arranged by the editors to address different facets of a common topic. Typically, the authors never meet one another, or even the editors; consequently, the authors have different goals and may envisage different audiences. Like *Religion and Ethnicity in Canada,* this book has been conceived quite differently. In both cases, under the auspices of the Centre for Studies in Religion and Society at the University of Victoria, the authors met twice to develop a common project and to enter into dialogue with one another. However, authors were also asked to bring their unique perspectives and methods to bear on their chapters in order to produce an original piece of research that fits within the traditional framework of sound scholarship.

To maintain this balance between the diversity of the authors and the unity of the book, as a group we developed a very loose template of core issues to discuss. These issues included:

- the changing nature of religious practices and ideas;
- the current demographic reality;
- the social, economic, and political inclinations of the individuals and groups involved;
- the history of migration to Canada;
- ethnographies and life histories;
- the major contemporary challenges facing each community;
- the extent of institutional completeness within each community;
- the structure of major communal organizations;
- racism and religious discrimination;
- the role of women;
- second-/third-/fourth-generation concerns; and
- the role of the community in the broader Canadian public arena.

What to expect

When we began discussions about the structure and focus of this book, we realized that we would need to make some difficult decisions about which groups to include and which ones to exclude. We adopted the guiding principles of size and the historical importance and continuity of the traditions in Canada. Unfortunately, space does not permit us to explore in depth some very interesting but numerically smaller groups, such as Doukhobors, Mormons (Church of Jesus Christ of Latter-day Saints), Hutterites, Seventh Day Adventists, Jehovah's Witnesses, Quakers, and the Salvation Army. Although some of these groups are mentioned in the chapters on evangelicals and the Eastern Christian traditions, we leave to the authors of a future volume a fuller discussion of the intersection between ethnic and religious identities in these and other smaller Christian traditions. As well, we hope that the complex relationship between Aboriginal Canadians and Christianity will be explored by other scholars. The central analytical focus in the current volume is ethnicity – a concept that is not clearly relevant in First Nations discourse. Consequently, we felt that a full discussion of the unique Aboriginal Christian community in Canada would be more appropriate in a separate book.

It is also worth noting here that while most chapters explore the role of ethnicity within a single and easily identifiable religious community (e.g., the Lutherans, Anglicans, etc.), in the case of four chapters we faced distinct challenges in delineating the boundaries of the subject matter. The history of Canada and the social reality of the linguistic divide between anglophones and francophones forced us to make some hard – and not infrequently arbitrary – decisions. In the case of the two chapters on the Roman Catholic community, the division we have suggested between Roman Catholics in English and French speaking Canada will no doubt seem intuitively correct to many readers. A third-generation English-speaking Italian Canadian Catholic in Montreal is officially a member of the largely francophone Quebec province of the church, although this community is explored in the chapter on English-speaking Canada; similarly, Franco-Manitobans find themselves in largely anglophone dioceses, although this community is mentioned in the chapter on French-speaking Canada. Myroslaw Tataryn faces perhaps the most daunting challenge of all of our authors, since he must address the place of ethnicity in the broadest religious category in this book, one that includes not only Canadians of Ukrainian Catholic background, but those of Orthodox Christian origins who trace their lineage to countries as distinct as Lebanon, Russia Lithuania, Ukraine, and Egypt. Similarly, Bruce Guenther must examine the place of ethnicity in the decentralized, heterogeneous, and highly dynamic conservative Protestant tradition, which includes – among dozens of others – Pentecostal, Baptist, Christian and Missionary Alliance, Nazarene, and some Mennonite churches. While there is a degree of arbitrariness in any interpretive category, as a group we decided that the communities and individuals we have gathered in these chapters share enough common features to justify these typologies.

Three chapters of this book (on Anglicans, Presbyterians, and the United Church of Canada) address the issue of ethnicity in those three pillars of Canada's Protestant establishment. The three communities share a long history on Canadian soil, British (and American) roots, an experience of religious and political leadership and privilege and, very recently, precipitous declines in membership and attendance. Because of their long history in Canada, their active involvement in Canadian public policy, as well as their ties to Canada's political and economic elite, these communities developed the strongest sense of a Canadian 'ethnic' identity; that is, they saw themselves as essentially Canadian communities, more and more distinguished from their British and American counterparts. Moreover, all three churches have been hard hit by the forces of secularization, losing members and participants since 1960. Each in its own way has had to struggle with declining prestige, influence, and resources. In this period of decline, immigrants from Asia, Africa, and Latin America have joined these churches, adding a new vitality. In fact, in most cases it might even be the case that without these newcomers the situation in each of these churches would be not merely serious, but dire indeed. Nonetheless, with the new vitality come fundamental challenges to both the historic ethnic profiles of these established communities and to the ways the denominations have over the twentieth century defined themselves as distinctly Canadian.

In theory, the story of religion and ethnicity among Anglicans ought to be a simple affair; it is 'the Church of *England*' after all. However, in Wendy Fletcher's chapter 4 on Canada's Anglicans, we see how this community now struggles to integrate an assortment of non-British ethnic groups. Once embedded in a Canada where politicians could earnestly declare, 'This is a British country,' the Anglican Church now struggles to find a place in a new, multicultural, multi-faith, and increasingly secular Canadian society. Fletcher notes that Anglicans are now losing members at an alarming rate. However, there is a tension within this community between the emerging 'discourse of loss' regarding their historic power, and the efforts – perhaps even the profound need – to welcome Anglicans from Africa and Asia. While often more dynamic, newer Anglican immigrant parishes tend to be quite theologically and morally conservative, and this often exacerbates divisions within a denomination still struggling with women's ordination, same-sex union, and other issues.

Stuart Macdonald tells a similar story of the Presbyterian Church of Canada. He points out that the easy identification of Canadian Presbyterianism with Scots (and highland Scots, at that) has always been an over-simplification. Moreover, like the Anglicans, the Presbyterians are losing ground. For example, the 2001 Census showed a drop of 35 per cent in the number of people identifying themselves as Presbyterian (compared with 1991 figures). Partly in an effort to respond meaningfully to this dramatic decline and partly in order to better reflect the tradition of multiculturalism in Canada, the Presbyterian Church of Canada has become very resourceful in accommodating diverse ethnic groups from around the world. In his chapter Macdonald also explores the Christian Reformed Church – another community that traces its roots to the Swiss Reformation. In this community, ethnic solidarity takes a back seat to religious identity, Macdonald explains. The post–Second World War Dutch immigrants adopted the English language as quickly as they could but also insisted on creating separate Christian social institutions (such as schools and labour unions) to accommodate their adherents' unique religious orientation.

Greer Anne Wenh-In Ng examines the United Church of Canada as a community in which the sense of a Canadian identity has become strongest. The United Church was born in 1925 out of the dream of creating a broad-based national church. As the nation became more open to multiculturalism, so too did the United Church of Canada. Ng highlights the denomination's Ethnic Ministry Unit as an example of an attempt to allow minority groups a forum of self-expression and self-determination in a church that has become thoroughly Canadian. She argues that the United Church finds that its progressive stances on social issues reflects Canadian values, but this sometimes brings the dominant church community into conflict with some of its immigrant congregations that are more conservative on social and sexual issues. However, on other issues – such as accommodation of diversity – it is the minority groups that challenge the church to become more inclusive and open.

The situation of the Roman Catholic community in Canada is more complex because, in comparison with the three mainline Protestant churches, it is much more divided by ethnicity and language. The French created the first Roman Catholic communities and, as Solange Lefebvre argues in her chapter, since then Roman Catholicism and the ethnic identity of Canadian francophones have been inseparable. In New France, Catholicism was the established religion and the church enjoyed many privileges. After the Treaty of Paris of 1763 (and even more so after the Rebellions of 1837 and 1838), the Roman Catholic Church became the dominant social framework of French Canadians. Since that time, there was – in Quebec as well as in francophone communities outside of Quebec – almost a fusion of francophone identity and Roman Catholicism. Given the paucity of francophone immigrants, the French-speaking Catholic community was remarkably homogenous until changes in Canadian immigration policies in the late 1960s led to increased ethnic diversity in Canadian cities, and until Quebec's National Assembly passed its famous Bill 101 in an effort to safeguard the French language and Quebec's distinct cultural identity. More profound than this new diversity was the shock of rapid secularization during Quebec's Quiet Revolution that saw the quite sudden collapse of the institutional power wielded by Roman Catholicism in that province. While this period of rapid modernization and secularization was unparalleled outside of Quebec, it is important to note that francophone Catholics had to face the challenges of increased diversity at the same time.

Despite working under one institutional roof, English-speaking Roman Catholics are almost another denomination altogether. Mark McGowan traces the development of this diverse community, which includes those communities we would expect to see – the Irish, Germans, Poles, and Italians – as well as more recently arrived groups from the Philippines, Vietnam, and China. The church's tradition of creating 'ethnic' missions and so-called national parishes that cater to each major ethnic community illustrates that it recognized the importance of the link between religion and ethnic identity. McGowan observes that, unlike mainline Protestants, Roman Catholics in English-speaking Canada lived on the margin of respectability – not quite sharing the power and prestige of the Protestant establishment, but still able to wrestle important accommodations from the Canadian state with regards to education and other interests. Consequently, Canadian Catholics – including newcomers – had, and still have, access to an impressive set of institutions ranging from schools and universities to hospitals and social service networks.

Canada's Lutherans have also lived on the margins of respectability. Part of that marginalization has come from the fact that other Canadians identified Lutherans with Germany, Canada's enemy in two world wars. Even Canadian Lutherans who were immigrants from Scandinavia were regarded with some suspicion. Perhaps even deeper was the resentment on behalf of Canada's Protestant elite about the Lutheran tendency to remain ethnically and religiously distinct. Bryan Hillis argues that this sense of being religiously and ethnically different is dissipating as Canadian Lutherans, who now include immigrants from all around the world, have developed a strong Canadian consciousness. Services in German, references to the homeland or 'old country,' as well as European traditions are less and less significant in the denomination and almost totally insignificant for younger Lutherans who have known nothing but Canadian culture.

In contrast, as Myroslaw Tataryn argues in his chapter on Eastern Christians, Orthodox communities have maintained a clear tie between their faith and ethic identity. Eastern Christians consist of a broad spectrum of ethnic groups, which include Serbs, Ukrainians, Russians, Armenians, and Syrians. The decentralized structure of Eastern Christianity also means that Eastern Christians do not have an overarching central church organization. As well, the fact that changes in immigration policies have led to fairly recent increases in some of these groups, not to mention the fact that in some cases these communities continue to draw their priests from the 'old country,' guarantees that religion and ethnicity remain inextricably bound.

Bruce Guenther's chapter on evangelical Christians demonstrates a different dynamic. Here a wide variety of ethnic groups is united in diverse church structures that claim to transcend any ethnicity. These churches may be independent or (more likely) gathered in a multitude of associations and fellowships such as the Pentecostal Assembly of Canada or the Evangelical Fellowship of Canada. Particular congregations may cater to certain ethnic groups such as the Chinese or Koreans, but most are open to any and all Christians. What is remarkable about these churches, Guenther argues, is their adventurous sense of innovation, shaping and reshaping their structures to adjust to new needs and realities. What also unites them is their distance from the Canadian cultural and religious mainstream and the fact that, unlike mainline churches, they are either growing or maintaining their membership numbers.

Finally, Royden Loewen's chapter on Canadian Mennonites revisits some of the fundamental issues of the whole book. When discussing the different discourses that one finds among Canadian Mennonites on the possible relations between religion and ethnicity, Loewen argues that for some Mennonites their religion is indistinguishable from their ethnicity. Others seek to affirm their ethnic heritage but free it from the shackles of what they perceive as an irrational and oppressive religiosity. Still others seek to affirm the universality of the Mennonite interpretation of Christianity, wishing to suppress any suggestion of an ethnic core to the tradition by arguing that the historically ethno-religious tradition is, in fact, universalist at its core. Finally, some more recent Canadian Mennonite groups, Loewen argues, display neither the traditional religious characteristics of the Mennonite faith tradition nor the European characteristics of the cultures traditionally associated with it.

Conclusion

The title of Loewen's chapter, 'The Poetics of Peoplehood,' reminds us of the socially constructed nature of religious and ethnic identity and solidarity, its changing nature, and its multiplicity of forms. Furthermore, his discussion of the many discourses of identity most clearly outlines what all the authors observe in their chapters. That is, there is no single relationship between religion and ethnicity in Canada. Instead, there is a plurality of relationships unique to each religious and ethnic community. Indeed, within any one church or group, there is a variety of approaches. Moreover, given the rapidity of social change as well as the ever-evolving nature of religion and of ethnicity, it should come as no surprise that these relationships are changing. In the 1950s, no one could have imagined that the fusion of Roman Catholicism and French Canadian identity could ever have come undone. Similarly, very few people would have imagined the current ethnic diversity of the Presbyterian Church. However, the great changes of the 1960s – most notably the changes to Canada's laws that allowed immigration from Asia, Africa, and Latin America, as well as the cultural revolution of the post–Second World War period that saw the rise of secularization, feminism, and other challenges to traditional Christianity – have overturned the old assumptions. Korean Presbyterians, Filipino Roman Catholics, Hungarian Reformed Christians, African Mennonites, and Chinese Anglicans are now permanent features of Canada's religious landscape. It is time that Canadians – both inside and outside the churches – understand the new reality and its enormous implications. The new diversity will certainly complicate and enrich both the churches and Canadian society. The multiplicity of voices will remind us that there are many ways to be Christian and to be human. The struggle to open public debate and Canadian culture to the contributions of these voices – we believe – will serve to make Canada a society in which social inclusion and open dialogue will replace the Eurocentric cultural and religious monologue that has marked Canada's history.

Notes

1 Another Slovenian Roman Catholic Church, Our Lady of the Miraculous Medal, opened in 1959 and served those Slovenian Canadians who settled in the suburban community of Etobicoke. Run by a Slovenian religious order, the Vincentian Fathers, along with the Sisters of Our Lady of the Miraculous Medal, it is Canada's largest Slovenian Roman Catholic parish. While the churches were the centre of the Slovenian-Canadian community, there was a variety of other organizations, summer camps, sports and hunting clubs (popular activities in Slovenia), as well as groups dedicated to the arts. One group of Slovenian entrepreneurs even bought a small ski club, Old Smokey, in Ontario's Beaver Valley. Although the club was open

to the public, its owners and most of it members were Slovenians, and they often arranged for a Slovenian priest to say Mass in a downstairs lunch-room.

2 In our *Religion and Ethnicity in Canada*, the authors explored the intersection of religious and ethnic modes of identification within the six major minority traditions. While our focus on minority traditions in that book might have implicitly supported the tendency to naturalize the European Christian communities in Canada (as though it were the 'normal' way to be), our plan was to devote the current book to the kinds of religious and ethnic diversity one finds in Canadian Christianity. For detailed tables on these changes within the major minority traditions, see Beyer (2005). See also Statistics Canada, 'Religions in Canada.'

3 *Paris 1919*, the comprehensive historical work by Canadian scholar Margaret MacMillan, documents the negotiations that took place after the First World War over how the victorious democracies ought to divide the spoils, rewrite the maps, and re-configure the societies previously in the orbit of the Ottoman and Austro-Hungarian empires. In these pivotal six months of discussions among the leaders of France, Britain, the United States, and Italy, there were virtually no debates about whether or not these nations had the moral right to play such determinative roles in the lives of whole peoples. Regrettably, and especially in the Middle East, we are still reaping the whirlwind that was sowed during those fateful months.

4 In fact, the current American 'empire,' especially as it is expressed in its occupation of present-day Iraq, may be more pernicious and powerful than the British Empire in the nineteenth century. The point is that it is structurally different. See, for example, Khalidi (2004).

5 Of course, this does not apply so readily to minority Christian denominations, such as the Mennonites, who, especially in the first period of their lives in Canada, organized themselves in terms of their resistance to the state and thus would not have championed the intimate connection between church and state that was so central to the Christianization of Canada.

6 See J.W. Grant (1977, 9–12). Grant calls this process 'transplanting Christendom,' that is, the recreation of the European norm where one political unit is coextensive with one church. Naturally, the religious situation in France and Britain was not monolithic: there were Protestants in France and Roman Catholics in England; both groups suffered discrimination and, from time to time, persecution.

7 While Protestants and a small number of Jews lived and traded in the colony, they were not allowed to worship publicly. Public offices and most

professions were limited to Roman Catholics during the French Regime (Crowley 1996, 3).

8 For the role of the church in New France, see Jaenen (1985).

9 In fact, the Church of England was legally established only in Nova Scotia, New Brunswick, and Prince Edward Island. In Upper and Lower Canada, it enjoyed de facto but not de jure establishment, despite the efforts of bishops Jacob Mountain of Quebec and John Stachan of York (Toronto). See Hayes.

10 These churches were historically the 'respectable' Christian communities that received special recognition from the Government of Canada. For example, their ministers were involved directly in public education, served as chaplains in the armed forces, prisons, and other federal institutions, and served on government boards and commissions. One could also include the wealthier Baptist, Reformed, and Lutheran congregations among them.

11 One element that has been ignored in histories of Canada was rampant anti-Catholicism. In Ontario, the Orange Order, an Irish invention to promote anti-Catholicism, thrived in the late 1800s and early 1900s. See J.R. Miller (1993). Roman Catholics struggled to define for themselves a place of legitimacy in this society. See McGowan (1999) for the example of the Irish in Toronto.

12 See Bramadat and Seljak (2005).

13 Of course all such attempts at periodization are somewhat arbitrary. The first period extends from the founding of New France until the *Act of Union* (1840) in which the clergy reserves were first dissolved (although it took another fourteen years for the final liquidation). The second period extends from the *Act of Union* to the 1960s. In French Canada, the British government gave special privileges to the Catholic Church after the Rebellion, since the higher clergy opposed the rebels. From the 1840s on, the church exercised a special role as the main pillar of French Canadian society until the Quiet Revolution in the 1960s – although the state effectively checked and trumped the church's power in the 1920s (Hamelin and Gagnon 1984, 1:442–3). The power of the churches in English Canada also began to wane after the First World War; however, secularization proceeded more gradually over the following decades. The 1960s marked the beginning of a period of more thorough and rapid secularization in both English and French Canada.

14 So, for example, the anticlerical Joseph Louis Papineau, head of the Parti canadien, never imagined a French Canada without Catholicism. Indeed his rebellion was led in the name of 'nos lois, notre langue, notre religion' (Balthazar 1986, 54–8). Likewise, when Egerton Ryerson called for the

establishment of 'neutral' public schools, he meant non-denominational Christian schools dominated by a Protestant culture (Dickinson 1997, 42).

15 Grant points out the boom in church numbers was centred in suburbia, while inner-city and rural churches declined in numbers. Sunday school attendance shot up, as did participation in study and prayer groups. The United Church of Canada alone built 1,500 new churches and church halls, as well as 600 manses between 1945 and 1966. However, Grant argues that the middle classes stayed loyal, but workers, especially unionized workers and low-income Canadians, dropped out (1972, 160).

16 While this point may appear obvious in the case of English Canada, it runs contrary to the traditional understanding of the French-Canadian elite, who were – according to assumptions still alive in the minds of many Canadians – supposed to be dominated by conservative church authorities dedicated to keeping the population on family farms. In fact, historians now agree that, since the First World War, the French-Canadian political and economic elite was guided more by liberalism – especially in the economic sphere – than conservatism. Most business people and politicians shared a belief in private property, liberty, economic growth, and 'progress.' See Roy (1988, 1993).

17 While the promotion of Christianity has been removed from all public schools in Canada (with a few exceptions in Alberta, for instance), state support for Christian and other religious schools still exists in the form of full support for Ontario's 'separate' school system for Roman Catholics, as well as partial support for religiously based independent schools, through grants and tax credits in provinces such as British Columbia and Quebec. One current source of considerable debate is the fact that Ontario continues to support only one 'public' (which was ostensibly Protestant until the 1960s) and one 'separate' Roman Catholic school system; all other forms of independent schools – religious or secular – are denied direct provincial support in Ontario (see Sweet 1997).

18 Currently, all but two of Canada's military chaplains are Christian, although they now serve an increasingly religiously diverse armed forces. Today there is only one rabbi, although during the Second World War, there were more. In December 2003, Captain Suleyman Demiray became the first Muslim chaplain in the Canadian Forces. See Rennick (2005) and Canada, National Defence (2006).

19 However, such a trajectory is by no means a reliable indicator of the future, as José Casanova indicates (1994). Casanova explores several situations in which religious groups suddenly moved from the margins to the centres of political life.

20 As Bruce Guenther notes in his chapter, only certain 'conservative' evangel-
    ical churches have escaped these dramatic declines. Contrary to popular
    perception, these groups have not all been growing; most have just been
    able to maintain their numbers, largely through reproduction and 'holding
    on to' their young people.
21 See Fuller (2001).
22 The authors in this book rarely use this term because it has somewhat pejo-
    rative connotations.
23 See Indian and Northern Affairs Canada (1996).
24 In 2003, the market research group CF Group conducted a survey of just over
    one thousand Canadians and found that roughly sixty per cent of people
    under thirty-five supported same-sex marriage, whereas the same propor-
    tion of people over sixty-five rejected it. See NFO WorldGroup (2003).
25 People are more likely to be aware of the quandary that secular Jews face
    when they say they are ethnically Jewish but have no interest in Judaism.
    Similarly, many Sikhs are debating the line between Sikhism and Punjabi
    ethnic identity. See the chapters by Ravvin and Mahmood in Bramadat and
    Seljak (2005).
26 Indeed the successful film by Winnipeg native Nia Vardalos, *My Big Fat
    Greek Wedding* (2002), plays precisely on this theme of the changing nature
    of Greek identity in North American society and the issue of intermarriage.
    However, the fact that the film was a comedy rather than a drama illus-
    trates that the penalties for betraying traditional Greek norms are likely to
    be milder now than ever before.
27 See the discussion of how people often become muddled when you ask
    them to delineate these two strands of their identities in Bramadat (2005b,
    1–2, 18–19).
28 For a discussion of these terms and debates, see Bramadat (2005a).
29 The scientific community has established that races – understood as exclu-
    sive, distinct, and genetically based groups – do not really exist. What do
    exist are groups of people who share certain physical commonalities and
    phenotypical similarities (dark skin, blond hair, etc.). While this concept
    has been discredited by geneticists, it retains tremendous social and politi-
    cal force in contemporary societies. Even opponents of race as a concept
    and racism as a phenomenon nonetheless have to continue to use these
    terms in order to address historical patterns of social organization that are
    based on what we might think of as the tyranny of genotypically and phe-
    notypically small differences (see Gould 1977).
30 James Walker (1997) documents how these exclusionary attitudes and val-
    ues informed even judicial decisions on fundamental rights and freedoms.

31 Kenneth McRoberts (1997) argues that this policy also sought to frustrate French Quebec nationalism.

32 Of course, others, such as journalist and novelist Neil Bissoondath (1994), argue that multiculturalism as a federal policy is in fact a way to manage and tame real cultural diversity. See Kymlicka (1998, 2005) and Biles (2002) on critiques of multiculturalism.

33 See Bannerji (2000), Comaroff (1987, 1996), Driedger (1996), Halli and Driedger (2000), James (1999), Mahmood and Armstrong (1992), Moberg (1997), and Sahlins (1995).

34 The genocide in Rwanda may offer us the most recent and provocative case study in the invention of tribal or ethnic consciousness; in this case, group tensions were exacerbated to the point of mass murder, even though the distinctiveness of these two groups (especially from one another) is a matter of speculation. See Dallaire (2003). The classic statement of the social construction of ethnic tradition as 'invention' is found in Hobsbawm (1983).

35 Of those people, some 6.7 million (23 per cent of the total population) reported Canadian only and some 5 million (16 per cent of the total population) reported it along with other origins. By comparison, almost 6 million people identified their ethnic origins as English, 4.7 million as French, 4.15 as Scottish and 3.8 million as Irish. (See the electronic document, http://www40.statcan.ca/101/cst01/dem026a.htm; accessed May 25, 2006.)

36 For example, the General Conference Mennonite Church consisted of Mennonite congregations in both Canada and the United States and had offices in Manitoba and Kansas. In 2002, Mennonite Church Canada and Mennonite Church USA were formed. Despite continued transnational links, this resulted in the creation of a uniquely Canadian Christian entity.

37 For an analysis of how interaction in such institutions creates the context for acts of communication between individuals that lead to the social construction of shared worlds of meaning and eventually ethnic and even national consciousness, see Deutsch (1962).

38 This is not the place to consider the debates about the definition of the term *religion*, but it is worthwhile to note that the main issues at stake are whether or not a religion needs to involve the worship of a divine being, whether it is reliant on an institutionalized centre, whether it is a social construction or a product of divine creation, whether scholars can translate insider theological claims into language that can be adequately understood by non-believers, and whether insiders can study these phenomena in a disinterested manner (see Arnal 2000; McCutcheon 1997). The category of religion is a largely Western intellectual invention, and thus, it is not an

accident that the way Westerners commonly use the term 'fits' Christianity well.

39 Of course, as Walter Capps (1995) suggests, religious studies scholars have had a wider perspective on religion for some time.

40 See Talal Asad's (1993) critique of anthropologist Clifford Geertz's definition of religion, for example.

41 Of course, the distinction between these two groups should be nuanced; there would also be evangelicals who would embrace the Roman Catholic emphasis on traditional morality.

42 For a discussion of the privatized nature of religion in Canada and the United States, see Bibby (2002) and Fuller (2001).

43 On the relationship between religion and social capital, see Bramadat and Biles (2005).

44 'Separate' (as opposed to public and private) schools denote state-chartered, publicly funded schools in which there is religious education (see Sweet 1997). Ontario's separate school system is unique in that it is guaranteed by the *Constitution Act* (1982). In Saskatchewan, Alberta, and the Northwest Territories, funding for Roman Catholic schools is also guaranteed by their charters. Manitoba also represents a special case, as separate schools – part of the province's charter – were suppressed for awhile but are now funded. While there is no provision for separate Catholic schools in Nova Scotia, New Brunswick, and Prince Edward Island, political compromises and administrative arrangements have resulted in separate schools in everything but name. The government of British Columbia funds Roman Catholic schools, like other private schools, up to 60 per cent the amount that public schools receive.

45 As a result of political upheavals in Africa, the Somali Muslim community in Canada has recently grown considerably, but many Somali Muslims are understandably preoccupied with basic survival concerns; in this sense, they are similar to the Cambodian Buddhists (McLellan 1999). While Canadian federal, provincial, and municipal integration agencies are always straining to keep up with demand, it is noteworthy that immigrants are not left to fend for themselves once they arrive. As such, while not enjoying the embedded privileges of an anglophone from a commonwealth country, the Somali woman in question would likely receive some community as well as governmental support.

46 These generalizations are of limited use, of course. In Canada there are probably some rich, multilingual Somali immigrants, and probably some traumatized, poor, illiterate British immigrants.

Works Cited

Airhart, Phyllis D. 1990. Ordering a new nation and reordering Protestantism, 1867–1914. In *The Canadian Protestant experience, 1760 to 1990*, ed. George Rawlyk, 98–134. Burlington, ON: Welch.

Arnal, William E. 2000. Definition. In *Guide to the study of religion*, ed. Willi Braun and Russell T. McCutcheon, 21–34. London: Cassell.

Asad, Talal. 1993. *Genealogies of religion: Discipline and reasons of power in Christianity and Islam*. Baltimore: Johns Hopkins University Press.

– 2003. *Formations of the secular: Christianity, Islam, and modernity*. Stanford: Stanford University Press.

Balthazar, Louis. 1986. *Bilan du nationalisme au Québec*. Montreal: L'Hexagone.

Bannerji, Himani. 2000. *The dark side of the nation: Essays on multiculturalism, nationalism, and gender*. Toronto: Canadian Scholars' Press.

Behiels, Michael D. 1985. *Prelude to Quebec's Quiet Revolution: Liberalism versus neo-nationalism, 1945–1960*. Montreal and Kingston: McGill-Queen's University Press.

Berger, Peter. 1967. *The sacred canopy: Elements of a sociological theory of religion*. Garden City, NY: Doubleday.

Bibby, Reginald. 1987. *Fragmented gods: The poverty and potential of religion in Canada*. Toronto: Irwin.

– 1993. *Unknown gods: The ongoing story of religion in Canada*. Toronto: Stoddart.

– 2002. *Restless gods: The renaissance of religion in Canada*. Toronto: Stoddart.

– 2004. *Restless churches: How Canada's churches can contribute to the emerging religious renaissance*. Kelowna, BC: Wood Lake Books.

Biles, John. 2002. Everyone's a critic. Special issue, *Canadian Issues / Thèmes canadiens* (Association of Canadian Studies) 1, no. 1 (February): 35–38.

Biles, John, and Humera Ibrahim. 2005. Religion and public policy: Immigration, citizenship and multiculturalism – Guess who's coming to dinner? In Bramadat and Seljak 2005, 154–77.

Bissoondath, Neil. 1994. *Selling illusions: The cult of multiculturalism in Canada*. Toronto: Penguin.

Boisvert, Matthieu. 2005. Buddhist in Canada: Impermanence in a land of change. In Bramadat and Seljak 2005, 69–88.

Bramadat, Paul. 2000. *The church on the world's turf: An evangelical Christian group at a secular university*. Oxford: Oxford University Press.

– 2005a. Beyond Christian Canada. In Bramadat and Seljak 2005, 1–29.

– 2005b. Toward a new politics of authenticity: Ethno-cultural representation in theory and practice. *Canadian Ethnic Studies* 37 (1): 1–20.

Bramadat, Paul, and John Biles, eds. 2005. The re-emergence of religion in international public discourse. Special issue, *Journal of International Migration and Integration* 6, no. 2.

Bramadat, Paul, and David Seljak, eds. 2005. *Religion and ethnicity in Canada*. Toronto: Pearson Longman.

Breton, Raymond. 1964. Institutional completeness of ethnic communities and the personal relations of immigrants. *American Journal of Sociology* 70 (2): 193–205.

Brown, Peter. 1988. *The body and society: Men, women, and sexual renunciation in early Christianity*. New York: Columbia University Press.

Brym, R.J., W. Shaffir, and M. Weinfeld, eds. 1993. *Jews in Canada*. Toronto: Oxford University Press.

Canada, National Defence. 2006. History of the Canadian Forces chaplaincy. http://www.forces.gc.ca/chapgen/engraph/history_e.asp?cat=1.

Capps, Walter. 1995. *Religious studies: The making of a discipline*. Minneapolis: Fortress.

Casanova, José. 1994. *Public religion in the modern world*. Chicago: University of Chicago Press.

Christie, N. 1990. 'In these times of democratic rage and delusion': Popular religion and the challenge to the established order, 1760–1815. In *The Canadian Protestant experience, 1760 to 1990*, ed. George Rawlyk, 9–47. Burlington, ON: Welch.

Clark, S.D. 1962. *The developing Canadian community*. Toronto: University of Toronto Press.

Comaroff, J. 1987. Of totemism and ethnicity: Consciousness, practice, and signs of inequality. *Ethnos* 52 (3): 301–33.

– 1996. Ethnicity, nationalism, and the politics of difference in an age of revolution. In *The politics of difference: Ethnic premises in a world of power*, ed. P. MacAllister and E. Wilmsen, 162–84. Chicago: University of Chicago Press.

Crowley, Terry. 1996. The French regime to 1760. In *A concise history of Christianity in Canada*, ed. Terrence Murphy and Roberto Perin, 1–55. Toronto: Oxford University Press.

Dallaire, Romeo. 2003. *Shake hands with the devil: The failure of humanity in Rwanda*. Toronto: Random House Canada.

Davie, Grace. 1994. *Religion in Britain since 1945: Believing without belonging*. Cambridge: Blackwell.

Deutsch, Karl. 1962. *Nationalism and social communication: An inquiry into the foundations of nationality*. Cambridge, MA: MIT Press. (Originally published 1953.)

Dickinson, Greg M. 1997. The chicken in the road: Constitution vs religion in Canadian schools. *School Business Affairs* 63 (5): 39–45.

Driedger, Leo. 1996. *Multi-ethnic Canada: Identities and inequalities.* Toronto: Oxford University Press.

Fuller, Robert. 2001. *Spiritual, but not religious: Understanding unchurched America.* Oxford: Oxford University Press.

Gellner, Ernst. 1983. *Nations and nationalism.* Oxford: Blackwell.

Gould, Stephen Jay. 1977. Why we should not name human races: A biological view. In *Ever since Darwin: Reflections in natural history,* 231–36. New York: Norton.

Grand'Maison, Jacques. 1970. *Nationalisme et religion.* Tome 2, *Religion et idéologies politiques.* Montreal: Beauchemin.

Grant, Agnes. 1996. *No end of grief: Indian residential schools in Canada.* Winnipeg: Pemmican.

Grant, John Webster. 1972. *The church in the Canadian era.* Toronto: McGraw-Hill Ryerson.

– 1977. Religion and the quest for a national identity: The background in Canadian history. In *Religion and culture in Canada,* ed. Peter Slater, 7–21. Waterloo, ON: Canadian Corporation for Studies in Religion.

Halli, Shiva, and Leo Driedger. 2000. *Race and racism: Canada's challenge.* Montreal and Kingston: McGill-Queen's University Press.

Hamelin, Jean, and Nicole Gagnon. 1984. *Histoire du catholicisme québécois : Le XXe siècle.* Tome 1, *1898–1940.* Montreal: Boréal Express.

Hayes, Alan L. n.d. Canadian Anglican history, 3: The establishment ideal. http://home.cogeco.ca/%7Ealhayes/anglicancanada/anglhist3.htm.

Herberg, Will. 1983. *Protestant, Catholic, Jew: An essay in American religious sociology.* Chicago: University of Chicago Press. (Originally published 1955).

Hervieu-Léger, Danièle. 2006. The role of religion in establishing social cohesion. *Eurozine,* http://www.eurozine.com/articles/2006-08-17-hervieuleger-en.html.

Hobsbawm, Eric. 1983. Introduction: Inventing tradition. In *The invention of tradition,* ed. Eric Hobsbawm and Terence Ranger, 1–14. Cambridge: Cambridge University Press.

Indian and Northern Affairs Canada. 1996. Report of the Royal Commission on Aboriginal Peoples. http://www.ainc-inac.gc.ca/ch/rcap/.

Jaenen, Cornelius J. 1985. *The role of the church in New France.* Ottawa: Canadian Historical Association.

James, C. 1999. *Seeing ourselves: Exploring race, ethnicity, and culture.* 2nd ed. Toronto: Thompson Educational.

Jedwab, Jack. 2003. Coming to our census: The need for continued inquiry into Canadians' ethnic origins. *Canadian Ethnic Studies* 35 (1): 33–50.

Khalidi, Rashid. 2004. *Resurrecting empire: Western footprints and America's perilous path in the Middle East*. Boston: Beacon, 2004.

Kymlicka, William. 1998. Finding our way: *Rethinking ethnocultural relations in Canada*. Toronto: Oxford University Press.

– 2005. The uncertain futures of multiculturalism. *Canadian Diversity* 4 (1): 82–5.

Lincoln, Bruce. 2003. *Holy terrors: Thinking about religion after September 11*. Chicago: University of Chicago Press.

MacMillan, Margaret. 2003. *Paris 1919: Six months that changed the world*. New York: Random House. (Original published 2001).

Mahmood, Cynthia, and Armstrong, S.L. 1992. Do ethnic groups exist? A cognitive perspective on the concept of cultures. *Ethnology* 31 (1): 1–14.

McCutcheon, Russell T. 1997. *Manufacturing religion: The discourse on sui generis religion and the politics of nostalgia*. Oxford: Oxford University Press.

McGowan, Mark G. 1999. *The waning of the green: Catholics, the Irish, and identity in Toronto, 1887–1922*. Montreal and Kingston: McGill-Queen's University Press.

McLellan, Janet. 1999. *Many petals of the lotus: Five Asian Buddhist communities in Toronto*. Toronto: University of Toronto Press.

McRoberts, Kenneth. 1997. *Misconceiving Canada: The struggle for national unity*. Toronto: Oxford University Press.

Miller, J.R. 1993. Anti-Catholicism in Canada: From the British Conquest to the Great War. In *Creed and culture: The place of English-speaking Catholics in Canadian society, 1750–1930*, ed. Terrence Murphy and Gerald Stortz, 25–48. Montreal: McGill-Queen's University Press.

Miller, Vincent J. 2004. *Consuming religion: Christian faith and practice in a consumer culture*. New York: Continuum4.

Moberg, M. 1997. *Myths of ethnicity and nation: Immigration, work and identity in the Belize banana industry*. Knoxville: University of Tennessee Press.

NFO WorldGroup. 2003. Public divided about definition of marriage. CBC. http://www.cbc.ca/news/background/samesexrights/gay_rights_poll2003b.pdf

Paquette, Jacques. Table 2: Non-Christian religions are growing. Canadian Heritage, http://www.pch.gc.ca/progs/multi/spmc-scmp/conference/02_e.cfm.

Ravvin, Norman. 2005. Jews in Canada: A travelling cantor on the prairies and other pictures of Canadian Jewish life. In Bramadat and Seljak, 111–32.

Rennick, Joanne. 2005. The chaplaincy in war and peace: Caring for all in a new context. Paper presented at the Chaplaincy in War and Peace Community

Seminar, Centre for Studies in Religion and Society at the University of
Victoria, 26 April.

Rioux, Marcel. 1976. *La question du Québec*. Montreal: Parti Pris. (Originally
published 1969.)

Roy, Fernande. 1988. *Progrès, harmonie, liberté: le libéralisme des milieux d'affaires
francophones de Montréal au tournant du siècle*. Montreal: Boréal.

– 1993. *Histoire des idéologies au Québec aux XIXe et XXe siècle*. Montreal: Boréal.

Sahlins, Marshal. 1995. *How natives think*. Chicago: University of Chicago Press.

Stackhouse, John. 1993. *Canadian evangelicalism in the twentieth century: An introduction to its character*. Toronto: University of Toronto Press.

Statistics Canada. 2001. Population by selected ethnic origins, by province
and terriroty (2001 Census). http://cansim2.statcan.ca/cgi-win/cnsm-
cgi.pgm?Lang=E&SP_Action=Result&SP_ID=30002&SP_TYP=5&SP_
Sort=1.

– n.d. Religions in Canada: Highlight tables, 2001 Census. http://www12
.statcan.ca/english/census01/products/highlight/Religion/
Index.cfm?Lang=E.

Swatos, William, ed. 1999. The secularization debate. Special issue, *Sociology
of Religion: A Quarterly Review* 60 (3).

Sweet, Lois. 1997. *God in the classroom: The controversial issue of religion in
Canada's schools*. Toronto: McClelland and Stewart.

Taylor, Charles. 1994. *Multiculturalism: Examining the politics of recognition*.
Ed. Amy Gutman. Commentary by K. Anthony Appiah, Jürgen Habermas,
Steven C. Rockefeller, Michael Walzer, and Susan Wolf. Ed. Amy Gutmann.
Princeton: Princeton University Press.

Walker, James. 1997. *'Race,' rights and the law in the Supreme Court of Canada:
Historical case studies*. Waterloo, ON: Osgoode Society for Canadian Legal
History and Wilfrid Laurier University Press.

2 Roman Catholics (Anglophone and Allophone)

MARK G. MCGOWAN

Introduction: Unity in Diversity

The caretaker unlocked the doors of the church for an old man and a teenaged boy, who had come to pay a visit. 'I was baptized here,' related my grandfather as he proceeded to lead me up and down the aisles of this massive gothic structure that dominated the hill overlooking the sleepy village of Formosa, Ontario. The Church of the Immaculate Conception had been the dream of Father Archangel Gstir, an Austrian-born Franciscan who founded the parish in 1861 and who envisioned building a grand structure for the local German Catholic community. He was ambitious enough to seek assistance from a charitable foundation sponsored by King Louis I of Bavaria and, although $2,000 was received, it would be Gstir's successor priests who would see the small wooden chapel replaced by the massive stone temple, now a place of history to an old man and wonder to a boy (Foyster 1981, 55). When the church was completed in the 1880s, it was said that three teams of horses could be driven side-by-side between the new walls and the frame of the old chapel that was torn down only after the superstructure of the new church had been completed around it (Kuntz 1980, 21–5). To the boy more accustomed to the modern architecture of post–Second Vatican Council churches in Canada, Immaculate Conception stood out as different and distinctly German with its hand-carved altars, highly lacquered pews, and hand-painted Stations of the Cross, each of which was identified in German in Gothic script, and vivid statuary. Even its cemetery spoke of its German past, with monuments dedicated to the lasting repose of families like Weiler, Zettel, Anstett, Rich, Schnurr, Kuntz, Becker, and Batte. This was sacred ground and undoubtedly German.

Figure 2.1. Formosa. German Catholics head to the shops after Sunday Mass at Immaculate Conception Church in Formosa, Ontario, in the late nineteenth century.

As a teen, I marvelled, and now as an historian, I still marvel at the Roman Catholic Church as a study in contrasts so evident when I compared this German Catholic rural enclave in Carrick Township revealed to me by my grandfather, with my own parish in what was to become suburban Ottawa. In 1962, in the semi-rural community of Bells Corners, the Archdiocese of Ottawa erected St Martin de Porres Parish to serve the growing commuter population in the recently built housing subdivisions west of the nation's capital (McEvoy 1998, 152–3). With its modern design dominated by a large triangular roof capped with a cross, St Martin's was aesthetically, artistically, and architecturally as foreign to the Formosa church as structures might be. The parishioners of these churches differed profoundly; St Martin's was a highly cosmopolitan parish of farmers, labourers, liberal professionals, and white-collar workers, many of whom were immigrants or second- and third-generation Canadians. Although the founding pastor, D.D. MacDonald, harkened from a time when the non-francophone church in Canada was dominated by bishops and clergy of Irish and Scots descent, these charter groups represented only a modest proportion of his parish. On any given Sunday at St Martin de Porres (named after a

Peruvian of mixed Spanish and Native ancestry), one could identify parishioners of Polish, Italian, Maltese, German, English, Ukrainian, Chinese, Trinidadian, French, Filipino, Lebanese, Croatian, Swiss, Dutch, and Goan backgrounds. St Martin's reflected not only the growing phenomenon of multicultural suburban Catholicism in the 1960s, but also the blending of diverse peoples under a common liturgy and in an English vernacular.

Both parishes speak loudly of the diversity of peoples in Canada's Roman Catholic churches. Such diversity is most apparent in the 'migrating generations' who seek to maintain their ethnicity by constructing their own distinctive church communities as the hub of their resettled communities. Such was the case with German settlers at Formosa who shared Father Gstir's dream of a German Catholic enclave in the wilderness. In time, the Formosa Germans demonstrated what so many other like-minded distinctive Catholic communities had: in an English-speaking-dominated church, in an English-speaking world, second- and third-generation Catholics would prefer the use of English, and these parishes would change accordingly. In the nineteenth and early twentieth centuries, the mosaic of Canadian Roman Catholicism would be united by a common Latin liturgy. In time, as the children and grandchildren of immigrants adapted to the exigencies of living and working in Canada, the daily use of languages would wane, although diversity in cultural traditions would still demarcate some Catholic communities from the anglophone mainstream. In contemporary Canada, in which the vernacular languages have subsumed the old Latin ritual (with some notable exceptions), the diverse people of the new church are still bound together by means of the Mass, a common hierarchy, and, until recently, a dynamic and demanding pope.

This chapter explores the struggle within Canada's largest Christian church to accommodate the diversity of its peoples, languages, traditions, and cultures within a single unified ecclesial community. The effort to seek a balance between the impulse to centralize and the liberty to allow groups to develop and grow with greater autonomy in Canada is just another variation of the historical tension imbedded in the church's very name: Roman Catholic. Throughout history the catholic (that is, 'universal') impulse of the church has been to embrace all nations, while the Roman (that is, specific to a certain place) character of the church has often sought to centralize or establish uniformity in belief and practice. In Canada these challenges facing the universal church have been made even more difficult by the sheer number of distinctive ethnic communities within Canadian Catholicism and by the fact that in Canada outside of Quebec until very recently, the Catholic population was often marginalized and discriminated against by the Protestant majority who believed they ought to, as it were, have dominion over English Canada. Over time Catholics moved from the margins in English Canada to the centre, sharing political, economic, and social success with their non-Catholic neighbours. These struggles between Catholicism and Protestantism, and the challenges brought to unity by diversity should also be seen against the broader canvas in which the Catholic Church's two principal charter groups – anglophone and francophone Catholics – have struggled to maintain a balance nationally between their sometimes competing visions of the church and the state.

History of Migration and Settlement

Although Roman Catholicism first came to the North American shores of Newfoundland and Labrador in the dragon ships of the eleventh-century Norsemen (Oleson 1963, 7, 32–3) and by means of Basque and Portuguese whalers and fishermen in the fifteenth century (Barkham 1982, 515–19; Teixeira 1999, 1076), Roman Catholicism is most frequently associated with the French settlements in Acadia and Quebec (see chapter 3). Despite their dominance of Canadian Catholicism from the seventeenth century onwards, however, francophone Catholics in the St Lawrence Valley welcomed only small groups of non-francophones into their midst. Irish-Catholic sailors, serving in the French navy, and Irish volunteers in the French army, visited and settled in New France, while assisting France in her wars against their common enemy – Protestant England. While their settlement was sometimes only temporary and their public presence often un-noticed, some non-francophone Catholics became prominent among the French, including Captain Charles Latouche McCarthy and Dr Timothy Sullivan (Sylvain), stepfather of Marguerite d'Youville (Guerin 1946, 41; Moogk 1974).

Less welcome were the Gaelic and English-speaking Catholic interlopers who navigated the coves and treacherous waters off Newfoundland in search of cod, the 'beef of the sea.' In fact, this annual flow of fishermen to *Talamh an Eisc* (The Land of Fish) quickly turned into a torrent, as Irish Catholics provided the first large mass migration of non-francophone Catholics to North America in the late eighteenth and early nineteenth centuries. Every year, fisherman from the southeastern counties of Ireland continued to travel to Newfoundland and its cod-rich Grand Banks. In the half century leading up to the collapse of the fishery in 1830, thousands of Irish Catholics, mostly English speaking, had built villages along the coasts of the Avalon Peninsula, Conception Bay, and Trinity Bay, or had set down roots in the port city of St John's (Houston and Smyth 1990; Mannion 1974). Throughout the nineteenth century some of these Irish Catholics, colloquially known as 'two boat-ers,' literally took one boat to sojourn in Newfoundland and then took a second boat to settle parts of the Mirimichi Valley, in New Brunswick, the shores of Cape Breton Island, or the coasts of Prince Edward Island (O'Grady 2004), or to join fellow Waterford and Wexford migrants who had already settled in Halifax, Nova Scotia (Punch 1981). By 1815, Irish Catholics were migrating to the interior Canadian colonies of Lower Canada (later Quebec) and Upper Canada (later Ontario). Attracted by the need for manual labour and cheap arable land, these 'pre-famine' Irish found themselves in the canal works on the St Lawrence River at Montreal, the dockyards of Quebec City, the 'dark druidic groves' of white and red pine in the Upper Ottawa Valley (Cross 1973), on the mosquito-infested swamps and sludge of the Rideau Lakes as they built a canal linking Kingston and Bytown (later Ottawa), or the farm-steads of central and southern Upper Canada.

By the mid-nineteenth century some 450,000 Irish had migrated to British North America. Not all of them remained in the colonies, nor were all of them Catholic. In Newfoundland, where Catholics would comprise close to half of the island's population, nearly all the Irish were Catholic. The same could be said of those who settled in Prince Edward Island and Halifax, Nova Scotia. Catholics in these colonies numbered 40 per cent and 25 per cent respectively, although each colony had multicultural Catholic communities of Irish, Scots, francophone Acadians, and the indigenous Mik'maqs. In New Brunswick, half of the Irish community was Catholic, while in Lower Canada Irish migration patterns brought Catholics primarily, who settled in the principal cities of Montreal and Quebec, and in small rural communities along the southern tributaries of the St Lawrence River. In Upper Canada at this time the Irish Catholic population comprised only about 40 per cent of the entire Irish migration to the colony and most were rural dwellers, inhabiting all regions of the colony from the Ottawa Valley to the rich farmlands adjacent to Lake Huron, in what would become Perth, Huron, and Bruce counties (McGowan 1999a, 738–42).

The largest single influx of Catholic Irish came in 1847 as a direct result of the mass starvation experienced in Ireland during the infamous potato famine – *gorta mor* – which lasted from 1845 to 1850. In Black '47 approximately 100,000 migrants streamed across the Atlantic out of British and Irish ports.[1] Most of these were Irish Catholic refugees who were among those small farmers and cottiers most fortunate to have compiled sufficient savings to make the horrendous six- to eight-week voyage across the Atlantic to British North America. Contrary to popular memory and some historical interpretations, only about 6,000 Irish migrants were subsidized by their landlords (O'Gallagher and Dompierre 1995, 340–56; Parr 1974, 101–13). The influx of these sick and weary travellers was insignificant in Nova Scotia, Prince Edward Island, and Newfoundland; the vast majority headed for New Brunswick (17,000) or the two Canadas (as many as 80,000). By year's end, approximately one-fifth of those passengers who had embarked on their journey to British North America had died. While many of the surviving Irish Catholics moved on to warmer climes in the United States, and did not significantly alter the settlement patterns established by their Catholic predecessors, the lingering memory of the horror witnessed by Canadians in 1847 would provide a lens through which Irish Catholics would be viewed hereafter, both by themselves and by their host community.

Many Canadians shunned them because of their sickness, denied them work, hoping they would leave, or discriminated against them in social life because they were perceived as ignorant and superstitious minions of the pope of Rome. The Irish would come to see themselves as the suffering servants of the faith with a providential mission to spread the Catholic faith in North America by means of the English language.[2]

Although the Irish would quickly become the largest non-francophone Catholic group in Canada, they would immediately encounter the presence and power of their Scots Catholic co-religionists. The number of Catholic Scots in British North America, in fact, was disproportionately larger than their population at home because of mass migrations that came in two waves between 1770 and 1850 from the Catholic-dominated tenancies in Inverness, Sutherland, Skye, Ross, Barra, and South Uist, among other areas in the western Highlands (Hornsby 1992, 411–12). In the 1770s, boatloads of Scots, both Catholic and Protestant, began to arrive in Nova Scotia and Prince Edward Island, although the peak of Highland migration to these colonies was not witnessed until 1801–3, when 5,854 arrived, all of whom hailed from the overpopulated

Figure 2.2: The Celtic cross memorial erected on Grosse Ile, the quarantine station, commemorating the thousands of Irish migrants and Canadian volunteers, clergy, and laypersons who lost their lives as the result of the Great Famine migration to Canada in 1847. (Photo: Mark McGowan)

western Highlands and islands (Bumsted 1981, 68–74). They would be joined by those fleeing land clearances, after 1815, those attached to North America–bound military units (Bumsted 1993, 82), and artisans and farmers who elected to migrate when the British economy slowed in the wake of the Napoleonic Wars. By the 1820s, non-francophone Catholics in the regions east and west of contemporary Quebec (excluding Newfoundland) soon found themselves under the domination of Scottish bishops.[3] Prior to the 1840s, these Scots prelates laid the episcopal grid for Catholics outside of Lower Canada while creating a positive atmosphere of rapprochement with local governments (Moir 1971).

As the Gaelic ascendancy slowly gave way to a 'Hibernarchy' (rule by the Irish) in most BNA dioceses by the middle of the nineteenth century, the Celtic Catholics were joined by several other non-francophone groups. Over a period of twenty years in the middle of the nineteenth century, nearly 20,000 Kashub Poles left the oppressive environment of Prussian-occupied Poland and carved out farmsteads in what is now Renfrew County in the Upper Ottawa Valley (Perin 1998, 5; Radecki 1976, 144). At roughly the same time, German migrants from Baden-Wurttemberg, Bavaria, Alsace, Lorraine, the Swiss Cantons, and Swabia ventured to Upper Canada either directly from the German states or after a brief sojourn in the United States. Catholics mingled with fellow German-speaking Lutherans, Prussian Poles, and Mennonites in Wellington and Waterloo counties, where their agricultural endeavours provided a hinterland for the burgeoning city of Berlin (now Kitchener). Farther to the west, in 1886 a small group of Black Sea German Catholics took root near the town of Leader, near Regina, in what is now Saskatchewan (Perin 1998, 8). To a lesser degree, migrants and sojourners from the Italian states began to arrive in small numbers in search of employment in Canada's major cities – Vancouver, Montreal, and Toronto – or in areas where employment building railways was available (Ramirez 1989, 6; Zucchi 1988, 81).[4]

Between 1890 and 1920, the diversity and sheer numbers of non-francophone Catholics increased dramatically. By the end of this great 'Laurier-Borden' phase of migration in 1920, nearly 450,000 Catholics in Canada could claim neither English nor French as their mother tongue – 12 per cent of the entire Catholic population (Perin 1998, 6). In response to the Canadian government's advertising campaign of 'The Last Best West,' the alleged closure of the American frontier, a dramatic upswing in the Canadian economy, the availability of resource-based jobs and the need for skilled workers, as well as the incentives provided by shipping companies and railways to service their shareholders, over 1 million immigrants entered Canada (Brown and Cook 1974, 49–82). Thousands of these hailed from primarily Catholic regions of central and eastern Europe. Notable among these new Catholic Canadians were approximately 35,000 Poles from the German, Russian, and Austrian area of occupation who ventured to the heartland cities of Montreal, Hamilton, and Toronto, to resource-based industries in Sudbury and Sault Ste Marie, to Winnipeg, the metropolis of the prairie west, to farmsteads in Manitoba and Saskatchewan, and finally to Edmonton, Alberta. As early as 1899, Poles in Winnipeg began to gravitate around the multi-ethnic Holy Spirit Parish, which, by 1904, became a Polish institution by the sheer force of their numbers.

Also prominent among this wave of mass migration were Catholic Italians, mostly from the southern provinces of Sicily, Calabria, Puglia, and Campania, a smaller number from the central regions of Molese and the Marches, and some from the two northernmost provinces of Friuli and Veneto. Although the vast majority of the migrants from the south were peasants, they tended to seek unskilled and semi-skilled employment in Montreal, Toronto, and Hamilton. Again in the interests of region and labour, between 1901 and 1920 close to 121,000 Italians had arrived in Canada (Ramirez 1989, 7), and although many had planned on merely sojourning in the New World, until their prospected 'fortunes' could carry them back home for a life of status and relative affluence, most ended up settling at the Canadian end of a migration chain that would continue to link the old and new worlds for the rest of the twentieth century.

This remarkable period of migration also witnessed the augmentation of Catholic ethnic communities and the introduction of new groups to Canada. In 1903, a small group of German Catholics, fearing the loss of their language and assimilation in the United States and led by Benedictine monks, ventured into central Saskatchewan and founded the St Peter's Abbey and Colony, near Muenster. By 1906, the population of the colony stood at 6,000; fourteen years later this number had increased by 50 per cent (Hubbard 1983, 156). The colony soon included the farms surrounding Humboldt and St Joseph. When combined with German migration to other Prairie provinces and Ontario, the Muenster settlers comprised a key component of the close to 40,000 Germans who entered Canada between 1871 and 1914 (McLaughlin 1985, 5).

Saskatchewan also hosted a group of Hungarian Catholic immigrants, led by the Count Paul Oscar Esterhazy, who encouraged Hungarian peasants to leave the poverty of their homeland and pursue a new life on farms in southeastern Saskatchewan (Kovacs 1982, 65–7). In Saskatchewan and Manitoba, Hungarian Catholics settled cheek-by-jowl with Calvinist compatriots who were quick to establish their own churches distinct from the Catholic majority (Patrias 1997, 7). Hungarian Catholic migrants also ventured to the industrial heartland of Ontario, settling in Toronto as well as Hamilton – a city that would become known later by the community as the 'Hungarian capital of eastern Canada' (Dreisziger 1982c, 102). In Toronto, however, Hungarians would be one group among a veritable 'little Europe,' as they lived among newly arrived Czechs, Slovaks, Ukrainians, Lithuanians, Syrians, Italians, Poles, and Maltese Catholics. In Montreal and Vancouver, Catholic authorities would scramble to assist Chinese Catholics who, although not new to Canada, given their work on the Canadian Pacific Railway, were new to the Catholic Church (Perin 1998, 12).

The outbreak of the Great War (1914–18) provided only a temporary stop to mass migration to Canada. In the 1920s and early in the Great Depression of the 1930s, Canada received additional numbers of Catholic immigrants, but mainly from the principal groups represented in the pre-war wave of migrants. Notable in their migration were Hungarians, whose nation was subdivided to the extent that only one-third of its original territory was left intact by the post-war treaties. Also notable were Flemish Catholic Belgians, who ventured to the Red River basin of Manitoba, where Belgians were already settled, Saskatchewan, where a number of Belgian communities were planned, and southwestern Ontario, near Delhi, where there was ready employment in the tobacco industry (Jaenen 1991, 15).

With the end of the Second World War in 1945, Prime Minister William Lyon MacKenzie King implemented changes to Canada's immigration policy in response to the needs of the Canadian economy, which was making a transition from wartime production to peacetime consumer capitalism. Moreover, the Canadian government urgently sought to accommodate the homeless refugees of the European theatre of the war and the communist 'liberation' in eastern and central Europe. In 1947, King announced a policy that, while stressing that migration was to be determined by the Canadian government according to its economic needs and protective of its social fabric and complexion, Canada would be opening its borders to the 'displaced persons' ('DPs') of Europe (Whitaker 1991, 14–17). Commencing shortly thereafter, Canada began admitting displaced persons according to a strategy based on the economic needs of various regions of the country. Over the ensuing decade, Canada witnessed the arrival of thousands of newcomers, many of whom were Catholics. Slovenians, Croatians, Lithuanians, Hungarians, Poles, and Czechs were admitted from regions not only devastated by war, but now under the control of Communist governments under the eye of the USSR. One Slovenian refugee family, the Ambrozics, a family of seven children aged seven to nineteen, spent three years in a displaced persons camp in Austria before being granted permission to move to Canada (Coursellis and Ferrar 2005, 11, 33, 169). The eldest son, Aloysius, would study for the priesthood and, within forty years, become one of Canada's most powerful cardinal archbishops. The Ambrozics and other families like them were joined by increasing numbers of Italians, Germans, Austrians, and Dutch who were seeking new lives. As well, throughout the 1950s the Dutch Catholics, who had been previously discouraged by their priests and bishops from migrating to 'Protestant' Canada, left famine and war-ravaged Netherlands to carve out farms amongst the Canadians who had been their liberators from Nazi occupation (Ganzevoort 1999, 447).

Many displaced persons sought out churches as their most comforting reference points in a new and strange country, where many did not speak the language or were engaged in labour far beneath their level of skill. The story of Matilde Van de Pas was a case in point. Maltilde was born in Holland and raised in Germany, and in the 1930s she married the Baron de Eszenasyi, a convert from Judaism whose family had been awarded its title in 1411 from Sigismund, the Holy Roman emperor-elect. Matilde had worked as a translator and language tutor among the diplomatic corps in Madrid prior to the Spanish civil war. With the onset of hostilities, she and her husband were sought by Franco's police and they escaped from Spain on the last train out of Hakka. During the Second World War, she and her husband escaped the Nazi invasion of Belgium, where they had been living, and narrowly eluded execution in Vichy France. The baron was finally captured and, as a Jewish convert, was killed. At war's end, the baroness, a devoted and deeply prayerful Catholic, sought refuge in the church. Through its network, she was sponsored by Oblate priests in Winnipeg, who employed her as a domestic. Matilde had never done such menial tasks in her life, and she recalls scrubbing the floors of Winnipeg churches in her 'alligator shoes.'[5] For her, however, the church was a refuge and a reference point, and from Winnipeg she ventured to Ottawa where she joined the

German Canadians being ministered to by a University of Ottawa professor and Oblate priest, Clemens Stoick, a group that eventually formed St Albertus Pfarrgemeinde (McEvoy 1998, 162). Matilde then sought employment commensurate with her skill as a linguist in the Foreign Language Section of the Carleton University library. Although the details of her story and her personal background were unique, Matilde's experiences of fleeing a shattered Europe as a displaced person, her strong Catholicity, and her sense of being undervalued were shared by many displaced persons, regardless of ethnicity.

The openings made to displaced persons and the needs of a booming economy in the post-war period made Canada's need for labourers insatiable. In the 1950s Catholic Portuguese from the mainland, Madeira, and the Atlantic archipelago of the Azores, ventured to Canada by the thousands. In the 1950s, Portugal was one of the poorest countries in Europe and the close to 17,000 Portuguese in Canada sought manual work in construction and railways (Januario and Marujo 2000, 97; Teixeira 1999, 1076). By the early 1960s, these post-war Catholic immigrants would be augmented by the arrival of members of their extended families, a phenomenon made possible by changes in Canadian immigration law that allowed landed immigrants and citizens to sponsor the migration of family members. Such provisions made it possible for Toronto to become one of the largest Portuguese cities outside of Portugal, a size that would be augmented by the arrival of nearly 10,000 Portuguese-speaking Brazilians since 1960 (Shirley 1999, 275). Montreal and Vancouver also contained substantial Portuguese communities (Lavigne and Teixeira 2000, 175–90).

Two exceptional cases of post-war refugees admitted to Canada had implications for the Catholic Church. In 1956, the short-lived Hungarian revolution was brutally repressed by Soviet forces. In an act of solidarity with those who opposed the rule of Communism over their homeland, Canada admitted, in one year, an unprecedented 30,000 Hungarians (Dreiszinger 1999, 663), many of whom were professionals and clerical workers. This brief but significant wave of Hungarians differed significantly in education and profession from the Hungarian labourers and farmers who had preceded them to Canada. Their arrival placed increased pressure on existing Hungarian Catholic communities and prompted the formation of new ones (Patrias 1997, 26). Similarly, in August 1968 Soviet tanks rolled into Czechoslovakia, ending the 'Prague Spring,' which had attempted to liberalize and humanize a repressive Communist regime. Again, on both humani-

tarian grounds and for reasons germane to the Cold War between
the Western democracies and communism, Canada admitted 21,000
Czechs and Slovaks (Jovanovic 1999, 400), the majority of whom had
ties to the Catholic Church, even though their homeland was officially
atheist. As had been the case with earlier migrants from their region,
Czechs and Slovaks tended to cluster in the city of Toronto, where
employment opportunities appeared to be better than in other regions
of Canada and where there were significant communities of their fel-
lows already in place. Geo-political considerations behind Canadian
generosity are not to be overstated. In 1973, when Salvador Allende's
socialist government in Catholic Chile was overthrown and Allende
and his followers murdered, Canada was less inclined to open its doors
to 'leftist' refugees (Whittaker 1991, 21). Canada began to admit Chil-
ean refugees, some of whom were Catholic and some who claimed
their ethnicity as Spanish. By the early 1990s, there were nearly 23,000
Chileans settled in Canada, two-thirds of whom were in Ontario and
Quebec (Diaz 1999, 348–50).

The changes in Canadian immigration policy in 1947 did little to offset the discrimination and near exclusion of Asian migrants from Canada. Chinese migrants had been charged a head tax as a prerequisite to
their entry into Canada and from 1923 to 1947 they had been excluded
entirely. The racially motivated atrocities committed by the Nazis
during the war, in addition to changing attitudes towards race and culture, internationally, made exclusionary policies in immigration an
unsavoury proposition to many Canadians in the late twentieth century.
In the 1960s, the creation of a point system for immigrants opened up
the door to large numbers of migrants from the Caribbean, South Asia,
Latin America, China, and Southeast Asia. The liberalization of immigration policies, as assured by the Green Paper of the early 1970s and the
subsequent *Immigration Act* of 1978, provided the easier entry of people,
including Catholics, from Hong Kong, the People's Republic of China,
Hong Kong, the Philippines, Sri Lanka, India, Goa, Korea, and Vietnam.
For the Vietnamese, the refugee provisions of the immigration policy
amendments of the 1970s were welcome. By 1975, the U.S.-supported
regime in Saigon finally succumbed to Viet Cong guerrillas and the People's Army of North Vietnam. A large proportion of Vietnamese Catholics were among the 53,000 boat people who fled the new communist
regime and were admitted as refugees to Canada. By 1991, there were
close to 80,000 Vietnamese in Canada, of which 10–15 per cent were
Roman Catholics, who quickly adopted English as their language of

communication. Viet still served as their liturgical language, where priests of their own culture were available (Fay 2005c, 2–6).

By the late 1970s and early 1980s, as a result of shifting immigration policy, the ethnic and racial composition of the Catholic Church changed dramatically. New Catholic Canadians from Asia were fast becoming the majority among those migrating groups. Anglophone parishes in inner city Toronto, Hamilton, Calgary, Edmonton, and Ottawa were now receiving large numbers of Filipinos, Goans, Koreans, and Chinese Catholics. The Filipinos have been the most prominent of the Asian Catholics. Figures from the 2001 Census indicated that Filipino migration, which has been 82 per cent Catholic, has created a Catholic community some 270,000 strong (2001). As a group they have come to dominate three parishes in downtown Vancouver and five more in the suburbs of Richmond and Burnaby, to the extent that St Patrick's Parish of Vancouver boasts a population that is close to 70 per cent Filipino (Fay 2005a, 32). In Winnipeg, Filipinos account for more than half of the population in several western (Driedger 2003, 195) and north end parishes. In Toronto, the largest Filipino settlement in Canada, their population of nearly 115,000 has become a dominant group in many downtown and suburban parishes. At Our Lady of Lourdes, St Thomas More (Scarborough), and Our Lady of the Assumption parishes, Filipinos comprise 50 to 70 per cent of the membership (Fay 2005a, 46).

The changes in immigration laws in the 1970s, especially those regarding refugees, precipitated a marked increase in Spanish-speaking Catholics from Latin America. Although there was a relatively large Argentinean Catholic community in Ontario dating from the late 1950s, the migration of skilled workers and professionals from Argentina was notable after the fall of Juan Peron in 1976 and during the Malvinas (Falkland Islands) war of 1980 (Rues-Bazan 1999, 213). More representative of Latin American refugees were the largely Catholic migrants from Nicaragua who were fleeing civil war in the 1980s (Kowalchuk 1999b, 1009–10) and Salvadorans who fled their country under similar horrific circumstances throughout the 1980s and 1990s. Collectively, both groups accounted for about 25,000 migrants, of whom about 80 to 85 per cent were Roman Catholic (Kowalchuk 1999b, 1111). Like their Latin American co-religionists from Peru, Guatemala, Mexico, Ecuador, and Brazil, most have opted to live in Ontario, specifically Toronto (Philips 1999, 452; Shirley 1999, 275). Today, it comes as no surprise that Cardinal Matthew Aloysius Ambrozic of Toronto can claim that, on any given Sunday, the Mass will be celebrated in at least thirty-five different languages within the Greater Toronto Area.

The Changing Nature of Practice and Ideas

While the Roman Catholic Church is one of the oldest ecclesial communities in the Christian tradition, the beliefs, rituals, devotional practices, and moral life that would be witnessed in Canada actually date from the Council of Trent of the sixteenth century. In response to the Protestant Reformation, Catholic bishops and theologians met at Trent, in the Holy Roman Empire, for three sessions (1545, 1547, 1562–3), where they effectively demanded reforms to the disciplines of the church and reaffirmed its central beliefs. So-called Tridentine decrees confirmed Catholic belief in the divinity of Jesus Christ, in both his divine and human persons, the triune God of the Trinity (God the Father, God the Son, God the Holy Spirit), and the Holy Roman Catholic Church as the body and spotless bride of Christ in the world. The council fathers also reiterated that God could be known through both the scriptures (Old and New Testaments of the Bible) and through the living tradition of the church. Moreover, by reiterating the belief that one's salvation depended both on God's grace and on the works that flowed from it and prepared one for a faithful response to this grace, Catholics struck back at the Protestant principle that humans were saved by the grace of God alone. The council reaffirmed that the divine presence was also made tangible in seven sacraments: baptism, Eucharist, confirmation, penance, matrimony, holy orders, and extreme unction.

In terms of discipline and daily practice, the council set a template that would endure for 400 years, until 1965. The *ecclesia docens* (church that teaches) formed a distinctive hierarchical pyramid with the pope, the bishop of Rome, at the apex of the episcopal power structure, with the bishops and clergy forming the successive levels beneath him. The bishops and clergy were exclusively male and, in the Roman Church, celibate. Lower still on the pyramid were male and female religious orders, which shared common values of poverty, chastity, and obedience, although they took on a variety of charisms (gifts and tasks) – cloistered, mendicant, educational, as well as education, health, and social service orientations. At the base of this power structure sat the Catholic majority, the laity, or the *ecclesia discens* (discerning church). Laypersons were expected to attend the Mass weekly and on holy days of obligation, fast on prescribed days of the week, offer tithes (a portion of their earnings) to the church, and participate in myriad devotional practices, including the veneration of saints and the practice of private piety. Catholic leaders, both francophone and non-francophone, in the British and French colonies that became Canada, would have recognized the decrees and devotional practices of the Council of Trent as the blueprint of their faith tradition in the New World.

Modern readers assume that Canadians were always deeply pious and that we have become progressively less religious. However, most Canadian Catholics adopted the disciplines and creedal reformulations of Trent only during the so-called ultramontane[6] revival of the mid-nineteenth century. In the eighteenth and early nineteenth centuries, Catholicism had been practised unevenly on the frontier for a variety of reasons: the paucity of priests to administer the sacraments, the lack of distinctive Catholic nodes of population outside of urban areas, the inability of settlers in the anglophone colonies to build costly churches, and, in the case of several of the Atlantic colonies, the continued imposition of discriminatory legislation that excluded Catholics from openly practising their faith, pursuing the liberal professions, and – until the 1830s in Prince Edward Island, New Brunswick, Nova Scotia, and Newfoundland – from serving in public office (J.R. Miller 1993; Rollman 1987).

Even when Catholicism was accorded some liberty in public profile and practice, particularly in Upper Canada and the Eastern Townships and Ottawa Valley of Lower Canada, local priests were frustrated by their flocks. Mass attendance was irregular, parishioners in the early nineteenth century in most colonies insisted on the lay control of church properties through elected church wardens or trustees, and their tithes and pew rents were paid irregularly. Moreover, missionary priests on the frontiers outside of the well-settled St Lawrence Valley, where institutional Catholicism had been well established, discovered to their horror that Catholics routinely averted the canon laws of marriage by marrying Protestants in the presence of Protestant ministers or civil magistrates, by cohabiting with partners of their choice, by selecting partners who were considered minors, or by marrying cousins (McGowan 2005, 57–83). Without strong institutional and episcopal structures in most of the British colonies outside of Lower Canada (Quebec), the moral disciplines of the Council of Trent regarding marriage and sexual behaviour were essentially a dead letter.

Roman Catholicism in Canada would undergo significant change and renewal in the mid-nineteenth century with the spread of the European ultramontane revolution to Canada. This enthusiastic renewal of Catholicism had many faces, including the vision of an institutional church that would be the central focus of Catholic life (see chapter 3 by Solange Lefebvre). Such vigorous clericalism, often referred to by its detractors as 'papal aggression,' featured the church's imposition of its authority in the civil sphere, the reaffirmation of the power of the clergy and the pre-eminence of bishops, the renewed focus on the absolute authority of the pope in matters of faith and morals, which culminated in the declaration of papal infallibility by the first Vatican Council in 1870, and the creation of a sacred Catholic 'separate world' in education, marriage, communication, and social life that would defend the faithful in the face of dangers posed by the 'modern world.' This vision of a sanitized, sacred, and exclusive community was encapsulated by Bishop Ignace Bourget's profession: 'Let each of us say in his heart, I hear my curé [parish priest], my curé hears the bishop, the bishop hears the Pope, and the Pope hears Our Lord Jesus Christ' (Bourget 1876). Such aggressive clericalism was complemented by a renewed commitment to Catholic missionary endeavour, a revival in Catholic religious orders, and the development of myriad devotional practices and religious confraternities for the laity. For Canadian Catholics, regardless of language or region, their religious practice for a century or more before 1965 would be marked by a reverence for ecclesiastical authority, membership in a parallel Catholic social and symbolic universe, and the regular practice of personal piety marked by the saying of the rosary, praying novenas, and marking the rhythms of one's life by the distinctive Catholic calendar of feasts, saints' days, and holy days of obligation to attend the Mass.

The ultramontane devotional revolution drew Scots and Irish Catholic women into confraternities for service and prayer in an effort by the church to evangelize the home and make churchgoers of their husbands (Clarke 1993). By the turn of the twentieth century, Irish and Scottish Catholic regions of Canada were noted for their high church attendance relative to other religious denominations (Fourth Census of Canada 1901).[7] In English Canada, in the same period, Catholic dioceses looked less and less to Europe for their clergy as local men became 'homegrown priests' because they were able to attend local Canadian seminaries. Likewise, young women from Irish, Scottish, and German families soon swelled the ranks of women's religious orders, creating religious congregations and institutes in which the majority Canadian members were directed by Canadian women. By the time of the Great War most Canadian dioceses outside of Quebec and outside of the Northwest missions were under the authority of Canadian-born men of Celtic descent.

The mass migrations of Catholics from southern and eastern Europe from 1896 to 1914 and from 1921 to 1939 added a greater breadth to forms of worship that had been dominated by Irish, Scots, French, or German traditions. The thousands of Italians, Hungarians, Poles, Ruthenians/Ukrainians, Austrians, Maltese, Slovaks, and Czechs, among other Catholics, provided an even greater richness in worship – as well as numerous challenges for the Anglo-Celtic leadership of the Catholic Church outside of Quebec. Most of these new Catholic Canadians came with neither priests nor an understanding of the Canadian principle of voluntarism, which allowed for church independence from the control of the state, but which also demanded that the believers themselves, and not the state, build their own churches and provide for their own clergy. For many Catholics, the idea that in this new country they would have to build a church, make a request to the local anglophone bishop for a priest who could speak their language, and then sustain him through weekly collections during the Mass, was burdensome, given their lack of experience in such matters and their limited means as newly arrived migrants.

Initially, local French Canadian and Anglo-Celtic bishops assigned these Catholic newcomers to existing parishes, following the Catholic practice of attending the parish within whose geographic boundaries one found oneself. In Toronto, this meant that Poles, Ukrainians, Maltese, Lithuanians, Italians, and other groups in the early 1900s were channelled into Anglophone 'Irish' parishes. If available, local or itinerant priests who spoke the language of a given group would conduct special masses. Such circumstances were not always ideal: Poles attending St Mary's Parish complained that their services were disrupted by rude altar boys who scampered about corners of the church trying to get a glimpse of their 'strange' rites, while one itinerant priest who had travelled to Toronto from Berlin (Kitchener) alerted the local ordinary, Bishop Denis O'Connor, that what appeared to be a sham priest had been visiting the local Slavic communities and had been observed charging money for the sacraments and smoking while hearing confessions.[8] In Winnipeg, Archbishop Adelard Langevin had instructed Ruthenian migrants to attend Holy Spirit Church, the local Polish parish. Given the historical animosity between Poles and Ukrainians, the experiment resulted in the alienation of the Eastern Rite

Ukrainians from the local bishop (Hryniuk 1988, 24–5; Perin 1990, 173–4).

With the bicultural reality of Canadian Catholicism having created a tradition of cultural accommodation, the Canadian bishops quickly accommodated the canonical erection of national parishes in their dioceses. An extra incentive was the home missionary work of Canada's Protestant majority, which appeared to be highly motivated to convert and assimilate these new 'popish' Canadians in order to preserve the Canadian Protestant way of life and prevent the growth of Catholicism (Grant 1968; cf. Carlson-Cumbo 1993, 155–76). Such threats prompted these bishops and their episcopal colleagues to establish the Catholic Church Extension Society to ensure the provision of adequate parish facilities and multilingual priests for Catholic immigrants (McGowan 1984; Pautasso 1989).[9]

Thus, because of historical circumstances inherent to the Canadian church and threats from Protestants outside of Quebec, the evolution of the national parish in Canada in the twentieth century was relatively smooth. After the First World War, national parishes – for Italians, Slovenians, Germans, Slovaks, Poles, and Irish, for example – were a natural part of the Canadian Catholic landscape (Jakesova and Stolarik 1999, 1174).

The national parish became a sacred space in which the liturgical and devotional traditions of the Old World could be preserved, and where the broader cultural interests of the community could be served and nourished. Hungarians in Welland, Ontario, or Stockholm and Kaposvar, Saskatchewan, would feel free in their national parishes to celebrate their distinctive Easter customs and rites of passage. For Hungarian Catholics the baptism of a child was the significant rite of entry into not only the Christian faith but also the Hungarian community. Baptisms were marked by *mulatás*, or merry-making, in which the entire extended family and village community participated, with the mandatory keg of beer to facilitate celebration. Similarly, these parishes hosted *lakodalom*, or weddings, which were noted for six groomsmen, four matrons of honour, and sometimes several days of celebration (Kovacs 1982, 71–2). St Patrick's in Toronto, originally an Irish parish, would, by 1908, become the hub of Italian Catholic devotional life and cultural *feste* in the city, when Italian migrants assumed control of 'old St Patrick's' (Our Lady of Mount Carmel) and the Irish and Germans continued their worship in a new church built close to the old site (Zucchi 1988). In the century that followed, Our Lady of Mount Carmel witnessed the departure of the Italians, to be replaced by the Portuguese, then Korean, and finally Chinese communities. While there has been considerable debate on whether national parishes were simply a way station for assimilation or a means of preserving a cultural and spiritual heritage (Tomasi 1970; Vecoli 1969), there is little doubt that these new parishes created an institutionalized cultural mosaic within Canadian Catholicism well before multiculturalism became the official policy of the Canadian government. By 1941, on any given Sunday or feast day in most major Canadian cities and towns, one could witness a degree of Catholic cultural diversity scarcely imagined by the French, Irish, or Scots Catholics who had dominated the cultural landscape of the church for the previous 300 years. In eastern Ontario, northwest of Trenton, for example, Thomas Bata's Czech shoe factory workers, once having fled the Nazi invasion of Czechoslovakia, had created the village of Batawa (1939) where they formed a distinctive Czech Catholic mission amidst a sea of Irish Catholics and Anglo-Protestants (Jovanovic 1999, 400).

The practice of establishing national parishes and using them to foster ethnic distinctiveness did not change appreciably for other immigrant groups who were to follow the central and eastern Europeans. Portuguese migrants established national parishes in Vancouver and several central Canadian cities, and enlivened these sacred spaces and their neighbourhoods with their Azorean customs and special feast days dedicated to Our Lady of Fatima and 'Christ of Miracles' (Teixeira 1999, 1080). In the process of building their own parishes in the 1950s and 1960s, Lithuanian Catholics persisted amidst the alleged 'coldness' of Canadian bishops and the 'irksome' opinions of many host Canadians that they were little more than 'Polacks' (Danys 1986, 298–302). In Montreal, the Lithuanian parish began in a rat-infested 'old Irish hall' in Verdun where the resident priest slept with a bag over his head to keep the rodents from scampering across his face. The Lithuanians, most of whom were of limited means, having left most of their worldly goods behind as Soviet troops 'liberated' their homeland, did not move to better quarters until the archdiocese agreed to assist the congregation with a loan for a new church. For Slovenian refugees after the Second World War, the national parishes they established in Toronto, Hamilton, Winnipeg, and Montreal provided a hub for Slovenian life in Canada. According to Cvetka Kocjanac, 'Church represents traditional Slovene values and rituals and provides community support, as do Slovene schools, credit unions, scout groups, choirs and youth groups' (Kocjanac 1999, 1185).

Other groups experienced recreating life without the anchor of the national parish. For post-war Dutch Catholic immigrants, who never established significant settlement clusters in urban areas, there was neither significant incentive nor critical mass to establish their own separate parishes. Consequently Dutch Catholics gradually assimilated into anglophone parishes (Ganzevoort 1999, 447). Similarly, Flemish Catholics from Belgium, scattered throughout Canada, established only one national parish, Sacred Heart, in St Boniface, although for a time after 1927, Capuchin monks, from their small monastery near Blenheim, Ontario, ministered to Flemish tobacco workers (Jaenen 1999, 265–8).

The liturgical and institutional rhythms of Catholic life among these immigrant and charter groups (Celts and French) within the church remained relatively constant until the 1960s. In 1959, having been pope for less than a year, John XXIII announced that the Vatican City would host an ecumenical council, gathering together all the bishops and leading thinkers of the church to engage in *aggiornamento* or updating. Over three sessions, which took place in successive autumns from 1963 to 1965, the Second Vatican Council prepared, argued, and promulgated sixteen documents that would dramatically change the face of Catholicism in Canada and internationally.[10] According to the new dogmatic constitution of the church, *Lumen gentium*, the word *church* would be defined as the 'people of God' and not as the hierarchy, the institution, or the clergy. These people of God, by merit of their baptism, were considered co-responsible for being the body of Christ in the world, meaning, at least in theory, the ideal of the church as a pyramid of greater and lesser vocations was to be considered anachronistic. The council empowered laity to be active in the world, and through its new pastoral constitution, *Gaudium et Spes*, made a clarion call for social justice, service to all humanity, and protection of the dignity of each human person. The council set aside the church's hostility to the modern world, calling instead for dialogue. Similarly, in *Dignitatis humanae*, the church revised its relationship to the state, calling for autonomy of the state and politics from church control, the freedom of religion from the state, and the freedom of individual conscience in the face of coercion from either state or church. The council changed the church's approach to missiology (replacing proselytization with witnessing the faith), called for greater ecumenical dialogue between the Christian communities of the world, and formally advocated dialogue with non-Christians, particularly Jews and Muslims. The ultramontane church that had attempted so vigorously to protest and secure the faithful from the evils of the world was, in theory at least, dead.

For most people in the pew, these changes remained abstract. It was the liturgical reforms of the Second Vatican Council that would touch their lives most directly. The uniformity of Latin throughout the Roman Rite was replaced by allowance of the Mass to be celebrated in the vernacular languages of the faithful. The Tridentine Mass was altered in favour of a liturgy that emulated the celebrations of the early church when the faithful gathered around 'the table of the Lord.' The priest no longer consecrated bread and wine into the body and blood of Christ with his back to the congregation, leading them to God, while droning his Latin in hushed tones. Now he stood at an altar table, positioned more closely to the assembly, no longer separated by an altar rail, and pronounced the words of consecration in Tagalog (Filipino), Cantonese, English, Polish, Maltese, or the language of any other Catholic group. The liturgy of the word included readings from the Old Testament, Psalms, Pauline and Pastoral Epistles, and all four Gospels. Such changes in the lectionary denoted the council's call for Catholics to break open the scriptures more readily. Local conferences of bishops were charged with putting these changes into effect, in addition to determining the local feast days and holy days of obligation. For Canada's bishops, the challenge would be to implement these changes in the most multicultural ecclesial community on the planet (save for the United States) while maintaining unity and respecting diversity.

The changes prescribed by the council were challenges enough in the best of times; for the Canadian church they coincided with the mass infusion of new Catholic Canadians. Prior to the council, at least the Latin liturgy had formed a bond linking dozens of ethnic communities housed under the umbrella of Catholicism. With the infusion of thousands of Tamil, Filipino, Chinese, Korean, and Latin American Catholics into the mix, the challenge of maintaining unity amidst such diversity was daunting, to say the least. With Easter, Christmas, and New Year's Day (Feast of the Solemnity of the Blessed Virgin Mary) honoured as the only remaining days of obligation, those in the diverse ethnic congregations, national parishes, and cultural congregations who wished to preserve distinctive feast days for patron saints and national festivals would have to do so within a church that now appeared to have withdrawn the rather rigid scaffolding that had supported voluntary associations, sodalities (devotional associations), popular devotional life, and church practice. Moreover, as arrangements were made, blueprints drawn, and architectural designs put into play in response to the liturgical changes, individual congregations would now be challenged as to how their sacred spaces could retain a sense of their distinctive cultures. For example, for the German descendants living in Formosa and area it meant compromise: the retention of their carved high altar, side altars, and Germanic art, but the inclusion of a new 'front' altar; eight kilometres down the highway in Walkerton, Sacred Heart Parish's mixed congregation of Irish, German, French, and Scots descendants witnessed the painting over of their frescoes, the dismantling of the high and side altars, the removal of the communion rail, and whitewashing of statues. Changes could be predicated on the will of the local priest, the budget of an individual parish, the mandates of a local bishop, or, perhaps, the steely will of a large ethnic community to retain what it could in their sacred and 'national' space.

Newer Catholic communities adapted to the changes reasonably well, given that many had already experienced the vanguard of the council's liturgical and pastoral changes before leaving their homeland. In Latin American parishes, the sounds of steel guitars and local hymns resonated in churches in Toronto and rural areas where migrant workers from Mexico, Nicaragua, Guatamala, or El Salvador gathered to worship (Basok 2003). Filipino Catholics retained their distinctive feasts *sinahulo* (The Passion of Christ), *Santcruzen* (St Helen's search for the true cross), or *Todos dos Santos* (All Saints), but managed them, not in national parishes, but in community clusters within existing anglophone parishes where by merit of their numbers they soon came to dominate (Chen 1999, 510). In recent times, Filipino and Tamil Catholics have revived the Marian piety indigenous to their own regions, but muted in Canada since the Second Vatican Council (Fay 2004, 15). The Filipinos in Vancouver, Winnipeg, and Toronto have also been prominent in their embrace of such modern Catholic lay spiritual movements as *Cursillo*, Marriage Encounter, Engaged Encounter, and Charismatic Renewal, in addition to transplanting their own movements: 'Couples for Christ,' The Christian Life Program, and prayer groups called *Bukas Loob sa Divos* (Opening up to God) or BLD. Although these groups remain almost exclusively Filipino, in 1994 Couples for Christ was formally recognized by the Archdiocese of Vancouver and, within three years, the Christian Life Program had spread from BC to Filipino communities in Calgary and Edmonton (Fay 2005b, 34–6, 46–9).

Since the 1980s there have been significant signs that the worship and leadership of the Canadian Catholic Church outside of francophone

Figure 2.3. St John the Evangelist Church, Whitby, Ontario (ca. 1959), illustrates the mid-twentieth-century innovation in Catholic church architecture with its 'inverted hyperbolic parabola design' roof made entirely of poured concrete. (Photo: Archives of the Roman Catholic Archdiocese of Toronto)

Canada is passing from the hands of the Anglo-Celts. These changes go beyond the sheer numbers of Filipinos, Goans, Tamils, and Chinese occupying the pews of traditionally 'Irish' or anglophone parishes, or the erection of distinctive and massive Chinese and Korean parishes in Vancouver, Toronto, and Montreal (Fay 2005a, 9–11). In the 1960s, Remi De Roo, a Manitoba-born priest of Belgian ancestry, was appointed bishop of Victoria (McNally 1990); shortly thereafter, Anthony Marrocco became the first bishop of Italian ethnicity to be appointed for Ontario. His appointment as auxiliary bishop of Toronto set a precedent that appeared orchestrated both in recognition of the size of Catholic ethnic constituencies and the priestly talent that was emerging from these same communities. In 1984, Anthony Tonnos, a Catholic of Lebanese ancestry, was named bishop of Hamilton; Richard Grecco, an Italian Canadian, was made auxiliary bishop of London and then Toronto; similarly Basilian priest Ronald Fabbro, another Italian Canadian, was elected bishop of London. Perhaps the most significant appointment, however, came in 1986, when Aloysius Ambrozic, the Slovenian

'DP,' was named auxiliary bishop of Toronto. On 17 March 1990 (St Patrick's Day), a date whose significance was not lost on some Irish Canadian observers, Emmett Carter passed the archdiocese to Ambrozic, making him the most powerful cleric outside of Quebec, and virtually assuring him the 'red hat' worn by members of the College of Cardinals. The 'Hibernarchy' had been broken, and if the newly appointed bishops with names like Exner (emeritus Vancouver), Weisgerber (Winnipeg), Colli (Thunder Bay), De Angelis (Peterborough), Sabatini (emeritus Kamloops), Wiesner (Prince George), or Mancini (Halifax) are any indication, church leadership will come, more and more, to resemble the ethnic complexion of those who fill the pews.

Current Demographics

The following tables represent the current Roman Catholic population of Canada and its provinces, noting the exceptionality of Quebec where the majority of Catholics are francophone (see Solange Lefebvre's chapter 3 in this book). Assuming that the vast majority of francophones (defined here as those who gave French as their mother tongue in the 2001 Census) are at least nominally Catholic, they have been removed from the total Catholic population considered in this data to offer an estimate of Canada's non-francophone Catholics. This crude calculation reveals that almost half of Canada's Catholics are non-francophone; given that this figure does not exclude non-Catholic francophones and francophones of no religion, the figures in table 2.1 assume a very conservative estimate of non-francophone Catholics. The actual percentage is likely much higher.

Table 2.2 identifies the principal non-francophone ethnic groups and their estimated proportion of Catholics, based on indicators derived from the *Encyclopaedia of Canada's Peoples* (Magosci 1999). Although incomplete, because of the way that the Census reports on ethnic groups on these schedules of the 2001 Census, one can estimate the size of specific Catholic ethnic communities on the basis of the number of respondents who indicated 'single' ethnic identity, as opposed to mixed identity, which certainly adds a level of complexity, so typical of trying to define one's culture in a multicultural country.

The tables underscore the incredible diversity of non-francophone Catholics in Canada and the strength of Catholicism outside its traditional Quebec bastion. What the tables fail to relate is the preponderance of these Catholics in Canada's major cities and the weakening of Catholic numbers in rural areas to such an extent that in dioceses such

Table 2.1. Francophone and non-francophone Catholics in Canada, 2001

Region	Catholics	Francophones	Total non-francophone	(%)
Canada	12,936,905	8,703,325	4,233,580	32.7
Newfoundland	187,440	2,110	185,330	98.7
Nova Scotia	328,700	34,025	294,675	89.6
PEI	57,080	5,665	51,415	90.1
New Brunswick	386,050	236,665	149,385	38.7
Quebec	5,939,715	5,761,765	177,950	3.0
Ontario	3,911,760	485,630	3,426,130	87.6
Manitoba	323,690	44,340	279,350	86.3
Saskatchewan	305,390	17,775	287,615	94.2
Alberta	786,360	58,645	727,715	92.5
BC	675,320	54,400	620,920	91.9
Yukon	6,015	890	5,125	85.2
NWT	16,990	950	16,040	94.4
Nunavut	6,215	395	5,820	93.6

Table 2.2. Selected ethnic groups, 2001 Census

Ethnic group	Population	Percentage RC	Estimated number
Chinese	936,210	10	93,621
Dutch	316,220	76	240,220
Filipinos	266,140	80	219,912
Germans	705,600	50	352,800
Hungarians	91,800	67	61,506
Irish	496,865	50	248,482
Italians	726,275	90	653,648
Poles	260,415	90	234,374
Portuguese	252,835	90	227,552
Scots	607,235	20	121,446
Spaniards	66,545	90	59,891
Vietnamese	119,120	15	17,868
Total			2,531,132

as London (Ontario) or Pembroke (Ontario/Quebec) some priests are covering three parishes on any given Sunday.

Institutional Completeness and Community Organizations

'Sacred' institutional completeness was a prescription of the ultramontane church that sought to insulate Catholic life in a parallel world from the cradle to the grave. For many Catholic immigrant communities, the local bishop's establishment of a national parish facilitated this creation of a separate Catholic universe, while providing a necessary reinforcement for an immigrant community's cultural activity and often the focus of its social, business, and neighbourhood life. When speaking during the mass migrations of the early twentieth century, Monsignor Alfred E. Burke, president of the Catholic Church Extension Society of Canada, was adamant that the priest was 'the first necessity of the church' who could take an area dominated by 'degenerate men' and make it 'blossom like a rose' (Burke 1909, 80). Burke and his Extension Society were dedicated to building chapels for immigrant Catholic communities and recruiting priests who spoke their native languages. Preferences were given to priests recruited from Europe, although the Canadian Catholic Extension Society proposed that anglophone priests with additional linguistic skills were a suitable fallback plan (McGowan 1984). The latter was certainly not the ideal, since some ethnic groups did not entirely trust priests from the host French and Irish/ Scottish communities, for fear they might be assimilated by their pastors regardless of their multilingualism or, in the case of Ukrainian Catholics, 'Latinized' (McGowan 1988, 1991; see Myroslaw Tataryn's chapter 8 in this book).

In time, Catholic ethnic groups were served pastorally by members of their own ethnic communities. In the Canadian West, the Oblates of Mary Immaculate, whose French priests dominated the missions to the First Nations peoples, formed distinctive Canadian 'provinces' (jurisdictions) for its Polish apostolate in Manitoba and Alberta, while the German Oblates did the same with an eye to the German communities spread out across Saskatchewan (Matejko 1982, 56–7). In Saskatchewan, the work of the German Benedictines at the Abbey of St Peter at Muenster was so important that, in 1921, the Vatican created Canada's only abbot nullius, a case where the abbot would assume the powers and role of a bishop within the defined territories surrounding the monastery. Other religious orders became associated with their compatriots and expatriates: the Scalabrini Fathers and the Franciscans were noted for their work with the Italians; the Vincentians and Salesians served Slovenian parishes and missions; Augustinian priests worked with German communities in eastern Canada and established a seminary in Ottawa; Redemptorist priests served a multitude of communities in their own language, including the Irish of Quebec, Germans in Toronto and Waterloo, and Ukrainians on the prairies; Resurrectionists served

Poles and Germans; and priests of the Society of Jesus were incultur-
ated in several communities, including the Hungarian, Slovenian, Slovak, and German.

While 'ethnic priests' administered the sacraments and maintained
the canon law in parishes, it was women belonging to religious orders
who often commanded the network of services that radiated from the
parish into the community. In the nineteenth and early twentieth
centuries, the convent and religious life offered a viable alternative
to motherhood, spinsterhood, or wage labour for immigrant women
(Danelywicz 1987). And, generally speaking, 'women religious' outnumbered male priests and brothers two to one. Women from Irish
religious orders – The Presentation Sisters and Sisters of Mercy in
Newfoundland, the Sisters of Charity in Halifax and Saint John, and
the Congregation of the Sisters of St Joseph and the Loretto Sisters in
Ontario – created the template for establishing and teaching in parochial
schools, the creation of social services, and the provision of medical care
open to Catholics and non-Catholics (McGahan 1995; Norman 1999;
Smyth 1992). After 1900, new Catholic Canadians were served by
women of their own ethnicity, including the Felician Sisters among the
Poles, Servants of the Little Jesus with the Croatians, Carmelite Sisters of
the Divine Heart among the Italians, Sisters of Social Service among the
Hungarians, and Sisters of the Immaculate Conception among the
Lithuanians, just to name a few.

Later, as religious orders declined in numbers because of fewer
recruits, many of those priests serving ethnic communities have been
drawn from dioceses in their countries of origin. In Vancouver there are
five Filipino priests, for example, and in Calgary twelve, while in Toronto, the home of Canada's largest Filipino community, there are
twenty-seven Filipino priests serving mainly in geographic parishes.
This pattern of recruitment is replicated across many Canadian dioceses for Tamil, Korean, Viet, Chinese, African, and Latin American
parishes. The decline in priestly vocations within the Canadian Catholic Church as a whole has made greater demands on these Asian-born
priests. In smaller dioceses and those in more remote areas of Canada,
Asian-born priests have gone beyond the boundaries of their specific
ethnic communities in order to serve in geographic parishes because
there are not sufficient numbers of Canadian-born priests to accommodate all parishes. In the Northern Ontario town of Kenora in the Diocese of Thunder Bay, for example, the parish of St Louis at Keewatin is
served by a priest from India, and the larger and older parish of Our

Lady of the Portage is directed by two Filipino priests. Both parishes serve a mixed anglophone population and many First Nations peoples. In the Diocese of Thunder Bay, there are simply not enough vocations to the priesthood among those young men who were born and raised in a diocese that stretches from the shores of western Lake Superior to the Manitoba–Ontario border. Similarly, in the larger Diocese of Calgary, geographic parishes depend heavily on priests recruited from eastern Europe and southern and eastern Asia (*Canadian Catholic Church Directory 2005*, 447–53). While these receiving congregations are grateful for the services of a priest, parishioners often complain that 'foreign' priests do not understand 'Canadian ways' or local traditions, or that because these priests speak English as their second or third language their homilies are too difficult to understand.

Historically, the importance of the national parish and 'national' priest in community development and institutional completeness within Catholic communities cannot be underestimated. Irish Catholic communities were among the first in Canada to illustrate this symbiotic relationship between church, people, and neighbourhood. In Toronto, the first Irish settlers congregated close to their parish church of St Paul's, in neighbourhoods aptly named 'Corktown,' 'Slabtown,' and 'Cabbagetown' (named after the pungent aroma of the ghetto around suppertime) (Careless 1984; Nicolson 1983). Even though these neighbourhoods failed to last more than a generation, Irish Catholics established community associations, both devotional and social, that had strong connections with the parish. Throughout the city, the St Vincent de Paul Society, parish athletic clubs, the Holy Name Society, Catholic Boy Scouts and Cadets, Girl Guides, the Catholic Mutual Benefit Association, the Apostleship of Prayer, Knights of Columbus (by 1912), and the Catholic Women's League (by 1919) helped to create a parallel universe for Irish Catholics distinct from their Protestant neighbours who formed a majority in the city. Through these networks emanating from the parish, Irish immigrants and their descendents could pray together, buy life insurance, play sports and recreate, engage in charitable work, and pledge abstinence from 'the demon of drink.' These networks were augmented by distinctive Catholic social institutions – St Michael's Hospital, St Joseph's Orphanage, The House of Providence (for the poor), St Michael's College, and state-supported Catholic schools. By 1900, supported by a strong network of Catholic businesses, Catholic weekly newspapers, and philanthropists, Irish Catholic Torontonians had a strong sense of their own safe Catholic world in what they sometimes called the 'Belfast' of North America (Clarke 1993; McGowan 1999b).

These Anglo-Celts, however, may also have created a template for integration and eventually assimilation into the Canadian mainstream. Irish Catholics came to share both the economic aspirations and the patriotic sentiments of the English-speaking Protestant community around them. By 1920, Irish Catholics had left the unskilled and skilled labour categories of their forbearers in the previous century and now could be found within the most skilled blue collar and influential white collar occupations. With more secure incomes, they had left the inner city in droves and were buying their own homes in practically every neighbourhood in the city. Increased contact with Protestants on the shop floor, in public events, and in local neighbourhoods increased the possibility of mixed marriages. By the 1930s at least one in every three marriages blessed by the Catholic Church was between partners who did not share a common Catholic creed. By the 1960s, the old Irish Catholic community was dispersed throughout the city and now engaged in the ecumenical spirit of the Second Vatican Council – a far cry from the sectarian bitterness that had been prominent in Toronto just a century before. The behaviour of Canadian-born generations of Irish Catholics appeared to be motivated by an impulse to fit in while retaining the essentials of the faith. Their shared language helped facilitate this process, but in general the integration with the broader community suggests behaviour soon to be seen within other Catholic groups, once Canadian-born generations came to embrace not only the English language, but Canadian political, economic, and social values. This pattern of Irish acculturation to the Canadian mainstream was slower in areas such as Ottawa, Montreal, and New Brunswick, where, as a double minority – linguistically in their church and religiously in their society at large – they tended to hold on to the unique badge of Irish identity longer (Moir 1971).

In more isolated rural areas this sense of Catholic institutional completeness has been easier to retain. Historically the Germans of the Muenster settlement in Saskatchewan were able to retain a high degree of their ethno-religious identity. The rhythms of the community were set economically by the planting and harvesting cycles, and socially by the strong presence of the church and its German clergy at its helm. Moreover, German-speaking Ursuline Sisters (Lauer 1979, 93–5) directed the local school, which conducted classes in English according to the law, but with German instruction daily (White 1978, 98). Similarly, the local health care facility was operated by an Austrian order of the Sisters of St Elizabeth (Lauer 1979, 96), and the Benedictines attempted to raise educational levels of the local population while nurturing their cultural identity (Perin 1998, 9). In short, local social institutions reinforced a sense of German culture and Roman Catholicism. By the 1960s, however, this tightly knit community's sense of itself would change with the secularization of health care, laicization of Catholic teachers, rural out-migration, and the Anglicization of the Canadian-born generations, as evidenced by the emergence of the *Prairie Messenger* as a local Catholic weekly, now published in a manner that reflected its English-language audience. According to local historian Bede Hubbard, the colonists' original hopes of 'escaping the American melting pot failed' (1983, 163). In 1998, Pope John Paul II terminated the diocesan status of Muenster and it became part of the Diocese of Saskatoon.

While institutional completeness has been defined in a variety of ways, the historical pattern remains similar across Catholic groups in Canada. Despite tight and exclusive associational networks, newspapers, businesses, social relations, and political affiliations that might radiate from parishes, the second and third generations of these Catholic groups acquire the English language of necessity and slowly adopt the norms of the society outside of their distinctive cultural world. Public schools, popular culture, and the urge to migrate to hubs of social and economic activity hasten the process. Today, the Italians of Copper Cliff are remnants of what once was an institutionally complete community near Sudbury (Stefura 1983) and Filipino parents are already beginning to regret the 'disrespectful habits,' consumptive behaviour, and language choices of their children (Fay 2005b, 50). Intergenerational change is also witnessed in ethnic parishes themselves as masses in the native tongue become fewer and are replaced by masses in English in order to meet the linguistic demands and a sense of 'relevance' to a new generation emerging from their groups.

Social Location, Historical and Present

'Immigration and ethnic affiliation (or membership in a cultural group),' wrote renowned sociologist John Porter, 'have been important factors in the formation of social classes in Canada' (1965, 73). He added that analysis indicated that Roman Catholics, many of whom were ethnically distinct, were under-represented in the higher income groups he examined (100–2). Porter's analysis seemed to confirm that what Max Weber and R.H. Tawney had postulated for Europe – that Protestants were among the most progressive socially and economically, while Catholics were more 'otherworldy' and more readily identified with poorer areas of southern Europe – appeared to have some traction in Canada. In 1943, A.R.M. Lower had talked about Canada as comprising two nations, the progressive British on the one hand and the 'peasant-spiritual' and less enterprising French Canadians on the other, whose attitudes to enterprise and opportunity were deeply rooted in Catholicism's medievalism (Lower 1943, 14, 23). These academic analyses confirmed in the minds of some Protestants their suspicions that Catholics in Canada were the nation's hewers of wood and drawers of water.

The early history and occupations of Catholic migration to Canada would leave few to doubt Porter, Weber, Tawney, or Lower. By the 1830s, Irish Catholic lumber workers or 'shiners' had cultivated a reputation for crudeness, alcoholism, and the ability to beat their competitors senseless with their fists or whatever could be picked up, swung, or hurled (Cross 1973). In cities like Hamilton, Montreal, Halifax, or Toronto, Irish Catholics were perceived as unskilled labourers who sometimes had 'the lowest rates of upward economic mobility' (Fingard 1999, 38; Katz 1975, 165; Raddall 1950, 145).

More rigorous statistical analysis has indicated, however, that such perceptions had very little basis in reality after 1871. After Confederation, Irish Catholics in urban centres were clearly moving into white collar and skilled jobs, leaving the unskilled and semi-skilled work to new migrants to the cities (Darroch and Ornstein 1980; Di Matteo 1996; McGowan 1999b). Moreover, according to the work of Donald Akenson (1984), Irish Catholics were more likely to be found in rural areas, owning their own farms and proving themselves highly competitive with their Protestant neighbours. In this way they were little different occupationally from Kashub Catholic farmers in Renfrew County, the Germans of Formosa and area, or the Poles, Germans, and Hungarians who had carved out huge block settlements in the prairie west. In the twentieth century, while new Catholic migrants flocked to these rural areas – as was expected of those whom Interior Minister Clifford Sifton termed 'peasants in sheepskin coats' – most of the new arrivals from southern and eastern Europe flocked to Canadian cities and engaged in the rising Canadian industrial complex. Italian Catholics settled in two clusters in Sydney, Nova Scotia, and engaged in the steel industry and manual labour in the coal mines. Unskilled jobs for men and women were plentiful for their Calabrian, Sicilian, and Apulian cousins in Hamilton, Toronto, Montreal, Winnipeg, Sudbury, Sault Ste Marie, and North Bay. Sudbury became the catch basin for mine workers, railway labourers, and forestry workers. Since the area was one of the world's leading nickel producers, the urban conglomeration of Sudbury, Falconbridge, Coniston, Copper Cliff, and Ramsey became, and remains, Canada's most symmetrically multi-ethnic city: one-third francophone, one-third anglophone, and one-third allophone (Stefura 1983). An integral part of this complex were Catholics engaged in blue collar work. Many Italian and Maltese workers came originally as sojourners, discovering later that it would take much longer to 'make their fortunes' and therefore sending for their wives and extended families (Portelli 2001, 59–63).

The ability to find work was often facilitated by family members who had already migrated and were settled, or, in the case of the Italians, the influence of *padrones*. These local middlemen were situated within the Italian *colonia* and were engaged by local businesses or industry to conscript labourers as they arrived in Canada (Harney 1981; Zucchi 1988). At times the role of the *padrones* became much greater than employment agents since they could claim greater sway over those young men that they had assisted in finding employment. Within their Little Italies, women took in boarders, did piecework, managed one another's children, or became wage labourers in local factories in order to supplement the family income. Both Terry Copp (1974) and Michael Piva (1979) have argued persuasively that because of the decline in real wages in the first decades of the twentieth century, most family budgets could be maintained only if both adults and children had the opportunity to engage in wage work. Other women could elect to become sisters in a religious order, which became a rare pathway to professionalism in teaching, health care, social service, or administration. The last route placed Catholic women among Canada's CEOs who presided over hospitals, health care networks, school boards, colleges, and major charities (Smyth 1999, 234–54). Few laywomen of any denomination ever attained this status until the end of the twentieth century.

Occupational status differed among Catholic immigrants in the latter half of the twentieth century. Post-war Catholic migrants from Europe tended to be highly skilled. Displaced persons, both men and women, complained that their level of skill or professional status was undervalued by Canadians, who required them to engage in semi-skilled and unskilled tasks in the burgeoning post-war economy. In 1956, however,

Hungarian refugees, many of whom were Catholic, were treated differ-ently. One hundred Hungarian engineering students were relocated to the Faculty of Engineering at the University of Toronto, while 200 students and twenty-nine professors from the School of Forestry at the University of Sopron, in Hungary, were permitted to recreate an autonomous branch of their school at the University of British Columbia (Dreisziger 1982b, 207). In this same period, Italian Catholics were now rising to buy out and establish their own construction companies and were poised to become a force to be reckoned with in the building trades and real estate development in central Canada. More recently Goan Catholics, having arrived from west India and east Africa, have become prominent as judges, corporate executives, physicians, and lawyers. Commenting on the community's collective drive and skill, a fellow non-Catholic Indian commented, 'If ever there were a colony on Mars, Goan Christians would be among the first to go there' (Wagle 1999, 613).

More recently Filipino Catholics have continued the pattern of highly educated Catholics moving into the Canadian labour market. While the first waves of Filipinas, in the 1960s, consisted of domestic servants who were engaged either as day servants or live-in domestics in middle-class and upper-middle-class Canadian homes, subsequent waves have fared differently. Because of the enormous stress placed on men and women to acquire a university education in the Philippines, many of the new arrivals in Canada have one or more university degrees. Unfortunately, Canadian business and Canadian universities do not consider the education offered in these Filipino institutions to be on par with a Canadian education. Many well-educated Filipinos engage in domestic work, white collar jobs, and manual labour until they have recertified in their professions as doctors, dentists, engineers, and teachers, or they have taken additional university-level qualifications to meet Canadian standards (Chen 1999, 503; Fay 2005b).

The success story of the Filipinos, Hungarians, Italians, and Goans is not representative of all new Catholic Canadians. Ecuadorian immigrants have experienced significant 'domestic stress' that they claim results from the pressures for men and women to overwork to make ends meet (Phillips 1999, 453). Mexican migrant workers venture to Canada annually to work in the farms (both family-based and corporate), orchards, and other agro-industries in Canada. By means of special business contracts between the Canadian government and Mexican partners, these workers have no rights to Employment Insurance,

unionization, or immigration to Canada with their families. In l
ington, Ontario, Mexican men spend half the year away from their families tending to and harvesting the tomato crop for which the region is
famous. The local Catholic Church is one of their meeting places, but
should it be sensed by their Mexican agents or their employers that
they are attempting to organize with the purpose of asserting their
basic human rights as workers, they can be summarily dismissed and
returned to Mexico and condemned to subsistence living (Basok 2003).
It has been reported that some Mexican workers at Holland Marsh,
Ontario, are not even permitted to leave their large farm on their free
time. Currently, the Ontario Conference of Catholic Bishops, in partnership with other concerned citizens and representatives of the Hispanic
communities, are seeking redress for workers, mostly Catholic, who
live in Dickensian conditions. These church workers have received a
frosty reception from businessmen and farmers who consider migrant
labour a necessity because Canadians refuse to undertake this work.

Racism and Discrimination

Discrimination falls essentially into three broad categories: religious
discrimination pitting Protestants against Catholics; linguistic discrimination between francophone, anglophone, and allophone Catholics;
and racial discrimination between Catholic visible minorities and Protestant, Catholic, and other members of the host societies. There is some
overlap between these categories at times, but each in itself deserves
an essay on its own. Rivalry between Catholics and Protestants dated
from the Reformation of the sixteenth century. These sectarian tensions
were part of the baggage brought to Canada by French, Irish, and Scottish Catholics and English, German, Scottish, and Dutch Protestants.
Neither side trusted the religious minorities – be they Huguenot
French (Calvinist) or Celtic Catholic – that seem to threaten the peace
and stability of each kingdom, always suggesting that the loyalties of
the minority to the Crown might be in question. When the English formalized their conquest of Canada in 1763, the Protestant Crown demonstrated remarkable restraint in weeding out the large Catholic
population of Canada. Moreover, when the half-hearted attempts to
assimilate His Majesty's 'papist' subjects failed, the passage of the *Quebec Act* in 1774 provided Catholics in Canada with rights that were not
accorded to Catholic subjects elsewhere in the British Empire (Neatby
1969).

Although there was official toleration of Catholics in His Majesty's newly acquired colonies of Upper and Lower Canada, civil rights to Catholics in the Atlantic colonies were not accorded fully by the Crown until the 1830s. By the mid-nineteenth century the civil rights and toleration accorded to Catholics did not easily translate into public toleration. The combination of the rise of Catholic ultramontanism in Europe (referred to as 'papal aggression' by many Protestants), the dysfunctional parliament in the United Province of Canada (1841–67) in which French Canadian Catholics were perceived to have an undue amount of influence, the re-establishment of the Catholic Church in the United Kingdom, the transplanted hatred between Irish Catholics ('the Green,' after the colour of Ireland) and Protestants ('the Orange,' after King William III of Orange, defender of Protestant rights), and the nagging issue of state support for separate Catholic schools pitted Catholic against Protestant in Canada. From the latter's perspective, one need only be reminded of Catholic 'superstition,' the 'priest-ridden' character of Catholic life, and the alleged supreme Catholic loyalty to the pope over everything else, to conjecture that the Catholic presence in Canada endangered liberty, freedom of conscience, progress, and the advance of enlightened British values and governance. For these reasons, sectarian violence erupted in St John's, Halifax, Saint John and Woodstock in New Brunswick, Montreal, Toronto, and other Ontario towns. This atmosphere of fear and the ethos of sectarian hatred, although often exaggerated in popular and historical accounts, helped, in the popular Catholic mind, to reinforce the boundaries between the two religions, thus buttressing the aforementioned parallel Catholic social universe in nineteenth-century Canada (Johnston 1984, 146–63; J.R. Miller 1993, 25–48; Moir 1993, 327; Smith 1963).

Ironically the growing awareness of Celtic Catholics themselves as anglophone Canadians in the 'greatest empire that has been' coincided in the early twentieth century with the mass arrival of European Catholic immigrants whose customs seemed as foreign to Irish and Scottish Catholics as they did to Canada's Protestants. While there were periodic flare-ups of Catholic–Protestant tension, when the latter often felt that the principle of 'equal rights for all, special privileges for none' (J.W. Miller 1978) was violated by state concessions to Catholic schools, Catholic assertion of the canon law over civil law, or ostentatious Catholic behaviour in 'Protestant streets' by means of parades and processions, the two sides discovered they had more in common than they thought. This was particularly true of anglophones who fought two world wars for Canada and Britain side by side, Protestant and Catholic. While inflammatory demagogues like the Baptist minister Thomas T. Shields of Toronto continued to rail against 'popery' in Canada, targeting such events as Ottawa's International Marian Congress in 1947, most Protestants had moved on.[11] In the wake of the Second Vatican Council, an ecumenical spirit spread across Canada. A cover of the *United Church Observer* even featured a photo of Pope John XXIII, hailing the Second Vatican Council reforms afoot in Rome (Moir 1993).

Each group living outside of Quebec has discovered that second and third generations are falling away either to an exclusive use of the English language or, worse, to the secular habits of a consumerist-capitalist and post-enlightenment culture in Canada. In 2006, Pope Benedict XVI cautioned the Canadian bishops about the growing secularism in Canada that he claimed was directly responsible for the closing of churches, the drop in Canada's birthrate, and a culture that is increasingly inimical to Christianity (Vatican Information Service 2006). Not even waves of new Catholic Canadians could halt the restructuring plans in many Canadian dioceses that witnessed the closure of churches and the amalgamation of parishes for lack of recruits to the priesthood.

Historically, new Catholic Canadians have also felt the sting of the slang that belittled them – 'dago,' 'pollack,' 'kraut,' 'bohunk,' 'DP' – because of their fractured English, their clustering in low-paying jobs, or parading customs and traditions that differed from those of Anglo-Celtic Canadians with whom they shared Canada's urban landscape. The discrimination meted out to displaced persons is a case in point. Highly skilled and professional Europeans were forced into menial work as a condition of their arrival and were left unappreciated and undervalued by Canadians who had 'welcomed' them. More recent Catholic immigrants from Asia have experienced discrimination based on race and colour. Highly skilled Filipinos living in the Greater Toronto Area have been queried by neighbours to explain how they can afford large homes and fine automobiles, as if dark-skinned Asians could not possibly possess the skills required by engineers, doctors, and lawyers (Fay 2005b). While such ignorant behaviour does not constitute a 'Catholic' problem per se, it reveals the struggle of Tamil, Filipino, Chinese, Goan, and Korean Catholics to break through stereotypes that would ghettoize them as capable merely of driving cabs, running convenience stores, becoming niche restaurant owners or laundry managers, or engaging in domestic service.

Challenges to the Church

While the Canadian Census continues to place Roman Catholicism as the largest Christian denomination, such statistics simply mask the numerical losses of the church, which have been offset in the short term by the influx of new Catholics from Asia and Latin America. Moreover, the statistics hide the incongruity between those who practise and those who still claim affiliation to the church for a variety of reasons: cultural attachment, the desire for rites of passage, or other more mysterious reasons (Bibby 2002, 46–8). The stark realities of these changes in membership and involvement, however, are evident. Suburbanization and rural depopulation have forced the closure of both inner city parishes in some dioceses and parishes in rural areas (Bibby 1987, 16–21). The dramatic decline in vocations for the priesthood among Canadian men has led to the importation of priests from abroad or the combining of parishes together to be served by one priest. The latter practice places enormous stress on older men who knew times when every parish had its own resident pastor and city parishes were served by a team of priests. Those days are gone. In the largely anglophone county of Pontiac, Quebec, one priest now serves congregations in Bristol, Quyon, and Bryson, a driving distance of thirty kilometres from one extreme to the other. A decade ago, each had its own priest.

The church faces more than just a numbers crisis. Among its own members, its youth, and with the public at large it faces a huge crisis of credibility. Scandals over the sexual and physical abuse of students in Newfoundland shook the local church to its foundations, forced its archbishop to resign, and sent shockwaves through the entire Canadian church. The abuse of young boys by the Christian Brothers at Mount Cashel Orphanage and other such scandals horrified and disgusted Catholics and non-Catholics alike. Slowly, local variations of these scandals came to the surface across the country, from BC to Nova Scotia. In 2005, the bishop of St George's, Newfoundland, was forced to place church properties on the open market so that the Episcopal Corporation could pay off the financial liabilities incurred by the sordid behaviour of one local priest. Figures of trust and authority have fallen. Trust in church leadership is low.

Such scandal is complicated by the debate that percolates over the Catholic Church's positions on social and ethical issues. Many young Catholics ask why women are not accorded equality, particularly in their access to the priesthood. Moreover, they ask how, if the church values the dignity of each human person and working for the common good, can the church stand back when the environment is degraded by rapacious corporations, workers are accorded less than the dignity they deserve in a globalized economy, and the gap between the developed world and the developing world grows wider by the day? Increasingly, Catholics are divided over social issues and ethical issues like abortion, euthanasia, same-sex marriage, birth control, premarital sex, and sexual diversity (Bibby 1987, 154–7). According to Catholic education specialist Father James Mulligan, in the battle between secular, consumer, and individualist culture and Gospel values, 'Quite frankly ... the culture is winning' (Mulligan 2005, 10). The greatest challenge to Catholics – of all ethnicities – may be to define clearly where the church should position itself in relationship to the seemingly unstoppable secularization and commercialization of Canadian society.

Second, Third, and Subsequent Generations

As I have already mentioned, the 'migrating generation' of many communities has expressed concern over whether their children and grandchildren will retain their historical language, their unique traditions, their folk culture, and their faith. Lithuanian elders, who for so long regarded endogamous marriage as a safeguard of faith and culture, have since the 1970s witnessed an increase in 'mixed' marriages (Danys 1986, 319), a factor that may be contributing to the dwindling attendance of youth at Sunday Mass (Danys 1999, 937). This latter phenomenon is likely due to the factor Danys suggests, as well as to the loss of the linguistic skills to participate fully in Lithuanian liturgy, hence alienation from religious ritual, and the general movement of younger Catholic Canadians away from the institutional church. Filipino Catholics have also expressed concern over the manner in which their children are conforming to the culture norms of Canada – social attitudes, dress, treatment of elders, and laxity in traditional values (Chen 1999, 507; Fay 2005b, 59). Similar fears of children falling away from the church or being assimilated into anglophone Canadian popular culture have been heard from the Spanish, Belgian, German, and Czech communities among others (Cazorla and Shubert 1999, 1216).

However, not all communities are necessarily pessimistic about second- and third-generation members retaining their culture and faith, or declining numbers, for that matter. Chinese Catholic churches in the Toronto area are actually growing as adults, both young and old, are appearing at Rite of Christian Initiation for Adults (RCIA) classes. Since 2000, in the Archdiocese of Toronto, average RCIA classes per parish can have up to about eighty-nine prospective converts; the Chinese Martyrs Parish boasts 500 neophytes per year and five times the annual average number of baptisms per parish in the archdiocese (Fay 2003, 84–5). Across town, at Our Lady of Mount Carmel Parish, there is a more modest group of 120 neophytes divided into four classes, two for Mandarin-speakers, two for Cantonese. In each parish, the Chinese congregations comprise Canadian-born Chinese, both Catholic and converts, Hong Kong and Taiwanese Chinese, Chinese immigrants from the 'official' Catholic Church in the People's Republic, and those Chinese from the underground Catholic Church in the PRC, which is in communion with the Holy See (Fay 2003, 85). In Richmond, BC, at Canadian Martyrs Parish, the RCIA program has 40 neophytes annually and sixty baptisms total per year (Fay 2005a, 11). Elsewhere in Richmond, at Corpus Christi Parish there are a remarkable four *presidia* (groups) of the devotional association the Legion of Mary. In most geographical parishes, the legion usually has only one group, usually comprising a handful of older parishioners. In Richmond, however, there is one in Mandarin, two in Cantonese, and one for Cantonese youth (Fay 2005a, 11).

The story is, perhaps, more mixed among Portuguese Catholic Canadians. On the one hand, the Portuguese in urban Canada can claim a remarkable level of institutional completeness with more than forty churches, close to 200 social and cultural institutions, and thousands of businesses. However, the principal Portuguese communities in Vancouver, Toronto, and Montreal are visibly concentrated in specific neighbourhoods where these associations, services, and shops thrive (Teixeira 1999, 1076). Places like Sousa's Restaurant, at Nassau Street and Bellevue Avenue in Toronto, became the hub of the community and a self-acknowledged 'family home for the Portuguese' (Marques and Medeiros 1984, 155). In Montreal, Portuguese immigrants, from the 1950s to the present, 'seized the opportunity to be architects of an urban space of their own' (Lavigne and Teixeira 2000, 187) by buying homes (both first and second residences) in the same quarter bounded by Avenue du Parc, Rosemount Boulevard, Rue St-Denis, and Boulevard Rene Levesque. Nevertheless, there are concerns that second- and third-generation Portuguese are not embracing all that the faith and culture entail. Many youth are avoiding membership in either faith or community associations – institutions that tended to reinforce the domesticity of

Portuguese women and were, in most cases, exclusively male in leadership (Teixeira 1999, 1077–81). Moreover, in Montreal, second-generation Azoreans embrace either English or French as their first language and have no inclination to return to the Azores. While Azoreans comprise 60 per cent of Portuguese immigrants, these trends among the youth signal a speedy demise of the traditional Azorean form of Portuguese life (Teixeira and da Rosa 2000, 201–2).

Political Muscle

In nineteenth- and early-twentieth-century Canada, few prime ministers would form a Cabinet without representation from the anglophone Catholic community. From 1867 to 1891, in the federal Parliament, Conservative John A. Macdonald maintained an eye on Irish Catholics through the agencies of Thomas D'Arcy McGee (Montreal), John Costigan (New Brunswick), or Frank Smith (Toronto). Wilfrid Laurier, Robert Borden, and William Lyon MacKenzie King maintained the tradition. It was a vestige of constituency politics and quid pro quo: the individual would pull in the vote from his constituency and expected fair treatment, if not better, from the government in return. Such characteristic ethnic politicking was not unusual at all levels of government, depending on the concentration of Catholics in any neighbourhood, county, or city, or on the agency of the Catholic community itself, which asserted its presence politically in order to secure favourable results on specific questions – often concerning schools.

The secularization of Canadian society, the multiplicity of ethnic communities – Catholic and non-Catholic – and the many new concerns taken into consideration in forming a Cabinet today have changed the presence of anglophone Catholics as 'Catholic' representatives. The old Irish constituents are spread thinly across the country, except in concentrations such as eastern Newfoundland where Irish Catholics still support Conservatives, harkening back to the Catholic opposition to Confederation in 1949 and its Liberal supporters (Fitz-Gerald 1999). Catholicism has come to be a transparent characteristic of Canadian politics. Six of the last eight prime ministers have been practising Catholics – Pierre Trudeau, John Turner, Joe Clark, Brian Mulroney, Jean Chretien, and Paul Martin Jr – but if one were to assess the connection between their legislative habits and their faith, one might not recognize much overt Catholicity in their policies (see chapter 11). Trudeau, a Jesuit-trained and deeply spiritual Catholic (English, Gwyn, and Lackenbauer, 2004) ushered in legislation to liberalize laws on abortion and homosexuality; Clark was openly pro-choice on matters of abortion; Mulroney's fiscal policies lacked any sense of the basic principles of Catholic social teaching; and, in 2005, Martin oversaw legislation to permit same-sex marriage in Canada, despite the public opposition of several Canadian bishops. In Canada, the privatization of religion has been evident most clearly in the public behaviour of Catholic politicians. Catholic politicians claim they should not impose their personal religious views on legislation that serves a multi-religious, multicultural, and ideologically pluralistic Canada (see chapter 11).

Catholic political candidates are identified less by their Catholicity than, perhaps, the cultural group from which they are elected. Non-francophone Catholics have emerged as new political players but not necessarily as 'Catholic' candidates. Italian Catholics on the island of Montreal have become a mainstay of the Liberal Party in federal and provincial elections, but also in referenda on sovereignty. Having narrowly lost the referendum of 1995, Quebec Premier Jacques Parizeau blamed the defeat on 'business and the ethnic vote.' Montreal Italians, among other groups, needed little persuasion to assume that he referred to them – not necessarily as Catholics, but as 'ethnics' and not Quebecois of *pur laine*. In 1988, Ray Pagtakhan, of Winnipeg North, became the first Filipino elected to the federal Parliament and the first appointed to Cabinet. His Catholicism had little to do with either appointment. The same might be said of Senator Frank Mahovlich (Croatian Catholic), Peter Kormos, MPP Ontario (Slovak Catholic), Paul Szabo, MP (Slovak Catholic), or Sergio Marchi, MP (Italian/ Argentinean Catholic). As each Catholic ethnic group roots itself in Canada, some members of that group will venture into the political arena. Whether their ethnicity or Catholicity will determine their election will very much depend on the issues at hand, the concentration of members of their own ethnic group in the constituency, and the needs of political parties and governments seeking to build alliances with specific groups of Canadians.

Conclusion

The ongoing challenge of Catholic ethnic groups to stake out a place within the Canadian Roman Catholic Church, while resisting the temptations of an increasingly secularized Canadian mainstream, is evident, in microcosm, at Canada's largest Catholic University. Situated in the heart of Toronto, the University of St Michael's College was founded in

1852 by Irish and French members of the Congregation of St Basil, whose mission it was to 'teach goodness, discipline, and knowledge,' to boys of Irish, Canadian, and American backgrounds. Today 'St Mike's' is responsible for the education of nearly 4,500 students registered in the University of Toronto's Faculty of Arts and Science. Approximately 60 per cent of these young men and women are Roman Catholic or from the Eastern Rites of the Church (see chapter 8) and many have graduated from Ontario's fully funded Catholic school system. At the annual June convocation, one can hear the names – Wojtowicz, Soares, Pangalilingam, Ljahovic, Busato, Wong, and McAuliffe – as college graduates receive their degrees from the University of Toronto. These names, among others, identify those students who form the warp and woof of student life: chaplaincy, choir, the 'Out of the Cold' program for the homeless, and ethnic student clubs. The last five student union presidents have been, in turn, Filipino, Spanish, Portuguese, German, and Iranian (Muslim). The language of everything at the college is English, though the Irish Catholic founding presence is evident only in the names etched in stained glass, a few retired faculty, and the Celtic Studies Program, which caters to a large number of students from outside of the college. As principal of the college, I recognize that it is these children and grandchildren of Catholic immigrants that sustain and nurture the Catholic life at St Mike's.

While St Michael's, as an institution of higher education, is renewed by new waves of Catholic ethnic groups, so too is the Catholic Church in Canada, broadly speaking. Moreover, just as the Catholic Church, in its mission 'to be in the world, yet not of the world,' walks the tightrope within a Canada where one's worship and religious views have become increasingly relegated to the private sphere, so too these students and their teachers encounter the tensions of being members of a Catholic college in Canada's largest secular teaching and research university. Issues of gay rights, abortion, euthanasia, assisted suicide, birth control, laissez-faire capitalism, the Da Vinci Code 'conspiracy,' or business ethics have sometimes created tensions between student leaders at St Michael's and the rest of the university. In an environment grounded in 'academic freedom,' these students, drawn as they are from a variety of backgrounds, advance Catholic perspectives on these and other issues in a fashion similar to that of their Irish and French forebears who, generations ago, advanced positions on human sexuality, coeducational residences, conscription, loyalty, eugenics, or 'the bomb.' This time-tested struggle for Catholics, once with Protestants and now with agents of secularization and consumerism, play themselves out on

Catholic campuses, in national Catholic organizations, and in parishes from coast to coast, in large urban centres like Vancouver and tiny villages such as Formosa.

In December, the valley in which Formosa sits nestled is blanketed with as much snow as Lake Huron can provide. Immaculate Conception Parish, where my grandfather was baptized, still towers over the village, which has changed considerably. The brewery has been revived but is owned by a corporation in Waterloo. The population is stable, but there are many more bedroom residents who spend the better part of the day at the Douglas Point nuclear facility. There are 600 parishioners who can choose from three English-language masses on a weekend, all of which will be celebrated by their Maltese Canadian priest. In one sense, this tiny hamlet in southwestern Ontario presents a case for the diversity of the Canadian church and, perhaps, a long-term prospectus of the character of Catholicism in English-speaking Canada. As Canadian society changes, and as generations of Canadian-born Catholics are offered more choices of places to live, occupations to pursue, dreams to follow, and values to embrace, perhaps the face of most individual parishes will look more and more like the multicultural place Canada has elected to be. One can only speculate on who will be in the pulpit and how many persons will be in those pews to imbibe this experience.

Notes

1 Eighth General Report of the Colonial Land and Emigration Commissioners, June 1848 (London, William Clewes and Sons, 1848, reel 1746: 15–17, CO 384/382, Colonial Office Records, Library and Archives Canada). The total emigration from British ports for 1847 was 106,812, although the commissioners reported that approximately 90,000 arrived at Quebec, 6 out of 7 of whom were Irish. When added to the 17,000 headed to New Brunswick and the 2,000 to Nova Scotia, the figure is close to 100,000 (97,492 to be exact).

2 Archbishop John Joseph Lynch, as reported in the *Irish Canadian*, 22 March 1871. See also Nicolson (1983).

3 Specifically William Fraser in Nova Scotia, who presided over both the Irish of Halifax and the Scots of eastern Nova Scotia and Cape Breton (Johnson 1971); Angus MacEachern, who governed multicultural Catholic communities in New Brunswick, PEI, and the Magdalen Islands (MacDonald 1987,

53–67); and Alexander Macdonell, who, from his base of operations among the Scots in Glengarry County, was responsible for all of Upper Canada and the upper Great Lakes (Bumsted 1993, 92–4; Rea 1974).

4 While these mid-nineteenth-century Catholic migrants tended to form strong community networks, the migration of single males cannot be underestimated. George Giesler, for example, left Biberach-an-der-Reiss in Wurttemberg, in the early 1850s in order to avoid military service. He was joined at Le Havre, France, by travelling companions Joseph Reichenbach, a fellow German Catholic, and Andrew Cuneo, an Italian (Canadian Census 1871). On board ship, Giesler learned the butchering trade – a skill he would soon ply among the farmers adjacent to the Upper Canadian village of Formosa, Carrick Township, Bruce County. When the three arrived at the port of New York, they elected to leave the United States, persuaded by the incentive of cheap land in Upper Canada. Over 150 years later, descendents of these three itinerant labourers still live in the town of Walkerton and its surrounding townships of Brant, Carrick, Culross, and Greenock, and share family legacies that included farming, small business, and law (Albert Giesler, interview with author, 1989).

5 Matilde Van De Pas de Goldis, Baroness Eszenasyi, interview with author, July 1984.

6 Literally *ultramontane* means 'over the mountains' and was coined in the Middle Ages to designate those Catholics who looked to the pope in Rome as their principal focus of loyalty. In the nineteenth century, ultramontane Catholics looked to Rome for stability, order, sensibility, and moral authority in a quickly changing world of competing 'isms.'

7 See vol. 1, table 8, 144–5; table 9, 146–53; table 11, 284–405; table 12, 406–13; crosstabulated with vol. 4, table 19, 361–95.

8 Father J. Schweitzer, CR, to O'Connor, 12 April 1907, Archbishop Denis O'Connor Papers, Archives of the Roman Catholic Archdiocese of Toronto (ARCAT).

9 In 1999, it was renamed Catholic Missions in Canada. See Catholic Missions in Canada (n.d.).

10 The documents varied in terms of authority. The Constitutions of the Council (The Dogmatic Constitution of the Church [*Lumen gentium*], the Pastoral Constitution on the Church and the Modern World [*Gaudium et spes*]; the Constitution on Divine Revelation [*Dei verbum*]; The Constitution on Sacred Liturgy [*Sacrosanctum concilium*]) are considered to be of higher authority than the 'declarations' and the 'decrees' of the Council.

11 *The Gospel Witness*, 8 May 1947.

94   Mark G. McGowan

Works Cited

Akenson, Donald H. 1984. *The Irish in Ontario: A study in rural history.* Montreal and Kingston: McGill-Queen's University Press.

Barkham, Selma. 1982. The documentary evidence for Basque whaling ships in the Strait of Belle Isle. In *Early European settlement and exploration in Atlantic Canada: Selected papers*, ed. G.M. Story, 53–95. St John's: Memorial University of Newfoundland.

Basok, Tanya. 2003. *Tortillas and tomatoes: Transmigrant Mexican harvesters in Canada.* Montreal and Kingston: McGill-Queen's University Press.

Bennett, Carol. 1987. *Peter Robinson's settlers.* Renfrew, ON: Juniper Books.

Bibby, Reginald. 1987. *Fragmented gods: The poverty and potential of religion in Canada.* Toronto: Irwin.

– 2002. *Restless gods: The renaissance of religion in Canada.* Toronto: Stoddart.

Bramadat, Paul, and David Seljak, eds. 2005. *Religion and ethnicity in Canada.* Toronto: Pearson Longman.

Brown, R. Craig, and Ramsay Cook. 1974. *Canada, 1896–1921: A nation transformed.* Toronto: McClelland and Stewart.

Bourget, Ignace. 1876. *Mandements de Montreal.* Vol. 8, *Bourget's Circular*, s. 8, 299, 1 February.

Bumsted, J.M. 1981. Scottish emigration to the Maritimes, 1770–1815: A new look at an old theme. *Acadiensis* 10:65–85.

– 1993. Scottish Catholicism in Canada, 1770–1830. In *Creed and culture: The place of English-speaking Catholics in Canadian society, 1750–1930*, ed. Terrence Murphy and Gerald Stortz, 79–99. Montreal and Kingston: McGill-Queen's University Press.

Burke, Alfred Edmund. 1909. The need of a missionary college. In *The First American Catholic Missionary Congress*, 77–84. Chicago: Hyland.

Byrne, Cyril, and Terrence Murphy, eds. 1987. *Religion and identity: The experience of Irish and Scottish Catholics in Atlantic Canada.* St John's: Jesperson.

Canadian Catholic Church Directory 2005. 2004. Montreal: Novalis.

Careless, J.M.S. 1984. The emergence of Cabbagetown in Victorian Toronto. In *Gathering place: Peoples and neighbourhoods of Toronto, 1834–1945*, ed. Robert Harney, 25–6. Toronto: Multicultural History Society of Ontario.

Carlson-Cumbo, Enrico. 1993. Impediments to the harvest: The limitations of Methodist proselytization of Toronto's Italian immigrants, 1905–1925. In McGowan and Clarke 1993, 155–75.

Catholic Missions in Canada. n.d. Our history. http://www.cmic.info/index.php?option=com_content&view=article&id=44&Itemid=86.

Cazorla, Antonio, and Adrien Shubert. 1999. Spaniards. In Magosci 1999, 1208–18.

Chen, Anita Beltran Chen. 1999. Filipinos. In Magosci 1999, 501–13.

Choquette, Robert. 1990. *De la crise à la concorde*. Ottawa: Editions L'Interligne.

Clarke, Brian P. 1993. *Piety and nationalism: Lay voluntary associations and the creation of an Irish-Catholic community in Toronto, 1850–1895*. Montreal and Kingston: McGill-Queen's University Press.

Copp, Terry. 1974. *The anatomy of poverty: The condition of the working class in Montreal, 1897–1929*. Toronto: McClelland and Stewart.

Coursellis, John, and Marcus Ferrar. 2005. *Slovenia 1945: Memories of death and survival after World War II*. New York: Tauris.

Cross, Michael S. 1973. The Shiners' war: Social violence in the Ottawa Valley in the 1830s. *Canadian Historical Review* 5:1–26.

Danelywicz, Marta. 1987. *Taking the veil: An alternative to marriage, motherhood, and spinsterhood in Quebec, 1840–1920*. Toronto: McClelland and Stewart.

Danys, Milda. 1986. *DP: Lithuanian immigration to Canada after the Second World War*. Toronto: Multicultural History Society of Ontario.

– 1999. Lithuanians. In Magosci 1999, 929–1038.

Darroch, Gordon, and Michael Ornstein. 1980. Ethnicity and occupational structure in Canada in 1871: The vertical mosaic in historical perspective. *Canadian Historical Review* 61:305–33.

Diaz, Harry. 1999. Chileans. In Magosci 1999, 374–454.

Di Matteo, Livio. 1996. The wealth of the Irish in nineteenth-century Ontario. *Social Science History* 20:209–34.

Dreidger, Leo. 2003. *Race and ethnicity: Finding identities and equalities*. Toronto: Oxford University Press.

Dreisziger, N.F., ed. 1982a. *Struggle and hope: The Hungarian Canadian experience*. Toronto: McClelland and Stewart.

– 1982b. Toward a golden age. In Dreisziger 1982a, 195–219.

– 1982c. The years of growth and change 1918–1929. In Dreisziger 1982a, 94–138.

– 1999. Hungarians. In Magosci 1999, 660–74.

English, John, Richard Gwyn, and P. Whitney Lackenbauer, eds. 2004. *The hidden Pierre Elliott Trudeau: The faith behind the politics*. Ottawa: Novalis.

Fay, Terrence, J. 1998. The Canadian messenger of the Scared Heart 1905–1927: Window on ultramontane spirituality. *CCHA Historical Studies* 64:9–26.

– 2003. The new faces of Canadian Catholics: Filipinos, Chinese, and Tamils. *Africana: Studio Extraeuropei Edstudio – Pisa*, 83–9.

– 2004. Canadian Tamil Catholics and their search for ultimacy, 1964–2004.

Paper presented at the conference 'Ultimate Reality and Meaning,' 21–3 December, University of Pune, India.

– 2005a. Chinese Catholics: Intelligent organizers. http://individual.utoronto.ca/historyhaven/ccvv.htm.

– 2005b. From the tropics to the freezer: Filipino Catholics acclimatize to Canada. *CCHA Historical Studies* 71:29–59.

– 2005c. Vietnamese Catholics: Sentimental family sensitivities, people over activity. http://individual.utoronto.ca/historyhaven/ccvv.htm.

Fingard, Judith. 1989. *The dark side of Victorian Halifax*. Porter's Lake, NS: Pottersfield.

FitzGerald, John E. 1999. Archbishop Roche, J.R. Smallwood, and denomination rights in Newfoundland education, 1948. *CCHA Historical Studies* 65:28–49.

Fourth Census of Canada. 1901. Ottawa: King's Printer.

Foyster, Kenneth. 1981. *Anniversary reflections, 1856–1981: A history of the Hamilton Diocese*. Hamilton: Griffin.

Ganzevoort, Herman. 1999. Dutch. In Magosci 1999, 435–50.

Grant, John Webster. 1968. *The church in the Canadian era*. Toronto: McGraw-Hill Ryerson.

Guerin, Thomas. 1946. *The Gael in New France*. Montreal: Private.

Harney, Robert. 1981. Toronto's Little Italy, 1885–1945. In *Little Italies in North America*, ed. Robert Harney and J. Vincenza Scarpaci, 41–62. Toronto: Multicultural History Society of Ontario.

Hornsby, Stephen J. 1992. Patterns of Scottish immigration to Canada, 1750–1870. *Journal of Canadian Historical Geography* 18:397–416.

Houston, Cecil, and William J. Smyth. 1990. *Irish emigration and Canadian settlement: Patterns, links and letters*. Toronto: University of Toronto Press.

Hryniuk, Stella. 1988. Pioneer bishop, pioneer times: Nykyta Budka in Canada. *CCHA Historical Studies* 55:21–42.

Hubbard, Bede. 1983. St Peter's: A German-American marriage of the monastery and colony. In *Visions of the New Jerusalem*, ed. Benjamin Smillie, 153–64. Edmonton: NeWest.

Jaenen, Cornelius J. 1991. *The Belgians in Canada*. Canada's Ethnic Groups Series. Ottawa: Canadian Historical Association.

– 1999. Belgians. In Magosci 1999, 257–70.

Jakesova, Elena, and Mark Stolarik. 1999. Slovaks. In Magosci 1999, 1168–79.

Januario, Ilda, and Manuela Marujo. 2000. Voices of immigrant women. In Teixeira and da Rosa 2000, 97–111.

Johnston, A.A. 1971. *A history of the Catholic Church in eastern Nova Scotia*. 2 vols. Antigonish: St Francis Xavier University Press.

Johnson, A.J.B. 1984. Popery and progress: Anti-Catholicism in mid-nineteenth century Nova Scotia. *Dalhousie Review* 64:146–63.

Jovanovic, Marek. 1999. Czechs. In Magosci 1999, 397–405.

Katz, Michael. 1975. *The people of Hamilton, Canada West: Family and class in a mid-nineteenth century city.* Cambridge, MA: Harvard University Press.

Kocjancic, Cvetk. 1999. Slovenes. In Magosci 1999, 1179–85.

Kovacs, Martin L. 1978. The Hungarian school question. In *Ethnic Canadians: Culture and education,* ed. Martin L. Kovacs, 333–58. Regina: Canadian Plains Research Centre.

– 1982. The Saskatchewan era, 1885–1914. In Dreisziger 1982a, 61–93.

– ed. 1983. *Roots and realities among Eastern and Central Europeans.* Regina: Canadian Plains Research Centre.

Kowalchuk, Lisa. 1999a. Guatemalans. In Magosci 1999, 626–630.

– Nicarguans. 1999b. In Magosci 1999, 1008–1012.

Kuntz, Herbert M. 1980. *History and stories of Formosa and area.* Formosa, ON: Private.

Lauer, Bernarda. 1979. Russian Germans and the Ursulines of Prelate, Sask. 1919–1934. *CCHA Study Sessions* 46:83–9.

Lavigne, Gilles, and Carlos Teixeira. 2000. Building a neighbourhood in Montreal. In Teixeira and da Rosa 2000, 175–90.

Lower, A.R.M. 1943. Two ways of life: The primary antithesis of Canadian history. *Report of the Canadian Historical Association,* 5–8.

MacDonald, Allan. 1987. Angus Bernard MacEachern, 1759–1835: His ministry in the Maritime provinces. In Byrne and Terrence 1987, 53–67.

Magosci, Paul Robert, ed. 1999. *Encyclopedia of Canada's peoples.* Toronto: University of Toronto Press.

Mannion, John. 1974. *Irish settlements in Eastern Canada: A study of cultural transfer and adaptation.* Toronto: University of Toronto Press.

Marques, Domingo, and Joao Medeiros. 1984. Portuguese immigrants in Toronto. *Polyphony* (Summer): 154–8.

Matejko, Joanna. 1983. Polish farmers in Alberta, 1896–1930. In *The Polish presence in Canada and America,* ed. Frank Renkiewicz, 48–62. Toronto: Multicultural History Society of Ontario.

McEvoy, Fred. 1998. The parishes. In *Planted by flowing water: The Diocese of Ottawa, 1847–1997,* ed. Pierre Hurtubise, Mark McGowan, and Pierre Savard, 49–175. Ottawa: Novalis.

McGahan, Elizabeth. 1995. The Sisters of Charity of the Immaculate Conception: A Canadian case study. *CCHA Historical Studies* 61:99–134.

McGowan, Mark G. 1984. Religious duties and patriotic endeavour: The Catholic Church Extension Society, French Canada and the prairie west, 1908–1916. *CCHA Historical Studies* 5:107–20.

– 1988. A watchful eye: The Catholic Church Extension Society and Ukrainian Catholic immigrants, 1908–1930. In *Canadian Protestant and Roman Catholic*

Missions, 1820s–1960s, ed. John S. Moir and Thomas C. McIntire, 221–43. New York: Lang.

– 1991. A portion for the vanquished: Ukrainian Catholics and Roman Catholics in Canada, 1891–1948. In *Canada's Ukrainians: Negotiating and identity*, ed. Stella Hryniuk and Lubomyr Luciuk, 218–34. Toronto: University of Toronto Press.

– 1999a. Irish Catholics. In Magosci 1999, 734–83.

– 1999b.*The waning of the green: Catholics, the Irish, and identity in Toronto, 1887–1922.* Montreal and Kingston: McGill-Queen's University Press.

– 2005. *Michael Power: The struggle to build the Catholic Church on the Canadian frontier.* Montreal and Kingston: McGill-Queen's University Press.

McGowan, Mark G., and Brian P. Clarke, eds. 1993. *Catholics at the gathering place: Historical essays on the Archdiocese of Toronto, 1841–1991.* Toronto: Canadian Catholic Historical Association / Dundurn.

McLaughlin, K.M. 1985. *The Germans in Canada.* Canada's Ethnic Groups Series. Ottawa: Canadian Historical Association.

McNally, Vincent. 1990. Victoria: An American diocese in Canada. *CCHA Historical Studies* 57:7–28.

Miller, J.R. 1978. *Equal rights.* Montreal and Kingston: McGill-Queen's University Press.

– 1993. Anti-Catholicism in Canada. In *Creed and culture: The place of English-speaking Catholics in Canadian society, 1750–1930*, ed. Terrence Murphy and Gerald Stortz, 25–48. Montreal and Kingston: McGill-Queen's University Press.

Moir, John S. 1971. The problem of the double minority: Some reflections on English-speaking Catholics in Canada in the nineteenth century. *Histoire sociale / Social History* 4 (7): 53–67.

– 1993. Toronto's Protestants and their perceptions of their Roman Catholic neighbours. In McGowan and Clarke 1993, 313–40.

Moogk, Peter. 1974. Timothy Sullivan. *Dictionary of Canadian biography.* 3:602–4.

Mulligan, James. 2005. *Catholic education: Ensuring a future.* Ottawa: Novalis.

Neatby, Hilda. 1969. Servitude de l'église catholique: A reconsideration. *CCHA Study Sessions* 36:9–26.

Nicolson, Murray. 1983. Irish Tridentine Catholicism in Victorian Toronto: Vessel for ethno-religious persistence. *CCHA Study Sessions* 50:415–36.

Norman, Marian. 1999. Making a path by walking: Loretto pioneers facing the challenges of Catholic education in the North American frontier. *CCHA Historical Studies* 65:92–106.

O'Gallagher, Marianna, and Rose Masson Dompierre. 1995. *Eyewitness: Grosse Isle 1847.* Sainte-Foy: Carraig Books.

O'Grady, Brendan. 2004. *Exiles and islanders: The Irish settlers of Prince Edward Island*. Montreal and Kingston: McGill-Queen's University Press.

Oleson, Tryggvi. 1963. *Early voyages and northern approaches, 1000–1632*. Toronto: McClelland and Stewart.

Parr, G. Joy. 1974. The welcome and the wake: Attitudes in Canada West to the Irish famine migration. *Ontario History* 66:101–13.

Patrias, Carmela. 1997. *The Hungarians in Canada*. Canadian Ethnic Group Series. Ottawa: Canadian Historical Association.

Pautasso, Luigi. 1989. Archbishop Fergus P. McEvay and the betterment of Toronto's Italians. *Italian Canadiana* 5:71–90.

Perin, Roberto. 1990. *Rome in Canada: The Vatican and Canadian affairs in the late Victorian Age*. Toronto: University of Toronto Press.

– 1998. *The immigrants' church: The third force in Canadian Catholicism, 1880–1920*. Canada's Ethnic Group Series. Ottawa: Canadian Historical Association.

Phillips, Lynne. 1999. Ecuadorians. In Magosci 1999, 451–3.

Piva, Michael. 1979. *The condition of the working class in Toronto, 1900–1921*. Ottawa: University of Ottawa Press.

Portelli, John. 2001. Father Fortunato Mizzi's contribution to Maltese Catholics in Toronto. *CCHA Historical Studies* 67:57–80.

Porter, John. 1965. *The vertical mosaic: An analysis of social class and power in Canada*. Toronto: University of Toronto Press.

Punch, Terrence M. 1981. *Irish Halifax: The immigrant generation, 1815–1859*. Halifax: International Education Centre, St Mary's University.

Raddall, Thomas H. 1950. *Halifax: Warden of the north*. London: Dent.

Radecki, Henry. 1976. *A member of a distinguished family: The Polish group in Canada*. Toronto: McClelland and Stewart.

– 1999. Poles. In Magosci 1999, 1056–75.

Ramirez, Bruno. 1989. *The Italians in Canada*. Canada's Ethnic Groups Series. Ottawa: Canadian Historical Association.

Rea, J.E. 1974. *Bishop Alexander Macdonell and the politics of Upper Canada*. Toronto: Ontario Historical Society.

Rollman, Hans. 1987. Religious enfranchisement and Roman Catholics in eighteenth-century Newfoundland. In Byrne and Murphy 1987, 34–52.

Rues-Bazan, Agueda. 1999. Argentinians. In Magosci 1999, 212–15.

See, Scott W. 1993. *Riots in New Brunswick: Orange nativism and social violence in the 1840s*. Toronto: University of Toronto Press.

Shirley, Robert W. 1999. Brazilians. In Magosci 1999, 273–82.

Smith, Neil Gregor. 1963. Religious tensions in pre-Confederation politics. *Canadian Journal of Theology* 9:248–62.

Smyth, Elizabeth. 1992. Congregavit nos in unum Christi amor: The Congregation of the Sisters of St Joseph, in the Archdiocese of Toronto, 1851–1920.
Ontario History 84 (September): 224–240.

– 1999. Professionalization among the professed: The case of Roman Catholic
women religious. In *Challenging professions: Historical and contemporary perspectives on women's professional work*, ed. Elizabeth Smyth, 234–54. Toronto:
University of Toronto Press.

Statistics Canada. 2001. Highlight tables, 2001 census. http://www.statcan.ca/
bsolc/english/bsolc?catno=97F0024X1E2001006.

Stefura, Mary, ed. 1983. Sudbury's people. Special issue, *Polyphony* 5, no. 1.

Teixeira, Carlos. 1999. Portuguese. In Magosci 1999, 1075–83.

Teixeira, Carlos, and Victor M.P. da Rosa, eds. 2000. *The Portuguese in Canada:
From the sea to the city.* Toronto: University of Toronto Press.

Tomasi, Silvano. 1970. The ethnic church and integration of Italian immigrants
in the United States. In *The Italian experience in the United States*, ed. Silvano
Tomasi, 163–93. Staten Island, NY: Centre for Migration Studies.

Vatican Information Service. 2006. Ad limina visit of the Canadian Conference
of Catholic Bishops (Atlantic Conference), 22 May, document 64, vis-
form@pressva-vis.va.

Vecoli, Rudolph. 1969. Prelates and peasants: Italian immigrants and the Catholic Church. *Journal of Social History* 3:217–68.

Wagle, N.K. 1999. Goans. In Magosci 1999, 612–15.

White, Clinton. 1978. Language, religion, schools and politics among German-
American settlers in St Peter's Colony, Saskatchewan, 1903–1916. *CCHA
Study Sessions* 45:81–100.

Whitaker, Reg. 1991. *Canadian immigration policy since Confederation.* Canada's
Ethnic Group's Series. Ottawa: Canadian Historical Association.

Zucchi, John. 1988. *The Italians in Toronto: Development of a national identity,
1875–1935.* Montreal and Kingston: McGill-Queen's University Press.

3 The Francophone Roman Catholic Church

SOLANGE LEFEBVRE

My grandmother was born in the small Quebec village of St-Édouard-de-Lobinière, shortly after midnight on the first of January 1900. Coming into the world at the turn of the century and growing up on a family farm near Quebec City, she found her childhood marked by poverty. As a young adult, she went to work as a cook for a wealthy family in New Bedford, Massachusetts. She liked living in the United States, but after some time, family obligations forced her to return home to Quebec. There, she met my grandfather, a francophone Catholic widower and father of two children. Eventually, my grandparents married and had six more children of their own, including my mother.

Like most women of her time and place, my grandmother was. a pious Catholic, devoted both to her family and to the work of charities in her parish, notably Les Dames de Sainte Anne.[1] She lived in Montreal's poor St-Henri district, made famous by Gabrielle Roy in her novel *Bonheur d'occasion* (1945), the first book written about city life in Quebec. Once her children were out on their own, my grandmother went to work for many years as a manager at the Greenberg general store where her boss was a Jewish man whom she liked very much. These were happy years for her.

Until her death in 1994, my grandmother cherished religious objects. In her bedroom, she kept a statue of the Sacred Heart of Jesus[2] and another of the Blessed Virgin Mary, the mother of Jesus. Her prayer book was always within easy reach on a small table in the living room. During her last days spent in hospital, she held a rosary in her frail hands.[3]

I grew up in one of Montreal's middle-class suburbs in the 1960s. It was an entirely francophone Catholic neighbourhood, quite unlike the one in the heart of Montreal where my father had lived and played as a child with English-speaking neighbours. Like my parents and grandparents, I was baptized into the Roman Catholic Church as an infant. As a girl, I received the sacraments of initiation: Reconciliation, First Communion, and Confirmation. My family and I attended Mass in the local school's gymnasium, where I participated in the liturgy, which, in the wake of the Second Vatican Council, had begun to drift from rather stiff formality toward a somewhat folksy cosiness. Mass was no longer said in Latin but in French and sometimes even included pop-rock music. But the family I grew up in was not truly pious. Though my mother was and still is a practising Catholic, she later has admitted to me that, during the sixties and seventies, she considered religion 'a crutch.' In Quebec during those years, the classic critics of religion (Freud, Marx, and Nietzsche) had become widely known, even in popular culture. When my family left the suburbs and moved to Montreal proper in the 1970s, we stopped going to Sunday Mass, less out of conviction than as the result of growing indifference and our fading sense of community. As a teenager, I found myself like so many others searching for meaning in life. I began to read esoteric books from a wide variety of religious traditions. In 1970s Quebec, the religious world had become a real marketplace. After more than a century of Roman Catholic monopoly on the religious life of French Quebeckers, there was suddenly a wealth of other options to explore. Following a number of discussions with a sympathetic Jesuit, I finally returned to my Roman Catholic roots. Two years later, after I had received a first degree in music, I began to study theology at the University of Montreal where eventually I would go on to become a professor. The university environment inspired me to become more ecumenical in my religious outlook and to take a more interdisciplinary approach to understanding the Christian faith. Subsequently, I went to Paris to complete my education in social anthropology at l'École des Hautes Études en sciences sociales.

One of my best doctoral students, Lamphone Phonevilay, was just a baby when he arrived in Canada in the early 1980s with the 'boat people' from what the French called Indochina (Vietnam, Cambodia, and Laos). His family members say that as they were fleeing the communist regime, Lamphone's loud crying threatened their lives. In Laos, his family was part of a French-speaking community, and that was why they chose to come to Quebec. The family is Roman Catholic and belongs to the Association catholique des Laotiens du Québec, which

FAİTES CELA EN MEMOİRE DE MOİ !

Figure 3.1. Reformed liturgy after the Second Vatican Council – from Latin to French. (Courtesy of *Vivre en Église*, journal of the Diocese of Montreal.)

now numbers a few hundred members. The family would join other Laotian Catholics five or six times a year to celebrate Mass in their native language and sometimes perform Buddhist ceremonies as well. They would gather at various churches in Montreal that occasionally gave them access to their spaces, and only recently began gathering regularly at St-François-D'Assise Church in the city's east end. Lamphone was integrated into the French-language public school system, which at the time was Roman Catholic. Today, he speaks French with a perfect Montreal accent and understands only snippets of his mother tongue, Laotian.

These three short life stories reflect the complex history of Roman Catholicism in French-speaking Canada.[4] The first offers a glimpse of the threads of tradition interweaving French Canadian culture and society with Roman Catholicism. However, my grandmother's story already gives hints that the threads of this close-knit fabric were beginning to unravel as Quebec developed into an urban, industrial society. My own life story illustrates the deep impression that secularization and the rise of individualism have made on Quebec society and Catholicism since the 1960s. Finally, the story of my Laotian student reinforces a dimension of the francophone Catholic story: French-speaking Catholics who are neither recent immigrants from Europe nor descendants of long-established French Canadian communities. Like many non-European immigrants, my student represents new challenges to an old religious community. These three stories, like those of Canada's other francophone Roman Catholics, are diverse yet interwoven in that they underline the special challenges faced by these ethnic, linguistic, and religious minorities in an environment that has at times been nurturing and at others inhospitable.

It is the very diversity of these stories that illustrates why it is so hard to characterize today's francophone Roman Catholic 'community' in Canada. The seeds of this community were sown over 400 years ago with the arrival of French explorers in the New World. For a time during the seventeenth century, the Roman Catholic Diocese of Quebec covered all of North America and ministered to a great variety of cultural groups.[5] That is why throughout the United States one finds so many traces of French culture, for example, in city names such as Detroit and New Orleans. However, historical events have dramatically altered this first and essentially French iteration of the North American story. Today, most people living in Canada and the United States claim English as their mother tongue, no matter what their ethnic origins and English is the lingua franca of the continent's business, social, and cultural affairs. However, the francophone presence is still alive – most obviously in Quebec with its French-speaking majority, but also in small enclaves such as Ponteix and Gravelburg in Saskatchewan, where visitors are fascinated to discover villages whose local inhabitants of French ancestry now speak only English. There are also sizeable French-language communities in cities with English-speaking majorities, such as St Boniface in Winnipeg, Manitoba, Ottawa in Ontario, Fredericton and Moncton in New Brunswick. Also, scattered across the Canadian landscape are 'mixed' communities where people of French ancestry live in both official languages, some of them, especially those in urban areas, progressively losing command of their mother tongue. Adding to this diversity, an influx of more recent French-speaking immigrants from other parts of the world has changed the traditional ethnic homogeneity of French-speaking Canadians. This has implications for the church because these 'new' French-speaking communities – albeit smaller in their numbers (sometimes a few hundred or fewer) – are often more fervent in their religious belief and practices.

Despite historical developments and recent trends in immigration, Catholics of French European origin whose families have been here for at least three generations are, without dispute, still in the majority.[6] At the turn of the nineteenth century, a few French immigrants came from Belgium to settle in western Canada and a few Christian Arabs from what is now Lebanon also integrated with the French-speaking population. After the Second World War, this latter stream of immigration increased. However, most immigrants to Canada – and even to Quebec – did not speak French. These 'allophones' (people who speak neither English nor French) were usually assimilated into the English-speaking community, including Quebec where the English-speaking community was a minority.[7] Because English was the majority language across Canada and the United States as well as the language of socio-economic success, most immigrants to Quebec sent their children to (Protestant) English-language schools. Consequently, until the late 1970s, 'the French-speaking population remained remarkably homogeneous in terms of both ethnicity and of religion' (Perin 1996, 230).

The passage of Quebec's Language Charter or Bill 101 in 1977 substantially changed both the province's school environment and its cultural landscape, since the charter required immigrant children to attend French schools. Catholic schools, mostly French-speaking, started to take in students from a variety of cultural and religious backgrounds. Bill 101 also required large-scale corporations in Quebec to operate in French, making French the language of upward mobility in the business world. As a consequence of these legal measures, a growing number of people now declare French to be the official language spoken in the home, even though it may not be their mother tongue. On the religious front, this has meant that in Quebec's large urban centres – and especially in Montreal – a large number of the French-speaking Roman Catholic parishes have become multi-ethnic. An increasing number of their parishioners are French-speaking Catholics from Europe, Africa, the Middle East, Asia, and South America. Some of these groups have formed their own parishes or 'ethnic missions' where they go for special masses, feasts, and so on, but most of them also regularly attend their local parish church (see parallels in Mark McGowan's chapter 2 on Catholicism in English Canada).

A Brief History

A brief history can do no more than give a general outline of how francophone Catholics came to define their religion as a pillar of their ethnic identity and solidarity.[8] It is essential to understand this development, not only because Catholicism had been there at the very foundation of the French settlement of what was later to become Canada, but also because, between 1840 and 1920, Roman Catholicism and French Canadian identity fused to encompass every dimension of life: personal psychology, family life, higher learning, and popular culture, as well as social, cultural, economic, and political life. It is impossible to do justice to the richness and diversity of all of Canada's French-speaking Catholic communities – Quebeckers, Acadians, Franco-Ontarians, Franco-Manitobans, Franco-Albertans, and Franco-Columbians, and various smaller communities, so I will focus on just a few as illustrative examples.

On 7 July 1534 a French priest accompanying the explorer Jacques Cartier came ashore on the Gaspé Peninsula and celebrated Mass for the first time in what was to become Canadian territory. In 1604, the first French colony in North America was founded in Moncton. European conquest of the continent began with the founding of Quebec City in 1608 by Samuel de Champlain and the establishment in 1642 of Ville Marie, now Montreal, by Sieur Paul de Chomedey de Maisonneuve.[9] French colonists arrived in the so-called New World, hoping to establish New France, an extension of their country of origin. Small in number at first (600 in 1645, 3,000 in 1663), by the end of the century they had increased to 15,000. This period was also distinguished by the emergence of a powerful clergy, mainly because, unlike their lay compatriots, the religious orders of men and women who came to New France were educated and competent enough to set up schools, help the needy, care for the sick, and act as political leaders. They were also loyal supporters of the French Crown.

However, the dream of recreating the French church on American soil came to an end in 1759. After years of conflict, the French and Canadian forces suffered defeat in 1759 on the Plains of Abraham in Quebec City, and Montreal fell a year later. The 1763 Treaty of Paris formalized the transfer of New France to the British Empire. At first, French Canadians worried about their future because Roman Catholics in Great Britain were forbidden to show any public expression of their faith. However, a strong parish structure backed by the astute political action of many religious men and women convinced British governors to tolerate the Catholic Church. In the Province of Quebec, Governor Guy Carleton had skilfully negotiated a policy instituting toleration for Catholicism, recognition of French laws, and access for Catholics to civil employment. In 1774, George III 'gave royal assent to the *Quebec Act*, which re-established French civil law, extended the borders of the country, exempted Canadians from the oath of the *Test Act*, and officially recognized the Catholic religion by allowing the church to collect tithes' (Chaussé 1996, 71). Governor Carleton even overlooked the few restrictions contained in the act.

While the Catholic Church survived the new Protestant administration, it would ascend to its fullest power only after the ill-fated rebellions of 1837 and 1838. The Quebec bishops sided with the British Empire against the 'patriots,' despite the fact that these agitators were mostly French Canadians. When the rebellions failed, the church gained great power and, in 1841, the *Act of Union* gave the church full legal standing in the United Canadas.

The new powers entrusted to the church by the British administration came at a propitious moment in the history of Catholicism. In response to the French Revolution and the spread of liberalism, Catholics around the world had adopted a conservative form of the faith, called ultramontanism.[10] Ultramontanists favoured a strong commitment to the pope and opposed other currents, such as Gallicanism in France, which instead asserted the supremacy of the state, ecumenical councils, or national churches. Generally conservative in its aims, ultra-montanism sought the restoration of the pope's spiritual powers and of social and moral order. In Quebec, ultramontanism provided French Canadians with a project and the confidence with which to carry it out. In Montreal, Bishop Jean-Jacques Lartigue and his successors forged strong ties between the Quebec church and Rome and dreamed of creating a model Christian society on the banks of the St Lawrence. Consequently, ultramontanism provided French Canadian Catholics with the psychological, cultural, and spiritual means to resist interference by the English Protestant political, economic, and religious elite.

After 1841, the family, the school, and the parish were united in their transmission of the Catholic faith among francophone Canadians. Consequently, 'most French Canadians shared a common religious expression wherever they might find themselves in North America' (Perin 1996, 198). From then on, the Catholic faith would penetrate all aspects of francophone Canadian society, inspiring the foundation of numerous religious orders and hallowing streets, cities, and villages with the names of real and apocryphal saints.

French Catholics and Canada's First Peoples

Of course, French Catholics did not move into an empty territory. Wherever they went, they ran into Canada's Aboriginal peoples, a variety of tribal societies large and small. From the very beginning, the French sought to convert the 'Indians' to Roman Catholicism. However, historical studies remind us that 'the First Nations did not insist on spiritual exclusivity' (Crowley 1994, 13) and so their 'conversions' did not necessarily constitute a rejection of traditional ways. Europeans of the seventeenth and eighteenth centuries often idealized Native peoples as *bons sauvages* (noble savages, thought to represent humanity in its natural state of purity and innocence). Indeed many missionaries saw Aboriginal peoples as central figures in their utopian quest of recreating the fervour of the primitive church and the simplicity of the apostolic church in New France. However, there was another, darker vision of Aboriginal peoples. For example, commenting on the missions of the Oblate Fathers, Saindon wrote in 1928 that the Aboriginal peoples were 'at the a-b-c stage of civilization, with no sense of society' (1928, 20).

Some missionaries respected the customs and languages of the Native populations and struggled to protect them when Europeans started to arrive in greater numbers. Others did not and, as a rule, Catholics, like most Christians, had a strong sense of religious exclusivity and superiority. Whatever the attitudes of particular individuals, studies show how dramatically the arrival of the French people modified the life, economy, and culture of Aboriginal peoples, notably in the creation of reserves to convert them to a sedentary life. In the settlements, epidemics devastated their populations, as did the alcohol trade, despite efforts by Catholic authorities to prohibit the trade in the eighteenth century. Ultimately it should be remembered that, though few in number during the seventeenth century (600 in 1645, 3,000 in 1663), French Europeans had already taken possession of most of the territory along the St Lawrence.[11] Contemporary reappraisals of the relations between missionaries and Native populations recognize the injustices done to the first inhabitants of this continent.

Reinforcement of the Links between Ethnicity and Roman Catholicism

Because of the unique situation of French Canadians after the British Conquest, Roman Catholicism and French Canadian ethnic identity became closely intertwined. Three socio-historical facts reveal the close bond connecting ethnicity and religion in French Canada. First, there is the indispensable support that French-speaking minorities across Canada received from Catholicism in their struggle to preserve their culture and their language. Second, there is the sense of 'nationhood' that has, to various degrees, marked the French-speaking communities scattered across Canada. Finally, there is the difficulty Protestantism has had in gaining a foothold in French Canadian settings. Across Canada, the crux of the French Canadian struggle for cultural survival has been to strengthen linguistic and educational rights. Until recently, this struggle took place in the colonialist climate that ruled the day, as described by Bramadat and Seljak in the first chapter of this volume. Under the French regime, Catholics monopolized public offices and most professions, excluding Aboriginal peoples and Protestants as untrustworthy inferiors. After the British Conquest, the situation was reversed, and in the parts of Canada where French-speakers were in the minority, they had to struggle for their rights and their survival against varying attempts to assimilate them. Gabrielle Roy (1909–1983), the celebrated Franco-Manitoban writer, opens her autobiography with these words: 'So when did I first realize that, in my own

country, I was destined to be treated as some sort of inferior being?'
(Roy 1984).

Ethnic Catholic groups from the British Isles, especially the Irish and
the Scots, often tried to weaken the French influence because they felt
themselves better suited to represent the interests of Catholicism to the
Protestant majority. Rome, too, had a general dislike for French-speaking bishops of a nationalist stripe and preferred 'the melting-pot model
advanced by their English-speaking colleagues' (Perin 1996, 222). Nevertheless, prior to the Second World War the lone Canadian cardinal
had always been a French Canadian.

National Consciousness in Quebec and French Canada

Overall, Catholic French Canada was a special case in the West. Its situation was somewhat similar to that of its ecclesial rival, the Irish Canadian Catholic community, or that of Ireland in Great Britain or Poland
in Europe (Baum 1991). It was also similar to that of other Catholic
national enclaves in broader federations, like the Slovenians, Croatians,
and Slovaks, where ethnic and religious identities fused under pressure
or threat from an external group defined as 'other,' both ethnically and
religiously. Most French Canadians were, up until the 1960s, convinced
that Roman Catholicism was the bedrock of French Canadian nationalism, which took so many forms during the twentieth century, most visibly in the Province of Quebec where it was seen at its most reactionary
and xenophobic as well as its most opened-minded and modern. The
concentration of a French-speaking majority on Quebec's vast territory
did favour the development of a certain national consciousness, even if
this did not lead to widespread political nationalism or calls for independence until the 1960s and 1970s. This political nationalism did
emerge eventually and some have observed that, by the 1960s, even the
Liberal Party of Quebec insisted that Quebec was the homeland of a
'distinct society.'

Rousseau and Remiggi (1998) interpret the marriage between French
Canadian society and Roman Catholicism as a the result of a religious
revival that sought to counteract the deep crises then plaguing Lower
Canada (the name originally given to the Province of Quebec, as distinguished from Upper Canada, or modern Ontario, its neighbouring
province). These crises loomed on all fronts: economic, political, demographic, cultural, and religious. Religion allowed the population to
cope with the major changes brought about by industrialization and

urbanization (a prominent phenomenon by 1930) in the early twentieth century and to emerge with confidence in its distinct status within the North-American environment.

The Acadians

From the very beginning, Acadia, the francophone community on Canada's east coast, constituted a special case in its relations with the British Empire. Ever since the old French colony was conquered by the British, Acadians have turned to their Roman Catholic faith as a source of hope and strength in their struggle to sustain their integrity as a people in North America. While living under British rule, Acadians negotiated as tenaciously for the right to protect their religious heritage as for the right to remain neutral in the conflicts between Britain and France. Whether in North America or Europe, exiled Acadians have clung to their ancestral faith. Even in Roman Catholic Louisiana, where no foreign Protestant power threatened them, Acadians were quick to establish their own churches and acquire priests to serve them, suggesting that their faith has always been an integral and enduring part of their sense of identity and never simply a mark of distinction defined against a ruling Protestant power.

After the Treaty of Utrecht (1713), when Acadians lost most of their territory, the clergy negotiated with the British to gain neutrality for Acadia in the midst of the conflicts opposing France and England. However, both a desire for land and a suspicion of all French Catholics led the British authorities to deport the Acadians from 1755 to 1763, scattering them throughout the east coast of the British colonies and elsewhere. After this disastrous exile, the Acadian ecclesiastical divisions were placed under the authority of English-speaking bishops, effectively separating them from the mother church in Quebec. Between 1783 and 1830, the civil and political rights of the Acadian population were expanded. The arrival of missionaries from France and Quebec reinforced the church. However, during their turbulent history, the lay Acadian Catholics had developed a strong spirit of independence, having run their churches without clerics for long periods. During the post-1840 era, Acadians began to leave the coastal regions of the Maritimes, opening up new districts in the interior, along the Gulf, in the lower St Lawrence region, as well as along the north shore.

As in the case of Quebec, historians disagree in their assessment of the significant power that the Acadian Church enjoyed: some authors view it negatively as the triumph of ecclesiastic control while others argue that the Acadian church played a significant role in the definition of Acadians' national consciousness (Thériault 1993). For example, French Canadian religious men and women led efforts in education, giving crucial support to the survival of Acadian culture in New Brunswick. They worked in the public school system and founded a number of private schools 'that gave students access to provincial teacher-training in their own language' (Perin 1996, 212). In 1864, the first Acadian *collège classique* was founded by the Holy Cross Fathers, and among its graduates one can find many leaders of the Acadian renaissance of the 1880s. All over Canada, the establishment of *collèges classiques* – high schools run by religious orders such as the Jesuits – would play a major role in educating the children of the influential French Canadian elite.

Catholicism is still an essential feature of Acadian culture – both in its collective life and in its folklore. A striking example is the fact that in 1881, Mary, the mother of Jesus, became the patron saint of Acadia under one of her numerous titles: Our Lady of the Assumption. Her feast day, 15 August, came to be celebrated as a 'national' holiday, as it still is: a solemn Mass is said, followed by recreational events and festivities (Chiasson, Cormier, Deschênes, and Labelle, 1993). The Acadian 'national' anthem is a religious song dedicated to Mary under one of her Latin titles, Maris Stella. The Acadian flag reproduces France's tricolour, but with a star on the blue stripe, symbolizing Acadia's French heritage while invoking Mary as Star of the Sea, that is, a star to guide sailors on their voyages (Thériault 1993, 68).

Other Francophone Communities across Canada

The francophones of Ontario and western Canada also have a unique history. For example, the latter included a community of French-speaking Metis (people of Aboriginal and non-Aboriginal origin) which, in 1817, had been entrusted to the care of Roman Catholic missionaries from Quebec. The Metis community lived in the Red River colony, where Anglicans ruled supreme over both Aboriginal people and Metis (Francis and Palmer 1992). After 1840, the Metis community increased its numbers with the influx of French Canadians and Acadians who had been encouraged to settle in the West by Canadian immigration agents operating in New England. The growing community also attracted a small number of immigrants from France and Belgium who arrived at the turn of the century.

Figure 3.2. Pilgrims gathered around the monument of Notre-Dame-de-l'Assomption, Rogersville, New Brunswick, 14 August 1982. (Collection of the Centre d'études acadiennes, E22088.)

The icon of this people's struggle for survival is the controversial figure Louis Riel. Born in St Boniface, Manitoba, in 1844, he led the Metis uprising of 1869–70, partly supported by the Catholic clergy. This revolutionary stirred the ire of Anglo-Protestants when he executed the Ontario Orangeman Thomas Scott. French Canadians pled for amnesty for Riel, and he was exiled to the United States. When he came back roughly fifteen years later to head the 1884–5 revolt in Batoche, Saskatchewan, he formed a new government – which failed – and he was hanged in 1885. Riel was a fierce opponent of the Anglo-Protestant usurpation of lands that had been granted to the Metis and, at the same time, a defendant of Catholicism and French culture in Manitoba and Saskatchewan. Although there is still debate surrounding the question of Riel's mental health and self-understanding during the final decade of his life, 'his creative doctrines had succeeded in indigenizing the Christian message and presenting it in a form that was meaningful and relevant to the Metis and the crisis their society was facing' (Huel 1996, 211). Riel's execution became a symbol of Anglo-Protestant oppression of French Roman Catholics for both the Metis and French Canadians. After his death, as Riel had anticipated, Catholicism and the French language became more and more marginalized in the West. Today, more than a century after his death, he continues to exert a powerful influence in Metis and Aboriginal identity and politics, especially in the Great Plains region.

While some francophone Canadians had moved to the prairies, the majority fleeing the economic hardships of the early twentieth century moved to the Ottawa valley, where they established their parishes and schools. Tensions with English-speaking Irish Catholics arose almost at once. As the latter formed the majority in Acadia and Ontario, they meant to put their own stamp on Catholicism (Cartwright 1978; Moir 1971). With the support of the Irish Canadian bishop M.F. Fallon of London, the Ontario government adopted Regulation 17 in 1912 abolishing French as a language of instruction. Despite these tensions, a Franco-Ontarian church emerged in the inter-war period against a backdrop of debates over schools and language (Choquette 1975, 1984; Gaffield 1987).

In the West, the Manitoba government – which had already replaced its bilingual, bi-religious school system with a single public system (in violation of the terms of its entry into Canada) – in 1916 also banned instruction in 'foreign languages,' including French. The Catholic bishop of Calgary, John Thomas McNally (1913–15), put all his weight behind similar unilingual education policies in his own province (Gagnon 1989; Ross 2003). At the ecclesiastical level, a similar battle raged; often dioceses and parishes with a French Canadian majority had no access to services in French. English-speaking Catholics and Protestants feared the strong religious revival in Quebec and the revolt led by Riel in the West and, as early as the end of the nineteenth century, they would form a common front against the assertion of French-language rights across Canada. However, when it came to protecting the religious identity of their schools, Catholic anglophones would sometimes join forces with their French-speaking co-religionists.

Fidelity to Catholicism

Perhaps the greatest sign of the strong link between French Canadian ethnic identity and Roman Catholicism across Canada is the failure of successive attempts to convert French Canadians to Protestantism.[12] Despite the fact that conversion, along with assimilation into English-language society – especially before 1960 – would have brought many advantages (because the main pathways to socio-economic success were dominated by English-language institutions), it was relatively rare. Some estimates maintain that 2,000 conversions had been achieved by 1850, and 20,000 by the end of the nineteenth century (Perin 1996, 193). In protest against such efforts, some Catholic clergy even participated in public burnings of Protestant Bibles. So strong was this resistance to Protestantism as it tried to break the links between religion, culture, and ethnicity that even to this day, when most francophone Quebecers do not practise their Roman Catholic faith, they do not convert to Protestantism in any great number.

The Framework of French Canadian Society

Since the nineteenth century, the Catholic Church has played a prominent role in public education, health care, and social services for French Canadians. During the nineteenth century, numerous religious communities came from France to reinforce the social power of the Catholic Church and bolster its ultramontane and Roman orientation, especially under the episcopate of Ignace Bourget in Montreal (1840–76). These religious communities worked all over Canada and in the United States. Most of French Canada's hospitals, schools, and social services were founded and run by religious orders, and at the turn of the twentieth century Quebec had the highest level of institutional health and social services in Canada (Perin 1996). The church also responded to the growing urbanization, industrialization, and secularization of society by forming new associations, such as labour unions, workers' groups, farmers' cooperatives, and athletic clubs. Parish priests worked for the social and economic development of their communities, sponsoring credit unions, electrification programs, and scientific farming techniques (Ryan 1966).[13] Outside Quebec and Acadia, the situation for francophone Catholics was more precarious. As Perin writes, 'Elsewhere the availability of services depended on restrictive provincial legislation and the ethnic allegiance of the local bishop' (203).

The result of this history is an astonishing network of francophone Roman Catholic institutions across Canada. In the Catholic Church Directory, published each year by Novalis, one can find details about the number of parishes, churches, and chapels, but also colleges, elementary schools, high schools, hospitals, homes for the aged, social services centres, nurseries, and refugee centres administered by Catholics in each diocese. One can also find a list of francophone Catholic hospitals and health associations on the website of Canada's bilingual Catholic Health Association. While most of Canada's social, health care, and education institutions have been progressively secularized since the 1960s, the institutional completeness of the Catholic Church is still remarkable, even if steadily declining. A look at the denominational school system illustrates these transformations.

The Association of Catholic Colleges and Universities in Canada, for example, counts two francophone universities among its nineteen members; ironically they are based in Ontario and not Quebec – Ottawa's Collège Dominicain de philosophie et de théologie and Sudbury's Jesuit-run Université de Sudbury. St Paul University in Ottawa – a Canadian Catholic university with a papal charter – is officially bilingual but French predominates. In Quebec, where one would expect to find the largest francophone Catholic universities, one finds instead two French Catholic faculties of theology embedded in secular universities: at Université Laval in Quebec City and at the Université de Montréal in Montreal. Both faculties also teach non-denominational religious studies.

The school system has been the main issue in debates on the remaining influence of the Catholic Church in francophone Canada. Education is officially a provincial jurisdiction and so the situation varies from province to province (Pratte 1999). In Newfoundland and Labrador, a constitutional amendment allowed the provincial government to replace the denominational public school system with a non-denominational one. Students receive a common religious education and, where parents consent to it, religious services and devotions can be held in the school. Prince Edward Island's public school system has no religious dimension, nor does British Columbia's. In Nova Scotia, public schools are not denominational, but the *Education Act* (S.N.S. 1995–6, c.1) states that 'a school board may permit persons to offer religious studies in its schools.' New Brunswick has a non-confessional public school system that nevertheless allows certain religious practices such as the recitation of prayers. Ontario runs a bilingual (though predominantly anglophone) public school system alongside a strong Roman Catholic school system that operates in both English and French. The boards of education of these two separate school systems are responsible for religious education. In Manitoba, Alberta, and British Columbia, we also find separate publicly funded Catholic schools, including French-language Catholic schools, that receive financial support ranging from 50 to 100 per cent of the amounts received by public schools.

In Quebec, until just recently, the Catholic and Protestant churches enjoyed the privilege of offering denominational instruction within their separate public systems. Then, as mentioned earlier, adoption of Bill 101, the 1977 French Language Charter, ushered in a period of growing diversity in Quebec's French-language schools, especially in greater Montreal. With the advent of the *Charter of Rights and Freedoms* (Quebec in 1975 and Canada in 1982), respect for freedom of conscience and religion became a matter of greater concern. After several years of debate,[14] the government succeeded in redefining the schools along linguistic lines (French and English) rather than religious lines (Catholic and Protestant). By 2008, religious education will take the form of a series of courses entitled Ethics and Religious Culture. For now, each school is expected to offer a neutral Spiritual Care and Guidance and Community Involvement Service for religious and non-religious students alike; denominational chaplaincy is no longer allowed.

Ethno-religious diversity is gradually transforming the francophone Canadian Catholic community, most notably in the field of education (Cardinal 2002). These changes often evoke fear, but does this fear spring from reluctance in historically established churches to share their symbolic monopoly? Might it stem from leaders' uncertainty about how to handle religious diversity? Or is it rooted in public wariness about unfamiliar forms of religious expression? Any or all of these reasons may come into play, in anglophone and francophone communities in Quebec and in the rest of Canada. However, in the case of

Franco-Catholic minorities, another reason may be awareness of the historical struggle for cultural survival and the all-too-recent strengthening or acquisition of linguistic rights across Canada, such as the right to have some publicly funded French separate school systems. A threatened francophone minority – united by religious and ethnic bonds – often offers only a chilly welcome to newcomers who speak French but do not share its religious and ethnic sensibilities. However, the current situation challenges this minority to learn to welcome a highly diverse population of francophone immigrants – notably, from Africa and Asia – capable of stopping the erosion of small francophone minorities still threatened by assimilation. Moreover, the larger francophone populations in Quebec, Ontario, and Acadia need immigration to compensate for the steady demographic decline caused by low birth rates and work-related movement to other parts of the country. Fortunately, this infusion is occurring at a time when younger generations are bringing new visions and experiences of diversity to their communities of origin, having developed strong friendships with individuals of other ethnic groups through school, during summer travel, or on the internet.

Contemporary Francophone Roman Catholics on the Move

The 1960s initiated a series of changes in francophone Catholic communities that had unexpected and unintended consequences. Modifications in immigration policy, transformations in anglophone and francophone Canadian cultures, religious reforms inaugurated by the Second Vatican Council, the rise of feminism and the human rights agenda all profoundly altered the religious life of French-speaking Roman Catholics in Canada. Some of the changes were undertaken with great care and consultation. However, most were the unanticipated effects of broader social changes that were, at the time, reshaping religious and social realities throughout Canada and other liberal democracies. Much attention has been paid to Quebec society's so-called Quiet Revolution of the 1960s. However since the 1960s the francophone Catholic Church has experienced its own Quiet Revolution. It is this revolutionary transformation to which we now turn.

Changes in Ethnicity, Language, and Religion

One of the most dramatic changes in the francophone Catholic community has been in its ethnic make-up. While it is still true that most francophone Catholics can trace their roots to France, this pattern is beginning to change. Should current immigration patterns remain the same, we can expect francophones who have no direct connection to France to exert a growing influence on the Catholic Church in Quebec and across Canada.

Before the 1960s, most francophone Catholic immigrants were of French stock and only a handful declared any other origin. In the 2001 Census, the great majority of French-speaking Catholics (6,138,731 out of 6,324,307) reported French as their mother tongue or first official language, showing that the Catholic francophone community attracts only a small number of allophone immigrants. In fact, in every Canadian province, francophone Roman Catholics born elsewhere are still mostly natives of France. Consequently, francophone immigration, for the most part, does not challenge the ethnic or racial make-up or self-understanding of the French-speaking Catholic community. This said, a reflection on some of the impending changes we can see on the horizon in the French-speaking Roman Catholic communities is worthwhile.

A Multi-Ethnic French-Speaking Catholic Community

Before the 1960s, Franco-Catholic communities across Canada were little concerned with ethno-cultural and religious diversity.[15] There were very few French-speaking immigrants not of French stock, and most allophone immigrants assimilated into the English-speaking majority. Moreover (as Mark McGowan points out in chapter 2), the Catholic Church has traditionally tried, whenever possible, to provide its diverse minority communities with services in their own language. Immigrants themselves have requested such services, and the ethnic parishes set up in response often preserve some rites and other religious traits derived from their region of origin (Perin 1998, 4). These ethnic communities may form either independent parishes and have their own church building or space, or missions, gathering a few times a year in space provided by another religious community group or parish. As a rule, minority groups do hold onto distinctive characteristics such as language and religion (Anctil 1984; Meintel and Fortin 2002). Consequently, few francophone Catholic parishes have had to face the challenge of integrating these ethnic minorities, beyond perhaps granting them access to their buildings.

The best example of this phenomenon is found in Montreal. As far back as 1986, Montreal's estimated 1.5 million Catholics already included more than 350,000 individuals whose mother tongue was not French and, of these, 225,000 were of Italian origin (Paquette 1986, 342). Since the adoption of Bill 101 in 1977, many of these Italians have mastered the French language. In 2005, the Diocese of Montreal had a list of forty cultural and worship communities in its territory. Of these forty, eleven use French as their first official language, thirteen use both official languages, and fourteen use only English. Among the French-speaking groups, for example, one finds Cambodian, Congolese, Copt, Haitian, Latin American, Laotian, Latvian, Lithuanian, Italian, Portuguese, Spanish, and Vietnamese missions. Among the bilingual group, one finds Portuguese (two), Italian (four), Hungarian, Lithuanian, Polish, Croatian, Japanese, Korean, and Chaldean missions.[16]

This new development raises the central question of how allophones who also speak French are transforming the francophone Catholic community. The case of my Laotian student, mentioned at the beginning of this chapter, serves as a perfect illustration of the nature of this transformation. Lamphone's mother tongue is Laotian; the language of the Laotian Catholic services he attends is Laotian – which he now only partially understands and speaks. Yet his mastery of French is perfect and it is in this language (and sometimes in English, his second official language) that he participates in Montreal's wider Catholic community.

To give another example, over the past twenty years, a once very homogeneous Catholic parish in east-end Montreal has seen its congregation gradually transformed by waves of immigration from Portugal, Latin America, Africa, and the Caribbean. In the parish's church, visible minorities now sometimes constitute the majority of children attending Sunday catechism. At other times, these children are with their families at ethnic missions or parishes.

In the rest of Canada – except for New Brunswick – allophone Canadians tend to adopt the English language, even among those groups, like the Spanish and Vietnamese, who might initially seem inclined to adopt French. As a consequence, as Father Doris Laplante, chancellor of the Diocese of Ottawa, explained to me in an informal conversation, in Ontario cultural missions are more common in English-speaking communities. In some French-speaking communities from the Caribbean, Africa, and the Middle East, parents will use French but their children tend mainly to speak English. Indeed, and predictably, when French is not the mother tongue, it proves to be the first official language spoken only in provinces with a heavy concentration of francophones. Everywhere else, English exerts a strong attraction as the first official language.

Figure 3.3. Trilingual Italian community of Montreal at St Joseph's Oratory, Montreal, September 2004. (Courtesy of *Vivre en Église*, Diocese of Montreal.)

A major challenge for French-speaking minorities in predominantly English-speaking provinces is how to attract immigrants willing to adopt French as their official language (Jedwab 2002). Sometimes they succeed. Thus, in an informal conversation a francophone from Edmonton tells of about 200 African families that have settled there and adopted French as their daily language. Many of these families are Catholic while the rest are Muslim. A further challenge in this context is how to welcome allophones who have adopted the French language into largely English-speaking communities.

New immigration patterns force us to rethink who makes up the Franco-Catholic community. While Franco-Catholics are, for the most part, descendents of immigrants from France, in major urban centres in Quebec (and elsewhere) they are also allophones who choose to speak French.

The Changing Nature of Religious Practice and Ideas

Religious change in the Canadian francophone community has been remarkable since the 1960s. Quebec surpassed other Western societies in the rapidity with which its institutions and values moved towards secularization. Used here in its very classical sense, the concept of secularization refers both to a decline in the influence of religious institutions over a society and to a differentiation between the public and private scope of this influence. The once ubiquitous presence of this influence in Quebec's public sphere would from now on be relegated to the private sphere: the hearth, the heart, and the faithful few. In this last respect, the so-called Quiet Revolution was quite dramatic because of the widespread notion or ideology of *rattrapage* or 'making up for lost time.' This ideology imagined Quebec emerging from the still smouldering ashes of its Christian past with astonishing rapidity and measuring up to modernity with remarkable facility. In fact, the change was not as rapid as it was believed to be at the time. Although religion held sway over their values and social life, Quebecers had already been constructing new models of industrial and scientific progress for several decades (Elbaz, Fortin, and Laforest 1996).

The religious change was all the more dramatic because, just as Quebec entered the revolutionary 1960s, the international Roman Catholic Church had begun a major reform with the opening of the twenty-first ecumenical council, known as the Second Vatican Council. Ferretti reminds us that the reforms initiated by the council would bring

wrenching changes to the Quebec Catholic Church. New practices were
introduced quickly, and many people felt unprepared for them. The
spiritual renewal advocated by the Second Vatican Council certainly
did help to eliminate 'routine practices,' but it also 'swept aside all
imprints of traditional popular piety. The new Christian paths were too
abstract' (Ferretti 1999, 162). On the other hand, some of the more committed and educated laity had been expecting broader and deeper
reforms, especially in the realm of power-sharing between the laity and
clergy as well as between men and women. The demand for such
reforms came largely from Catholic Action, a lay movement that
greatly influenced the political thought of French Canadian intellectu-
als during the twentieth century. Using the *collèges classiques* as its
forum, it helped to educate a lay and religious elite who would play a
major role in the transformations of Quebec society (Boismenu et al.
2005; Seljak 1996).

The 1960s introduced confusion and dissent into many areas of
church life. For example, religious communities of nuns, brothers, and
priests faced a decline in their social and intellectual influence. Many
left, and the remaining members of the religious orders sought to redefine their mission. The sexual revolution, unleashed by new methods of
birth control, provoked a split between many Catholics and the Roman
Curia, especially in the aftermath of Pope Paul VI's 1968 encyclical
Humanae Vitae. Ever since, there has been constant tension between
conservatives and reformists surrounding this issue (Gauvreau 2005).
More crucially, many elements of Catholic institutional life suffered
dramatic decline in the council's wake, such as vocations, attendance at
Mass, confession, and the number of converts. We can see that the parish structure had already begun to crumble after the Second World War.
For Catholics, the parish had been a pivotal space where social and religious life converged. Urbanization and increased mobility gradually
eroded this link to a sacred space that relied on regular participation in
parish activities. Quebec Catholicism had entered into crisis.

In Canada's other francophone communities, the shockwaves of the
secularization of the 1960s were not felt so directly. In view of the 1987
synod on the mission of the laity, the Canadian Catholic bishops
launched a vast survey and comparative analysis of Catholic anglophones and francophones from Canada's four regions (the Maritimes,
Quebec, Ontario, and the West) (Gingras 1993). This survey revealed
that Quebec Catholics tended to stray from the national average on all
points, notably showing the lowest rate of attendance at Sunday wor-

ship. Catholics from the West led in the importance accorded to personal prayer, books, magazines, extra-parish courses, and ways of practising the faith, while Quebecers are to be found at the opposite end of this scale. French-speaking Catholics generally accord more importance to social justice, and also differ slightly from anglophones in claiming that the church has not changed enough. Quebec Catholics stand out as being the most demanding on the issue of lay involvement. Catholics in the Maritimes go against the tide by adopting a more positive vision of the current state of Catholicism. More recently, another study took a sombre look at the disaffection of the younger generations (Poirier, Poirier, and Poirier 2003).

In his comparative studies, Reginald Bibby mentions the 'magnitude' of the drop-off in church attendance in Quebec from the 1970s on. In the first 'severe crash,' attendance dropped from 88 per cent in the mid-1950s to 42 per cent by 1975 and it then fell further to 28 per cent by 1990. He observes a similar 'measure of disenchantment with the Catholic Church' in the other provinces, but the decline has been less dramatic and attendance still remained at 37 per cent in 1990, partly as a result of Catholic immigration (Bibby 2002, 17–18). Ferretti (1999) agrees that Roman Catholicism has been particularly marginalized in the province of Quebec. However, all the authors agree that there exists a certain dynamism on the issues of social justice and political transformation in all of Canada's French-speaking Catholic communities.

As in other Western societies since the Second World War, French Catholicism in Canada has been facing a crisis in its institutional life and its transmission of the faith. Given the immense authority of the Catholic Church in the period preceding the Second World War, it should come as no surprise to see today's Franco-Catholic Quebec torn by ambivalence, struggling with a combination of resentment and nostalgia. Most French-speaking Catholics in Quebec are more non-conformist than their counterparts in the rest of Canada. They are reacting to the strict control that the Catholic Church exercised over the province for many decades prior to the 1960s. In the last twenty years, Quebec has been characterized as fertile ground for a cultural and popular Catholicism that manifests 'itself as a spiritual quest, an emotional experience and an affirmation of perennial values, with weak ties to the Church' (R. Lemieux 1990, 162). As in other Western countries, the relation of Catholics to their religious institution became more individualized (Grand'Maison, Baroni, and Gauthier 1995; Roof, Carroll, and Roozen 1995).

Theological and Social Dynamism

Despite declining numbers in religious vocations, practice, and attendance, the francophone Catholic community is not moribund. In fact, it has undertaken ambitious projects of innovation and renewal. Since the 1960s and 1970s, francophone dioceses, especially in Quebec and Ontario, have been training and hiring numerous lay people, mostly women, to fill pastoral roles such as preparation for initiation to the sacraments, religious education, responsibilities in the dioceses, pastoral services in schools, and optional denominational religious instruction classes for both children and teenagers. This change has provided significant career prospects for students educated in various fields of theology, particularly in those concerned with practical or pastoral dimensions. At the same time, the Second Vatican Council left in its wake numerous organizations or institutions dedicated to catechetical and liturgical renewal, adapting them to contemporary culture and new modes of communication. A large number of organizations devoted to pastoral activity in the social sphere as well as many grassroots communities, all run by dynamic, socially engaged Christians, have been active since the 1970s. To complete this portrait of pastoral activity, one should also mention, among other services, the religious publishing houses in Quebec and Ontario.[17] More recently, theological and practical initiatives surrounding inter-religious dialogue have produced much that may be useful to Canada as it deals with growing multiculturalism. New programs of study and courses, for example, have been created at St Paul University (Ottawa) and at the Faculty of Theology and Religious Studies at the University of Montreal on conflict resolution and inter-religious dialogue, while the bilingual Canadian Centre for Ecumenism, founded in Montreal in 1963, facilitates understanding and cooperation among believers of various Christian traditions and world religions. Among various tools and activities, it publishes the quarterly journal *Ecumenism* and maintains a website (www.oecumenisme.ca).

Women in the Catholic Church

Nowhere is this francophone Catholic dynamism and innovation more evident than in the changing roles for women in what is often seen as a patriarchal and paternalistic church. Women have been pillars of the Catholic Church in the Americas since the foundation of New France.

There were usually more female than male members of religious orders because religious life then offered them 'in addition to opportunities for education and work, advantages of self-direction that were not otherwise available to most women' (Crowley 1996, 45; Perin 1996, 213). They were, however, not usually found on the front lines of the feminist movement along with lay women, struggling to gain advantages for all women, notably access to education. However, many religious communities made education their central mission and were highly successful in teaching basic skills. Others ran hospitals, did social work, and laboured as missionaries all over Canada and the Americas.[18] Male religious authorities often felt that their powers and prerogatives were threatened by these dynamic nuns and sometimes reacted by trying to interfere with the nuns' efforts. Some sociologists even see Quebec's Quiet Revolution of the 1960s as the triumph of male technocrats who finally succeeded in marginalizing women's religious orders. Nicole Laurin, for example, shows how, prior to the 1960s, religious sisters organized Quebec's health care system along novel matriarchal lines, harmonizing many often competing forces: domestic economy and capitalism, family and bureaucracy, science and religion. The new technocratic state of Quebec, along with the male clerics, undermined the work of the women who had, until that time, built an elaborate social system. If the social order that replaced the pre-1960s system was more effective in material productivity, Laurin (1996) would say its bureaucratic logic impoverished its social and cultural spirit (see also Juteau and Laurin 1989).

I have already mentioned the new opportunities for church service and leadership open to women as pastoral agents, but it is also worth considering developments in feminist theological discourse after the Second Vatican Council. Three groups in particular reveal the broad lines of contemporary trends in this area. Femmes et ministère (Women and Ministry) is a reformist group of active church women advocating equality between men and women, including women's ordination (Baroni, Bergeron, Daviau, and Laguë 1995; Caron 1991). In 1988, they published *Les soutanes roses : Le portrait du personnel pastoral féminin au Québec* (The Pink Soutanes: Portrait of Female Pastoral Associates in Quebec – soutanes being the robe traditionally worn by priests), which attracted media attention (Bélanger 1988). Since their creation in 1982, they mobilized hundreds of women, mainly pastoral agents, through their conferences and publications. Another group, L'Autre parole (The

Other Word), founded in 1976, which published in 2004 the hundredth issue of their journal of the same name, is an association of more radical feminists, less numerous but very active. They go as far as advocating the creation of a women's church since they see the current Roman Catholic Church as quintessentially and irrevocably patriarchal (Couture 1995; M.-A. Roy 1996). A third group, l'Association des Religieuses pour la promotion des femmes (Association of Women Religious for the Promotion of Women), created in 1986, gathers 130 members from fifty communities and publishes the *Bulletin Reli-Femmes*.

Under the pontificate of John Paul II, the Catholic feminist movement was weakened in Canada as well as in the United States. However, there are now more and more women working as theologians and as pastoral agents, and a majority of them wish to gain more power in the church. If the groups involved in the feminist movements mentioned above represent only a very small minority of the broader population of Roman Catholics, their publications and their symbolic significance should not be underestimated. In general, many francophone Catholics, especially in Quebec, espouse their views on the role of women in the church.[19] Ironically, while the women in these groups represent a minority among church leaders, they probably represent the views of the majority of parishioners.

Hopes, Disappointments, and Challenges

The dynamic optimism of the francophone Catholic Church was sometimes challenged during the long pontificate of John Paul II (1978–2004). The Polish pope's attitudes were complex in that he adopted quite progressive positions on some questions while remaining adamantly conservative on others. He seemed to pursue a dual project of political, democratic emancipation underpinned by strict consolidation of the church's moral and religious doctrine. Moreover, this consolidation was accompanied by a centralization of ecclesial power in the papacy (S. Lefebvre 2005a, 2006). As head of the Church for twenty-seven years, John Paul II appointed bishops who were certainly more conservative than many of their predecessors.

Although many people loved and admired John Paul II, many disagreed with his teachings, particularly on sexual morality. In this regard, one finds varying degrees of support for the pope's positions. For example, churchgoing Catholics tend to be more conservative than those who do not regularly attend Mass (Talin 2006). In both groups, a majority (albeit more strongly among the latter) support the ordination of women and allowing priests to marry. An even larger majority support the use of contraception. On the issues of abortion and homosexuality, Roman Catholics are more divided in their views. Still, the province of Quebec is more favourable toward same-sex marriage and abortion than Catholics in the rest of Canada (Centre for Research and Information on Canada 2004; Deglise 2002; Presse Canadienne 2004).

While today Catholic bishops in Quebec generally defend the Vatican's official position on these matters in public, during the 1970s and 1980s francophone Canadian bishops, many of them from Quebec, were well known for their progressive positions. Mgr. Bernard Hubert, former bishop of a diocese near Montreal, once told me in an informal conversation, 'When Canadian bishops attended international Catholic meeting, some colleagues, smilingly, would say, "OK! We're going to hear about improving women's condition in the Catholic Church again!"' While he was proud of the progressive stance taken by Franco-Catholics on questions such as women's priesthood and contraception, he could not hide a certain resignation and battle fatigue in the face of the pope's and the Curia's resistance to discussing the matter in the church. Many ecclesiological hopes of the 1970s and 1980s dissipated under John Paul II's long reign. The critical questions many Catholics asked after the Second Vatican Council about matters of ecclesiology, women, and sexual ethics were simply not at the top of John Paul II's agenda. A new generation of more conservative bishops emerged, facing the challenges resulting from an increasing disengagement of Catholics (for example, parish mergers, church closures, and the reduction of pastoral staff for lack of money). Under these conditions, the critical and progressive side of francophone Canadian Catholicism became less audible in the broader public arena. Most of the church's efforts became focused on children's Christian initiation and the reorganization of parishes in the face of dwindling resources (Assemblée des évêques catholiques du Québec 1992). What can the Franco-Catholics expect of Pope Benedict XVI? Certainly he represents a more discreet papacy, lacking John Paul II's charismatic appeal and dedication to religious mobilization. Benedict XVI is deeply committed to the reconciliation of the Eastern Orthodox and Roman Catholic churches as well as the reaffirmation of the importance of tradition and continuity. Minor changes regarding the marriage of priests, contraception, and AIDS might be anticipated (S. Lefebvre 2006).

Conclusion

Like their co-religionists in several Western countries, Franco-Catholics in Canada today live with the paradox of a collective attachment to their religious institutions and a strong belief in individual choice. This stance has resulted in tension within the Catholic community between the development of stimulating pastoral and theological projects (several examples of which have been mentioned) and the loss of momentum brought about by secularization – interestingly, this is a greater challenge in Quebec than anywhere else in Canada. Symptoms of this crisis include declining interest in religious vocations and dwindling church attendance (except on major feast days or traditional rites of passage such as baptism, weddings, and funerals). Francophone communities outside Quebec report a similar phenomenon, albeit on a smaller scale. We also encounter tensions between, on one hand, the abiding faith expressed in the development of bold and valuable theological projects and pastoral practices and, on the other hand, the growing challenges of basic survival that diminish the real impact of these projects and practices. Of course, it is important to interpret these difficulties as products of both enhanced individualism and the secularization of society.

Still, historically and culturally, Franco-Catholicism has played an important role in the individual and communal lives of millions of Christians throughout Canada. Communities across Canada have been deeply marked by francophone culture and religion and still show signs of its influence in their churches, place names, schools, and other institutions. Immigrants present a challenge to Franco-Catholics. Francophone minorities are striving to attract and welcome visible minorities into a religious culture that had been, until quite recently, almost entirely homogeneous and very much on the defensive. Everywhere in Canada, until the 1960s, francophone communities were so exclusively defined that they have only recently become able to constructively integrate newcomer ethnic communities. In this regard, since the Quiet Revolution the ethnic profile of Quebec's Roman Catholic churches has been changing with astonishing speed. How exactly that community will respond to such rapid change in already difficult circumstances remains to be seen. Certainly, immigration represents an opportunity for Roman Catholicism, a chance to strengthen francophone communities generally and in Quebec, particularly, to revitalize shrinking communities with an influx of people who do not share attitudes developed as the result of the province's somewhat ambiguous historical and religious heritage. French-speaking immigrants are already bringing new life to Quebec's Franco-Catholic landscape.

Notes

1 Among the saints venerated by the Catholic Church as models of spirituality and virtue, St Anne holds a prominent place as the mother of the Blessed Virgin Mary. She is the patron saint of Brittany, the region in France from which many of the French colonists in New France had come. Because of this connection, St Anne also became the patron saint of the province of Quebec. On popular religion in French Canada, see Lacroix and Simard (1984).
2 In the seventeenth century, the French mystic Mary Margaret Alacoque is believed to have had a vision of Jesus showing his heart, a symbol of divine love; she felt it was her mission to spread devotion to the Sacred Heart of Jesus, and this devotion grew in popularity. In Quebec, it was so popular that the sacred heart motif found its way into some of the province's early folk art. However, since the 1960s, many Catholics find this portrayal of Jesus too sentimental. Consequently, the popularity of this devotion has declined dramatically, but here and there it still survives.
3 The rosary (in French called *chapelet*, meaning 'petit chapeau' or 'little hat') has been in use since the twelfth century. In the Middle Ages statues of Mary, the mother of Jesus, used to be crowned with roses symbolizing prayers. From this custom emerged the string of beads, which today is known as the rosary.
4 Historical developments make it difficult to use one term to describe francophone Canadians. Originally, the French-speaking inhabitants of New France were called 'les habitants' or 'les Canadiens' in order to distinguish them from those who lived in the colony temporarily until returning to France. When the colony became part of the British Empire, the population became 'les Canadiens' and later still 'French Canadians.' From the 1840s to 1950s, French Canadian nationalists most commonly imagined that their community – united by a common language and a common faith – stretched across Canada and into the United States. In the 1960s, there arose a political and more secular version of this nationalism that focused on the state apparatus of the Province of Quebec, the only state that French Canadians could control. From that time on, there emerged a 'Quebecois' identity, limited to francophones in Quebec. Since the 1980s, some have

included all residents of the Province of Quebec in the term. However, its more common use refers to francophone Quebecers. In this chapter, I will refer to them as French Quebecers to distinguish them from anglophone and allophone (those who speak neither French nor English as a first language) Quebecers.

5 The term *diocese* is derived from the Greek *dioikèsis*, which refers to housekeeping tasks. In the Roman Empire where Christianity was born, a diocese was an administrative division. The word was taken up by the church to designate a 'portion of the people of God entrusted to a bishop' or a 'local church' linked to the universal church located on a given territory.

6 Globally, Statistics Canada reports that the Canadian francophone population is still mostly composed of people of French ancestry: 'In Quebec, 80% of its population aged 15 years and older in 2002 were in Canada for at least three generations. The third generation or more in this province was composed mainly of those of French descent' (Statistics Canada 2003, 7).

7 Perin observes, 'Although half a million new immigrants settled in the province of Quebec between 1945 and 1965, only a tiny fraction of them were French-speaking (44,000 from France and an undetermined number of the 11,000 immigrants from Belgium)' (1996, 230).

8 To adequately treat the historical and contemporary situations of French-speaking Catholics in Canada would be a complex and demanding project. In fact, it would mean covering 400 years of history and reviewing the vast literature documenting them. On this period, see Choquette (1984), Dumont, Grand'Maison, Racine, and Tremblay (1982), Hubert (2000), L. Lemieux (1968), Murphy and Perin (1996), and Voisine (1984).

9 The first diocese was established in Quebec City in 1674, and the first bishop of Quebec and of North America, François Montmorency de Laval, was given authority over most of the territory that today covers Canada and the United States. That is why to this day the archbishop of Quebec City is considered to be the primate of the Roman Catholic Church in Canada. We should also remember that a French Catholic colony was established in 1699 in Louisiana, with New Orleans declared as its capital in 1718. It was at that time part of the Diocese of Quebec.

10 The word *ultramontanism* comes from the Latin words *ultra* (beyond) and *montes* (mountains), the mountains in question being the European Alps. It signifies loyalty to the pope in Rome – that is, beyond the mountains. For a fuller discussion of this phenomenon, see McGowan's chapter 2 in this volume.

11 In 1991, Reverend Douglas Crosby, OMI, president of the Oblate Conference of Canada, wrote a formal apology on behalf of his order for many of

the injustices perpetrated against Aboriginal peoples. After the celebrations of the five hundredth anniversary of the arrival of Europeans on the shores of America, the Oblates, he said, wanted to 'show solidarity with many Native people in Canada whose history has been adversely affected by this event' (Crosby 1992).

12 In the twentieth century, the first Canadian census taking into account the correlation between religion and ethnicity revealed that only 2.6 per cent of Protestants were of French origin (15.5 per cent in Quebec, 43 per cent in Ontario, 30 per cent in the West). They belonged to the major denominations. Conversion, immigration, and intermarriage were cited among the factors of this increase. The Catholic Church used many tactics in opposing the development of French Protestantism, but the main obstacle encountered by French Protestantism was, after all, the potential converts' reluctance to join an English-speaking congregation. In their book on the history of Protestantism in Quebec since 1960, Smith, Peach, and Lougheed (1999) reflect on the difficulties Protestant churches face in maintaining their French-speaking congregations without an infusion of outsiders. Guenther addresses this complex issue in his chapter on Canadian evangelicals in this book.

13 Ryan (1966) shows that during this crucial period in Quebec's economic development, the clergy were motors of economic growth and modernization and not barriers to change as the official story often says.

14 Ministère de l'éducation (1999). For the debate on religion in schools in Quebec, see, for instance: Brodeur, Routhier, and Caulier (1996), Charron (1995), Lefebvre (1998, 2000), Ouellet (2005).

15 There are, however, historical examples of attempts to spread the French language. In 1904, a community of 200 Chinese Catholic converts in Montreal were put in the care of an English-speaking Sulpician. But soon after, sisters belonging to the Missionaries of the Immaculate Conception founded a trilingual school (Cantonese, English, and French) (Helly 1987). A few other schools of this type sprang up in Quebec, such as those set up in 1912 for some Italian communities, for example (Perin 1998, 14).

16 In the English-only groups one finds Italian (six), Polish (three), Tamil, Filipino, Slovak (two), and Czech missions. Some of these minorities have their own parishes, while others gather a few times a year in one or another parish.

17 For example, in Quebec (Montreal), notably Fides, Éd, Paulines, and Médiapaul; in Ontario, Novalis (Ottawa) and Prise de Parole (Sudbury).

18 Of course, missionary work – to communities abroad and to Canada's Aboriginal peoples – is now understood differently by members of these

same female religious communities. They understand their work in terms
of interfaith dialogue and social justice work among some of the world's
poorest populations.

19 For example, during the Synod of the Catholic Montreal Diocese (1995–8),
nearly 60 per cent of the participants recommended women's ordination
(M. Lefebvre 1999).

Works Cited

Anctil, Pierre. 1984. Double majorité et multiplicité ethnoculturelle à Montréal.
Recherches sociographiques 25 (3): 441–50.

Assemblée des évêques catholiques du Québec. 1992. *Risquer l'avenir: Bilan
d'enquête et prospectives*. Montreal: Fides.

Baroni, L., Y. Bergeron, P. Daviau, and M. Laguë. 1995. *Voies de femmes, voies de
passage*. Montreal: Éditions Paulines.

Baum, Gregory. 1991. Catholicism and secularization in Quebec. In *The church
in Quebec*, 15–47. Ottawa: Novalis.

Bélanger, Sarah. 1988. *Les soutanes roses: Le portrait du personnel pastoral féminin
au Québec*. Montreal: Bellarmin.

Bibby, Reginald. 2002. *Restless gods: The renaissance of religion in Canada*. Toronto: Stoddart.

Boismenu, Gérard, Michel Brûlé, Solange Lefebvre, Claude Lessard, and Pierre
Noreau, eds. 2005. *Ruptures et continuité de la société québécoise: Trajectoires
de Claude Ryan*. Montreal: Faculté des études supérieures, Université de
Montréal.

Brodeur, Raymond, Gilles Routhier, and Brigitte Caulier, eds. 1996. *L'enseigne-
ment religieux: Questions actuelles*. Quebec: Novalis.

Canadian Catholic Church Directory 2005. 2004. Montreal: Novalis.

Cardinal, Linda. 2002. Droits linguistiques, droits des minorités, droits des
nations: De quelques ambiguïtés à clarifier avant de parler d'avenir. In
L'Alberta et le multiculturalisme francophone: Témoignages et problématiques, ed.
Claude Couture and Josée Bergeron, 51–61. Edmonton: Centre d'études
canadiennes de la Faculté St-Jean.

Caron, Anita, ed. 1991. Femmes et pouvoir dans l'Église. Montreal: VLB Éditeur.

Cartwright, D.G. 1978. Ecclesiastical territorial organization and institutional
conflict in Eastern and Northern Ontario, 1840–1910. *CHA, Historical Papers*,
176–99.

Centre for Research and Information on Canada (CRI). http://www.cric.ca/
pwp_re/double_poll/religion_en.ppt.

Charron, André, ed. 1995. *École et religion*. Montreal: Fides.

Chaussé, Gilles. 1996. French Canada from the Conquest to 1840. In Murphy and Perin 1994, 56–107.

Chiasson, Anselme, Charlotte Cormier, Donald Deschênes, and Ronald Labelle. 1993. The Acadian folklore. In *The Acadians of the Maritimes: Thematic studies*, ed. Jean Daigle, 649–705. Moncton: Centre d'études acadiennes.

Choquette, Robert. 1975. *Language and religion: A history of English–French conflict in Ontario*. Ottawa: University of Ottawa Press.

– 1984. *L'Église catholique dans l'Ontario français du dix-neuvième siècle*. Ottawa: Presses de l'Université d'Ottawa.

Couture, Denise, ed. 1995. *Les femmes et l'Église, suivi de la Lettre du Pape Jean-Paul II aux femmes*. Montreal: Fides.

Crosby, Douglas. 1992. Apology statement. In *Études Oblates de l'ouest*, no. 2, ed. Raymond Huel et al., 259–62. Queenston, ON: Mellen.

Crowley, Terry. 1996. The French Regime to 1760. In Murphy and Perin 1996, 1–58.

Deglise, Fabien. 2002. Sondage – Un Québec distinct jusque dans ses pratiques religieuses. *Le Devoir*. 22 July. http://www.ledevoir.com/2002/07/22/5776.html.

Dumont, Fernand, Jacques Grand'Maison, Jacques Racine, and Paul Tremblay, eds. 1982. *Situation et avenir du catholicisme québécois: Entre le temple et l'exil*. Montreal: Leméac.

Elbaz, Mikhaël, Andrée Fortin, and Guy Laforest, eds. 1996. *Les frontières de l'identité: Modernité et postmodernisme au Québec*. Sainte-Foy: Presses de l'Université Laval.

Ferretti, Lucia. 1999. *Brève histoire de l'Église catholique au Québec*. Montreal: Boréal.

Francis, R. Douglas, and Howard Palmer, eds. 1992. *The prairie west: Historical readings*. Edmonton: Pica.

Gaffield, Chad. 1987. *Language, schooling and cultural conflict: The origins of the French language controversy in Ontario*. Montreal and Kingston: McGill-Queen's University Press.

Gagnon, Anne. 1989. The Pensionnat Assomption: Religious nationalism in a Franco-Albertan boarding school for girls, 1926–1960. *Historical Studies in Education* 1 (1): 95–117.

Gauvreau, Michael. 2005. *The Catholic origins of Quebec's Quiet Revolution*. Montreal and Kingston: McGill-Queen's University Press.

Gingras, François-Pierre. 1993. Divergences ou convergences ? Les laïcs anglophones et francophones dans le catholicisme canadien. *Studies in Religion / Sciences religieuses* 22 (1): 75–92.

Grand'Maison, Jacques, Lise Baroni, and Jean-Marc Gauthier. 1995. *Le défi des générations*. Montreal: Fides.

Helly, Denise. 1987. *Les Chinois à Montréal, 1877–1951*. Quebec : Institut québécois de recherche sur la culture.

Hubert, Ollivier. 2000. *Sur la terre comme au ciel: La gestion des rites par l'Église catholique du Québec (fin XVIIe – mi-XIXe siècle)*. Quebec: Les presses de l'Université Laval.

Huel, Raymond. 1996. *Proclaiming the Gospel to the Indians and the Métis*. Edmonton: University of Alberta Press.

Jedwab, Jack. 2002 Immigration and the vitality of Canada's official language communities: Policy, demography and identity. http://www.ocol-clo.gc.ca/html/stu_etu_imm_022002_e.php#.

Juteau, Danielle, and Nicole Laurin. 1989. La sécularisation et l'étatisation du secteur hospitalier au Québec, 1960 à 1966. In *Jean Lesage ou l'éveil d'une nation*, ed. R. Comeau, 155–67. Sillery: Les presses de l'Université du Québec.

Lacroix, Benoît, and Jean Simard, eds. 1984. *Religion populaire, religion de clercs?* Quebec: Institut québécois de recherche sur la culture.

Laurin, Nicole. 1996. Le projet nationaliste gestionnaire: De l'hôpital des religieuses au système hospitalier de l'État. *Les frontières de l'identité: Modernité et postmodernisme au* Québec, ed. Mikhaël Elbaz, Andrée Fortin, and Guy Laforest, 95–104. Sainte-Foy: Les presses de l'Université Laval and L'Harmattan.

Lefebvre, Marcel. 1999. *Le Synode diocésain de Montréal: 1995–1998, la dernière étape, l'Assemblée synodale (24–25 octobre et 28–29 novembre 1998)*. Montréal: Fides.

Lefebvre, Solange. 1998. Autres regards sur la laïcité. *Théologiques* 6 (1): 3–7.

– 2000. *Religion et identités dans l'école québécoise*. Montreal: Fides.

– 2005a. John Paul II – A celebration: His impact on Canada. *Globe and Mail*, 2 April.

– 2006. Conflicting interpretations of the council: The Ratzinger-Kasper debate. In *The new pontificate: A time for change?* ed. Erik Borgman, Maureen Junker-Kenny, and Janet Martin Soskice, 95–105. Concilium 42, no. 1. London: SCM.

Lemieux, Lucien. 1968. *l'Établissement de la première province ecclésiastique au Canada, 1783–1844*. Montreal: Fides.

Lemieux, Raymond. 1990. Le catholicisme québécois : Une question de culture. *Sociologie et société* 22 (2): 145–64.

Meintel, Deirdre, and Sylvie Fortin, eds. 2002. The new French fact in Montreal:

Francization, diversity, globalization. *Canadian Ethnic Studies / Études ethniques au Canada* 34 (3): 1–4.

Ministère de l'éducation. 1999. *Laïcité et religions: Perspective nouvelle pour l'école québécoise, Report from the task force on the place of religion in the school.* Quebec: Ministère de l'éducation, Gouvernement du Québec.

Moir, John. 1971. The problem of a double minority: Some reflections on the development of the English-speaking Catholic Church in Canada in the nineteenth century. *Histoire sociale / Social History* 7:53–67.

Murphy, Terrence, and Roberto Perin, eds. 1996. *A concise history of Christianity in Canada.* Toronto: Oxford University Press.

Ouellet, Fernand, ed. 2005. *Quelle formation pour l'éducation à la religion.* Quebec: Presses de l'Université Laval.

Paquette, Mario. 1986. Les communautés ethniques et rituelles dans le diocèse de Montréal. In *L'Église de Montréal, 1836–1986*, 342–65. Montreal: Fides.

Perin, Roberto. 1996. French-speaking Canada from 1840. In Murphy and Perin 1996, 190–259.

– 1998. L'Église des immigrants: Les allophones au sein du catholicisme canadien 1998–1920. Ottawa: La société historique du Canada.

Poirier, Donald, Norma Poirier, and Sébastien Poirier. 2003. Rapports intergénérationnels en matière religieuse entre jeunes adultes et aînés francophones et Anglophones du grand Moncton: Étude exploratoire. *Francophonies d'Amérique* 16:107–17.

Pratte, Sonia 1999. *La place de la religion dans les écoles publiques des provinces anglo-canadiennes: Rapport de recherche.* http://www.meq.gouv.qc.ca/REFORME/religion/etude4.pdf.

Presse Canadienne. 2004. Sondage Léger Marketing: Le pays est très divisé sur le mariage entre conjoints de même sexe. *Le Devoir* 25 May. http://www.ledevoir.com/2004/05/25/55263.html.

Roof, Wade Clark, Jackson W. Carroll, and David A. Roozen, eds. 1995. *The post-war generation and establishment religion.* Cross Cultural Perspectives. Boulder: Westview Press.

Ross, Sheila. 2003. Bishop J.T. McNally and the anglicization of the Diocese of Calgary, 1913–1915. *CCHA Historical Studies* 69:85–100.

Rousseau, Louis, and Frank W. Remiggi. 1998. *Atlas historique des pratiques religieuses: Le Sud-Ouest du Québec au 19ème siècle.* Ottawa: Ottawa University Press.

Roy, Gabrielle. 1945. *Bonheur d'occasion.* Montreal: Pascal.

– 1984. *La détresse et l'enchantement.* Montreal: Boréal Express.

Roy, Marie-Andrée. 1996. *Les ouvrières de l'Église.* Montreal: Médiaspaul.

Ryan, William. 1966. *The clergy and economic growth in Quebec, 1896–1914.* Quebec: Presses de l'Université Laval.

Saindon, Émile. 1928. *En Missionnant: Essai sur les missions des Pères Oblats de Marie Immaculée à la Baie James.* Ottawa: Imprimerie du Droit.

Seljak, David. 1996. Why the Quiet Revolution was 'Quiet': The Catholic Church's reaction to the secularization of nationalism in Quebec after 1960. *CCHA Historical Studies* 62:109–24.

Smith, Glenn, Wesley Peach, and Richard Lougheed. 1999. *Histoire du protestantisme au Québec depuis 1960.* Montreal: La Clairière.

Statistics Canada. 2003. Ethnic diversity survey: Portrait of a multicultural society, content overview. Catalogue no. 89-593-XIE. Ottawa: Statistics Canada.

Talin, Kristoff. 2006. *Valeurs religieuses et univers politiques: Amérique du Nord et Europe.* Quebec: Presses de l'Université Laval.

Thériault, Léon. 1993. The Acadianization of the Catholic Church in Acadia. In *The Acadians of the Maritimes: Thematic Studies,* ed. Jean Daigle, 431–66. Moncton: Centre d'Études Acadiennes.

Voisine, Nive, ed. 1984. *Histoire du catholicisme québécois.* 3 t., 4 vol. Montreal: Boréal.

4 Canadian Anglicanism and Ethnicity

WENDY FLETCHER

You would think that the story behind the relationship between the Anglican Church of Canada and ethnicity would be straightforward. After all, its roots lie in the Church of England and it has the root word *anglo* right in its title. The story of the Anglican Church of Canada unfolds within the larger story of the global Anglican community.[1] The Canadian church developed, as did much of the larger global Anglican community, from the colonial activity of the British Crown, which sought to disseminate this uniquely English religion, along with English economic, political, and cultural power around the world. Anglicanism began as the Church of England, which was a church born from the Protestant Reformation of the sixteenth century. Linked to the intellectual and spiritual energy of the Continental Reformation (see Bryan Hillis's chapter 7 on Lutheranism in this book), England completed its separation from the Roman Catholic Church in 1534 after the pope refused the request of the King of England, Henry VIII, to grant a divorce from his wife, Catherine of Aragon. Prior to the dispute over Henry's divorce, England's monarchy had remained largely loyal to the pope. However, when the pope refused to grant his divorce, Henry was able to use the emerging Protestant Reformation as a vehicle to achieve his own political ends. Under Henry's direction, the church in England became the Church of England, which was organized in a way quite different from its predecessor: no longer was the pope the final authority in the English church. Instead, the British monarch became de facto and de jure head of the church. This linking of royal and ecclesial power set the stage for much of what would come later in the Anglican story. When Britain began colonizing in the eighteenth century, the Anglican religion – ostensibly the state religion of Britain – became an integral part of what would later be known as Canada. It was not until the latter part of the nineteenth century, however, that the church in Canada became its own autonomous church, relating to England out of respect rather than from structural necessity. Nonetheless, the influence of the British political and religious hierarchy remained considerable in Canada until the second half of the twentieth century. Historically, the Anglican Church of Canada represented a middle ground between the Roman Catholic Church with its global reach, structure, and ambitions on the one hand, and the United Church of Canada, with its indigenous and autonomous Canadian national identity on the other hand. As one might expect, this historical position has complicated discussions within the church on same-sex relationships and the appropriate nature of the relationship between the Canadian, British, and global communions. As this chapter indicates, it remains to be seen how this rapidly evolving church might resolve the challenges produced by the fact that the Canadian church is reliant on non-European immigrant communities that do not necessarily share with the established community (composed mainly of British descendents) the same relationship with the historical British origins of the church.

Despite the location of Anglican religion within British religious history, untangling the relationship between Anglicanism and ethnicity is a complex undertaking, particularly given that it is a denomination imbued with historic privilege. The threads of dominant culture and marginalized 'other.' weave themselves around each other in historically complicated ways. My own story is a case in point. I was raised originally in Brantford, Ontario, by a third-generation Canadian mother of Scottish Baptist origins and a father who was the child of English Anglican immigrants. The home I was raised in was one of comfort and privilege. There was little distinction made between Anglican Christianity and Christianity as such, the common good and political conservatism. My family of origin was observably small *r* racist when it came to First Nations persons. I knew as child that 'they' were not like me and definitely 'they' were less than I was.

I was often puzzled by how my father's family treated my mother. It was clear to me that they thought there was something wrong with her, but I could never determine what it was. By all accounts and from outward appearance, she looked the model of a middle-class Anglican matron. However, her marginalization in my father's family was unrelenting. My father died when I was twelve and since we had little to do with my father's family thereafter we were somewhat freed from the judgement of the Fletcher family.

I had never met my mother's parents. She herself was raised by her Scottish Baptist grandparents. Her mother had died young and her father, although alive and living in the same city as we, was persona non grata. I was told he was a 'bad man' and we never had contact. I knew his name but that was all. My mother died when I was twenty-eight. At the time of her death her own origins were not at all clear to me.

In my work in Vancouver, I work regularly with a First Nations woman who had always seemed very familiar to me. One day several years after we met, I was sitting in a meeting puzzling about why she looked familiar. Of whom did she remind me? And then I realized – it was my mother. That realization catalyzed a journey of discovery. Many years after my mother's death, as part of my academic and pastoral work, I became involved on behalf of the church in research on a residential school known as the Mohawk Institute. I was traumatized deeply by the horror of what I found. My small *r* racism went careening into the dumpster, as I understood for the first time the unbelievable history of systemic racism in which we as a society have historically participated. One day as I was pursuing my research, I found myself sifting through lists of student names from various years of the school's history, when I encountered the name of my maternal grandfather, along with his date of birth and his school-assigned number. The shock of recognition was followed by further research, which confirmed that in fact my mother's father, whom I had never met, this 'bad man,' had in fact been of First Nations ancestry. My grandfather had been a member of the Mohawk First Nation. He had attended the Mohawk Institute residential school at the turn of the twentieth century, when conditions were horrific. My discovery explained my mother's marginalization in my father's family.

My own experience demonstrates for me that the pursuit of understanding in the arena of religion and ethnicity in Canadian culture is a complex undertaking. Definitely there are patterns in the construction of our corporate religious identities that follow fairly predictable lines of ethnic heritage, language, and religion, but those patterns must themselves be understood against the backdrop of acculturation, marriage, and procreation, all of which were marked by and at times independent of religion and ethnicity. Given the dominant immigration patterns at work in contemporary Canada (see chapter 1 of this book), the relationship between Anglican and ethnic identities is likely to become increasingly complex (Radner and Turner 2006, 29; Williams 2003, 18–23).

Historical Context

The beginning of the story for Canadian Anglicans sets the tone. We find ourselves at the beginning of the story as a tradition that appeared homogenous and privileged. However, when we look between the covers of that story we find considerably more complexity. It might be said that Canadian Anglicans have never quite recovered from the radical act of disestablishment in 1854 Canada associated with the liquidation of the clergy reserves, an act that abruptly challenged and reshaped denominational self-understanding. In Britain, members of the Church of England enjoyed the place, power, economic solidity, and privilege of life as a state church (Sykes 1998, 112). When Anglican clergy and lay people crossed the Atlantic to make new lives for themselves in the New World, they brought with them a religion the privilege of which was both assumed by adherents and protected by the state.[2] Moreover, within the Anglican sphere in Britain, the English sought to dominate a larger religious community that was ethnically heterogenous, including Irish, Scottish, and Welsh populations. This diversity put non-English British Anglicans into a minority position defined by language and ethnicity. This institutionalized discrimination engendered hostilities within the larger Anglican community that migrated with them wherever they travelled.

The new world of British North America, however, ultimately demanded things from its citizens that were different from the established traditions that emerged in Britain. When the colony that was to become Canada began, Anglican privilege was assumed and, it appeared, assured. However, by 1867, with the development of Canada's earliest constitutional form, the *British North America Act*, the disestablishment of the single state church formed the cornerstone of what would become the ethos of the new country of Canada.

As noted by John Webster Grant (1998) and observed in chapter 1, in this period of 'plural establishment' Canada saw the deconstruction of a way of managing social and political power that had been inherited from the British experience. From the beginning of British settlement there had been a close affinity between politics and religion for Anglicans as the named religion of the British government. In British North America, the close affinity between the established church and the forces of political conservatism coalesced. This began most notably after the American Revolution with the arrival of the United Empire Loyalists who immediately moved into centres of Canadian power. With the aid of the Anglican Church, tightly knit and narrowly focused oligarchies were organized (Hayes 2004, 11). These pockets of power rooted in Upper Canada (a jurisdiction created by the *Constitutional Act*, 1791) became known as 'Family Compacts.' They represented the close alignment of the Anglican Church, the Tory Party, and the professional and mercantile upper classes, united to preserve the traditional values and mores of late-eighteenth-century Britain. Although grounded in a policy of religious toleration, the privileged position of Anglicanism was protected through its designation as the official or established religion of the colony.[3] The *Constitutional Act* had given one-seventh of all public land to the Church of England as clergy reserves, and the income generated from these properties was intended to finance the building of churches and the maintenance of clergy. Moreover, only clergy of the Church of England had the legal right to register births, marriages, and deaths – an important function before the creation of municipalities. This alignment of power gave rise to a graded and hierarchical society that was understood at the time to be necessary to manage and overcome the lawlessness and disorder that were often features of frontier settlements (Hayes 2004, 19).

The Family Compact did not stand in the landscape unchallenged, even from within. For example, the Irish Anglican Bishop Hume Cronyn was appointed by the archbishop of Canterbury to develop a new diocese southwest of Bishop John Strachan's Toronto. Intent on expressing the particularity of the Irish evangelical Anglican variant, which was less linked to social, economic, and political privilege, Cronyn established a diocese that represented a counterpoint of resistance to the Anglo-Catholic, English elitism of Toronto (Houston and Smythe 1980, 27). The hostility between Cronyn and Strachan demonstrates a degree of heterogeneity within the apparent homogeneity of the nascent Canadian Anglican world.[4]

With the development of the *BNA Act* of 1867, Anglicanism became one religion among many. Already in response to the rebellions of 1837 and 1838, the Crown had taken way the Church of England's monopoly on the clergy reserves. In 1841, it split half of the money between the Church of England and the Church of Scotland and gave the rest to the other denominations. In 1854 the clergy reserves were finally liquidated – and thus ended the land-based economic advantage and the concomitant supportive taxation system in place for Anglicans until that time – signalling the end of any hope for Anglican establishment in Canada. As one denomination among many, Anglicanism would need to adjust itself to its dramatically reduced privilege.

As such, from the moment of Confederation in 1867, although Christianity was certainly privileged in a number of ways (see chapter 1 of this volume), Canada did not have an established religion in the European sense of a single denomination identified as the state's official religion. Anglicanism was thus set to live in the world of denominational competition. Nonetheless, Anglicans continued to be well represented, perhaps even over represented, in the halls of political and social power for many decades.

The impact of immigration on the balance of power in the new country cannot be underestimated. A severe depression in the early 1890s gave way to a period of unprecedented prosperity. This economic boom was part of a larger global economic expansion spurred by the expansion of the British Empire and its global economic activities (between 1890 and 1910 the GNP of Canada increased by 122.7 per cent). An increase in ship building, a cycle of wet years from 1899, and improved prairie farming techniques inspired a dramatic increase in immigration, especially to the western part of the country from the turn of the last century. To put this in perspective, in 1896 fewer than 17,000 immigrants entered Canada. Between 1901 and 1911 more than 1 million people went to the Prairies (Grant 1998, 92).

The source of this and later immigration had a major impact on the development of Anglicanism, as the vast majority of early immigrants came from the United States (where all the free land had already been claimed) and from Britain. This did not mean that all settlers in this period were Anglicans, but a significant proportion of them were. As such, the absolute and relative increase in the denomination's membership numbers led to the continuation of the community's political and economic influence in Canada.

The relevance of immigration to church life in the early part of the twentieth century cannot be underestimated. Between 1898 and 1914 and then again between 1919 and 1939, an increasing number of immigrants to Canada came from eastern Europe, bringing with them forms of Christianity (and other religions, of course) that would assume a minority place in the Canadian landscape. However, for the most part, the immigration patterns that characterized especially the first half of the twentieth century meant (with the notable exception of Quebec) the reinforcement of British descent domination in religious expression, language, culture, and social norms. During this period, Protestant immigrants considerably outnumbered Roman Catholic immigrants, and this religious imbalance shaped the relations between political and religious spheres in English-speaking Canada (Hayes 2004, 39).

All of the major Protestant churches of the time enthusiastically embarked on a mission to immigrants with a clear set of goals in mind, including recognizing and meeting the needs of strangers in a strange land; encouraging non-Christians to convert (Protestants generally assumed that Roman Catholics and what we are calling in this book Eastern Christians were all in need of conversion); and imparting Canadian values, attitudes, ideals, and lifeways as well as a strong sense of citizenship to the newcomers. The desire to Canadianize new immigrants through religious and social assimilation moved to the front of the churches' agendas prior to the First World War. For Anglicans, this focus was expressed through urban social missions embodying both charity and advocacy for new immigrants in their social dislocation, as well as political action that attempted to introduce and then inculcate ethical norms reflective of British dominant culture (Woolverton 1984, 86). The moral reform agenda, as expressed in efforts to protect Sunday as a day free from work as well as those to curb gambling, prostitution, and alcohol consumption, quickly rose to the top of the church's agenda, outstripping the objective of conversion. During this time, the Anglican Church understood its role to be a former and framer of culture as well as religion.

In my research on women's voluntary work, I encountered a woman who, like her mother, had spent her life engaged as a volunteer for the Anglican Church. She tells the story of going with her mother as a young girl to protest the consumption of liquor by marching with many other women from the Woman's Auxiliary of her church in front of a well-known drinking establishment, carrying a placard denouncing the social evil of alcohol consumption. She said, 'My mother taught me that it was a church woman's obligation to teach others what it meant to be a good citizen, which meant a good Canadian, which meant a good Christian, which meant no drinking alcohol!' (interview 3, 26 October 2005).

The outbreak of the First World War in 1914 also strengthened the Anglican voice on the Canadian landscape. Virtually without exception, the Church of England in Canada expressed enthusiastic support for that war. The few voices raised in support of pacifism were overwhelmed by this support throughout the rest of the church (Grant 1998,

76), and the reasons were obvious. For Anglicans, the English monarch is understood to be the head of the church. Although Canada had formally disestablished the Church of England, the monarch of England was still the titular head of the Canadian parliamentary system. He or she was also the head of the Anglican religion in Canada and the rest of the world. As such, for Canadian Anglicans the legal differentiation between church and state might have been accepted as a defining feature of Canadian society, but was actually contrary to the polity of the church, based as it was on an earlier model.

For Anglicans, the First World War became a holy war. The monarch had called his people to war, and for many Anglicans there was not a measurable separation between a call to secular war and to religious war. Although the Anglican population of the day included many recent British immigrants who had always maintained close ties to the motherland, the war appealed to sentimental ties of kinship, both literal and metaphoric, for many Canadian-born Anglicans as well.

Ironically, of course, participation in the war ultimately undermined the social reform agenda which had so dominated the church's self-concept prior to the war (Hayes 2004, 43). Soldiers returned from the theatre of war having lived lives of relaxed standards on alcohol, church observance, and sexual activity. They also returned traumatized by extraordinary violence and experience of human evil. Disillusionment, loss of faith, and loss of trust in a church that had summoned them to participate in war as an act of faith all worked to undermine the social and religious agenda of the church. From the end of the war, the demographics of church involvement and affiliation for Anglicans began to shift demonstrably (Radner and Turner 2006, 42).

In an attempt to interpret the historical forces involved in this recent period, I conducted several oral history interviews with Anglicans who were alive during the transformations I have outlined. One such interviewee, Robert, tells the story of his grandfather who had fought in the First World War. He had been raised in the church. His father had been an Anglican priest. He himself had been involved in all kinds of youth work at the church. Yet, when he returned from the war he refused ever to set foot inside a church. Even for the weddings of his children and grandchildren he would not to go to church. When I interviewed Robert, he explained,

> I don't think he ever got over what happened to him in the war. He used to say that the church told him God wanted him to go to war. What he saw in the war made him believe that there was no God. He never wanted to be a

hypocrite – so he never went back inside a church. He wasn't willing to pretend something that wasn't real for him anymore. (Interview 9)

In the aftermath of the First World War, it became increasingly common for people to turn their backs on Anglicanism as they sought to make sense of their lives. In fact, the only time this pattern appears to have abated was immediately after the next world war. In the wake of the Second World War, the Church of England in Canada, along with all other Protestant churches, experienced something of a boom in membership. As Canadian society expanded economically and in population, an unprecedented period of church building and expansion began (Grant 1998, 160).

The Anglican Church did not support the Second World War as enthusiastically as it had the First. That is not to say that the church spoke against participation. Its members still participated – after all, the overlap between identification with one's church, country, king, and God were deep and substantial – but with a relative lack of zeal. Perhaps because the church had not summoned people to war as it had in 1914, Anglicans were more open to allowing the church to respond to its needs in the aftermath of the Second World War (Grant 1998, 56). Notable nostalgia surfaced among veterans who wanted to make up for lost years. It appears that things such as church participation and Sunday school represented a form of normalcy they wanted for themselves and their children.

According to the Anglicans I have interviewed, after the Second World War, the predictable desires to reorder a world made disorderly during the war and to return to pre-war values dominated the Anglican imagination. My interview subjects also indicated that the culture of conformity so prevalent in English Anglican culture was also fuelled by perhaps one of the most pervasive characteristics of the post-war era in Canada – anxiety. The threat of the Cold War and its attendant atomic destruction, accompanied perhaps by residual guilt from the aftermath of wartime activities, all appeared to have contributed to the nostalgic desire to return to a mother church. Of course, this nostalgia – both for the relative innocence of pre-war values and the idealized church that people began to imagine must have been intimately associated with these orderly and righteous ideals – may never have actually existed in such pristine states. However, what is important is that in the imaginations and narratives of the people I interviewed, the popularity of these concepts was a crucial precursor to the post-war boom in the church.

The Anglican Church made an effort to respond to the rapidly shifting demographics and affluence that began to characterize Canadian society after the war. It responded with enthusiasm to the desire for social conformity as a value and for a culture in some ways reminiscent of the turn of the twentieth century (Grant 1998, 113). Social conformity according to values of a dominant English-speaking culture was something the church was uniquely suited to provide.

Unfortunately, these values were often articulated at the expense of other people and communities. One older man who had fought in the Second World War as a German soldier (and then after the war immigrated to Canada) tells of his experience attempting to settle in rural Canada:

> It must have been twenty-five years before some of my neighbours stopped calling me that dirty Hun. I tried my best to be a good neighbour: I assumed they were always right and tried my best to fit in. But still, when they were angry or upset or the crops had a problem and I would go into town, it would be the same thing every time. Somehow it was my fault – if it weren't for that dirty Hun ... (interview schedule 21)

Despite the appearance of a post-war boom, current demographic analysis shows that the growth in the Anglican community was more particular and not as universal as one might at first assume (see, for example, the chapter by Bramadat and Seljak in this book; see also Radner 2006, 28). The boom of Anglican Christianity was largely a phenomenon of suburbia, where families with small children were most heavily concentrated and where the effects of increased affluence were most obvious. Veterans returning from the war received veterans' benefits to assist with the financing of both post-secondary education and homes, both of which facilitated movement into the middle class. This new capacity for more people to own their own homes fuelled a construction boom in the suburbs that were coming to characterize Canadian society. It was in suburbia that Anglicans built their new churches, halls, and clergy residences. In contrast, in small towns, the number of Anglicans grew only slightly, and in rural areas as well as the inner city the church actually declined (Grant 1998, 122).

This epoch of suburbanization and growth left its mark on the character of Anglican life. The culture of this era laid the groundwork for roughly thirty years of rapid decline in which Canadian Anglicans are currently living. For example, a near obsession with material security led people to invest in pension plans and save for the future. This post-war attitude toward security and conservatism was also reflected in the church. There was also a notable shift from what Anglican insiders would call a 'mission-based' to a 'ministry-based' mindset in virtually all mainline Protestant denominations. In practical terms, this meant that in Canadian Anglican seminaries, ministry became professional-ized and pastoral care became its primary focus (Berton 1965). Congre-gational adherents and their leaders paid very little attention to those outside of local congregations.

This transformation was accompanied by growth in conservative theologies and attitudes within the Anglican Church. In their quest for stability, returning veterans asked for a theology that would mirror the stability they felt a world of warfare lacked. In this period we witnessed also the increasing popularity of neo-orthodoxy, a theological move-ment that rejected the basic optimism of classical liberal theology and called for an explanation of the human story in a radical doctrine of sin and grace. This movement interpreted theological questions through classic doctrine and moved the church away from its earlier relatively liberal discourse of social change. As well, as consumer culture and lei-sure time expanded, Christianity – not just Anglicanism, but most other mainstream forms – became increasingly oriented toward individual needs and interests.

Each of these developments worked to shape church culture in ways that limited its inclination to be progressive, visionary, or resistant to cultural trends. Increasing demands on churches (not just the Anglican churches) for personal services such as marriage, counselling, and bap-tism also contributed to its transformation. Paradoxically, as the church struggled to give people what they asked for, it found it could not keep pace with the surrounding culture (Berton 1965).

By the mid-1960s the Anglican Church of Canada realized that some-thing had changed. It began to see that the boom that it had experi-enced in places – specifically, in the burgeoning suburbs – in the 1950s had not been sufficient to rescue it from the fact that in the lives of its members and in Canadian society as a whole, the church was losing ground. As a result, the national body of the church, its General Synod, asked noted Canadian author Pierre Berton to study the situation and write a reflection on what was happening to Canadian Anglicanism. At Berton's request the research mandate was expanded to reflect gener-ally on Canadian Protestantism. His findings, published as *The Comfort-able Pew* in 1965, were challenging for the church. Berton argued that the church was in decline because its leadership had abdicated responsibility for grappling with the genuine issues of people's lives in a way that spoke meaningfully to their experience. The religious establishment, he said, had become tyrannical, dominating church life with its own agenda for survival and excluding the marginalized or different. The church too often argued the rightness of its position and failed to listen to the struggles of those who were looking for answers, and it had failed to communicate its messages in ways that were meaningful to the culture. Finally, Berton argued, because the church over-valued tradition and feared revolution, it was stuck in the paradox of its own irrelevancy (Berton 1965).

The picture Berton painted in 1965 was a harbinger of what was to come. As we shall see, despite efforts to recover, the church continues to lose its members at an alarming rate, and the underlying questions raised by Berton have remained unanswered.

Current Demographics

Creating a contemporary demographic profile of Canadian Anglicans from statistics is not a simple matter. Unlike some other denominational traditions, there is no relationship between the submission of statistics to its national body and funding from this body. With no direct incentive for the accurate reporting of numbers to the national church (the body that historically has gathered data on the Anglican constituency), the figures that do exist have been collected from parishes and dioceses in an empirically unreliable manner, to say the least (Larmondin 2000). It is not that the church has not cared about gathering statistics. In 1893, its national body (the General Synod) formed a committee on statistics that continued its work until 1969. After that point, statistics were gathered by the Administration and Finance Committee of the General Synod. However, despite the best efforts of this committee, the church can produce no reliable data on the number of its members. Nonetheless, with these limitations in mind, I can still offer the following comments on Anglican demographics.

First, the figures released by Statistics Canada (which collects information about religious affiliation every ten years) are at variance with the figures reported by the Anglican Church. This discrepancy is a product of the fact that the church does not count its members in the same way as Statistics Canada. The church determines membership from figures in parish rolls counted at the local level. It tracks the number of members, identifiable financial contributors, youth activities, Sunday school participation, baptisms, confirmations, marriages, and funerals, paid and unpaid (non-stipendiary) clergy, and paid staff in diocesan offices. It also looks at the financial situations of parishes and dioceses. It monitors trends and on occasion asks for analysis of those trends. Statistics Canada, however, simply accepts the way people identify themselves. The 2001 census indicates that there were approximately 1,950,802 Anglicans in Canada, while the church itself registered a total membership of 650,977 (Larmondin 2000).

The discourse of loss one hears among Anglicans on the topic of declining church numbers is best illustrated in a report presented to church leaders by marketing analyst Keith McKerracher (also a member of the Anglican Church of Canada Communications and Information Resources Committee). At the October 2005 Canadian House of Bishops (a semi-annual meeting of all active Anglican bishops from across the country), McKerracher used statistics gathered by the national church and his own research to illustrate the effects of the current declining membership trends in Canada and announced that 'the last Anglican will leave the church in 2061' (De Santis 2005). The response of church leaders to this prediction was varied. Some were delighted that a clear statement of the urgency and immediacy of church decline had reached the bishops. Others felt that McKerracher's analysis was alarmist and did not take account of the fact that declining birth rates among the church's traditional constituency – white Anglo-Americans and Anglo-Canadians – were more responsible for this decline than the church's actions and attitudes (De Santis 2005).

Other statistical data collected prior to McKerracher's report, however, indicate that his findings are not alarmist. Rather, they document a trend of decline since the 1970s moving toward the eventual and perhaps inevitable end of an Anglican presence in Canadian society. For example, at its trienniel national meeting of the General Synod in 2001, Bishop Thomas Collings presented a report that provided some analysis of statistics gathered by the national church between 1970 and 2000. His findings supported two perceptions: first, the number of affiliated Anglicans is declining; second, the church has expended considerable effort trying to keep the institution afloat, despite the persistent trend toward dramatic decline (2001). Thus, while not predicting a definitive outcome, Collings identified trends that would lead to McKerraher's hypothesis of church demise several years later.

Between 1970 and 2000 the total number of people on church rolls fell by roughly 40 per cent, or 475,593 people. The decline indicates a persistent trend. In fact, between 1990 and 2000 alone, roughly 20 per cent of Anglicans fell off the church rolls. The Canadian census presents a rosier picture. For example, Statistics Canada claims that that the decline for Anglicans between 1990 and 2000 was approximately 10 per cent. Again, this discrepancy is likely a function of the fact that Statistics Canada's figure indicates merely how many people identify themselves as Anglicans, rather than how many have any involvement in the church itself. Such identity claims may say as much about the enduring historical and symbolic links between Canadian society and the Anglican tradition as they do about the commitments of individuals, although this speculation is difficult to corroborate (see the Solange Lefebvre's chapter 3 on Roman Catholicism in Quebec, and Bramadat and Seljak's chapter 1, for a discussion of similar forces at work in Roman Catholic self-description in Quebec).

Other figures are also troubling to Anglican insiders. For example, the number of those who have been confirmed (have made a confession of faith as an adult or young adult) declined dramatically in those thirty years. In fact, the number of confirmations in the year 2000 was some 75 per cent less than the number of confirmations recorded in 1970. Moreover, baptisms (the rite of initiation into the Christian faith that marks the beginning of membership) declined by 54 per cent in this same period. Perhaps most striking of all and not unrelated to the above-mentioned statistics is the decline in the number of youth in the church: between 1970 and 2000 the number of young people involved in youth groups dropped by 89 per cent. To put it another way, for every young person in the church in 2000, there were almost ten in 1970. During this same period the number of children in Sunday schools dropped by 66 per cent (Collings 2001). Perhaps even more notable is the fact that of the 650,977 total members on parish rolls in 2000, only 214,176 (about one-third) were identifiable regular financial contributors. This means that slightly more than 200,000 individual contributors alone support the entire infrastructure of the work at all levels of the Anglican Church of Canada.

The ongoing decline of membership in the Anglican Church, particularly among the young, does not mean that the church has not attempted to recover its former numerical strength. In fact, the opposite is true. While membership has declined, the church has attempted to maintain an infrastructure that had been developed for a much larger membership. Despite a 42 per cent decline in membership in recent decades, there was only a 17 per cent decline in the number of Anglican congregations. As well, there has been only a statistically small decline in the number of paid clergy. The data indicate only small random fluctuations in clergy figures in those thirty years. In fact, with the addition of the category of non-stipendiary (unpaid) clergy, the overall number of parish clergy in the period of membership decline actually increased by 20 per cent (Collings 2001).

As parishes have struggled with the challenges of dramatic decline, diocesan offices and the national church have attempted to support these struggles by developing new program initiatives and resources. This has meant that the number of paid clergy on diocesan staff has increased by 132 per cent in the thirty-year period under consideration and the number of paid lay staff in said offices has increased by 5 per cent. However, despite efforts to help the church survive and thrive, the demographics indicate that these attempts have been insufficient to stem the tide of decline (Collings 2001). As noted elsewhere in this volume, it is not that Canadians have ceased to ask traditionally 'spiritual' questions. It is, rather, that people, particularly in a younger age bracket, are not moving toward the Anglican Church to find answers to questions they have about the meaning of their own lives and the ethical questions that confront them.

The crisis depicted by these figures speaks to a trend we are witnessing within many mainstream churches (see the chapters on the United Church and the Presbyterian Church). Such a commonality is not, however, particularly consoling for Anglicans. After all, there is no indication in data gathered since 2000 that the trend noted here has abated; in fact, McKerracher argues that it has persisted (De Santis 2005).

Contemporary Issues

Much of the church's energy over the past decades has been devoted to the questions of survival and identity that significant decline have generated. The focus on survival has competed with several controversial issues that, in their turn, have compounded the complexity of addressing the question of what has happened to Canadian Anglicanism. Four particular issues have dominated the stage of church politics and decision making and have, in their own way, contributed to struggles over decline and identity. These struggles include the ordination of women, human sexuality (with particular reference to sexual orientation and the blessings of same sex unions), the church's relations with First

Nations communities, and the impact of ethnic diversity on the church. I now turn my attention to this last matter, although this issue can be best understood in terms of its relationship with the other challenges I have listed.

By way of a preamble to this section, I should note that current demographics indicate that global Christianity is undergoing dramatic transformations. As Christianity declines in the Northern Hemisphere, it continues to grow rapidly in the so-called two-thirds world of the Southern Hemisphere (Jenkins 2002, 95). Anglicans are not immune to this trend. There are currently more Anglicans living in Africa than in all of the rest of the Anglican Communion combined. As Jenkins (2002) indicates, in each region and nation in which it takes root, Christianity becomes theologically and socially distinctive. Since Anglicanism is growing almost exclusively in regions associated with conservative cultural, political, and ethical norms, the fastest growing form of Anglicanism in the world tends therefore to be more theologically and ethically conservative than much of Canadian Anglicanism, which has tended to pursue a traditional middle ground in both theological and ethical matters (Fletcher-Marsh 1995). In Canada this means that the only real numeric growth in the Canadian Anglican Church currently is among newcomers whose distinctive form of Anglicanism is often far more conservative than the dominant historical form one finds in the churches in which these immigrants settle. Over time, this will have an effect on the way Anglicanism evolves in Canada. Already the impact of the changes in the ethnic composition of the church is quite evident in two lively debates: the role and rights of women and the church's approach to homosexuality.

The ordination of women to the priesthood has been one of the most controversial issues to arise in Christian circles during the twentieth century. For Anglicans at the global level, this issue is still a matter of debate, although for Canadian Anglicans it is now a matter of contemporary history (see Fletcher-Marsh 1995), since women have been allowed to serve as priests in Canada since 1976 (Fletcher-Marsh 1995, 2002).

To put these changes in their proper historical context, I should observe that at the turn of the twentieth century, Canadian society struggled with the questions that the first wave of feminism raised about the place and inclusion of women in society.[5] However, the Canadian Anglican Church did not begin to address the question of women's inclusion in the church until well after second wave feminism had further changed the broader culture in the late 1960s. In fact, the church did not want to move further until an international audience through the Lambeth Conference in 1968 brought pressure to bear on the Canadian church to consider the ultimate issue of women's ordination (and such discussions really began in earnest in the early 1970s).[6] Prior to this time, women who wanted to serve the church as paid employees often found themselves serving in ministries on the peripheries of the Canadian Anglican world (Fletcher-Marsh 2002).[7]

Anglicanism in the modern era modelled its understanding of gender roles on the values and mores of Victorian England. Although Canadian and British gender expectations differed in some ways, what we might call the 'gender project' of Canadian Anglicanism was fundamentally a colonial inheritance of British origin; that is to say, these rigid notions about womanhood that made such an impression on Anglicanism and the broader culture were features of what we might call Victorian era British ethnicity. The Victorian woman who was also the Canadian Anglican woman was defined by virtue on several levels. She lived within a distinct and limited sphere of domesticity; she was devoted to home and hearth; she was a helpmate for her husband and a constant caretaker for her children; she was the emotional heart of her home and became for the family its font of moral virtue and religiosity. Any commitment to the church was an expression of her domestic virtue in the ecclesial or para-ecclesial spheres.

Up until the 1960s the dominant model for Canadian Protestant womanhood was the Victorian woman, understood within the confines of women's domestic sphere. The fact that the Canadian church did not consider the question of the full inclusion of women in ordination until it had been asked to by its predominantly English parent body, would probably surprise some Canadians who might assume Canadians would be more 'progressive' on this matter than the British would be. Moreover, this fact signals the extent to which Canadian Anglican ethos and life were still strongly linked to a romanticization of its British heritage. Even though the Church of England had moved beyond its earlier understanding of the subordinate role of women, Anglicans in Canada nostalgically clung to the model that dominated the nineteenth and early twentieth centuries.

Paradoxically, however, Canada eventually moved much more quickly toward the full inclusion of women in the ministries of the church than did their English counterparts. The decision of the Canadian church to move toward gender integration – and to move there much more quickly than the English church was able to do in the arena of ordination – ultimately indicates a growing separation of consciousness and identity from the colonial parent body. Canadian Anglicanism was an identity increasingly differentiated from English Anglicanism. In fact, the Canadian church took action to ordain women to the priesthood in 1976, many years ahead of the Church of England's decision in 1992. Canadian willingness to take this action and risk a breach of the Communion demonstrates its increasing institutional autonomy and signals a new day in its relationship with the culture of its ethnic origins. It is interesting to note that the growing autonomy and progressive development of the Canadian church (relative to the British church) corresponded to the leadership of the first Canadian-born Anglican archbishop, Ted Scott, who served as primate of the Anglican Church of Canada between 1971 and 1986.

In short, the Canadian Anglican Church was reactive rather than proactive on the issue of full inclusion of women in the polity of its church. It lagged behind both Canadian culture and the Church of England on the issue of including women in leadership positions. However, on the question of the ordination of women, once the wheels were finally set in motion in Canada, the decision-making process went fairly rapidly, especially when one considers the Victorian sensibilities that worked against such innovations.[8] Nonetheless, progress toward the full integration of women (not just ordained women) throughout the church was limited (and is perhaps not yet completed) and often obstructed by powerful stakeholders within the church itself.

There are still sectors in the broader Anglican Communion that reject the notion of ordaining women to the ministry. Here English – or to be more precise, Victorian – history, ethnicity, and the different ways the Anglican message has been interpreted in cultures around the world determine the way these communities respond to questions on the full inclusion of women in the church. As increasing numbers of Anglicans from other parts of the world immigrate to Canada, Anglican attitudes here are likely to shift. Given that Anglicans in most of the rest of the world hold considerably more conservative views on this particular issue, it seems likely that Canadian Anglican opinion will probably shift in that direction as well.

It is a common view within the Canadian Anglican community that Anglicans from Asia tend toward a more conservative view of ethics, social praxis, and theology. As we shall see, this is certainly the case with the matter of the blessings of same-sex unions. However, in women's ordination, there are notable and interesting exceptions. For example, the Chinese Anglican Church was ahead of not only Canada but the Communion as a whole. In 1944, the bishop of Hong Kong ordained the first woman to the priesthood in the Communion. At the hands of Bishop Baker, Florence Li Tim Oi became the first woman in the world to be admitted to the Anglican priesthood. It is generally agreed that this happened as a result of the exigencies of war; Baker needed a priest to provide the sacraments in an area where no clergy were available. Since no ecclesiastical decision making was undertaken, the action was locally determined and simply accomplished. In 1945 after the end of the war, the archbishop of Canterbury threatened to remove Baker as bishop of Hong Kong if he did not laicize Reverend Oi. Baker refused. Unwilling to be the cause of an ecclesiastical rupture, Reverend Oi herself simply disappeared from the ecclesiastical scene in Hong Kong, migrating first to mainland China, and then, after the 1960s Cultural Revolution in China, settling in Canada where she served as a priest in the Diocese of Toronto (Fletcher-Marsh 1995).

One might imagine this action to have been a random act disconnected from the Chinese cultural context. However, in 1971 when the Anglican Consultative Council found that there was no impediment to the movement of member churches toward ordaining women, the church in Hong Kong immediately proceeded to ordain two further women to the priesthood and has ordained women ever since (Fletcher-Marsh 1995). Nonetheless, there are still Asian dioceses and congregations that categorically refuse to welcome the ordained leadership of women. While one wants to avoid generalizations, in the matter of the reception of women's leadership Anglican communities from Asia, Africa, and parts of the Caribbean have been historically (and most are still) more resistant to the full inclusion of women than those from North America and western Europe.

The complexity of relationship between ethnicity and attitudes toward women's place in the community is further illustrated by the African experience. As I mentioned earlier, there are more Anglicans in Africa, indeed within the Ugandan Church *alone*, than in *all* the other national churches of the Communion outside of Africa *combined*. Therefore it stands to reason that the approach that African Anglicans take to many issues will significantly affect the direction of global Anglicanism. Since African immigration into the Canadian church is numerically significant, the impact of the African perspective on this national scene will be increasingly important. Within the African Church itself reception of the idea of the ordination of women is mixed. The Ugandan Church and the Church of Kenya were among the first to ordain women in the late 1970s. However, in other parts of Africa, such as Zimbabwe, the ordination of women is still not accepted by Anglicans (Fletcher-Marsh 2002). In November 1998 I went to Zimbabwe as delegate representing the Anglican Church of Canada. I was asked through the staff of the World Council of Churches if I would like to preach while there. I agreed and was assigned to preach at the Anglican Cathedral in Harare. The day before I was to preach, I received a note at my table in the Assembly, telling me that I had been reassigned. I would now preach at a small Methodist Church in a neighbouring town. When I asked WCC staff people why I had been reassigned, I was told that the local Anglican leaders had not realized that 'the reverend doctor' was a woman. However, in the case of Zimbabwe, it is important to note that while the ordination of women is not accepted, other forms of women's leadership in groups, such as the Mothers' Union, thrive (Fletcher-Marsh 2002), a fact that reminds us just how complex are the relationships between ethnicity and religion, especially when one considers this powerful interaction in terms of women's latitude within the church.

The controversial matter of the blessing of same-sex unions has made the debates within the Anglican world over women's roles look minor and pacific indeed. In an attempt to be pastorally sensitive to the needs of gays and lesbians, North American dioceses have been asking whether or not church teaching and practice in marriage and sexuality needs to change. The North American Anglican churches in particular have lagged slightly behind the surrounding secular culture in their approach to this issue, but they have been well ahead of the larger worldwide Anglican Communion. To put this contrast in context, though, it is important to note what happened in June 2007 at the General Synod meeting of the Anglican Church of Canada. At this meeting in Winnipeg, an official motion that would allow dioceses to decide whether or not to bless same-sex unions (not to conduct the weddings, but to bless those unions performed by civil authorities) was rejected. However, the vote was extremely close: lay delegates voted seventy-eight to fifty-nine in favour of the motion; clergy also voted sixty-three to fifty-three in favour; however, the House of Bishops voted twenty-one to nineteen against this measure. So, even though the majority of those voting actually favoured the blessing of same-sex unions, since all three bodies had to accept the motion for it to pass, it was defeated (Anglican Church of Canada 2007).

The Canadian Anglican debate on this issue demonstrates a further separation of Canadian Anglicanism from its colonial parent. The decision of the Diocese of New Westminster in British Columbia to proceed with the blessing of the unions of same-sex couples triggered not just a national but indeed a global debate within the broader Anglican Communion. Discussion arose within the global Communion on whether the Anglican Church of Canada should be severed from the rest of the Anglican world because of this decision, which has led to significant conflict though not a fatal breach in the Communion. The 2007 vote at the meeting in Winnipeg was indeed very close; however, given the increasing power of relatively conservative ethnic minority newcomers in the church, it is unclear what will happen if or when the national Anglican community is asked to vote on this matter again. The contrast and tension between the established liberal Anglicans and the relatively conservative newcomer Anglicans reflects the larger uncertainty within the church on the direction in which Canadian Anglicanism will evolve.

Anglicanism has always made room for adaptation to the surrounding cultural context; this tradition of adaptation is reflected in the great diversity one finds within the worldwide Anglican Communion. The movement to bless same-sex unions, especially in Canada, reflects a decision that had been several decades in the making. In 1976, the same year that the Canadian church moved to ordain women, the forty bishops of the House of Bishops established a task force to study the issue of homosexuality. Work on the issue in various contexts has been ongoing ever since. In 1998, 2001, and 2002, the Synod of the Diocese of New Westminster voted to offer same-sex blessings. In May 2003, Michael Ingham, the diocesan bishop, issued a rite of blessing of covenanted same-sex unions. The first blessing took place a few days later.

The complexity of this issue mirrors the complexity of the evolving Anglican identity. For much of its history Anglicanism has been deeply bound to its roots in British descent heritage. That ethnic legacy has been in many ways the guiding force in the way Canadian Anglican identity has emerged and become coherent. However, as an adaptive tradition, local and regional cultures have often led to significant metamorphoses in Anglicanism. The blessing of same-sex unions in Canada illustrates this tendency, just as the 2007 rejection of the motion indicates the power of the larger institution to curtail innovation.[9] Both forces are at work here.

As immigration of African and Asian Anglicans into the Canadian ecclesiastical landscape continues, the impact of immigration on the church with reference to this issue is likely to be significant. The diversity of attitudes among Asian and African churches on the issue of women's leadership has been noted earlier. Such diversity, however, is not apparent on the issue of homosexuality. Despite the existence of homosexual persons and subcultures in Asian and African cultures, the churches in these areas have consistently stigmatized homosexuality as an aberrant behaviour.

The opposition of most Canadian immigrant communities – particularly those from Africa and Asia – to the practice of homosexuality is quite notable in the Canadian Christian landscape; elsewhere in this book one finds many examples of the relative conservatism on sexual matters among African and Asian congregations. After the Diocese of New Westminster made its decision to proceed with the blessing of same-sex unions, all Chinese Anglican congregations in the diocese left and sought affiliation with African Anglican churches who share their opposition.[10]

However, it is prudent to avoid assumptions about the ways ethnic minorities will interpret gender issues. When the debate over the blessing of same-sex unions gripped the broader Canadian Anglican Church, within one Chinese congregation that left the Diocese of New Westminster under the leadership of its Asian clergy, a group remained that felt that their loyalty to the national church was more important than their sympathy with the decisions of other New Westminster Anglicans who decided to bless same-sex unions. As such, while not supporting the blessing of same-sex unions, this group sought an Asian member of clergy to lead them in forming a new Chinese Anglican congregation that would remain as part of the Diocese of New Westminster. It would surprise many people to learn that the priest they found to lead them was an Asian woman.

The Asian cultural context serves as one backdrop for interpreting Anglicanism's colonial past and present. In fact, in no instance is the involvement between Anglicanism and colonial power more visible than in the case of Anglican relationships with First Nations peoples for the last several centuries. Most notably, the Anglican partnership with the federal government to run residential schools for First Nations children has left a legacy that the church is attempting to acknowledge and transcend.

Following the 1759 British victory over the French forces on the Plains of Abraham in present-day Quebec, the French formally ceded

Quebec to the British in the 1763 Treaty of Paris. In the 1763 Royal Proclamation, the British outlined among other things an understanding of
how they would relate to First Nations persons in the new land. The
proclamation announced a policy of friendship. The Anglican Church
as the established religion of the British government adopted this policy. This policy of friendship meant that ethnic or, to use a concept more
appropriate for Aboriginal discourse, national variety was encouraged
within the development of local Anglicanism. Indigenous clergy were
sought or cultivated; the prayer book and the Bible were translated into
indigenous languages by English-speaking clergy, who first had to
learn the new languages. Some indigenous ritual elements (for example, drumming) were not only allowed but encouraged as part of the
Anglican liturgy.

By the time Canada became a nation in 1867, the attitude of the dominant culture had shifted. From friendship, governing bodies moved to
a policy of 'civilization' and ultimately to assimilation (Milloy 1999, 41).
In keeping with its historic partnership with government, the Anglican
Church again generally mirrored the policy of the government in its
own practices and involvement with First Nations people. As such, as
the government moved to delimit the rights and freedoms of First
Nations persons, so too did the Anglican Church. For example, in
residential schools the use of First Nations languages was no longer
tolerated, reflecting a larger policy developed by government and reinforced by churches to move toward eradication of all signs and practices of Native culture. Indigenous clergy were no longer sought. All
indigenous tribal rituals were eliminated from the liturgy. In some
instances in the northwestern parts of the county, clergy even participated in the symbolic cutting down of totem poles. First Nations persons were taught that such practices were evil and an obstacle to
salvation.

Early mission work in Canada ran along denominational lines. The
Anglican Church developed missions in many First Nations communities, as did other denominations in regions of the country. Given the
communal nature of indigenous communities, whole villages converted to Anglicanism following the example of the elders of their village. Residential schools similarly followed this denominational
pattern.

When the government was ready to initiate the residential school
experiment in 1870, the Church of England in Canada signed on as one
of its four church partners (Milloy 1999, 12). This meant that the mis-

sionary organ of the Anglican Church, the Missionary Society of the Church of England in Canada, would manage several government-owned residential schools. Churches received a per capita grant from the government to oversee the implementation of government policy in the schools as well as their daily management. The Missionary Society also supplemented the school by providing necessities such as warm boots and socks, and on occasion providing workers through the Woman's Auxiliary (Fletcher-Marsh 2002, 73).

As we now know, the residential school experiment was a dismal failure. It was grounded in the twin assumptions that Native persons were inferior to their European-descent neighbours, and that only removing children at an early enough age from the influence of Native culture, custom, and parentage would facilitate their transformation into Canadian (read: Europeanized) citizens. However, the schools often failed to provide effective education. Moreover, because of chronic underfunding by the Canadian government, they often failed to provide the necessities of life. As such, they profoundly deprived many generations of students.

Duncan Campbell Scott, working for the Department of Indian Affairs early in the last century, was responsible for the 'Indian problem.' His attitude reflected the dominant ethos when he stated, 'Education is the answer to the Indian problem – education, education until there is no Indian left' (Milloy 1999, 39). To be a citizen of Canada, a human being under the law, meant transcending an Indian identity. Scott continued, 'I want to get rid of the Indian problem ... Our objective is to continue until there is not a single Indian in Canada who has not been absorbed into the body politic and there is no Indian question and no Indian problem' (46).

In the mid-1960s, the Canadian government considered closing its residential schools. Opposing this move George Luxton, the bishop of Huron, wrote, 'There is not much hope for this generation of Indians. But if we persist in our efforts perhaps their grandchildren may be raised up to the level of a servant class' (Fletcher 2004, 6). Even when the government had begun to repent of its assimilationist practices, there were many in Anglican Church leadership who still believed in the colonial model of relating with First Nations people. The assumption of racial inferiority that had undergirded early government policy was alive and well in parts of the Anglican Church well past the middle of the twentieth century.

By the 1990s the church's self-understanding had changed. It began to repent of its earlier work in partnership with government and in 1992 the primate of the Anglican Church of Canada, Michael Peers, offered a formal apology to First Nations people for the church's collaboration with residential schools. Since the mid-1990s the national Anglican Church has worked to overcome the harm caused by residential schools by creating partnerships with First Nations peoples, many of whom are Anglicans.[11] This work aimed toward healing and reconciliation has taken several forms, including the development of a healing and reconciliation fund that supports the cost of projects developed by First Nations leadership. Each year the Anglican healing fund allocates many tens of thousands of dollars to support local indigenous projects aimed at healing and reconciliation. Gradually, and ironically not unlike they did in the eighteenth century, Anglicans have begun to seek indigenous candidates for the priesthood; First Nations tribal practices have again been welcomed by many as part of Anglican liturgy; and First Nations languages are increasingly part of ecclesial practice. In each of these shifts we observe the reintegration of First Nations peoples into church life.

The cost of litigations initiated by residential school survivors and involving both the church and government as defendants produced a climate of concern among many Canadian Anglicans. The legal expenses incurred by the church have predictably led to a significant financial crisis. As one diocese dissolved as the result of bankruptcy and the national church moved toward the same end, the Anglican Church of Canada signed an agreement with the federal government. This agreement, ratified in March 2003, stipulated that the Federal Government of Canada agreed to pay 70 per cent of compensation to be awarded to plaintiffs while the church would pay 30 per cent up to a maximum of $25 million. This $25 million is to be paid jointly by all dioceses of the Canadian church as a sign of whole church accountability. With this agreement the church both admitted its responsibility for work in the schools and made a deal that would save it from bankruptcy.

The agreement caused great distress among Anglican indigenous leaders. For example, the Anglican Circle for Indigenous People denounced the agreement the day after it was signed, citing their sense of betrayal at the church's decision to make a deal with the government, its old partner in exploitation of First Nations communities. Most disturbing in the agreement was the requirement that the church oppose any attempt by school survivors to make claims for loss of culture. The official 2003 agreement covered claims only for sexual and physical abuse. Despite the church's commitment to reconciliation, ulti-mately its survival meant that it chose to realign itself with its former partner in the residential school policy. The anger that this re-partner-ing produced in First Nations communities toward the church will take many years to transcend.

The federal government did in fact move past that agreement and in November 2005 agreed in partnership with former students, legal counsel for churches, the Assembly of First Nations, and other Aborig-inal organizations to sign an agreement in principle that resolves all outstanding residential school claims. This agreement and the issues that attend it involve such key elements as 'common experience pay-ment' to all survivors and a truth and reconciliation process (Anglican Church of Canada 2005; Department of Justice Canada 2005). It is designed to produce some form of justice since, in the eyes of so many Aboriginal people, many years of court battles have failed them. How-ever, work continues among Anglican First Nations organizations and the national church to negotiate a form of self-government for First Nations Anglicans through the election of a First Nations bishop who will be responsible for the pastoral care of First Nations Anglican com-munities across the country.

Conclusion

mainstream Church

The complexity of the relationship between ethnicity and Anglicanism in Canada cannot be overestimated. However, in order to do justice to this kind of analysis, ethnicity must be brought into conversation with issues of geography, race, class, culture, ethics, theology, the history of missionary activity overseas, regional specifics, and globalization, since all of these forces work together. While this makes it very difficult for us to make clear generalizations about, for example, the impact of non-European ethnic communities on the Anglican Church in Canada, there is arguably a tendency toward moral and gender conservatism within these newer communities. As these communities find a place within the dominant Canadian Anglican community that is itself still strug-gling to redefine its relationship with its own colonial heritage, we will likely witness complex mutual post-colonial religious redefinition. Here we are observing not simply the standard phenomenon of new-comer communities adjusting to a singular mainstream religious ethos, but rather a vast web of mutual readjustments: of the newcomer Angli-cans to the existing religious ethos they find in the Canadian church, of the mainstream Anglicans to the arrival of newcomers who bring with them distinctive articulations of a putatively universal heritage, and finally of mainstream Anglicans to the ambiguous legacy of their British forebears.

In order to understand the salience of ethnicity within the Canadian Anglican community, I should perhaps return to where I began this chapter. In my own family narrative, we find that my maternal grandfather rejected Christianity with a vengeance after his experience in the residential school system, but later in life did in fact move back toward Anglicanism. However, when he returned to the church he took his relearned wisdom from longhouse practice with him. And me? I continue to puzzle out the meaning of my own story, as a woman raised as an English-descent Anglican who at mid-life finds that her actual history is quite a bit more complicated than she had assumed. As for the Anglicans, in keeping with and in contradistinction to what my parents taught me as a child, they are not – and they are – like me.

Notes

1 For more on the history of the transformation of Anglicanism from a 'national church' into a global communion, see Duffy (2003), Kaye (2003), and Sachs (2003). For a look at Anglicanism from a North American perspective, see Holmes (1982), Karterberg (2001), and Noll (2002).
2 For more on the Anglican Church in the New World and how it changed according to its social context, particularly Quebec, see Reisner (1995).
3 In fact, the Church of England was legally established only in New Brunswick, Nova Scotia, and Prince Edward Island. Nevertheless, in Upper and Lower Canada it enjoyed the privileges of establishment. See Hayes (2004).
4 For more on Stachan's worldview, see McDermott (1983).
5 First wave feminism refers to the movement in the early part of the twentieth century that was aimed at the enfranchisement of women and their inclusion in contemporary culture. Second wave feminism refers to the next wave of social energy that coalesced around actualizing the full inclusion of women in Western societies in the 1960s and early 1970s. Germinal texts that elaborate this phenomenon include Betty Friedan's *The Feminine Mystique* (1963), Simone de Beauvoir's *The Second Sex* (1952), and Mary Daly's *The Church and the Second Sex* (1985).
6 The Lambeth Conference is a gathering of all Anglican bishops once every ten years, convened by the archbishop of Canterbury. However, while the

archbishop of Canterbury is a titular head, he has no overarching authority. The Anglican Consultative Council provides a venue for churches to talk together on issues at the level of consultation and education. It is important to note that in the Anglican world, national churches are not obliged to adhere to the decisions of the Lambeth Conference or the Anglican Consultative Council. On the Lambeth Conference, see http://www.lambeth conference.org/.

7 An example was the Bishops' Messengers, an order of women who practised pastoral ministry in the most geographically far-flung reaches of the country where ordained men were often unwilling to go. Another example included women workers in varieties of urban settings who worked among the poor, particularly women and children, funded not by the church itself but by the Woman's Auxiliary.

8 The primate, the titular head of the Canadian church, convened a commission that prepared a report for the 1973 meeting of the national decision-making body, the General Synod. That report contained both a majority and a minority position. After some deliberation, all members of the commission except one male cleric had concluded that the ordination of women should proceed. The majority position considered both theological and sociological reasons for this recommendation. Subsequently, the General Synod of 1973 voted to proceed with the ordination of women, achieving the necessary two-thirds majority. Rather than proceeding immediately, the matter was then referred to the House of Bishops for further consideration. When the issue returned two years later to the General Synod of 1975, it was again ratified by a two-thirds majority, this time with even stronger support than in the 1973 decision (Fletcher-Marsh 1995).

9 On this issue, see the Anglican Communion Official Website, *The Windsor Report 2004*, produced by the Lambeth Commission on Communion. See also Linzey and Kirker (2005).

10 Since Anglicans believe that bishops are the successors of the original apostles, they need a legitimate bishop in order to remain in the Anglican communion as well as to ordain clergy. The Chinese groups in question have affiliated with the Diocese of Rwanda. See Canadian Info Society.

11 Although First Nations membership in Anglican communities is dwindling (as it is in other mainstream denominations), their presence in the Canadian Anglican landscape is still numerically significant. Although the church does not gather statistics that would measure this exactly, I estimate that more than 15 per cent of the Anglican population overall are of First Nations ancestry, and in some northern Anglican communities this figure would be roughly 90 per cent.

Works Cited

Anglican Church of Canada. 2005. Residential schools agreement: Q&A. http://www.anglican.ca/Residental-Schools/qa-2005-11-23.htm

– 2007. Blessing of same-sex unions defeated. http://www.anglican.ca/news/news.php?newsItem=2007-06-24_ssb.news.

Anglican Communion Official Website. The Windsor Report 2004. http://www.anglicancommunion.org/windsor2004/index.cfm

Berton, Pierre. 1965. *The comfortable pew: A critical look at Christianity and the religious establishment in the new age*. Toronto: McClelland and Stewart.

Beauvoir, Simone de. 1954. *The second sex*. New York: Vintage Books.

Bryant, Darryl, ed. 2001. *Canadian Anglicanism at the dawn of a new century*. Lewiston, NY: Mellen.

Canadian Info Society. Conservative Anglicans prepare to celebrate their 'common cause.' http://www.canadianchristianity.com/cgi-bin/na.cgi?national updates/060824anglican

Collings, Thomas. 2001. Preliminary analysis of church stats, in the record of proceedings of the 2001 General Synod. General Synod archives, Toronto.

Daly, Mary. 1985. *The church and the second sex*. Boston: Beacon.

Department of Justice Canada. 2005. Healing the past: Addressing the legacy of physical and sexual abuse in Indian residential schools. http://www.justice.gc.ca/en/dept/pub/dig/healing.htm.

De Santis, Solange. 2005. Bishops examine church growth. *Anglican Journal* 131(10): 13.

Duffy, Eamon. 2003. *Anglicanism and the Western Christian tradition: Continuity, change and the search for communion*. Norwich: Canterbury.

Fletcher, Wendy. 2004. The Canadian experiment with social engineering – A historical case: The Mohawk Institute. In *Historical Papers: Canadian Society of Church History*, 133–50.

Fletcher-Marsh, Wendy. 1995. *Beyond the walled garden: Anglican women and the priesthood*. Toronto: Artemis.

– 2002. *Like water on rock: Gender integration in Canadian Anglicanism*. Toronto: Artemis.

Friedan, Betty. 1963. *The feminine mystique*. New York: Norton.

Grant, John Webster. 1998. *The church in the Canadian era*. Vancouver: Regent College Publishing.

Hayes, Alan. 2004. *Anglicans in Canada: Controversies and identity in historical perspective*. Urbana: University of Illinois Press.

– n.d. Canadian Anglican history, 3: The establishment ideal. http://home.cogeco.ca/%7Ealhayes/anglicancanada/anglhist3.htm.

Holmes, Urban T. 1982. *What Is Anglicanism?* Toronto: Anglican Book Centre.

Houston, Cecil G., and William Smyth, eds. 1980. *The sash Canada wore: A historical geography of the Orange Order in Canada.* Toronto: University of Toronto Press.

Jenkins, Phillip. 2002. *The next Christendom: The coming of global Christianity.* Oxford: University of Oxford Press.

Karterberg, William. 2001. *Modernity and the dilemma of North American Anglican identities.* Montreal and Kingston: McGill-Queen's University Press.

Kaye, Bruce. 2003. *Re-inventing Anglicanism: A vision of confidence, community, and engagement in Anglican Christianity.* Adelaide, Australia: Openbook Publishers.

Larmondin, Leanne. 2000. Chasing the elusive statistics. http://www.anglican.ca/news/php?newsItem=2002-02-03_ll.news

Linzey, Andrew, and Richard Kirker, eds. 2005. *Gays and the future of Anglicanism: Responses to the Windsor Report.* The Bothy, UK: O Books.

McDermott, Mark. 1983. The theology of Bishop John Strachan: A study in Anglican identity. PhD diss., St Michael's College.

Milloy, John. 1999. *A national crime: The Canadian government and the residential school system, 1879 to 1986.* Winnipeg: University of Manitoba Press.

Noll, Mark. 2002. *The old religion in a new world: The history of North American Christianity.* Grand Rapids, MI: Eerdmans.

Radner, Ephraim, and Philip Turner. 2006. *The fate of communion: The agony of Anglicanism and the future of the global church.* Grand Rapids, MI: Eerdmans.

Reisner, M.E. 1995. *Strangers and pilgrims: A history of the Anglican Diocese of Quebec, 1773–1993.* Toronto: Anglican Book Centre.

Sachs, William. 2003. *The transformation of Anglicanism: From state church to global communion.* Cambridge: Cambridge University Press.

Sykes, Stephen, ed. 1998. *The study of Anglicanism.* London: SPCK.

Williams, Rowan. 2003. *Anglican identities.* Cambridge, MA: Cowley.

Woolverton, John Frederick. 1984. *Colonial Anglicanism in North America.* Detroit: Wayne State University Press.

5 Presbyterian and Reformed Christians and Ethnicity

STUART MACDONALD

The Presbyterian and Reformed Christian traditions in Canada share a common heritage of the unique Protestantism inspired by John Calvin, Ulrich Zwingli, and other Swiss Reformers. Despite popular ideas that these churches are ethnically homogeneous, they have always been diverse. Portraits of three different congregations illustrate the point.

St Timothy's

The church sits in the middle of a Toronto suburb on a winding boulevard. The architecture suggests to the observer that it was built sometime after the Second World War in that period of massive expansion of Christian churches into the suburbs of Canada's cities. There are cars lining the street but the parking lot is surprisingly empty with the 10:30 service soon to begin. Inside the church the praise-band warms up. The sound technicians adjust the volumes and check PowerPoint for the hymn lyrics. As the service progresses, I discover many things that make St Timothy's – a Korean Presbyterian Church situated in a large metropolitan area – unusual. For example, I discover why the parking lot is so empty. There will be several services held today at St Timothy's, including the 10:30 English-language service, a Korean-language service at 1:00, and an evening Korean-language service. Each will involve different participants. Those already here have parked their cars on the street because they do not wish to be blocked in by those arriving for the 1:00 p.m. Korean service. I learn that while we are in church the youth of the congregation are holding their own worship service (not Sunday school) in the adjoining gymnasium. The children's time focuses on a simple catechism – a mode of teaching out of fashion in many congregations but used effectively here as the children learn the basics of the Ten Commandments. So much about the congregation feels familiar to one who grew up in a European Canadian Presbyterian church – and yet so much of what I see reflects a different way of being Presbyterian.[1]

The Ghanaian Presbyterian Church

The choir processes into the church wearing black robes, the female members wearing mortar boards. There is a rhythmic swaying as the choir moves up the aisles, singing the hymn in Ga, one of the languages of Ghana. A call to worship led by the minister is followed by more prayer and more music. The church pulses with music. Members sing, and some dance. Some dancers wear Western style clothes, while others wear more colourful African clothing. Many dance with white hand-kerchiefs in their hands, the handkerchiefs moving to the tempo of the drums. The Bible is read in three languages: English, then Twi and Ga, two of the main languages of Ghana, the West African country from which most members of this Toronto congregation, a partnership of the Presbyterian Church of Ghana and the Presbyterian Church in Canada, have come. The sermon is primarily in English, but throughout it the guest minister intersperses sentences in Ga. The sermon is longer than one would now find in many European Canadian Presbyterian churches, running over half an hour, but the congregation remains attentive and responsive.

Worship takes place in a building recently opened in the west end of Toronto. Rather than building a series of smaller churches throughout the Greater Toronto Area, the Ghanaian Presbyterians have worked together to create one congregation and to worship in one setting, despite differences in language and tribal heritage that typically divide the Ghanaian community. Three to four hundred adults have come from throughout the city. Their children and youth are involved in edu-cation and worship in classrooms in other parts of the building. The ushers do not pass plates through a seated congregation (the custom in most churches). Instead, several Plexiglas boxes are wheeled to the front of the church. As the choir and church band lead in music, mem-bers of the congregation each come up the aisles and place their finan-cial contributions into the offering boxes. The choir, ministers, and guests are all welcomed – and expected – to come forward with their offering. The service lasts over three hours.[2]

Grace Christian Reformed

'Do you know what is special about next Friday?' the minister asks the children at the front of the church. He has a poppy on his white shirt and holds another in his hands. Several of the children put up their hands, until the one who the minister names answers, 'Remembrance Day.'

A Canadian small town the Sunday before Remembrance Day. The theme of the children's talk – war and its human cost – is not unusual. But for members of this congregation, one could sense this is an absolutely vital theme to be discussed this day, something they want their children and grandchildren to know – even though there are no plaques on the walls naming those who served and died in either the First or Second World War. Such plaques do not exist because this congregation was established after the Second World War – but many of the grandparents at worship that day know only too well the experiences of war. Many survived the Second World War in the Netherlands, which was invaded and occupied by Nazi Germany. They remember occupation, fear, hunger, and the joy of being liberated by Allied troops, many of them Canadian.

The service continues. The music is a blend of traditional hymns and more contemporary praise songs. The minister conducts the service in a warm, informal fashion, making it similar to many congregations in the town. Many of the features of the service could be found in other congregations anywhere, but the children's story that Sunday clearly identifies the Dutch heritage of the congregation – and how ethnicity continues to shape it.[3]

Religion and Ethnicity

In all of these examples, ethnic identity shapes the music chosen, the progression of worship, the stories told, the locations of the buildings, the languages spoken and sung, and countless other practices. At the same time, ethnicity is rarely subjected to analysis or even casual discussion – either in the churches or in academia. The reason, one suspects, is that assumptions have been made both by those inside these churches as well as those outside, that there is nothing to study.

According to what one might call the master ethnic narrative about Presbyterians in Canada, the community has been understood as mono-culturally Scottish. The Scots have indeed been a very important component of Canadian Presbyterianism but are by no means the only ethnic community within that tradition. Scottish ethnicity competed from the beginning with others, and eventually with a Canadian ethnicity that is now being challenged on the one hand by recent immigration and on the other by the re-emergence of symbols and celebrations of Scottish ethnicity. Those in the Presbyterian Church in Canada exist in an increasingly ethnically diverse church but one where the dominant ethnicity is still under negotiation (is it Canadian? is it Scottish?).

The experience of the Christian Reformed Church – another Reformed or Calvinist tradition – tells another story altogether of the relationship between ethnicity on the one hand and language, nationality, and theological principles on the other. In the Christian Reformed Church, theology and religious values function in ways similar to the ways ethnicity often functions in other churches, in that they act together as the touchstone for group identity and solidarity. In the Christian Reform denomination, it is the particular theological understanding of the Calvinist tradition that has been transplanted to Canada, and this more than language and ethnicity has made the Christian Reformed Church distinctive.

To illustrate the development of these two communities, I begin by identifying the tradition and its origins in the sixteenth century, and by defining terms such as *Presbyterian* and *Reformed*. I then look at the contemporary demographics of each of the major denominations under study, before turning to a brief discussion of how each came to Canada and the ethnic issues involved in that history. Given the current variety of ethnic identities among Presbyterians in Canada, it is necessary to look separately at selected traditions within the Presbyterian tradition that stand alongside the British and Irish traditions with which most Canadians are familiar. I examine how Presbyterians have come to see themselves as essentially Canadian. Finally, I explore the challenges facing the Reformed churches in Canada amidst the increased ethnic diversity of Canadians (both inside and outside of the churches).

For me, such a study is not purely an academic enterprise. Ethnically, I am the child of a Scottish-immigrant father who came to Canada after the Second World War and a second-generation Scots Canadian mother. While our family has mixed religious origins – Plymouth Brethren, Scottish Episcopalian, United Church – I was raised in a Presbyterian church in a small Ontario town. Although I have never been a member of the Christian Reformed Church, I count among my friends many active members of this denomination, and I have spent many hours discussing with them the similarities and differences between our traditions. My observations of the Christian Reformed Church are thus those of a sympathetic outsider, and of the Presbyterian Church in Canada are those of a participant and a historian. As an ordained minister in the Presbyterian Church in Canada, I serve as associate professor of church and society in one of the theological colleges of that denomination. My academic background is in history; so, I cannot begin to understand a contemporary situation without examining its beginnings and development. It is to history we now turn.

What Is Presbyterian? What Is Reformed?

The Reformed movement, of which Presbyterians are one part, arose in sixteenth-century Switzerland. In this period of religious ferment, individuals and cities broke with the Catholic tradition and attempted to reform the church. While these reformations happened in parallel with Martin Luther's more famous attempt at reform in Germany, they rapidly took on a character of their own. Ulrich Zwingli in Zurich, John Calvin in Geneva, and other leaders such as Martin Bucer in Strasbourg developed a distinct understanding of theology and of church governance that separated them not only from the Catholic tradition, but also from the Lutherans and Anabaptists (MacCulloch 2003, 133–47, 174–84, 230–45, 348–82). The Reformed tradition is similar in many ways to the Lutheran tradition with its emphasis on the authority of scripture, recognition of only two sacraments, and acceptance of married clergy, but has developed different understandings of doctrine. For example, Reformed Christians took the Lutheran emphasis on scripture a step further, arguing that only those things explicitly mentioned in the Bible should be practised. This led to the banning in some countries of celebrations such as Christmas, for which no scriptural justification was found. The Reformed tradition has strongly emphasized the doctrine of predestination, present in earlier Western theology and shared with Luther – namely that God chooses whom God will save. This emphasis countered the popular piety of Luther's day, which suggested that people needed to ensure their salvation and that of their loved ones through acts of piety, including financial contributions. Later, Lutherans placed less emphasis on predestination and did not develop the same interpretations of it as did later Calvinists (see Bryan Hills's chapter 7 in this volume).

Reformed doctrine was codified in creeds (e.g. the Helvetic Confession, the Westminster Confession) in the sixteenth and seventeenth centuries. Different creeds have had greater importance in some areas of Europe than in others. The Westminster Confession, for example, has been more influential on the Reformed tradition in Britain than on the Continent. Historical developments since the seventeenth century have also contributed to differences among Reformed communities. The thought of Abraham Kuyper (1837–1920), for example, has dramatically affected Reformed Christians in the Netherlands. Kuyper was a minister, theologian, and prime minister of the Netherlands (1901–5) who was crucial in developing the idea of separate Christian institutions or pillars within the Netherlands. Kuyper's ideas had little impact on the Reformed tradition in the British Isles.

One distinct feature of this Reformation, which came to be identified primarily with John Calvin, was the creation of a system of church organization whereby a council of elders governed each church. In some models these church consistories or sessions were independent, while in others they were linked into networks with a hierarchy of church courts (MacCulloch 2003, 171). The ideas of the Swiss Reformation were influential through many parts of Europe. The organizational structure was adaptable in different circumstances and allowed the Reformation to be successful in France, England, Ireland, and Germany where the Reformed Christians were a minority without state support, as well as in Scotland and the Netherlands where the movement gained official status. Recent scholarship has highlighted how effective Reformed ideas were in eastern Europe, including Hungary, Poland, and Lithuania (MacCulloch 2003, 329–33, 442–49). The Reformed tradition has always been an international movement. At the same time, its dominant status in Scotland and the Netherlands has meant that there is a strong connection between ethnicity and religion in both nations.

While many in the Reformed community trace their origins directly to Europe in the sixteenth century, increasingly Reformed Christians around the world place emphasis upon the nineteenth-century missionary movement. It was in the nineteenth century that, for the first time, Presbyterian and Reformed Christians became widely involved in evangelism or mission, overseas and within Canada to ethnic communities (including to those who were Roman Catholic, Orthodox, or Jewish) and to Aboriginal Canadians.[4] The overseas Presbyterian and Reformed missionary efforts were sufficiently effective that their members now live on all continents. Particular areas of concentration include Korea, Taiwan, Ghana, Nigeria, Malawi, and South Africa, but

Reformed Christians also can be found in Pakistan, Iraq, Egypt, and the Caribbean. As immigrants arrive in Canada from these countries, they retain and recreate here their unique forms of the Reformed tradition.

The largest Reformed denominations in Canada are the Presbyterian Church in Canada and the Christian Reformed Church. The former has been, since its foundation in 1875, a crucial part of the Protestant establishment. The current Presbyterian Church in Canada grew out of the approximately one-third of Presbyterians who stayed out of the union in 1925 that brought together Methodists, Presbyterians, and Congregationalists to form the United Church of Canada (see Greer Anne Wenh-In Ng's chapter 6 in this volume). The 2001 census noted that 409,830 persons – or roughly 1.4 per cent of the Canadian population – identified themselves as Presbyterians. Between 1991 and 2001, the number claiming to identify with the tradition declined by 35.6 per cent – the highest rate of decline of any of the roughly twenty-five major Christian denominations measured by Statistics Canada.

Members of the Christian Reformed Church came to western Canada and parts of Ontario in the first decade of the twentieth century from the United States, and the denomination remained relatively small until the immigration to Canada from the Netherlands in the aftermath of the Second World War. Since then the Christian Reformed Church has grown dramatically, with 76,665 adherents noted in the 2001 census (Hofman 2004, 11–31; Statistics Canada 2001). Another feature of the Christian Reformed Church is that it is bi-national, with many of its major institutions being in the United States.

Although I am discussing here the two largest denominations within this broader Reformed tradition, there are other often fairly autonomous Reformed denominations in Canada, including the Canadian Reformed Church, Free Presbyterians, theologically conservative Presbyterians with links to American denominations, and Korean Presbyterian denominations.

The Demographics of Diversity

While rooted in the same theological traditions, the Presbyterian Church in Canada and the Christian Reformed Church are distinguished by different ethnic profiles.[5] According to the 2001 Census, the Christian Reformed Church almost exclusively (98.6 per cent) is comprised of people who are not 'visible minorities.' In numerical terms, of 76,660 Christian Reformed in the census, only 1,070 identified as visible minorities.[6] Moreover, no single visible minority community makes up more than 1 per cent of the Christian Reformed community. In contrast, of the 409,830 persons who identified themselves as Presbyterians in the 2001 Census, 29,705 (7.25 per cent) are visible minorities, with the remaining 92.75 per cent being non-visible minorities. By far the largest visible minority among Presbyterians are Koreans, at 13,105 (3.2 per cent) of the total. Next are Black Presbyterians at 5,860 (1.4 per cent), followed by the Chinese 3,565 (0.9 per cent), and South Asians 2,855 (0.7 per cent). The census records also note 420 Japanese, 310 Filipino, and 275 Latin American Presbyterians, as well as lesser numbers of Arabs, Southeast Asians, and so-called West Asians (people from, for example, Iran and Afghanistan).[7]

Immigration and the Presbyterian Church in Canada

The ethnic diversity of the Presbyterian tradition as reflected in census statistics is not limited to the Presbyterian Church in Canada. There are, as noted earlier, distinct Korean Presbyterian denominations (such as the North American Korean Presbyterian Church) that have been established in Canada in recent years, reflecting the denominational diversity in Canada and the religious complexity within the Korean context. Even so, the Presbyterian Church in Canada is a diverse denomination. Worship is conducted in an estimated seventeen languages (MacLachlan 2005b, 41). A recent (November 2005) issue of the *Presbyterian Record* highlighted the new church building for the Ghanaian Presbyterian church in Toronto (my visit there was described in the introduction to this chapter). At the same time, the article referred the perception of the Presbyterian Church in Canada as a Scottish denomination (MacLachlan 2005a, 16–18). This is a common perception, but the historical reality is more complex.

The origins of the Presbyterian Church in Canada were largely American. American Presbyterians were crucial, as United Empire Loyalists and as later settlers, in the Niagara Peninsula in Southern Ontario and in other parts of British North America. The Americans brought a particular kind of evangelical and revivalistic faith to these areas, such as pioneer missionary Robert McDowall, who was sent from an American Dutch Reformed denomination (Moir 2003b, 28–30). Early Scottish settlers in Canada include Highland migration to Pictou County and disbanded Highland soldiers in Quebec. Later waves of Scottish immigrants would gradually come to dominate the Presbyterian traditions in Canada, but the American contribution should not be forgotten. The importance of the early American immigrants to the Presbyterian tradition tended to be obscured by these later immigrants and by the backlash against things American caused by the war of 1812 and the Upper Canadian rebellion (Moir 2003a).

To speak of Scots as a single ethnic group is also somewhat problematic. It would be more accurate in the eighteenth and nineteenth centuries to talk of two distinct Scottish ethnic communities divided by language and culture, and, at times, mutual antagonisms – Highlanders and Lowlanders. Most Scots and most Scottish Presbyterian immigrants to British North America were Lowlanders, people who came from the more fertile southern regions of north Britain. Lowlanders spoke a dialect of English and brought with them a variety of customs. Lowland immigration is often overshadowed by the emigration of Highland Scots, perhaps because Lowlanders were more similar in language and culture to English and American immigrants. Highlanders, however, spoke Gaelic and came from a pastoral (cattle-raising) culture. Religiously, Highlanders were divided between Roman Catholics and Presbyterians. (See also Mark McGowan's chapter 2 on anglophone Roman Catholics.) Highland and Lowland Scots were quite distinct and did not always get along. To cite but one example, the prominent secessionist minister Rev. William Proudfoot, who ministered around London, in Upper Canada, in the early nineteenth century wrote in his diary about his Highland Presbyterian neighbours, 'These ignorant Highlanders are a hindrance to improvement wherever they go – about them there is an obstinacy which nothing can move and then the Gaelic – alas for the Gaelic!' (Gordon 1993, 47). Indeed, the attitude of many Lowlanders towards Highlanders throughout the nineteenth century and into the twentieth century was racist (MacLeod 2000, 125–78).

If the contribution of Lowland Scots has been neglected in the study of Canadian Presbyterianism, another ethnic group – the Irish – has been all but forgotten. The Irish, largely (though not exclusively) from Northern Ireland, comprised a significant group, establishing congregations in areas such as Cavan and Monaghan townships southwest of Peterborough and in other areas (Grant 1988a, 83, 125, 232). In Kingston, Ontario, there was an Irish Presbyterian church alongside two ethnically Scottish churches (Cossar 2000, 3), and Cooke's church in Toronto was also an ethnically Irish church.[8]

Presbyterianism in colonial Canada was thus more diverse than has been recognized, with significant contributions being made by American and Irish ethnic groups, as well as both the distinctive Highland and Lowland Scots. To contemporary Canadians, the divisions between these ethnic communities might seem trivial, but they were considered of much greater importance in the nineteenth century (Gregg 1892, 240).

While these origins have left their mark on Canadian Presbyterianism, new developments changed the face of the church in unexpected ways that make the simple equation of Presbyterianism with its British and Irish roots problematic. The denomination has been here long enough that, while individuals may be able to trace their family name to a particular country, the contact with that country may be extremely attenuated. As is the case throughout Canada and in most religious groups, over generations inter-marriage has created individuals who can choose from multiple ethnicities. The denomination, as an institution within a particular environment, also takes on a life of its own and is thus somewhat distinct from that of the country from which people emigrated. I sit writing this chapter in a building that was constructed nearly 100 years ago to house a theological college that has itself been in Toronto for 160 years. While the founders and some of the faculty may have been Scottish, it would be ludicrous to speak of it still as a 'Scottish' college when, among other factors, Koreans and Korean Canadians comprise approximately 20 per cent of the student body. Similarly, while the origins of the Presbyterian Church in Canada may be Scottish, events in Canada – from the creation of a national denomination in 1875, to the settlement of the West, to the crisis over remaining out of the United Church in 1925 – have all contributed to the Canadian-ness of the Presbyterian Church in Canada.[9]

Presbyterians find themselves confronted with a simple question: is the major 'ethnic' identity of the Church now 'Canadian'? When did Canadian become an ethnicity? We are reminded of our understanding of ethnicity as an identity of a group with a 'sense of attachment to a particular place, a history, a culture (including a common language, food, clothing, etc.)' (see chapter 1 of this book). Ethnicity is thus constructed or determined by those within the community itself, as well as imposed by those outside the group. It is important to recognize that, until recently, the Canadian Census encouraged people to focus on their families' ethnic origin – even when it might not have had much personal meaning for the individuals being surveyed. When given an opportunity to state Canadian as one of the possible ethnicities (as Canadians have been able to do only since 1991), a significant number have chosen to do so. Indeed, as Derrick Thomas has noted, in the 2001 Census 'more than half of the 11.7 million persons who reported "Canadian" described their ancestry as *exclusively* Canadian without mentioning any other ethnic connection' (Thomas 2005, 2; see the discussion in chapter 1 of this book). We will return to this matter later, but it is important to note the long presence of a Canadian ethnicity within the Presbyterian Church in Canada.

Ethnicity and the Christian Reformed Church

The Christian Reformed Church came to Canada largely through the United States as American Dutch immigrants moved into the Canadian prairies in search of affordable farmland (Hofman 2004, 11–20). In 1946, there were fourteen Christian Reformed Church congregations in Canada, which were one part of the much larger denomination with congregations throughout the United States. The denomination had taken the step in 1918 of making English the official language of its synod, and since that time had worked to move all of its publications (Church school, worship materials, and newspapers) from Dutch to English (Van Ginkel 1982, 41, 49–50). As the historian Aileen Van Ginkel has noted, because the denomination had worked so hard to become 'Americanized' – or 'Canadianized,' as the case may be – it was greatly challenged by the wave of post–Second World War immigration from the Netherlands (Van Ginkel 1982, 53). The new immigrants from the Netherlands settled throughout Canada, initially in farming areas but, as time went on, also in Canada's expanding urban centres (26). Between 1945 and 1968, approximately 750,000 people left the Netherlands, 38 per cent of whom came to Canada. Reformed Christians were disproportionately represented among those who chose to come to Canada, particularly in the earliest phases of immigration (11–15). The impact of this immigration can be seen by the fact that by 1960, there were 124 new congregations established in the Christian Reformed Church (29, 57).

The Christian Reformed Church, a bi-national denomination with the bulk of its resources and membership in the United States, faced an enormous challenge with this post–Second World War immigration of people from the Netherlands into Canada. The challenges were to help the immigrants to settle and find the resources – human and material – to staff and build the new congregations. As Joanne Van Dijk has noted,

'The Christian Reformed Church in North America sent salaried home missionaries and fieldmen to help recent immigrants find work and housing' (Van Dijk 2001, 59). A network of assistance to the immigrants was established to help them move into a new life and also to connect with a Christian Reformed congregation, or, in many cases, help to establish one (Hofman 2004, 34–48). Until 1952, the supply of ministers came largely from the United States, but from 1952 to 1960 an estimated fifty ministers arrived from the Netherlands (Van Ginkel 1982, 67).

Established congregations that had already moved to English-language services moved temporarily back to Dutch services, but the goal to worship exclusively in English remained. For example, many churches held Dutch services in the morning and English services in the evening or would offer a sermon outline in Dutch before preaching in English (Van Ginkel 1982, 60). Newly established congregations began in Dutch, but moved rapidly to services in English. For example, at First Christian Reformed Church in Victoria (established in 1952) portions of the published Sunday worship bulletin were in English by 1956. By 1960 worship services on the first Sunday of the month were conducted in English, and there was a decision a year later to celebrate special services such as Christmas in English (Ruitenbeek-Ott 1999, 66–9).

A more serious challenge to the Christian Reformed Church was the desire to bring the immigrants who came from different Reformed denominations in the Netherlands into a single Canadian denomination. After all, Reformed Christians in the Netherlands were divided into the state church (the Dutch Reformed Church), the Reformed Church of the Netherlands, the Liberated Reformed Church of the Netherlands which had in 1944 broken away from the Reformed Church of the Netherlands, and a variety of other, more conservative, Reformed denominations (Van Ginkel 1982, 14–23; Hofman 2004, 48–52).[10]

Other established Canadian churches with Reformed roots, notably the United Church of Canada and the Presbyterian Church in Canada, were seen by the Christian Reformed Church in Canada as competitors for the new immigrants (Ruitenbeek-Ott 1999, 61) for several reasons. The Dutch Reformed Church in the Netherlands encouraged its members who immigrated to Canada to join the United Church of Canada (Van Dijk 2001, 64). The Presbyterian Church in Canada was interested in attracting immigrants from the Netherlands and sent a minister to the Netherlands to encourage immigrants to join them. Presbyterian officials assigned to welcome immigrants handed out pamphlets in

Dutch to immigrants from the Netherlands (Ruitenbeek-Ott 1999, 47–8). Christian Reformed Church ministers responded by criticizing these denominations, stressing the differences between the United Church and the Presbyterian Church in Canada and what Calvinism was like in the Netherlands (Van Ginkel 1982, 118). Despite these warnings from Christian Reformed ministers, many immigrants chose to ignore this advice. The 1961 Census indicates that 24.1 per cent of those from the Netherlands identified with the United Church of Canada, 4.1 per cent identified as Presbyterians, and 24.2 per cent were noted as other – which would include the Christian Reformed Church (Statistics Canada 1961, 1.3–8:1.2).

The greatest challenge, however, was the approach to religion and life that the immigrants brought from the Netherlands, which was very different from the understanding in the Christian Reformed denomination in North America in 1946. Rather than building institutions for all members of society in the Netherlands, the four different divisions or pillars within society – Roman Catholic, Dutch Reformed, orthodox Calvinists, and others – established their own set of institutions (schools, political parties, trade associations, etc.). Immigrants brought a model to Canada that permitted individuals to live in relative isolation from members of other 'pillars.' Individuals often patronized stores of fellow *zuil* [pillar] members. Class differences could cut across the pillars, but unlike other models of society which propose horizontal segmentation by class the Netherlands experienced vertical segmentation by religious belief (Ruitenbeek-Ott 1999, 9).

This model, which owed a great debt intellectually to Abraham Kuyper (Van Ginkel 1982, 61), was brought by the post–Second World War immigrants to Canada. As Aileen Van Ginkel (1982) and Laura Ruitenbeek-Ott (1999) have each argued, religion for the new immigrants was thus the core determinant of identity – their 'faith and a neo-Calvinist world-view were far more important than a national heritage rooted in the physical world' (Ruitenbeek-Ott 1999, 104). That is, Calvinist immigrants identified along theological lines and not necessarily with all who shared a common Netherlands heritage. This vision also contrasted with the understanding of the North American Christian Reformed, as exemplified in the Canadian congregations and by the American-trained ministers who served in Canada. Christian Reformed members in North America had absorbed the temperance movement's condemnation of alcohol and smoking and were struck by the attitudes of the new immigrants, who thought nothing of either drinking or smoking but could not understand why those already in Canada had not yet built Christian schools (Van Ginkel 1982, 60–1). Van Ginkel (1982) has explored this tension, examining the differences between the American ministers, who focused on the church as the central institution that they believed the immigrants should establish, and the Dutch ministers, who supported many of the new immigrants' desires to rapidly establish the kinds of parallel institutions they enjoyed in the Netherlands.

Discussions of ethnicity and the Christian Reformed Church have focused on these themes of institutional completeness and the role that religion has played. The effects of the trauma of living under Nazi occupation during the years of the Second World War immediately prior to immigration has also received some attention (Mary Vander Vennen 1980; Mark Van der Vennen 1988). There has been no discussion of the different languages and cultures brought from the Netherlands by post-war immigrants. The main linguistic divide was between those who spoke Frisian and those who spoke Dutch. Within the Christian Reformed Church the decision made to move as rapidly as possible to worship in English meant this divide was not permanent.

It is also not clear how many immigrants from the Netherlands chose to join the more established Reformed churches already in existence in Canada, such as the Presbyterian Church in Canada or the United Church of Canada, rather than the Christian Reformed Church. However, the suggestion that immigrants began in the Christian Reformed Church then later moved into the Presbyterian Church in Canada or the more liberal United Church (Ruitenbeek-Ott 1999, 77) seems reasonable, particularly once they developed greater fluency in English.

However, for those who chose to join the Christian Reformed Church, language was not the sole motivation. The understanding of Christianity embraced by immigrants from the Netherlands was markedly different, theologically and culturally, from what existed in post–Second World War, mainstream Canadian Protestantism (Hofman 2004, 95–108). One important aspect of this vision was the establishment of distinctively Christian institutions. This agenda was pursued where the existing social institutions were implicitly Christian. For example, Christianity had an extremely privileged place in Ontario schools well into the 1960s. Yet immigrants from the Netherlands and their ministers did not perceive these institutions as sufficiently Christian, so they established their own schools where their particular understandings of Christianity would be expressed, just as they had been in the schools they had known in the Netherlands (Van Ginkel 1982, 148).

Ethnicities in the Presbyterian Church in Canada

If the dominant culture historically within the Presbyterian Church in Canada has been defined by British and Irish ethnicities, the denomination has also had a long-standing tradition of establishing or allowing the establishment of distinct congregations based upon language or, in some cases, ethnicity. Some of the earliest examples were Gaelic-speaking congregations. In the late nineteenth and early twentieth centuries, Canadian Presbyterians began mission work to Aboriginal Canadians and to immigrants (Bush 2000). The attempt clearly was to assimilate new immigrants and Aboriginal Canadians into a British culture. At the same time, what is fascinating is the willingness to allow for linguistic and cultural heritage to continue as a means to that end. Presbyterian missions involved Icelandic and other Scandinavian, Hungarian, Ukrainian, and, later, Italian communities. Because of their strong Reformed heritage, Hungarians were obviously of interest to the Presbyterian Church in Canada; at the same time, their language allowed them to remain a linguistically based subculture within the church.

James Robertson, the famous mission superintendent to western Canada, was more worried about effective ministry on Canada's prairies than about maintaining a Scottish ethnicity:

> To be a Presbyterian a man must not of necessity talk Gaelic, or broad Scotch, or hail from Ulster. The lack of an adequate revenue prevented us from undertaking this work in the past; the time, however, has come for broadening the scope of our work, and so showing that Presbyterianism is not a creed of race or locality; but adapted for all nationalities and races. (Bush 2000, 125)[11]

The Presbyterian Church in Canada began to create ethnic congregations. The presbytery of Hamilton, for example, established Hungarian, Italian, and Ukrainian congregations, all prior to 1950 (Bailey 1990, 142, 147, 153). Peter Bush describes the model developed on the Canadian prairies after mission superintendent James Robertson's success among Icelandic immigrants:

> Instead of seeking to assimilate the ethno-cultural grouping into an existing English speaking congregation, they sought to find a spiritually gifted individual who spoke the language of the people group they were seeking to reach. Through mentoring and some formal course work, this individ-

ual was trained on the job to be the minister of the new ethnic congregation. Over time it was hoped that the congregation would be drawn ever
more closely into the Presbyterian Church. (Bush 2000, 123–4)

The result of these missions was the creation of ethnic congregations
that have co-existed with the traditional Presbyterian communities for
decades. While certain ethnicities have dominated in the Presbyterian
Church in Canada, at least a limited degree of ethnic diversity has been
a constant. Given this reality, it seems important to more fully discuss
selected communities.

Chinese Presbyterians

Presbyterians began mission work among the immigrant Chinese workers in the late nineteenth century when they first came to Canada
because of the gold rush, then were recruited to help build the Canadian
Pacific Railway (Toronto Chinese Presbyterian Church 1980, E15). Official and unofficial racism among Canadians, however, led to restrictions
on immigration and complete exclusion from 1924 to 1947. A new immigration policy in 1967 ended the restrictions, but the close regulation
(and periods of exclusion) shaped the growth of the Chinese population
in Canada (Lai, Paper, and Paper 2005, 90). The Presbyterian mission to
Chinese immigrants began with literacy programs in 1892, and the first
congregation was founded in Victoria that same year (Moir 2004, 167),
while another was founded in Toronto in 1903 by Rev. Ng Moon Hing,
making it one of five such missions (Moir 2004, 167; Toronto Chinese
Presbyterian Church 1980, E16). These missions were small, a result of
the restrictions on emigration. The Chinese community was dominated
by the male labourers who had been allowed to enter during or before
the periods of exclusive legislation – the fact that among the 600 Chinese
in Toronto in 1910 there were only ten families (Toronto Chinese Presbyterian Church 1980, E16) is evidence of these regulations. Chinese
Presbyterians worshipped in Cantonese, and moved to an English-language service only in 1972 (Toronto Chinese Presbyterian Church 1980,
E10, E12). Since the changes to Canadian immigration laws in 1967, the
community has expanded numerically and has grown as an ethnic
group within the Presbyterian Church in Canada. In Toronto, new congregations have been established out of the original Toronto Chinese
Presbyterian Church. With continuing Chinese immigration, Taiwan-
ese- and Mandarin-speaking congregations have also been established
within the Presbyterian Church in Canada.

Korean Presbyterians

In the Presbyterian Church in recent years Koreans represent by far the most significant ethnic group to arrive in Canada. Korean immigration to Canada began in the 1960s, with the first significant numbers and families arriving in and after 1965. (For a further discussion on Asian immigration, see the Bruce Guenther's chapter 10 on evangelical Christians.) This immigration depended on encouragement from the government of Korea as well as the changes in the mid-1960s that endeavoured to deracialize Canada's immigration laws (Yoo 2002, 36, 38). The first Korean immigrants began worshipping in Toronto's Knox Presbyterian Church, a major Canadian church with a strong evangelical and mission orientation. The first Korean Presbyterian church in Toronto was established in 1967, and continuing immigration has led to the expansion of this community. The 2001 Census indicated that of 100,660 Koreans, 13,105 identified themselves as Presbyterians (2001 Census). By 1985 the Korean Presbyterians were the largest visible ethnic community in the Presbyterian Church in Canada. What is also true is that while many Korean Presbyterians affiliated themselves with the Presbyterian Church in Canada, many others did not. In 1999 Andrew Lee estimated that there were 250 Korean congregations representing fifteen to twenty different denominations, but only fifty (one fifth) were affiliated with existing mainstream Canadian denominations (Lee 1999, 19–20).

The immigrant experience has been difficult, and many who were middle-class professionals in Korea have experienced downward social mobility because they were not able to find equivalent jobs with similar salaries in Canada, and turned instead to other occupations, such as running variety stores, in order to make a living. Koreans established linguistically based congregations, often meeting in the afternoon within existing European Canadian congregations until they acquired the financial resources to build or purchase their own facilities. As these gatherings (like all church gatherings) often included food, there were some tensions over the use of kitchen facilities between the Korean congregations and the host congregations. Korean ministers also found that operating within Canadian presbyteries was difficult, as business was conducted in English. While the youth who immigrated or were born in Canada became more proficient in English, continuing immigration from a variety of age groups meant that Korean services were still necessary. Many Korean congregations have thus continued to have a strong Korean-speaking ministry, while developing an English-speaking ministry for the so-called 1.5 generation (those born in Korea but raised in Canada) and second generation (those born in Canada). Some also welcome European Canadians into their English-language worship services, even removing *Korean* from the church name in an effort to reach out beyond the founding ethnic group.

While part of the Presbyterian Church in Canada, Korean congregations are unique in important ways. Korean churches have tended to focus resources on young people's ministry far more than in other parts of the denomination. Moreover, Korean congregations continue to focus on overseas mission work and on evangelism among non-Christians. Another feature of the Korean tradition – which Koreans of all Protestant denominations share – is the importance of early morning prayer services, which originated as part of the great evangelical revival in Korea in 1903–10 (A. Anderson 2004, 2, 37).

As the number of Korean Presbyterians and Korean Presbyterian congregations grew within the Presbyterian Church in Canada, there was a move to establish separate presbyteries based upon language rather than the customary geographic boundaries.[12] Among the reasons given for their creation was that it would encourage participation from ministers who spoke only Korean and who were often unable to participate in English-language presbyteries. Andrew Lee, who participated in the creation of the Korean-language presbyteries and was the administrator on the national staff of the Presbyterian Church in Canada responsible for Korean ministries, has noted that the 'governing body of the PCC requests that ethnic groups integrate as soon as possible, but they do not understand people's sentimental behaviour and their cultural traditions, ethos, and life patterns' (Lee 1999, 86). In moving to linguistically based presbyteries, the Presbyterian Church in Canada was doing what other denominations, including Presbyterians in the United States as well as members of the United Church of Canada, had already done. In 1997 two linguistically based Korean presbyteries were formed, for eastern Canada and for western Canada. The name chosen for these presbyteries reflects the vision of these communities: 'Han-Ca,' which consists of *Han* (Korean) and *Ca* (Canadian).

The creation of two linguistically based presbyteries has been a milestone in the history of the Presbyterian Church in Canada, a departure from the tradition of organizing churches based upon geography. In the denomination's statistics for 2004, Han-Ca West had sixteen congregations with 1,375 members, while Han-Ca East had seventeen congregations with 4,150 members. This makes Koreans a significant segment of the 124,000 on the denomination's official national membership rolls (Presbyterian Church in Canada 1995, 816, 818). It is worth asking whether the whole of the Presbyterian Church in Canada has been transformed by the presence of this significant number of Koreans or whether two parallel institutions exist under a single roof.

Separate linguistic presbyteries – and congregations – certainly have been an effective short-term solution, but long-term issues remain. For example, one wonders if they have not introduced new questions of fairness. At the moment most congregational governing bodies (sessions) operating within the Han-Ca system also function in Korean. How will power be shared with the younger, English-speaking members of the second generation? Are Korean Canadian ministers who work in English-speaking ministries and are not fluent in Korean at a disadvantage in a Korean-speaking presbytery, just as the Korean-speaking ministers were in the English-speaking presbyteries before the creation of Han-Ca? In Korean culture where Christianity has reinforced as well as challenged the traditional valuing of age over youth, of men over women, these are important questions (Soh 1993, 54). Andrew Lee noted that, even before the creation of the Korean-language presbyteries, the second-generation members were 'joining neither a Korean nor English congregation' (Lee 1999, 20). Have these new presbyteries, with their greater linguistic and cultural grounding, been able to address this problem?

Koreans began arriving in large numbers just as the Canadian Presbyterian church moved into numerical decline. Membership has dropped steadily since the mid-1960s, and the number of Presbyterians noted by the census has also seen dramatic decline – between the 1991 and 2001 census, the largest (35 per cent) of any major tradition in Canada. This decline only reinforced what the editors of this book have called a 'discourse of loss' within the denomination, and this has fed into a sense that something is dramatically wrong within the Presbyterian Church in Canada.[13] For Korean Presbyterians, there is no reason to adopt what we might call the ethnically Canadian culture of the denomination, as that seems to be a way to ruin. By way of an explanation for this conviction, we should recall that the Korean church brought a different heritage from Korea, in theology, approach to scripture, and the place of women in the church. Indeed, the more evangelistic approach of Korean Presbyterians is reinforced by the common perception among Koreans that the Canadian church, which places less emphasis upon active evangelism toward non-Christians, has declined precisely because of its failure to spread the gospel. Korean Presbyterians did not experience the denomination when it was robust and membership was increasing. The response of Korean Presbyterian congregations has been to work independently of the national bureaucratic structures in order to achieve what they perceive as their central task, which is mission work, both overseas and also with Aboriginal communities in Canada. As the largest ethnic community within the Presbyterian Church in Canada and with linguistically distinct presbyteries, the Korean Presbyterians will likely remain a very powerful but distinct force within the Presbyterian Church in Canada.

Caribbean, Black, and African Presbyterians

Caribbean, Black, and African Presbyterians represent a variety of cultures, including those that the census identifies as Blacks as well as descendants of South Asian indentured labourers who moved from India to the West Indies. Caribbean Presbyterians (South Asian and Black) originate principally from Guyana and Trinidad and are the product of the significant nineteenth-century Presbyterian missionary effort to what had been British colonies. Black Presbyterians are a mix of those who are Canadian-born, from Africa, and from the Caribbean. As Caribbean immigrants have arrived in Canada, they have moved into existing Presbyterian churches or into the United Church.

For the most part, however, Presbyterians from the Caribbean have not formed their own congregations but have integrated into mainstream congregations. In his study of the integration of Guyanese Presbyterians into a Canadian Presbyterian congregation, Robert Anderson (1992) notes that while the Presbyterian missions in Guyana made the Presbyterian Church in Canada an obvious choice for immigrants to Canada, the move into existing Canadian congregations has not been without its difficulties. Coming from a culture where whites had historically dominated, many Caribbean Presbyterians grew up understanding that whites should be in change. In Canadian Presbyterian churches, members of these communities often would remain separate, even at the joint coffee hours, with Guyanese members chatting to each other while European Canadians formed separate circles. Despite the challenges, Caribbean Presbyterians have gradually transformed these congregations. One distinguishing feature of Caribbean Presbyterians is the importance of family, and the importance of blessings – of new homes, major purchases, and other life events. There are now congregations in major urban areas where the congregational culture blends Caribbean, Guyanese, and European Canadian forms of Presbyterianism.

Presbyterians from Africa represent a newer community of immigrants, distinct from each other and in many ways distinct from Caribbean and Canadian-born Blacks. Ghanaian Presbyterians are one large group from Africa, but there are many others from throughout the African continent, and the differences in language and culture are significant. For example, Portuguese-speaking Africans from Angola may find more in common with other Portuguese-speaking Presbyterians from Brazil than with French-speaking Presbyterians from the Congo or English-speaking Presbyterians from Ghana. African Presbyterians represent a growing community – and notably growing in Quebec, as Africans who speak French find a home in that province – but the divisions along linguistic and cultural lines are also worth considering.

As we have seen, there have long been congregations established within the Presbyterian Church in Canada on the basis of language, ethnicity, or some combination of both. Other immigrant groups have, like those from the Caribbean, found a home in existing congregations. Throughout most of the denomination's history, these congregations have been on the margins of the denomination. Given continuing immigration patterns from Africa, Asia, the Caribbean, and other parts of the world where the number of Reformed Christians is growing and now surpass those in Europe and North America, one anticipates these communities will grow in Canada. Given this pattern, it is important to recognize this diversity, as ethnic congregations continue to grow in importance as membership and attendance decline among those born in Canada.

The Presbyterian and Reformed World in Canada

As one would expect, the new diversity in the Presbyterian communities is affecting the institutional life of the denomination. Historically, most members of the Presbyterian Church in Canada saw themselves as members of the Protestant establishment and expected all institutions in Canadian society to reflect their values. It was assumed that universities, schools, the laws of Canada, and other social institutions should all support the values of the Protestant tradition as the church determined them. The dramatic recent shifts in Canadian culture and demographics seem to have caught them off guard, and there is a discourse of loss within the denomination.

One notable difference between the dominant established, largely anglophone Canadian group (for whom there is no term, and to which I have referred as European Canadian), and those who are usually termed 'ethnic Presbyterians,' is that Presbyterians in congregations that are more ethnically distinctive or who worship in a language other than English have had a much stronger sense of the need to build and protect their own institutions. For these communities, the church becomes not only the place for worship, but the context in which one's culture is affirmed. For example, Hungarians are able to preserve both their language and culture as they worship together. Similar things could be said of Arab, Korean, Taiwanese, Chinese, and Ghanaian Presbyterians.

The Christian Reformed Church offers a better example of 'institutional completeness,' rapidly building a complete network of social institutions after the Second World War. As has already been noted in chapter 1, institutional completeness refers to the extent to which one can function within that culture without needing to step outside it. While language was not the glue holding the Christian Reformed Church culture together, the church and other institutions provided remarkable cohesion. The bi-national model that the Christian Reformed Church in Canada had embraced prior to the massive post–Second World War immigration inspired them to work within and transform existing institutions. However, this model was rejected in the 1950s and replaced by a model of creating parallel institutions as they had existed in the Netherlands (Van Ginkel 1982, 82, 113). We see this change when we consider the development of schools associated with the Christian Reformed Church. There were only 3 Christian Reformed schools in 1945, 33 in 1960, and 114 by 1985 (Van Ginkel 1984–5, 45). Next to churches, Christian schools have been the most popular institution created by those in the Christian Reformed Church. Aileen Van Ginkel has stressed the role of ministers from the Netherlands in promoting this vision of parallel institutions, including educational institutions: 'With the thinking and experience of Kuyperian Calvinism behind them, the Dutch ministers sought to establish a Christian front against secularism in Canada' (1982, 116). *Secular* was often understood as meaning different from the Calvinist vision that the ministers and their members had experienced previously.

The variety of parallel institutions was impressive. For example, a

'Calvinist Cadet Corps' for boys and 'Calvinettes' for girls were established as an alternative to the mainstream Canadian organizations such as the Boy Scouts or Girl Guides, or even the overtly religious Boys Brigade and Canadian Girls in Training (Van Ginkel 1982, 135). When it came time to attend university, one could go to Calvin College (a large Christian Reformed Church university in the United States), The King's University College in Edmonton, Alberta, or, as of 1982, to Redeemer College (now Redeemer University College) in Ancaster, Ontario. And if one wished to pursue post-graduate education, the Institute for Christian Studies in Toronto was available.

By the 1960s, young people could attend school with Christians from their denomination, worship with them on Sunday, and belong to youth organizations supported by the church. If issues of social justice were of concern, they could explore them through Citizens for Public Justice. If they worked, they could join a Christian labour union.[14] This creation of parallel religious institutions, as Van Dijk has noted, stands in sharp contrast with Dutch Roman Catholics who did not create their own parallel institutions but had joined 'existing Catholic institutions' or otherwise assimilated (Van Dijk 2001, 60).

While Citizens for Public Justice and Redeemer University College are certainly not restricted only to those of Christian Reformed background or Dutch ethnicity, in reality these have been places where, until recently, Dutch/Frisian folk dominate – despite the explicit intentions of people from these institutions. Their founders hoped that they would inspire other Canadians to join, but, in practice, this has taken time: 'As long as they perceived themselves to be and/or were perceived by others to be Dutch, few non-Dutch people joined the Christian Reformed Church or its associated organizations' (Van Ginkel 1982, 162).

The institutional separateness is quite remarkable, as it was achieved – as already noted – despite the fact that all of these groups normally functioned in the language of the dominant culture. To maintain this institutional autonomy, it was necessary to use or develop a theological rationale, which might be more significant than any structures based on language. Languages tend to fade away, but it is not clear yet that such theological rationales will.

The Role of Women

One consequence of the Canadianization of the Presbyterian Church of Canada has been the changing attitude towards women and their leadership in the church. As part of the dominant cultural group, the Presbyterian Church in Canada moved to give women full rights and privileges in the life of the church at roughly the same time that the broader Canadian culture was dealing with these issues. The Presbyterian Church debated the entire issue in the 1950s and into the 1960s, originally rejecting the notion, but finally approving in 1966 the ordination of women as both ministers and elders (members of the sessions or councils that govern each congregation) (Moir 2004, 255–6, 263–4). Of course, formal equality for women in leadership has been more slowly realized than the official decision would suggest. Some ethnic communities have easily accepted women in leadership, as among Chinese, Black, and Hungarian Presbyterians. However, women's leadership has been very difficult for the Korean community, shaped as it has been by the values of traditional patriarchal Confucian culture (Soh 1993, 54). In very recent years, women have been ordained as ministers, but there is still a struggle with leadership at the congregational level and with acceptance.

In the Christian Reformed Church the move to bring women into leadership was slower and was one of several issues that led some congregations in Canada to break away from the national organization. Because of the centrality of the Bible in Reformed churches, debates revolved around different interpretations of various scriptural passages. For example, some argued that a literal reading of the Old and New Testaments precluded the ordination of women, and texts from the New Testament were used to argue that in general women must remain subservient to men within and outside of the church. Debates over these sorts of theological and scriptural issues have been more important than, say, Dutch ethnicity in shaping the role of women in the Christian Reformed Church. These debates involved the entire Christian Reformed Church denomination, in Canada and the United States (Hofman 2004). Discussions on the ordination of women began in 1970. By 1978 the synod of the church agreed to ordain women as deacons, the lowest of the three orders of leadership (minister, elder, and deacon). Despite this decision, future Synods delayed ratifying it and instead established new committees to study 'the headship of men over women in marriage and its implications for the church' (Christian Reformed Church n.d.). In 1984, a committee again argued for the ratification of the 1978 decision, but again it was delayed by further studies. In 1990, this next study argued for opening all offices to women, and although this recommendation passed there were again delays in implementation. The Christian Reformed Church Synod went back and forth on the issue until 1995. At that time, the Synod recognized the two opposing positions and then allowed each classis (regional body) to decide for itself whether to allow congregations in their jurisdiction to open all church offices to women for five years. At the moment, eighteen of forty-seven classis, or 38 per cent of those in the denomination in the United States and Canada, have opened offices to women (Christian Reformed Church n.d.).

Generational Concerns, Current Issues

The Christian Reformed Church has been remarkably successful at maintaining the involvement of its members. However, this community has not been immune to the decline in religious identification and membership that is being witnessed in most Canadian Protestant churches. Between the 1991 and 2001 census, the Christian Reformed denomination saw a decline of 9.5 per cent in identification. While certainly not as potentially devastating as the 35.6 per cent loss faced by Presbyterians, it is still a trend that deserves to be studied. Current and future immigration patterns do not seem to be favouring the Christian Reformed tradition. Immigration from Europe has declined, with more immigrants coming to Canada from Africa, the Middle East, and Asia (Beaujot and Kerr 2004, 124). Even if emigration from the Netherlands were to suddenly return to numbers seen in the immediate post-war period, it is not clear that the Christian Reformed Church would benefit. The sending culture in the Netherlands has become dramatically more secular in the last half century. Put simply, new immigrants who have never gone to church in the Netherlands are not likely to start participating in a church once they arrive in Canada. However, the situation might change, should more immigrants arrive from countries linked historically to missionary work undertaken by the Christian Reformed tradition in North America or the Netherlands.

The challenges facing the Presbyterian Church in Canada are somewhat different. One key question that it faces revolves around its ethnic self-understanding: is the denomination Canadian, or Scottish and should become Canadian? This is not a new debate. As we have already seen, missionary superintendent James Robertson called upon Canadian Presbyterians to move out of being a church looking only to Scottish and Irish immigrants, and look to all Canadians. But he was not the first to call upon Canadian Presbyterians to think of themselves as

Canadian first. One of the earliest calls for a more Canadian orientation came from William Proudfoot, himself an immigrant from Scotland in 1846: 'We are too Scotch – our habits, our brogue, our mode of sermonizing are all too Scotch' (Moir 2003a, 175). I will consider the empirical data shortly, but for now it is noteworthy that the perception continues over a century and a half later that Scottish ethnicity is dominant in the denomination. In reference to post–Second World War construction of new churches in the suburbs, Geoff Johnson wonders 'whether the post-war developments made a significant difference in the ethnic makeup of the church as first and foremost the church of Scottish and Ulster immigrants and their descendants' (Moir, Johnston, McLelland, and Johnston 2005, 199–200). His observation on its ethnic make-up might be accurate, but to no small degree because so many, admittedly similar, ethnic groups are included as if they were only one – Scottish (Highland/Lowland); Ulster or Northern Irish; and their descendants (Americans, Canadians).

The question naturally arises, why is the Presbyterian tradition portrayed as so monolithically Scottish? One reason clearly is that the Scots were and remain a major ethnic community within the Presbyterian Church in Canada. Continuing waves of Scottish immigrants may also have contributed to a sense of a continuing Scottish hegemony, even as the majority of those in the denomination became indigenized. The data on ethnicity in the 1961 census are very telling: in 1961, 85 per cent of Presbyterians were of 'British' ethnicity – as defined by responses to the question 'To what ethnic or cultural group did your ancestor (on the male side) belong on coming to this continent?' (Statistics Canada 1961, Religion by ethnic groups 1 [3], ix). What may be more surprising was the extent to which other European ethnic groups were represented: French (2 per cent), German (3 per cent), Dutch (2 per cent), and Scandinavian (1.4 per cent), all represented the larger ethnic and linguistic heritages that had become part of the Presbyterian Church in Canada. The numbers were also significant – the 3 per cent German ethnicity, after all, represents over 26,000 people (Statistics Canada 1961, 1.3–8:1, Table 110). Unfortunately, the category 'British' was not broken down into its constituent parts (English, Welsh, Scottish, Irish) in the published reports, so it is difficult to know what percentage of these immigrants were indeed Scottish. The same census also produced an analytical study of the effects of post-war immigration on the Canadian population, including religious denominations, indicating that in 1961 76 per cent of Canadian Presbyterians were native born, 14 per cent were pre-war immigrants born elsewhere, and 10 per cent were post-war immigrants. Within each of these categories the British were a dominant group, but the percentage born in Canada is worth noting (Kalbach 1970, 162–7).

By 1961, the vast majority of those in the Presbyterian Church in Canada were born in Canada. Other indicators, as noted in chapter 1 of this book, can also suggest when the denomination might best be understood as ethnically Canadian. It was in the nineteenth century that Canadian Presbyterians built their own theological colleges to supply their own ministers and began to establish their own missions overseas. The decision of four separate bodies to form a denomination united regionally and theologically in 1875 also demonstrates a Canadianness. Enthusiastic support of national endeavours such as First World War and Second World War, and participation in rallies opposing Quebec separation at the time of the 1995 referendum (Hiller 2000) are signs that Presbyterians define themselves as Canadians. By such criteria, the Presbyterian Church in Canada has long been an ethnically Canadian denomination.[15]

Still, the perception that the Presbyterian Church in Canada is an ethnically Scottish denomination remains and may indeed be reinforced by specific celebrations of ethnicity in Presbyterian congregations that are distinctly 'Scottish' and claim a place of privilege. These celebrations would include Robbie Burns suppers, Tartan Sundays, and celebrations of the 'Kirking of the Tartan.' It would be fascinating to know how many of these events are of long standing and how many are of more recent origin. Pictures in the denominational magazine seem to give the impression that they are ubiquitous and of venerable Scottish lineage. However, historians, sociologists, and other academics alert us to the socially constructed nature of identities and the traditions that define them. Eric Hobsbawm calls such practices 'invented traditions,' which he defines as a 'set of practices, normally governed by overtly or tacitly accepted rules and of a ritual or symbolic nature, which seek to inculcate certain values and norms of behaviour by repetition, which automatically implies continuity with the past' (Hobsbawm 1983, 1). Both Scottish country dance and Highland dance include features indicative of invented traditions (Morrison 2003), as do other elements of Highland culture (Nairn 1981; Trevor-Roper 1983).[16] In terms of Canada, Ian McKay offers insight into how the Scottishness of Nova Scotia was invented, reminding us that Nova Scotia was an ethnically mixed province of Germans, English, Irish, Scots, and other ethnic groups that

– under the direction of a powerful provincial premier who had a desire to promote tourism – became a province perceived as 'essentially Scottish' (McKay 1992, 6). Even more, the Scottish identity that was created focused on the Highlander rather than the Lowlander, even though both groups had immigrated to the province (McKay 1992, 27).

Important parallels to these cultural processes continue to occur in the Presbyterian Church in Canada. It is notable that certain symbols of Scottishness are resurfacing or being introduced to the church community for the first time. For example, some congregations have a long history of the formal suppers (complete with ritual toasts and speeches) in honour of the Lowland Scottish poet Robert Burns. In other cases, Burns suppers are being introduced for the first time. More notable are services that celebrate the 'Kirking of the Tartan,' an invented tradition that deserves a more lengthy description.

During the Second World War, a chapter of the St Andrew's Society in the United States approached Peter Marshall, a Scottish immigrant who became a prominent American minister, and, in the words of his son, 'asked him to create a religious service for them. The result was the "Kirking o' the Tartan" service, which has become an annual event for St Andrew's Society chapters everywhere' (Marshall 2005, 114). The first service was conducted in Washington DC, and in more recent years has come to be celebrated in a variety of Canadian congregations. In one Ontario congregation it was first introduced in 1994 and has become an annual celebration. The service begins with bagpipers leading standards with tartan banners representing various Highland clans (tribal groups) into the front of the church where they and national flags are received. 'God Save the Queen' is sung before the service and 'O Canada' at the conclusion. During the service, the Lord's Prayer is recited in English and Scottish dialect. The high point of the service is a prayer blessing the tartans. A piece of tartan is either placed on or covers the Bible. The underlying ritual that the service purports to recreate is the time when tartans were banned in Scotland, and Highlanders supposedly took a piece of tartan each year into the church to have it blessed. Regardless of historical issues (did this really happen?), the tradition is broadly considered to be ancient (even when it has been introduced only within the last two decades) and serves several functions. One is to affirm the identity of those who are Scottish and those who wish to claim to be Scottish.[17] It also embeds that identity within a particular religious community, implying that the denomination is the caretaker of that heritage. And, given that no other heritages – Dutch,

American Presbyterian Revivalist, Northern Irish, or Korean – are celebrated, it privileges the Scottish Highland tradition, saying loudly and
clearly, 'This is a Scottish denomination,' just as a piper at the border of
Nova Scotia implies, 'This is a Scottish province.' Pictures of such celebrations included in denominational magazines reinforce the implied
message that the denomination is essentially Scottish, and those of
Northern Irish, Canadian, Chinese, Ghanaian, or Korean ethnicity are
not part of the dominant denominational culture. The obvious question
is, why?[18] Why, at a moment of great transition in the ethnicity of the
Presbyterian Church in Canada, is one ethnicity being privileged in this
way? Do Canadian Presbyterians hope to reach out to new immigrants
from Scotland (few in number)? Are they hoping to reach out to lapsed
adherents, whether from Scotland or with some vague Scottish memory, and, through the vehicle of a yearly service to reignite an ethnic
connection with the church and thus to garner support? Such questions
need to be explored further. The growth of these ethnic celebrations is
fascinating.

    However, this nostalgia for an essentially Scottish nature of the church
has to compete with a different understanding of the Presbyterian tradition as essentially Canadian. Presbyterians have been in Canada long
enough to develop their own ways of being and their own culture.
Events such as the resistance to the church union in 1925 have been more
formative than any event in Great Britain. The major theological figure
in the twentieth century has not been Scottish, but rather a Swiss theologian (Karl Barth) mediated through a Canadian (Walter Bryden).
Canadian Presbyterians have developed a pragmatic approach and
have largely abandoned a meticulous creedalism grounded in documents such as the Westminster Confession of Faith. The tradition is as
likely, if not more likely, to respond to developments south of the border
than those across the Atlantic Ocean. For example, the contemporary
statement of faith written in the 1980s was inspired and owed a great
debt to a similar statement produced in the United States (Presbyterian
Church in Canada 1982, 3).

Conclusion

As we have seen, ethnicity is an important factor in the broader
Reformed Christian tradition, both among Presbyterians and those in
the Christian Reformed Church. However, ethnicity functions in different ways. Those in the Presbyterian Church in Canada exist in an

increasingly ethnically diverse church but one where the dominant ethnicity is still under negotiation (is it Canadian? is it Scottish?). In the Christian Reformed Church, religion functions in a way similar to that of an ethnic identity, in that it acts as the touchstone for a group of people. In the Christian Reformed denomination, it is the particular understanding and shape of the Calvinist tradition that has been transplanted to Canada, and this, more than language and ethnicity, has made the Christian Reformed Church distinctive. Given the changing nature of Canadian society, the shifting patterns of immigration, and the marvellous capacity of religious communities to adapt to new realities, it is clear that ethnicity will continue to play a significant role in the evolution of the Reformed tradition on Canadian soil.

Notes

1 This visit took place on 26 October 2005.
2 The visit took place 22 January 2006.
3 This visit took place on 6 November 2005.
4 For more on the relationship of Presbyterians and Aboriginal peoples in Canada, see Bush (2004), Grant (1978), and McKay and Silman (1995).
5 In its published reports, the census has one category for those who refer to themselves as Presbyterian. The Presbyterian Church in Canada is historically the largest Presbyterian denomination in Canada, and the assumption has traditionally been made that most of these individuals would relate to it. There are also other Presbyterian denominations with which one could be associated. In recent years with the establishment of a large number of Korean Presbyterian denominations, as well as independent congregations and congregations affiliated directly with denominations in Korea, the proportion affiliated with the Presbyterian Church in Canada has gone down.
    The census allows several options under 'Reformed.' Christian Reformed is the largest, but Canadian Reformed and other Reformed are also noted.
6 All census figures for 2001, unless otherwise specified, arise out of a custom table 2001 Census – Statistics Canada E00870, which Brian Clarke and I use in our exploration of religion in the census.
7 Calculations based upon 2001 Census – Statistics Canada E00870 indicate that Roman Catholics also have a visible minority population of 7.3 per cent of their total. Filipino, Black, and Latin American are among the largest visible minority groups among Roman Catholics. Presbyterians are thus as diverse in terms of visible minorities as are Roman Catholics, although the

differing concentrations in visible minority communities and overall numbers are noteworthy.

8 Canadian church historian John Webster Grant has noted the contribution that the Irish made to Presbyterianism, as well as how little it has been studied: 'The Irish were also far more formative of Presbyterianism than later Presbyterians have been inclined to acknowledge. They furnished much of the constituency of the United Secession Church and came to dominate the United Synod in later years; after 1838, when it established mutual relations with the Synod of Ulster, even the Church of Scotland admitted Irish ministers' (Grant 1988a, 83; see also 125, 232).

9 For more on the complex relationship of Presbyterianism to ethnic identity in specific historical and geographical contexts in Canada, see Klempa (1992). For studies on this relationship in specific historical and geographical contexts, see Bennett (1998), Bridgman (1978), Brouwer (1979), Burnger (1990), Bush (1997), Dickey (2002), Klempa (1992), Mack (1992), Osborne (2004), Papp (1996), Ruggle (1984–5), and Stanley-Blackwell (1997).

10 In Canada the Christian Reformed Church took immigrants from all three traditions (Van Ginkel 1982, 15, 23).

11 Note that Robertson mentions the Irish (Ulster), as well as noting the two Scottish language groups. There is an important discussion in the literature on the extent to which culture and religious faith were confused in these ventures, and the extent to which efforts to reach out were intended to force new immigrants into a Canadian Protestant mould. See Bush (2000, 122–57) Moir (2004, 164–9).

12 The Presbyterian Church in Canada was by the late twentieth century unaware of its earlier experimentation with something similar involving Ukrainians in the early part of the century (Bush 2000, 144–9).

13 The dramatic drop in census membership in the Presbyterian Church in Canada needs to be seriously considered, on its own and in light of losses among other Canadian religious denominations, such as the Salvation Army (–21.9 per cent) and the Pentecostals (–15.3 per cent). Presbyterian losses have only compounded previous census losses. Membership has also, as noted in the text, declined. For those active in congregations, both membership and census decline should be of concern, with the former being of greater significance. Census decline demonstrates the extent to which Presbyterian is no longer a brand that many in Canada identify with or possibly even recognize.

14 The Christian Labour Association of Canada was established in 1952 as a separate Christian union, and arguments were made that belonging to other, secular institutions was morally wrong (Van Ginkel 1982, 137–9).

15 Literature on the Presbyterian Church in Canada wavers on when the
denomination became Canadian. Moir (2004) and Reid (1976) both seem to
argue for a Scottish influence in the nineteenth century that became more
Canadian over time, but also stress a continuing Scottish presence. Moir,
Johnson, and McLelland (2005) would date the change later.
16 Nairn explores the impact on Scottish nationalism of a school of Lowland
literature (the Kailyard school) as well as aspects of the Highland tradition,
which he refers to variously as 'tartanry' or the 'tartan monster' (1981, 165).
Hugh Trevor-Roper also explores invented Highland tradition. Paul Bramadat offers an important caution, that we not invalidate these traditions
over supposedly authentic traditions (Bramadat 2005). See also MacDonald
(1988).
17 A recent study indicates that being Scottish has gone from being 'the least
popular white ethnic identity' in the United States to being a popular identity in recent years, the movie *Braveheart* being one factor in the transformation (Stenhouse 2005).
18 It has long been argued that Scottish ethnicity was used in opposition to
church union. See Moir, Johnson, and McLelland (2005, 131), and Reid
(1976, 126–7). Grant (1988b, 168) notes another, different, use of Scottish
ethnicity: 'The Presbyterians, who in reaction against the unspoken Canadi-
anism of the United Church had made a good deal of their Scottish inheritance, now [the 1950s] found it expedient to play it down.'

Works Cited

Anderson, Allan. 2004. *An introduction to Pentecostalism*. Toronto: Cambridge
University Press.
Anderson, Robert K. 1992. Identification of elements to consider in the integra-
tion of families of Caribbean origin with a traditional Presbyterian congrega-
tion, with special reference to the descendants of indentured labourers from
South Asia. DMin diss., Toronto School of Theology.
Bailey, Thomas Melville. 1990. *Wee kirks and stately steeples – A history of the Pres-
bytery of Hamilton: The Presbyterian Church in Canada 1800–1990*. Burlington:
Eagle.
Beaujot, Roderic, and Don Kerr. 2004. *Population change in Canada*. 2nd ed. Don
Mills: Oxford University Press.
Bennett, Margaret. 1998. *Oatmeal and the catechism: Scottish Gaelic settlers in Que-
bec*. Montreal and Kingston: McGill-Queen's University Press.
Bramadat, Paul A. 2005. Toward a new politics of authenticity: Ethno-cultural

representation in theory and practice. *Canadian Ethnic Studies* 37 (1): 1–20.

Bridgman, Harry John. 1978. Three Scots Presbyterians in Upper Canada: A study in emigration, nationalism and religion. PhD diss., Queen's University, Kingston, Ontario.

Brouwer, Ruth Compton. 1979. 'Their hope … sorely tried': Presbyterian foreign and home missionary concerns about the treatment of South Asians in Canada, 1907–1925. *Canadian Society of Presbyterian History Papers* (1979): 15–40.

Brunger, Alan G. 1990. The distribution of Scots and Irish in Upper Canada, 1851–71. *Canadian Geographer* 34 (3): 250–8.

Bush, Peter. 1997. 'Why should the church confine her labour to those who may show a Presbyterian pedigree?' The Presbyterian Church responds to non-English-speaking immigrants in western Canada, 1896–1925. *Canadian Society of Presbyterian History Papers* (1997): 22–33.

– 2000. *Western challenge: The Presbyterian Church in Canada's mission on the prairies and North, 1885–1925*. Winnipeg: Watson & Dwyer.

– 2004. The Native residential school system and the Presbyterian Church in Canada. *Presbyterian History* 48 (1): 1–4.

Christian Reformed Church. Women in ecclesiastical office. http://www.crcna.org/pages/positions_women_office.cfm.

Cossar, Bruce. 2000. Church union in Kingston. *Canadian Society of Presbyterian Church History Papers* (2000): 1–13.

Dickey, Tom. 2002. Chapel Place Church: The Middle East comes to Markham, Ontario. *Presbyterian Record* (April): 24–6.

Gordon, Robert John. 1993. The attitude of the clergy to Highland settlers in Upper Canada. *Canadian Society of Presbyterian History Papers* (1993): 43–59.

Grant, John Webster. 1978. Presbyterian women and the Indians. *Canadian Society of Presbyterian History Papers* (1978): 21–37.

– 1988a. *A profusion of spires: Religion in nineteenth-century Ontario*. Toronto: University of Toronto Press.

– 1988b. *The church in the Canadian era: Updated and expanded*. Burlington: Welch.

Gregg, William. 1892. *Short history of the Presbyterian Church in the Dominion of Canada: From the earliest to the present time*. Toronto: Blackett Robinson.

Hiller, Harry H. 2000. Civil religion and the problem of national unity: The 1995 Quebec Referendum crisis. In *Rethinking church, state, and modernity: Canada between Europe and America*, ed. David Lyons and Marguerite Van Die, 166–85. Toronto: University of Toronto Press.

Hobsbawm, Eric. 1983. Introduction: Inventing traditions. In *The invention of tradition*, ed. Eric Hobsbawm and Terrence Ranger, 1–14. Cambridge: Cambridge University Press.

Hofman, Tymen E. 2004. *The Canadian story of the CRC: Its first century.* Belleville: Guardian Books.

Kalbach, Warren E. 1970. *The impact of immigration on Canada's population.* Ottawa: Dominion Bureau of Statistics.

Klempa, William. 1992. There's more to a Presbyterian than meets the eye. In *The burning bush and a few acres of snow: The Presbyterian contribution to Canadian life and culture,* ed. William Klempa, 1–12. Ottawa: Carleton University Press.

Lai, David Chuenyan, Jordan Paper, and Li Chuang Paper. 2005. The Chinese in Canada: Their unrecognized religion. In Bramadat and Seljak 2005a, 89–110.

Lee, Andrew Shung Kap. 1999. A model of ministry for Pacific Asian congregations in the mainline churches: The development of the language/cultural presbytery. DMin diss., St Stephen's College.

MacCulloch, Diarmaid. 2003. *The Reformation: A history.* New York: Viking.

MacDonald, Norman. 1988. Putting on the kilt: The Scottish stereotype and ethnic community survival in Cape Breton. *Canadian Ethnic Studies* 20 (3): 132–46.

Mack, Barry. 1992. Canadian Presbyterians and guardian angels. In *Amazing grace: Evangelicalism in Australia, Britain, Canada, and the United States,* ed. Mark A. Noll, 269–92. Montreal and Kingston: McGill-Queen's University Press.

MacLachlan, Amy. 2005a. Looking for growth in all the right places. *Presbyterian Record* (November): 16–21.

– 2005b. The changing church. *Presbyterian Record* (November): 41–2.

MacLeod, James Lachlan. 2000. *The second disruption: The Free Church in Victorian Scotland and the origins of the Free Presbyterian Church.* East Linton, UK: Tuckwell.

Marshall, Peter J., ed. 2005. *The wartime sermons of Dr Peter Marshall.* Dallas: Clarion Call Marketing.

McKay, Ian. 1992. Tartanism triumphant: The construction of Scottishness in Nova Scotia, 1933–1954. *Acadiensis* 21 (2): 5–47.

McKay, Stan, and Janet Silman. 1995. *The First Nations: A Canadian experience of the Gospel–culture encounter.* Geneva: World Council of Churches.

Moir, John S. 2003a. Loyalties in conflict: Scottish and American influences on Canadian Presbyterianism. In *Early Presbyterianism in Canada: Essays by John S. Moir,* ed. Paul Laverdure, 174–89. Gravelbourg, SK: Gravelbooks.

– 2003b. Robert McDowall: Pioneer Dutch Reformed Church missionary in Upper Canada. In *Early Presbyterianism in Canada: Essays by John S. Moir,* ed. Paul Laverdure, 28–40. Gravelbourg, SK: Gravelbooks.

– 2004. *Enduring witness: A history of the Presbyterian Church in Canada*. 3rd ed. Burlington: Eagle.

Moir, John S., Geoffrey D. Johnston, Joseph C. McLelland, and John A. Johnston, eds. 2005. *No small jewel: A history of the Synod of Southwestern Ontario, the Presbyterian Church in Canada*. Toronto: Presbyterian Church in Canada.

Morrison, Cecily. 2003. Culture at the core: Invented traditions and imagined Communities, part 1: Identity formation. *International Review of Scottish Studies* 28:3–21.

Nairn, Tom. 1981. *The break-up of Britain: Crisis and neo-nationalism*. 2nd ed. London: NLB/Verso.

Osborne, Brian S. 2004. *Rock and the sword: A history of St Andrew's Presbyterian Church, Kingston, Ontario*. Kingston: Heine.

Papp, Maria. 1996. *To the Hungarian Canadians ... The story of your people*. Trans. Violet Kasza and Helen Kovacs. Welland: Paper House.

Presbyterian Church in Canada. 1982. *Living faith: A statement of Christian belief*. Winfield, BC: Wood Lake Books.

– 1995. The acts and proceedings of the one hundred and twenty-first General Assembly of the Presbyterian Church in Canada, Waterloo, Ontario, 4–9 June. http://www.presbyterian.ca/webfm_send/56.

– 2004. Confessions and apologies. http://www.presbyterian.ca/nativeministries/confessions.

Reid, W. Stanford. 1976. The Scottish Protestant tradition. In *The Scottish tradition in Canada*, ed. W. Stanford Reid, 118–36. Toronto: McClelland and Stewart.

Ruggle, Richard E. 1984–5. The Presbyterian churches of the Scotch Block, Esquesing Township in the nineteenth century. *Canadian Society of Presbyterian History Papers* (1984–5): 135–61.

Ruitenbeek-Ott, Laura Renata. 1999. Religion and ethnicity: Dutch immigration and the First Christian Church of Victoria, British Columbia, 1952–1961. MA thesis, University of Victoria.

Soh, Chungsee Saran. 1993. *Women in Korean politics*. 2nd ed. Boulder: Westview.

Stanley-Blackwell, Laurie. 1997. 'Tabernacles in the wilderness': The open-air communion tradition in nineteenth- and twentieth-century Cape Breton. In *The contribution of Presbyterianism to the Maritime Provinces of Canada*, ed. Charles H.H. Scobie and G.A. Rawlyk, 93–117. Montreal and Kingston: McGill-Queen's University Press.

Statistics Canada. 1961. Census of Canada. Ottawa: Statistics Canada.

– 2002. Ethnic diversity survey: Portrait of a multicultural society. 85-593-XIE. Ottawa: Statistics Canada.

Stenhouse, David. 2005. Plaid it again, Uncle Sam. *Scotsman*, 23 March. http://
thescotsman.scotsman.com/s2.cfm?id=308332005.

Thomas, Derrick. 2005. 'I am Canadian.' *Canadian Social Trends* (Spring): 2–7.

Toronto Chinese Presbyterian Church. 1980. *70th Anniversary memoir: 1910–
1980*. Toronto: Toronto Chinese Presbyterian Church.

Trevor-Roper, Hugh. 1983. The invention of tradition: The Highland tradition
of Scotland. In *The invention of tradition*, ed. Eric Hobsbawm and Terence
Ranger, 15–41. Cambridge: Cambridge University Press.

Vander Vennen, Mark. 1988. Multi-generational transmission of war-induced
trauma: Its effects on family structure and process. Unpublished MS, MEd,
OISE.

Vander Vennen, Mary. 1980[?]. The long shadow of war. Christian Counselling
Service.

Van Dijk, Joanne. 2001. The role of religion in the postwar settlement patterns
of Dutch Canadians. *Canadian Review of Sociology and Anthropology* 38 (1):
57–74.

Van Ginkel, Aileen Marilyn. 1982. Ethnicity in the reformed tradition: Dutch
Calvinist immigrants in Canada 1946–1960. MA thesis, University of Toronto.

– 1984–5. Assimilation, transformation, or opposition? Patterns and models
for the cultural integration of the Dutch Calvinist community in Canada.
Canadian Society of Presbyterian History Papers 1984–85: 42–58.

Yoo, Young-Sik. 2002. Canada and Korea: A shared history. In *Canada and Korea:
Perspectives 2000*, ed. R.W.L. Guisso and Young-Sik Yoo, 9–39. Toronto: University of Toronto Press.

6 The United Church of Canada: A Church Fittingly National

GREER ANNE WENH-IN NG

It shall be the policy of the United Church to foster the spirit of unity in the hope that this sentiment of unity may in due time, so far as Canada is concerned, take shape in a church which may fittingly be described as national.
        – *Basis of Union* (1925), the founding document of the
                                                        United Church of Canada

On 10 June 1925, at the Mutual Street Arena in Toronto, over 8,000 representatives from four church bodies – the Congregationalists, the Methodists, two-thirds of Presbyterian congregations, and the Association of Local Union Churches – gathered to bring into being the first organic church union in the Western world, the United Church of Canada. This chapter provides a sketch of how the result of that church union – Canada's largest Protestant denomination[1] – has attempted to live out that vision of its founders, to become 'a church ... fittingly described as national.'

When the United Church was established as a 'national' church, the nation, or 'imagined community' (to use the term of Benedict Anderson [1996]) that the founders had in mind consisted of white, Protestant descendants of immigrants from the British Isles. The victims of these imaginings were Aboriginal peoples, French Canadians, non-Protestants, non-Christians, and recent immigrants. Moreover, because the concepts of both church and nation were imagined in essentially male terms, women were also marginalized. Today, the church still sees itself as 'national' but imagines the community quite differently. It is composed of men and women, of francophones, Anglophones, and allophones, people of all races, people of mixed religious heritages, homosexuals and heterosexuals, members of the First Nations, as well as immigrants and refugees. This re-imagining has had a profound impact on the United Church as it struggles to find its place in an increasingly secular, multicultural, and multi-faith society.

I write both as a latecomer to and as an insider of the United Church, since I originated from one of its founding bodies, the Congregational-ists, my home church being the China Congregational Church in Hong Kong. As a first-generation immigrant beginning her life in Hong Kong and then moving with her family to Canada in 1970, I will approach issues of identity, generation, gender, and racism from the perspectives of my academic fields of theology and religious education. As a young adult convert to Christianity who grew up in an average middle-class Chinese household with its blend of Confucian, Daoist, and (in my case far less prominently) Buddhist sensibilities and values, I will pay atten-tion to the possibility of 'multiple religious belonging' in the religious/ spiritual life of non-European United Church Christians. Given that I have been directly involved in the struggle of the United Church to come to grips with ethnic and racial diversity in Canadian society and church life, my commitment both to the church and to multiculturalism will be clear.[2]

A Canadian Christianity, a Christian Canada

The movement for church union among the three major Protestant denominations in the late nineteenth century was motivated by several factors, the most obvious of which was the desire to end division and competition among themselves and to become a truly 'united and unit-ing church,' especially in the fields of foreign missions, social services, and outreach to Aboriginal people. Another factor was pressure com-ing from the grass roots, in particular, local 'union churches' of the western provinces that for practical purposes and sheer survival had already been joining forces and worshipping together. Their members appeared determined to continue in this way, whether or not the national denominations came together.[3] A third factor – and one that gained urgency at the turn of the new century – was the challenge posed by the arrival of large numbers of non-Anglo-Saxon immigrants from Europe. In particular, those from eastern and southeastern Europe, who were either Roman Catholic or perceived as being only nominally Christian, were felt to be a threat to the emerging and still fragile 'Canadian' (i.e., mainly Anglo-Saxon) identity rooted in Protes-tant Christian ideals. Only a strong, national Protestant church with consolidated human and material resources could undertake the task of

206   Greer Anne Wenh-In Ng

'Christianizing' and 'Canadianizing' these newcomers with any hope of success (Vipond 1992).

The new church saw its 'call' or special mission as that of building up the Canadian nation, but a Canadian nation that centred mainly on its ethnic elements from Britain and a nation the citizens of which spoke chiefly English. This close relationship between the United Church and English/Anglo Canada was to continue for well over six decades, and the dominant Anglo elements of the church only reluctantly allowed themselves to be challenged after 1967 by the gradual emergence of a country characterized by immigration policies more favourable to prospective citizens from non-European home countries.[4] Another result of this assumption was that the church neglected ministry support to French Protestants for decades, confirming in the minds of both anglophones and francophones that the United Church was an 'English Canadian' institution. If the United Church generally ignored francophones, its attitude to Aboriginal peoples was more pernicious. It adopted a paternalistic understanding of Canada's first peoples, hoping to Christianize and Canadianize them by assimilating them.

United Church Structure and Belief

Before understanding the interaction of the United Church and ethnic identity, it is useful to understand what sets the church apart from other denominations. The United Church is a 'conciliar' church, governing itself by a series of 'courts' or levels of church governance rather than by bishops and archbishops. It inherited these unique administrative and governing structures from its founding denominations. From the Congregationalists came the local 'congregation' or 'pastoral charge' (two or more neighbouring congregations sharing financial resources and pastors together). From the Presbyterians came 'presbyteries,' clusters of local churches within a geographical area; they exercise 'oversight' to the congregations in their area, including oversight and 'discipline' of its ordained ministers or, as they are known today, 'ministry personnel.'[5] From the Methodists came a number of more or less geographical regional groupings called 'conferences' from British Columbia to Newfoundland and Labrador, which screen and ordain or commission its professional paid ministry personnel. A national elected body known as the 'General Council' meets regularly (originally every other year, but since 1997 every three years) to decide on policy and directions for the whole church.[6] Administratively, the national office is known as the General Council office.

Besides church governing structures, the founding denominations also passed on a summary of their faith convictions in the form of the Twenty Articles of Faith of the Basis of Union. The 'Reform' heritage of Presbyterians, Methodists, and Congregationalists meant that scripture remained the central authority for the new church's beliefs. Article 2 expressed an understanding of the Bible as 'containing the only infallible rule of faith and life.' One of the first acts of the young church was to appoint a committee of Christian Doctrine to come up with a more contemporary statement of faith, which eventually appeared in 1940. In 1968, 'A New Creed' appeared.[7] In all these statements of faith, scripture remained the central authority, but modern biblical scholarship, with its less literal, historical-critical approach, has changed the way that scripture is read.[8] After the 1960s, the church transformed traditional doctrines in response to more liberal and radical theological voices, including those of process theology, Latin American liberation theology, Black and Hispanic theologies, as well as feminist and Third World theologies. This theological evolution has sometimes been a source of tension between members and congregations that embrace such openness and those who adhere to more traditional and conservative views. Among the latter are the majority of so-called ethnic minority congregations in the United Church, leading – as we shall see – to occasional disagreements between those faith groups and the denomination's stance on some social issues.

Supporting 'Ethnic Ministries' in the United Church of Canada

At the time of church union, earlier home mission efforts established by the Methodist and Presbyterian churches (including their women's missionary societies, which had been very active in work among 'Orientals' in British Columbia) joined forces to carry on work among the influx of 'strangers within our gates' (Woodsworth 1972).[9] In the cities, this mission work manifested itself in the All People's Mission headed by J.S. Woodsworth for a time in Winnipeg, and Church of All Nations (Vancouver, Toronto, Hamilton). These missions continued to exist well into the middle of the twentieth century, with thirty-six of them across the country in the 1950s. These multi-ethnic missions existed until their individual ethnic and linguistic groups and congregations left to build their own places of worship. The Church of All Nations in Toronto, for instance, housed separate Czech, Finnish, Hungarian, Japanese, and Ukrainian congregations from the 1940s through to the 1960s as well as holding Sunday evening 'international' worship services in English (MacKay and Smith 1963). Because prior to 1961, Canadian immigration legislation gave decided preference (in descending order) to British, American, north European, and south European applicants, however, the 'face' of the United Church until and including the post-war baby-boomer church expansion period was still predominantly white and western European, even if it was less exclusively Anglo-Saxon. According to Roland Kawano – the United Church's national Congregational and Mission Support officer for ethnic and other ministries from the mid-1980s to the mid-1990s – the Board of Home Missions looked upon All Nations and All Peoples centres as transitional vehicles to assist non-Anglo groups to assimilate into Canadian society. The board assumed that they would no longer be necessary when the English-speaking children and grandchildren of their members eventually joined the ethnically Anglo dominant United Church congregations of their neighbourhood. 'The literature of Home Missions,' declare Kawano and Komiyama, 'clearly recognizes that these transitional congregations were a real form of nation building' (Kawano and Komiyama 1989, 23).

Until the early 1970s, so-called ethnic ministries in the United Church were organized under the paternalistic care of the Board of Home Missions along with 'Indian' missions. Such work covered both minority European and non-European 'Oriental' congregations and 'missions.' These ethnic minority congregations and missions – including the early established Japanese and Chinese groups in Vancouver and Toronto, Black missions like the Union United Church in Montreal, outreach to Chinese in Winnipeg and Calgary, and post—Second World War Japanese missions in Montreal, Hamilton, and Toronto – continued to live in the shadow of the denomination's mainstream from 1925 until the board was restructured out of existence in 1972. In that year, all work with non-Anglo, non-Franco, and non-Aboriginal United Church congregations and missions, renamed 'ethnic ministries,'[10] was folded into the newly structured national Division of Mission in Canada with diminished focus and resources.

For over two decades after 1972, clergy and lay leaders of ethnic minority congregations struggled to gain recognition and support at the national level of the United Church. Such support was particularly needed in the early 1970s, the period during which Koreans fleeing the political turmoil of the Korean War had begun to come to Canada. Among these newcomers was Sang Chul Lee, who eventually became the United Church's first Asian Canadian moderator in 1988. The elimination of overt racial and country-of-origin discrimination in Canada's immigration legislation and the integration of the now famous 'point' system into the immigration regulations in 1967 led to a 'second wave' of Chinese immigration as well as a 'first wave' of Koreans, Filipinos, and West Indians (Knowles 1997, 145–60; Li 2003, 22–37). It is often surprising to observers just how numerous Protestants were among the large influx of non-European, visible minority groups after 1967 and especially since the 1980s. Evidence of this influx was the mushrooming of Chinese and Korean places of worship in Canada's cities, including churches from more evangelical Christian traditions, as noted in Bruce Guenther's chapter 10 in this volume. Although generally not much aware of the existence of the United Church of Canada before their arrival (except for some of the Korean Presbyterian Christians mentioned in the 'Diaspora and Transnational Identities' section below), some of these immigrant Christians eventually sought a connection with the United Church. The result was seen in the gathering of the first Korean worshipping groups in Vancouver, Toronto, and Montreal, as well as the increased presence of Caribbean and Filipino Protestants in a number of urban mainstream Anglo congregations such as Lakeview United in Vancouver and St Matthew's United and Saint Luke's United in Toronto. These 'second wave' Chinese Protestants from Hong Kong and parts of Southeast Asia began to further change the composition of the existing Chinese congregations. The 1970s and 1980s also saw the beginnings of Taiwanese groups in Toronto and Vancouver.

In 1982, at the national biennial meeting of General Council, the United Church's highest 'court,' the denomination acknowledged its responsibility to these ethnically diverse groups and a few years later appointed Rev. Dr Roland Kawano as part-time staff for these ethnic minorities. Already instrumental in getting the church to recognize its ethnic congregations, May Komiyama, a member of the Nisei (English-speaking second-generation Japanese) congregation of Vancouver's Japanese United Church continued her advocacy role as chair of the newly formed Ethnic Ministries Working Unit. In 1994 and after two years of church-wide consultation and intense theological reflection, a national structure for supporting Ethnic Ministries, i.e., ethnically and culturally specific 'minority' groups within the United Church, was finally approved by General Council. The Ethnic Ministries Council was inaugurated in 1996, with Rev. Richard Chung-sik Choe as its general secretary. At present, all non-Anglo, non-francophone, and non-Native United Church congregations and missions come under its wing by belonging to one of the ethno-cultural specific congregational groupings called 'associations' (Japanese, Chinese, Korean, and Filipino) or 'coalitions' (Black, African, Taiwanese, and European congregations together).[11] Renamed the Ethnic Ministries Unit (EMU) after further restructuring of the national office in 2002, it aims to 'nurture and support the ministries of Ethnic Ministries congregations and ethnic minorities of the United Church of Canada to participate fully and faithfully in the Church's life and mission as a developing, growing, and gifted presence.'[12]

Governed by a group of dedicated volunteers and with a staff of six, the Ethnic Ministries Unit provides a context for sharing common concerns and for developing national programs and resources relevant to the needs of its member congregations. The EMU has produced translations of significant church documents into heritage languages as well as original publications by ethnic minority writers in order to add their voices to the whole denomination.[13] Official regional groupings of churches known as 'presbyteries' across the country often call upon their staff to assist in interpreting United Church policy matters to Ethnic Ministries congregations and their clergy or to help address conflicts. It has developed successful national gatherings for women (such as the 'Sounding the Bamboo' biennial conferences), youth and young adults, as well as for men.[14] The Ethnic Ministries Unit also cooperates with the Ethnic Ministries Committees of five of the United Church's thirteen regional Conference offices. The unit has made contributions to the internal deliberations and operations of the United Church as well as to its liturgical life, such as Asian language translations of the denomination's 1968 'A New Creed,' as well as some key prayers in both its 1996 hymn book *Voices United* and its 2000 book of worship *Celebrate God's Presence.* These contributions help to bring ethnic and cultural diversity in a concrete form into the worship life of the United Church's whole membership.

Hailed by Paul Bramadat as 'an example of a religious community that is making an effort to engage one of the great challenges and opportunities in the contemporary metropolis – ethnic diversity – in a creative manner' (Bramadat 2005, 60), this national body appears to be unique among Canada's Protestant churches.[15] In an effort to understand the current state of the United Church ten years after the beginning of the work of the Ethnic Ministries Unit, let us take a look at three contemporary congregational portraits in this Canadian denomination.

Newcomers to the United Church Today

New Taiwanese Mission in British Columbia

Asked how he ended up worshipping at Amazing Grace Taiwanese Mission in Fraser Presbytery in the Lower Mainland of British Columbia, Lobo Liang recalled how, as a newcomer to Canada in the 1990s, he had to adjust both his living style and career expectations: 'Like many other young professionals from Taiwan, I was in a new country, with a new language, a new culture ... We had to start by taking low-income jobs, like working in the supermarket – whatever we could find.' He met up with a small group of Taiwanese young adult Christians looking for a church home. 'The need for companionship and support made it easy to invite friends along,' Liang said, and Amazing Grace began to grow. When asked how non-Christians decided to join the church, he said, 'A lot of it has to do with the way our minister makes us feel at home in Canada. Church activities include celebrations of the Lunar New Year, the Dragon Boat Festival, and the Mid-Autumn Festival. He made us realize that there is one common Creator' (personal interview, 13 February 2006).

Rev. Brian Tsai, minister of Amazing Grace, agreed that it was important for his congregants to make connections with their home culture so as to ease the transition from Taiwan to Canada. 'They need a God of hope, a God of love,' he explained. 'Families bring their children for worship together on Sunday, where the use of three languages and dialects – Taiwanese, Mandarin, and English – takes place almost naturally' (personal interview, 14 February 2006). The strategy of integrating the ethno-cultural heritage of Chinese Canadians is different from past missionary approaches in Taiwan and other Asian countries, where Christian converts were enjoined to give up their religio-cultural heritage, and any attendant practices were deemed by missionary teachers to be unacceptable to the converts' new Christian identity. The more open attitude at Amazing Grace stems from Rev. Tsai's own theological convictions, which he confesses tend to be more 'liberal' than those he left behind in Taiwan. In the case of Amazing Grace, therefore, there seems to be a good 'fit' between the needs of the ethnic group and the 'ethos' of the United Church.

Ministry to the Chinese in the Greater Vancouver Area

Chinese immigration to Canada, and especially to the city of Vancouver, has exploded in recent years. According to the 2001 Census, there are 1.1 million Chinese in Canada. Moreover, those census figures also show that 40 per cent of all immigrants coming to Canada between 1991 and 2001 were born in the People's Republic of China. In the census metropolitan area of Vancouver, the Chinese population represented 17 per cent of its total population in 2001: many among that 17 per cent were Chinese from the People's Republic of China ('mainland China'). United Church leaders within the Vancouver presbyteries of the British Columbia Conference realized the timeliness and urgency of expanding ministry among this new population. A 'mission' or satellite place of worship, already put in place in the densely Chinese suburb of Richmond by the Chinese part of Chown Memorial and Chinese United Church, received a 'diaconal minister'[16] in order to meet this need.

In 2002, a project called 'Ministry to the Chinese in the Greater Vancouver Area' was established to 'spread the [Christian] gospel to Chinese people, both Cantonese and Mandarin speaking ... working in cooperation with existing Caucasian [mainstream Anglo] congregations' (Wong 2003, 74). This three-year pilot project was headed by the locally trained and newly ordained United Church minister Rev. Marion Man Wai Wong. Herself a 1990s arrival from Hong Kong, where she taught secondary school English, Wong began by inviting Chinese newcomers to Canada to her English as a Second Language classes. Since these groups met on the premises of local United churches (Oakridge United Church in Central Vancouver and Wilson Heights United Church in Burnaby), Wong soon found that these learners were curious about Christianity, God, and Jesus (77). In response, Wong added a women's group that read and studied the Bible in Mandarin. In time, Sunday worship services in Mandarin and Cantonese were also added.

With the end of the funding period for this experimental ministry in 2005, there is no doubt that the United Church presence among Chinese newcomers in the Greater Vancouver Area has been noticeably reduced. However, attempts are being made by individual mainstream white United Church congregations to carry out similar work on a much smaller scale and in a less systematic way.

Hungarian Congregations in the United Church

Historically, the largest influx of post–Second World War Hungarian immigrants and refugees came to Canada after the Hungarian revolt of 1956. Both of the Hungarian language communities – peopled by Protestants of the 'Reformed tradition' who find an affinity in the Presbyterian strand of the United Church, and who in previous decades had been the target of mission outreach by the United Church – are being served by recently arrived Hungarian clergy still in the process of being formally 'admitted' as United Church ministers. For example, in Winnipeg, Rev. Geza Szemok ministers in both Hungarian and English to a congregation consisting of 'old-timers' from the 1956 revolution period and more recent arrivals, often Hungarian families arriving 'from Scandinavia to the United Kingdom to South America to Australia' (personal interview, April 2006). It is the children from this latter group that fill the Sunday school and for whom Rev. Szemok is planning to organize Hungarian language classes. With an estimated Hungarian Canadian population of at least 50,000 in Canada in 2006, 4,000 of whom live in Winnipeg (including the 'lost generation' of the children of the old-timers), one of Rev. Szemok's challenges is to locate them and to invite them to join or rejoin the congregation. Increasingly, too, culturally and ethnically mixed married couples (one partner of whom is Hungarian) are choosing this congregation as their religious home. The longer-term vision of the pastor is to help this congregation become a more multicultural faith community that is open to all people.

The Hungarian United Church in Montreal, founded in 1926 by Rev. Michael Feher, had moved into its own building in the Mount Royal district while under that minister's forty-year leadership. Its numbers have surged recently, largely as a result of the sizable number of new Hungarian immigrants gaining direct admission to Quebec because of their Romanian background and the proximity of the Romanian language to French. Many of them well-educated professionals, these newcomers have helped to increase the number of Hungarians in Quebec to over 3,000 (interviews with Rev. Laszlo-Atilla Gyorgy, current minister, and Mary White, spring 2006). The need in a strange land for ethnically familiar social circles as well as the need to network for employment opportunities helps to motivate an increasing number of these individuals and families to seek out a Hungarian congregation. Activities such as the celebration of the grape festival in the fall and the observance of a pre-Lent carnival fulfil both cultural and religious needs. At the same time, accommodating to unique North American holidays such as Mother's Day and Father's Day is easier to accomplish when one lives among people of the same cultural background. The community in such instances acts both as a safe haven to celebrate the culture of the 'old country' but also as a means for adapting to Canadian culture.

Can the same be said of their religious acculturation to the type of Christianity practised by the United Church of Canada, and even to Christianity itself? Both Rev. Gyorgy and Mary White point out that many recent immigrants are relative newcomers to Christianity as a result of fifty years of Communist rule, during which religion was discouraged and had to be practised in secret. In terms of a strong identification with the United Church of Canada, Mary White explains that the Montreal Hungarian congregation has a history of adhering strongly to its Reformed Calvinist roots and has always appreciated the relative freedom with which it has been able to do so underneath the larger United Church 'umbrella.' Rev. Gyorgy is appreciative of the Methodist strand in the heritage of the United Church and hopes to broaden the congregation's outlook while remaining faithful to the Reformed traditions.

Because of new immigration, Hungarian United Church Christians are the only church newcomers of European descent in a position of growth or rejuvenation in 2006. In other European minority congregations, members of the more 'Canadianized' generation who arrived when they were young but now have reached middle age, either began attending English-speaking churches or stopped going to church altogether, like so many other Canadians. Typical is the United Church's only Welsh congregation, Dewi Sant in Toronto, which saw its highest influx of immigrants in the 1930s (Humphreys Jones 1982); predictably, it is currently at the point of asking itself how much longer it can remain viable as a congregation (interview with Nest Pritchard, who joined the church in 1972 after emigrating in the 1960s). Because of both reduced immigration from Europe after 1961 and the aging of the current members, one finds that overall these congregations have been diminishing in size and vigour.

New immigration to urban areas is still the driving force that stimulates growth of non-Anglo segments in the United Church – in the present case, immigration from Taiwan, mainland China, and Hungary and Romania. What is new is that, rather than gathering solely in ethnically and linguistically defined congregations, many of these immigrants choose to worship in neighbourhood United churches dominated by Anglo-Canadians. This recent development is discussed in the following section.

Developing Ethnically Diverse Congregations

Beginning as an Anglo-majority congregation established in the heyday of post–Second World War church growth, Willingdon Heights United Church in Vancouver, not unlike many others of its era, has found itself in the early twenty-first century diminishing in both numbers and financial sustainability as the result of an aging membership and dramatic demographic changes in the ethnic make-up of its neighbourhood. With the closing of its doors in sight, the congregation decided to invite another, more viable Christian group –the Korean-speaking, non-denominational Sung Soo Congregation – that was in need of its own worshipping space and in search of a Canadian denomination with which to align itself, to join forces with them. This finally happened in 2004 after over a year of 'getting to know you' negotiations. As a result of such a merger, Rev. Charles Ahn found himself needing to reassure 'old-timers' that they have not lost their church. At the same time, he began to encourage newcomers to learn what it was like to practise one's Christian faith 'the United Church way.' Both segments have had to learn to worship a little differently, such as learning to recite a central prayer of the faith, the Lord's Prayer (or 'Our Father') simultaneously in English and Korean during Sunday worship. For the newcomers to Willingdon Heights, it involved learning how to 'sing one's faith' from the contemporary United Church hymn book *Voices United* (1996) at weekly evening 'hymn sings.' The two segments are also learning to serve or 'minister' to each other mutually. Newcomers, who are usually younger, volunteer hours and hours to carry out much-needed maintenance and repairs of the church building; the mostly Anglo old-timers in turn offer ESL lessons to the newcomers. The merging of these two groups into one congregation has made the church reach its goal of becoming financially viable. Furthermore, as a result of the new Korean presence, Willingdon Heights is increasingly seen as a congregation that welcomes a wide variety of newcomers, thus attracting Filipinos, Caribbean Blacks, and Pacific Islanders to its Sunday worship and programs. By shifting its attitude from a defensive 'fortress mentality' to one of welcoming its ethnically diverse neighbours, this congregation has become a model for a denomination that aspires to become an 'intercultural church' (Milne 2006, 27).

In Toronto's Davenport-Perth Community Church, Mary Egbedeju breathlessly apologized for being late as she rushed into the busy alcove where I was waiting for her. 'I've just come out of an adult literacy class,' she explained. 'It's one of the ways I am trying to improve myself.' Mary came to Canada from Nigeria over six years ago and works as an educational assistant in one of Toronto's public schools. She lives in a community housing complex close by and has been coming to Davenport-Perth Community Church since she arrived. In the late 1980s, the church solved its financial crisis by giving land adjacent to the church to the city of Toronto to build a health and community centre in return for maintenance of the church building. According to the congregation's mission statement, 'Davenport-Perth Community Church is a church of and for the community.' It also affirms that the church, which is 'made up of many diverse cultures and ethnic backgrounds,' 'must be present in the world connecting with the struggles, hopes and experiences of people in the community.' It celebrates such diversity with contemporary and non-traditional music and worship styles, using songs from around the world often accompanied by a host of 'global' musical instruments. Moreover, Black History Month is celebrated every February. Also, Shawan Johnson, a board member who is Ojibwa, has found a home at this inclusive congregation where he is able to hold sweetgrass ceremonies and participate in Native drumming as an expression of his faith – something he could not even dream of in his previous congregation, the non-denominational but largely evangelical Street Connection. In 2006, Davenport-Perth Community Church was approximately half white and half non-white, with more of the latter attending weekly worship services.

A Variety of Models

Both Willingdon Heights and Davenport-Perth communities faced rapidly declining membership and thus were unable to continue in ways these originally majority Anglo congregations had always existed and functioned. Across Canada, many strong, Anglo-dominant United Church congregations have faced similar challenges, providing contemporary examples of the decline discussed in the opening and closing chapters of this volume. Response to loss and threatened loss have been varied. Some congregations have merged with other struggling congregations in their neighbourhoods. Others, such as First United Church in Hamilton, Parkdale, St Matthew's and Newtonbrook in Toronto, have exemplified the denomination's commitment to social service and social justice by decreasing their worship space in order to build seniors' residences or affordable housing. Frequently, the 'discourse of loss' discussed by Bramadat and Seljak in chapter 1 is in evidence.

Other congregations in similar declining membership have experimented with merging with ethnic minority congregations. For example, Toronto's Centennial United Church (with a largely European-descent majority) in 1986 merged with the by then stronger English-speaking Nisei congregation of the Toronto Japanese United Church (which had been worshipping in Centennial's building since 1954 when they moved from their location in the Church of All Nations). In Vancouver, Chown Memorial United Church (also with a European-descent majority) merged with the Vancouver Chinese United Church in the mid-1990s to the mutual benefit of both congregations. (At that time, the Vancouver Chinese United Church needed more physical space, both indoors for meetings and programming and outdoors for parking, for its expanding membership – a need not being met by its Chinatown location, but which the suburban location of Chown Memorial could satisfy.) However, Vancouver's Lakeview United Church took another approach; after receiving a growing number of Filipino immigrants throughout the 1980s, it remade itself as the Lakeview Multicultural United Church. It is now led by a Filipino Canadian lay pastoral minister. Saint Luke's United Church in downtown Toronto, on the other hand, while not adopting an explicitly 'multicultural' nomenclature, has a Sunday school consisting of mostly Filipino children and youth, as well as an ethnically mixed (Filipino and English-Canadian) church choir, and is developing a largely Filipina women's group. Led by a Korean Canadian minister, it is also attracting worshippers from a large variety of ethnic communities. However, it is worth noting that at Saint Luke's the numerically smaller Anglo-Canadian members seem to have retained control over the governing structures.

What is new, therefore, is that church mergers are bringing together culturally diverse congregations. Many of the remaining, predominantly white, urban, United Church congregations find themselves becoming more culturally diverse, either simply because of demographic changes or more intentionally by shifting their mission to reach out to new immigrants in their area. Occasionally some, like Davenport-Perth, are combining social outreach with their ministry to new

Canadians. If this trend continues, more mainstream, ostensibly white congregations will become increasingly ethnically diverse.

While these congregations may be becoming increasingly diverse ethnically, they still struggle to organize their internal structures in order to invite all their members to 'participate fully,' as the United Church's Anti-Racism Policy Statement of 2000 obliges them to do. It is uncertain that they can create just internal structures and modes of operation as well as finding ways to 'speak to the world' – the other two strategies of the Anti-Racism Policy Statement. In other words, to what extent can such new configurations of faith communities share power and leadership equitably, or would the dominant 'host' element still retain the 'reins' of the congregation? Will newer members feel themselves to be 'perpetual guests' who may be warmly invited into a home, but are never considered part of the household sufficiently to feel they can 'move around the furniture'?[17] Such a challenge is expressed profoundly by the fact that the Ethnic Ministries Revisioning Task Group set up in preparation of its tenth anniversary in 2006 to reflect on its place in the denomination concluded it needed to try moving the United Church towards formally declaring itself a culturally diverse, intercultural denomination. The Task Group's proposal, entitled 'A Transformative Vision for the United Church of Canada,' was affirmed at the denomination's Thirty-Ninth General Council in August 2006, in Thunder Bay, Ontario. By this action, the United Church committed itself to 'becoming an intercultural church, and that intercultural dimensions of ministries be a denominational priority in living out its commitment to racial justice, where there is mutually respectful diversity and full and equitable participation of all Aboriginal, Francophone, ethnic minority, and ethnic majority constituencies in the total life, mission, and practices of the whole church.'[18]

According to the Task Group's report, *A Transformative Vision for the United Church of Canada*, the term *intercultural* was deliberately chosen over the more common *multicultural* in recognition of some of the problems connected with the latter term. For example, many felt that since the establishment of the federal policy in 1971, multiculturalism tended to concentrate on the celebration of cultural diversity ('song and dance' and food) to the neglect of addressing inequality of power and wealth. Moreover, Aboriginal peoples do not see themselves as one of Canada's ethnic minority groups (Ethnic Ministries Revisioning Task Group 2006, 579). As used in the task group's proposal, *intercultural* stresses several features of the new relationships it envisioned: justice, mutuality, and equity, as well as the expectation that traditionally dominant Anglo-Celtic members (the 'ethnic majority constituencies' who usually do not see themselves as being 'ethnic groups') will recognize the need to foster these mutual and equitable relationships envisioned for the broader church (579–90).

As the three congregational portraits of newcomer congregations demonstrate, it appears that in these early years of the twenty-first century, immigration and existing ethnic diversity (of new immigrants and of the Canadian-born descendents from earlier immigration) will continue to change the face of the United Church of Canada. This new reality will pose important new challenges to the church. For example, how will newcomers relate to their Canadian home church while still remaining attached to their 'home country'? Will the traditional ideas about gender, intergenerational dynamics, authority, and morality that characterize the ethnic minority congregations clash with the relatively liberal attitudes of the mainstream churches? How will conflicts and tensions within and among ethnic minority United Church communities themselves and between them and the still predominantly white, liberal denomination be resolved? And, for a denomination that has formally adopted an anti-racism policy in 2000, how will the Canadian church be able to address both the systemic or institutional racism inherent in its structures and culture as well as the 'white privilege' that accompanies it?

A National Church in a Bilingual Canada

One challenge to the United Church's traditional Anglo-Canadian identity has come not from recent immigrants but from long-time francophone residents. In its early years, the United Church ignored or at least discounted the large francophone community in Canada and consequently refused to provide support for ministry among French Protestants. In fact, a non-denominational French Canadian Missionary Society, La Grande Famille, had come into existence in 1840 but had been dissolved in 1875 (Tanner 1931, 147). The great expectations raised by the possibility of a renewed La Grande Famille in 1925 did not materialize, in spite of the more than sixty places of worship still in the province of Quebec in 1927 (see United Church of Canada 2007). Francophone ministries within the United Church came under the purview of the Board of Home Missions, where they 'languished in relative anonymity' (Kenny 1989a, 10) while the board committed itself to mission work in South and East Asia as well as Europe. Locally, each francophone church became part of their local and regional church governing structures.

Without a supportive national structure after church union, francophone congregations, which were minorities in their presbyteries, often experienced isolation and powerlessness. That is why the formation of the Zone Pastoral Francophone in Quebec in 1971 was understood to be a harbinger of positive change. The zone 'sought to preserve a principle sacred to the francophone Protestant community: the right to make its own decisions and to minister to francophones within the United Church' (Kenny 1989, 10). In 1985 the formation of a francophone presbytery, the Consistoire Laurentien, within the Montreal and Ottawa Conference, enshrined this principle.

In 2002, the church created a national Unit for Ministries in French with a two-pronged agenda of promoting ministries in French within the United Church, and increasing the visibility of the United Church in francophone society. Its strategies called for greater support of francophone ministries with appropriate resources, including original resources for mission, worship and formation, education with a distinct francophone minority perspective, as well as timely translations into French of United Church documents (such as official policy statements and news releases). The unit also sought the promotion of bilingual worship services within existing anglophone congregations in addition to developing new francophone places of worship in and outside Quebec (Gagnon 2006, 14).

To support French-language communities, the United Church publishes a monthly magazine called *Aujourd'hui Credo*, which celebrated its fiftieth anniversary of publication in 2004.[19] Moreover, the church has undertaken to translate its hymn book into French with a projected publication date in 2008. These new development efforts are also aimed at serving French-speaking newcomers to Canada from Africa (Nigeria, the Republic of Congo), and the Caribbean (Haiti). So, even as the church works to become more open to francophone Canadians, that community itself is becoming more ethnically diverse. One sign of the church's changing attitude to francophones and its traditional identification with English Canada is its decision to stay out of the debate over the 1995 Quebec referendum on sovereignty. Instead of coming out in favour of 'national' unity (where the nation is imagined as a federalist Canada), it allowed congregations and their leaders to express their concerns through ecumenical prayer vigils and similar activities at the local and regional levels (Hiller 2000).

Transnational Identities in the United Church

As the ethnic make up of the United Church evolves, the church has to deal with new forms of transnationalism.[20] From their very beginnings, the components of the United Church of Canada had to deal with transnationalism, such as Methodists who had strong ties to Great Britain or the United States and Presbyterians with connections to Scotland. However, the post-1960s immigration posed new challenges for the United Church of Canada. I would like to explore how transnationalism affects ethnic groups and individuals within the United Church both in their ethno-cultural self-identity and their identity as United Church Christians.

There is no doubt that for most of the first-generation immigrants in these groups, sustaining attachments to more than one place is natural, since many of them still have family members, friends, and work or business associates in their countries of origin. Increased ease of travel and efficient and inexpensive means of communication have enabled these new Canadians to keep up transnational links both physically by actual visits and socially, emotionally, and politically via the mass media, the Internet, and personal communication. Furthermore, economic globalization in the 1990s has given rise to a phenomenon known as transnationalism, the maintenance of several 'national' identities (Ong 1999). One example of this phenomenon are the so-called astronauts, that is, primary breadwinners of Chinese Canadian immigrant families who elect to maintain active business or professional ties in both Canada and their former homelands (Hong Kong, Taiwan, or countries in Southeast Asia). Such an ability to connect with their 'homelands' was certainly denied to members of the earliest Chinese community in Canada not only because travel and communication were difficult and expensive, but because Canada's racist immigration policies prevented them from becoming citizens or bringing their families.[21]

The main challenge of maintaining transnational religious identities is finding a way to sustain sufficient attachment to two places – each of which may be steeped in religious, spiritual, and personal meaning. In the case of Asian astronauts who are Christian, it may mean maintaining the ties to their home congregations in Hong Kong or Taiwan (which in the case of United Church persons could well be Methodist, Presbyterian, or Congregational ones) while they try to integrate into their newly adopted Canadian congregations. This attachment to a 'home church' after emigration can generate a diasporic mentality, whereby one's spiritual home is still seen as being lodged 'elsewhere' than Canada. Whereas a certain amount of nostalgia is understandable (witness the existence of a group of Torontonians calling themselves the 'Canadian Fellowship of former China Congregational Church Members' who have been gathering twice a year for two decades), unwillingness to relinquish the past may indicate either a tenacious clinging to valued religious traditions or a reluctance to become 'full citizens' in the adopted country and religious community. For both the individuals and for the United Church of Canada, such 'dual religious citizenship' – not to mention the astronaut phenomenon – is a new challenge.

Although the denomination – and its component parts (Methodists, Congregationalists, Presbyterians) – has a long history of mission work in China and Korea, in parts of Africa, and in the Caribbean, technically the church is strictly Canadian and thus has no denominational sibling institution operating outside of Canada.[22] By contrast, other Canadian mainstream church bodies such as the Roman Catholic, Anglican, Presbyterian, and Lutheran churches – which are world Christian bodies with common ways of worship, governing, and believing – are readily identifiable by name by new immigrants because these churches have been active around the world for centuries. The major adjustments facing most Christian immigrants are, at least, not complicated by their having to join an entirely 'new' church, whereas this sometimes daunting obstacle is faced by those who join a United Church congregation.

The lack of an equivalent global denominational presence of the United Church in lands of potential emigration to Canada therefore has implications both for membership and recruitment, since 'transfer of membership' from one overseas denomination to the United Church of Canada cannot be assumed, and since new members cannot be expected to have any recognition of, not to say any loyalty to, the denomination. So, while the very 'Canadianness' of the United Church in the past may have facilitated growth by attracting newcomers interested in joining an explicitly 'Canadian' church, in the contemporary period marked by high immigration, the church may not be as attractive to those immigrants who are more drawn to ethno-religious communities that allow them to maintain a more robustly transnational identity.

Another challenge for immigrants to Canada is the pressure to assimilate into the dominant anglophone or francophone European-based culture of Canada. This often means the gradual dilution of specific ethnicities as younger generations increasingly come to view their nationality as 'Canadian.' For white Canadians, this usually poses few problems. For 'visible minority' persons, on the other hand, things are not so simple. Because of the their facial features and the colour of their skin, even fourth- or fifth-generation Canadians from visible minorities – such as Black Canadians with Loyalist roots stretching back to the eighteenth century as well as descendents of Japanese and Chinese Canadians who came to Canada well over a hundred years ago – are still frequently assumed to be relative newcomers (West 2003). A similar frustration faces third-generation Japanese Canadians whose Nisei (second-generation) parents deliberately raised their children to assimilate into the majority population as much as possible because of the Niseis' own bitter internment experience as enemy aliens during the Second World War. Many of these Sansei (third-generation Japanese Canadians) and their mixed-race children – the result of 'out marriage' rates among Sansei as high as 75 per cent – often choose to identify themselves as 'Canadian,' but are still perceived by outsiders to be 'Japanese' (Makabe 1998). Unlike Canadians of European descent, visible ethnic minorities cannot choose to become, or to appear, 'Canadian' so easily (Song 2003, 118).

In the post-colonial era, however, more and more ethnic minority groups in Canada (and in Britain and the United States) are refusing to 'abide by the meanings, discourses and stereotypes which are foisted upon them by the wider society' (Song 2003, 141). One form of this resistance can be insisting on keeping one's 'ethnic' name, as Rev. Hanns Skoutajan, a German-speaking Czech refugee who came to Canada as a ten-year-old, chose to do when pressured by his teacher to change 'Hanns' to the Anglicized 'John.'[23] Similarly, in the early 1990s, I reclaimed my Chinese given name 'Wenh-In,' in addition to my English one, 'Greer Anne,' by which I had been known both personally and professionally (and not only in English-speaking situations) until then.[24] The fact that I felt I could 'come out' only as recently as in the early 1990s is evidence of the long-lasting effects of colonization and internalized racism whereby I was trained to give higher value to the colonizer's language and culture, English, and to devalue my own.

Inter-Generational and Gender Considerations

Another challenge all immigrants to Canada face is tensions between old values and lifeways and those they find here. When coming to Canada, a predominately liberal democratic society that focuses on individual rights, newcomers find a society that often espouses values that appear to clash with those of their home culture. Generally speaking, first-generation immigrant parents and grandparents tend to place a high value on a more communal, interdependent, and traditional way of relating, as opposed to the more individualistic, independent, and modern Western values espoused by the second and third generations who were born and raised in Canada. The former are also more used to a more hierarchical model of relating in family and community life, with older people taking precedence over younger people, with males taking precedence over females, and with parental authority being treated as sacrosanct. While these hierarchical social structures may have been the norm elsewhere, many members of the younger genera-tion, growing up and going to school in Canada, find it difficult to embrace these ways. The tendency toward egalitarianism and individ-ualism one can witness among younger, more acculturated members of minority families, communities, and churches, may cause consterna-tion and even conflict, especially in those of East Asian origin (Korean, Chinese, Japanese, ethnic Chinese-Vietnamese, Taiwanese) where the Confucian hierarchical values continue to be practised.

A unique situation in which religion and ethnicity co-mingle in a complex manner is found in the Korean community where, in the immigration wave of the 1970s and 1980s, an unusually large number of teenagers accompanied their parents to Canada. These young immi-grants, who belong to what demographers call the '1.5 generation,' are caught between the old and new worlds. Writing of his own 1.5 experi-ence, Rev. Chung-sik Choe describes his experience as a 1.5 Korean as being 'not quite sure who I was, although I knew who I was not' (Choe 1995, 16). In confrontations with their elders, his generation found themselves 'despised and corrected, but never understood' (16). Even-tually finding solidarity with other members of the 1.5 and subsequent generations, he decided to become an agent of change for both his com-munity and the United Church by working towards 'a new community identity' rooted in the cultural diversity of Canadian society (16).

Each group will deal with the tension posed by the opposing values (hierarchy versus egalitarianism, patriarchy versus gender equality, and so on) differently, based not only on its specific cultural traditions but also its religious heritage, including its tradition of scriptural inter-pretation. More conservative Christians tend to stay closer to the hier-archical values, reinforcing them with biblical sanction. Such is the case in many contemporary Korean Canadian congregations (Hertig 2002).

Others will use the scriptures to interpret Christianity as a resource for liberation, and as a vehicle for greater gender equality through feminist biblical interpretation (G. Ng 1996c, 1999). Such differences could influence behavioural norms in the home, including the extent to which female family members are encouraged to enter a profession, as well as whether women in Canadian churches are encouraged to engage in ministry leadership.

One area where the United Church of Canada challenges traditionalists both within the denomination and within the broader Christian tradition in Canada is its ordination of women. This is a long-standing tradition in the denomination. Lydia Gruchy was the first woman ordained in the United Church of Canada. Her ordination in 1936 at St Andrew's United Church in Moose Jaw, Saskatchewan, after a long and fierce struggle, was the first not only in the United Church, but apparently also the first in any major denomination in North America (Taylor 1999, 119). The fact that this event took place only eleven years after the young church was founded makes it quite remarkable, though the prevailing gender views of the time still required women employed in the church to give up their professional ministry positions when they got married, much as the case with other 'career' women. Indeed, Rev. Gruchy herself never married, and spent the rest of her ministerial life on rural pastoral charges in Saskatchewan (personal interview, Rev. Nettie Hoffman, 7 November 2006).

Even more remarkable, though hardly known to more than a handful of history buffs burrowing in the depths of the United Church Archives, is the story of Dr Victoria Cheung. Canadian born and educated at the Oriental Home and School for Girls in Victoria, British Columbia, in the early twentieth century, she proceeded to Toronto to study medicine under the sponsorship of the Presbyterian Women's Missionary Society (this was before two-thirds of Presbyterian churches went into church union to help form the United Church in 1925). At a time when even most middle-class women of the dominant culture did not attend university, she became the first woman physician to enter the residency program at the Toronto General Hospital after graduating with a medical degree. By the year of church union, she was stationed in the mission hospital in Kongmoon in southern China, thus fulfilling her dream of being a missionary doctor in her ancestral land.[25]

This tradition continues. Since 1993, the United Church has held a national biennial conference named 'Sounding the Bamboo,' a forum to promote fellowship among women of ethnic minority groups. Beyond encouraging networks and training women for leadership, the 'Sounding the Bamboo' conference has provided a safe space for exploring faith, gender, and justice topics usually not dealt with adequately, if at all, in participants' sometimes rather conservative congregations. Topics include sexism and gender roles in church and home, domestic violence, as well as racism in one's workplace and Canadian society. One of the conference's main goals is to develop participants' potential for leadership. With a dedicated staff and generous funding, the conference has drawn together sixty to eighty participants every two years, meeting in different locations across Canada. The conference provides opportunities for ethnic minority women of the United Church to get to know one another, to develop their leadership potential, share their struggles and joys, and build community across great distances. A strategy of appointing women from local congregations of each conference site to form the planning team has helped to identify women who could be integrated into national committees or task groups, bringing ethnic minority women's perspectives and concerns to the wider church. Out of its regular participants, several individuals have taken up formal theological training and been ordained or commissioned to professional ministry in the United Church.[26] For a congregation or even a whole ethnic group that expects women to hold only traditional service roles, it is still challenging to encourage ethnic minority women to assume professional leadership. Consequently, even some of those who are fully trained can find pastorates only outside their own ethnic communities. They are not welcome in most of the United Church's ethnic minority congregations with sizeable immigrant populations (for instance, Korean, Chinese, Taiwanese, Ghanaian, and Ugandan), or even in second- and subsequent generation English-speaking 'sub-congregations,' which are governed by church councils or official boards dominated by ancestral language–speaking first-generation elders and members. The only exception is in the Japanese Canadian United Church community, two of whose churches are currently (in 2007) served by ethnically Japanese women pastors and one (in an amalgamated Japanese-Anglo congregation) by a non-Japanese white woman pastor.

Tensions between Ethnic Ministries Congregations and the Denomination

There is no doubt that the existence of ethnic minority communities within the United Church has challenged the denomination. Beyond gender, two issues that affect these minority communities directly illustrate this point: the church's commitment to social justice and its openness to interfaith dialogue. The response of members of these ethnic minority communities to these two issues is complex. For example, given that members of minority communities are often recent immigrants and refugees, their main concerns centre on the socio-economic challenge of finding employment, settling their families, and educating their children (with the exception of those from the middle and professional classes who, for fear of political instability, left Hong Kong in large numbers before the end of British rule in 1997). Issues such as the plight of Canada's Aboriginal peoples or global warming may seem rather abstract and removed from their day-to-day struggle for survival. On the other hand, those among them who have experienced and still experience material deprivation most frequently support the church's efforts to alleviate poverty and to pressure the government to address the issue seriously. Similarly, many members of these groups are recent arrivals in Canada and some of them are still waiting to bring their families over to Canada; they certainly appreciate the church's ground-breaking work on the rights of refugees and immigrants. Again, as in the ways these communities respond to the question of women's roles, theological orientation may affect how a particular group responds to the social justice orientation within the church. If a congregation reads scripture from a highly individualistic or moralistic perspective, then they will likely perceive those who are concerned with the social and political dimensions of the biblical texts as inappropriately 'politicizing' the faith.

Nowhere is this tension more evident than in the more conservative attitude of ethnic minority congregations towards gays and lesbians, when confronted with the much more progressive, some would say radical, stance of the broader denomination. As early as 1988, the United Church's Thirty-Second General Council decided as the highest court of the church to remove barriers to the ordination and commissioning of gay and lesbian ministerial candidates. In the years following, it was active in supporting the move towards legalizing same-sex marriage which resulted in the Canadian federal government's legislation to this effect in 2005. The general response of the ethnic minority congregations was to distance themselves from their denomination's stance, partly out of a genuine difference of opinion, but partly also out of a desire to maintain their peer standing among the even more conservative Christian churches of their ethnic communities. An example from the Chinese United churches will illustrate this point. Meeting in 2004 in Moose Jaw, Saskatchewan, the eleven-member congregations and missions of the United Church's Chinese Association drew up a statement to be released to the Chinese-language religious press, which said in part, 'We insist that Canada and other cultural and religious traditions ... legally define marriage as [the union between] one man and one woman,' even while 'we sympathize with those who have experienced prejudice and unequal treatment as a result of their sexual orientation' (United Church of Canada 2004a, 1–2).[27]

This cautious, at times sceptical, approach to progressive or social gospel discourses within the church is also evident in the way some factions respond to the United Church's very liberal position on interfaith dialogue. After decades of preaching an exclusivist understanding of the gospel and condemning non-Christian (and non-Protestant) faiths, by the middle of the 1960s the church had adopted an attitude of tolerance and even appreciation for other faith communities. For recent immigrants, especially those from Asia, this new openness may pose challenges, since some of the world religions now being more actively 'appreciated' by the United Church may be among those that dominated their country of origin; in fact, these newly repositioned and newly appreciated non-Christian traditions could have been personally rejected by some newcomers when they became Christians or when they immigrated to Canada.

Social Justice and Inclusion

'Social Christianity,' declares one of the contributors to the United Church's volume celebrating its seventy-fifth anniversary in 2000, 'is the heart and soul of the United Church of Canada' (Reeve 1999, 105). An inheritance of its founding denominations, this passion found expression during the Depression in a deep criticism of government and business. Some of the church's clergy members even began a movement called 'Fellowship for a Christian Social Order,' led by biblical scholar R.B.Y. Scott. Making strategic use of its national network, the young church could disseminate information and harness its clergy and membership in its causes. Seeing 'evangelism' and 'social service' as two sides of the same coin, this church soon came to be in the vanguard of prodding the federal government towards adopting social policies that enabled society to take responsibility for all citizens. Between the 1950s and early 1970s, under the leadership of secretaries of the board such as J.S. Woodsworth (first leader of the Co-operative Commonwealth Federation, the CCF, later to become the New Democratic Party), James Muchmore, and Ray Hord, the United Church mobilized public support for guaranteed income supplement for low-income pensioners, the construction of senior citizens' homes, the recognition of labour unions, the provision of fair wages and decent working conditions, a more equitable distribution of the country's wealth by a progressive taxation system, the provision of a 'social safety net' for Canada's poorest families, and, most famously of all, universal health-care insurance.

The United Church has not shied away from political involvement. For example, in the 1950s, during the height of the anti-communist campaign in Canada and the United States, its General Council called for the recognition of 'Red' China against prevailing public sentiment in Canada. In the sixties, it was the first national body to recommend publicly the welcoming of young American draft resisters during the Vietnam War (MacDonald 1984, 90). In the 1970s, the United Church came more and more to work collaboratively with other Christian denominations, especially the so-called PLURA churches (Presbyterian, Lutheran, United Church, Roman Catholic, Anglican), in specialized 'ecumenical coalitions' for justice (Lind and Mihevc 1994). Thus programmes such as Interchurch Committee on Human Rights in Latin America and the Interchurch Committee on Refugees came to advocate for human rights both locally and globally, and a coalition such as the Task Force on the Churches and Corporate Responsibility worked to challenge those corporations with investments in countries that 'aid and abet oppressive regimes in other countries' (MacDonald 1984, 90). These inter-church groups would also collaborate with secular groups such as Project North that speak for land claims of Canada's Native peoples. The United Church continues such ecumenical justice work within the 'umbrella' coalition called KAIROS, the Ecumenical Justice Network of the Canadian Churches.[28]

Like Kairos, the United Church had devoted significant resources for groups working on Aboriginal rights, poverty, ecology, global economic issues, international human rights, refugees, and immigration. Naturally, these last two areas are of particular interest to many newer members of the United Church of Canada's ethnic communities. For example, during the 1970s, the church helped congregations and individuals sponsor and re-settle refugees from Chile after the brutal military coup there. In the 1980s, the church worked on behalf of the

Vietnamese 'boat people,' followed by influxes of refugees from Central America (Nicaragua, Guatemala, El Salvador), and African countries such as Uganda and Ghana. In the 1990s there were emergency cases from Bosnia and other troubled regions of the world. For the congregations, sponsoring refugees and helping to settle immigrants is a way of practising hospitality to the 'stranger' as commanded by Jesus and major figures in the Old Testament stories. At the same time, members of these sponsoring churches also have to learn to interact with persons from different cultures. Sometimes they even venture to learn new languages, as Port Wallis United Church in Dartmouth, Nova Scotia, did, learning basic Spanish as part of their preparation for welcoming a Colombian family (Carlisle 2005, 32). Because refugee families often may not be Protestant (or even Christian), sponsorship is sometimes an invitation not only to an inter-cultural, but also an inter-faith encounter, as members of Kamloops United Church discovered when they began sponsoring Vietnamese refugees in the late 1970s (32). The challenge is for sponsors to engage in such interactions with respect rather than condescension, which is difficult to do, given the historical legacy of ethno-centric missionary activities in Canada and abroad and also given uneven power relations between established, middle-class members of the United Church and refugees who often arrive in Canada penniless, traumatized, and disadvantaged.

In recent years, refugee resettlement work and social justice issues have become more intertwined, leading the church to engage in advocacy for the humane and just treatment of refugees and refugee applicants, including those who apply for refugee status within Canada after they have entered the country. When such applications are not successful and individuals are ordered deported to a home country situation that poses danger to their life, occasionally they may decide to go into hiding. Some publicly seek sanctuary within church buildings, which as sacred spaces have been historically considered inviolable by law-enforcers. For example, in 2002, the Union United Church of Montreal, Canada's oldest Black congregation, offered sanctuary to an Ethiopian mother and her three children whose claim had been denied. The family lived in the church for well over a year, until December 2004, when the minister of immigration and citizenship gave them permission to stay on humanitarian grounds. Another congregation, St Andrew's–Norwood United Church in St Laurent, Quebec, provided sanctuary to a professor from Bogota, Colombia, and his wife and daughter for over a year, until summer 2005 (Shepherd 2004).

Commitment of the United Church to Inter-Faith Dialogue

Involvement with refugees and immigrants of different faith traditions highlights the church's commitment to social justice and social service as well as its new openness to inter-faith dialogue. It is in these dialogues that one can see some of the ways in which Christianity and ethnicity interact in the Canadian Christian community. In 1966, a report of the Commission on World Mission urged that 'the Church should recognize that God is creatively and redemptively at work in the religious life of all mankind' (United Church of Canada 1966, 435). Since then, the church has committed substantial human and financial resources to the dialogue with representatives of the world's major faiths, including the establishment in the early 1970s of a portfolio for Interfaith Dialogue in the denomination's newly formed Division of World Outreach. Several important church-wide studies have resulted in significant documents, including *Mending the World* (1997) that expanded the understanding of ecumenism (a term with Greek roots meaning 'the whole inhabited earth' but had in fact generally referred only to relationships among Christian bodies) to include faiths groups other than Christian. *Bearing Faithful Witness* (2003) addressed United Church–Jewish Relations and *That We May Know Each Other* (2004b) took on United Church–Muslim relations. These initiatives demonstrate that the United Church of Canada has developed the post-colonial consciousness described by Bramadat and Seljak in chapter 1 of this volume. Religious chauvinism and triumphalism most often accompanied the European project of colonization. These efforts to validate the religions of other peoples – especially the faith of Jews and Muslims, which Christians have denigrated for centuries – reveal a remarkable change in the church's outlook and a new and more positive openness to the many ways in which religion, ethnicity, and culture interact in Canada and around the world.

The Role of Ethnicity in Inter-Faith Dialogue

Ironically, the United Church's openness to world religions has caused tensions for members of those ethnic communities traditionally identified with religions other than Christianity. There is debate, for example, among Asian Canadian Christians about the way non-Christian traditions are and ought to be represented within the United Church. For example, the conversions to Christianity of many Korean, Vietnamese,

Chinese, and Japanese Canadians had involved a great deal of personal sacrifice. Two examples of such sacrifices are the disruption of harmonious relationships with family members (because these family members remained non-Christian) and the relinquishing of the practice of ancestor veneration (because it was viewed by missionaries as pagan and thus forbidden). For this reason, many Asian Canadian United Church members perceive the very idea of returning to those non-Christian religions as threatening and insulting. A recent case in one of the United Church Conferences illustrates the seriousness of this dilemma.

At the 2006 annual meeting of the Toronto Conference, a group of Korean pastors protested the opening worship service led by a Buddhist. To highlight the conference's theme, 'Journeying as Pilgrims in a Multi-Faith World,' the president of the conference had invited an ordained Buddhist master with past Methodist ministry experience to engage the 500 or so delegates in inter-faith reflection. The opening worship included readings and prayers deeply rooted in Christianity; the sermon also reflected this context. However, the rest of the prayers and some of the ritual elements were Buddhist; for example, a gong was sounded to signal the beginning and ending of worship.

Speaking on behalf of the fourteen Korean United churches in the country (the eastern region of the Korean Association happened to be meeting immediately following the conference's annual meeting), the officers of the Korean Association expressed shock at what had occurred. In a letter to the executive secretary of Toronto Conference dated 13 June 2006, the Korean Association of the United Church wrote, 'We feel strongly that it was inappropriate for the Conference leaders to have given a Buddhist monk the main leadership role in the service ... This incident stirred confusion in our Christian identities, and created crises for Christian evangelism and mission ... not only for the Korean United Church, but especially for many ethnic United Churches.' The letter requested clarification of the incident and 'an apology to prevent such events from occurring again.'

The Korean pastors were very clear that they worship the biblical God, and that God alone. This incident illustrates an interesting phenomenon: the pastors have come to identify Christianity per se with the form of Christianity they encountered in Asia as they were struggling to distinguish themselves from their Buddhist neighbours. Like many such Christians, they adopt a faith strongly influenced by the highly exclusivist Christianity of the Asian missionary context. Consequently, they have not been frequently exposed to the new openness to inter-faith dialogue that so clearly marks the United Church's approach to religious diversity in Canada. As such, it must have been highly disturbing for such worshippers to find themselves at a service in which their co-religionists were expressing such openness to Asian religions.[29] To add to the complexity of the situation, these pastors' response was not the only one that resulted from the incident of the conference opening worship; a minority of Korean Canadian pastors wanted to register their dissent from the association letter and align themselves with the United Church position vis-à-vis inter-faith dialogue. This illustrates the range of theological positions that can occur within even the same ethnic group in the United Church.

Native Spirituality and the United Church

No account of the present-day United Church of Canada's new attitudes to other faiths and other peoples would be complete without some reference to its relationship with Canada's First Nations communities. After decades of participation in the Canadian colonial project, the United Church began to come to terms with the moral problems inherent in their intimate involvement in the assimilation of First Nations peoples. In 1986, the church officially apologized to First Nations peoples in a statement delivered by then moderator Robert Smith at the church's Thirty-First General Council at Laurentian University in Sudbury, Ontario. In part, the apology read, 'Long before my people journeyed to this land your people were here, and you received from your Elders an understanding of creation and of the Mystery that surrounds us ... We did not hear you when you shared your vision. In our zeal to tell you the good news of Jesus Christ we were closed to the value of your spirituality' (Bougton and Chevalier 2005, 6).

Beyond the recognition of past injustices in its involvement in residential schools, the United Church is hoping to contribute to the promotion of respect for the spiritual traditions of First Nations peoples. Native spirituality was one of the multiple spiritualities introduced in the 1997 'Sounding the Bamboo' conference. It is also the focus of the latest in the United Church's inter-faith studies under the title 'Circle and Cross' (formerly the Task Group on the Relationship of the United Church to Aboriginal Spirituality). The name 'Circle and Cross' expresses the sense of balance Aboriginal Christians seek in their integration of their traditional spirituality and Christianity as well as iden-

234   Greer Anne Wenh-In Ng

tifies the process the task group developed in a series of talking circles in regional gatherings across the country. These circles were used to establish a respectful dialogue between Aboriginal Christians and their non-Aboriginal counterparts in United Church congregations. Circles began with a teaching from a Native elder and were facilitated by a circle-keeper. Four such gatherings were held across the country, in Alberta, Manitoba, Ontario, and British Columbia. By the time of the last gathering in British Columbia on Gitksan territory, it became obvious that what had started off as an 'inter-religious' project also had to take into account the fact that First Nations Christians had to wrestle with the tensions, contradictions, and complementary wisdom of both their traditional spirituality and Christianity. In other words, not unlike those Asian United Church members who had been socialized into an exclusive Christianity but are beginning to question the erstwhile wholesale rejection of the religious and cultural traditions of their ancestors, some United Church members of Aboriginal communities are coming to see and experience, in the midst of much soul searching and community confrontation, the possibility of honouring both sets of traditions they have inherited.

The United Church and Residential Schools

The damage done to First Nations peoples by Christians was certainly not limited to refusing to honour their spiritual traditions. One of the most harmful institutions in which the churches participated was the residential school system. Residential schools for Native children came into being at the turn of the twentieth century as a more effective way of 'civilizing' and 'Christianizing' the young; in fact, it is important to note that these two processes were always understood to be co-terminus. By 1915 the federal government had come to an agreement with several churches (Roman Catholic, Anglican, Presbyterian, and Methodist) whereby it would provide full funding for building and maintaining such schools and the churches agreed to take responsibility for administering them. Laws were passed requiring children between the ages of five and sixteen to attend these boarding schools (usually established away from Native communities in or near a town) for ten months of the year, away from their families and communities. The United Church inherited this project from its founding denominations. There were thirteen such United Church residential schools in 1927, six in 1951, and four in 1966, with the last one, the Port Alberni School in

British Columbia, closing only in 1973 (Taylor 1999, 147–8). The schools were part of a systemic attempt to resolve the 'Indian problem' by forcibly integrating students into white European society. The process involved erasing First Nations' languages, cultures, and spiritualities – not to mention the physical and sexual abuse inflicted on many, and the emotional and psychological trauma on all.

With regards to residential schools and respect for First Nations, it seems that centuries, not decades, separate the United Church of today from that of the 1960s. For example, the Very Rev. Stan McKay, a Cree from Fisher River reserve in Manitoba, became the Church's first Aboriginal moderator, from 1992 to 1994. Rev. McKay's grandparents spent their entire childhood in the United Church–run Brandon Residential School in Manitoba. His parents sent him and one sister to Birtle Indian Residential School (run by the Presbyterians), as there were no other options for an education. McKay made it a special mission during and after his years as moderator to address the church's troubled relations with First Nations peoples.

Efforts within the church to resolve the legacy of the residential school era have reflected a relatively recent post-colonial and, many would argue, more authentically Christian approach to First Nations people. When victims of abuse at the nation's residential schools began to reveal their painful experiences in the early 1990s and to bring lawsuits forward against both the government and the church, the United Church began its difficult journey of repentance and reparation by establishing a Healing Fund of $1.2 million in 1994. It formed a Residential Schools Steering Committee and assigned national staff to address the issue, including training 'accompaniers' to support victims in Alternative Dispute Resolution hearings as an alternative to lawsuits. In 1998, under the leadership of then moderator the Right Rev. Bill Phipps, the Executive of the General Council brought forward a second apology specifically for the harm done by the church's involvement in its residential schools.[30] The church committed itself to working through legal cases and working out compensation packages. It gave regular 'Residential School Updates' on its website to keep the whole church informed. Under its Justice, Global, and Ecumenical Relations Unit, it explored educational opportunities and provided funding for local congregational initiatives in Aboriginal justice, and developed resources to educate the whole church (see United Church of Canada 2001, 2004c). It assigned 'Right Relations' as its mission study theme for three years, culminating with a special edition of its mission magazine *Mandate* in May 2005 (Bougton and Chevalier 2005) to enable congregations to observe the twentieth anniversary of the 1986 Apology. It also took the lead in calling other church leaders and government representatives to work with Aboriginal leaders and the Assembly of First Nations in round table forums to move toward establishing a 'Truth Telling, Healing, and Reconciliation' process well into 2005.

The United Church also participated in the negotiations leading to the Residential Schools Settlement Agreement that the federal government announced in the spring of 2006, a multi-party, comprehensive package in which the Aboriginal voice was central. Each former residential school survivor would receive a lump sum of $10,000 without litigation, plus $5,000 for each year of school attended, in addition to legal compensation for proven cases of abuse. The United Church agreed to sign this Residential Schools Settlement and to commit $6.89 million as its part of the financial compensation. That more than half of this amount has had to come out of the church's national reserves at a time of dwindling membership, as well as the fact that the church began paying out compensation to recipients in its former residential schools even before the federal and provincial governments did so, both speak to the seriousness with which the church takes its obligations. The denomination also committed to participation in the Truth and Reconciliation Commission to be set up as part of the agreement. As the United Church's General Council officer for residential schools put it, 'It is to the work of healing, justice-seeking, and reconciliation that we must now turn our attention and our resources. This work will challenge our theological and cultural assumptions as well as our pocketbooks, but it offers the promise of transformation.'[31]

It must be said that while many people within the mainstream of the Church support these kinds of inter-faith dialogue and reconciliation gestures with First Nations peoples, these efforts to make room for the spiritual traditions of First Nations peoples causes tensions for many newcomers. Some of them feel that they arrived after the colonial period and neither they nor their ancestors participated in the colonization of Canada and the damage done to so many First Nations peoples. Others also feel that the scriptures and tradition affirm the exclusive validity of Christianity.

The post-colonial sensitivity behind the Circle and Cross Task Group promotes a broader sensitivity to issues of inter-culturalism within the United Church of Canada. There is potential for this vision of Circle and Cross to dovetail with the Ethnic Ministries Unit's efforts to ensure that the church becomes intentionally 'inter-cultural.' In essence, together these projects have the potential of redefining the character and composition of the imagined community or the nation in what aspires to become Canada's 'national church.'

Conclusion

The United Church's early vision for a church that is 'fittingly national' focused on the task of bringing about a dominion of an English Canadian Christianity 'from sea to sea.' Its original intent of being a united and uniting church by seeking to amalgamate with other mainstream (anglophone) church bodies became less realistic, however, after union talks with the Anglican Church broke off in 1975. In any case, the values of both the church and Canadian society changed, and United Church Christians began to see the original intent as too imperialistic. Rather than viewing diversity as something to be overcome, as the church's founders did, there is at present 'a shift toward a greater appreciation of "difference" which runs counter to the dominant cultural assumptions at the time of church union' (Airhart 2000, 26). As ethnic diversity in Canada becomes more visible, more heterogeneous, and more recognized as part of Canadian identity, perhaps it is time for the United Church to be seeking an alternative interpretation of *national*. The Very Rev. Peter Short, the most recent past moderator, poses the dream of such an alternative in a whimsical letter to the United Church's first moderator, Dr George Pidgeon: 'I long for the day when francophones are welcomed to a place at the heart and on the lips of the church; when First Nations peoples stand and speak among us as founders, teachers and leaders ... when new Canadians are instrumental in shaping a changing church for a changing country' (Short 2006, 20).

The fact that the Thirty-Ninth General Council over which Short moderated in Thunder Bay in August 2006 did commit itself to becoming an inter-cultural church is an indication of the willingness of the church to be open to an alternative interpretation of *national*. The goal is for Aboriginal ministries, French ministries, ethnic minorities, and ethnic majorities to learn to participate fully as they make decisions and interact in a mutually respectful manner with one another in the whole life and work of the United Church. The new challenge facing the United Church, therefore, is for this once Anglo-dominant Protestant denomination to re-conceptualize what it means to be 'fittingly national' in a radically inclusive manner in this new century, and for all its ethnic elements, both minorities and majorities, to act together to bring about such a transformation. It is an enormous challenge, of course, but it is not greater than was church union in 1925.

Notes

1 The 2001 census gives 2,939,125, or 12 per cent, as the number or percentage of persons claiming affiliation with the United Church, with the next non–Roman Catholic denomination, the Anglican Church of Canada, at 2,035,500 or 8 per cent.
2 Some of my publications on the topic include G. Ng (1989, 1993, 1995, 1996a, 1996b, 1996c, 1996d, 1996e, 1998, 1999, 2000, 2003, 2004a, 2004b), Ng and Kim (1997).
3 For details and analysis of the church union movement, see Grant (1967) and Silcox (1933).
4 A word about terminology may be in order here. Although historically speaking the term *English Canada/Canadians* used to be sufficiently unambiguous in referring to the 'non-French' part of Canada, its current use in the same sense is problematic, since such a term also covers English-speaking immigrant groups and their descendents from a variety of ethnicities. In this chapter, therefore, the term *Anglo-Canadian* will be employed when referring to the ethnically Anglo-Saxon/Celtic elements within English Canada. In a similar effort to be more precise, the terms *francophone* and *anglophone* when applied to the contemporary scene will refer literally to French-speaking and English-speaking Canadians, regardless of country of origin or ethnicity, inside Quebec and elsewhere.
5 Currently 'ministry personnel' covers not only ordained persons, but also diaconal ministers who are not ordained but 'commissioned' and yet also belong to the 'order of ministry.' The term also includes a category known as 'lay pastoral ministers,' as well as lay educators and pastoral care staff known as 'staff associates.' All of these categories of 'ministry personnel' are presbyters of their respective presbyteries and all are under pastoral oversight and discipline of Presbytery.
6 These governing structures have continued till the present (2006) in spite of some modifications and adjustments since 1925. For instance, there have been several realignments within and between conferences for more efficient functioning as well as the addition of a thirteenth conference in the form of the All Native Circle Conference in 1988.

7 The full text of this new United Church Creed in English may be found in the United Church hymn book *Voices United* (1996, 918), in French (919), and in Cree, Japanese, Korean, Taiwanese, Chinese, and Tagalog (922–7).

8 A more contextual and communal approach to scriptural authority came with the 1992 report *The Authority and Interpretation of Scripture.* Affirming the Bible's 'foundational authority,' the statement takes into consideration contextual and human factors such as the reader's social, cultural and theological assumptions as well as the call to be liberated and transformed. See United Church of Canada 1992, 6–35.

9 A study book for young adults in the newly formed denomination referred to 'sixty-eight nationalities now represented in our Canadian population.' See foreword to Stephenson and Vance (1929).

10 The term *ethnic ministries* is problematic in that it inferred that only those groups outside the mainstream Anglo and Franco Canadian communities had an identifiable 'ethnicity.' The adoption of this term therefore bespoke the denomination's unconscious assumption about who was to be considered an unconditional – or unhyphenated – Canadian, a stance that rendered its own British and French ethnicities invisible to themselves by 'othering' those outside its pale, as Bramadat and Seljak argue in the introductory chapter of this volume.

11 Since 2005, in addition to the associations and the coalition, a 'movement' known as The Journeys of Black Peoples in the United Church of Canada has emerged. This group includes self-identified members of African heritage in any United Church congregation across the country.

12 The phrase *and ethnic minorities* was added into its original mandate by the Ethnic Ministries Council in 2000. See 'General Council Office Structure: Ethnic Ministries Unit Profile,' http://www.united-church.ca/organization/gco/em.

13 These include *Tales of Interracial Marriage* (1993), *Generations Trying to Live Together* (1995), *Fire from the Ashes* (1995), *Birthing the Promise* (1997), and *Our Roots, Our Lives* (2003). See 'United Church Publications: Ethnic Ministries Books,' http://www.united-church.ca/sales/publications/em.

14 Such conferences include the four Chinese youth and young adult conferences 'United Hands across Canada' from 1997 to 2000, the Millennium Youth Camps in Waterton Park, Alberta, in 2000 and 2002, and a series of three men's conferences in 1999, 2000, and 2001 specifically for male clergy, male lay leaders, and young men, respectively.

15 See Mark McGowan's chapter 2 in this volume for a parallel development in the non-francophone Roman Catholic Church in the form of culturally and linguistically specific 'national parishes' (as opposed to the usual heter-

ogeneous geographical local parishes). These range from Irish parishes in Quebec from the mid-nineteenth century on, through a variety of European parishes such as Italian, Polish, Slovenian, and Portuguese since the 1920s, to the more recent Filipino, Vietnamese, Chinese, and Korean parishes as a result of the new waves of immigration from Asia.

16 In the United Church, diaconal ministers are professional ministry personnel who have been commissioned into a ministry of 'word, education and pastoral care' rather than ordained into a ministry of 'word, sacrament and pastoral care.' Both belong to the 'order of ministry' and are subject to pastoral oversight from Presbytery.

17 This image was employed by Isaac Kawuki-Mukasa in a presentation to launch his *Belonging: Constructing a Canadian Theology of Inclusion* at Metropolitan United Church, Toronto, on 5 June 2005. In the metaphor provided by Biles and Ibrahim (2005, 161–3), the authors ask when new Canadian Christians can shift from being guests invited to a potluck dinner to being dinner planners and eventually to being hosts. Until such a shift happens, this trend in the corporate life of the United Church will not move beyond the equivalent of the 'song and dance' stage of Canada's multiculturalism policy.

18 From 'Proposed Statement of Faith,' http://www.united-church.ca/files/organization/gc39/workbook1_commissions.pdf, 149.

19 According to David Fines, editor-in-chief of *Aujourd'hui Credo*, in an interview with the author on 18 September 2006, it is the second-oldest among French Protestant magazines established in Canada. Its mission statement speaks of providing a 'Christian Reformed and ecumenical perspective on spiritual, social, and cultural matters reflecting the interests, concerns. and needs of United Church congregations' (author's translation).

20 The term *diaspora* has been used to describe the communities making up United Church Ethnic Ministries congregations, especially the Black and Chinese groups dispersed from their original homelands (Djao 2003; G. Ng 1999). Paul Bramadat has argued that the term *diaspora* is usually applied in reference to non-white groups, implying that such 'diasporic' communities do not 'naturally' belong in Canada and that their 'real' home is elsewhere. While the term is unproblematic as a self-description, because of its 'othering' connotations the term (as it is applied to others) has been contested. For example, Bramadat argues that using the term *diaspora* only in terms of non-European groups (no one speaks of English Canadians living in an 'English diaspora') tends to render invisible the fact that all groups in Canada may be understood as ethnic groups (though of course it is more diffi-

cult to use this definition when speaking of First Nations communities). It also tends to diminish the complexity of the attachments that Canadians maintain with other 'homelands' (2005a, 14–17).

21 For a succinct account of the history of Chinese immigration to Canada, see Lai, Paper, and Paper (2005, 89–90).

22 A notable exception is the Bermuda Presbytery, which, owing to historical ties, is still a member of the United Church's Maritime Conference.

23 The Rev. Skoutajan shared this personal experience with me during our years as ministerial colleagues at St James-Bond United Church, Toronto, 1980–1.

24 The name 'Wenh-In' is represented by two Chinese characters, *Wenh* meaning 'to sing or recite,' and *In* meaning 'to smile.' Not only classmates and friends, but even my parents would refer to my siblings and me by our English names, even when conversing in Chinese-Cantonese with their peers, so colonized were we in Hong Kong.

25 For a succinct, vivid account of Dr Cheung's days in Kongmoon through the challenging circumstances of the Second World War and the changes brought by the revolution that established the People's Republic of China in 1949, see Sinclair (1993).

26 Among these are the Rev. Amy Lee, composer of the conference theme song 'We Are Many, We Are One,' and Jung Hee Park, now a diaconal minister working in London Conference, who shared her struggles as a theological student with young children in her story 'Welcoming Our Differences' (Park 2003).

27 Until this document is posted in the archives of the United Church, readers may contact http://www.united-church.ca/local/archives/using.

28 See http://www.kairoscanada.org/.

29 The situation of these Korean pastors stood in sharp contrast with that of the invited speaker, Fred Ulrich, a person born with multi-religious and multi-ethnic roots, being of Metis and German-Iroquois-Winnebago heritage. His exposure to Christian religious traditions such as Methodist, Quaker, and German Brethren as well as to Native traditional ways has probably made an internally diverse personal identity both real and natural for him. The fact that he currently offers medicine bundle therapy, sacred circle, and medicine wheel rituals while being pastor of the Manitoba Buddhist Church indicates that he has integrated the Native and Buddhist strands of his identity into a comfortable balance. Religious plurality has been embedded into his multi-faceted ethnicity.

30 For the text of this apology, see 'United Church Social Policy Positions: 1998

Apology to First Nations (1998),' http://www.united-church.ca/beliefs/
policies/1998/a623.

31 For full text of this new release, see United Church of Canada (2006). For
quarterly updates from the United Church's Residential Schools Steering
Committee, go to http://www.united-church.ca/communications/news-
letters/residentialschools/.

Works Cited

Airhart, Phyllis. 2000. A 'review' of the United Church of Canada's 75 years.
Touchstone (September): 19–31.

Anderson, Benedict. 1996. *Imagined communities: Reflections on the origin and
spread of nationalism.* London: Verso.

Biles, John, and Humera Ibrahim. 2005. Religion and public policy: Immigration, citizenship, and multiculturalism: Guess who's coming to dinner. In
Bramadat and Seljak 2005, 161–3.

Bougton, Noelle, and Rebekah Chevalier, eds. 2005. One more step: Living in
right relationship 20 years after the United Church's apology to First
Nations peoples. Special issue, *Mandate* 56 (2).

Bramadat, Paul. 2005. Revisioning religion in the contemporary period: The
United Church of Canada's Ethnic Ministries Unit. *Canadian Diversity /
Diversité canadienne* 4 (3): 59–62.

Bramadat, Paul, and David Seljak, eds. 2005a. *Religion and ethnicity in Canada.*
Toronto: Pearson/Longman.

– 2005b. Toward a new story about religion and ethnicity in Canada. In Bramadat and Seljak 2005a, 222–34.

Choe, Richard Cung-sik. 1995. Power to name ourselves. In G. Ng 1995,
16–17.

Djao, Wei, ed. 2003. *Being Chinese: Voices from the diaspora.* Tucson: University of
Arizona Press.

Ethnic Ministries Revisioning Task Group. 2006. *A transformative vision for the
United Church of Canada.* 39th General Council 2006, 13–19 August 2006,
Thunder Bay, Ontario. Record of Proceedings 2006. Toronto: United Church
of Canada.

Executive of Toronto Conference. 2006/7. Minutes of the Executive Committee
of the Toronto Conference of the United Church of Canada 13 September
2006 Meeting. Toronto.

Gagnon, David-Roger. 2006. Les nouvelles des paroisses. *Aujourd'hui Credo* 53
(3): 14.

Grant, John Webster. 1967. *The Canadian experience of church union*. London: Lutterworth.

Hertig, Young Lee. 2002. *Cultural tug of war: The Korean immigrant family and church in transition*. Nashville: Abingdon.

Hiller, Harry H. 2000. Civil religion and the problem of national unity: The 1995 Quebec Referendum crisis. In *Rethinking church, state, and modernity: Canada between Europe and America*, ed. David Lyon and Marguerite Van Die, 166–85. Toronto: University of Toronto Press.

Humphreys Jones, J. 1982. *The Welsh Church in Toronto: 75 Years (1907–1982)*. Toronto: Dewi Sant Welsh United Church.

Kawano, Roland, and May Komiyama. 1989. Ethnic congregations in the United Church. Special issue, *Mandate* 20 (4): 22–5.

Kawuki Mukasa, Isaac. 2005. *Belonging: Constructing a Canadian theology of inclusion*. Toronto: Kamu Kamu.

Kenny, Gary. 1989a. The mosaic and the church: A look at what's happening in the United Church. *Mandate* 20 (4): 7–10.

– 1989b. Welcome to Canada: A brief history of Canada's peoples. *Mandate* 20 (4): 3–7.

Knowles, Valerie. 1997. *Strangers at our gates: Canadian immigration and immigration policy, 1540–1997*. Toronto: Dundurn.

Lai, David Cheunyan, Jordan Paper, and Li Chuang Paper. 2005. The Chinese in Canada: Their unrecognized religion. In Bramadat and Seljak 2005, 89–110.

Li, Peter S. 2003. *Destination Canada: Immigration debates and issues*. Don Mills, ON: Oxford University Press.

Lind, Christopher, and Joseph Mihevc. 1994. *Coalitions for justice: The story of Canada's interchurch coalitions*. Ottawa: Novalis.

MacDonald, Clarke. 1984. The United Church. In *Spirit of Toronto: 1834–1984*, ed. Margaret Lindsay Holton, 84–92. Toronto: Image.

MacKay, J.I., and J. Lavell Smith. 1963. One lord, one door, one people: The Church of All Nations, Toronto. Toronto: United Church of Canada/Victoria University Archives.

Makabe, Tomoko. 1998. *The Canadian sansei*. Toronto: University of Toronto Press.

Milne, Mike. 2006. *Reaching out to new neighbours: Congregations that welcome change and are stronger for it*. United Church Observer (April): 27–8.

Ng, David, ed. 1996. *People on the way: Asian North Americans discovering Christ, culture, and community*. Valley Forge, PA: Judson.

Ng, Greer Anne Wenh-In. 1989. The dragon and the lamb: Chinese festivals in the life of Chinese Canadian/American Christians. *Religious Education* 84 (3): 368–83.

– ed. 1993. *Tales of interracial marriage*. Toronto: Division of Mission in Canada, United Church of Canada.
– ed. 1995. *Generations trying to live together*. Toronto: Division of Mission in Canada, United Church of Canada.
– 1996a. The Asian North American community at worship: Issues of indigenization and contextualization. In David Ng 1996, 147–75.
– 1996b. Asian North American relationships with other minority cultures. In David Ng 1996, 228–37.
– 1996c. Asian socio-cultural values: Oppressive and liberating aspects from a woman's perspective. In David Ng 1996, 63–103.
– 1996d. One faith, one baptism – one liturgy? Worship in a multicultural, multifaith context. *Reformed Liturgy and Music* 30 (3): 28–31.
– 1996e. Towards wholesome nurture: Challenges in the religious education of Asian North American female Christians. *Religious Education* 91 (2): 238–54.
– 1998. Toward gender justice: Challenges in human living from a Confucian-Christian perspective. *Ching Feng* 41 (3–4): 345–61.
– 1999. Crossing oceans, crossing disciplines: Doing theology as Asians in diaspora. In *Ecumenism in Asia: Essays in honour of Feliciano Carino*, ed. K.C. Abraham, 1–11. Bangalore: Board of Theological Education of the Senate of Serampore College.
– 2000. Diversity and difference in the work of gender justice. *Making Waves* 1 (1): 13–22.
– ed. 2003. *Our roots, our lives: Glimpses of faith and life from Black and Asian Canadian women*. Toronto: United Church.
– 2004a. Reading through new eyes: A basic introduction to reading scripture from a feminist, postcolonial perspective for anti-racism work. *Making Waves* 4 (2): 27–9.
– ed. 2004b. *That all may be one: A resource for educating toward racial justice*. Toronto: Justice, Global and Ecumenical Relations Unit, United Church of Canada.
Ng, Greer Anne Wenh-In, and Kim Uyede-Kai, eds. 1997. *Birthing the promise: Advent reflections and worship resources from many cultural realties*. Toronto: United Church.
Ong, Aihwa. 1999. *Flexible citizenship: The cultural logics of transnationality*. Durham, NC: Duke University Press.
Park, Jung Hee. 2003. Welcoming our differences. In G. Ng 2003, 78–81.
Reeve, Ted. 1999. The heartbeat of the church. In *Fire and grace: Stories of history and vision*, ed. Jim Taylor, 105–10. Toronto: United Church.
Shepherd, Harvey. 2004. From torture in Colombia to sanctuary in Montreal.

United Church Observer. http://www.ucobserver.org/archives/sep04_cvst2
.shtml.

Short, Peter. 2006. A heart-to-heart with George. *United Church Observer*
(March): 18–21.

Silcox, E.C. 1933. *Church union in Canada: Its causes and consequences.* New York:
Institute of Social and Religious Research.

Sinclair, Donna. 1993. Victoria Cheung. *Touchstone* 11 (3): 37–43.

Song, Miri. 2003. *Choosing ethnic identity.* Cambridge: Polity.

Stephenson, F.S., and Sara Vance. 1929. *That they may be one: An introduction to
the study of the work of the Board of Home Missions of the United Church of Canada.* Toronto: Committee on Literature, General Publicity and Missionary
Education of the United Church of Canada.

Tanner, J.U. 1931. French Protestantism in Quebec. Report of the Board of
Home Missions. *United Church of Canada Year Book 1931,* 146–7. Toronto:
United Church of Canada General Offices.

Taylor, Jim, ed. 1999. *Fire and grace: Stories of history and vision.* Toronto: United
Church.

United Church of Canada. 1992. *The authority and interpretation of scripture: A
statement of the United Church of Canada.* Theology and Faith Committee,
United Church of Canada. Toronto: United Church.

– 1996. *Voices united.* Toronto: United Church of Canada.

– 1997. *Mending the world: An ecumenical vision for healing and reconciliation.*
Toronto: Committee on Inter-Church and Inter-Faith Relations, United
Church of Canada. http://www.united-church.ca/partners/interfaith/
mtw/ecumenism.

– 2001. *Justice and reconciliation: The legacy of Indian residential schools and the
journey toward reconciliation.* Toronto: Division of Mission in Canada, United
Church of Canada.

– 2003. *Bearing faithful witness: United Church–Jewish relations today.* Toronto:
Committee on Inter-Church and Inter-Faith Relations, United Church of
Canada. http://www.united-church.ca/partners/interfaith/bfw.

– 2004a. Report of the Chinese Association, Ethnic Ministries, United Church
of Canada.

– 2004b. *That we may know each other: Statement on United Church–Muslim relations today.* Toronto: Committee on Inter-Church and Inter-Faith Relations,
United Church of Canada. http://www.united-church.ca/files/sales/publi-
cations/400000126_finalstatement.pdf.

– 2004c. *Toward justice and right relationship: A beginning – A resource for congregations.* Toronto: Justice, Global and Ecumenical Relations Unit, United
Church of Canada.

246   Greer Anne Wenh-In Ng

- 2006. United Church agrees to sign Residential Schools Settlement Agreement. http://www.united-church.ca/communications/news/releases/060502
- 2007. Unit for Ministries in French Mandate. http://www.united-church.ca/organization/gco/umif.

Vipond, Mary. 1992. Canadian national consciousness and the formation of the United Church of Canada. In *Prophets, priests, and prodigals: Readings in Canadian religious history, 1608 to present*, ed. Mark G. McGowan and David B. Marshall, 167–87. Toronto: McGraw-Hill Ryerson.

West, Wanda. 2003. Black and Canadian. In G. Ng 2003, 101–3.

Wong, Marion Man Wai. 2003. Walking on water. In G. Ng 2003, 74–7.

Woodsworth, James S. 1972. *Strangers within our gates or coming Canadians*. Toronto: University of Toronto Press. First published 1909.

7 Outsiders Becoming Mainstream: The Theology, History, and Ethnicity of Being Lutheran in Canada

BRYAN HILLIS, WITH ASSISTANCE FROM CHRISTIAN LIEB AND PAUL DEBLOCK

In 1912, Susanna Jackle and her nine children ranging in age from two to twenty made their way by train from Montreal after suffering a week's worth of seasickness on the ocean crossing from northern Europe. They were on their way to a new home in Saskatchewan. Susanna hustled her children into action when she saw the long-awaited sign for the town of McLean, where they were to meet her husband Lorenz, who had travelled to Canada almost one year earlier. Once they had all disembarked, Susanna was perplexed that Lorenz was not there. She double-checked her notes. Though they were a couple of hours late, it was the right date and Lorenz had written that Canadian trains did not always run on time. The children anxiously looked around for signs of their father, but to no avail. No one at the train station spoke German, let alone their dialect.

Finally the railway agent, having watched the confusion, approached the mother. As they attempted to communicate, one of the older boys ran up and asked what the *Man* after *McLean* on the railway sign meant. Within a few minutes, the railway agent realized that the family had disembarked one province too early, as they were to have travelled to McLean, Saskatchewan, not McLean, Manitoba. So began life in Canada for a rather typical European immigrant family that shared with many others the dislocation of arriving in a new land of great promise, only to find things were not quite as they had hoped.

The story continues, as it did for many immigrant families of Lutheran faith. After eighteen months of hard labour on a neighbouring farm, Bertha, one of Susanna's daughters, married Adam Maier. Six children followed, with the family eventually settling in Kayville, Saskatchewan. Olga, the eldest daughter, brought English home from school and, together with her siblings, taught it to her eager parents. However, German continued to be the language of religion, as the Lutheran missionary held services for them in the language, if not always the dialect, of the homeland. The children learned *Luther's Small Catechism*, a small handbook of Christian ethics and theology penned by Martin Luther in sixteenth-century Germany. They also memorized Bible verses and, of course, were confirmed – all in German.

One of the daughters, Alma, moved to Regina in 1943, where she worked as a secretary. She attended Lutheran services at Grace Lutheran Church, where she had the option of German or English services. When she married Samuel Victor Hillis of Irish Methodist background in 1951, they attended English Lutheran services. Vic took the required adult education classes and was confirmed as a Lutheran. Their three children went to Sunday school, began two years of confirmation classes at twelve years of age, and underwent confirmation at fourteen years of age. I am one of those three children.

Our Lutheran religious affiliation was an important part of our lives, even as the fact that we were Canadian rather than German or Irish became important to us. German services continued to be held at Grace Lutheran, but by the 1970s fewer than fifty people attended them on an average Sunday. I have since married, as has my sister, and we have brought our spouses into the Lutheran faith through adult education and confirmation; our children have taken or will soon take their course of instruction for confirmation, though the Lutheran Church has adapted and the standard two years of weekly three-hour instruction has been shortened. Our children still learn *Luther's Small Catechism*, memorize a very small number of Bible verses, and are certainly aware of the significance of Martin Luther, but they have little knowledge of their German heritage. Being Lutheran is important to them, although it is a challenge for them to remain Christian in a world where swim meets and ballet performances are very likely to occur on Sundays. My brother has married a Roman Catholic woman, which just one generation earlier would have been relatively unusual and, only a few years before, in fact caused great emotional distress for my cousin who had married a Catholic man; by the time my brother and his wife married, there was little controversy, even though my sister-in-law remains Catholic.

So runs one rather typical Lutheran family history in Canada. However, the picture is not complete until we understand what it is that makes a Lutheran. We need to know some of the history and unique theological perspective of Lutheranism, and we need to understand how it became associated with a variety of ethnic communities in Europe and, later, around the world. More precisely, we need to know how Lutheran identity in Canada has evolved to the present day.

What Does It Mean to Be Lutheran?

Martin Luther was not the first reformer of the medieval church, but for those of us who have come to be called by his name, he was the great reformer from which all the rest of Protestantism issued.[1] The main plank in Luther's platform of theological reform was what Lutherans refer to as 'justification by grace alone through faith.' Luther argued against what he called 'works righteousness,' the idea that we could do good works to save – or justify – ourselves in the eyes of God. Based on a reinterpretation of Romans 1:17 ('The righteous shall live by faith'), Luther concluded that no work of our own is able to put us right with God; rather, salvation is the free gift of a righteous God who alone 'justifies' or saves us. Our salvation then is not earned but is freely given through God's grace. Ever since the sixteenth century, Lutherans have sought refuge in this central doctrine of justification, often in contradistinction to what they perceive as the 'works righteousness,' especially of Roman Catholics, but also of Anabaptists and other religious groups (Braaten 1990).

A number of supporting theological ideas accompany this central one. First is the idea that God's perfect revelation came to humanity in his *Logos* or Word, namely Jesus Christ. Since so few were physically able to witness Christ's presence here on earth, the next best witness is that of the Bible. Lutherans often refer to this principle as *sola scriptura* (scripture alone), the idea that all matters of faith must be checked against the Bible as the best reflection we have of God's incarnate Word, Jesus Christ. For this reason, Luther translated the entire Bible into German so that the average literate person could read it. Since everybody can read God's Word, Luther used the phrase the 'priesthood of all believers' to articulate his conviction that we can all understand and interpret God's Word for ourselves. The priesthood of all believers is an abiding aspect of contemporary Lutheran theology, especially among some ethnic groups in which individual piety is emphasized. As significant an idea as this is, Luther also emphasized the special leadership of a trained, well-educated clergy responsible for the leadership of the flock (Althaus 1966); when there is no member of clergy, Lutheran congregations find themselves in difficulty.[2]

Luther did not confine himself to purely spiritual questions. As the history of the Reformation unfolded, it became clear that restraint by secular authorities might also be needed. When other reformers, like Thomas Műntzer, began leading an uprising of the peasants against the rulers, Luther wrote vehemently that they were confusing the two 'kingdoms' of the secular and the spiritual. According to Luther, the rule of grace upon which the entire church should be based, cannot be the modus operandi for the secular kingdom, where the law with its emphasis on restraint and justice, even punishment, must rule. Hence, Luther squelched any thoughts he was trying to establish a theocracy (Braaten 1983). Even for Lutherans today, this theology of 'two king-doms' has been interpreted in various ways. For example, Lutheran pietism, wherein one's individual salvation and personal religious experience are emphasized (Evenson 1974) often to the neglect of social activism, is one such interpretation and has resulted in a common per-ception that Lutherans are social conservatives (Braaten 1983, 1990; Hertz 1976; Threinen 1977).

As the Reformation movement fractured in Europe, Lutherans pro-duced confessional and instructional documents to facilitate discussion with the papal emissaries as well as with the more radical movements (Gritsch 2002). These were collected in what are now called *The Book of Concord: The Confessions of the Evangelical Lutheran Church*.[3] Aside from the Small Catechism (the best known of these documents), few Cana-dian Lutherans actually read much of the rest of the Confessions. Sem-inary students may read them as part of their academic training but the Confessions seldom figure prominently if at all in Sunday sermons. However, denominational hierarchies and convention resolutions con-stantly make reference to them for a number of reasons. First, the foun-dational doctrines of Lutherans are expounded there. The criteria for *adiaphora*, or activities or items neither prescribed nor forbidden by scripture, are also described (Tappert 1959). These distinctions help Lutherans understand what is critical to their faith, even non-negotia-ble (justification by grace through faith), and what can be considered in its historical context (customs, rules, traditions, ways of worshipping, social practices such as prohibitions against dancing and gambling). Second, though Luther had written only a few of the documents of the Confessions, less bombastic theologians, like Luther's good friend and spokesman Melanchthon, had penned the rest, giving the Confessions a conciliatory tone indicating openness to further dialogue, even with Roman Catholics. Hence, while the Confessions are hailed by some as the bedrock upon which Lutheran theology is founded, they are equally viewed by others as indicators of the dynamic, progressive faith of the Reformation (Gritsch 2002 and interviews with pastors).[4]

Early Immigration and History of Lutherans in Canada

Lutheran historians like to make the point that Jens Munck, a Danish Lutheran sea captain, had his pastor, Rev. Rasmus Jensen, preside over Lutheran services in what is now Churchill, Manitoba, in 1619, a full six years before the Jesuits arrived in Quebec and eight months before the Pilgrims arrived in what became the United States (Cronmiller 1961; Eylands 1945; Schultz 1966; see also chapters 2 and 3 of this volume).[5] The next significant record of Lutherans in Canada occurs in 1749 when the British, having built a stronghold at Halifax, brought over 2,000 immigrants to settle the fledgling colony, among whom were 1,825 German-speaking Lutheran farmers and vinedressers from Würtemberg and other small central European territories (McLaughlin 1985; cf. Stuart MacDonald's chapter 5 in this book on the way Nova Scotia was eventually 're-imagined' as essentially Scottish). By 1753 a German Lutheran congregation was established at Lunenburg, so named possibly for the town of Lüneburg whence most of these German settlers originated. When 35,000 United Empire Loyalists, loyal to the British cause but not necessarily British, fled to Nova Scotia and the Great Lakes region during the American Revolution, many were Lutheran, though the exact number is difficult to establish (Bassler 1990; Bausenhart 1989; Eylands 1945).

Loyalists continued to populate these areas, but when plans called for a Church of England building in Halifax, the 'stubborn Germans' (Schultz 1966) refused to cooperate. The congregation managed to 'call' or ask a German Swiss cleric by the name of Burger to be their pastor. However, Burger found the more substantial salary of Anglican clergy (200 pounds sterling per year) too great a temptation and received Episcopal ordination. Hoping to keep as many of his German Lutheran flock as possible, he translated the Anglican service into German and was returning from England with a German Bible and prayer books when he disappeared. His German Lutheran congregation, feeling betrayed by their pastor, thought he had probably received his just reward of shipwreck (Schultz 1966).

Variations of the story were common in the early Lutheran congregations of Upper Canada. Sometimes a congregation had no choice but to ask an Anglican clergyman to lead services, and often the congregation found itself joining the Anglican communion. Other times 'clerical tramps' or uneducated pretenders of low morals led worship for a time until their true colours showed (Cronmiller 1961; Schultz 1966). Missions were even established in Quebec where some Loyalists chose to settle, but again a lack of qualified pastors for the flock resulted in 'many a promising field [being] lost to the Church' (Cronmiller 1961). Not until the mid-1800s, when immigrant congregations began calling pastors from American Lutheran conferences and seminaries, did some stability arise in the pastoral ranks. Even so, receiving a call to the Canadian wilderness was a difficult one for American pastors from the more established Lutheran areas of New York and Pittsburgh; having that pastor stay in the Canadian wilderness was certainly not guaranteed if, after a year or two, another call came from the more settled areas of the United States (Bachmann and Bachmann 1989; Cronmiller 1961; Eylands 1945; Schultz 1966).

An Era of Expansion, 1850 to 1920

David Pfrimmer identifies the next period of Lutheran development from 1850 until about 1920 as the 'Era of Expansion' (Pfrimmer 1986). In central Canada, expansion went together with consolidation, as German-speaking immigrants continued to arrive from eastern European countries and Scandinavian congregations gathered in southern Ontario, particularly Waterloo County. At the time of Confederation in 1867, about 70 per cent of non-British and non-French immigrants to Canada were Germans, who played an essential part in establishing Lutheran churches (McLaughlin 1985). At the time of the first Canadian census in 1871, only 1,623 Scandinavians resided in Canada, so the vast majority of the 37,935 Lutherans reported at the time were likely to be Germans (Leacy 1983).

With the *Dominion Land Act* of 1872 and its offer of 160 acres for any male immigrant twenty-one years of age or older, western Canada was open for business. Close to 1 million immigrants arrived from Britain, the United States, and rural regions of eastern and southeastern Europe between 1900 and 1914. Lutherans in eastern Canada and the United States supported the fledgling congregations of similar ethnic backgrounds by sending missionaries and pastors to support the work in the Canadian west. By 1861, there was enough of a critical mass for the Evangelical Lutheran Synod[6] of Canada to be organized (Cronmiller

1961; Schultz 1966). The name of this denomination should not betray the fact that Lutherans were still very much divided along linguistic and ethnic lines. The Augustana Evangelical Lutheran Church was dominated by Swedes, most of whom had immigrated to Canada after a stay, often of a generation or two, in America. The Suomi Synod was Finnish in background, while the American Evangelical Lutheran Church was Danish. Hauge's Synod as well as the more obviously named United Norwegian Lutheran Church and Norwegian Synod, were all Norwegian by heritage, while the Ohio, Iowa, and Buffalo synods were predominantly German in background as was the pietist Lutheran Free Church. The Icelandic Synod was also aptly named, though not until there was a critical mass of Icelanders in Manitoba did this synod assume the ethnic name. Danes could be found in the American Evangelical Lutheran Church as well as the United Evangelical Lutheran Church (Evenson 1974). Congregations served by the Lutheran Church–Missouri Synod, originating in the United States, were almost entirely German in background.

Within each of these groups individual congregations typically would hold on to their original language as long as there were enough members more comfortable in it. Congregations whose membership came to Canada by way of the United States worshipped in English much more readily than others whose members came directly from Europe (Schultz 1966).

Retaining one's native language became a greater challenge for German Lutherans during the First World War. As foreigners who spoke the same language as the enemy and who largely kept to themselves, German Lutherans, like all German Canadians, were treated as 'enemy aliens,' even though as Germans they represented more than one in every twenty Canadians and counted as the third-largest ethno-cultural group. German schools were banned, the teaching of German as a second language disappeared even from universities, mobs pillaged properties owned by Canadians of German descent, and no fewer than twenty-four camps were set up to intern 8,600 Germans and Austro-Hungarians. Berlin, Ontario, the 'cultural and industrial nerve centre of German-speaking Ontario,' swallowed a bitter pill when, under the influence of 'coercive patriotism,' it was renamed Kitchener (Meune 2005) in honour of the British general who had died aboard his ship when it struck a German mine. This treatment of German Canadians as second-class citizens continued for some time after the war (Herzer 1946).[7]

Despite such troubles, Lutherans retained their native languages much longer than one might expect, in part because pastoral care was usually available in the mother tongues as seminarians trained either in Europe or America. When Waterloo Lutheran Seminary opened in 1911, Canadian Lutherans finally had a source for their own clergy. The opening of educational institutions on Canadian soil, originally meant to prepare young men for training leading to seminary and the ministry, such as Camrose Lutheran College (1910), Concordia College in Edmonton (1921), and Luther College in Melville, Saskatchewan (1913, later relocating to Regina), also played a role in educating and integrating a Lutheran public into Canadian culture.[8]

Second World War to the Present

The Second World War was not nearly as difficult for Canadian Lutherans, even as they increasingly lost the use of their mother tongues – another aspect of the 'discourse of loss' the editors of this volume discuss in their chapters. First, it was far easier for other Canadians to understand what the Lutherans were saying, as more spoke English. *The Lutheran Hour*, a weekly broadcast consisting of hymns, biblical readings, and a sermon, and the *Davey and Goliath Show*, a claymation children's television series, raised the profile of Lutherans and showed how mainstream Lutheran values really were (Herzer 1946). Finally and probably most importantly, Lutheran men and women signed up for military service in the same proportions as other Canadians. To support this work, the Lutheran denominations worked together to establish the Lutheran Service Board in 1941, which cooperated with the Army and Navy Board in registering men, and supplying them with religious pamphlets, Bibles, and prayer books (Herzer 1946). Lutherans were finally working with the Canadian establishment.[9]

Predominantly Lutheran groups, such as Danes, Finns, Swedes, Norwegians, and Icelanders, significantly increased their numbers in Canada after the end of the Second World War. By far the single largest group among them, however, was the Germans, with close to 200,000 immigrants during the peak years of 1951 to 1957. In fact, German Lutherans were responsible for about half of the 50 per cent increase of Lutherans in Canada between 1951 and 1961, from 444,923 to 662,744 (Leacy 1983; Schmalz 2000). The great volume of German immigration can be explained by two factors: the demographic and economic situation in Germany after the war wherein thousands of displaced ethnic Germans from elsewhere in Europe returned to Germany, as well as the involvement of the Canadian Lutheran World Relief and Canadian Christian Council for the Resettlement of Refugees in organizing migration from Europe.

Given the difficult economic situation of Germany, there was a widespread desire in the population to leave Europe for a fresh start and better opportunities overseas (Freund 1994). The Canadian Lutheran World Relief was a coordinated effort by almost all Lutheran groups in Canada to help people in Europe after the war. Founded in 1946, the organization initially focused on the distribution of food, clothing, and other necessities, primarily in Germany and Austria. However, when ethnic Germans from outside Germany were initially rejected as refugees by the International Refugee Organization in London, the Canadian Lutheran World Relief got involved (Sauer 1993). Horace H. Erdman and T.O.F. Herzer of the Canadian Lutheran World Relief met with Prime Minister Mackenzie King in February 1947; by May, the Canadian government acknowledged that ethnic Germans were eligible again for immigration (Steinert 1995). With the adjustments in immigration policy, the Canadian Lutheran World Relief, together with the Canadian Christian Council for the Resettlement of Refugees, brought ethnic Germans and others who were not recognized as refugees by the International Refugee Organization to Canada. By the mid-1950s, more than 35,000 immigrants had arrived in Canada with the financial help of the Canadian Christian Council for the Resettlement of Refugees (Steinert 1995).[10] In the 1950s and 1960s, the ethnic churches were an important factor in the establishment of support networks for new immigrants, especially in places where ethnic clubs did not exist. Good Shepherd Lutheran Church in Victoria, which offered both German and English worship services, is a good example of this double function of material and spiritual help. The Canadian Immigration Department would inform Rev. Bergbusch of new German arrivals in Victoria so that he could meet them, without regard to their religious affiliation. Good Shepherd's members then functioned as a network that donated household items and helped the new immigrants find a place to live and work. Often these new immigrants were considered to be Lutherans solely by virtue of being a member of one of the European ethnic communities historically associated with Lutheranism (e.g., Germans, Swedes, and Danes).

Declining Ethnic Diversity and Declining Numbers

Lutherans have never been a dominant component of Canadian Christianity, currently comprising only 2 per cent of the Canadian population, as figure 7.1 and table 2.1 indicate.

As the previous history illustrates, Lutheran demographics have been dominated by immigration from northern European countries, particularly Germany and Scandinavian countries. Figure 7.2 confirms this finding, together with the place of origin and aging of Lutherans relative to the Canadian population.

These immigration patterns were reflected in the ethnic denominational structures. Until the 1960s, there were at least as many Lutheran denominations as there were ethnic groupings. However, in the 1960s, Lutherans regarded themselves less as ethnic Lutherans and more as Canadian Lutherans. Mergers occurred to support this perception. In 1963, the Lutheran Church in America – Canada Section was organized as a result of the United Lutheran Church in America (itself a union of thirty-four denominations including those of German, Swedish, Icelandic, Finnish, and Danish extraction) joining with congregations of Estonian, Latvian, Lithuanian, Slovak, Volga (Russian), and Transylvanian (Romanian) German stock. The American Lutheran Church in Canada, composed of Scandinavian (particularly Norwegian) and German synods and conferences became the indigenous and autonomous Evangelical Lutheran Church *of* Canada in 1967 (Bachmann and Bachmann 1989). In 1985, the Evangelical Lutheran Church of Canada and the Lutheran Church in America – Canada Section decided to work together, becoming in 1986 the Evangelical Lutheran Church *in* Canada, the largest denomination of Lutherans and fourth-largest denomination overall in Canada.

The more conservative Lutheran Church–Missouri Synod, based in the United States, had been a very active missionary agency in Canada, with four Canadian districts organized as mission fields. Almost entirely of German descent, these districts had declined earlier to join the other Canadian Lutheran bodies in the merger that led to the creation of the Evangelical Lutheran Church in Canada because of their strongly held position, inherited from their American parent denomination, that organizational union should not take place until there is full agreement in all doctrinal matters. In 1987, this federation of Canadian districts of the Lutheran Church–Missouri Synod became the Lutheran Church–Canada, an autonomous Canadian entity with

Figure 7.1: Lutherans in Canada by number and percentage (analysis courtesy of Paul DeBlock)

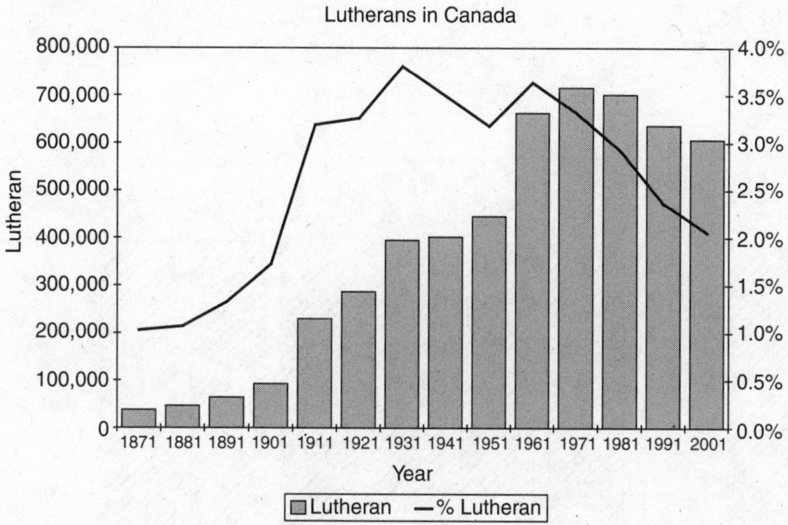

Lutherans in Canada

Table 7.1. Lutherans in Canada

Year	Canada	Lutheran	% Lutheran
1871	3,689,257	37,935	1.0
1881	4,324,810	46,350	1.1
1891	4,833,239	63,982	1.3
1901	5,371,315	92,524	1.7
1911	7,206,643	229,864	3.2
1921	8,787,949	286,458	3.3
1931	10,376,786	394,920	3.8
1941	11,506,655,	401,836	3.5
1951	14,009,429	444,923	3.2
1961	18,238,247	662,744	3.6
1971	21,014,885	715,740	3.3
1981	24,014,885	701,320	2.9
1991	26,908,950	636,205	2.4
2001	29,546,745	606,490	2.1

Source: Statistics Canada (2001).

Figure 7.2: Place of origin and age of Lutherans in Canada (analysis courtesy of Paul DeBlock)

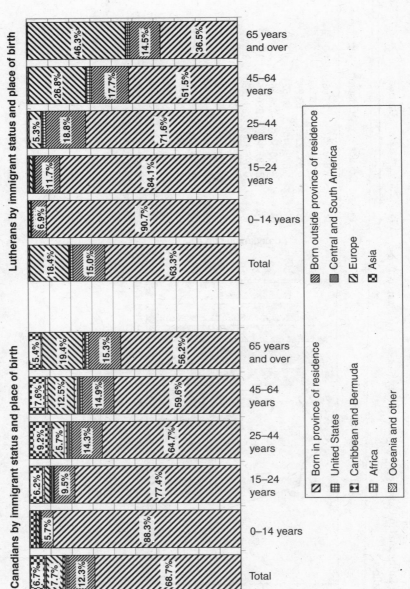

Lutherans by immigrant status and place of birth

Canadians by immigrant status and place of birth

Legend:
- Born in province of residence
- United States
- Caribbean and Bermuda
- Africa
- Oceania and other
- Born outside province of residence
- Central and South America
- Europe
- Asia

Source: Statistics Canada 2001

strong links to the Lutheran Church–Missouri Synod. This was another indication that Lutherans in Canada were shedding their ethnic ties and assuming a Canadian identity. For the rest of this chapter, *Lutherans* in Canada will refer primarily to the membership of the Evangelical Lutheran Church in Canada and Lutheran Church–Canada denominations that constitute approximately 96 per cent of the population of Lutherans in Canada.[11]

As with most denominations, many more people claim to be Lutheran than actually attend the services of or hold membership in a denomination. The Lutheran Council of Canada[12] publishes a directory indicating denominational membership on the basis of information provided to it by the denominations. From those data, the Council counted 279,537 Lutherans in Canada, while the 2001 Statistics Canada Census reported 606,590 people who called themselves Lutherans. There are important reasons why the census reports more than twice as many Lutherans as the churches themselves.

The Evangelical Lutheran Church in Canada and Lutheran Church–Canada measure membership from those who are baptized.[13] Both denominations also keep track of who is confirmed because, while confirmation is not a sacrament, it is a very special ceremony in the life of a Lutheran in which, usually after a period of study, one is recognized as an adult member of the congregation.[14] In confirmed membership, the numbers are even lower than the figure reported by the Lutheran Council of Canada: 58,525 in the Lutheran Church–Canada (2005), and 135,750 in the Evangelical Lutheran Church in Canada (2005), for a total of 194,275 in 2001. Having been confirmed means one is more likely to be active as a Lutheran, but all churches struggle with how to keep young people involved after confirmation. Many young people, recognizing the importance of confirmation as a Lutheran rite or simply wanting to appease their parents, take their confirmation training and become confirmed but rarely attend church after that. One telling statistic is the number of those who commune (that is, take the Lord's Supper or Eucharist) once per year; in 2001, the Evangelical Lutheran Church in Canada recorded that 84,963 of its members took communion; 31,693 members of the Lutheran Church–Canada took communion, for a total of 116,656.[15] Reginald Bibby's (2002) statistics on weekly attendance support these figures.[16]

The 2001 Census figures also indicate that between 1991 and 2001, the numbers of people identifying as Lutherans declined from 636,205 to 606,590 – a 5 per cent decrease. The only province where any sizable

Lutheran population experienced an increase was Alberta (137,145 to 142,475) – an increase of 4 per cent.[17] At the same time, the median age for the Canadian Lutheran population was 43.3, the fourth-highest among mainstream religious groups,[18] whereas the median age of all Protestants is 42 and for all Canadians is only 37 (Statistics Canada 2003). Hence Lutherans are over-represented in the 55 and over age group; like most mainstream Protestant denominations, Lutherans are 'disproportionately old,' as Bibby writes. Bibby shows that Lutherans, like so many other denominations, can expect their weekly attendance to continue to drop (from 80,000 to 50,000 in 2015) as their aging members die off (Bibby 2002). Bibby also notes that fewer teens are identifying as Lutherans and fewer teens are attending Lutheran worship services than in other denominations.

These declining figures also constitute the greatest challenge for Lutheran denominations. Church leaders, such as past Bishop Ray Schultz of the Evangelical Lutheran Church in Canada (2001–7) and President Ralph Mayan of the Lutheran Church–Canada, also reflect this discourse of loss, expressing concern about the post-modern and secular nature of Canadian society. They argue that Canadians feel no particular loyalty to any one denomination but increasingly choose their religion 'à la carte' (Bibby 1987). Attendance records confirm this insight; like other Canadians, many Lutherans now regard Sunday less as a day of rest and more as a day of leisure where children's organized activities, shopping, and even work barely pause. In particular, young Lutherans do not seem to be looking for fulfilment of their spiritual lives in the church, even if they have undergone the rite of confirmation. In the new context of pluralism and post-modernism, few people believe that any one church or denomination has all the answers, so they search and create their own spirituality – if they remain active in such a quest at all (Kuhn 2005; Swait 2003).

Also significant is the fact that generations of ethnic (typically northern European) Lutherans, who were at least nominally Lutheran, are aging and dying. Their children grew up speaking English and assumed a Canadian identity, an identity without specific religious affiliation. As ethnic identity dissipated, so too did loyalty to the Lutheran Church. Interviews I conducted in November and December of 2005 with pastors, bishops, and district presidents of the Evangelical Lutheran Church in Canada and Lutheran Church–Canada corroborate this fact.[19] To a person, even those who had a strong sense of their own ethnic background and that of the church agreed that the ethnic heritage of their congregations was not a significant part of their congregational life. However, some ethnic tendencies survived. There was a 'certain feel' to some of the congregations, evidenced often by ethnic food and jokes on social occasions, though even the jokes about 'Sven' and 'Ole' occur with less frequency as people become aware that such jokes do not mean as much to the younger generation and to those members outside the dominant ethnic group. Congregations of German heritage preferred a full, musical liturgy as found in the *Lutheran Book of Worship*, while Norwegian congregations preferred a spoken liturgy. Similarly, congregations of a Norwegian pietist background were often opposed to having their clergy wear vestments. Each ethnic group tended to have its favourite hymns, which they would sing in the original language if they could, though English translations overshadowed them in time. Working with the quiet Norwegians could mean that disputes often festered, with clergy unaware of the problem, whereas German congregations would tell the pastor quite pointedly their difficulties and state, half-mockingly of themselves but with a view to justifying their concerns, 'We're German so we're stubborn.' There were cheerful Danish congregations and more dour ones, depending on the type of Danish Lutherans they counted as ancestors. And there were certain ethnic festivals that were still celebrated, such as St Lucy's Day (13 December) among Scandinavians in Alberta, even if the pastor could not lead or even participate (interview, Pastor Daryl Olson [Bethlehem, Outlook], 7 December 2005). However, all the pastors interviewed agreed that these distinctions were dissipating over time as congregations lost their ethnic European traditions with each passing generation. All thought that retaining a sense of being Lutheran was still relatively important in these ethnic communities, but even this declined as ethnic identities diminished.[20]

Some aspects of aging ethnic populations and the challenges of contemporary society are evident in what have been called the 'worship wars.' In the 1960s, like other denominations, Lutherans experimented with folk and rock services and the use of instruments in order to appeal to younger people. Country gospel, jazz services, and polka liturgies all had their day. Liturgies were revised, 'praise bands' were used, and new worship books were developed. Many resisted, predictably those of the older generation who had just given up their own European worship language of choice and were not happy losing many familiar hymns. In most Lutheran congregations where there remains a strong European influence, there is still a heavy reliance on the traditional *Lutheran Book of Worship.*

The modernization of Canadian society has challenged the traditional Lutheran communities in other ways as well. Public debates on the role of women, religious pluralism, post-colonialism (and especially Christianity's implication in the mistreatment of Canada's first peoples), and same-sex marriage all reveal some of the fault lines in the contemporary Canadian Lutheran community – divisions that run along ethnic as well as ideological and religious lines.

Lutheran Women

Women have always been an important part of the work of the Lutherans churches in Canada. Despite the fact that women played an important role in the immigration and settlement of Canadian Lutherans, they were not allowed to lead in the political life of the congregation or denomination. Until 1975, ordination to the priesthood was closed to them. Female leadership was evident in the teaching of Sunday school and Vacation Bible School courses to the extent that, by the mid-1970s, it was unusual to find a male teacher.[21] Lutheran women were heavily involved in the women's societies, which accomplished social welfare functions within the community. Women's societies also tended to play a disproportionate role in the missions programs, raising money in support of overseas missionary work through teas, craft sales, and other functions. Finally, the results of a study indicating that mothers play a more significant role than fathers in the religious training of the children (Jones 1999) would sound very familiar to Canadian Lutherans of the past and present.

The two major Lutheran denominations hold different opinions on the ordination and leadership of women. In the larger, multi-ethnic, more mainstream Evangelical Lutheran Church in Canada, the place of women reflects the increasingly egalitarian values embraced by many people in the surrounding culture. Since 1975, women have been able to seek ordination and to assume leadership. In this denomination, more and more women are being ordained each year; for example, women comprised 44 per cent of those receiving ordination in 1998 (Kuhn 2005). Still, of the 855 active pastors in the Evangelical Lutheran Church in Canada in 2003, only 117 (13.7 per cent) were female, in part because women tend to come to the pastorate later in life, and thus the figures do not yet reflect their high involvement in seminary programs (Kuhn 2005).

In contrast, the Lutheran Church–Canada does not allow the ordination of women; women are also not allowed to assume any role that might place them in a position of authority over men – a policy based on LCC's conception of the order of creation and the words of biblical passages that are interpreted to support that order (for example, 1 Timothy 2:11–14).[22] This theological perspective reflects that of the Lutheran Church–Missouri Synod, the American denomination responsible for the missionary efforts and development of the Lutheran Church–Canada and to which the Lutheran Church–Canada continues to look for theological leadership. Mary Todd argues that the Missouri Synod, in seeking to retain its theological and German immigrant identity in the face of American religious freedom, vested its authority in the male clergy. The question of ordaining women has not been officially addressed in a direct way, and the 'absence of women in the debate over women's service has been striking' (Todd 2000, 264). The same holds true for the Lutheran Church–Canada. Like its American counterpart, it is almost entirely of immigrant German origin and has assumed a sectarian, prophetic stance against its surrounding culture.

Even with this explanation, it is baffling why women's voices are still not heard in the Lutheran Church–Canada. There are at least three possible explanations for the absence of women's issues (e.g., concerning ordination) or even of women's voices on such issues. First, perhaps both the leaders and the female members of the Lutheran Church–Canada agree that the question has been answered by the biblical argument from the created order, noted above. Second, perhaps Lutheran Church–Canada women may simply not realize they are not able to become ordained; one woman I spoke with asked her Lutheran Church–Canada pastor how to go about becoming ordained and was surprised to discover that she could not because she was a woman.[23] Third, it may be that women of the Lutheran Church–Canada perceive that the fight to change the rules would simply not be worth the conflict, and might not be resolved in their lifetimes. The last is the most likely reason, as Canadian women know only too well the influence of the Lutheran Church–Missouri Synod in the affairs of the Lutheran Church–Canada and, until there is movement in the American body, it is highly unlikely there will be changes in the Lutheran Church–Canada. Whatever the reason, there does not appear to be significant controversy surrounding women's ordination in the Lutheran Church–

Canada. For instance, in the *Planning Conference Research Survey Report*, 2003, the place of women in the Lutheran Church–Canada does not even register as an issue. Nevertheless, it may be an ominous sign that, of the respondents to the report, only 26.4 per cent responding were female, even though proportionately there are just as many women in the Lutheran Church–Canada as in the rest of Canadian society. It will be interesting to watch this issue as the Lutheran Church–Canada continues to shed its ethnic German origins and determines its place vis-à-vis its parent body of the Lutheran Church–Missouri Synod.

Lutherans Relating to Others

In general, Lutherans have become more confidently engaged in public debates in the past few decades. They feel that they have a strong theological background to bring to bear on all public issues, but, even in the more publicly engaged and socially progressive Evangelical Lutheran Church in Canada, national leaders have to be careful about making too many pronouncements on political life for fear that they will be criticized for mixing the two kingdoms of the church and the secular. Hence, even with the social justice, or 'social change' (Bramadat 2005) agenda of the Evangelical Lutheran Church in Canada, one will rarely find the Evangelical Lutheran Church in Canada speaking out on social or political issues unless they do so in concert with the Canadian Council of Churches or Kairos Canada – an umbrella group for social justice coalitions among a number of Christian churches.[24] Through its membership in the Lutheran World Federation, the Evangelical Lutheran Church in Canada also has a voice in international affairs and works on international issues or crises; however, the Lutheran World Federation, a federation of national churches, does not make any of its pronouncements binding on its members.[25] The Lutheran Church–Canada has more difficulty participating in such broad ecumenical councils and coalitions because of its insistence that there must be doctrinal agreement before there is fellowship with other groups of Christians.[26] This position is a result of the strong influence of the American Lutheran Church–Missouri Synod.

By contrast, through its membership in the Lutheran World Federation, the Evangelical Lutheran Church in Canada was a signatory to the Joint Declaration on the Doctrine of Justification with the Roman Catholic Church in 1999.[27] In this declaration, Lutherans and Catholics agreed to lay aside their historic condemnations of each other and agreed that they have a common understanding of justification or how we are made right in our relationship with God. This understanding is similar, if not identical, to Luther's articulation of this doctrine in the sixteenth century.[28]

The Evangelical Lutheran Church in Canada has also entered a relationship of 'full communion' with the Anglican Church of Canada through the Waterloo Declaration of 2001. By this agreement, clergy of either denomination can preach or administer the sacraments of Baptism and Holy Communion (hence the term *full communion*) in both the Evangelical Lutheran Church in Canada or the Anglican Church of Canada (Evangelical Lutheran Church in Canada 2001; Anglican Church of Canada 2000; see also Wendy Fletcher's chapter 4 on Anglicanism). Certainly the ELCIC's and the LWF's conciliatory approach to other Christian communities is in harmony with the multicultural ethos that is familiar to so many Canadians.

Informally, Lutheran pastors in rural areas will speak of the good relationships they as pastors and their congregations enjoy with other Christian denominations. Whereas in the past it was common for small though lively rural centres to have many churches, including multiple Lutheran churches of various ethnic backgrounds, the declining rural population means that most rural parishes find it difficult to attract ministers, let alone to retain them. Ecumenical cooperation then is not only desirable but necessary if rural parishes are going to hear a sermon prepared by someone with theological training. Hence, cooperation between Lutheran parishes in neighbouring towns, even of different ethnic heritages or denominational backgrounds, has occurred for years. For the same reason, ecumenical cooperation between Lutherans and other denominations in any area has also become necessary. It is not uncommon then for Lutherans to share their facilities and buildings with other denominations, especially in rural areas. Since the Waterloo Declaration instituting full communion with the Anglican Church of Canada, the Evangelical Lutheran Church in Canada congregations have sometimes called one member of clergy to serve both the Anglican and Lutheran congregations in small centres. Ecumenical cooperation also occurs between Presbyterian, United Church, and even Roman Catholic congregations when the need arises, often bringing together congregations of different ethnic heritages, though this occurs less among the relatively ethnically homogenous Lutheran Church–Canada. Although contemporary forces of secularization and urbanization are forcing especially rural Lutherans to cooperate with communities with divergent ethnic and Christian backgrounds, Lutheran theology remains strong among pastors who serve in mixed or community churches.

Lutherans and Canadian Aboriginals

As an ethnic and introverted group, Lutherans have, in general, been oblivious to the Canadian Aboriginal population. Not having been a part of the mainstream church establishment (see chapters 2, 3, and 4), Lutherans were not involved in the residential school system. Their mission work in Canada was limited to the newly arrived immigrants of similar European ethnic background. As a result, only rarely will one find an Aboriginal person in a Lutheran congregation. Other factors are probably relevant here. As Pastor Lindsay Hognestad of Trinity Lutheran in Regina said, 'It is perhaps not so much that Lutherans do not know how to deal with Aboriginal people, although that would be to some extent the case, but it seems clear to me that in general we don't know what to do with the poverty they represent' (interview, 15 November 2005). Pastor Kim Sherwin, who was married to a Cree man some years ago, said there was no question that there were degrees of discrimination among Lutherans, as there are among the rest of the Canadian population, though she also noted that this is not a part of official Lutheran doctrine (interview, 1 December 2005). Of late, Lutherans are attempting to reach out to Aboriginal communities overtly through, for example, the Circle of Life Lutheran Native Ministry in Regina, sponsored by the socially progressive Evangelical Lutheran Church in Canada. However, Rev. Frank Armistead, pastor at Circle of Life, notes that there are only two dedicated Aboriginal ministries in Canada within the Evangelical Lutheran Church in Canada; his conclusion was that support for Aboriginal ministries at the national level was weak, even while local congregational support for his own Regina ministry was high. Armistead also noted that the problem is that Lutherans do not really know whether they should be attempting to engage in dialogue with Aboriginals or to convert them (interview, 21 February 2006). The Lutheran Church–Canada has also been a partner with Evangelical Lutheran Church in Canada in Lutheran Association of Missionaries and Pilots (LAMP), a mission outreach to the Inuit and northern Aboriginal communities, but even this ministry has struggled during the past few years because resources have been scarce, and because there has been confusion about its primary mandate with Aboriginal peoples – an understandable problem for a church body only just discovering it should be considering its ministry to and with Aboriginal peoples.

Lutherans and Same-Sex Marriage

Same-sex marriage is another issue concerning which Lutherans displayed both their ethnic sectarian as well as their more accommodating tendencies. In the multi-ethnic Evangelical Lutheran Church in Canada, the matter received extensive study. A motion was drafted for the 2005 General Convention favouring the blessing of same-sex unions, and that motion was defeated. Given the progressive social activism of the Evangelical Lutheran Church in Canada, the issue is certain to reappear, but for now the issue of same-sex marriage is laid to rest, according to then national Bishop Ray Schultz (interview, 23 November 2005).[29] Evidence that this issue is still front and centre for the Evangelical Lutheran Church in Canada was the motion passed in its Eastern Synod in the summer of 2006 condoning same-sex marriage. The National Church Office ruled that this action threatens the unity of the church but has also suggested a task force to bring recommendations to the next General Convention of the national body. On the other hand, the Lutheran Church–Canada (which is predominantly German) has had no doubt about its opposition to same-sex blessings, as its 2002 letter to Prime Minister Jean Chrétien indicated. For these Lutherans, homosexuality is a sin, condemned in the Bible; consequently there can be no question of blessing same-sex unions. Its *Planning Conference Research Survey Report* of October 2003, written by Michael Swait, indicates the denominational concern that 'the changing moral acceptability of homosexuality [is] an emerging threat to the Lutheran Church–Canada' (Swait 2003). As with the place of women in the church, discussed above, the Lutheran Church–Canada regards its opposition to the blessing of same-sex unions as one way in which it can take a prophetic stand against what its members and leaders perceive to be the insidious moral changes associated with an increasingly secular and permissive Canadian society. Its roots as an ethnically homogeneous denomination on the outside of mainstream Canadian culture have given the Lutheran Church–Canada a great deal of practice in articulating such a stance. However, the multi-ethnic, more mainstream, and relatively liberal Evangelical Lutheran Church in Canada struggles with the issue, like many other Canadians, as public opinion polls indicate (Religious Tolerance 2003).

New Dimensions in Lutheran Ethnicity

As the history of Lutheran immigration to Canada briefly outlined above indicates, Lutherans have traditionally been associated with northern European countries and North America, where those northern Europeans found a home. Where Lutherans made a home, they did their best, as their numbers allowed, to provide education for their young, residences for the old, and services for others.[30] As listed in the 2003 *Lutheran Churches in Canada* directory, published by the Lutheran Council in Canada,[31] there are twenty-three church camps, four seminaries, three liberal arts colleges, five high schools, one Bible college, thirty-three parochial schools, and eighty-one senior residential and health-care facilities across Canada. In the Kitchener-Waterloo area of Ontario, where the Lutheran population is most densely concentrated, a series of eight 'community opportunities' associations have been established, involving everything from child care to employment centres. Though in certain instances Lutherans may have priority in gaining access to these opportunities, these services are provided as a service to the community and are not limited to Lutherans, if for no other reason than there are not enough Lutherans to fill them.

Service to the community has often involved serving new immigrants, even if they were not from the traditional northern European groups. As Lutheran missionary efforts of the twentieth century have matured, especially in Africa, Asia, and South America, and as growth in Christianity is occurring mostly in the Southern Hemisphere (Jenkins 2002), Lutheran populations have increased in previously unfamiliar terrain. According to the Lutheran World Federation (2006), there were 69.8 million Lutherans in the world in 2005, of whom 15.0 million lived in Africa, 7.4 million in Asia and Australia, and another 1.1 million in South America. This combined total of 23.5 million is still fewer than the combined total of the 46.1 million Lutherans in Europe (38.0 million) and North America (8.1 million), but the pattern has been for Lutheran populations in the Northern Hemisphere to decrease and those in the Southern Hemisphere to increase. These shifts in populations have been reflected in recent years in the ethnic diversity of Lutherans in Canada as the numbers of Lutherans arriving from the Southern Hemisphere increase.

The first indication of this shift in ethnic populations in Canada is given in the form of statistics from the two largest denominations. Whereas in former years worship services conducted in languages other than English would have been solely in the languages of northern Europe (Finnish, German, Icelandic, Slovak, Swedish, Norwegian) and the Baltic (Estonian, Latvian), currently three of the sixteen congregations hosting non-English services in the Lutheran Church–Canada do so in Asian languages (Chinese and Korean), while another two host French and Spanish services. The same sort of picture emerges in the Evangelical Lutheran Church in Canada, where of the thirty-seven non-English-speaking worship centres seven are of Asian heritage (five in Cantonese and one each in Vietnamese and Mandarin) while the rest are of northern European and Baltic origin.[32] The Evangelical Lutheran Church in Canada has also recognized the importance of its ethnic ministries by establishing four separate conferences for its German, Swedish, Latvian, and Chinese constituencies. Each conference operates under its own constitution and reports directly to the assistant to the national bishop.[33]

While it is true that Canadian Lutherans still have a strong sense of their history of northern European immigration within their congregations, particularly in the larger centres where services are held in German, Swedish, and Latvian, it is equally true that Lutherans are looking to make the newest immigrants to the country feel welcome, just as their ancestors had extended welcomes to European immigrants.More than any statistical analysis, a brief illustration of four examples of this new dimension among Canadian Lutherans demonstrates the increasingly dynamic relationship between religion and ethnicity among Canada's Lutherans.

St John's Lutheran, Toronto, Ontario

St John's Lutheran in downtown Toronto was a struggling congregation of older European, predominantly German, members in the 1980s. Once a vibrant congregation of over 1,000 members sponsoring services for immigrants of Estonian, Latvian, and Lithuanian heritage, the congregational numbers of this Lutheran Church–Missouri Synod–parish declined after 1960 as so many of its members moved to the suburbs. In 1987, Pastor Michael Drews arrived and, following his predecessor, developed a ministry that helped new, especially Tamil, refugees to gain access to government services, find appropriate clothes, and seek employment. Soon Drews found his congregation hosting worship services in Tamil. This immigrant ministry expanded in 1989 to include a newly arrived Eritrean pastor, looking for a Luthe-

ran church. By the time Nancy Vernon Kelly wrote about the congregation in 1996, the congregation was hosting worship services in English,
Tigrinya (the language of Eritrea), French (so as to serve various immigrants of African origin), and some South African languages. Some of
the congregations and worship services had a less than Lutheran identity in liturgical format and were less rigid regarding some Missouri
Synod rules (Kelly 1996).[34]

When I spoke with Pastor Drews in 2005, he indicated that the main
emphasis of the church remained the same – to minister to new immigrant communities – but that some of those communities had changed.
The South Africans were gone and the Congolese community had come
and gone, starting up their own congregations with their own worship
style. A ministry to Ethiopians in their native Oromo language had
begun. Another outreach had begun among the Tamil population with
Dr Tilly Chandulal, a graduate of the Evangelical Lutheran Church in
Canada's Waterloo Lutheran Seminary, who helped the predominantly
Hindu population with social programs such as English as a Second
Language and exercise classes for seniors, and acting as a resource for
people in various 'life situations' (death, abuse, alcoholism, drug use,
etc.). In acting as a friend to these new immigrants, the church hoped
but did not expect to win new converts to the Christian faith.

Drews also had great hopes for training clergy in ethnic ministries
through an Internet service emanating from the Ethnic Immigrant Institute of Theology at Concordia Seminary in St Louis, Missouri.[35] Nevertheless, St John's Lutheran remains limited in its financial resources and
was encouraged by the English District administration to sell its valuable real estate and carry on its ministry elsewhere. Its members have
refused and currently are looking at other options that would provide
additional income for the church while serving its immigrant population (interview with Pastor Drews, 28 November 2005).

Faith Evangelical Lutheran Church, Surrey, BC

Pastor Kwang Soo Kim is the pastor at Faith Evangelical Lutheran
Church of Surrey, BC. When Kim arrived in 1992, this small, struggling,
English-speaking congregation had a minimum of activities. In 1993,
Kim convinced the congregation to start mission work among the Koreans in the larger Vancouver area, and an active Bible study and worship
service for Koreans soon developed. In the course of his work, Kim met
a Chinese Lutheran man who was eventually ordained as an associate

pastor working among the Chinese population. In 1999, Kim recognized a need for ministry to the Hispanic people in his area and encouraged a pastor friend to conduct worship services in Spanish. As a result, there are English, Chinese, Korean, and Spanish services at Faith Evangelical Lutheran Church, comprising four 'worshipping fellowships,' as Kim calls them. Kim is also training lay people of Hispanic, Hindi, and Mandarin backgrounds and has received funds from the Lutheran Church–Canada to hire a lay woman – a Hindu convert to Christianity – as an evangelist. At the time of writing, there were four families at Faith holding regular Sunday evening *satsang* or gatherings in Hindi and English.

Pastor Kim notes that most of his English-speakers are Lutheran by heritage but that only one Chinese family was Lutheran in Hong Kong. Although no direct Chinese translation of the *Lutheran Book of Worship* is available,[36] Kim has incorporated what he considers important Lutheran features such as the Confession and Absolution,[37] scripture readings, and Lutheran hymns into the Chinese worship services. For the Hispanic fellowship, they have been able to follow a Lutheran liturgy much more closely because of the similarity to Catholic liturgies with which the Central and South American worshippers were already familiar. Moreover, like Toronto's St John's congregation, on festival days Faith Lutheran brings all four worshipping fellowships together for joint worship services, followed by a pot-luck lunch where ethnic foods are shared.[38] Other occasions where the four ethnic fellowships are brought together include multicultural night,[39] talent night, and Bible trivia night. Kim notes that the kind of ethnic tensions one might see between Chinese and Koreans were not evident in his church (interview with Pastor Kwang Soo Kim, 2 December 2005).

Rhenish Lutheran Church, Markham, Ontario, and Toronto Chinese Lutheran Church, Scarborough, Ontario

Pastor David Tin is the dean of the Toronto Conference and chair of the Chinese Ministry Conference of the Evangelical Lutheran Church in Canada, which reports directly to the National Convention and bishop of the Evangelical Lutheran Church in Canada. Tin notes that there are fourteen Chinese congregations across Canada in the Evangelical Lutheran Church in Canada, though not all of them have distinct Cantonese or Mandarin worship services. Pastor Tin is sure that the vast majority of Chinese Christians in Canada were not Lutheran or even

Christian before their arrival in Canada, but found the church to be a good place for fellowship with other people of Chinese background. The Lutheran Church was welcoming and family oriented, so there was a natural fit.

Tin leads two Chinese Lutheran congregations. Rhenish Lutheran Church began its work among Chinese people in Scarborough in the 1970s as an extension of the mission work of a German mission society, the United Evangelical Mission, formerly the Rhenish Mission, which had been active in mainland China and Hong Kong. The church moved to Markham in 2005. Toronto Chinese Lutheran Church began in Markham in 1988 as a Cantonese-speaking congregation and moved to Scarborough in 2005. With a variety of constituencies speaking English, Cantonese, Mandarin, and Tamil, the congregation recognized the opportunity for a multicultural ministry and currently has ministerial workers assigned to each of the communities. Besides sharing Pastor Tin, the congregations also jointly participate in learning events, vacation Bible schools and, together with other Chinese Lutheran congregations in the area, youth programs, special worship, and retreat events.

Tin has also made accommodations for his Chinese congregants. Because the *Lutheran Book of Worship* has not been translated directly into Chinese, the liturgy has been pieced together for his congregation, as it has for Kim's. Moreover, the position of an elder – a position held usually for two to five years in a Lutheran church – was regarded by Tin's Chinese congregants as a life-long position – an idea Tin suggested was rooted in the Chinese respect for the wisdom of the elder. To accommodate this view, the parish has adapted the title of elder and added some life-long positions to the congregational structure. Tin stressed that all of these accommodations reflect the multicultural mandate of his congregation (interview with Pastor Tin, 7 December 2005).

Zion Lutheran Church, Saskatoon, Saskatchewan

Pastor Boyd Molder is the senior pastor at Zion, a large downtown congregation of predominantly Norwegian pietist Lutherans. There are approximately twenty baptized members of Chinese heritage, and on any given Sunday there will be between thirty and forty Chinese people in the English worship service. On the second Sunday of every month, the second lesson, gospel reading, and Communion are translated into Cantonese. The Chinese congregation also has its own services later in the morning, led by seminary student Jeremy Chen, but many Chinese Lutherans enjoy the English service, where they can improve their English. English as a Second Language is another service available to this new immigrant community. Molder says that most of the Chinese members were not Christian or Lutheran before attending Zion but joined through personal and family contact with one or two people in the community who were. As Chen is training to be a Lutheran pastor, he tries hard to integrate the Lutheran liturgical style into the Chinese worship services. Most members of his Chinese congregation tend to be baptized as adults because, as Molder speculates, the original members were most familiar with adult baptism as practised by the Christian and Missionary Alliance Church –an active missionary church in China. Pastor Bolder is not aware of conflict or discrimination between the Norwegian and Chinese groups in his congregation, though he is also careful to ensure that the worship life of the older Norwegian group has not been altered too much – a point he says he would have had to be careful about, regardless of whether the Chinese congregation was there (interview with Pastor Boyd Molder, 20 November 2005).

Our four illustrative examples of these relatively new ethnic congregations demonstrate some interesting trends. First, most of the immigrant peoples attending these Lutheran congregations were not Lutheran before they arrived in Canada but were attracted by the fact that the church afforded an opportunity for getting together with others of similar ethnic background. They were also attracted by the welcoming attitude of those in the Lutheran churches and the emphasis on family life among Lutherans.[40] The place afforded to women in these churches seemed to be acceptable to these newcomers, too; all the pastors of the ethnic congregations interviewed noted that while the women in their communities were not necessarily vocal in public, there was little question that they were in charge at home and in the religious lives of their families. Some accommodations were made for all the ethnic congregations, sometimes out of necessity (such as use of alternate liturgies for lack of an adequate Chinese translation of the *Lutheran Book of Worship*) and other times to enhance outreach (such as relaxing closed communion in the Lutheran Church–Canada and related congregations). Overall, however, these accommodations were minor. In fact, the new ethnic congregations seemed to enjoy, even appreciate, the structure that they were participating in as members of the Lutheran community. Pastor Tin cautioned against making too many accommodations, as one risks 'watering down the richness of our Lutheran tradition and theology,' which his congregation finds attractive (interview with Pastor Tin, 7 December 2005).

The Lutheran pastors ministering to these new ethnic congregations and the church leaders of each denomination were unanimous in thinking that the new ethnic congregations and their members were more socially conservative (see chapters 4 and 6 on the Anglican Church and the United Church for a similar perception.) They thought this emphasis was due, in part, to the socially conservative culture of the countries of origin. However, the pastors also thought it likely that the new immigrants came to the Christian faith as a result of the efforts of evangelically minded missionaries, many of whom were not Lutheran but from other conservative denominations such as the Christian and Missionary Alliance (see Bruce Guenther's chapter 10 on evangelical Christianity). Consequently, for example, most of these new Lutherans are opposed to the blessings of same-sex unions. Moreover, these pastors claim divorce is very negatively viewed, among the Chinese immigrant community in particular. This social conservatism extends even to the understanding of the place of children; in the last ten years, the Evangelical Lutheran Church in Canada has admitted, even encouraged, unconfirmed children to participate in Communion, but immigrant families resisted, not out of theological conviction (which is the reasoning for this exclusion among the more traditional Lutheran congregations), but out of a sense that children are not to act on their own in matters such as religion. In short, these new ethnic communities act a great deal like the Lutheran ethnic communities that came to Canada in the 1800s and early 1900s; the congregations are gathering places where those of similar ethnic backgrounds are able to assume shared values.

Dr Alan Lai, professor of religious education at the Vancouver School of Theology, ordained minister of the Evangelical Lutheran Church in Canada, and himself an immigrant from Hong Kong, notes some significant differences between immigrants practising as Lutherans in Canada. While those who came as Norwegian Lutherans, for instance, were strongly loyal to the idea of being Lutheran, such is not the case for most Chinese immigrant converts. Becoming a Christian was a big enough step; assuming loyalty to one particular subsection of that tradition is simply not very compelling, particularly when the missionary who brought one to faith was probably non-Lutheran and had a worship style that was likely quite different from that found in the Lutheran congregations.[41] Finding comfort in the community of the faithful, making connections with friends of the same ethnic heritage, and receiving the gospel of Christian acceptance and forgiveness were far more important than being attached to a particular form of that Christian message. In fact, Dr Lai noted that importing traditional Lutheran terminology, such as 'justification by grace through faith,' can in fact pose more difficulties, especially if such language is counterintuitive, as it sometimes is to a population like the Chinese, concerned with self-development and doing good works (interview, 15 March 2006).[42] Still, whether the concept is called justification or grace or forgiveness or acceptance, this idea, so central to Lutheran theology, is always cited as significant in drawing new immigrants to Lutheran churches.[43]

Lai also notes that second and subsequent generations of visible minority immigrants face a common challenge of blending in with the dominant culture – a difficulty not faced by previous generations of Lutherans of northern European heritage. Second-generation visible minorities, while speaking perfectly accented Canadian English, will continue to be asked 'Where do you come from?' just because they belong to a visible minority. This seeing one's neighbour as an 'other,' even within the Canadian Lutheran community, will continue to be an issue as churches help their members 'cope with discrimination' (interview, 15 March 2006; see also Greer Anne Wenh-In Ng's chapter 6 on the United Church of Canada).

Language is another important ethnic marker among new immigrants in Lutheran congregations. As with their northern European predecessors, new immigrant Lutherans try to learn English at the earliest opportunity while preserving their national language in various ways, for the first generation at least. For example, Cantonese and Mandarin worship services are welcomed in Saskatoon but so too is the opportunity to learn English through worship services. Amongst those with whom Pastor Tin works, new immigrants look to learn English, reserving the language of the country of origin for home use and perhaps also congregational use where possible. By the time of the second generation, there is more incentive to participate in the English of the congregation because the comfort level in English is that much higher. In fact, according to Pastors Hung and Voo of Vancouver, second-generation Lutherans of Asian heritage in Vancouver demanded English services (personal interviews). Again, theirs is very similar to the experience of Lutherans of European heritage in past decades and indicative of the Lutherans readily integrating into Canadian culture, even while retaining their ethnic roots. As Stuart MacDonald indicates in chapter 5 on Presbyterianism, when an ethnic group is in such a minority, church can become a place where one's culture is actually affirmed, as was the case, for instance, at Zion Lutheran in Saskatoon. One can argue that this experience in itself is characteristically Canadian, at least among Lutherans since they first arrived in Canada.

Concluding Remarks

As the Canadian Lutheran churches in the 1970s considered merging, Norman Threinen, historian of Canadian Lutherans, particularly the Lutheran Church–Canada and its antecedents, edited *In Search of Identity: A Look at Lutheran Identity in Canada.* The contributors to that volume made many important points. Vincent E. Eriksson noted that the changes in Canada's immigration patterns have challenged the security and identity of Canadian Lutherans (Eriksson 1977). William Hordern noted that there is a double crisis for the Canadian Lutheran church as it is caught between remaining relevant and distinctive on the one hand and maintaining its identity on the other (Hordern 1977). These words remain true today as membership figures continue to shrink and fewer people identify themselves as Lutheran in the federal census. In the past, so much of being Lutheran was tied up with being German or Scandinavian that it is difficult to imagine how optimistic one can be about the future of such a small group as the Lutherans in Canada, when more of these descendants think of themselves first as Canadians and second as members of other ethnic communities. Moreover, since being Canadian appears to be defined in increasingly postmodern, post-institutional terms that have no necessary links to religious affiliation, Canadian Lutherans will likely continue to participate in the discourse of loss that Seljak and Bramadat have observed within so many Christian denominations.

However, Canadian Lutherans appear to have hope in two areas. First, while Canadian Lutherans have been historically tied to specific ethnic communities, the ethnic congregations discussed briefly above are good indications of the deep influence of multicultural policies and traditions and the affinity that Canadian Lutherans have with strangers in a new land. A related source of optimism for Lutheran insiders may be derived from the facts that there are more Lutherans in Africa alone than in all of North America (Granquist 2003), and that Lutherans have a history of ministering to new immigrants. Given the shifts we have witnessed in Canadian immigration policies, these facts may bode well for Canadian Lutherans.

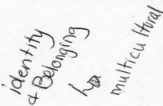

Second, what has remained strong, even through this period of declining church involvement, has been the theological continuity of the Lutheran faith. Lutheran young people continue to receive the rite of confirmation after being educated in the teachings of the Bible, as understood through the lens of *Luther's Small Catechism*, just as were my grandmother, mother, siblings, and children. Lutherans continue to talk about justification by faith and strive to understand God's will as it relates to scripture, even as this theological language is reinterpreted in light of the new multicultural and multi-faith Canadian reality. Bishops recommend to their pastors that they read Kelly Fryer's *Reclaiming the 'L' Word: Renewing the Church from Its Lutheran Cord*, a book that tries to reinterpret the most significant principles of the Lutheran Confessions for a multicultural North American world in an effort to make ethnic peoples of all descriptions, not just European, welcome in the Lutheran Church. Although the Lutheran Confessions are not well known among believers, they continue to be a theological anchor for interpreting the faith in new contexts, even if the line between *adiaphora* and essentials continues to blur.[44]

In short, Lutheran identity in Canada is evolving and is not limited by the original Scandinavian and German ethnicities that accompanied it. Lutherans continue to immerse themselves in Canadian culture and to become part of the Christian mainstream, trying to discern what is vital to their Christianity and what can be discarded as *adiaphora*, all the while retaining their Lutheran identity as rooted in their theology, history, and the Confessions. In doing so, they consider themselves part of the continuing reform of the church, first started by their founder, Martin Luther.

Notes

1 Though the veneration of Luther has diminished in recent years, a barometer of his stature in Lutheran circles was the popularity of a 2003 Hollywood movie entitled *Luther* starring Joseph Fiennes and Peter Ustinov.

2 The significance of this problem is noted in several histories for various geographical areas – Baglo and Beglo (1995), Evenson (1974), Herzer (1946), and Threinen (1989) – as well as Kuhn (2005).

3 The confessions were published as the *Book of Concord* in 1580 and later subtitled *The Confessions of the Evangelical Lutheran Church* (Tappert 1959). The ambiguous nature of the Confessions became prominent as Lutheranism

spread to the Scandinavian countries where, tied as they were to historical contexts, they were not accepted in their entirety (Gritsch 2002).

4 Interviews were conducted as follows: Pastors Carla Blakely, Dennis Hendricksen, Bob Leeson, and Orville Kaminski (Christ Lutheran, Regina), 10 November 2005; Pastors Wayne Garmon and Lindsay Hognestad (Trinity Lutheran, Regina), 15 November 2005; Pastors Sid Haugen and Jeff Tank (Our Savior's Lutheran, Regina), 16 November 2005; Pastor Boyd Molder (Zion Lutheran, Saskatoon), 30 November 2005; Pastor Kim Sherwin (Buchanan/Norquay/Melville), 1 December 2005; Pastor Daryl Olson (Bethlehem, Outlook), 7 December 2005. Interviews with pastors of new immigrant congregations are noted separately later.

5 Unfortunately, no amount of Lutheran worship saved the expedition, as most of Munck's crew died of scurvy, dysentery, and other diseases, with only four of the original crew surviving the winter before they sailed back to Denmark the next year.

6 *Synod* means literally 'walking together.' In North American Lutheran history, the word is used to denote any group of Lutherans who have formed an organizational structure wherein they meet regularly to make decisions for that group. What causes these Lutherans to organize together can be the result of different factors: (1) they may occupy a common region, as in the case of the New York and Pittsburgh synods mentioned here; (2) they may have a common ethnic background, as in the case of the Suomi (Finnish) or Augustana (Swedish) synods; or (3) they may have a common historical, ethnic, and geographical background, like the Lutheran Church–Missouri Synod that had its origins in Missouri, with a large number of German settlers who had a strong missionary impulse, resulting in missionary outposts in places as far removed as the northern borders with Canada.

7 C.F. Walther, superintendent of the Alberta-BC district of the Lutheran Church–Missouri Synod at the time described the situation: 'The lot of our church in the Northwest in 1918 has been worse than at any time during the war years. Hatred has grown and increasingly the people are made to suffer actual persecution at some places though the government is making every effort to protect them' (Herzer 1946, 37).

8 Still, particularly among the German congregations, it took another generation before there were more worship services, for instance, held in English than in German. Edward Thomas Hedlin's study (1963) provides good evidence of this.

9 A similar phenomenon occurred among the Canadian Irish when they signed up in proportions similar to the rest of the Canadian population while the Irish in Ireland were less enthusiastic. See McGowan (1999).

10 Members of the CCCRR were the Baptist Convention of Ontario and Quebec, Canadian Lutheran World Relief, Canadian Mennonite Board of Colonization, Catholic Immigration Aid Society, German Baptist Colonization and Immigration Society, Latvian Relief Funds of Canada, and Sudeten Committee.
11 On their chief distinguishing features, see Lutheran Church–Canada / Evangelical Lutheran Church in Canada (1998). Of the 1,002 Lutheran congregations in Canada, 961 are Evangelical Lutheran Church in Canada (627) or Lutheran Church–Canada (342), with the remaining 41 being of the Association of Free Lutherans (6), Church of Lutheran Brethren (7), Danish Lutheran Church Abroad (6), Canadian Association of Lutheran Congregations (3), Church of the Lutheran Confession (1), Latvian (3), and Wisconsin Evangelical Lutheran Synod (15) (Lutheran Council in Canada [2003]).
12 The Lutheran Council of Canada is 'an agency through which Lutheran church bodies in Canada are able to work together in matters of common interest and responsibility.' Having no paid staff of its own, the Council is responsible primarily for coordinating joint efforts of military and prison chaplaincies, Scouts and Guides, and the publishing of the Lutheran Directory (Evangelical Lutheran Church in Canada [2003]).
13 Once baptized, you are a member of that church until you either die or transfer to another denomination.
14 In the Lutheran Church–Canada, one is normally not allowed to take communion until after confirmation.
15 Statistics on those who commune are not perfectly accurate, as the tabulation is based on attendees self-recording their visit, usually by completing and submitting a printed card at the time of communion. However, some people forget, others do not know they should be doing this, and others do not like to provide this record.
16 Although Bibby's statistics are extrapolations, they are based on the most current census figures (2002).
17 PEI and Newfoundland also experienced increases, but these were minimal: PEI from 115 to 170 and Newfoundland from 415 to 535.
18 The only mainstream denominations with a higher median age were the Presbyterians at 46, Anglicans and United Church at 44.
19 See note 4 for a list of these interviews.
20 Interviews with pastors as noted in note 4 above. Compare this with Myroslaw Tataryn's chapter 8 on Orthodox Christianity, where ethnicity outlasts religious adherence.
21 Men tended to lead confirmation courses, not so much because their gender

uniquely qualified them to do so, but because confirmation was viewed to be the purview of the pastor, given his seminary training.

22 'Let a woman learn in silence with full submission. I permit no woman to teach or to have authority over a man; she is to keep silent. For Adam was formed first, then Eve and Adam was not deceived, but the woman was deceived and became a transgressor' (New Revised Standard Version of the Bible). The one exception the LCC allows to this passage is the role of teacher, so long as the males under the authority of women in this role are not yet adults.

23 Interview with Pastor Carla Blakely, 21 February 2006. Pastor Blakely since joined the Evangelical Lutheran Church in Canada so she could become ordained.

24 The Lutheran Church–Canada is not a member of the Canadian Council of Churches.

25 For more on the Lutheran World Federation, see http://www.lutheranworld.org.

26 For this reason, the Lutheran Church–Canada does not participate in the Lutheran World Federation. Sister churches of the Lutheran Church–Canada with whom there is adequate doctrinal agreement can be found under 'Other Lutheran Resources,' http://www.lutheranchurch.ca/other.html.

27 The actual date of this signing was 31 October, the date that Martin Luther posted his '95 Theses' for general discussion, by tradition, on the door of the Wittenberg church. See Vatican (1999a, 1999b) and Lutheran World Federation (1999).

28 Interestingly, this Joint Declaration was cited recently in a statement issued by the Lutheran World Federation and sent by the Communication Office of the Evangelical Lutheran Church in Canada to church members. In July 2007, the Vatican's Congregation for the Doctrine of the Faith issued 'Responses to Some Questions regarding Certain Aspects of the Doctrine on the Church,' which emphasized the long-standing doctrine that the title *church* is not to be extended to 'Christian communities' like the member bodies of the Lutheran World Federation. Lutheran World Federation's General Secretary Rev. Dr Ishmael Noko issued a statement on 11 July 2007 noting LWF's dissatisfaction with 'Responses' and citing the Joint Declaration, which its signers recognized as a 'decisive step forward on the way to overcoming the division of the church.' Noting that he hoped ecumenical discussion could continue, Noko stated clearly that Lutheran churches do not accept the understandings of church found in the 'Responses' (Lutheran World Federation 2007).

29 Bishop Schultz also notes that same-sex marriage is simply not an issue for

young people in the Evangelical Lutheran Church in Canada because most young people in the Lutheran church condone same-sex blessings.

30 Significant historical examples are those depicted by Roy Grosz in Ontario (1989) and Ragna Steen and Magda Hendrickson in Alberta (1944).

31 The Lutheran Council in Canada is a cooperative venture of the Lutheran Church–Canada and the Evangelical Lutheran Church in Canada to coordinate chaplaincies in the military, among Scouts and Guides, and in correctional institutions. It also publishes this directory occasionally.

32 Of the nineteen Lutheran congregations in Quebec, only one hosts French-language services, according to denominational officials of the Lutheran Church–Canada and the Evangelical Lutheran Church in Canada. Most of the Quebec congregations host services in English; however, two congregations host services in German, and one each in Danish, Finnish, and Chinese.

33 A complete listing of these non–English-speaking congregations was provided to the author by the head offices of each denomination. To summarize, in the Evangelical Lutheran Church in Canada, worship services continue to be held in the following languages: German (sixteen), Finnish (seven), Cantonese (five), Estonian (five), Danish (three), Latvian (three), Hungarian (one), Lithuanian (one), Mandarin (one), Swedish (one), and Vietnamese (one). In the Lutheran Church–Canada, the following information was provided: German (six), Korean (two), Mandarin (two), Slovak (two), Spanish (two), Cantonese (one), Estonian (one), French (one), Finnish (one), and Polish (one).

34 For instance, closed communion (the practice of limiting communion to those of the same denomination) was relaxed and women were allowed to become elders. St John's is a member of the Lutheran Church–Missouri Synod, English District. The Missouri synod is divided into 35 districts of which two are non-geographical including the English district formed in 1911 as a district of English-speaking Lutherans in a predominantly German denomination (Nelson 1980, 266). Over the years, the English District has been among the most liberal of the districts. When the Lutheran Church–Canada formed, the English District congregations in Canada decided they would remain with the Missouri Synod.

35 Concordia is the largest seminary of the Lutheran Church–Missouri Synod.

36 Pastor Allan Lai, professor of religious education at Vancouver School of Theology, offers an explanation for this apparent deficiency. Lai says having a literal translation of the *Lutheran Book of Worship* would be very impractical, given its European and North American roots. In Hong Kong, *Lutheran Book of Worship* equivalents exist as a result of the work of various denominations, including Lutheran clergy (interview with Dr Lai, 15 March 2006).

37 Pronouncement of forgiveness by the pastor.
38 Pastor Kim listed the festival days as Easter, Thanksgiving, Reformation, Christmas, New Year's, Chinese New Year's, and February 'Friendship Sunday.'
39 On such occasions, the ethnic communities of the church share a pot-luck dinner.
40 In support of this it can be noted that, according to the 2001 Census ('Selected Demographic and Cultural Characteristics [104], Selected Religions [35A], Age Groups [6] and Sex [3] for Population, for Canada, Provinces, Territories and Census Metropolitan Areas, 2001 Census–20% Sample Data'), Lutherans have a lower rate of divorce, common-law marriage, and single parenthood than the national average and most mainstream Protestant denominations.
41 Dr Lai noted these same evangelical influences are evident in the worship style of many Chinese Lutheran congregations where praise songs and an unstructured liturgical style are common.
42 Dr Lai's observations were corroborated by the author's conversations with all the pastors responsible for ethnic ministries noted here, especially Pastor Tin of Unionville, Ontario.
43 In addition to the pastors and Dr Lai already mentioned, I interviewed Pastors Richard Hung (25 April 2006) and Samuel Voo (2 May 2006), who lead Lutheran churches in the Vancouver area. They both cited this idea as being central to why new immigrants and even their children and grandchildren attend Lutheran churches.
44 In 2005, the *Lutheran Handbook* was published. This is a book intended for general readership, poking fun at Lutheran identity, even while instructing the reader in the basics of the Lutheran faith. Even though this is an American publication, it resonates with Canadian Lutherans. For instance, on the cover is a caricature of a winking Martin Luther, whose explanation summarizes the meaning of theology to a Lutheran: 'The wink on Luther's face indicates that even though theology is serious stuff, we should nonetheless remember that it is not our theology that saves us, but Jesus Christ. Therefore, our life in the church can be buoyant, and our theological wranglings can be done with a sense of humor and love for our neighbor.'

Works Cited

Althaus, Paul. 1966. *The theology of Martin Luther.* Philadelphia: Fortress.
Anglican Church of Canada. 2000. Called to full communion: The Waterloo

Declaration. http://www.anglican.ca/primate/communications/water-loo.htm.

Bachmann, E.T., and Mercia B. Bachmann. 1989. *Lutheran churches in the world: A handbook*. Minneapolis: Augsburg Fortress.

Baglo, Gerinand E. 1962. *Augustana Lutherans in Canada*. Canada Conference of the Augustana Lutheran Church.

Bassler, Gerhard P. 1990. Silent or silenced co-founders of Canada? Reflections on the history of German Canadians. *Canadian Ethnic Studies* 22 (1): 38–46.

Bausenhart, Werner. 1989. *German immigration and assimilation in Ontario, 1783–1918*. New York: Legas.

Beglo, Barton, ed. 1988. *A time for building: Essays on Lutherans in Canada*. Kitchener: St Mark's.

Beglo, Barton, and Jo N. Beglo. 1995. *By faith: Lutherans in Ottawa and the valleys*. Ottawa: St Peter's.

Bibby, Reginald. 1987. *Fragmented gods: The poverty and potential of religion in Canada*. Toronto: Stoddart.

– 2002. *Restless gods: The renaissance of religion in Canada*. Toronto: Stoddart.

Braaten, Carl E. 1983. *Principles of Lutheran theology*. Philadelphia: Fortress.

– 1990. *Justification: The article by which the church stands or falls*. Minneapolis: Fortress.

Bramadat, Paul. 2005. Re-visioning religion in the contemporary period: The United Church of Canada's Ethnic Ministries Unit. *Canadian Diversity* 4 (3): 59–62.

Cronmiller, Raymond. 1961. *A history of the Lutheran Church in Canada*. Toronto: Evangelical Lutheran Synod of Canada.

Eriksson, Vincent E. 1977. Rationale for an indigenous Lutheran Church in Canada. In Threinen 1977, 33–47.

Evangelical Lutheran Church in Canada. 2001. Called to full communion (the Waterloo Declaration). http://www.elcic.ca/What-We-Believe/Waterloo-Declaration.cfm.

– 2003. Report of the Lutheran Council in Canada. http://205.200.236.76/website//docs.nsf/0/F666B592B55A9C6B86256D250067FD2B.

Evenson, George O. 1974. *Adventuring for Christ: The story of the Evangelical Lutheran Church of Canada*. Calgary: Foothills Lutheran.

Eylands, Valdimar J. 1945. *Lutherans in Canada*. Winnipeg: Icelandic Evangelical Lutheran Synod in North America.

Freund, Alexander. 1994. Identity in immigration: Self-conceptualization and myth in the narratives of German immigrant women in Vancouver, B.C., 1950–1960. MA thesis, Simon Fraser University.

Fryer, Kelly. 2003. *Reclaiming the 'L' word: Renewing the church from its Lutheran cord*. Minneapolis: Augsburg.

Granquist, Mark. 2003. North American Lutheranism and the new ethics. In *Lutherans Today: American Lutheran identity in the 21st century*, ed. Richard Cimin and William B. Erdmans. Cambridge, UK: Erdmans.

Gritsch, Eric W. 2002. *A history of Lutheranism*. Minneapolis: Fortress.

Grosz, Roy N. 1989. *Mission and merger: Wheels of change – A history of the Eastern Canada Synod*. Kitchener, ON: Eastern Synod of the Evangelical Lutheran Church in Canada.

Hawkins, Freda. 1988. *Canadian and immigration policy: Public policy and public concern*. Montreal and Kingston: McGill-Queen's University Press.

Hedlin, Edward T. 1963. *The language transition in the Canada District, ALC*. Chicago: Lutheran School of Theology at Chicago-Maywood Campus.

Hendrickson, Magda, and Ragna Steen. 1944. *Pioneer days in Bardo, Alberta, including sketches of early surrounding settlements*. Tofield, AB: Historical Society of Beaver Hills Lake.

Hertz, Karl H. 1976. *Two kingdoms and one world*. Minneapolis: Augsburg.

Herzer, John E. 1946. Homesteading for God: *A story of the Lutheran Church (Missouri Synod) in Alberta and British Columbia 1894–1946*. Edmonton: Commercial.

Hordern, William. 1977. Interrelation and interaction between Reformation principles and the Canadian context. In Threinen 1977, 19–32.

Jenkins, Philip. 2002. *The next Christendom: The coming of global Christianity*. Oxford: Oxford University Press.

Jones, Frank. 1999. Are children going to religious services? *Canadian Social Trends* catalogue no. 11-00813–16.

Kelly, Nancy V. 1996. The development of a diverse urban congregation in Canada: The death of business-as-usual at St John's Lutheran Church in Toronto. *Consensus* 22 (1): 57–80.

Kuhn, Kenneth C. 2005. *Millennium study of pastoral leadership needs*. Winnipeg: Evangelical Lutheran Church in Canada.

Leacy, F.H., ed. 1983. *Historical statistics of Canada*. Ottawa: Canadian Government Publishing Centre.

Lutheran Church–Canada. 2005. *Summarized statistics 2001*. Winnipeg: Lutheran Council in Canada.

Lutheran Church–Canada / Evangelical Lutheran Church in Canada. 1998. Where Canada's Lutherans stand. http://www.lutheranchurch.ca/CTCR/LCC-ELCIC.pdf.

Lutheran Council in Canada. 2003. *Lutheran Churches in Canada 2003*. Winnipeg: Lutheran Council in Canada.

Lutheran World Federation. 1999. Justification. http://www.lutheran-world.org/Special_Events/LWF-Special_Events-Justification.html.

– 2006. Lutheran World Federation 2005 membership figures. http://www.lutheranworld.org/LWF_Documents/LWF-Statistics-2005.pdf.

– 2007. LWF dismayed by Vatican document despite significant ecumenical results. http://www.lutheranworld.org/News/LWI/EN/2064.EN.html.

McGowan, Mark. 1999. *The waning of the green: Catholics, the Irish, and identity in Toronto, 1887–1922*. Montreal and Kingston: McGill-Queen's University Press.

McLaughlin, K.M. 1985. *The Germans in Canada*. Canada's ethnic groups, 11. Ottawa: Canadian Historical Association.

Meune, Manuel. 2005. Berlin, Canada. *Queen's Quarterly* 112 (2): 283–90.

Nelson, E.C. 1980. *The Lutherans in North America*. Philadelphia: Fortress.

Pfrimmer, David. 1986. Who are the Lutherans? *Ecumenism* (81): 3–7.

Religious Tolerance. 2003. Canadian public opinion polls during 2003. http://www.religioustolerance.org/hom_maro.htm.

Sauer, Angelika E. 1993. A matter of domestic policy? Canadian immigration policy and the admission of Germans, 1945–1950. *Canadian Historical Review* 74 (2): 239–40.

Schmalz, Ron. 2000. A statistical overview of the German immigration boom to Canada, 1951–1957. *Deutschkanadisches Jahrbuch / German-Canadian Yearbook* (2000): 4.

Schultz, Erich R.W. 1966. Tragedy and triumph in Canadian Lutheranism. Lutheran Historical Conference: Essays and Reports 1112–144.

Statistics Canada. 2003. *2001 Census: Analysis Series Religions in Canada*. Ottawa: Statistics Canada.

Steinert, Johannes-Dieter. 1995. *Migration und Politik: Westdeutschland-Europa-Übersee, 1945–1961*. Osnabrück: Secolo Verlag.

Swait, Michael. 2003. Lutheran Church–Canada Planning Conference research survey report. http://www.lutheranchurch.ca/resources/LCC_Survey_2003.pdf.

Tappert, Theodore G. 1959. *The Book of Concord: The confessions of the Evangelical Lutheran Church*. Philadelphia: Fortress.

Threinen, Norman J. 1977. *In search of identity: A look at Lutheran identity in Canada*. Winnipeg: Concorde.

– 1989. *Like a mustard seed: A centennial history of the Ontario District of Lutheran Church–Canada (Missouri Synod)*. Kitchener, ON: Ontario District LCC.

Todd, Mary. 2000. *Authority vested: A story of identity and change in the Lutheran Church–Missouri Synod*. Grand Rapids, MI: Eerdmans.

Vatican. 1999a. Joint declaration on the doctrine of justification. http://

www.vatican.va/roman_curia/pontifical_councils/chrstuni/documents/
rc_pc_chrstuni_doc_31101999_cath-luth-joint-declaration_en.html.
– 1999b. Pontifical Council for promoting Christian unity: Lutheran World
Federation. http://www.vatican.va/roman_curia/pontifical_councils/
chrstuni/sub-index/index_lutheran-fed.htm.
Wisconsin Evangelical Lutheran Synod. WELS statistical reports. http://
www.wels.net/cgi-bin/site.pl?2601&collectionID=827.

8 Canada's Eastern Christians

MYROSLAW TATARYN

If you have driven across the Canadian prairie between Winnipeg and Saskatoon you have noticed how ubiquitous are both the grain elevators and the onion-domed Ukrainian churches. You may have wandered the streets of the Danforth neighbourhood in Toronto and been surprised by storefronts promoting the sale of trinkets and Christian icons. Or perhaps you were exploring Montreal and left the Metro Henri-Bourassa, only to discover Arabic and French signage announcing the Cathedral of St Maron. These encounters signal the vitality of Eastern Christians throughout Canada. However, few Canadians appreciate the complexity of the Eastern Christian world or its particular manifestation in Canada. As a married Ukrainian Catholic priest, I have often faced complete bewilderment when I assert with complete accuracy that I am a Catholic priest and I am married. 'So you must be Orthodox!' is the insistent response of those who think they really understand. 'No, in fact I am a Catholic in union with the pope, but we maintain Orthodox traditions, so we have married priests,' I explain. Bewilderment slowly gives way to grudging acceptance, but seldom understanding. Years ago, while working as a chaplain in a major Toronto health centre I was asked to give the names of a few approachable Orthodox priests who could be called upon to minister to Orthodox patients in the hospital. My response to the simple request bewildered my supervisor: a two-page document providing an outline of which ethnic group and/or Orthodox jurisdiction could be ministered to by which priest – without causing a veritable international incident. This is not to suggest that Eastern Christianity is awash in tribal or provincial antagonisms. Rather, it is an indicator that the terms *Orthodox* and *Eastern Christian* mask very complicated realities and sets of relationships.

Figure 8.1. Protection of the Holy Mother of God Ukrainian Orthodox Church, St Julien, Saskatchewan, hovering over the prairie skyline north of Saskatoon. (Photo by author)

Although Eastern Christians have been part of the Canadian Christian world for over a century, they are in fact little understood and too often overlooked in any discussion of religion in Canada. They present to the student a confusing and rather exotic panoply of ethnicities, religious denominations, and jurisdictions. This chapter is an attempt to bring some clarity and some detail to the very term *Eastern Christian* and to the reality of Eastern Christians in Canada.[1]

The term *Eastern Christian* is undoubtedly problematic and was coined to conglomerate those branches of the Christian world that historically developed quite independent of both the ancient Church of Rome (Roman Catholicism) and the churches of the Reformation. It is, in other words, a term referring to the 'otherness' of these Christian churches: they are other than the Christians of the West (the Christians of the West being the authors of the distinction) (Tataryn 1998).

Christian history begins in the eastern Mediterranean world with the birth of the Christian communities of Jerusalem, Antioch (in today's Syria), and Alexandria (in today's Egypt). Simultaneously, other Christian communities, comprising Jews and others, emerged in the West, most particularly in Rome. The gradual Christianization of the Roman Empire did not reduce this diversity in the early Christian community, but rather led to a formalization of identities and an establishment of hierarchies. As a result, at the Council of Chalcedon, 451, the Christian churches in attendance recognized five major 'sees' (from the Latin word for 'seat,' as in an area under the jurisdiction of a bishop or archbishop) in the Christian world: Rome, Constantinople, Alexandria, Antioch, and Jerusalem. These five centres are viewed as historic 'mother' churches for all other Christian communities.

Significantly, only one of the major sees recognized in this important fifth-century meeting – Rome – is geographically located in the western part of the empire and thus renders all the other churches eastern. For most of the two millennia of Christian history Rome's purview was limited to western Europe; thus, it is closely associated with the development of western European culture. The expansion of the Church of Rome and, after the sixteenth century, the Protestant churches, is a phenomenon that corresponds to the period of European colonial expansion. The other churches, called Eastern, have a much more diverse life. They have historically taken root from the Middle East, south through Egypt to Ethiopia, east through Mesopotamia to China and on to India, and north through Asia Minor to the Balkans and on to the Slavic lands in eastern Europe. This growth was completed by the tenth century and

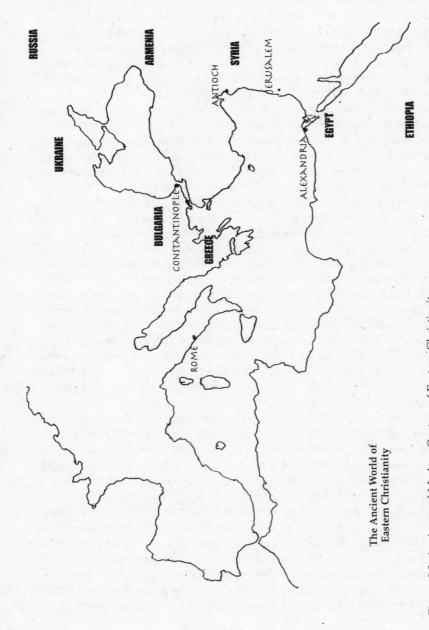

The Ancient World of
Eastern Christianity

Figure 8.2. Ancient and Modern Centres of Eastern Christianity
Note: City names represent ancient Christian centres/sees. Countries of origin for Eastern Christians are designated in
block letters.

involved the indigenization of Christianity within local cultures. As a result, Eastern Christian cultures are deeply marked by local cultural characteristics, such as Ukrainian Easter eggs and Ethiopian liturgical dance.

Some of these Eastern Christian communities were at one time the state religion of the nations in which they were based, but then eventually became a minority, often oppressed and repressed. Members of the Greek Church (with its see in Constantinople – modern-day Istanbul), for example, went from enjoying the privileges of belonging to the imperial church to being a repressed majority under the Turks by the thirteenth century. Similarly, the Russian Orthodox Church had for centuries been the church of the Russian Empire, but it became a repressed and controlled church within the officially communist Soviet empire. As these Eastern churches slipped into a less favourable status vis-à-vis the state in the fifteenth and sixteenth centuries, they were often additionally challenged by the expansion of Roman Catholicism. Struggles between Roman Catholicism and Eastern Christianity over influence in the Balkans and eastern Europe date to the seventh century but became more widespread as a result of the Counter Reformation within Roman Catholicism. The resulting tension often led to the creation of new forms of Eastern Christianity, today referred to as Eastern or 'Greek' (the latter term connotes the early liturgical language, rather than ethnic or national identities) Catholicism. Eastern Catholic churches have maintained their strong ethnic associations, and many of their historic traditions, but have accepted varying aspects of Roman Catholicism. As a result, as a Ukrainian Catholic I am a Catholic priest (in union with Rome) yet I preside at a liturgy that is very similar to that celebrated in a Ukrainian Orthodox Church (which is not in union with Rome), and I am married. There is therefore no easy template by which to describe these churches, and each has been marked by the vicissitudes of its own particular history.

To further complicate matters, dismal social, political, and economic conditions have resulted in almost continual waves of emigration from traditional homelands. This last experience has led many Eastern Christian believers – with their unusually complex and heterodox religious traditions and trajectories of development – to Canadian soil. Although experiencing the loss of their homeland, they attempted to hold on to their religious heritage. The first instance of Eastern Christians in Canada dates from the eighteenth century, when Russian Orthodox clerics came across the Bering Strait to minister to Russian settlers along the Alaskan panhandle and to proselytize the Inuit. There was marginal success among the indigenous people, and most of the Russian settlers gradually moved south into what is today the United States. There was no lasting marker then of Russian Orthodoxy on Canada's west coast. Nonetheless, the Slavic form of Eastern Christianity is the first, and (since the immigration of Ukrainians to Canada in the last decade of the nineteenth century) remains the dominant form of non-Western Christianity in Canada.

Ukrainians in Canada

In Canada, the Ukrainians are certainly the most commonly recognized ethnic group associated with Eastern Christianity. Immigrants from western Ukraine, religiously dominated by Ukrainian (or Greek) Catholicism,[2] began to come to Canada in significant numbers in 1891, in response to the government's promise of free land. A smaller number of immigrants from the Bukovinian region of Ukraine were more commonly adherents of the Orthodox Church under the jurisdiction of Moscow.

Ukrainians in Canada first settled on the prairies and so their churches dot the landscape and their culture has helped form the unique Western Canadian identity. Rooted in an ancient Christian tradition that divided into Eastern Catholic and Eastern Orthodox forms in 1596, these new Canadians mainly adopted the Catholic form. On the vast prairies, however, their initial dilemma was not a choice between Eastern Orthodoxy or Eastern Catholicism, but rather a dire shortage of any clergy. In a publication from 1899, one of the settlers wrote,

> Life here is very good for our bodies; there is no physical deprivation, but what of that, when there are great deprivations of the soul. There is enough to eat, drink, and wear. But our soul is poor, very poor. This is because it has nothing to eat or drink, nothing from which to live, no roof to stand beneath. It can only shelter itself under strangers' roofs and listen to them, but it does not hear and does not understand. (Yereniuk 1989, 110)

Others wrote of the settlers' attempts to continue a regular liturgical life without a cleric present:

> Our poor settlers consulted among themselves and decided to meet every

Sunday and sing at least those parts of the liturgy that were meant to be sung by the cantor (*diak*). Since our house was large enough, that was where the meetings were held. On Sunday mornings everyone hurried to our house the way one would to church ... And so it was that we were able to gratify, at least partially, the longing of our souls. (Yereniuk 1989, 110)

The lack of pastors for the settlements meant that these new Canadians were often subject to proselytizing by Russian Orthodox clerics based in the United States and Protestant missionaries based in Central Canada. The story of the Edna Star colony is a prime example of externally initiated strife. Simply desiring adequate pastoral care, the community received itinerant pastors of both Ukrainian Catholic and Orthodox persuasion (the services would have been essentially identical). The community chose to purchase land and erect a church in the name of parish trustees. However, the Roman Catholic bishop of the area insisted (and threatened sanctions if his wishes were not respected) that the land must be registered in the name of the diocese (consistent with civil regulation at the time). This claim on community property by a 'foreigner' (non-Ukrainian) was perceived as aggressive and passionately denounced by the majority of the community. However, Catholic members objected to the Orthodox claim to make the church, built in 1899, formally Orthodox. The conflicting claims resulted in a protracted series of court cases that were ultimately resolved by a Privy Council decision in London, England, in 1907, granting the land and church to the Orthodox community on the basis of registered ownership of the property by the parish trustees (J. Petryshyn 1985, 130). In this very early crisis the interconnection of religious and ethnic identities was clearly at the forefront.

The confusing question of religious identity meant that the settlers' communities were often susceptible to disreputable figures. For example, in 1903 a 'Bishop' Seraphim was able to claim a reported 55,000 members for his All-Russian Patriarchal Church, unaligned with anyone, despite his public claims to being under the jurisdiction of the Church of Moscow. This confusion facilitated the rise of an Independent Greek Church from the Seraphimite church by drawing faithful out of the orbit of the Ukrainian Catholic Church. Early allies of Seraphim were a group of graduates of the Presbyterian Manitoba College who were able to 'provide wise leadership beyond Seraphim' (Martynovych 1991, 190, 174). Seeking to capitalize on the dearth of Ukrainian Catholic priests and religious anarchy in the settlements, the Presbyterian Home

Figure 8.3. Crossroad markers established by the first Eastern Christian settlers on the prairies are still ubiquitous on country roads.

Missions, in collaboration with former supporters of the Seraphimites, established this 'Protestant Orthodox' Church. Among the organizers were prominent figures in the Ukrainian community: Cyril Genik, an immigration agent; John Bodrug, a teacher; and John Negrych, a teacher and editor of the newspaper *Kanadyisky Farmer* (Canadian Farmer). Established at a synod in Winnipeg on 26 January 1904 with the sponsorship of the Presbyterian Church of Canada, the new church gained great popularity in the period before the First World War; however, it dwindled out of existence by the mid-1920s.

The persistent struggle within the community to sustain religious life, consistent with the community's history and self-identity, led to an acute crisis in the period 1915–18. The result was the creation of a uniquely Canadian Orthodox Church: the Ukrainian (Greek) Orthodox Church of Canada, established in Saskatoon in July 1918 mainly by disaffected Ukrainian Catholics. Thus by the 1920s Ukrainian immigrants and their children were dispersed among three ecclesial entities: the dominant Ukrainian (Greek) Catholic, the emergent Ukrainian (Greek) Orthodox, and the Russian Orthodox whose North American jurisdiction dated to the first eighteenth-century settlers. These three ecclesial units dominated the religious life of the over 170,000 Ukrainian immigrants to Canada between 1891 and 1913 (Martynovych 1991, 3). These settlers overwhelmingly resided in so-called block settlements on the prairie. Although the census of 1921 records that there were 106,721 Ukrainians in Canada, Matiasz comments that in fact 'for many of the immigrants to Canada at the turn of the century national identities were meaningless' (1989, 220).[3] Thus, although ostensibly presented as a unified ethnic group, it is apparent that Ukrainians were divided by religion and terms of ethnic self-identification.

Immigration patterns for Ukrainians have been well documented and discussed. In brief, the first wave of immigration commenced in 1891 and roughly concludes with the end of the First World War. The second period is from the First World War to the end of the Second World War. The census of 1941 indicates that 305,929 persons identified themselves as Ukrainian. Again, given the problems of self-identification, this figure is probably low; however, it will provide a base for comparison with the number of persons self-identifying as either Greek Orthodox or Ukrainian (Greek) Catholic in 1941 (325,793).[4] As the result of periods of concentrated immigration, the number of Ukrainians in Canada increased, but data from the 1971 census allow Yuzyk to suggest that only 52.2 per cent of Ukrainians adhered to either the Ukrainian Catholic or Orthodox Church (Yuzyk 1980, 175). This trend was verified by the more detailed data available from the 2001 Census. The total single- and multiple-ethnic-origin respondents who identified as Ukrainian in 2001 were 1,071,055 (although only 326,195 were single-ethnic-origin respondents to the query on immigrant status). However, when we look at the responses to the question of religious affiliation, there is a sharp drop in the numbers. If we maximize possible affiliation with traditional churches, there are only 539,515 adherents (50.4 per cent). Because both 'Greek Orthodox' and 'Orthodox not included elsewhere' would include non-Ukrainians, the percentage of adherents is in reality well below 50 per cent and probably at a maximum of 25 per cent.[5] Wolowyna notes that 'the addition of multiple ethnicities increased significantly the number of Ukrainians in Canada; it had little or no effect on the number of Ukrainians in the two traditional denominations' (Wolowyna 2001). In other words, Ukrainians, who represent the largest ethnic group in Canada with historical ties to the Eastern Christian churches, have over the years more readily maintained an association with their ethnicity than with their traditional religious affiliation.

Ukrainians have been in Canada for over a century. Over that time they have had to endure discrimination, internment during the First World War, and political and religious conflicts that threatened the community's cohesion. However, they have not merely survived; they have in fact built an extensive network of support institutions to maintain their sense of ethnic identity and cohesion. In 1899 young community activists in Winnipeg organized a 'reading club' to promote education and community advancement independent of narrow denominational interests (Martynovych 1991, 266). Cultural and educational societies sprang up throughout the prairies, and as the number of young men who could benefit from a university education increased, a movement started to establish male residences in Edmonton, Saskatoon, and Winnipeg open to all Ukrainians, regardless of their religious denomination. The Ukrainian community wisely attempted to benefit from an initially progressive public school education policy by nurturing school attendance and the growth of the number of Ukrainian school teachers.[6] The defence and expansion of Ukrainian bilingual schools dominated the community's concerns prior to the First World War. Provincial teachers' associations became extremely important vehicles for community building. The effort to bolster the bilingual schools sometimes resulted in tensions with unsympathetic clergy, who attempted, unsuccessfully, to dissuade manifestations of what they perceived as 'nationalism' among their parishioners (Martynovych 1991, 271). Nonetheless, Martynovych notes that 'Catholic parishes were also the first stable organizations' in many centres, and secular priests (that is, ordained men who were not members of religious orders), when they arrived, facilitated cultural activities (272). Swyripa suggests that the end of bilingual schools in 1917 meant that Ukrainian women assumed a much greater role in the community than prior to the First World War. Citing a 1915 letter from a woman, Swyripa notes, 'Her sex, she said, had to shoulder its domestic and maternal responsibilities, and answer the challenge to Ukrainians' national existence that the abolition of bilingual schools presented' (Swyripa 1993, 52). It seems that the gradually increasing imperative of ethnic self-preservation supplanted community voices for women's equality (56–7). The anti-bilingual schools agenda that 'the greatest object of education is not to teach children to read and write, but to make good citizens of them' (Martynovych 1991, 366) was countered by the institutionalization of the mother's role as nurturer of ethnic identity.

This political agenda of the community was also expressed in print. The first Ukrainian Canadian newspaper was *Kanadyisky Farmer* (Canadian Farmer), established in 1903, and quickly joined by *Ranok* (Morning) in 1906 and *Chervonyi Prapor* (Red Flag) in 1907. The first denominational newspaper, *Kanadyisky Rusyn* (Canadian Ruthenian – the English form of the Latin word used for Ukrainians) was launched in 1911. Still today the Ukrainian community in Canada has numerous Ukrainian-language weeklies and a number of denominational newspapers (all of which are now bilingual).

In the inter-war years the complexity of the political climate in the Ukrainian Canadian community radically intensified. Nationalist groups fought for community influence. One of the most significant community organizations, established in 1927, was the Ukrainian Self-Reliance League, which was born of nationalist intelligentsia, tinged with agrarian socialism, and strongly supported by leaders of the Ukrainian Greek Orthodox Church (Gerus 1991, 158). Its purpose was to enlighten the community, build ethnic cohesion, and support the homeland's struggle for liberation. Other organizations arose as well, all nominally nationalist but ranging in their view of the manner in which the liberation struggle should take place and the role of the churches in community life. While there was much division in the community, Ukrainian Canadians could agree on some things, such as their unanimous condemnation of the Soviet-sponsored Labour-Farmer Temple Association. Disarray among the non-communist organizations was finally, at least nominally, overcome in 1940 with the creation of the Ukrainian Canadian Committee – renamed the Ukrainian Canadian Congress in 1989 – which served as a coordinating agency for Canada's Ukrainian community. The two traditional churches played prominent roles in this organization from its very inception.

Ukrainian communities also quickly engaged in the political life of their new country. Winnipeg, for example, 'has consistently, since 1911, elected Ukrainians to public office' (Wiseman 1991, 348). Ukrainian Canadians have now been elected as provincial premiers (for example, Roy Romanow in Saskatchewan) and have held senior Cabinet positions in provincial and federal governments (for example, Michael Starr as minister of labour under Diefenbaker and Don Mazankowski as deputy prime minister under Mulroney). They have been appointed lieutenant-governors and even governor general (Ramon Hnatyshyn, 1990–5). Ukrainians Walter Tarnopolsky and John Sopinka have made lasting impressions upon Canadian jurisprudence. Yet one of the most important contributions of the Ukrainian community to Canada's political culture has undoubtedly been the concept of multiculturalism. The 'father' of Canada's multiculturalism is undoubtedly Paul Yuzyk (Bociurkiw 1978, especially 104). In his first speech as a parliamentarian on 3 March 1964 he declared,

> The Indians and Eskimos have been with us throughout our history; the British group is multicultural – English, Scots, Irish, Welsh; and with the setting up of other ethnic groups, which now make up almost a third of the population, Canada has become multicultural in fact … In keeping with the ideals of democracy and the spirit of Confederation, Canada should accept and guarantee the principle of the partnership of all peoples who have contributed to her development and progress. (Yuzyk 1987)

His efforts, along with those of Albertan Manoly Lupul and other representatives of Canada's ethnic communities, shifted the focus of the Royal Commission on Biligualism and Biculturalism beyond the two languages and cultures. The fourth volume of the commission's report recommended a federal policy of multiculturalism. On 8 October 1971, Prime Minister Trudeau formally announced in the House of Commons his government's formal adoption of all the recommendations of the fourth volume of the Report.

Today Ukrainian Canadians participate in Canadian public and private life with no sign of lingering discrimination. Their institutions dot the country and enhance both the life of the ethnic community and broader Canadian society.

Greeks in Canada

Winnipeg native Nia Vardalos and her hit movie *My Big Fat Greek Wedding* probably brought the Greek heritage into the consciousness of more people in North America than anything else throughout the over 200 years of Greek presence on this continent. Yet, in the film, that heritage was represented as somewhat quaint and odd. So while the movie was likely a boon for the Greek community in that it ended a long period of virtual popular invisibility, it also promoted flat images of Greek culture and Greek religious tradition.

Historically, Greeks are the ethnic group most strongly associated with Eastern Christianity. From the perspective of the Western Christian world, the largest Christian 'other' was Byzantium, or the Byzantine Empire, the Hellenic inheritor of the ancient Greek civilization. Byzantium flourished throughout the fourth to twelfth centuries while Western Europe underwent the ascendancy of the Germano-Frankish peoples and the Dark Ages. Although many Eastern Christians, most notably Armenian, Assyrian, and Coptic Christians, did not acquiesce to Byzantine power, many people in the West assumed that all Eastern Christians were the children of Byzantium. As local centres of Christian power declined, the Byzantine emperors asserted their control over such centres as Alexandria and Antioch, thus imposing a strong Hellenic facade on relatively autonomous, local, indigenous forms of Christianity.[7] *Greek* often became synonymous with Chalcedonian[8] or Eastern Christianity. When the Byzantine form of Christianity took hold in Slavic lands such as Bulgaria, Serbia, Ukraine, and Russia, the church was often termed a 'Greek' Church. This nomenclature was transported to the New World and thus Ukrainians, Russians, Serbians, and Bulgarians were often viewed as adherents of the 'Greek Church.' However, our focus here will be on ethnic Greek communities that in Canada, rather overwhelmingly, support the Orthodox Church. Currently in Canada most Greeks belong to the Greek Orthodox Metropolis of Canada and are as such under the jurisdiction of the Ecumenical[9] Patriarchate of Constantinople.

The Greek Canadian experience did not commence with the fanfare of free land in the West that enticed Ukrainian settlement. Rather, Greeks arrived for a wide variety of reasons. The first Greek immigrants to Canada left their homes in the late 1820s to escape the hardships of the revolution in Greece against the Turkish colonizers (Chimbos 1980, 22). A more significant period of immigration commenced at the beginning of the twentieth century. Pizanias identifies these pioneers as 'single men who worked as labourers and lived together in or near boarding houses ... Soon after their arrival, some sent for wives from their villages, a few went home to be married, and a rather large number married non-Greek women' (Pizanias 1991, 383). The 1911 Census data showed 3,614 persons of Greek origin – a figure that rose slowly to 11,696 by 1941. However, the largest immigrant growth occurred between 1961 and 1971 when the number grew from 56,475 to 124,475. After 1971, growth stabilized, so that according to the 2001 Census 215,105 Canadians claim single or multiple Greek origins.[10] The nearly inextricable relationship between Greek ethnicity and Greek Orthodoxy is demonstrated in this last census, where 158,305 participants self-identified as Christian Orthodox (73.6 per cent of total Greek ethnic respondents). However, there is a significant divergence between the 91.5 per cent who have single ethnic origin (131,605 of 143,785 identify as Orthodox), compared with only 37.4 per cent (26,695 of 71,325) who have multiple ethnic origin. People of single Greek ethnic origins strongly support close adherence to the traditional religious group, whereas having mixed ethnic origins significantly increases the probability that the respondent will attend another religious community. In other words, Orthodoxy serves to bolster ethnic identity even more in Canada than in Greece. Theodore Saloutos writes about the Greek immigrant to the United States: 'Absence from his ancestral home, the fear that he might never see it again, the thought of losing his nationality and of dying in a strange land, caused him, at least for a time, to embrace his religion with a fervor that he never had in Greece' (Chimbos 1980, 72). Given the brief history of the Greek community in Canada, this dynamic suggests that, although initially identifying with the Greek Orthodoxy is an important element of Greek ethnic identity, this quickly changes with inter-ethnic marriage.

The first organizations of Greek immigrants in Canada were initiated by the clerics of the Greek Orthodox Church. Parish life incorporated philanthropic organizations, youth groups, and cultural and social clubs. In the mid-1920s, the first Canadian chapter of the American Hellenic Educational Progressive Association, a secular Greek cultural organization first founded in the United States in 1922, was organized in Toronto. It did not have mass appeal, but attracted businessmen and professionals (Chimbos 1980, 78). Other organizations followed, including local school groups, labour associations, social service organizations, as well as social clubs or coffeehouses (*kafenion*) (84). Greek Canadians have developed a vibrant press that represent the gamut of the political spectrum. Published in Toronto, Montreal, or Vancouver, these newspapers include *Hellenic Canadian Chronicles*, *Greek Canadian Weekly*, *BHMA*, and *Patrides*. The Greek community has become a strong member of Canada's ethnic mosaic.

Russians in Canada

As mentioned earlier, the first Eastern Christians to arrive in North America and the first to establish an ecclesiastical jurisdiction were the Russian Orthodox. We have already seen that it is difficult to decipher accurately the data on ethnic self-identification of the East Slavic group for the first part of the twentieth century, since attendees at Russian Orthodox services would have included Russians, Ukrainians, Serbs, Romanians, and possibly even Greeks. Most commentators agree, however, that attendance at Russian Orthodox services in that period was not so much an expression of ethnic identity as a historic tie to the church 'in the old country.' The language of the services would have been Slavonic and therefore comprehensible for most East Europeans. Those Ukrainians who came from the territories of the old Russian Empire were also accustomed to attending the Russian Orthodox Church and so upon arrival in Canada they requested services from the Russian Orthodox bishop of San Francisco. Members of these ethnic groups would have attended Russian Orthodox services out of their historic ties to imperial Russia; they were not necessarily ethnically Russian. Most ethnic Russians arriving in Canada in the early part of the twentieth century were in fact Doukhobors. Fleeing religious persecution in tsarist Russia, and with the assistance of Leo Tolstoy, over 7,000 Doukhobors arrived in the North-West Territories (now Saskatchewan) in 1898. Although they originated in Russia, the Doukhobors (literally, the 'Spirit wrestlers') are not an Eastern Christian community in the way I have been using this term. In fact, they are more akin to Anabaptist churches (see Royden Loewen's chapter 9 on Mennonites in this book), who focus strongly on simple, non-materialist living, liturgical minimalism, and celebration of the Bible. Their history is a significant part of the story of Christianity in Canada, especially on the prairies.[11]

Ethnic Russians who would have more closely identified with the Russian Orthodox Church arrived in small numbers in the late nineteenth century. Ancestrally Russian Canadians are highly assimilated into the general population. Census data (with all the provisos mentioned above) show a population of Russians in Canada of approximately (probably just under) 100,000 for the better part of the twentieth century, although it is virtually impossible to draw significant conclusions about their adherence to Russian Orthodoxy. By 2001, only 20,205 single origin respondents identify with the Orthodox Church (28.5 per cent) and only 4.9 per cent of multiple origin respondents identify with the Orthodox Church. Among single origin respondents, almost as many identify as having no religious affiliation (19,425) as identify with Orthodoxy (Statistics Canada 2003). This disengagement of ethnicity and religious affiliation can also be noted in the history of the Russian Orthodox jurisdictions in Canada. There are currently three Orthodox jurisdictions in Canada that have at least a historical connection to the Russian Church. The oldest, and probably smallest (the available data are unreliable), is that of the Patriarchate of Moscow. Today, this community represents twenty-two parishes and missions, most of which are located in Alberta. Its centre is St Barbara's Cathedral in Edmonton, built on the site of the home of Canada's first resident Russian Orthodox priest, Jacob Korchinsky. This particular jurisdiction has consistently maintained its unity with the Patriarchate of Moscow, and its adherents are mainly descendants of original Bukovynian (now in Ukraine) settlers.

The Bolshevik revolution of October/November 1917 had a significant impact on Russian Orthodox life outside the Soviet Union. In response to the suppression of the Russian Orthodox hierarchy in the USSR, a portion of the hierarchy that found itself in western Europe after the revolution declared itself 'The Russian Orthodox Church Outside Russia' (ROCOR). In 1927, a synod held in the Serbian town of at Sremski Karlovtsi established the so-called Russian Synodical Church. Canonically it saw itself as awaiting the return of a properly elected patriarch to the see of Moscow, and it is only since the deterioration of the Soviet Union in 1989 that this church is once more in dialogue with the Church of Moscow to normalize relations. The primate of the Russian Orthodox Church Outside Russia resides in Holy Trinity Monastery in Jordanville, NY, and the church has an extensive network of parishes worldwide. There is a Canadian diocese, although currently it is administratively divided between eastern and western Canada and the responsible bishops reside in the United States. The church has approximately twenty parishes across the country and anecdotal evidence suggests that many of its clergy are converts to Orthodoxy and of non-Slavic ethnicity. Nevertheless, the flavour of the church is strongly Russian, perhaps best symbolized by Holy Trinity Monastery, where all the guest rooms, in addition to icons have photos of the last tsar's family on the walls (this branch of Russian Orthodoxy canonised the tsar and his immediate family in 1981, whereas the Russian Orthodox Church in Russia completed this process in 2000). ROCOR is commonly regarded as the most conservative and emotionally attached to the old Russian Orthodox imperial ideal.

The third jurisdiction is that of the Orthodox Church in America. Again, responding to the situation in the Soviet Union in the 1920s and the increasingly confused state of Orthodoxy in Canada with the birth of the Ukrainian (Greek) Orthodox Church in 1918, many previously Russian Orthodox parishes affiliated with Moscow chose to establish the so-called Metropolia (referring to an administrative or regional unit) of North America. This effectively meant administrative autonomy from their mother church in Moscow, now increasingly manipulated by the Soviet government. This Metropolia, attempting to establish a clear North American (yet simultaneously Russian) identity, went through a number of upheavals with communities joining and leaving. Over the years, its ethnic make-up has varied on the basis of local events and geographic concentrations (Lowig 1989). The continuing state of confusion was even marked in the Metropolia's official name: Russian Orthodox Greek Catholic Church of North America. After a number of initiatives in the 1960s, the Moscow Patriarchate granted the Metropolia the status of an autonomous church in 1970. At its first council, this newly autonomous church renamed itself the Orthodox Church in America. Today this jurisdiction prides itself on having parishes representing various ethnic groups (Russian, Ukrainian, Romanian, Bulgarian, etc.) and 'ethnic associations primarily ... on the level of reminiscences' (217). It sees itself as a church open to all persons, regardless of ethnic origin. Its mission statement clearly identifies it as 'the local autocephalous Orthodox Church,' meaning self-ruling in North America, and grants the church the evangelical goal 'to preach ... to the peoples of North America and to invite them to become members of the Orthodox Church' (Orthodox Church in America 1990).

The Orthodox Church in America has the largest number of adherents in Canada and so has a large network of local communities. Often the parishes have services in English and the members are a mix of persons who have an ancestral connection with Russian or Ukrainian settlers or persons who are converts to Orthodoxy and find that the muted ethnic character of these parishes facilitates their participation in an Orthodox community.

Other Communities

Canada's multicultural mosaic has provided a most fertile terrain upon which many other Eastern Christian communities have been able to build a home. It would not be an exaggeration to suggest that no other country in the world includes such a broad representation of Eastern Christians as does Canada. For the purposes of simplicity, these communities will be divided into three groups: Oriental Orthodox, Arab Orthodox/Catholic, and East European.

Oriental Orthodox refers to those Christians who did not accept the decisions of the Council of Chalcedon in 451. Territorially they developed during the first four centuries of the Common Era, in southern Egypt, Armenia, areas of East Syria, and Ethiopia (points more peripheral to Constantinople, thus designated Oriental). Today members of all of these groups have very recently migrated to Canada. Within the Oriental Orthodox community, 67 per cent of Syrians,[12] 65.5 per cent of Egyptians, and 53.6 per cent of Armenians have arrived in Canada since 1971 (Statistics Canada 2003). The Ethiopian community is even newer: 73.3 per cent of single Ethiopian origin Canadians arrived after 1981, and 68.3 per cent of the total Ethiopian populace in Canada (including Muslims, Christians, and others) arrived here after 1981. Few Canadians realize that Ethiopia has been an officially Christian state since the fourth century, accepting Christianity from Alexandria (Egypt). Indeed Ethiopian Christians claim to have over 35 million members of their church, and that would make them the second-largest Orthodox Church in the world (Angelfire). Ethiopian Christians are establishing communities in urban centres across Canada and at times are attracting Jamaican Rastafarians[13] (Magocsi 1999, 499). Canada is home to a population of over 20,000 single-ethnic-origin Egyptians, of whom almost half self-identify as Orthodox (9,870 of 26,150). As we have seen earlier, the relative number decreases with multiple ethnic origins (2,785 of 15,160). Nonetheless, Orthodox Egyptians (or Copts) number the largest religious group among single-ethnic-origin Egyptians. The religious leader in many of these communities has come to play a role far beyond that of spiritual head. Magocsi notes that this role has 'expanded to include that of organizer, provider of social aid, and promoter of cultural traditions. The religious institutions receive more support from the community than do socio-cultural ones' (460). However, even here (as is common with many immigrant groups) 'attendance is highest immediately after the immigrant arrives in this country' (460). A similar situation exists for Armenians. Among single-ethnic-origin Armenians (total 27,175), 16,250 or 59.8 per cent identify as Orthodox. Again, this relative strength declines in multiple origin respondents (30.1 per cent), albeit not as dramatically as with the Egyptian sample. Among Syrians, the number of Oriental Orthodox is difficult to ascertain, since a significant proportion of Syrians belong to the Orthodox Church or Melkite (Greek) Catholic Church. Of note in the Canadian scene is the fact that the strongest religious adherence is not to either form of Orthodoxy but to Roman Catholicism (38.7 per cent of all respondents and 34.5 per cent of single-ethnic-origin respondents). The second strongest religious group represented within the Syrian Canadian community is Islam and thus Orthodox Christians are in third place.

Arab Christians who are either Orthodox or Eastern Catholic can be found among those identifying themselves as Syrian, Lebanese, or Palestinian on the Canadian census. Reportedly the first Arab immigrant to Canada was the nineteen-year-old Lebanese Abraham Bounadere, who arrived in Montreal in 1882 (Abu-Laban 1980, 1). The Arab population in Canada grew very slowly, although significant numbers had already arrived by 1970. Among single origin Lebanese Canadians, of which there were 93,895 in 2001, 11,750 identify as Orthodox (12.5 per cent). In addition, those Lebanese who are Melkite or Maronite Catholic would fall within the 35,135 who identified as Catholic. The Melkites are those formerly Orthodox Christians who, like Ukrainian Catholics, entered into union with Rome. The Maronites are a Christian community that lived in isolation in the Lebanese mountains and preserved their unique form of Christianity in spite of first Orthodox and then Muslim dominance.[14] The Melkite Catholics arriving in Montreal in 1892 were accompanied by their own priest, Father Boutros Shamy, and they celebrated their liturgies in Notre-Dame de Bonsecours (Abu-Laban 1980, 133). The Melkite communities have had a bishop since 1981. Currently the Canadian Catholic Conference of Bishops suggests there are approximately 9,600 Melkite Catholics in Canada, in eight parishes or missions (Canadian Conference of Catholic Bishops, 2008). The number of Maronite Catholics is smaller, at 4,100.[15] Although the first parish was established in Toronto in the 1920s (Abu-Laban 1980, 135), they are concentrated mainly in Quebec. Today they have fourteen parishes or missions. Palestinian Orthodox Christians do not constitute a significant proportion of the Palestinian Canadian community (10.8 per cent of single ethnic origin); however, this community is noteworthy since most people identify Palestinians exclusively with Islam. Although Syrian Canadians were mentioned above, it is important to note that the Syrian or, more accurately, Antiochian Orthodox Church has an established network of twenty parishes across the country. These communities date back to the 1890s when they were part of the Russian Orthodox Church's Syrian Mission; now they are organized under the Antiochian Patriarchate. Magocsi notes that early Syrian communities often 'related more to its Canadian religious counterpart than to its homeland compatriots' (1999, 1243), which practically meant a high degree of religious assimilation – that is, becoming Roman Catholic, Russian Orthodox, or Anglican. However, post-war immigration has often increased the size of the Orthodox or Melkite communities sufficiently that the parishes are able to operate in Arabic, whereas previously they functioned in English and French (1245).

The third and final group is east Europeans such as Bulgarians, Macedonians, Romanians, Serbs, Slovaks, and Yugoslavs. In all of these communities there are a significant number of Eastern Christians, as reflected in table 8.1.

Bulgarians, many of whom were ethnically Macedonian Slavs, first arrived in Canada in 1903. The largest group settled in Southern Ontario, although many gradually moved west to work on the railway. The first Orthodox priests arrived in 1907 (Magocsi 1999, 289). Serbians began arriving in Canada prior to the First World War and the first parish was established in Regina in 1912 (1144). Tensions within all these Eastern European communities over their relationship with the mother church in a communist state often led to deep divisions. Serbs, Bulgarians, and Romanians at various times after the Second World War had competing communities in Canada, depending on whether their members wished to maintain ties with the mother church or sever them as a sign of anti-communist community sentiment.

Following what is emerging as a general trend, adherence to an Eastern Christian Church is strong among single-ethnic-origin respondents

Table 8.1. Eastern Christians from eastern Europe, 2001

	Total pop (% Orthodox)	Single ethnic origin (% Orthodox)	Multiple ethnic origin (% Orthodox)
Bulgarian	15,190 (50.8)	8,465 (71.9)	6,730 (24.1)
Macedonian	31,265 (69.1)	16,790 (85.0)	14,475 (50.6)
Romanian ·	131,830 (31.1)	53,320 (63.7)	78,505 (8.9)
Serb	55,540 (76.0)	39,205 (89.8)	16,330 (42.6)
Yugoslav	65,505 (22.7)	26,880 (43.0)	38,625 (8.6)

Source: Statistics Canada (2001).
Note: Census data for Slovaks are not available. However, Canadian Conference of Catholic Bishops (2000) states that there are 10,000 Eastern Catholic Slovaks in Canada.

but weakens in the multiple-ethnic-origin group. There is, however, a striking variation in the degree of decline: Macedonians and Serbs do not lose touch with their Orthodox affiliation as readily as Romanians and Yugoslavs. Vasiliadis comments that the 'Orthodox Church has always been a primary parameter of nationalism in Eastern Europe and the Mediterranean ... Religion has always been as strong a political formula in Macedonia as nationalism' (1989, 187). In fact, he suggests that the establishment of the ethnically Macedonian, Bulgarian Orthodox parish in Toronto in 1911 was a vehicle to 'repulse the efforts of the Greeks, Catholics, Protestants and Canadian society' in assimilating the fledgling Macedonian community (188). This role of the Macedonian parish, albeit affiliated of necessity with the Bulgarian Orthodox Church, as protector of Macedonian identity meant that tensions were inherent in the community between the laity and their ecclesial leadership, usually perceived as 'Bulgarian government representatives' (222). This tension resulted in 1940 in a split in the Toronto community between those more inclined to accept pro-Bulgarian clergy and those more resolutely opposed to such influences (Petroff 1995, 144). Strife continued among the communities and their relationship with the official Bulgarian Orthodox Church in Bulgaria (Magocsi 1999, 291). Nonetheless, the religious affiliation within the Macedonian community sustained their ethnic self-identification.

Transforming Identities

Upon arrival in Canada, most Eastern Christians closely associate ethnicity and religion. However, the connection is neither necessarily absolute nor enduring. For many of the identified ethnic groups, 'Orthodox' or 'Eastern Catholic' would have been a fundamental char- acteristic of their ethnic identity upon arrival in Canada. This may explain the high level of adherence among single-ethnic-origin repre- sentatives and new immigrants in the groups I have discussed. How- ever, the significant slippage that we often see in later generations or in multiple-ethnic-origin respondents suggests that the degree to which adherence to the traditional church marks ethnic identity declines, and at times quite dramatically so. Moreover, the very nature of both reli- gious practice and ethnic identity may change over time. In his study of ethnic identity, Wsevolod Isajiw suggested that the attributes identified as 'characteristic of the specific ethnic group are present among second or subsequent generations,' but they 'may or may not be the same as those found among the first generation' (1990, 34).

Ann Swidler has suggested that religion should be viewed as part of a cultural 'tool-kit' that provides resources for individuals and communities to negotiate their identities and actions (1986, 273). The high incidence of attachment to an ancestral church among first-gen- eration and single-ethnic-origin Canadians suggests that these reli- gious communities ground a new community and its extension in a new land over time. However, as the group accommodates to the new setting and its members commence to intermarry, the role of religion in the life of the individual and the community changes. Those who maintain a connection with their traditional church are far more likely to be children of single ethnic parents than of ethnically mixed marriages.

What aspects of the ancestral church prove less useful for individuals and communities as they negotiate their identities in new settings? Although we are considering an array of disparate ethnic groups and contexts, it is possible to identify several consistent factors that compli- cate the retention of re-created Eastern Christian faith traditions in Can- ada: community divisions over calendrical debates, use of the ethnic language in church services, unclear connection to established Cana- dian churches, a symbol system that is not easily transferable to the Canadian context, the traditional power of the clergy, and a dominant patriarchy that stifles the equalization of gender relations. Readers will notice that homosexuality, same-sex marriages, and homosexual clergy are not mentioned in this account of the emerging issues facing these Christians. While these issues are hotly debated in many of the other denominations and traditions discussed in this book, Eastern Christians have yet to address these matters openly in their churches or at the national level of their denominations.

Calendar

Many Eastern Christians arrived in Canada with not only a unique ecclesiastical foundation, which conceivably could easily be accommodated within the array of Canadian Christian churches, but also with a unique ecclesiastical calendar.[16] For the first millennium of the Common Era, Christians in the Roman Empire commonly used the Roman calendar of Julius Caesar (thus called Julian). In the sixteenth century astronomers suggested that the calendar was in fact slightly inaccurate and so in 1582 Pope Gregory XIII decreed the adoption in western Europe of the adjusted calendar, now termed the Gregorian. Orthodox countries did not accept the papally decreed corrected calendar. Although the Melkite Church had adopted the Gregorian calendar (the dominant calendar in use around the world) at the end of the nineteenth century, and the Syriac Church allowed their compatriots in North America to move to this calendar in the 1930s, the dominant Ukrainian churches steadfastly held to the Julian calendar until the 1960s. Today, the scene is diverse. Some churches have adopted the civil (Gregorian) calendar, others use the civil calendar for fixed feasts and the Julian calculation for Easter, and a third group holds to the Julian calendar. Such diversity even exists within a single denomination: the Ukrainian Catholics do not have a consistent calendar for all their parishes. Although the question of calendar may seem a simple matter of astronomical accuracy, it has in fact resulted in great tensions and antagonism within the various churches, perhaps because calendrical debates become lightning rods for other tensions in these ethno-religious communities related to power and prestige.

Although the controversy exists throughout the world, in Canada this question is especially divisive for Greek and Ukrainian parishes. Among Greek 'old calendarists,' loyalty to the Julian calendar is most often a sign of a conservative attachment to Orthodox practices and a rejection of what is regarded as an accommodation to the 'secular' world (Chimbo 1980, 96). They are a minority within the Greek community and have ecclesiastically aligned themselves with the Russian Orthodox Church Outside Russia (Orthodox Wiki). Although clearly beginning as a conservative Greek movement, this group today (in North America at least) has taken on many of the demographic characteristics of their compatriot Russian arm: a high number of non-Greek and non-Russian converts, a claim to an 'authentic,' pan-national Orthodoxy, a very exclusivist attitude towards other Christians, and a maintenance of the traditional liturgical language (liturgical Greek or Slavonic). Moves to accept the Gregorian calendar in Ukrainian Canadian communities began in the 1960s on the prairies. Parishes of mostly second- and third-generation Canadians were gradually favouring the adoption of the Gregorian calendar. While no officially binding decisions were made, parishes led by the two dominant male religious orders (Order of St Basil or Basilians and Congregation of the Redeemer or Redemptorists) haphazardly began to move to the Gregorian calendar. In eastern Canada, where post–Second World War immigrants dominated, the Julian calendar was and still is dominant. Although Canada was spared some of the excesses of this conflict experienced in the 1970s in the United States, many parishes continue to be divided over this issue. Most recently, the Cathedral Parish in Saskatoon revisited the calendar dilemma, debating adoption of the Gregorian calendar, adoption of a unique calendar proposed by the pastor, or continuing to function with the Julian calendar while also holding services on Christmas and Easter according to the Gregorian calculation. When this issue surfaces in these communities, of course, it becomes enmeshed in historic and new tensions over language, cultural heritage, and the appropriate relationship with the now free church in Ukraine. The Ukrainian Orthodox Church in Canada seems comparatively impervious to this conflict, seeing its preservation of the Julian calendar as an assertion of the authenticity of its ancient Ukrainian Christian tradition. Among many Ukrainian communities then, adhering to the Julian calendar is perceived as a method for maintaining a unique ethnic and ecclesiastical identity. Seemingly trivial issues to the outsider take on critical significance to the community, challenging it to struggle with the question of what is and is not central to its religious identity in the new cultural context of Canada.

Language

Beyond calendrical questions, Orthodox communities dispute the relationship between their ethnic heritage and their Orthodoxy. Syrian Orthodox Christians arrived in Canada in the period before the First World War and were served by the Syrian Mission of the Russian Church. In the inter-war period there were 'sharp disputes over maintenance of loyalty to the Russian Orthodox Church as opposed to entering the jurisdiction of the Antiochian Patriarchate' (Abu-Laban 1980, 132). This conflict sharply split the community in Montreal. Similarly, political opposition to or acceptance of Orthodox churches in Soviet-dominated eastern Europe often translated into conflicts between Bulgarian and Rumanian Orthodox communities in Canada. While today these hostilities seem to have subsided, the previous discord meant that many members left for other Christian churches or ceased to participate in any church at all.

The relationships among ethnic language retention, ethnic identity, and adherence to a traditional church are complex. Although 'ethnic language has been often considered one of the most socially significant ethnic patterns' (Isajiw 1990, 49), exactly how it is to be gauged is unclear. The question is further complicated by imprecise definitions of all the terms involved: how much use of a given language constitutes retention? is ethnic identity a matter of self-perception alone? and what in fact constitutes adherence to a religious community (regular attendance, financial support, self-identification)? Once more, Eastern Christians do not present a consistent pattern. Although Arab Christians quickly adopted English and French as liturgical languages, such accommodation was not always sustained. St Elijah's Parish in Ottawa also returned to the use of Arabic, almost exclusively, whereas Montreal's St-Saveur Melkite Parish continues to favour French. The return to the use of Arabic often had to do with an influx of new Arab immigrants (Abu-Laban 1980, 142). Abu-Laban concludes, 'These religious institutions have been flexible regarding their language of worship and this has, undoubtedly, enhanced their adaptive role vis-à-vis Arab Canadians' (143). For Greek Orthodox Canadians the relationship between language retention, ethnic identity, and church attendance is unclear. Although generally the Greek community is marked by language retention and a strong sense of ethnic identity (which typically involves self-identification as Orthodox), in one study of Greeks in Montreal this did not mean high levels of church attendance. In fact, although 57 per cent of respondents used Greek at home, had Greek spouses (94 per cent), and attended mostly Greek events (80 per cent), only 13 per cent of the respondents went to church every Sunday (Gavaki 1991, 374). This is not to suggest that the respondents' self-identification as Orthodox is disputable; rather, the very sense of being Orthodox probably cannot be identified simply with church attendance. Similarly, language retention in this context cannot easily be associated with the liturgical language (Greek) but rather with the overall place of language in the community's construction of its self-identity. Being Greek would seem to include maintaining ethnic familial and social ties, self-identifying with Orthodoxy, and language retention, but not necessarily church attendance.

For the Ukrainian community, language retention or loss often corresponds closely to ethnic identity and religious association. Isajiw has noted, 'For Ukrainians in particular, the language seems to have a special significance as mother tongue. In the second generation, Ukrainians reported the highest rate of language retention as mother tongue of all groups' (Isajiw 1990, 88). The high degree to which Ukrainians wish to retain their mother tongue is confirmed by Kuplowska and it is associated with a desire to 'maintain traditions and customs' (Kuplowska 1980, 153). Finally, language retention, ethnic identity, and adherence to traditional churches have been validated in the study of Ukrainians. David Millett has found that 'the church's continued use of the Ukrainian language "has provided a core around which organizations devoted to fine arts, recreation and politics have clustered" ... [However] as a result of greater use of English, changes in language habits were often accompanied by transfers to English language churches such as the Roman Catholic or United Church' (Kalbach and Richard 1980, 83).

The traditional churches often provide one of the few venues in which the language can be practised regularly. Kuplowska found that outside of the home, the greatest use of Ukrainian takes place with 'clergy and close friends.' However, this research also suggests that this venue is becoming less significant: 'One-fourth of the Ukrainian sample claimed no association with any church' (Kuplowska 1980, 151). As a result Kuplowska suggests the 'Ukrainian-language churches will gradually disappear' (153). What this prognosticator was unable to foresee was the radical political change in eastern Europe with the concomitant new wave of Ukrainian immigration from Yugoslavia, Poland, and, finally, Ukraine. The last especially has meant that Ukrainian churches in Canada have been able to address a perennial clergy deficit by staffing parishes with newly immigrated priests from Ukraine. The result is a rather anomalous situation: parishes that have effectively migrated to English as the liturgical language are now led by clergy who speak only Ukrainian. The implications of this extraordinary turn of events are still unclear. Nonetheless, even the Ukrainian Orthodox Church in Canada, which has steadfastly maintained Ukrainian as its sole liturgical language, has since 2005 (and after years of debate) begun to consider developing bilingual liturgical texts for use in Canadian churches. This new openness indicates that the church is attempting to accommodate the increasing number of new Ukrainian-speaking immigrants and clergy as well as to continue to cultivate Ukrainian literacy among its Canadian-born members.

Symbolic Worlds

Another source of tension for Eastern Christian communities and their adherents in Canada is the lack of popular understanding of how the Eastern Christian churches fit into the Christian family so dominated in Canada by the many western European forms of Christianity. From the time of their first arrival in Canada, the Eastern Christians experienced varying degrees of prejudice and thus socio-economic discrimination. The Eastern Christian appeared in Canada as what anthropologists term the 'other'; that is, the dominant Western Christian communities (Roman Catholics and Protestants) perceived Eastern Christians to be in dire need of Christianization and civilization (the two were thought to be concomitant, as Bramadat and Seljak indicate in the first chapter of this book). Clearly, this notion was as much attached to their ethnic origin as it was to their religious forms. The ostensible inadequacies of Ukrainians and their form of Christianity were unequivocally articulated by many a commentator (Olender 1989, 191–3). This patronizing attitude was a product of the Anglo-Celtic imperial ideal of Canada's destiny and, hence, a response to the Slavic ethnic identity of the immigrants. Anglo-Canada was very much in concord with the Presbyterian Church's diagnosis that these peasants were to be Christianized since they were ignorant victims of 'priestcraft' and 'superstitious ceremony' (191). Such slanders readily affixed themselves to Ukrainians because their liturgical forms appeared to some outsiders to be far more exotic than those of Protestants or even Roman Catholics. 'The Rev. Dr A.J. Hunter, a medical missionary to Ukrainians in the Teulon, Manitoba, area for over forty years, decried the Eastern-rite liturgy as the supreme form of ritualistic worship; Rome "pales before it" and Anglicanism "becomes almost invisible"' (193). Although these criticisms gradually grew milder among established Western Christian commentators, Eastern Christians have continued to be misunderstood and mistreated. In a 1971 study of social studies textbooks in Ontario schools, McDiarmid and Pratt found 'negative social attitudes towards and stereotyping of

Figure 8.4. The twelfth-century Vysh-horod Icon of the Mother of God (aka Vladimirska), one of the most famous creations of Eastern Christians.

Arabs, which of course would have included Eastern Christians' (Abu-Laban 1980, 90).

Canadians, and Westerners in general, tend to associate Christianity and related favourable qualities with Western rather than with Eastern Christians. The core curriculum of the United Church of Canada's Sunday school textbook does not even acknowledge the existence of Arab Christians. If and when their existence is acknowledged, Eastern Christians do not receive favourable treatment. A recent survey of Ontario school teachers, for example, shows that 'the picture given of Eastern Christians was one of rigid dogmatism, deceit and hypocrisy – in short, of Byzantine deviousness' (Abu-Laban 1980, 90–1).

Arab Christians are therefore doubly condemned. First, Christian Arabs suffer from 'guilt by association' because most Arabs are Muslim (McDonough and Hoodfar 2005, 137–8). Then, if recognized as Christian, they are denigrated as somehow unduly conservative and dishonest. As subsequent generations desire to enter the Canadian mainstream, adherence to an unusual, albeit Christian, church does not facilitate easy entry into the dominant socio-cultural and political environment. In their legitimate pursuit of social and economic latitude, some people may therefore become attracted to churches – such as the Anglican or United churches – that are more closely identified with the cultural mainstream.

More generally, it is important to consider the fact that the broader Canadian culture is clearly a product of Western Christian dominance. The Ukrainian onion-domed churches come from a very different cultural setting and symbolic reality. Upon entering an Eastern Christian church, one might be struck by its 'foreignness.' It is physically, visually, and aromatically different from a Western Christian church and from what a secular North American would expect to encounter in a Christian church. This meeting of symbolic worlds has produced awe and admiration but also conflict, cross-fertilization, and, one must admit, confusion.

Many adaptations to the North American setting have sparked critics to charge that Orthodox communities have lost their soul in conforming to what they perceive as Western Christian styles. Keleher argues that iconography is 'a crucial expression of Orthodox approaches to God, the universe, the nature of humanity, salvation and union with God' (1989, 47), and so cannot be altered in its classical style to the new setting. He provides examples of how the symbolic world of Orthodoxy has been adapted to the Canadian mainstream in ways that betray 'authentic' Orthodoxy. Keleher aims a particularly pointed barb at the iconography that has developed as a product of what he calls 'a pseudo-renewal like that of Roman Catholicism, marked by a secularized worship and the loss of a sense of sacredness.' 'These churches,' he writes, 'invariably seem bare and empty' (51). Without passing judgement on Keleher's assessment, one finds that his critique does suggest a radical dissonance between the symbolic world of Orthodoxy and the contemporary Canadian (Western) world. This dissonance is the source of internal crisis within Eastern Christian churches. To what extent should Eastern Christian churches adapt to the Canadian cultural and symbolic environment? Keleher suggests that iconography of a given style is normative for 'authentic' Orthodoxy and yet he implicitly admits that many do not find that this tradition bears cultural or symbolic meaning. Younger generations of Eastern Christians find themselves increasingly distanced from the ordered sacred space identified by Goa[17] and Keleher. Both authors seem to associate adherence to Eastern Christianity with the maintenance of historic forms. Consistency with the past is the barometer that demonstrates, for them, an 'authentic' Eastern Christianity.

Not all Orthodox Christians agree. In a discussion of traditional architecture, Zuk prefers to see the dynamic of creative interaction and evolution. His study concludes positively: 'A new stylistic interpretation, in the contemporary manner, and the development of new creative configuration and articulation types must be aimed for if this tradition is to continue' (Zuk 1989, 46). Swyripa suggests that even in the structuring of interior space, innovation is already coming to dominate. However, the manner in which this space is being constructed does not reflect simple identification with the home country, or the ancestral church, or even the new world. Adaptation implies uniting elements of the inherited with elements of the new setting, producing something that self-identifies with the inherited but is in fact a new form of it and more consonant with the dominant culture (cf. Isajiw 1990, 34). Swyripa asserts, 'The mobilization of history and expressions of secular consciousness in the Prairie region's (im)migrant churches reveal that many ethnic groups identify simultaneously as diasporas, in communion with the homeland, and as Canadians with roots in the local community' (Swyripa 2004, 341). Isajiw and Swyripa would agree that the very pliability of the symbolic world of Eastern Christianity allows it to adapt to the Canadian setting and thus to sustain itself as both a fitting representative of the inherited tradition that is simultaneously able to adapt itself and its historic forms and messages to the new context.

Structures of Power

One might argue that the two most difficult and intimately interrelated challenges to the survival of Eastern Christianity relate to power within the communities. Perhaps as a function of their cultural origins, perhaps due to common historic developments within the representative churches, the issues of clergy power and a dominant patriarchy confound the Eastern Christian churches in Canada. On both of these issues there is a clear disconnect with the attitudes of the dominant society and even with many other Christian churches in Canada. Gavaki notes that within Montreal's Greek community 'the main target of challenge and dispute is the authority and the power of the father' (1991, 371). This preferential status for males corresponds to reports on family life among Arabs (Abu-Laban 1980, 165) and Ukrainians (Swyripa 1993, 252). These communities have historically supported the dominance of men in roles of institutional decision making. This view is clearest when one focuses on the churches and how their roles of authority function. While all Western churches – Roman Catholic and Protestant – have engaged during the last hundred years in public discussions about the ordination of women (with mixed results), no Eastern Christian Church (Catholic or Orthodox) has even considered this issue.

Closely related to this matter, of course, is the fact that many Eastern Christian churches in Canada continue to struggle over the exercise of the clergy's influence in non-religious activities. Chimbos describes the priest's prestige in the Greek community, which would correspond to the reality in many other Eastern Christian communities: 'The priest, by virtue of his ecclesiastical appointment, has been the head of the parish, a position which involves civic as well as spiritual leadership' (1980, 80). Although this is the inherited model that once functioned to support and encourage the homeland community in its struggles against an oppressive majority (for Greeks the Turks, for Ukrainians the Poles), today in Canada the power of the priest is a source of great tension. 'The centralized authority of the priest has been resented by many Greek Canadians who see it as unnecessary intervention in the civic affairs of the Greek community' (Chimbos 1980, 91). Even in the Ukrainian community where there is an extensive secular community infrastructure and an ostensibly non-religious coordinating body (the Ukrainian Canadian Congress), its first leaders were heavily associated with church life. The first president (1940) was the rector of the Ukrainian Catholic Cathedral in Winnipeg, Rt Rev. W. Kushnir, and the vice-presidents were the lawyer Wasyl Swystun, one of the initiators of the establishment of the Ukrainian Orthodox Church, and S.W. Sawchuk, a Ukrainian Orthodox priest (Dreisziger 1991, 339). The role of the lay, but church-associated, Brotherhood of Ukrainian Catholics and the Ukrainian Self-Reliance League as senior members of the congress confirms this religious influence. However, it must be noted that the Ukrainian (Greek) Orthodox Church in Canada, established in 1918, had a noted anti-clerical strain, born of its discontent with the episcopacy and priests of the Ukrainian Catholic Church. Thus, although the church had its clergy and hierarchy, there has often been a historical tension between the clergy and the lay-dominated 'consistory' – the body that ostensibly governs the church (Yereniuk 1989).

Nonetheless, in these male-dominated and often highly clericalized communities, the largest marginalized group are women. This social ostracization is accentuated and evidenced by the common precept and practice among Eastern Christian communities barring women from the area around the church altar (Kucharek 1989, 73). This stricture is still often cited, but with discretion, to validate the lack of a role for women near the altar. With the arrival of Ukrainian-born clergy in Canada, the issue of women's participation in liturgy is retreating even more into the background. Although these new clergymen are young, they come from a cultural environment where women are totally excluded from any formal liturgical role. Consequently, instances emerge where Canadian women who have historically changed the altar cloths are being permitted only to iron the altar cloths, which are then replaced on the altar by the priest.

Although the effect of such strictures and conduct on the level of adherence among young women to the churches has not been studied, a quick survey of parish women's organizations reveals an aging membership. The authors of *Building the Future*, prepared for the Ukrainian Canadian Congress, reflected on the exclusion of women from decision making in community organizations:

> The very limited impact of the women's movement in mainstream society ... on our organizations and their members [is] a major reason for women's historical and continued subordinate role in community life ... By exclud-

ing women from decision-making structures we fail to recognize issues that are of particular concern to women. This limits the involvement of women in our community's development, since many women choose to work in the mainstream women's movement where their specific concerns are addressed. (Swyripa 1993, 253)

The lack of desire by religious leaders to address this question in any systematic way will not likely bode well for their communities.

Creating New Identities

Notwithstanding sources of stress and tension, Eastern Christianity continues to live and even thrive in Canada. I would like now to offer three examples of how Eastern Christians have adapted to the contemporary Canadian scene and are dealing with the question of ethnicity.

In January 1987 an idealistic young couple, Roberto and Jane Ubertino, chose to live out their Christian vocation with an evangelical fervour and tension. Together with some friends and volunteers they opened the St John the Compassionate Mission in the midst of a public housing project in a downtown neighbourhood in Toronto. The mission, which at the time was associated with the Ukrainian Catholic Eparchy of Toronto, endeavoured to create a prayerful environment in the midst of a troubled community; it would be a place where a Christian devotion to silence and prayer combined with the gospel call to service. Initially serving as a place to drop in, receive a warm meal once a week in a community setting, and perhaps participate in vespers or divine liturgy, the mission grew into a vibrant community of compassion and prayer, now in communion with the ecumenical patriarch. While it began in close relationship with the Ukrainian Catholic suburban parish of St Demetrius in Weston, today the mission is part of the Carpatho-Russian Orthodox Diocese and constitutes its 'Canonical, Pan-Orthodox, all English-speaking parishes.'[18] At both St John's Mission and the parish community of St Silouan the Athonite, one experiences no sense of ethnic association, although the Orthodox reality would be clear to people familiar with this tradition. The community is an interesting experiment in what is perhaps a uniquely indigenous Canadian Orthodox parish.

Father Larry Kondra's experience in the St John the Compassionate community led him to start a similar project called Welcome Home in a troubled neighbourhood in downtown Winnipeg, Manitoba. Welcome

Home also attempts to witness Eastern Christianity (specifically, Ukrainian Catholicism) in a Canadian urban setting, but here, given the dominance of an Aboriginal population in the area, the residents of Welcome Home have tried to wed certain Eastern Christian elements with aspects of indigenous culture. The prominent placement of an icon of seventeenth-century Aboriginal Roman Catholic Kateri Tekakwitha and the use of the traditional four colours in the chapel to mark the four directions are examples. Both the Toronto and Winnipeg communities provide promising examples of re-rooting Eastern Christianity in a contemporary Canadian milieu.

A unique experiment in Eastern Christianity exists in a small renovated building (formerly a radio station) in Saskatoon, Saskatchewan. Unlike any community mentioned thus far, Holy Covenant Evangelical Orthodox Church has no ethnic ties to Eastern Christianity. It is a community of former Protestant Canadians who gradually came to identify themselves as Orthodox, in spiritual communion with the ancient Eastern Christian churches. The genesis of this community lies with the evangelical Protestant group Campus Crusade for Christ and the efforts of Peter Gilquist, who in 1973 established the New Convenant Apostolic Order in Chicago. Subsequently this community went through spiritual searching and concluded that in order to be faithful to the Patristic Church it needed to grow closer to the historical expression of that church as they saw it, which could be found among the Orthodox churches. However, this insight led to ruptures among congregations and in 1988 some members of the movement joined the Antiochian Orthodox Church (which is the foundation of the Saskatoon parish of St Vincent of Lérins). Others remained as the Evangelical Orthodox Church (EOC). In 2002 many of the remaining EOC parishes in the United States entered into the Orthodox Church of America. Once again, the Holy Covenant community in Saskatoon steadfastly maintained its autonomy. Today there are only four parishes of the Evangelical Orthodox Church (O Great Mystery 2004), and one of them is the Holy Covenant community. This parish displays a fascinating mix of Eastern Christian iconography and theological sensibility, with traditional Mennonite hymnography, evangelical witnessing, and an interesting form of the Liturgy of St John Chrysostom. There is no reference to any specific ethnic background in this community; in fact, one might say it is thoroughly mainstream Canadian. Yet it attempts to express a very grassroots and contemporary form of Eastern Christianity. It has struggled with the question of women in the hierarchy and has chosen to limit women to the deaconate (being validated in this view by historic precedent within the Eastern churches). The community is a neighbourhood church and although its bishop, Jerold Gliege, has ongoing contact with other EOC parishes, it is essentially a church of the neighbourhood community. As a result, its future beyond its Saskatoon neighbourhood is unclear.

While the previous examples show how Orthodoxy can be defined apart from its traditional ethnic frameworks or in relation to a more generalized Canadian ethnicity, the experience of St Demetrius the Great Martyr Byzantine Ukrainian Catholic Church in Toronto demonstrates how Orthodoxy and ethnicity still inform one another in certain communities. Researchers have found that religious institutions can have an immense impact on 'keeping the immigrant's personal association within the boundaries of the ethnic community' (Kalbach and Richard 1980, 81). There is perhaps no better example in Canada of a religious institution providing its members with activities across the whole age spectrum than St Demetrius. Although the above mentioned communities all have ways of allowing their members to live out their lives in the context of the faith, most often these will be in the form of a parish sponsoring language classes, a Saturday school, and perhaps a seniors' club or apartment building. Since its inception in 1959, the St Demetrius community has attempted to demonstrate that an Eastern Christian parish can be wholly integrated into the Canadian social fabric while maintaining its Eastern Christian life and respecting its Ukrainian heritage.

St Demetrius Parish began as a mission of the Toronto Cathedral parish of St Josaphat and sought to address the spiritual needs of second- or third-generation Ukrainian Canadians who had perhaps been alienated from the established Toronto parishes because of the dominance there of Ukrainian as the functional language and a highly politicized post–Second World War immigrant population. St Demetrius Parish was the first in the Eparchy of Toronto to accept the Gregorian calendar. Led by the Canadian-born priest John Tataryn (no relation to this author), the parish was inspired by the excitement of the Roman Catholic reforms initiated by the Second Vatican Council. It instigated intentional attempts at reform, including an all-English liturgy, guitar accompaniment for the choir, and a circular church building without the traditional *iconostasis* or wall of icons separating the church sanctuary from the nave.

The 1960s saw the parish grow and thrive to become one of the largest Eastern Catholic parishes in North America. It established its own credit union (which has now merged with Ukrainian (Toronto) Credit Union, a local men's association (rather than join the Brotherhood of Ukrainian Catholics), a youth club, and a branch of the Ukrainian Catholic Women's League. By the 1970s the parish's ongoing self-reflection led it to a renewed vision of its purpose and it turned to a more conscious appropriation of its Eastern Christian tradition. Concurrently, the community entered on its most ambitious project, a Ukrainian Catholic day school. In 1975, St Demetrius Ukrainian Catholic School became part of the Etobicoke Catholic Board of Education. The school's reputation quickly grew and it was soon filled to capacity, even attracting non-Ukrainian students.

The 1970s also saw a renovation of the church in a fusion of contemporary elements and Eastern flavour: a low metal-framed *iconostasis*, icons but on stained glass with a combination of Ukrainian and Canadian motifs, and a novel dove-like tabernacle. The artist Jaroslava endeavoured to marry the folk spirit of her glass paintings with the stained glass technique and the demands of Eastern Christian iconography. The result is fascinating. Although decried by traditionalists (Keleher 1989, 52), it has over the years sustained the liturgical life of one of the most vibrant Eastern Christian communities in the country. It was in the 1970s that the pastor laid the foundation for further growth. Nurturing contacts with local civic and political leaders, he positioned the parish so that it was able to benefit from government programs and in 1984 the parish opened the St Demetrius Residence for seniors. This seniors' complex serves the needs of those wishing to continue independent living but in an apartment, for those who are beginning to require some assistance in daily living but can still maintain a high degree of autonomy. Significantly, from the perspective of language and adherence to tradition, the new residential community presented a new challenge for the pastor because most of the residents were Ukrainian-speaking and adhered to the Julian calendar. Interestingly, adapting to the needs of his community, Father Tataryn introduced services in the residence chapel in Ukrainian and according to the Julian calendar.

As the community grew, concessions to these new needs were also made in the parish church. Expansion of St Demetrius culminated in the construction in 1994 of the Ukrainian Canadian Care Centre, a nursing home complex on the expansive St Demetrius parish grounds. From baptism to death one can find institutional support and service at St Demetrius Parish. However, one does not necessarily have to be Ukrainian to enjoy these services. Rather, St Demetrius emphasizes a broadly Canadian Eastern Christian heritage, albeit with a strong historical connection to the Ukrainian community. The leadership of St Demetrius continuously attempts to emphasize the community's solidarity with not only other Ukrainian parishes, but with other Eastern Christians and other Christians as a whole. The view is that they are a community rooted in the Ukrainian tradition, but open to all. This ability to be simultaneously Eastern Catholic, Canadian, and Ukrainian was demonstrated by the parish's hosting an event entitled 'Glory of the East' in order to familiarize church members with other Eastern Christians and thus to foster solidarity among these believers.

In unique and remarkable ways, all three of the instances presented – St John the Compassionate Mission, Holy Covenant Evangelical Orthodox Church, and St Demetrius Byzantine Ukrainian Catholic Church – witness the vitality of Eastern Christianity in Canada, as well as its ability to transfigure itself in the service of its communities. Significantly, these communities appear to be marked by the diminishing power of ethnicity as a determinative force. This is not to suggest that this is inevitable, but rather to demonstrate that no matter how historically tied Eastern Christian churches have been to their culture and nation of origin, they are able to transform and recreate themselves in contemporary Canada. In other words, loss of ethnic identity need not necessarily lead to loss of religious identification. The adaptability demonstrated by Eastern Christians in the first millennium is being once more demonstrated in Canada. Although not without detractors who see in these adaptations betrayals of authenticity, for others it is part of the genius of the East. However, the integration of these communities into the Canadian reality has challenged the long-standing relationship between ethnic and religious forms of identity within this community.

Conclusion

This overview of Eastern Christianity in Canada has provided a glimpse of the array of Eastern Christian communities in Canada. It is not possible to speak uniformly of how they have adapted to Canada, or to speak simplistically of their role in the retention or perhaps more accurately recreation of ethnic identity. However, the churches are not simply agents in a community's attempts to sustain its mother tongue or adherence to an ethnic inheritance. Most of the churches discussed have demonstrated aspects of retention and adaptation, but also of loss. Although studies such as those of Abu-Laban, Chimbos, and Isajiw suggest that adherence to these churches may retard social integration, even a superficial look at a community such as St Demetrius in Toronto belies such an absolute assertion. Clearly the diversity of Eastern Christianity globally has become problematic for Eastern Christians as they attempt to formulate unified positions on such issues as Christian ecumenism and inter-religious dialogue. Similarly, this lack of unity in Canada and internationally militates against any comprehensive effort to establish a unified Orthodox/Eastern Catholic presence in the Canadian religious mosaic. These restraining currents also adversely affect Eastern Christian communities as they wish to retain their younger members, especially women. An inability to address changes in contemporary women's self-understanding is a major roadblock to growth and the indigenization of their religious message in North America. The strongly conservative official stance on same-sex relationships represents a similar challenge to the Eastern Christian tradition's integration into mainstream North American society. Nonetheless, continuing waves of new immigrants allow the churches to sustain themselves numerically if not, in all instances, to grow. Of course, this study is not exhaustive and has simply attempted to demonstrate that much remains to be analysed and written about the Eastern Christian world in Canada and its negotiation of ethnic and religious identity.

Notes

1 An immediate caveat is in order. There are Eastern Christians in Canada who regrettably will receive no notice other than this brief mention. I speak here of those Eastern Christians who are ethnically from the Indian subcontinent and are members of the ancient Syro-Malabar Church and the Syro-Malankara Church (there are both Catholic and Orthodox communities). Canada is home to followers of these churches, which hearken back to the legendary missionary activity of the 'Doubting' Apostle Thomas. However, their numbers are small and they are virtually unmentioned in the literature. As Canada becomes home to more people from southeast Asia, these communities will become an increasing presence within the already very diverse community of Eastern Christians.

2 Ukrainian Catholicism is a form of Eastern Christianity finding its origins in the 1596 Union of Brest, when the majority of bishops on the territory of contemporary Ukraine and Byelorussia changed jurisdictions from the patriarch of Constantinople (then under the Turks) to the bishop of Rome. Other Eastern Catholic churches formed at roughly the same time as the

result of segments of Orthodox ecclesiastical provinces opting for union with Rome.

3 The problem of self-identification is often historically perplexing. Such is the case with Ukrainians in Canada who self-identified under various names: Ukrainians, Galicians, Ruthenians, Austrians, Bukovinians, etc. When one looks at the census data on country of origin, the picture is even murkier. For example, Statistics Canada data on country of origin show almost an equal number of persons of Russian origin (100,064) as of Ukrainian origin (106,721) in 1921, yet all analysts would agree that the number of ethnic Ukrainians would have far exceeded the number of Russians in Canada at the time. On the 1921 Census data, see Wolowyna (1985).

4 The actual number of Ukrainians holding these religious affiliations would be fewer since, for example, in 1941 we already have 11,692 persons of Greek origin in Canada and they would self-identify to a high degree as Greek Orthodox. For example, Yuzyk (1980, 175) offers a figure of 241,781 for Ukrainians who adhere to either the Greek Catholic or the Greek Orthodox Church.

5 The work of demographer Oleh Wolowyna (2001) suggests that already in 1991 adherents to the two traditional Ukrainian Churches was half of those self-identifying as single Ukrainian ancestry.

6 Sources for the study of Canada's early experiments in bilingual schools are Crunican (1974), Jaenen (1970), Lupul (1974), and Skwarok (1958).

7 The local autonomy of churches was sustained through the structure of synods, or assemblies of local bishops who effectively governed local affairs, while deferring to the patriarch in fundamental matters of faith.

8 Adhering to the Council of Chalcedon, 451.

9 A title here referring to the *ekumene* or global.

10 See http://www40.statcan.ca.proxy.lib.uwaterloo.ca/101/cst01/dem026a.htm, accessed 2 November 2005.

11 A valuable resource can be found in Klymasz and Tarasoff (1995); see also Rak (2004). Also refer to http://www.civilization.ca/cultur/doukhobors/dou01eng.htm, accessed 2 November 2005.

12 See Magocsi (1999, 1242) for a discussion of the difficulty in dealing with early census data concerning Syrians.

13 Rastafarianism is a social and religious movement conceived as resistance to colonialism, particularly in Jamaica. The first communities identified the Ethiopian Emperor Haile Selassie (Prince Ras Tafari Makonnen) as a god and the embodiment of their belief in a new African homeland, Ethiopia (Religious Movements Homepage Project 2005).

14 See electronic document http://www.newadvent.org/cathen/10157b.htm, accessed 12 July 2006.
15 Electronic document, http://www.cccb.ca/Oriental-Rites.htm?CD=92&ID=35, accessed 12 January 2006.
16 See electronic document http://www.smart.net/~mmontes/ortheast.html, accessed 10 January 2006
17 Goa judges that the introduction of Western Christian practices into Eastern Christian communities in Canada 'diminishes the Eastern Christian symbolic tradition' (1989a, 33).
18 See St John the Compassionate Mission 2007.

Works Cited

Abu-Laban, Baha. 1980. *An olive branch on the family tree: The Arabs in Canada.* A history of Canada's peoples. Toronto: McClelland and Stewart.
Angelfire. History of the Ethiopian Orthodox Tewahido Church homepage. http://www.angelfire.com/ny3/ethiochurch/.
Bociurkiw, Bohdan. 1978. The federal policy of multiculturalism and the Ukrainian-Canadian community. In *Ukrainian Canadians, multiculturalism, and separatism: An assessment,* ed. Manoly R. Lupul, 98–128. Edmonton: Canadian Institute of Ukrainian Studies.
Breton, Raymond, Wsevolod W. Isajiw, Warren E. Kalbach, and Jeffrey G. Reitz. 1990. *Ethnic identity and equality: Varieties of experience in a Canadian city.* Toronto: University of Toronto Press.
Canadian Conference of Catholic Bishops. 2000. New eparch named for Catholic Slovaks in Toronto. http://www.cccb.ca/site/content/view/942/1062/lang,eng/.
– 2008. List of Eparchies. http://www.cccb.ca/site/component/option,com_wrapper/Itemid,1235/lang,eng/.
Chimbos, Peter D. 1980. *The Canadian odyssey: The Greek experience in Canada.* A history of Canada's peoples. Toronto: McClelland and Stewart.
Crunican, Paul. 1974. *Priests and politicians: Manitoba schools and the election of 1896.* Toronto: University of Toronto Press.
Dreisziger, N. Fred. 1991. Tracy Philipps and the achievement of Ukrainian-Canadian unity. In Luciuk and Hryniuk 1991, 326–41.
Gerus, Oleh W. 1991. Consolidating the community: The Ukrainian Self-Reliance League. In Luciuk and Hryniuk 1991, 157–86.
Goa, David J. 1989a. Cosmic ritual in the Canadian context. In *The Ukrainian*

religious experience: Tradition and the Canadian cultural context, ed. David J. Goa, 23–35. Edmonton: Canadian Institute of Ukrainian Studies.

– ed. 1989b. *The Ukrainian religious experience: Tradition and the Canadian cultural context*. Edmonton: Canadian Institute of Ukrainian Studies.

Isajiw, Wsevolod W. 1990. Ethnic-identity retention. In *Ethnic identity and equality: Varieties of experience in a Canadian city*, ed. Raymond Breton, Wsevolod W. Isajiw, Warren E. Kalback, and Jeffrey G. Reitz, 34–91. Toronto: University of Toronto Press.

Jaenen, Cornelius J. 1970. *Ruthenian schools in western Canada, 1897–1919. Paedagogica Historica* 10 (3): 517–541.

Kalbach, Warren, and Madeline A. Richard. 1980. Differential effects of ethno-religious structures on linguistic trends and economic achievements of Ukrainian Canadians. In W.R. Petryshyn 1980, 78–96.

Keleher, Serge. 1989. Ukrainian Church iconography in Canada: Models and their spiritual significance. In Goa 1989b, 47–55.

Klymasz, Robert B., and Koozma J. Tarasoff. 1995. *Spirit wrestlers: Centennial papers in honour of Canada's Doukhobor heritage*. Ottawa: Canadian Museum of Civilization.

Kucharek, Casimir. 1989. The roots of 'Latinization' and its context in the experience of Ukrainian Catholics in Canada. In Goa 1989b, 69–79.

Kuplowska, Olga M. 1980. Language retention patterns among Ukrainian Canadians. In W.R. Petryshyn 1980, 134–60.

Lowig, Evan. 1989. The historical development of Ukrainians within the Orthodox Church in America: A comparative study. In Goa 1989b, 209–18.

Lupul, Manoly. 1974. *The Roman Catholic Church and the north-west school question*. Toronto: University of Toronto Press.

Luciuk, Lubomyr, and Stella Hryniuk, eds. 1991. *Canada's Ukrainians: Negotiating an identity*. Toronto: University of Toronto Press.

Magocsi, Paul Robert, ed. 1999. *Encyclopedia of Canada's peoples*. Toronto: University of Toronto Press.

Martynovych, Orest T. 1991. *Ukrainians in Canada: The formative period, 1891–1924*. Edmonton: Canadian Institute of Ukrainian Studies.

Matiasz, Sophia. 1989. Three parishes: A study in the ethnic use of religious symbols. In Goa 1989b, 219–29.

McDonough, Sheila, and Homa Hoodfar. 2005. Muslims in Canada: From ethnic groups to religious community. In *Religion and ethnicity in Canada*, ed. Paul Bramadat and David Seljak, 133–53. Toronto: Pearson Longman.

O Great Mystery. 2004. Where are they now? http://www.ogreatmystery.com/eoc/now.

Olender, Vivian. 1989. Symbolic manipulation in the proselytizing of Ukrainians: An attempt to create a Protestant uniate church. In Goa 1989b, 191–207.

Orthodox Church in America. 1990. Mission statement of the Orthodox Church
in America. http://www.oca.org/MVmission.asp?SID=1.

Orthodox Wiki. Old calendarists. http://www.orthodoxwiki.org/
Old_Calendarists.

Petroff, Lillian. 1995. *Sojourners and settlers: The Macedonian community in Toronto to 1940*. Toronto: Multicultural History Society of Ontario / University
of Toronto Press.

Petryshyn, Jaroslav. 1985. *Peasants in the promised land: Canada and the Ukrainians, 1891–1914*. Toronto: Lorimer.

Petryshyn, W. Roman. 1980. *Changing realities: Social trends among Ukrainian
Canadians*. Edmonton: Canadian Institute of Ukrainian Studies.

Pizanias, Caterina. 1991. After the odyssey, Babylon: The social construction of
ethnicity in the Hellenic diaspora. In *Proceedings of the First International Congress on the Hellenic Diaspora: From Antiquity to Modern Times*. Vol. 2 of *From
1453 to Modern Times*, ed. John M. Fossey, 379–89. Amsterdam: Gieben.

Rak, Julie. 2004. *Negotiated memory: Doukhobor autobiographical discourse*. Vancouver: UBC Press.

Religious Movements Homepage Project. 2005. Rastafarianism. http://
religiousmovements.lib.virginia.edu/nrms/rast.html.

Skwarok, J. 1958. *The Ukrainian settlers in Canada and their schools*. Edmonton:
Basilian.

Statistics Canada. 2001. Ethnic origin (232), Sex (3) and single and multiple
responses (3) for population, for Canada. http://www12.statcan.ca/
proxy.lib.uwaterloo.ca/english/census01/.

– 2003. Selected demographic and cultural characteristics (105). http://
www.statcan.ca/bsolc/english/bsolc?catno=97F0010XIE2001040.

St John the Compassionate Mission. 2007. Homepage, http://www
.stjohnsmission.org/.

Swidler, Ann. 1986. Culture in action: Symbols and strategies. *American
Sociological Review* 51:273–86.

Swyripa, Frances. 1993. *Wedded to the cause: Ukrainian-Canadian women*. Toronto:
University of Toronto Press.

– 2004. The mother of God wears a maple leaf: History, gender, and ethnic
identity in sacred space. In *Sisters or strangers? Immigrant, ethnic, and racialized women in Canadian history*, ed. Marlene Epp, Franca Iacovetta, and
Frances Swyripa, 341–61. Toronto: University of Toronto Press.

Tataryn, Myroslaw. 1998. What is Eastern Catholic theology? Beyond classi-
cism towards liberation. *Logos* 39 (1): 89–107.

Vasiliadis, Peter. 1989. *Whose are you? Identity and ethnicity among the Toronto Macedonians*. New York: Abrahams.

Wiseman, Nelson. 1991. Ukrainian-Canadian politics. In Luciuk and Hryniuk 1989, 342–61.

Wolowyna, Oleh. 1985. Trends in the socio-economic status of Ukrainians in Canada, 1921–1971. In J. Petryshyn 1985, 53–77.

– 2001. Religion and ethnicity of Ukrainians in Canada. Mohyla Lecture, St Thomas More College, Saskatoon, 16 November.

Yereniuk, Roman. 1989. Church jurisdictions and jurisdictional changes among Ukrainians in Canada, 1891–1925. In Goa 1989b, 109–27.

Yuzyk, Paul. 1980. Religious denominations. In *A statistical compendium on the Ukrainians in Canada, 1891–1976*, ed. William Darcovich and Paul Yuzyk, 165–211. Ottawa: University of Ottawa Press.

– 1987. The senator's special work on multiculturalism and human rights. http://www.yuzyk.com/multicult-e.shtml.

Zuk, Radoslav. 1989. Sacred space in Ukrainian Canadian experience: Tradition and contemporary issues. In Goa 1989b, 37–46.

9 The Poetics of Peoplehood: Ethnicity and Religion among Canada's Mennonites

ROYDEN LOEWEN

Introduction

The question of religion and ethnicity is deeply vexing for many Mennonites in Canada. Their history, focused as it is on a small, closely knit, once-persecuted, migrating people of Swiss, Dutch, and German descent has produced all the features of ethnicity. Those features include a strong sense of peoplehood undergirded by a common history and genealogical interests for Mennonites generally, and distinctive dialects and clothing styles for the conservative, or 'old order' branches. Yet their religious ideals, emphasizing the permanency of Christ's teachings on pacifism, humility, and service stands in opposition to ethnic identity. Indeed, ethnicity in this instance is seen as a distraction from true Christian faith. Most Mennonites have at some point debated the issue of whether they are both an ethnic and a religious group, solely a religious group, or singularly an ethnic group.

Even the media present fundamentally different images of Mennonites, each representing a different mix of ethnicity and religion. As the holder of the chair in Mennonite Studies at the University of Winnipeg, I occasionally have been asked by the media to respond to current issues relating to Mennonites. Given my own experiences of the Mennonite lifeworld, I have developed a particular sensitivity to differences within that community: I farm as a hobby, but clearly work in a city; I associate closely with a relatively progressive Mennonite community, but have numerous old order cousins in both Canada and Mexico; I am writing a history of European-descended Mennonites in North America, but it is meant to appeal to first- and second-generation Asian and African Mennonites. I am aware that today's Mennonite faith is not a simple copy of the culture of my ancestors. The Mennonite World Conference reports more Mennonites in Africa than in North America (452,000 compared to 451,000 in 2003), as many in India as in Canada (127,348 compared to 127,851), and fewer in Europe, the birthplace of the Mennonite tradition, than in any other continent.

Questions I have been asked by the Canadian media about the 'typical' Mennonite illustrate the complexity of this dynamic mix of religion and ethnicity. The *Western Producer* magazine has asked about the seemingly inordinate commitment among modern, rural, and small town Mennonites in Manitoba to charity and especially their support for the Mennonite Central Committee (hereinafter MCC), a service agency whose program of peace-building, refugee settlement, and disaster relief has global reach. The *New Canadian* magazine has asked me to respond to award-winning Mennonite writers who are highly critical of their ancestral religious faith, cite leaders for repressive and misguided zeal, but embrace the esoteric elements of Mennonite agrarian life. *En Route* magazine was curious once about Ontario's single Old Order Mennonite women who wear aproned dresses and white bonnets, whose faith separates them from technology and modern fashion, but who nonetheless eagerly engage in the business of selling handcrafts to consumer-crazed tourists. *CBC Radio One* asked a common question about Mennonite men who served as conscientious objectors during the Second World War, wondering how it affected their sense of masculinity and how mandatory alternative service extricated them from close-knit rural communities. Numerous other queries have focused on Mennonites and ethno-tourism, drug-running, acculturation, entrepreneurship, politics, and inter-ethnicity.[1]

While these various queries are directed to newsworthy events of national Canadian interest, they also reflect the different ways in which Mennonites are identified. Indeed, the queries come with presuppositions about who is a Mennonite and what makes a Mennonite a Mennonite. The small town Mennonites, for example, often see ethnicity and religion as natural companions, while Old Order Mennonite women use ethnic traits to shore up religious practice. Meanwhile, conscientious objectors often rejected ethnicity as a diversion from true faith, and novelists have sometimes expressed a deep disdain for inherited religious practices.

Historically, Canadian Mennonites as a people have possessed both a religious and an ethnic identity. Most scholars of the Mennonites seem to agree on this position, even though some suggest that the term *peoplehood* is more appropriate than ethnicity to denote the social and cultural underpinnings of being Mennonite (Urry 2006). Using ethnicity in the particular sense outlined above, it is clear that in their history, religion most often informed the Mennonites' sense of ethnicity, while ethnicity often guarded their faith. Over time the two cultural phenomena intersected in a dynamic and even synergistic manner. In this regard, of course, Mennonite identity is like other ethnicities, which, as Bramadat and Seljak point out in the first chapter of this book, consist not of primordial or essentialist qualities, but historically conditioned cultural constructions. As in other cases, we should allow for, and even expect, 'the appearance, metamorphosis, disappearance, and reappearance of ethnicities' (Conzen, Gerber, Morawska, Pozetta, and Vecoli 1992, 38).

Ethnicity among Mennonites certainly has evolved over time. Even today the phenomenon is kaleidoscopic, presenting itself in various and disparate forms, some suggesting disappearance, others rejuvenation, and others endurance and persistence that intimate that it is a 'natural and timeless category' (Sollors 1989, xiv). In their everyday life, Mennonite men and women hold and practise disparate identities, and Mennonite scholars – historians, social scientists, literary critics, theologians – intensely debate the merits of ethnicity, one form over the other, or indeed the very existence of it. In this regard, both lay people and scholars have generated narratives of ethnicity, participating in what Hayden White refers to as 'poetic acts' (x). Those narratives can be actual writings, but they can also be imagined identities, codes of conduct, religious symbols, material artefacts, or social relationships. These 'narratives' reflect concerns of meaning and destiny; they seek to make sense of life, project order, instil hope, and create bonds of community. Ethnicity for Canadian Mennonites is a cultural construction, established by time, tempered by space, and conditioned by social interaction. It intersects dialectically with religious teachings that are themselves in flux. The dynamic intersection of the two constitutes a 'poetic act' for the Mennonites.

Historical Narrative as Ethnic Marker

At the root of today's debate about Mennonite ethnicity is a venerated narrative of Mennonite history. Mennonites have read, researched, written, and conveyed these accounts and thus generated the basic cadence of their peoplehood. That history begins with Mennonites as a religious group known as Anabaptists, the 're-baptizers,' consisting of people of various cultural backgrounds. The Anabaptist beginning is usually placed in 1525 in Zurich, Switzerland, but then, as the story goes, Anabaptistism spread rapidly to Austrian, south German, Dutch, and north German regions. The Anabaptists are said to have constituted the radical wing of the sixteenth-century Protestant Reformation. They emphasized adult believers' baptism, discipleship of Christ (especially pacifism and a simple lifestyle), and a community-centred or communitarian view of the church. An especially powerful early Anabaptist teaching, rooted in medieval Catholic monastic discipline, separated Christ's disciples from a fallen world and called them to constitute nothing less than the Kingdom of God in small, exclusive fellowships or communities here on earth. A seemingly contradictory positive view of the human condition suggested to Mennonites that people were not essentially sinful, but through *Nachfolge Christi*, literally 'following Christ,' they could create the Kingdom of God on earth (Snyder 1995). Over time a biblically based, pacifist Anabaptism was codified. The voluminous pastoral writings of Menno Simons, the Dutch Roman Catholic priest who converted to Anabaptism in 1536, were important in the crystallization of Anabaptist thought, but so too were numerous catechisms and statements of faith, most notably the Swiss Schleitheim Confession of 1527 and the Dutch Dordrecht Confession of 1632. With the publication of Thieleman van Braght's *Martyrs' Mirror* in 1660, Mennonites began appropriating their own history as part of their Protestant sub-identity and found in the stories of martyrdom in the sixteenth century a 'golden age,' a measure of complete and pure religious commitment.

This standard account of Anabaptism overlooks the complex, multifaceted, and dynamic nature of the movement during the first generation. Some groups were violent and apocalyptic, others emphasized universal love, some supported participation in government, some were rural and others urban, some leaned to mysticism and others to biblical authority. Numerous groups were spawned and many disappeared. Although this chapter's focus is on the Mennonites, two other Anabaptist groups survived. One was the pacifist and communalist Hutterite community, a group with Austrian origins also known as the Hutterian Brethren. Named after Jacob Hutter, a hat-maker, this movement took the biblical teaching of Acts 2:44 to insist that true followers of Christ must share all material goods; Hutter's execution by burning at the stake in 1536 was a powerful congealing moment for this group, but it also foreshadowed times of severe persecution that eventually sent it eastward to imperial Russia, then to the Dakota territory in the United States in the 1870s, and to Manitoba and Alberta during the First World War. A second group, the Amish, had its beginning in 1693 when it separated from the Mennonites and took root mostly in Alsace and Lorraine, the German-speaking provinces of eastern France. Named after their leader, Jacob Ammann, this group emphasized a peaceful and simple lifestyle, one that resisted modern fashions and technology, insisted on uniformity of dress and untrimmed beards for men, and the strict shunning of any member who accepted new fashions or technologies. It too eventually came to North America, especially to Pennsylvania and Ohio, but in 1824 an Amish community was founded in southern Ontario. Although migration patterns ensured interaction with the much larger Mennonite community, the Hutterites and the Amish developed into groups quite distinctive in dress, dialect, teachings, and history from most Mennonites and thus have not been covered in detail in this chapter.

If the histories of the sixteenth-century Anabaptist beginnings emphasize purity of beginning, the historical narratives of later centuries focus on the Mennonites' uneasy relationship with the state, their efforts to build cohesive, agrarian, pacifist communities, and their many migrations to secure these aims. They also focus on the process by which both the Swiss and the Dutch Mennonites evolved into ethnoreligious groups. They tell of intense persecution of both the Swiss and the Dutch Mennonites that drove them into the countryside and to neighbouring countries that welcomed craftspeople and farmers. Many Swiss Mennonites, for example, found refuge in the Palatinate region of southern Germany, before migrating in large numbers (alongside the Amish) to Pennsylvania after 1711. The Dutch Mennonites found refuge in England and northern Germany, but especially in northern Poland's Vistula River delta region and in and around the city of Danzig or Gdansk. Between 1788 and 1804, the majority of the Dutch Mennonites (alongside the Hutterites) migrated even farther east to the steppes of present-day Ukraine, in those days South or New Russia. In each of these places, the groups sought peace and tolerance, and created close-knit agricultural communities where religious teaching emphasized separation from worldly ways of fashion, power, and militarism.

This context produced the conditions for the evolution of ethnicity. Mennonites shared cultural practices, artistic expressions, and foodways, as well as clothing styles and architectural traditions, the last two often accorded special religious meaning. The Mennonites also developed particular dialects, consisting of their native language (Swiss German for the Swiss and Flemish for the Dutch) amalgamated with the language of their hosts (West Prussian Low German for the Dutch in Poland and Palatine German for the Swiss). During the eighteenth century when the Swiss in south Germany migrated to Pennsylvania and the Dutch Mennonites in Poland/West Prussia began moving to Russia, these cultural practices and dialects were transplanted in new settings and took on even stronger ethnic qualities. Sociologist E.K. Francis argues that the political arrangement in imperial Russia, in which Mennonites created their own mini-commonwealth, was especially important in the evolution of a Mennonite ethnicity. In fact, by the mid-nineteenth century, argues Francis, 'it became possible for one to be a Mennonite and yet not to be a member of the Mennonite church' (1955, 104). Meanwhile, in Pennsylvania the Swiss Mennonites took a similar, albeit distinctive, approach. 'As an ethnic identity,' writes Steve Nolt, 'Pennsylvania German-ness provided [the Mennonites with] a distinct and primary sense of ordering one's world, establishing distance from surrounding, mainstream American society' (1999, 490). Mennonites thus had become a migrant people with a particular cultural script, one that spoke about social borders, historical imagination, and religious faithfulness, but also one that spoke of peoplehood and community cohesiveness.

Transplanted Codes of Ethnicity

These disparate informal codes of Mennonite ethnicity were transplanted to Canada, where they were reformulated. Swiss Pennsylvania Mennonites first migrated to Upper Canada after the American Revolution, but in sizeable numbers only after 1800. They came speaking the Palatine Pennsylvania German (nicknamed 'Pennsylvania Dutch') and embraced the distinctive set of foodways, clothing fashion, vehicular styles (especially the blue-coloured Conestoga Wagon), architectural forms, musical traditions, folk medicines, and artistic expressions they had honed in eighteenth-century Pennsylvania (Beck 2004; Bergey and Hunsberger 1986). The purchase of a large block of land from (according to some historians, uninformed) Six Nations Aboriginals allowed Mennonites to create separate, homogeneous communities (Good 2001). A creative and energetic early leader, Benjamin Eby, rewrote German hymns, pencilled a German catechism, and created a network of

German-language, church-run schools and church conferences in three distinct communities in Upper Canada. As an entrepreneur, he also spearheaded the building of a small town at first called Ebytown, which later, reflecting its large German population, became known as Berlin (and was eventually renamed Kitchener). Nevertheless, the Mennonites' 'Pennsylvania Dutch' dialect and sectarian faith shielded them from the large mid-century influx of German Catholics into Waterloo County and from British Canadian immigrants in neighbouring counties (Fretz 1989).

When the Dutch Mennonites came to Canada from imperial Russia in three distinct waves in the 1870s, 1920s and 1940s (and even as they continue arriving today in a series of prolonged chain migrations from Mennonite colonies in Latin America or via Germany from Low German–speaking places in Kazakhstan or Uzbekistan), they bore distinctive ethnic features that they replicated in close-knit communities. Their arrival in southern Manitoba in the 1870s came after treaties with Aboriginal people and their settlement on land reserves. The subsequent availability of farmland allowed the Mennonites significant social distance from other Euro-Canadian settlers. Numbering about 7,000 persons, speaking their Low German dialect, and settling on exclusive Mennonite land blocks, the East and the West Reserves, these Mennonites made a significant cultural impact. On their own 'reserves' they replicated old world farm villages, including conjoined house-barns, and recreated their institutions – schools, fire insurance agencies, mutual aid societies, and farm village councils. Geographer John Warkentin notes that 'perhaps nowhere in North America [had] a peasant culture from Europe been so completely re-established'; it was, he said, a 'virtual transplanting' (2000, 1). E.K. Francis argues that even after the break-up of their farm villages between 1900 and 1920, Manitoba Mennonites 'remained a distinct ethnic group,' in large measure because of geographic 'concentration and segregation in definite areas of habitat' that allowed for 'strict endogamy, and a body of differentiating traits (including folk dialect and church language), certain folkways and a consciousness of kin and of common descent' (1955, 105, 106). Other historians have also emphasized the way the First World War set the German-speaking pacifist Mennonites apart from the wider, intensely patriotic Canadian society; Mennonite youths hastened to be baptized to qualify for military exemption, an act that reinforced their separateness from wider Canadian society.

Even though recorded histories of Mennonite settlement and progress emphasize the role of men, oral tradition accords a significant role to women in maintaining household cultures and unique folk traditions. True, their churches were overtly patriarchal, but the Swiss Mennonite women of Ontario and the Dutch in Manitoba enjoyed an egalitarian inheritance system and a set of teachings about agrarian self-sufficiency that provided women with important status in everyday life. In Manitoba, for example, the transplanted institution of the *Waisenamt*, usually credited with providing loans to the poor, was in fact more directly linked, as its name 'The Orphans Bureau' suggests, to the enforcement of a religiously sanctioned and elaborate inheritance practice under which boys and girls who lost a parent shared equally in that parent's estate. Moreover, both wives and husbands received only half of the farm property after the death of their spouse. This system encouraged a high degree of matrilocality, a phenomenon in which the bride attracted the groom to come to reside in her village, providing the young wife with status not found in predominantly patrilocal societies. Women in these communities also attained status by their active roles in self-sufficient farm households, working the dairy and poultry sectors of the farm, activities that not only provided them with the status of economic productivity, but with acknowledged roles in the maintenance of social boundaries (Loewen 1999; 2001). Moreover, women also taught moralistic Low German folklore and even the subversive comical 'street songs' to their children, stories that they handed down to succeeding generations (D. Klassen 1989).

Unlike the earlier migrants, the second and third waves of Dutch Russian Mennonites embraced a High German ethnicity. Both groups, those who arrived between 1923 and 1930 as victims of the Russian Revolution and those who came between 1948 and 1952 as refugees of the Second World War, found it advantageous to speak High German. James Urry argues that integration into a modernizing Russia had encouraged these Mennonites to cultivate the formal High German, a more forceful social boundary from their Slavic neighbours than the earthy everyday Low German. Then, too, these Mennonites had encountered and developed certain loyalties to the German state; it was the German army that occupied the Mennonite colonies in Ukraine during both the time of the Russian Revolution and Second World War, restoring Mennonite religious culture and social order. Some of these Mennonites even toyed with National Socialism and its idea of a global German *Volk*. This affinity with things German, however, had its limits. Urry writes that, with the passage of the anti-German laws in Russia, many 'Mennonites attempted to prove their "Dutch" ancestry, ransacking family archives for Old Dutch books and journals' (1983, 249) and that after the Second World War, in order to get to and stay in western Europe, Mennonites 'often claimed Dutch ancestry, crossing into the Netherlands and [thus] eventually found new homes in Canada or Paraguay' (255).

Nevertheless, the High German language was a crucial ethnic marker for these early twentieth-century immigrants and they eventually engaged in rancorous church struggles to protect the *Muttersprache* or mother tongue from disappearing (Ediger 2001). Part of the struggle involved expanding church conferences with numerous congregations and supporting institutions, especially the Conference of Mennonites in Canada (also known as the General Conference or the GCs) and the more pietistically inclined Mennonite Brethren (the MBs). These conferences in turn supported youth societies, mission boards, mutual aid associations, and church choirs, all of which reinforced the High German language (Ediger 2001; Ens 2004).

The history outlined above captures not only the slow evolution of a Mennonite ethnicity, but, as noted, a historical narrative that became a crucial component of that ethnicity. Mennonite history books emphasize the Mennonites' beginning as Anabaptists, the radical wing of the Protestant Reformation, a purely religious movement. These narratives also show how the Mennonite people developed over time in secluded agrarian communities. Here their faith was undergirded by an evolving ethnicity, by the Pennsylvania German culture for the Swiss Mennonites in Ontario, the agrarian Flemish–Low German for the Dutch Mennonites who arrived in southern Manitoba in the 1870s, and the more urbanized High German for Mennonites who arrived from the Soviet Union in the 1920s and 1940s.[2]

Mennonites and Symbolic Ethnicity

Most Canadian Mennonites were deeply affected by mid-twentieth-century social developments. During the Second World War, a third of all Mennonite young men answered the draft into military service and many of these eventually left the Mennonite communities. During the Great Depression, many Mennonites had begun moving from farms to towns and cities, a movement that gathered pace during and after the Second World War. By the 1970s, rural and conservative Mennonites had become a minority within the wider Mennonite world. In the towns and cities especially, Mennonites accepted the technologies, consumerism, popular culture, and political involvement of modern Canada and thus in their day-to-day life became indistinguishable from other middle-class Canadians. In their religious faith, most continued as Mennonites, attending churches that emphasized the idea of emulating the life of Christ, signalled by adult baptism and non-resistance. Outside of their church life, most Mennonites revised their identities along the lines of what some scholars have dubbed a 'symbolic ethnicity' (Gans 1979). These new ethnic identities were certainly no less authentic than 'visible ethnicities,' but they were more adaptable, easily attached to weekend events or discarded when interest waned (Bramadat 2005). They easily complemented Canadian middle-class values and identities, and Canada's evolving embrace of official multiculturalism and symbolic ethnicity associated with that policy.

Among Ontario Mennonites this reconsideration of ethnicity had begun early. Encounters with the wider world – working and trading in an industrial, market economy, voting in liberal democratic elections, participating in 'outside' projects, clubs, and groups – began with regularity by the second part of the nineteenth century (Regehr 2000). By this time many had fully accepted the English language and assimilated into the wider Canadian society by joining other evangelical churches (Loewen 1999). They had even shown new ways of expressing their ethnicity in the English language, especially in genealogy and local history books. For example, as early as 1895, Ezra E. Eby of Waterloo, Ontario, had produced a mammoth English-language genealogical record and family history that featured no fewer than 8,494 family biographies in short paragraphs, beginning with the Albright family and ending with the Widemans. Eby's book provided a mental genealogical map, giving an indelible place in this matrix to every single Waterloo County Mennonite. Similar early ethnic markers in the English language lay in local history books that at once describe Mennonites as a distinctive people and placed them within Canada's national narrative. Mabel Dunham's *Trail of the Conestoga* told the story of the coming of the Swiss American Mennonites to Upper Canada in the early nineteenth century. It portrayed the family of Christian and Nancy Eby – Nancy 'an industrious housewife' who 'knew how to hold her tongue,' Christian a man who 'walked in the ways of his fathers,' with a 'heart ... as large as his home' and a 'reputation for piety and hospitality' (1926, 4, 7). Especially significant was the book's portrayal of Mennonites as good Canadians, an impression made the stronger by a preface highlighting the Mennonites' 'initiative, patience and self-sacrifice' by none other than William Lyon Mackenzie King, Canada's sitting prime minister. In time, this celebration of the distant past became the mainstay of a Swiss Mennonite ethnicity, whether it was expressed in books bearing such titles as *Three Pennsylvania German Pioneer Homesteads in Ontario*, annual Waterloo County German cultural festivities, or folklore fragments (see Beam 1995; Beck 2004).

Similar patterns of symbolic ethnicity evolved among Dutch-descendent Mennonites during the first half of the twentieth century. Many of these Mennonites embraced commercialized agriculture in new farm communities in the Hague-Osler and Swift Current regions of central and southern Saskatchewan, around Coaldale in southern Alberta, around La Crete in Alberta's far north, and in BC's Fraser Valley, especially at Yarrow and Abbotsford. Even more Mennonites created working- or middle-class worlds in towns and cities, near traditional Mennonite communities, especially in Kitchener-Waterloo (Ontario), Steinbach, Winkler, and Altona (Manitoba), Rosthern (Saskatchewan), and Abbotsford (British Columbia). Many others moved to large cities, especially to the prairie centres of Winnipeg, Saskatoon, Calgary, and Edmonton.

Like the Swiss-descendent Mennonites, the Dutch have come to express their ethnicity in ways remarkably different from in the past. Today, most no longer speak Low German or even understand High German. Most participate in Canada's political culture, accept electronic media, emphasize college and university education, and work in the urban-based manufacturing, retail, and service sectors. Their ethnicity thus is usually symbolic, expressed in genealogy, local history, museum artefacts, art, and literature. For example, the Mennonite Heritage Village in Steinbach, Manitoba, toured by some 70,000 visitors each year, features a replicated Dutch Russian Mennonite farm village complete with a house-barn, white wood-sided church, and large fully-operational Dutch windmill. When it was established in 1967, its founder promised a 'show window on the past' and a measure of the cultural distance Mennonites had travelled over time (Loewen 2006, 66). Low German Ukrainian foodways are another aspect of this twentieth-century ethnicity. In local Dutch Russian Mennonite–owned restaurants across Canada, one can now order 'Mennonite' food, consisting of a smoked pork 'farmer's' sausage, double-bun zwieback, as well as pasta, pastry, and pierogi dishes adapted during the Mennonites' Russian Ukrainian sojourn (Voth 1991). I have personally ordered the 'Mennonite' pierogi dish, known as *varenikje* in restaurants in La Crete (Alberta), Hague (Saskatchewan), Winkler (Manitoba), and Aylmer (Ontario). Finally, the Mennonite community today supports numerous local genealogy committees, family history days, and even online resources such as GRANDMA (Genealogical Registry and Database of Mennonite Ancestry), all charting the bloodlines of Mennonites. Huge clan gatherings energize the search for these relations. Mennonites now joke that the very first question one asks after being introduced to a stranger is, 'Are you related to so-and-so?' The celebration of people's links to the past and to one another through the past is a dominant feature in their symbolic ethnicity.

In a certain sense, this new ethnicity is also a gendered category. On the one hand, few differences appear in the way men and women have assimilated the wider Canadian society. Feminist historians argue that only in the 1950s and 1960s did women from the urbanizing Old Mennonite church in Ontario fully rebel against the wearing of distinctive dress, the uniform white bonnets required by Mennonite church leaders after 1911 (M. Epp 1990). One especially important means of helping them discard these ethnic markers and also in assimilating Mennonite women to middle-class, English-language culture of urban Canada was the practice of leaving their family farms to work as maids in Winnipeg, Saskatoon, Vancouver, and Calgary. Here Low German became a secondary language and middle-class behaviours were learned (Derksen-Siemens 1999; Esau-Klippenstein 1989). Then, too, declining fertility rates among Mennonite women, ironically going back to the 1950s when the rest of Canada experienced the baby boom, meant that the worlds of these women now increasingly resembled those of their suburban counterparts in other denominations. Certainly, like the women of other ethno-religious groups, Mennonite females gained significant new rights within their communities after the 1960s. Women's progress, however, was uneven. In the largest of the denominations, the Conference of Mennonites in Canada (the so-called GC Mennonites), women pastors were first accepted in the 1970s. By contrast, other denominations such as the Mennonite Brethren accepted female senior pastors only in 2006, while the Evangelical Mennonite Conference lifted a moratorium on discussing the issue only in 2006, despite influential calls from within the conference for female leadership (G. Redekop 1996; A. Thiessen 2002). Among 'old order' Mennonites – the Old Order Mennonites per se as well as Chortitzer, Holdeman, Sommerfelder, and Old Colony groups – and among their distant cousins, the

Amish and the Hutterites, women were accorded even less of a public profile, although women in some of these denominations voted well before women of the more modernist groups (Kraybill and Bowman 2001).

Mennonite women from each of the various groupings – old order, middle-class, and progressive – have come to place cultural meaning in the material and bodily world, in both ordinary and subversive ways. Post–Second World War era Mennonite women guarded a home-based ethnicity, especially through the nurture of 'Mennonite' foodways – the artefact of symbolic ethnicity with the longest longevity. Mennonite women refugees of this era in particular, argues Marlene Epp in an article tracing the 'semiotics of zwieback,' gave special meaning to food preparation and earned a sense of satisfaction in managing one of the Mennonites' only truly celebrated and self-indulgent activities, overeating (M. Epp 2004). Pamela Klassen similarly suggests that southern Manitoba 'Mennonite women from all groups ... construct ... Mennonite identity through their work in the kitchen'; they find it in 'bre[a]d in the bones' or in the 'material specificity of [their] lives and history,' which is for 'birth or non-birth Mennonites ... a fundamental layer of sacred experience' (1994, 230).

A survey of articles in Canadian Mennonite periodicals for 2005 suggests that even as town- or city-based Mennonite women entered the work force, this gendered view of 'sacredness' not only held, but took on, a public role in Mennonite congregations. An August 2005 article in the *Canadian Mennonite* magazine announced a new cookbook titled *Simply in Season* that 'shows the importance of eating local, seasonal food and invites readers to make choices that offer security and health for their communities, land, bodies and spirit' (*Canadian Mennonite* [hereafter *CM*] 1 August 2005, 19). The cookbook's two female authors had united Mennonite foodways with a concern for their communities as well as for the environment. These ethical concerns were also reflected in congregational life. Many congregations served fair trade coffee before or after services, for example.

A crucial element in this urban-based ethnicity for Mennonites today is the presence of familiar social institutions that can guide one throughout the life cycle. In the cities in which they constitute sizeable minorities – Winnipeg, Saskatoon, Kitchener, or Abbotsford – Mennonites are able to live in virtual Mennonite urban villages and can move fairly easily within the confines of their own institutions. Many Mennonite children throughout Canada attend Mennonite schools. In Abbotsford they attend Mennonite Educational Institute or Columbia Bible College, in Calgary the Menno Simons Christian School, in Saskatchewan Rosthern Junior College, in Kitchener Rockway Mennonite Collegiate or Conrad Grebel University College. In Winnipeg, they can attend one of two private elementary schools, and then go on to either the Mennonite Brethren Collegiate Institute or Westgate Mennonite Collegiate before perhaps attending Canadian Mennonite University or enrolling in courses at Menno Simons College or in the Mennonite Studies program at the University of Winnipeg.

As the life cycle progresses, other institutions stand ready to serve Mennonites. Young families can obtain loans at Mennonite-related institutions; for example, they can use the Mennonite Savings and Credit Union, with branches in six towns and cities in Ontario, and in Winnipeg they can bank at the one-time exclusively Mennonite Crosstown Credit Union or at the city branch of the Steinbach Credit Union. More established families, with money to spend, can take Mennonite vacations, perhaps the Toronto-based Mennonite Roots Tour, which sends ethno-tourists on a riverboat on Ukraine's Dniepr River, among singing and festive Mennonites in the shadow of one-time prosperous Mennonite villages. People with fewer resources can save money and order the *Mennonite Your Way* home-hosting guide that lists 1,600 homes in forty countries willing to take Mennonite overnight guests for nominal fees.

Throughout Canada, Mennonites can petition provincial and federal 'Mennonite' politicians, even 'Mennonite' cabinet ministers. In several of the cities they can seek genealogical grounding at Mennonite archives, one of the oldest of which is Winnipeg's Mennonite Genealogical Inc. Moreover, anywhere in Canada, retiring Mennonites can order Mennonitica online, 'Mennonite Hour A Cappella' music from mennomedia.org, or Mennonite history books from mennonitebooks.org, or create a will through Mennonite Foundation of Canada (Dyck 1999). In addition, the elderly can find 'Mennonite' seniors' homes. In Abbotsford, BC, they obtain housing in Menno Terrace East consisting of ninety-five suites on six floors, complete with a wellness centre, underground parking, and private decks, all financed through the Mennonite Benevolent Society. In Leamington, Ontario, seniors can purchase condominiums at Leamington Mennonite Home and Apartments that include 'rest home services' and 'long term care residence.' In Manitoba they listen to daily funeral announcements on radio CFAM whose broadcast range easily covers Winnipeg, and they can have their funerals pre-arranged by Klassen Funeral Home (*CM, Mennonite Brethren Herald* [hereafter *MBH*]) As well, some urban Mennonites intentionally or unintentionally conduct business almost exclusively with Mennonite carpenters, plumbers, electricians, grocers, contractors, dentists, doctors, butchers, and accountants. Thus, one can say that in particular cities and towns in Canada, Mennonites exhibit a high degree of what Raymond Breton calls 'institutional completeness.'

Other new mechanisms of Mennonite ethno-cultural expressions include those linked to the communications revolution and to the spread of popular culture among urban Mennonites. Some are traditional expressions, reflecting new levels of wealth in the Mennonite community that now affords concert halls – such as the $3.5 million performing arts centre that opened at the private Mennonite Collegiate Institute in the small town of Gretna, Manitoba, in November 2004 (*CM* 10 January 2005, 9). Across Canada, numerous choirs, orchestras, and theatre groups put on concerts, plays, and even gala balls for formally dressed Mennonites. Other cultural expressions, however, are much more popular. Throughout the 1990s and into the twenty-first century, young Canadian Mennonites each summer flocked to the youth 'festival of music,' *MennoFolk*, located outdoors near Willowgrove Farm, Ontario, and billed as an 'opportunity for Mennonite artists to display their talents' (*CM* 27 June 2005, 29). In 2005 the Mennonite Central Committee offered Canadian youth the compact disc recording of Hispanic American Cruz Cordero's rap of *Martyrs Mirror*–based 'Anabaptist martyr tales' and 'stories of modern peace makers' (*CM* 27 June 2005, 13).

Then, too, 'Mennonite' films have become popular: *The Radicals* traces the Anabaptist beginnings in Switzerland; *And When They Shall Ask* recounts suffering in the Soviet Union; *Migration North* offers a backgrounder on newly arrived working-class Low German Mennonites from Mexico; *Mennonites of Manitoba*, a Prairie Public Television production, celebrates Mennonite adaptation to modernity; and *The Pacifist Who Went to War* depicts two brothers, John and Ted Friesen, who parted ways in their youth over the question of conscientious objection to wartime military service.

Finally, numerous Web-based programs have arisen, including the Global Anabaptist Mennonite Encyclopedia Online (GAMEO) and the genealogical aid GRANDMA described above. Others are Mennolink, found at www.mennolink.org, or the Third Wave Café at www.thirdway.com, which describes itself as 'a web site for anyone wishing to know more about Mennonites,' whether theological, historical, or genealogical (*CM* 10 January 2005, 22). They also include the award-winning site created by Winnipeg's Conrad Stoesz, www.alternativeservice.com, inviting visitors to consider the merits of conscientious objection to war. By 2005 'Mennoblogs' were on the rise, numbering at least two dozen and carrying such names as Menno Melange, Reasonably Jovial Scripts, Jared Tracker, and Edgework Update. Among various concerns, these personally operated websites solicited support for overseas relief efforts or were used by pastors to test sermons (*CM* 18 April 2005, 8).

Old Order Ethnic Constructions

In sharp contrast to this symbolic ethnicity of urban, progressive Mennonites are the highly visible 'old order' Mennonites who even today practise a more overt 'everyday ethnicity.' These Mennonites consist of the Old Order Mennonites, or 'horse and buggy' Mennonites in southern Ontario (indistinguishable for many Canadians from the similarly conservative Amish groups) as well as Beachy Amish, Markham-Waterloo, Rosedale, and Nationwide Conservative Mennonite groupings, usually of Swiss American descent. They also include the Dutch-descendant, Low German–speaking Old Colony, Reinlaender, Sommerfelder, Kleine Gemeinde, and Holdeman groups located in rural districts throughout English Canada. Many of these 'old order' Mennonites have roots in late nineteenth-century struggles to resist modernization. Although this chapter does not deal specifically with other 'old order' Anabaptist groups like the Amish and Hutterites, they too have developed visible customs that counter modernity and enhance a strong sense of ethnicity (Kraybill and Bowman 2001).

Certainly the most visible of the more traditional Mennonite groups are the so-called Old Order Mennonites founded in the 1890s after a schism in the main Swiss American or Old Mennonite Church in Ontario. Various branches of the Old Order Mennonite Church still enforce specific 'old fashioned' clothing styles for both men and women, denounce electricity and motorized power as worldly, embrace German as the language of worship, ban any political involvement, and wrap it all within the Pennsylvania Dutch dialect and folklore (Fretz 1989, Horst 2000; Martin 2000). Their picturesque farms especially possess religious meaning. Nancy-Lou Patterson argues that the very landscape and spatial arrangement of these farms give expression to fundamental aspects of Swiss Mennonite cosmology. The house and barn stand as symbols of symbiotic male–female relationship in the face of a hostile world; the fences further reinforce this distance, for the boundaries define the farm as a separate cosmos, away from the 'wilderness' of the worldly city. Here exists a 'spiritual state of blessedness, of Pietistic enjoyment of the divine presence ... embodied in this landscape of ... order and stability, created and inhabited by Swiss-German Mennonite settlers' (1984, 50).

Old order ideas also can be found among Dutch-descendent Mennonites. They are especially apparent among the descendants of the 1920s and 1940s emigrants to Latin America who have migrated back to the homeland and now live in scattered communities from Nova Scotia (Pauls 2004) to northern Alberta (Neufeld, Friesen, Wiebe, Friesen, and Pruyser 1989), and especially in southern Ontario (Plett 2000). These groups also have roots in late-nineteenth-century separations from more progressive churches. At the time, conservative secessionist groups emphasized simple agrarian lifestyles, parochial German-language education, and distinctive dress, including black kerchiefs and dresses for the women. The most conservative of these groups, the Reinlaender or Old Colony Mennonite church, also emphasized the sacredness of farm village–based communities and forbade car ownership when it made its debut. In 1922, after Manitoba and Saskatchewan enforced their public school legislation, some 7,000 of these Old Colony Mennonites made a dramatic exodus from Canada, transplanting their village-farms, horse-drawn culture, and German-language, church-run schools to the Mexican states of Chihuahua and Durango. Later, smaller groups founded similar settlements in Paraguay, and in time Old Colony Mennonites spread to British Honduras in 1958 and to Bolivia, especially after 1967. Today, some 50,000 descendants of these emigrants have claimed their birthright and returned to their ancestral home of Canada. Here many of them practise an overt Mennonite ethnicity, complete with the Low German dialect and distinctive, simple dress code for both women and men.

Discourses of Ethnicity

Mennonites in Canada today cultivate a complicated relationship with ethnicity. In general terms they can be divided between those urbanized, English-speaking people who embrace dimensions of a 'symbolic ethnicity' supported by a high degree of 'institutional completeness,' and the more rural, Low German– and Pennsylvania Dutch–speaking 'old order' Mennonites. This dichotomy, however, simplifies complex and evolving cultural phenomena as these ethnicities are shaped by gender, class, age, and geography. Most significantly they are affected by religious differences within today's Mennonite community.

Indeed, these faith differences have produced a rigorous and sometime acrimonious debate within the Canadian Mennonite community, not only on what ethnicity means for Mennonites, but what it should mean. Some scholars such as Calvin Redekop (1984) have seen an 'identity crisis' that challenges the very survival of the Mennonites' 'great tradition.' Census records suggest a significant decline among religiously 'practising' Mennonites, from 207,970 in 1991 to 191,465 in 2001, an 8.1 per cent decline (Statistics Canada 2003). The fact that 'old order' and rural groups grew strongly during the 1990s, through natural increase and immigration of Low German Mennonites from Latin America, means that the decline among self-identifying urban Mennonites may well be significantly greater than 8.1 per cent. In any case, the difference between the 1991 and 2001 figures, as well as anecdotal evidence, suggests that there is a growing number of 'non-practising' Mennonites, some of whom think of themselves as 'ethnic' Mennonites – a category for which the current census form does not allow. Some measure of secularization or religious affiliation switching among Canadian Mennonites is afforded by a comparison of the census record and telephone book surveys of traditional Mennonite surnames. Such a survey of the 2005 Winnipeg telephone directory, followed by an extrapolation of the number of people represented by those names and then a comparison of that figure to the number of self-declared Winnipeg Mennonites in the 2001 Census, is revealing. It suggests that the number of secularized Mennonites or ethnic Mennonites with no religious Mennonite affiliation in the city was as high as 31 per cent of persons (39,000 to 27,000) who were identified in some way as Mennonite or of Mennonite background.[3]

Just who, then, is and is not a Mennonite? And just how are ethnicity and religion intertwined for them? A review of the literature that raises, debates, or ponders this question – that is academic analysis, creative literature, or written defences (apologias) – is instructive. These texts suggest six rather distinct approaches to the relationship between religion and ethnicity among Canadian Mennonites. Without a doubt the idea that there are precisely six sets of ideas on Mennonite ethnicity simplifies a complex discourse on a constantly shifting and kaleidoscopic ethno-religious world. However, it is an attempt to identify the multidimensional state of modern Mennonitism and raises the question of whether an 'essential' Mennonite in fact exists.

In the first of these discourses, ethnicity is embraced while religious tradition is de-emphasized, soundly critiqued, or sometimes rejected outright. This approach can be found especially among writers echoing the thinking of many urbanized dwellers who no longer self-identify as Mennonites in religious terms, and seldom attend church or identify with any religion. The best known of these writers are the celebrated Mennonite novelists and poets of national prominence who see the inherited Mennonite religious practice as conformist and patriarchal, but celebrate Mennonite ethnicity as primal and life-giving. Canada's most celebrated Mennonite novelist, Rudy Wiebe, pioneered the overt criticism of Mennonite religiousness, especially of hypocrisy and self-serving power, in his 1962 *Peace Shall Destroy Many*. But in a sense he wrote the novel from the inside out, even didactically, while 'editor of the largest Mennonite English [news]paper in Canada,' an editor who 'had preached in most of the 20 Mennonite Brethren Churches in Winnipeg' (R. Wiebe 1987, 15). Younger urban writers, especially those with roots in prairie Canada, have been much more overtly critical of Mennonite religiousness and, as writers, have more often stood outside the Mennonite church.

Consider the works of Miriam Toews, Patrick Friesen, Di Brandt, Magdalene Redekop, and David Bergen. Miriam Toews's popular novel *A Complicated Kindness* castigates Mennonite religiousness as narrow and moralistic, caricatures Menno Simons as an apocalyptic killjoy, and villainizes the preacher called The Mouth, but quotes warm and ironic phrases in Low German and celebrates the 'complicated' but loving bonds of the Mennonite family. Patrick Friesen, best known in Mennonite circles for his poetic attack on the religious practice of excommunication and ostracization in *The Shunning*, similarly applauds earthy Low German culture. In his self-reflective 'I Could Have Been Born in Spain,' Friesen writes, 'I love those voices that talk of the real world, not the ones we have manufactured out of ideas of authority and arrogance,' that is, the religious voices (Friesen 1988, 105). Poet Di Brandt subversively suggests that she 'got saved,' not through the manipulation of Mennonite church institutions that produced only empty and guilt-ridden religious aching, but by 'getting lost,' that is recognizing the abusive authority of the Mennonite father who argued for non-resistance and truth, but in effect was violent and duplicitous and lacked imagination (1988). What is redeeming, she writes in her 2000 essay 'The Poet and the Wild City' and restates in her 2007 collection of essays, *So This Is the World & Here I Am in It*, are her deep ties to rural life and attachment to earthy and even primal farm life as well as to the matriarchal Low German culture (Brandt 2002, 2007). In 'Through the Mennonite Looking Glass,' Magdalene Redekop also criticizes mainstream Mennonite religious life. The bride of the 'conventional Jesus,' the modern Mennonite Church, is like an abused 'geriatric worn out bride'; a better model for redemption, writes Redekop, is a 'woman speaking Low German on the prairie' who 'may arrive, sooner than the man, at a place where all ranks and hierarchies are flattened, where being Mennonite has to do, not with an organized body of reasoned beliefs but rather with something disorderly and wild' (1988, 242, 247). And David Bergen's first novel, *A Year of Lesser*, is described by reviewer Al Reimer as displaying 'an atmosphere of charismatic Christianity' in which a 'cast of Mennonite characters, from teenagers to the middle-aged, go their sinful ways, smoking pot, drinking heavily and fornicating with casual abandon' (Reimer 1997, 263). These displays of a dysfunctional religious culture may well be shocking to many Mennonites, but the popularity of these works also suggests that they represent the thinking of thousands of Canadians of Mennonite descent who are either cool or antithetical to religious faith of any stripe.

A second, distinct set of writings by mostly urbanized Mennonites, those linked to overtly Canadian evangelicalism, also openly celebrates a Mennonite ethnicity, while showing a disinterest and even distain for traditional Mennonite religiousness. Its stance, however, is dramatically different from literary figures who parody religion and disparage it for its patriarchal and conformist religious values. The evangelicals' main problem with Mennonite religious practice lies with the liberal thought and social activism among many Mennonites, especially within the Mennonite Central Committee (MCC) and Canada's largest Mennonite denomination, Mennonite Church Canada. Evangelicals also believe that any linkage of religious faith to Mennonite ethnicity will make that faith unattractive to mainstream Canadians or members of other ethnic groups. This concern is recognizable among churches, especially in the large Mennonite Brethren (MB) denomination, in which many congregations name themselves 'community' and not 'Mennonite' churches. It is most prevalent today among large non-Mennonite evangelical churches – often linked to Alliance, Baptist, and Free Church denominations – that have been growing exponentially in the heart of Mennonite communities such as Steinbach and Winkler,

Manitoba (*Carillon*, 7 September 2006, 6A; Werner 2006). Historically the trend has exhibited itself in the Mennonite Brethren in Christ Church, which renamed itself United Missionary Church in 1947, as well as in the Evangelical Mennonite Brethren church, which redubbed itself the Fellowship of Evangelical Bible Church in 1987.

Calvin Redekop's *Leaving Anabaptism* represents a broad discourse that names this transition and offers an overt criticism of it. Redekop traces the history of the Evangelical Mennonite Brethren from its nineteenth-century beginnings as a peace church to the 1990s. He observes that 'in 100 years the renewal movement to return to the "faith of the fathers" reject[ed] its historical heritage and mov[ed] towards mainline North American evangelicalism and fundamentalism' (C. Redekop 1998, 178). The move, he argues, was a short-sighted response to stagnant growth: 'With no culprit in sight, self-hatred ... was a way out' (191); they named their Mennonite beliefs as the cause for the stalemate, making the false assumption that 'Mennonitism excludes missions' (163).

Despite the evangelicals' rejection of a 'Mennonite' faith designation, they often support ethnic Mennonite events such as Low German plays and historical societies, serve 'ethnic' foods at church functions, and partake in ethno-tourism in Ukraine or Paraguay (Glendinning 2006). In *A People Apart* John Redekop, one of the most influential Mennonite Brethren leaders in Canada, argues that the word *Mennonite* indeed refers to an ethnic group, and not a religious designation. The Mennonite Brethren people, he argues, are evangelical and pacifist; they may be Anabaptist perhaps, but religiously they should not be labelled 'Mennonite.' To be Mennonite is to affirm and even celebrate a Frisian Flemish ethnicity, apparent in family ties, foodways, and dialect. As such, ethnicity is seen as a gift from God. However, the category of 'Mennonite' is only the most prominent of several ethnicities in the Mennonite Brethren denomination that includes Chinese and French Canadian chapters. Separating himself from many other evangelicals, John Redekop warns that the problem with naming churches as 'Mennonite,' ostensibly an 'ethnic' designation, is that it not only undermines the mission of converting people to Christianity, it means that the church also loses the very opportunity to spread the idea of Anabaptist biblical non-resistance to members of other ethnic groups (J. Redekop 1988).

A third way of dealing with Mennonite ethnicity is expressed by urban dwellers whom we might call 'neo-Anabaptists.' Like the evangelicals, these urban thinkers also separate ethnicity from religious faith. They wholeheartedly support naming their faith a Mennonite or Anabaptist one, but they are guarded on Mennonite ethnicity. This stance has its grounding in the most influential article on Mennonites in the twentieth century, American Mennonite Harold S. Bender's 1944 'The Anabaptist Vision.' In it, Bender argued that modern Mennonites were the inheritors and champions of a progressive, peace-oriented, religious faith articulated by brave, university-educated, Anabaptist radicals of the sixteenth century. Over the years a new religious concern, the 'recovery of the Anabaptist vision,' became the mission of Canadian Mennonite preachers, Sunday school teachers, Bible college professors, and seminarians alike (Hershberger 1957). Today, numerous organizations, from MCC, to Mennonite Disaster Service, Mennonite Economic Development Agency, and others take the 'Anabaptist vision' as the very embodiment of a Christianity that has relevance in the wider society (Marr 2003). Even mission boards emphasize that the word *Mennonite* connotes an open door, a Christian denomination that venerates the everyday 'following' of Christ and is not merely an expressed 'faith' in Christ. The promise of the 'Anabaptist vision' for the modern Mennonite is simple: in the nineteenth and early twentieth centuries, Mennonites were an isolated and secluded people, but with the 'Anabaptist vision' they have found a raison d'être in the very towns and cities they once shunned, and this vision can transform urban, post-war society.

Representative of numerous works advocating this 'neo-Anabaptist' orientation was the popular 1981 book *Anabaptism: Neither Catholic nor Protestant* by Walter Klaassen, a Mennonite professor at Conrad Grebel College in Waterloo, Ontario. The sixteenth-century 'Anabaptists were radical,' he wrote, 'not simply because they were more biblicist, but also because ... they were dangerous people, their views of church and state challenged positions held and supported by authorities ... They were revolutionary ... in non-violent ways ... bring[ing] about change ... [that would] more nearly [be] representative of God's will' (Klaassen 1981, 9). This thinking spurred MCC Canada to voice opposition to military collusion with the United States and capital punishment in Canada during the 1970s, and emboldened gay and lesbian Mennonites to seek recognition among Mennonite churches during the 1990s (Biesecker-Mast 1998; Regehr 2000).

A generation after Klaassen's book, a 'neo-Anabaptist' culture has firmly rooted itself in the religious landscape of Canadian Mennonites.

In a 2005 article entitled 'Who Is a Mennonite?' Gerald Gerbrandt, president of Canadian Mennonite University, answers that it is 'first and most importantly to ... be a Christian,' and specifically one who cultivates the very religious characteristics Bender outlined in 1944: 'discipleship ... brotherhood, and an ethic of love and non-resistance.' The consequent faith is not expressed in 'ethnic goods, a style of dress, or the Low German language ... in [a] Mennonite pavilion' at ethnic or multicultural festivals (*CM* 31 October 2005, 6, 7). Sociologist Leo Driedger has taken the lead, with numerous books, in arguing that this 'neo-Anabaptist' thinking has particular appeal to urban Mennonites. They have left so-called ethnically defined, 'backward,' or isolated worlds and have adopted a progressive, globally oriented, Anabaptist, faith-based social agenda. They are educated, progressive on women's issues, politically engaged, media savvy, and youth-oriented.[4]

The neo-Anabaptist rejection of Mennonite ethnicity and embrace of a social activist agenda has had a variety of other consequences. In an ironic twist, some writers suggest that the new urban Mennonites have become so de-ethnicized and engaged in left-of-centre politics that they have come to constitute a brand new category of Mennonites, the muppies or 'Mennonite Urban Professionals' (Lesher 1985). But it has also meant an expansion of Mennonitism beyond old ethnic borders.

An especially striking example of the 'neo-Anabaptist' orientation can be found among Aboriginal Mennonites. Their congregations and related institutions rose from the missionary work of Mennonite conscientious objectors during the Second World War, subsequent missionary activities, and more recent efforts to secure social justice for Native Canadians (Block 2006, Doell 2007; M. Wiebe 2001).[5] Peter Campbell, a former chief of the Oji-Cree reserve of North Spirit Lake, Ontario, has written that as a student in the only Mennonite-run residential school in Canada, the Poplar Hill Development School, he experienced bitter loneliness, but also 'instructive' and 'endearing' times, which eventually led him to join an Aboriginal-Mennonite church. An increasing openness among Mennonite missionaries, argues Alvina Block, allowed Aboriginal converts to practise a syncretic religiousness (2001, 48). Given what they observed as 'superstitions, and backwardness,' the Mennonite missionaries at Pauingassi, 300 kilometres north of Winnipeg, at first dubbed Aboriginal peoples as 'heathen.' Later the same missionaries acknowledged 'native religions and art forms as authentic expressions of the Algonquian faith in the Kitchi Manitou' and worked to restore 'native pride which had almost vanished' (52). The broader implications of this shift in thinking has been recognized by activist Menno Wiebe, who calls for 'an honourable encounter of two peoples ... where communications have been mutual ... result[ing] in a two-way, horizontal relationship (M. Wiebe, 21).

The 'neo-Anabaptist' focus can also be seen among those who describe a globalized Mennonite religiousness. Writers linked to the Mennonite World Conference (MWC) in Strasbourg, France, celebrate the 1.3 million baptized adult Mennonites worldwide, and especially in African and Asia, as a transnational people, not bound in any way to Eurocentric ethnicities. John A. Lapp and C. Arnold Snyder, the series editors of the MWC-sponsored Global Mennonite History Series write in the foreword to its first volume, *Anabaptist Songs in African Songs*, that Mennonites have joined the worldwide phenomenon in which 'membership in the fast-growing churches of the global south [have] ... surpass[ed] that of the older northern heartlands' (Lapp and Snyder 2006, vii). Some scholars even suggest that true Mennonites or Anabaptists cannot be found in Canada as they can in Africa, Asia, and South America; in the first they conform to middle-class values and only 'preen [themselves] with the bright feathers of a heroic tradition,' while elsewhere they live in poverty and are often 'persecuted ... by repressive governments' (*MBH* 4 November 2005, 12, 13). Certainly, as Canadian Mennonites thought of themselves as belonging to a global fellowship of Mennonites they also distanced themselves from the old Low German and Pennsylvania German ethnicities.

Not all Mennonites separate faith and ethnicity as do the three groups of predominantly urban writers considered above. In fact a fourth group of writers intentionally link a Mennonite faith and a Mennonite ethnicity. They see such a nexus among 'old order' or conservative rural Mennonites – Conservative, Holdeman, Old Colony, Old Order, Sommerfelder, and other Mennonites. Given the high fertility and youth retention rates among these conservative rural Mennonites, their importance has increasingly caught the eye of modern Mennonite academics (Kraybill and Bowman 2001). Donald Kraybill and Carl F. Bowman are American social scientists, but their work includes studies of Canadian branches of Old Order groups. Winfield Fretz, William Janzen, and others have also written sympathetically of these non-conformists. They describe their distinctive dress codes especially – usually a prayer kerchief, uncut hair, and modest, print dresses for women, and dark trousers and necktie-less shirts (and sometimes beards) for the men – and explain how through these ethnic markers the conservatives express 'simplicity in Christ,' communitarian unity, and separation from worldly society. The visible nature of this conservative faith is also apparent in simple, wooden church structures, a rejection of musical instruments, and often an adherence to a German dialect. What progressives call markers of ethnic identity, the 'old orders' see as religiously significant, so much so that they are ready to shun those who abandon the old ways.

Other writers include 'old order' members themselves, apologists for the faith. Isaac Horst, author of *A Separate People: An Insider's View of Old Order Mennonite Customs and Traditions*, argues that the 'horse and buggy' Mennonites of Ontario have adopted a set of visible cultural symbols as a result of their religious commitment to 'discipline, obedience and discipleship' (Horst 2000, 29). He is unrelenting on the need for Mennonites to constitute a visible people, with religiously informed artefacts, and to underscore this idea he quotes the scripture passage, 'If any one loves the world, the love of the Father is not in him' (16). In this book Old Order Mennonites 'come to Christ' (110) and they 'look to Christ' (122), while urban, middle-class Mennonites seek in Christianity a 'crown without a cross' (174). Old Order religiousness requires ethnic distinction.

A fifth group of Mennonites may well represent a large, quiet majority, Mennonites for whom Mennonite ethnicity is 'symbolic' and without religious significance, but seems to exist almost naturally alongside Mennonite religious faith. Paul Toews, a Canadian-born professor at a Mennonite Brethren–operated university in California, defends Mennonite ethnicity: 'Ethnicity emerges out of a people's experience' as it is simply a 'historic category ... not easily erased or changed like analytical categories or policies.' Indeed, any effort to do so 'implicitly contains a denial of complexity and ambiguity' (1987, 145). In fact, posits Toews, the urban postmodern Mennonite 'is returning to a more richly elaborated system in which people live in a hierarchy of multiple, overlapping and indistinct categories' (147). The postmodern Mennonite expects to see ethnicity exist alongside faith and feels comfortable observing other identities evolve alongside of or within the broader Mennonite identity, including the identities of Italian Catholics, Greek Orthodox Christians, or German Lutherans. Most progressive Mennonites, he argues, position their religious faith within endogamy, employ familiar insider lingo, particular architectural conventions, a strong awareness of a common history, and an interest in genealogical mapping. In fact, argues Toews, urban Mennonites are especially drawn to churches with a strong, honest sense of ethnic background. Conversely, they are able to see through the false claims that 'faith exists without cultural forms' and are repelled by unrealistic attempts to exorcize old ethnicities (1988, 46, 47).

Numerous writings seem to describe a Low German Mennonite ethnicity without needing to distance it from religious belief. This latter concern is especially evident in attempts to maintain or revive old dialects, such as the Dutch Mennonites' Low German. In British Columbia, Reuben Epp has published numerous works on the history of this dialect, unravelling particular Flemish, West Prussian, Ukrainian, and English influences, as well as accounting for specific 'Chortitzer' and 'Molotschna' accents (R. Epp 1987). In Manitoba a group of university professors led an ambitious attempt to produce an edited series of the literary works by Low German humorist Arnold Dyck and created a formal lexicon of Low German (Doerksen, Epp, Loewen, Peters, and Reimer 1988; R. Epp 1996). But Jack Thiessen is the most ambitious of these scholars: in 2003 he produced a 520-page dictionary, one that earned him the designation of 'one of the most talented lexicographers' in Canada (Considine 2004, 247).

Other writings by acculturated Mennonites establish an easy link between ethnic language and religious belief. Armin Wiebe's *The Salvation of Yasch Siemens* won the Stephen Leacock award for humour for his innovative employment of Low German syntax in a story of a young Mennonite farmer seeking to earn respect in a southern Manitoba farming community; religious metaphor and symbolism are interwoven into the story without the searing criticism seen in most other Mennonite fiction. Doreen Klassen's anthropology, *Singing Mennonite: Low German Songs among Mennonites*, identifies 200 bawdy street songs that possess 'no moralistic vocabulary'; nevertheless, she argues, the songs embrace 'traditional communal goals,' criticize 'socially unacceptable behaviour,' and idealize 'the creation and maintenance of communal unity and harmony, based on a traditional moral code' (D. Klassen 1989, 11, 12). The most overt expression of the linkage between ethnic language and religion, though, can be found in the recently translated Low German Bible. *De Bibel* was translated in 2003 by Manitoba Mennonites J.J. Neufeld and Ed Zacharias into the Old Colony dialect and jointly published by Kindred Press (Winnipeg) and United Bible Societies (Miami). It was then distributed among Canadian-descendent Old Colony Mennonites throughout Latin America, even though it met with opposition from many Mennonites who insisted that High German and not the Mennonite Low German was the traditional language of religion.

A sixth comment on Mennonite faith and ethnicity regards newly arrived immigrants in Canada who call themselves Mennonites, but resonate with neither a Mennonite ethnicity nor with Anabaptist pacifist and communitarian religious ideals. These self-identifying Mennonites, argue scholars, do so for reasons of friendship, gratitude, and even a strategy of integrating into a highly respected social sector of middle-class Canada. The fact is that many Korean, Vietnamese, Chinese, Lao, Hmong, and Spanish immigrants recently have joined urban Mennonite churches as members or Mennonite conferences as congregations. Mennonite Church Canada, for example, is a home to approximately forty immigrant congregations whose services are not English, French, or German. The Mennonite Brethren denomination lists eleven Asian Canadian congregations across Canada, most in British Columbia.

These newcomers raise questions about the term *Mennonite* in both its ethnic and religious sense. Clearly, these churches have no collective memory of Low German or Pennsylvania Dutch identity, and help to support the idea among those Euro-Canadian Mennonites who argue that Mennonites are no longer 'ethnic.' Moreover, some of their own members and a number of scholars also argue that these newcomers have not generally accepted Anabaptist religious ideas. Like many other Asian immigrants to North America, argues sociologist Daphne Winland, Hmong Mennonites in Ontario have used a North American 'religious affiliation as a mechanism of integration,' labelling themselves 'Mennonite' out of gratitude to their hosts for their 'support and guidance' and because they saw the Mennonite 'emphasis on community solidarity, family values ... and mutual aid' as compatible with 'their traditional values and lifestyle in Laos' (1992, 96, 104).

Accounts of Asian Mennonite churches published in Mennonite news magazines seem to support these findings. In 2005, the *Mennonite Brethren Herald* published a story of octogenarian Rev. Enoch Wong, said by some to be the 'pope of the Chinese Mennonite Brethren churches'; the news story praised Rev. Wong as a 'godly' man who was an especially committed evangelical, a 'man with a frail back and big smile [who] has won so many hearts to Christ' (*MBH* 25 November 2005, 26); significantly, Wong's accolades were delivered in overtly evangelistic language. The *Canadian Mennonite* in 2006 reported on Pastor Kuaying Teng of the Lao Mennonite Church in St Catharines, who argued 'for many [refugee] people, their sponsors were Mennonite, so they were Mennonite.' However, he explained, '30 per cent of the lay leaders don't know what a Mennonite is' (*CM* 13 November 2006, 4). In view of this ongoing problem, Mennonite Church Canada offered a twelve-week 'multicultural leadership training' course in 2006 that included a unit on Anabaptist History and Theology (*CM* 7 February 2006, 22). Clearly one could identify as 'Mennonite' without fully embracing the history, ethnicity, or even distinctive religious teachings of Canadian Mennonites.

Conclusion

In the Canadian Mennonite world, ethnicity and religion are intertwined in a dynamic and pliable manner. This intersection matters, affecting the way in which Mennonites imagine themselves. The question of ethnicity is woven into the narratives that give meaning and purpose to their lives; ethnicity sets the cadence and rhythm of the language of life, and it is part of the poetry of Mennonite existence. Mennonites may have begun in the sixteenth century as a religious group, but their own teaching about separation from worldly society and their demarcated agrarian worlds over the centuries generated distinctive cultural voices. Those cultures in turn eventually gave a particular tone to their religious faith. During the pioneer eras in Canada, both the Dutch Russian Mennonite and the Swiss American Mennonite ethnic identities were boldly written into their religious outlooks in such a way that they could not be disentangled from the pulse of everyday life.

Today the role of ethnicity in the lives of Canadian Mennonites differs from group to group, and community to community. For many people Mennonitism is a matter of faith and not ethnicity, while for others it is the very opposite; for still others, the two are related in at least some fashion. Indeed, many Mennonites worry that the language of ethnicity might undermine the broad appeal and special genius of the Mennonite faith and they celebrate the assimilation of one-time Low German– and Pennsylvania Dutch–speaking Mennonites into the broad culture of English Canada. Other progressive Mennonites happily intertwine ethnicity into the language of peoplehood, especially as it provides voice and place in a cacophonous, postmodern, and multicultural world. Many rural, conservative, 'old order' Mennonites embrace ethnic symbols as the very means by which to articulate an inherited faith.

The discussion above suggests that Mennonites of today cannot eas-

[handwritten: 6]

[handwritten: seem to have found there place]

ily erase the language or the reality of ethnicity from their lives. The wider Canadian society has taken note of contesting scripts of Mennonitism. Canadian media seem fascinated by 'old order' customs, the plain dress, pre-industrial technology, private schools, and agrarian pursuits. However, Canadians also recognize among progressive Mennonites the existence of cohesive communities, marked by specific social behaviour, historical memory, artistic or literary expression, and debates on cultural authenticity. Canadian Mennonites themselves are aware of past or present ethnic dimensions. They recognize that perspectives are constructed realities; if they are written into their very lives, they can also be expunged from those lives.

The meaning of ethnicity has changed for Mennonites over the centuries and especially during recent decades, leaving a complex array of 'ethnic' voices. A survey of how Mennonitism is understood today, however, indicates that the variety of voices is not only a consequence of the passage of time, but of disparate perspectives in a postmodern world. Whether distinguished by time or tempered by space, the ethnic imagination among Mennonites is a 'poetic act.' It announces a particular narrative in an increasingly complex world. Whether it sharpens the articulation of religious faith, or presents itself in a vocabulary of temporality, ethnicity matters. It is an integral component in the narrative of Canadian Mennonites.

Notes

1 The list easily continues: *Reader's Digest* has asked me to comment on investigative pieces on 'Mennonite' drug runners – shady characters who have no connection to church life, who arrive from Low German–speaking colonies in Mexico with vans stuffed with marijuana, ready to deal with motorcycle gangs; *CBC Online* called about the Mennonites' distant cousins, the Hutterites, who recently won an Alberta court case allowing them to use photo-less drivers' licences and thus keep biblical commandments and the Anabaptist emphasis of Christ-like humility; the *Winnipeg Free Press* has asked about Mennonite ethno-tourism in Ukraine; *CTV* has enquired about Mennonite institutional completeness; *Prairie Public TV* interviewed me on the Mennonites' historicity, and the *Montreal Gazette* on Mennonite immigrants.

2 Importantly, Canadian Mennonite society today is no longer divided along these three lines, but along lines of relatively progressive, English-speaking,

and urbanized Mennonites (of Dutch, Swiss, and German decent) and conservative, agrarian 'old order' and Low German– or Pennsylvania 'Dutch'–
speaking Mennonites.

3 Research conducted by author. In this research the number of Mennonite
households in the 2003 Winnipeg telephone directory that bore recognizable
Dutch North German and Swiss 'Mennonite' surnames (110 different names
in total, the most common being Doerksen, Dueck, Dyck, Enns, Friesen,
Giesbrecht, Harder, Hiebert, Hildebrandt, Janzen, Kehler, Klassen, Loewen,
Martens, Neufeld, Penner, Peters, Reimer, Rempel, Sawatsky, Schmidt,
Schulz, Thiessen, Toews, and Wiebe, or variations of those names) was
counted. It was assumed that some names, such as Schulz and Schmidt, were
also typical German Canadian names, but it was also assumed that the list of
110 names was incomplete, meaning that the number of 'Mennonite' households was probably not inflated. With an average number of household residents of three (assuming that 'Mennonite' households were similar in size
to the average for Winnipeg households, a number derived by dividing Winnipeg's population by the total number of phone numbers), the number of
'ethnic Mennonites' living in Winnipeg was calculated.

4 Leo Driedger (1998, 2000) argues that the urban experience of Mennonites
has rescued the community from an 'ethnic' dead end and allowed it to
regain its socially engaged, Christo-centric, Anabaptist vision.

5 At a conference held at the University of Winnipeg in 2001 and in its
proceedings published in the *Journal of Mennonite Studies*, a dozen papers
explored the evolving relationship from these encounters.

Works Cited

Beam, C. Richard, ed. 1995. *The Thomas R. Brendle collection of Pennsylvania
German Folklore*. Vol. 1. Lancaster, PA: Historic Schaefferstown.

Beck, Irwin. 2004. *MennoFolk: Mennonite and Amish traditions*. Waterloo: Herald.

Bender, Harold S. 1944. The Anabaptist vision. *Mennonite Quarterly Review*
18:67–88.

Bergen, David. 1996. *Year of Lesser*. Toronto: HarperCollins.

Bergey, Lorna, and Albert I. Hunsberger. 1986. *Three Pennsylvania German
pioneer homesteads in Ontario: The families and their way of life*. Waterloo:
Pennsylvania Folklore Society of Ontario.

Biesecker-Mast, Gerald. 1998. Mennonite public discourse and the conflicts
over homosexuality. *Mennonite Quarterly Review* 72:275–300.

Block, Alvina. 2001. Mennonite missionary Henry Neufeld and syncretism among the Pauingassi Ojibwa, 1955–1970. *Journal of Mennonite Studies* 19:47–64.

– 2006. Changing attitudes: Relations of Mennonite missionaries with Native North Americans, 1880 to 2004. PhD diss., University of Manitoba.

Bramadat, Paul. 2005. Toward a new politics of authenticity: Ethno-cultural representation in theory and practice. *Canadian Ethnic Studies* 37:1–20.

Brandt, Di. 1988. How I got saved. In Loewen 1988, 26–33. Kitchener: Herald.

– 2002. The poet and the wild city. *Journal of Mennonite Studies* 20:89–104.

– 2007. *So this is the world & here I am in it.* Edmonton: NuWest.

Considine, John. 2004. Mennonite Low German dictionary: A review article. *Journal of Mennonite Studies* 22:247–58.

Conzen, Kathleen Neils, David A. Gerber, Ewa Morawska, George E. Pozzetta, and Rudolph J. Vecoli. 1992. The invention of ethnicity: A perspective from the USA. *Journal of American Ethnic Studies* (Fall): 3–43.

De Bibel. 2003. Winnipeg: Kindred.

Derksen-Siemens, Ruth. 1999. Quilt as text and text as quilt: The influence of genre in the Mennonite Girls' Home of Vancouver, 1930–1960. *Journal of Mennonite Studies* 17:118–30.

Doell, Leonard. 2007. Mennonite COs and the United Church in northern Aboriginal communities. *Journal of Mennonite Studies* 25:125–36.

Doerksen, Victor G., George K. Epp, Harry Loewen, Elisabeth Peters, and Al Reimer, eds. 1988. *Collected works: Arnold Dyck: Werke.* Vol. 3. Winnipeg: Mennonite Historical Society of Manitoba.

Driedger, Leo. 1998. *Mennonite identity in conflict.* Lewiston, NY: Mellen.

– 2000. *Mennonites in the global village.* Toronto: University of Toronto Press.

Dunham, Mabel. 1924. *The trail of the Conestoga.* Toronto: MacMillan.

Dyck, John. 1999. *A foundation like no other: Mennonite Foundation of Canada, 1973–1998.* Winnipeg: Mennonite Foundation of Canada.

Eby, Ezra. 1971. *A biographical history of early settlers and their descendants in Waterloo Township 1895.* Waterloo: Eby. First published 1895.

Ediger, Gerald. 2001. *Crossing the divide: Language transition among Canadian Mennonite Brethren, 1940–1970.* Winnipeg: Kindred.

Ens, Adolf. 2004. *Becoming a national church: A history of the Conference of Mennonites in Canada.* Winnipeg: Canadian Mennonite University Press.

Ens, Anna. 1996. *In search of unity: Story of the Conference of Mennonites in Manitoba.* Winnipeg: Canadian Mennonite Bible College Press.

Epp, Frank H. 1982. *Mennonites in Canada: A people's struggle for survival.* Toronto: Macmillan.

Epp, Marlene. 1990. Carrying the banner of nonconformity: Ontario Mennonite women and the dress question. *Conrad Grebel Review* 8:237–58.

– 2001. Pioneers, refugees, exiles and transnationals: Gendering diaspora in an ethno-religious context. *Journal of the Canadian Historical Association* 12:137–54.

– 2004. The semiotics of zwieback: Feast and famine in the narratives of Mennonite refugee women. In Epp, Iacovetta, and Swyripa 2004, 314–40.

Epp, Marlene, Franca Iacovetta, and Frances Swyripa, eds. 2004. *Sisters or strangers: Immigrant, ethnic and racialized women in Canadian history.* Toronto: University of Toronto Press.

Epp, Reuben. 1987. Plautdietsch: Origins, development and state of the Mennonite Low German language. *Journal of Mennonite Studies* 5:61–72.

– 1996. *The spelling of Low German and Plautdietsch: Towards an official Plautdietsch orthography.* Hillsboro, KS: Reader's Press.

Esau-Klippenstein, Frieda. 1989. Doing what we could: Mennonite domestic servants in Winnipeg, 1920s–1950s. *Journal of Mennonite Studies* 7:145–66.

Francis, E.K. 1950. The Russian Mennonites: From religious group to ethnic group. *American Journal of Sociology* 54:101–7.

– 1955. *In search of utopia: The Mennonites in Manitoba.* Altona, MB: Friesen.

Fretz, J. Winfield. 1989. *The Waterloo Mennonites: A community in paradox.* Waterloo: Wilfrid Laurier University Press.

Friesen, Patrick. 1988. I could have been born in Spain. In Loewen 1988, 98–105.

Friesen, Rudy. 2004. *Building on the past: Mennonite architecture, landscape and settlements in Russia/Ukraine.* Winnipeg: Friesen.

Gans, Herbert. 1979. Symbolic ethnicity: The future of ethnic groups and cultures in America. In *On the making of Americans: Essays in honour of David Riesman,* ed. H. Gans, 193–220. Philadelphia: University of Pennsylvania Press.

Glendinning, Lesley. 2006. Low German Mennonite drama as a subversive activity: Five plays by Manitoba women. *Journal of Mennonite Studies* 25:23–38.

Good, Reginald. 2001. 'Lost inheritance': Alienation of Six Nations' lands in Upper Canada. *Journal of Mennonite Studies* 19:92–103.

Hershberger, Guy F., ed. 1957. *The recovery of the Anabaptist vision: A sixtieth anniversary tribute to Harold S. Bender.* Scottdale, PA: Herald.

Horst, Isaac. 2000. *A separate people: An insider's view of Old Order Mennonite customs and traditions.* Kitchener: Herald.

Klaassen, Walter. 1981. *Anabaptism: Neither Catholic nor Protestant.* Waterloo: Conrad.

Klassen, Doreen. 1989. *Singing Mennonite: Low German songs among the Mennonites.* Winnipeg: University of Manitoba Press.

Klassen, Pamela. 1994. What's bre[a]d in the bone: The bodily heritage of Mennonite women. *Mennonite Quarterly Review* 68:229–47.

Kauffman, J. Howard, and Leland Harder. 1975. *Anabaptists four centuries later: A profile of five Mennonite and Brethren in Christ denominations.* Kitchener: Herald.

Kraybill, Donald B., and Carl F. Bowman. 2001. *On the backroad to heaven: Old Order Hutterites, Mennonites, Amish, and Brethren.* Baltimore: Johns Hopkins University Press.

Lapp, John A., and C. Arnold Snyder. 2006. Preface. In *Anabaptist songs in African hearts: A global Mennonite history,* ed. Alemu Checole, Bekithemba Dube, Doris Dube, Michael Badasu, Erik Kumedisa, Barbara Nkala, I.U. Nsasak, Siaka Traore, and Pakisa Tshimika, vii. Kitchener, ON: Pandora.

Lesher, Emerson L. 1985. *The muppie manual: The Mennonite urban professional's handbook for humility and success.* Intercourse, PA: Good Books.

Loewen, Harry, ed. 1988. *Why I am a Mennonite: Essays on Mennonite identity.* Kitchener: Herald.

Loewen, Royden. 1999. *From the inside out: The rural worlds of Mennonite diarists, 1863–1929.* Winnipeg: University Manitoba Press / Manitoba Records Society.

– 2001. *Hidden worlds: Revisiting the Mennonite migrants of the 1870s.* Winnipeg: University of Manitoba Press.

– 2006. *Diaspora in the countryside: Two Mennonite communities and mid-twentieth-century North America.* Toronto: University of Toronto Press.

Marr, Lucille. 2003. *The transforming power of a century: Mennonite central committee and its evolution in Ontario.* Kitchener: Pandora.

Martin, Donald. 2000. *Old Order Mennonites of Ontario: Gelassenheit, discipleship, brotherhood.* Kitchener: Pandora.

Neufeld, Bill, Tena Friesen, Jake B. Wiebe, Jake P. Friesen, and Mary Ann Pruyser. 1989. *A heritage of homesteads, hardships and hope, 1914–1989: La Crete and Area.* La Crete, AB: La Crete Then and Now Society.

Nolt, Steve. 1999. A 'two-kingdom' people in a world of multiple identities: Religion, ethnicity and American Mennonites. *Mennonite Quarterly Review* 73:485–501.

Patterson, Nancy-Lou. 1984. Landscape and meaning: Structure and symbolism of the Swiss-German Mennonite farmstead of Waterloo Region, Ontario. *Canadian Ethnic Studies* 16:35–52.

Pauls, Karen. 2004. Northfield Settlement, Nova Scotia: A new direction for immigrants from Belize. *Journal of Mennonite Studies* 22:167–84.

Plett, Delbert F. 2000. *Old colony Mennonites in Canada: 1875–2000.* Steinbach, MB: Crossway.

Redekop, Calvin. 1984. The Mennonite identity crisis. *Journal of Mennonite Studies* 2: 87–103.

– 1998. *Leaving Anabaptism: From Evangelical Mennonite Brethren to Fellowship of Evangelical Bible Churches*. Telford, PA: Pandora.

Redekop, Gloria. 1996. *The work of their hands: Mennonite women's societies in Canada*. Waterloo ON: Wilfrid Laurier University Press.

Redekop, John. 1987. *A people apart: Ethnicity and the Mennonite Brethren*. Winnipeg: Kindred.

– 1988. Ethnicity and the Mennonite Brethren: Issues and response. *Direction* 17:3–16.

Redekop, Magdalene. 1988. Through the Mennonite looking glass. In Loewen 1988, 226–53.

Regehr, T.D. 1996. *Mennonites in Canada, 1939–1970: A people transformed*. Toronto: University of Toronto Press.

– 2000. *Peace, order and good government: Mennonites in politics in Canada*. Winnipeg: Canadian Mennonite Bible College.

Reimer, Al. 1997. Review of David Bergen's *A Year of Lesser*. *Journal of Mennonite Studies* 15: 265–66.

Snyder, Arnold. 1995. *Anabaptist history and theology: An introduction*. Waterloo: Pandora.

Sollors, Werner. 1989. Introduction. In *The invention of ethnicity*, ix–xx. New York: Oxford.

Statistics Canada. 2003. *2001 Census: Analysis Series; Religions in Canada*. http:// www12.statcan.ca/english/census01/Products/Analytic/companion/rel/ pdf/96F0030XIE2001015.pdf.

Thiessen, Arden. 2002. *The biblical case for equality: An appeal for gender justness in the church*. Belleville, ON: Essence.

Thiessen, Jack. 2003. *Mennonite Low German dictionary*. Madison: Max Kade Institute for German-American Studies.

Toews, Miriam. 2003. *A complicated kindness*. Toronto: Knopf.

Toews, Paul. 1987. A people apart or pulling apart a people. *Journal of Mennonite Studies* 5:144–49.

– 1988. Faith in culture and culture in faith: The Mennonite Brethren in North America. *Journal of Mennonite Studies* 6:36–50.

Urry, James. 1983. Who are the Mennonites? *European Journal of Sociology* 24:241–62.

– 2006. *Mennonites, politics and peoplehood: Europe, Russia, Canada, 1525–1980*. Winnipeg: University of Manitoba Press.

Voth, Norma Jost. 1991. *Mennonite food and foodways from south Russia*. Vol. 2. Intercourse, PA: Good Books.

Warkentin, John. 2000. *The Mennonite settlements of southern Manitoba*. Steinbach, MB: Steinbach Hanover Historical Society. First published 1960.

Werner, Hans. 2006. *Living between worlds: A history of Winkler.* Winkler, MB: Winkler Heritage Society.

Wiebe, Armin. 1984. *The salvation of Yasch Siemens.* Winnipeg: Turnstone.

Wiebe, Menno. 2001. From Bloodvein to Cross Lake: A 25 year synthesis. *Journal of Mennonite Studies* 19:13–24.

Wiebe, Rudy. 1962. *Peace shall destroy many.* Toronto: McClelland and Stewart.

– 1987. The skull in the swamp. *Journal of Mennonite Studies* 5:8–20.

Winland, Daphne. 1992. The role of religious affiliation in refugee resettlement: The case of the Hmong. *Canadian Ethnic Studies* 24:96–119.

10 Ethnicity and Evangelical Protestants in Canada

BRUCE L. GUENTHER

In 1993 *Maclean's* magazine surprised the nation with its cover-page declaration: 'God is Alive: Canada is a Nation of Believers' (Rawlyk 1996; Swift 1993). Using the results of an extensive Angus Reid survey, it became clear that theorists who had predicted the demise of religion in modern technological societies had badly underestimated the persistence of religion in the life of the nation. The cover story indicated that, despite declining levels of participation in religious institutions, vestiges of basic Christian beliefs continue to be held by the majority of Canadians. While the Angus Reid research confirmed the precipitous decline in membership and attendance taking place within mainstream denominations (as described in chapters 4–6 by Wendy Fletcher, Stuart Macdonald, and Greer Anne Wenh-In Ng in this book), it also drew attention to a collection of so-called conservative evangelical denominations that have defied this trend.

Evangelical Protestants have, since the 1960s, transformed Protestant demographics by forging one of the most robust religious movements in Canada. By the end of the 1970s it became apparent to scholars that the number of people regularly driving to church included more evangelical than mainline Protestants (Bibby 1987, 14–15, 106–8, 113–16; Jantz 1991; Motz 1990; Oliver 1979; Stackhouse 1993, 3–6, 199). Despite a common perception that evangelical growth in Canada has been generated primarily by proselytization and defections from mainstream denominations, a closer analysis identifies other factors, including slightly higher than average birth rates, the ability to retain a higher proportion of their children and geographically mobile members within the church, and the higher level of expectations placed upon members (Bibby 1987, 27–31; 2002, 40).

Evangelical Protestants are an ethnically diverse collection of persons who are active in more than 100 denominations and a wide range of so-called para-church organizations and institutions that are not directly tied to a specific denomination (see the Appendix, Table 10.1). Together, evangelicals make up a substantial proportion of the Canadian population. Depending on the source one consults, 8–12 per cent of Canadians are evangelical Protestants.[1] Research indicates a 2 per cent increase during the past decade, with the strongest numerical growth coming from new ethnic immigrant groups (Bibby 1993, 23–5; Van Ginkel 2003).

This chapter explores the place of ethnicity within the evangelical Protestant community in Canada and highlights the multicultural diversity of that movement and how it has changed. Many of the patterns of ethnic identity in Canadian society shaped the life of evangelical Protestant denominations, although the same patterns are not always evident within each denomination. For example, prior to 1961 most evangelical Protestants, like most non-Aboriginal Canadians, had their roots in Europe. Changes in immigration policies during the 1960s brought an increasing diversity of ethnic groups to Canada; more than 75 per cent of immigrants who came to Canada during the 1990s are allophones, that is, individuals whose mother tongue is neither English nor French.[2] This new diversity is reflected in evangelical Protestant churches; on any given Sunday evangelicals in Canada can be heard engaging in worship in well over thirty languages.

At first some evangelical Protestants worried that Canada's new immigration policies would further 'dilute' the historic Christian predominance and influence in the country and accelerate secularization. These evangelicals discovered that their fear of dilution was unfounded: while the influx of immigrants, particularly in the second half of the twentieth century, brought adherents of other religions to Canada, it also added significant numbers – and significant ethnic diversity – to evangelical Protestant denominations. For example, by the end of the twentieth century the largest visible minority in Canada were Asians, with the majority settling in or near the urban centres of Toronto and Vancouver. The greatest ethnic diversity among evangelicals is also found in these two urban regions, with the Chinese representing the fastest growing and most dynamic component of the increasingly diverse world of evangelical Protestantism in Canada. R. Stephen Warner's observations about changes in American society are equally true in Canada: the entry of recent immigrants has resulted not so much in the de-Christianization of Canadian society, but in the de-Europeanization of Canadian Christianity (Bibby 1993, 20–8; Warner 2004). Moreover, the changes in immigration patterns have slowed the rate of certain aspects of secularization: immigrants to Canada are much more likely to attend religious services than their Canadian-born counterparts (Clark and Schellenberg 2006, 2).

What Is an Evangelical?

Despite its increased visibility within Canadian society, the sheer size and diversity of the evangelical Protestant world often leaves observers perplexed. It is helpful, therefore, to take a brief look at the religious movements that have, over time, given meaning to the term *evangelical*. The word is derived from the Greek word *evangel*, or 'gospel,' referring to the 'good news' of the Christian religion. The sixteenth-century Protestant reformers used it to describe their program of doctrinal reform, which emphasized justification by faith, the priesthood of all believers, and the authority of the Bible. These distinctive emphases were intended as a critique of medieval Roman Catholicism, which (according to Protestants) emphasized good works, the priesthood of small numbers of ordained male believers, and the authority of ever-evolving traditions in the church. At the time, the term *evangelical* was essentially synonymous with Protestant.

As Protestantism developed during the eighteenth century, the label was adopted by some Protestants in Britain and North America to distinguish themselves from those Protestants who putatively did not share the same emphasis on spiritual vitality as evidenced by a conversion experience, participation in evangelism, and a rigorous approach towards personal holiness. The most prominent leaders associated with the evangelical 'awakenings' occurring during this period included George Whitefield, an eloquent speaker with a flair for the dramatic, John Wesley, an evangelist whose organizational genius led to the creation of Methodism, and Jonathan Edwards, a prominent American pastor and theologian. The movement spread to Nova Scotia through the efforts of New-Light evangelists such as Henry Alline and Methodists such as William Black (Rawlyk 1984). At the same time, the label *evangelical* was applied to a particular group within the Church of England that was sympathetic with the emphases of the Methodist revival.

The religious 'awakenings' of the eighteenth century laid the foundation for widespread religious revivals in the nineteenth century, collectively known as the Second Great Awakening.

The camp meetings organized by Methodist circuit-riding preachers, the new methods of evangelism introduced by Charles Grandison Finney, and the evangelistic activity of Baptists resulted in spectacular displays of religious enthusiasm. Common concerns often transcended denominational differences, giving rise to hundreds of cooperative initiatives in the form of voluntary societies that furthered causes such as temperance, stricter observance of Sunday as a holy day of rest, prison reform, and the abolition of slavery. The capacity of evangelical Protestants to adapt and adjust the presentation of their message to changing cultural environments helped evangelicalism to become the prevailing religious orientation among Protestants in North America during the nineteenth century. In Canada, a largely white, English-speaking, Anglo-Saxon evangelical hegemony led by, but not limited to, the Baptists in the Maritimes and the Methodists in Upper Canada had a deep impact on anglophone regions. A general moral, theological, and social consensus among evangelical Protestants was the foundation for numerous interdenominational initiatives designed to Christianize Canada, making it truly 'his dominion.' This prompted at least one Canadian historian to identify the nineteenth century as 'the evangelical century' (Gauvreau 1991).

The evangelical Protestant cultural hegemony gradually came undone during the early part of the twentieth century as the Protestant world became more theologically diverse, and as Canadian society began to feel more fully the impact of the Industrial Revolution. After decades of negotiation, in 1925 the Methodists, Congregationalists, and two-thirds of the Presbyterians merged to form the United Church of Canada (see Greer Anne Wenh-In Ng's chapter 6 in this book). This event brought together several theological and ethnic traditions into one group to create the largest Protestant denomination in the country. Although the Methodists had been one of the most aggressively evangelical Protestant groups in the nineteenth century, leaders within the new United Church of Canada gradually distanced themselves from earlier evangelical impulses in favour of a more liberal theological orientation that prioritized commitment to social service over conversion and ecumenism over doctrinal unity (Airhart 1992; Wright 1990).

As the evangelical orientation diminished within some of the mainstream Protestant denominations, it gained new strength from sources including new immigrants, fundamentalism, the holiness movement, and Pentecostalism. Large groups of new immigrants, mostly from Europe, migrated to Canada during the first half of the twentieth century, particularly to western Canada where large areas of open prairie were settled by immigrants who did not speak English. By the mid-1930s the population of the four western provinces numbered just over 3 million, with only half of the population indicating that they were of British origin. The other half comprised more than fifty different – albeit mostly European – ethnic groups. Without any established religion in the region, a religious free-for-all ensued. Some of these immigrants had been influenced in other places by evangelical Protestant ideas and emphases that were reflected in the denominations they established in Canada.

Examples of these immigrant-based denominations include the Evangelical Covenant Church (Anderson 1995), the Swedish Baptists, now known as the General Conference Baptists, and the Evangelical Free Church (Hanson 1984), all of which were started by immigrants from Scandinavia. By 1931, Scandinavian immigrants in western Canada numbered more than 228,000. German-speaking immigrants helped form denominations such as the German Baptists, now known as the North American Baptist Church (Woyke 1976), and the Mennonite Brethren, whose early members arrived in North America in several distinct migrations (Toews 1975; Toews and Enns-Rempel 2002; see chapter 9 by Royden Loewen in this book). Many incoming Dutch-speaking immigrants found their way into various Reformed Church denominations (see chapter 5 by Stuart Macdonald in this book). Still other immigrants made contact with the Baptists, whose history in Canada dates back to the eighteenth century. The Baptist Union of Western Canada started congregations among at least nine different ethnic groups during the first half of the twentieth century, particularly during the 1930s (McLaurin 1939). In addition they assisted the German, Swedish, Hungarian, and Ukrainian Baptists in organizing their own associations.

These immigrant-based denominations often began in difficult pioneering conditions made worse during the economically depressed 1930s. Some began as missionary extensions of a larger denominational body in the United States. Many did not use the English language – at least not at the outset. As these denominations became more established, and as they made the transition to using English, they became more aware of others with whom they shared a common evangelical theological and social ethos. Together, these immigrant-based denominations represent an important strand within the larger Canadian evangelical Protestant tapestry.

A second strand in the twentieth-century reconfiguration of evangelical Protestantism was a movement that became known as fundamentalism, which was a catalyst for division within many Protestant denominations in the United States, generating considerable antagonism in many regions. The influence of this movement spilled over into Canada, although it was never as divisive as it was south of the border (Rennie 1994). In the United States, many Protestant denominations fought bitter disputes over the acceptance of Darwinian evolution and new critical methods for studying the Bible. A group of evangelicals particularly concerned about defending orthodox Christianity against the influence of 'modernism' and theological liberalism became known as fundamentalists. The label was derived from the publication in 1910 of *The Fundamentals*, a series of books outlining what the authors considered to be foundational Christian beliefs; the term gained even more public circulation during and after the infamous Scopes 'Monkey Trial' in 1925. The distinct ethos and identity of fundamentalism were shaped by the legacy of nineteenth-century revivalism, an emphasis on holy living, attempts to defend the accuracy and authority of the Bible, and a rather pessimistic theological schema known as dispensational pre-millennialism – referring to Christ's return to earth at the end of the current age (or dispensation), which would usher in a new millennium.

Increasingly alienated from most Protestant denominations, and dismayed by the loss of cultural influence, the fundamentalist evangelicals abandoned some of their more militant battles and poured their energy and resources into establishing a broad network of special-purpose organizations and institutions promoting missions, evangelism, and personal holiness. For many people, this network became a kind of surrogate denomination that paralleled the dominant liberal Protestant culture. Beginning in the 1940s, the fundamentalist movement gradually divided into two streams: the more inclusive neo-evangelicals, who reappropriated the label *evangelical*, and the fundamentalists, who preferred to remain more distinct from the surrounding culture.

One of the ways the fundamentalist movement manifested its influence in Canada was through the establishment of trans-denominational organizations and educational institutions. A notable example is Prairie Bible College, located in Three Hills, Alberta, which was started in

1922 by L.E. Maxwell and by the end of the 1940s had become the largest Bible school in the world. The trans-denominational environment created by this network became a potent force accelerating the 'Canadianization' of members within many of the ethnic immigrant-based denominations mentioned above. The English-speaking religious world of trans-denominational fundamentalism was compatible enough, and therefore attractive to culturally alienated immigrants (and children of immigrants) who were interested in making a transition from their former ethnicity to a newer, more socially desirable Canadian ethnicity (Burkinshaw 1995, 160–2; Carpenter 1997, 11, 141–60; Guenther 2001, 357–67; Marsden 1980, 194–5, 204–5; see also the discussion in the first chapter of this book of the emergence of *Canadian* as an 'ethnic' self-identification). The appeal to a spiritual unity and doctrinal 'essentials' within trans-denominational institutions that transcended all other denominational, theological, and ethnic differences served as a powerful, albeit inadvertent, engine of acculturation. Both ethnic characteristics and theological emphases unique to particular denominations, such as the Mennonite commitment to peacemaking, were minimized and sometimes discarded. The widespread and long-term strength of trans-denominational evangelicalism in western Canada suggests that the trans-denominational religious orientation embodied within Bible schools and mission organizations may have been a more effective agent for immigrant acculturation than the deliberate, and often coercive, attempts on the part of the Anglo-Saxon mainstream Protestant establishment to homogenize newcomers.[3]

Another group of evangelical Protestant denominations, loosely known as the holiness movement, emerged out of Methodism during the late nineteenth century. This strand was made up of groups that had left Methodism but continued to perpetuate and popularize John Wesley's message of sanctification, which emphasized the ongoing work of the Holy Spirit in the life of a Christian after conversion and held out the possibility of achieving perfection. The holiness movement was at the outset a 'come-outer' movement, drawing many of its members from those who were disgruntled about transitions taking place within mainstream denominations.

One of the earliest expressions of the holiness movement was the Salvation Army, which began its work in Canada in 1882. Started in London by William and Catherine Booth, dissident Methodist ministers, the group became known for its work among the destitute and needy, and its military-like organizational structure. Their rather brash tactics attracted attention and opposition, and their persistence helped them to become both a church in the institutional sense and a highly reputable social service agency (Moyles 1977). Another example is the Holiness Movement Church founded by Ralph Horner, who claimed that he had experienced the blessing of 'entire sanctification' and that God had endowed his ministry with irresistible 'cyclones of power' (Whiteley 1997). Still other examples include the Free Methodist Church, which today has more than 140 congregations (Kleinsteuber 1984), the Church of the Nazarene with almost 200 churches (F. Parker 1971), and the Christian and Missionary Alliance. The Christian and Missionary Alliance was started as a missionary-sending society by Albert Simpson and John Salmon, a young Scottish immigrant. It eventually became a denomination with one of the most rapid rates of growth in the country; it now has more than 425 congregations (approximately 20 per cent are primarily non-white) across Canada with a membership of over 130,000 people (Reynolds 1981, 1992).

Out of the holiness movement came one of the most significant, and fastest growing, international religious movements during the twentieth century. The movement's expectation that the Holy Spirit would work in believers' lives subsequent to conversion laid the foundation for Pentecostalism, with its emphasis on the supernatural gifts of the Holy Spirit such as speaking in tongues and divine healing, and a worship style characterized by emotional spontaneity and exuberance. The movement dramatically reshaped evangelical demographics by producing a host of new denominations and shaping the experience of many within non-Pentecostal denominations. By the end of the twentieth century, Pentecostals numbered approximately 500 million globally, or about 25 per cent of all Christians (Burgess and McGee 2002). In Canada the movement began in 1906 at the East End Mission in Toronto. This rescue mission and 'faith healing home' served as the hub for an informal network of Pentecostal ministries that extended the movement's influence to other regions. During the 1920s, evangelistic and healing campaigns in cities such as Winnipeg, Vancouver, and Montreal drew large crowds and considerable media attention. These events featured people such as the inimitable Aimee Semple McPherson, one of the most famous women in North America at the time, and Charles Price, a respectable British-born Congregationalist minister. The Pentecostal Assemblies of Canada (PAOC) was formally organized in 1919 and has become not only the largest Pentecostal denomination in Canada, but also the largest evangelical Protestant denomination, with more than 250,000 members and 1,100 congregations (Larden 1971; Miller 1994).

From the outset, the PAOC has incorporated a variety of ethnic groups: during the 1930s at least three separate conferences – the Slavic Conference, the Finnish Conference, and the German Conference – were organized within the larger denominational framework. Currently almost 300 PAOC congregations conduct services in languages other than English, including over twenty in Korean, more than forty in Spanish, and more than ten in Portuguese. The inauguration of the PAOC was followed by the formation of almost twenty additional Pentecostal denominations in Canada. As a whole, Pentecostalism has consistently been one of the fastest growing religious movements in Canada.[4] Almost 19 per cent of its membership is made up of visible minorities, one of the highest percentages among evangelical Protestant denominations. In the past two decades a significant component of Pentecostal growth in Canada has come from new immigrants, thereby strengthening transnational links within one of the most vigorous global religious phenomena in the past century (Wilkinson 2006).

During the first half of the twentieth century, many of these new evangelical Protestant denominations were satisfied to remain on the periphery of Canadian culture, focusing their energy primarily on evangelism and missionary activity. The decade of the 1960s marked a watershed for evangelical Protestants. As the strength of their numbers grew, and as they became more educated and affluent, so too did their desire for recognition, respectability, and influence within Canadian society. They began acting more like insiders within the cultural mainstream, with a sense of responsibility for the character of Canadian society. John G. Stackhouse Jr describes how they created 'a network of interlocking institutions comprised of a mutually supportive fellowship of organizations and individuals' (1991, 248; 1993, 177–204). Having established an impressive number of institutions in Canada, particularly schools, they came together because of common concerns in higher education, in order to form a self-conscious evangelical identity and to exert their collective influence within the political arena. The organization that best represents and embodies such collaborative interests is the Evangelical Fellowship of Canada. Started in 1964, it now comprises forty affiliated denominations, nearly 100 ministry organizations and institutions, and approximately 1,100 local church congregations (Fieguth 2004; Stackhouse 1993, 165–73). It operates the Centre for Faith and Public Life in Ottawa, and regularly organizes roundtables, forums, and commissions that educate, train, and facilitate partnerships among evangelical groups in Canada. Several initiatives, such as the Aboriginal Ministries Council, the Global Mission Roundtable, and Intercultural Ministries specifically engage multicultural issues. The momentum of the evangelical movement and its vast institutional resources represent significant attractions for incoming immigrants.

Evangelicals in Contemporary Canadian Society

The contemporary significance of evangelicalism as one of the few forms of Christianity in Canada that is growing – or at least not shrinking – has attracted the attention of some scholars and the media. Words such as *mosaic* and *kaleidoscope* have been used to describe the bewildering diversity of groups that are now associated with evangelical Protestantism, prompting scholars and pollsters to search for a more concise definition for the distinctive traits of the movement. A commonly used approach is illustrated by the descriptive quadrilateral developed by the British historian David W. Bebbington (1989, 1–19). Despite the considerable diversity among evangelicals, he argues there are at least four continuities or qualities that create a kind of conceptual unity, if not always an actual unity, and that define the essence of evangelicalism. None of the four characteristics is unique to evangelicals, but the emphasis placed on them sets evangelicals apart from other Christians. Evangelicals are *conversionists*, meaning that people become Christians by repenting and personally experiencing what the Protestant reformers called 'justification by grace through faith.' It is common to hear evangelicals describe their conversion experience as 'accepting Jesus as their personal Saviour,' or having a 'personal relationship with Jesus.' For many evangelicals, evidence of this 'relationship' is the primary criterion for identifying a 'real' Christian. Second, they are *crucicentric*, that is, at the centre of their theological scheme is the understanding that atonement was made to God for human sin by the death of Jesus Christ on the cross. Third, they are *biblicist*, that is, they have a particularly high regard for the Bible, considering it to be inspired by God and the final authority in all matters of Christian faith and practice. Many evangelicals consider the Bible to be the 'word of God.' Fourth, evangelicals are *activists*, meaning that genuine conversion will be accompanied by a new motivation for doing good and for holy living. This explains the time and energy evangelicals devote to personal piety, missionary efforts, and a multitude of philanthropic projects.

A survey done by Ipsos-Reid in 2003, which used Bebbington's definitional grid, offered a helpful demographic snapshot of evangelicals in Canada. Approximately 65 per cent were married, compared to only 46 per cent of non-evangelicals in Canada. Fewer of them were divorced or living common-law (7 per cent divorced, 4 per cent living common-law, compared to 10 per cent non-evangelicals divorced and 14 per cent non-evangelicals living common-law). The percentage of evangelical Protestants who lived as singles or had never been married was substantially lower than among non-evangelicals (17 per cent, compared to 25 per cent among non-evangelicals). A comparison of household size and levels of education showed very little difference between evangelical Protestants and the larger Canadian population. Annual household income revealed some variation: approximately 39 per cent of evangelical Protestant households had an income between $30,000 and $59,999, compared to 46 per cent of non-evangelicals, and fewer evangelical Protestant households (34 per cent) had an income greater than $60,000, compared to 39 per cent of non-evangelicals. The survey showed that evangelical Protestants were distributed across Canada, although the proportion varied considerably from region to region. An almost equal number of evangelical Protestants could be found in western Canada (42 per cent) and in Ontario (43 per cent); the remaining 15 per cent were located in Atlantic Canada (9 per cent) and in Quebec (6 per cent). Evangelical Protestants attended religious services with substantially greater frequency than most other Canadians (66 per cent attend at least once a week, compared to 8 per cent of non-evangelicals), and manifested significantly higher levels of volunteerism and charitable donations (Van Ginkel 2003).

As their numbers increased, and as they grew more active within Canadian society, evangelical Protestants became more visible, and points of contact with other Canadians became more common. For example, during the 1990s a combination of curiosity and astonishment drew hundreds of thousands of people to Toronto from all parts of Canada and around the world to experience the 'Toronto Blessing.' Their destination was the Toronto Airport Christian Fellowship, a remarkable charismatic congregation led by John Arnott and located near Pearson International Airport. Observers watched worshippers break into boisterous outbursts of laughter, uncontrollable fits of shaking, sudden weeping, and strange utterances, as they claimed to be experiencing the 'signs and wonders' of the Holy Spirit. Claims of emotional and physical healing were common. Originally linked to the Vineyard movement, an international and multicultural Pentecostal phenomenon, the congregation became of one of the largest tourist destinations in Toronto.

During the same decade those watching the political arena witnessed the debut of the populist Reform Party in western Canada, which eventually became the Canadian Alliance Party and more recently the Conservative Party. Thus far, every leader of this evolving political movement – beginning with Preston Manning, then Stockwell Day, and more recently Stephen Harper, who became prime minister of Canada in early 2006 – has been a devout evangelical Protestant. The religious affiliation of these leaders, and their more open stance on encouraging faith-based perspectives in Canadian politics, has created some consternation and discomfort among those whose image of Canada is characterized by the privatization and marginalization of religion that Bramadat and Seljak discuss in the first chapter of this book (see also Bramadat 2005; Bramadat and Seljak 2005, 6–7). Moreover, many members of the Reform/Conservative Party have been critical of the multiculturalist policies in Canada. The Reform Party's criticism during the 1990s, and the linkage between evangelical Protestants in western Canada and the Reform Party, created the perception among some that all evangelical Protestants are opposed to multiculturalism. However, surveys have indicated that evangelicals generally show a higher level of support for immigration than the general population; this response is in part due to the immigrant roots of many evangelical Protestants (*Faith Today* 1988; Nelles 1989). Moreover, not all evangelical Protestants supported the Reform Party.[5]

Another recent issue that brought evangelicals into the public arena developed in the late 1990s when Trinity Western University, the privately funded evangelical institution at which I teach, found itself at the centre of a case before the Supreme Court of Canada. At issue was the refusal by the British Columbia College of Teachers in 1996 to approve the university's teacher education degree program. This rejection was based on the university's 'community standards,' which require students to refrain from sexual behaviour outside of a heterosexual marriage relationship. Following the lead of several lower courts, the Supreme Court of Canada also ruled in favour of Trinity Western University in 2001. Aside from the significance of the ruling for defining the meaning of religious freedom in Canada, the media attention during these protracted court battles gave many Canadians a glimpse of a campus community that is a multicultural microcosm of evangelical Protestantism in British Columbia. The campus brings together more than 3,500 students along with 500 staff and faculty, creating a mixture of people from more than seventy denominations and forty-five ethnic groups. Started in 1962 as a two-year liberal arts college, the school shifted to a four-year program in 1977. As part of a strategy for obtaining broader recognition for its programs, it applied for admission to the Association of Universities and Colleges of Canada, and in 1984 was accepted. The transitions within this institution illustrate well the trajectory of many evangelical post-secondary educational institutions in North America that were interested in elevating their academic standards in order to obtain recognition from the larger public universities, and to address a general neglect of serious intellectual inquiry among evangelicals (Guenther 2004; Noll 1994; Wuthnow 1989, 142–86).

Still other Canadians encounter evangelical Christians by watching the daily television show *100 Huntley Street*, by listening to radio broadcasts distributed by the Canadian office of the American-based organization Focus on the Family, by reading the historical romance fiction of Janette Oke, an Albertan author whose seventy books have sold more than 27 million copies, or by listening to interviews with celebrity athletes such as Canadian hockey legend Paul Henderson, Canadian Football League veteran Mike 'Pinball' Clemens, and Olympic speedskating champions Catriona Le May Doan and Cindy Klassen (K. Stiller 2006). People on public university campuses encounter evangelical Christians through the activities of large organizations such as InterVarsity Christian Fellowship (Bramadat 2000) and Power to Change (formerly known as Campus Crusade for Christ). Many urban Canadians searching for a new church visit local 'community churches,' where denominational connections are obscured, where the nondescript architecture is more reminiscent of a movie theatre than a cathedral, and where worship services are carefully choreographed, technologically enhanced productions complete with stage lighting, live band music, and PowerPoint visuals. Custom built for a suburban, middle-class audience, and often patterned after Willow Creek Community Church in South Barrington, Illinois, near Chicago, these large so-called megachurches have become common in most Canadian cities and suburbs.

As evangelical Protestants have become more involved and visible within Canadian society, they have also faced suspicion and prejudice. For some people, the label *evangelical* conjures up a range of negative images. It evokes memories of the scandalous actions during the 1970s and 1980s of several prominent smooth-talking but sleazy television evangelists who preyed on gullible viewers for profit. Many Canadians have encountered zealous, but sometimes insensitive, evangelical Christians who buttonhole others, insisting on knowing whether they have been 'saved' or 'born-again,' not unlike Ned Flanders in the animated sitcom *The Simpsons*, or some of the characters depicted in Brian Dannelly's movie *Saved* (2004). Still others are alarmed by the presence of evangelical Protestants in politics, fearing that they might be an extension of the powerful 'religious right' in the United States, and that they will use political power to impose their morality on others (Barlow 2006; Haskell 2005; McDonald 2006; Reimer 2003; Simmie 2006). Still others assume all evangelicals are fundamentalists, a problematic simplification made worse by the considerable symbolic power of the label *fundamentalist* to evoke negative images of extremism and violence. The Canadian theologian Clark Pinnock has noted how the term is often one of opprobrium and abuse: 'Fundamentalists must be one of the few remaining minorities in our otherwise permissive society that one can safely ridicule without fear of rebuke' (1990, 42). For good reason many evangelical Protestants resent such negative and inaccurate stereotypes, and find the prejudice and intolerance behind them offensive (Davenport 2005; Matthews 1995; Stackhouse 1995b, 2005).

What is missing from both positive and negative public perceptions of evangelical Protestants in Canada is any serious consideration of their cultural and ethnic diversity. I have selected four very different examples, each serving as a window to offer glimpses of the changing multicultural dynamics among evangelicals. Each of these communities has its unique characteristics, but each can be seen as contributing to the larger movement. In the conclusion, I offer a brief look at how the new diversity among evangelicals is changing the nature of their participation in public life in Canada.

Asian Evangelicals

Although a significant number of Chinese came to Canada during the nineteenth century in search of gold and employment, harsh and restrictive immigration policies including a series of head tax bills starting in 1885 and the *Chinese Immigration Act* in 1923 discouraged further immigration from China during the first half of the twentieth century. This position began to change dramatically in the 1960s when country of origin was removed as a criterion for entry into Canada, and Chinese started arriving in greater numbers. Specific events also spurred Chinese immigration; for example, for several decades prior to the return of Hong Kong to China in 1997, a steady stream of immigrants came to Canada looking for a greater degree of political stability. Another wave of immigrants from China arrived in Canada following the Tiananmen Square massacre in 1989. The successive waves of immigration during the second half of the twentieth century have helped their total number surpass 1 million, or 3.5 per cent of the total Canadian population (Chui, Tran, and Flanders 2005). In only five years, between 1996 and 2001, the total number of Chinese Canadians increased by 20 per cent. (It should be noted that in 2001, 25 per cent of people of Chinese heritage in Canada were Canadian-born.) While some immigrants have returned to Hong Kong, the influx shows no sign of abating, as many Mandarin-speaking immigrants from mainland China continue to seek entry into Canada.

By far the largest concentrations are found in Toronto and Vancouver, with almost 75 per cent of the Chinese population in Canada living in these two metropolitan centres (Canadian Social Trends 2003). Taken together, Chinese dialects (mostly Cantonese and Mandarin) represent the third most common mother tongue reported in the 2001 Census (Chui, Tran, and Flanders 2005, 27, 29). In 2001, 9 per cent of Toronto's total population was Chinese; some areas in the Greater Toronto Area, such as Markham, are now 30 per cent Chinese. In the Vancouver region, more than 40 per cent of residents in Richmond are Chinese, making it the area with the highest concentration of Chinese people in Canada. The large numbers concentrated in these regions, and the substantial financial resources within this immigrant community (a significant proportion of Chinese immigrants are well-educated professionals), have made it possible to develop a Chinese cultural infrastructure within specific regions. This change has led to the flourishing in these areas of Chinese architecture, restaurants, shops, social clubs, media outlets, and the frequent public use of Chinese dialects.

More than 26 per cent of the Chinese in Canada identify themselves with some form of Christianity. This group represents the fastest growing and most dynamic component of the increasingly diverse world of evangelical Protestantism in Canada. Although the first Chinese church in Canada was established in 1892, Canadian policies and attitudes insured that Chinese immigrants and churches remained few. Because of the enormous influx of immigrants, the number of Chinese congregations in Canada has grown rapidly, from about 30 in the 1950s to more than 230 in 1990, and more than 350 at the beginning of the twenty-first century.[6] A handful of congregations, such as Scarborough Chinese Baptist Church, contain several thousand members, but most number several hundred. Recent estimates suggest that approximately 70,000 people, or 7 per cent of the Chinese population in Canada, attend evangelical churches regularly (Mak 1993).

Chinese Christians are distributed among a range of denominations. Evangelical Protestant denominations with a substantial number of Chinese congregations include various Baptist groups, Christian and Missionary Alliance (Ka-Lun 1998), Pentecostal, Associated Gospel churches, Evangelical Free, Methodist, and Mennonite Brethren, as well as numerous independent congregations. Following the start of their first Chinese congregation in Regina in 1961, the Christian and Missionary Alliance have added almost fifty more within three decades (1993). Chinese-speaking adults comprise 10 per cent of the denomination's membership in Canada (Fieguth 1993). The first Mennonite Brethren Chinese congregation began as an outreach ministry in the early 1970s (Kwan 2001, 2–8). Now there are seventeen Chinese churches in British Columbia alone, with nine operating English ministries. Together their membership constitutes more than 10 per cent of the Mennonite Brethren membership in the province.

Despite Chinese Christians' distribution among, and involvement in, various Canadian-based denominations, common ethnic ties remain a powerful bond reflecting the strong commitment to community that is part of Chinese culture. The sheer size of the Chinese community, along with the extensive Chinese cultural infrastructure in and around Vancouver and Toronto, makes it both possible and desirable for Chinese Christians in these regions to maintain significant involvement within their own ethnic community. Chinese evangelicals have established a parallel religious institutional infrastructure that includes a wide range of para-church initiatives such as periodicals (*Canadian Chinese Churches News*, *Herald Monthly*, and *Chinese around the World*), television shows such as *Showers of Blessing*, major events such as the Chinese Missionary Convention of Canada, which started in 1982, and the formation of a Canadian branch of the international Chinese Coordination Centre of World Evangelism in 1988. In addition, leaders from Chinese congregations have established their own interdenominational leadership networks; for example, nearly 100 Chinese church leaders from various denominations meet monthly as the Greater Vancouver Chinese Ministerial. A similar association operates in Toronto. Among other initiatives, this group coordinates a combined Cantonese, Mandarin, and English Bible conference that annually attracts several thousand people. In addition to interdenominational ministerial associations, Chinese leaders in several denominations have organized denominational ministerial networks; this is true both for the Mennonite Brethren in British Columbia and the Christian and Missionary Alliance. These specifically Chinese initiatives have helped to create and maintain international links with a global Chinese diaspora, but the time, energy, and resources necessary to sustain them often make it difficult for Chinese church leaders to accept roles within Canadian denominational structures (Wilkinson 2000).

The size of the Chinese Christian community and the demand for trained pastors have prompted several evangelical theological institutions in Canada to develop educational programs specifically for Chinese students. A good example is Tyndale University College and Seminary in Toronto, which started the Hudson Taylor Centre for Chinese Ministries in 2000. Six years later, in partnership with Association of Canadian Chinese Theological Education, this same school inaugurated the Canadian Chinese School of Theology. Financial resources along with trained leaders have made it possible for Chinese churches in Canada to launch their own outreach programs to people within their own ethnic group in Canada and to the larger Chinese diaspora around the world. For example, the Chinese Mennonite Brethren congregations in Vancouver sent missionaries to Venezuela in the 1990s to start Chinese churches in Porte la Cruz and Caracas (Kwan 2001, 7).

What may appear from a distance as a homogenous ethnic community of Chinese churches is, in fact, quite diverse. Within the Chinese community in Vancouver, there are at least six (probably more) distinct subcultural groups that remain somewhat separate from each other. Immigrants who arrived in Canada during early part of the twentieth century, generally from China's Cantonese-speaking Toyshan Province, make up one group. More recent Hong Kong immigrants fall into two socio-economic groups: the very wealthy and the middle class. Taiwanese immigrants who speak Mandarin are culturally and socio-economically distinct from less wealthy Mandarin-speaking immigrants from mainland China. The sixth group is made up of immigrants from Southeast Asia, including Indonesia, Singapore, and Malaysia (Johnstone 2002; Nagata 2003). To some extent, membership within different Chinese churches tends to follow these groupings. The task of leadership

within Chinese congregations is complicated further when congregations become a mixed collection of new, predominately Mandarin-
speaking immigrants, older first-generation, mostly Cantonese-speaking immigrants, and second- and third-generation Canadian-born
English-speaking Chinese.

Contributing still further towards the diversity within Chinese congregations are the cultural differences between generations as gradual
integration into Canadian culture takes place. The first generation of
immigrants often have the most difficulty learning a new language and
adjusting to a new way of life, and therefore may feel the cultural transitions as a loss of identity. However, retaining the language and culture of a former way of life frequently threatens to jeopardize their
relationship with the second- and third-generation Canadian-born
younger Chinese, who have become thoroughly familiar with the
English language and Canadian culture through school and work, and
who often wish to shed an exclusively Chinese ethnicity. Congregations
that are slow to adjust often lose a significant proportion of their young
people (Chong 1997). Inter-generational tensions are sometimes escalated further when the Chinese cultural value of giving honour and
respect to the elderly and to community leaders collides with the more
individualistic and democratic North American values accepted by the
youth. For example, recent arrivals might think that challenging a minister is disrespectful, while others see the absence of discussion with the
minister as a failure to exercise proper leadership (Matthews 1997, 23).

A common strategy for addressing the inter-generational and multicultural diversity is to organize language-specific services. These multiple services are symbolic indicators of the cultural transitions taking
place within Chinese congregations. Many of the older Chinese congregations have begun English-language services, marking the inevitable
–but often painful and difficult – transition within immigrant communities, from the predominance of one language (and culture) to another.
The high value that the Chinese generally place on education has
helped them adapt to such changes more readily than other immigrant
groups, but the ongoing influx of new immigrants prolongs the transition (Friesen 1987; Whysall 1988).

Some leaders in Chinese churches welcome the introduction of multiple services, particularly English-language services, and have hired
white English-speaking staff as part of a strategy for keeping Canadian-
born Chinese young people from leaving the church, and as a way to
signal that the congregation is interested in becoming more multicul-

tural. A number of older Chinese congregations have removed the word *Chinese* from their church name. Other leaders, however, argue that ethnic homogeneity is essential for attracting new Chinese immigrants who might see in such communities a way to cushion the shock associated with immigration. Such disagreements illustrate a debate currently taking place more generally among evangelicals, between those who think church planting is most effective when focused on specific ethnic groups and those who think the ideal ought to be the creation of intentionally multicultural congregations (Browne 2001; Clements 1997; Ghosh 2006; Seim 1999). Some suspect that the preference for ethnic homogeneity may be a subtle form of racism, even though the majority of Chinese in Canada live in close proximity to, and interact with, people of other races and ethnicities (Jones 2000).

While Chinese immigrants make up the largest proportion of Asian immigrants in Canada, Asians from other countries including Korea, the Philippines, Vietnam, and Japan have also added diversity to the evangelical Protestant melange. The most notable numerically are the Koreans and the Filipinos. For example, approximately 75 per cent of the 100,000 Koreans in Canada identify themselves as Christian, with Protestants outnumbering Catholics. As a result, Korean congregations in Canada often serve as community centres for incoming immigrants. The most popular denominational affiliations are with those denominations that sent missionaries to Korea during the last century, with the highest concentrations of Koreans among the Presbyterians, Methodists, United Church of Canada, and Baptists. Korean evangelicals have earned a reputation for their intense piety, zealous commitment to early morning prayer meetings, and missionary zeal, but like other immigrant congregations they too struggle with inter-generational tensions (Couto 2000). The Filipino population in Canada is three times larger than the Korean population, with the vast majority identifying themselves as Roman Catholic. Nonetheless, the raw number of Filipino Protestants and Korean Protestants is similar, with the highest concentrations distributed among the Baptists, Adventists, Churches of Christ, and Pentecostals.

Black Evangelicals

Historical disputes over slavery and civil rights are often considered by Canadians to be a part of American history, and yet a long history of racism, oppression, and systemic disadvantage is also a part of the heritage of many Blacks in Canada (Walker 1980; Wink 2000). Currently Blacks are the third-largest visible minority group in Canada, numbering over 660,000, 68 per cent of whom describe themselves as Christian. As highlighted in a recent documentary, *Seeking Salvation: A History of the Black Church in Canada*, churches have played a significant role in the Black communities in Canada.

The presence of several Black congregational networks makes up a significant part of the ethnic and racial diversity among evangelical Protestants in Canada. One of the oldest and largest is the African United Baptist Association in Atlantic Canada. With historical roots dating back to the formation of the first African Baptist church in Canada (Cornwallis Street Baptist Church), this association was formed in 1853 by Black Loyalists, former American slaves who accepted the British government's offer of freedom and land in Nova Scotia. Black settlers were attracted to the Baptists in part because of their emphasis on the independence of local congregations. The decision to maintain a separate network of Baptist churches allowed for a greater degree of freedom and participation in church life on the part of their members than would have been possible within a predominately white denominational structure. In addition to starting churches, Blacks organized their own schools and voluntary societies, which served as vital centres of social life at a time when Blacks were often refused access to the amenities and opportunities available within predominately white communities. To this day 40 per cent of Blacks in Atlantic Canada, and 9 per cent of all Blacks in Canada, belong to Baptist churches (Kylie 1998).

Leaders in Black churches are quick to point out that common race does not necessarily mean common ethnicity. In addition to those families that have been in Canada for many generations, a new influx of Black immigrants during the last half of the twentieth century from places such as the Caribbean and Africa has brought more ethnic diversity to the Black population (Milan and Tran 2004). For example, the second-largest expatriate Haitian community in the world can be found in Montreal; this community has organized some of the largest Protestant churches in the city. A significant number of these immigrants find their way into Pentecostal churches, preferring the movement's more expressive, emotional style of worship. Approximately 9 per cent of all Blacks in Canada worship in Pentecostal congregations.

Although most Black congregations are now affiliated with larger, more ethnically and racially diverse denominations, many still prefer to maintain some degree of separation. Despite Canada's official encouragement of multiculturalism, Black leaders state that they continue to face subtle forms of systemic or institutional racism, which is most evident in the inability of many in their communities to access the same economic and educational opportunities available to whites. As a result, there is a higher degree of poverty among Black communities, including the indigenous Black community, which has been present in Canada for more than two centuries. Because of these experiences, Black evangelical churches are often more vigorously involved in social activism than their white counterparts.

Francophone Evangelicals

Throughout much of Canadian history, it has generally been understood that French-speaking Canadians were Roman Catholic, while English-speaking Canadians were Protestant. Although never entirely accurate, nowhere has this general picture changed more dramatically in the last fifty years than in Quebec. Beginning in 1960, the newly elected Liberal Party set in motion a process of secularization within the province – a process later dubbed the Quiet Revolution – that significantly reduced the Roman Catholic Church's influence in Quebec culture and politics. It was a time of massive social change as the province rapidly moved towards cultural and political modernization (see chapter 3 in this book by Solange Lefebvre; Baum 2000; Gauverau 2006; Seljak 2000).

Levels of participation within the Roman Catholic Church began to plummet rapidly, from over 85 per cent in some regions prior to 1960 to less than 5 per cent in some urban areas as Quebecers began to explore a myriad of other religious options. Although several French evangelical Protestant denominations had been active in Quebec since the conclusion of the First World War, they struggled to survive, frequently encountering suspicion and enduring hostility as 'sectarians.' Their difficulties as a beleaguered and sometimes even persecuted minority nurtured a strident non-compromising mentality that often led them to embrace a cultural isolation that has diminished only recently (Wingender 2005). The diminishing influence of the Roman Catholic Church and the acceptance of religious pluralism, however, created unprecedented growth opportunities for evangelical Protestants after 1960.

Interest in Quebec among evangelicals in the rest of Canada increased significantly following Expo '67, a major international fair hosted in Montreal. This interest was sparked in part by the sponsorship of an evangelistic centennial project called the Sermons from Science pavilion, an alternative to the more broadly ecumenical Christian pavilion at the same fair. The project required cooperation from numerous evangelical organizations from across the country. At first the Sermons from Science pavilion was treated as a kind of embarrassing anomaly from the fringes of Canadian Christianity; attendance statistics, however, indicate that it was one of the most popular pavilions, with more than 840,000 visitors (Miedema 2005; Smith, 1988, 238–42; Stackhouse 1993, 114–20). After Expo closed, the pavilion continued to show its films until 1975, partly at the invitation of the City of Montreal and partly in response to invitations from numerous Roman Catholic schools. The public exposure, the relatively new experience of working together, and the desire to respond to new opportunities prompted evangelicals in Quebec to form a bilingual organization called Christian Direction / Direction chrétienne, which continues to be an important service agency to evangelicals in Quebec. The interest created outside of Quebec by the success of the pavilion precipitated an influx of evangelical workers financed by a variety of evangelical denominations. These English-speaking workers learned French and started churches, thereby contributing to the growth of French evangelical Protestantism during the 1970s and 1980s.

According to the 2001 Census, approximately 5 per cent of Quebecers (350,000) can be identified as Protestant. More than half (between 180,000 and 190,000) are associated with an evangelical Protestant denomination. Census results can be misleading: not all francophone evangelicals identify themselves as Protestant, which is seen by some as an exclusively anglophone label. Moreover, census numbers do not offer an accurate indication of how many people actually participate in Protestant churches. Other research shows that only about 1 per cent of the Quebec population (81,250) attends a Protestant church with any regularity, the majority (about 80 per cent) of these people showing up at evangelical congregations (Buchanan 2004). The best estimates suggest that there are now slightly more than 40,000 French-speaking evangelicals in Quebec, representing less than 0.6 per cent of the population.

From fewer than 50 French-speaking congregations in 1950 distributed among half a dozen denominations, the francophone evangelical movement grew to more than 350 French-speaking congregations distributed among approximately thirty denominations by the late 1990s

(Smith 1995, 235–6). (Almost all French-speaking evangelical Protestant congregations are located in Quebec, despite pockets of francophone populations in other provinces.) The largest denominations include the Eastern Ontario and Quebec division of the Pentecostal Assemblies of Canada, with more than eighty-five French-speaking congregations, the Association d'Églises baptistes évangéliques (Fellowship of Evangelical Baptist Churches) with sixty congregations, the Christian (Plymouth) Brethren with more than forty congregations, and the Union d'Églises baptistes françaises au Canada with more than twenty congregations. More than 65 per cent of the French-speaking congregations are located in small cities or rural areas of the province.[7] A demographic analysis shows that only 10 per cent of the membership of this movement have completed a university degree (in comparison to 15 per cent of the general population in Quebec), and the majority work in blue-collar occupations.

Despite impressive proportional gains in membership in recent decades, evangelical Protestants in Quebec remain a much smaller minority of the overall population than in other parts of the country. A variety of factors can be identified: the lingering associations between both Québécois identity and Roman Catholicism, even though most Quebecers do not attend church regularly. Upstart Protestant groups have had a difficult time overcoming historic stigmas of sectarianism within the province. Despite a high interest in spirituality, Quebecers display a higher level of distrust towards all forms of organized religion than other Canadians. The 'salvation only' message preached by many evangelical groups is perceived as inadequate for addressing social problems (Buchanan 2003b). Francophone evangelicals do not have the same institutional resources enjoyed by their anglophone counterparts in other provinces and they work in a cultural environment that has had less exposure to Christian literature, radio, television, and conferences (Bibby 2004, 24, 56). Notable, however, is the Pentecostal success: their more intensely emotional, spontaneous, and experiential approach has resonated more readily with Québécois culture.

The decade of the 1970s was tumultuous for Quebecers, beginning with the FLQ crisis, which prompted the federal government to invoke the *War Measures Act*, followed by the election of the first separatist Parti Québécois government in 1976. Thousands of English Quebecers left the province. Tensions between English and French Quebecers, and between Quebec and other parts of Canada, escalated, especially during the 1980 and 1995 referendums. These political differences were felt within evangelical churches: English-speaking evangelicals both inside and outside of Quebec uniformly opposed Quebec independence; French-speaking evangelicals, however, were more divided on the matter of Quebec national sovereignty, much to the consternation of their English-speaking counterparts (Koop 1995b).[8]

The frustration and animosity felt by Canadians outside of Quebec towards Quebec nationalists were often shared by evangelical Protestants. During the years of heightened tension, financial support from the rest of Canada for French-speaking evangelical ministries in Quebec declined, prompting a more urgent effort by French-speaking evangelicals to recruit and train indigenous francophone leaders. Evangelical Protestantism in Quebec has, therefore, gradually become more Québécois in leadership and less dependent on personnel, ministry models, and resources from outside the province. In addition, the reduction in financial support from outside the province pushed French-speaking evangelical denominations towards creating networks that facilitated better communication, allowed an exchange of resources, coordinated collaboration in the planning of large public events, and helped present a more unified public voice. Examples of greater cooperation include the formation of the Alliance francophone des protestant évangeliques du Quebec in 1995, a French parallel to the Evangelical Fellowship of Canada, and the negotiation of a cooperative program agreement in 2005 between the École de théologie évangélique de Montréal, a Mennonite Brethren school that has operated for more than a decade as the Protestant sector of the Faculty of Theology at the Université de Montreal, and the Institut Biblique V.I.E., a Christian and Missionary Alliance school located in Ste-Foy, Quebec (Hoyer 1987). Evangelical Protestants claim to share a common commitment to a spiritual unity that transcends other differences and warn about the dangers of giving ultimate allegiance to nationalism; because of their political and cultural differences, anglophone and francophone evangelicals have on numerous occasions tried to organize events designed to facilitate deeper understanding, greater cultural and historical awareness, and reconciliation between the two communities.[9]

Always an important financial and cultural centre in Canada, the metropolitan area of Montreal has gradually acquired the reputation of being one of the most cosmopolitan and multicultural cities in the world. The region makes up almost half of Quebec's population. Despite the fact that less than 7.5 per cent of the population claims no religious affiliation, one of the lowest percentages for a Census Metropolitan Area in Canada, less than 10 per cent of the population attends church once a month or more (Smith 1995, 242–59). With fewer than 100 congregations in the Montreal area, French-speaking evangelical Protestants remain a distinct religious minority within this metropolitan region. Ongoing immigration has added to this challenge: more than 15 per cent (530,000) of the population in the Montreal area is allophone, representing almost 170 different linguistic and ethnic groups. There are evangelical Protestant churches within approximately thirty of these ethnic communities, most notably among the Spanish, Haitian, Italian, Chinese, and Portuguese. As a result, French-speaking evangelicals now face the additional challenge of relating to a multiplicity of other language groups within Quebec.

Aboriginal Evangelicals

Since they originated only in the twentieth century, most evangelical Protestant denominations have not been directly implicated with the historic controversies created by Christian leaders who worked alongside government officials in negotiating treaties, restricting Aboriginal populations to reserves, and operating institutions such as residential schools (Grant 1984). Despite this lack of direct complicity, relatively few evangelical Protestant denominations have managed to draw substantial numbers of Canada's Aboriginal people into their fold. Most Aboriginal Christians have maintained their affiliation with older mainstream denominations such as the Anglicans and Roman Catholics. Although evangelical missionaries have been present among Canadian Aboriginals for decades,[10] the historic legacy of forced relocation, racism, and cultural oppression, along with political differences surrounding self-government and land claims settlements, has made it difficult for Aboriginal peoples to integrate comfortably into new, predominately white evangelical denominations (Redekop 1988).

The Pentecostal movement, however, represents a remarkable exception to this pattern (Tarr 1987). Observers suggest that the movement's more emotional, spontaneous worship style, together with the expectation of visible manifestations of supernatural phenomena, has close affinities with the world view of many First Nations people. The 2001 Census reported that 3.4 per cent (nearly 19,000) of Canada's 'Registered/Treaty Indians' called themselves Pentecostal, a proportion nearly three times greater than among the general population in Canada.[11] Several thousand more identified themselves as Baptist and

Moravian. Other evangelical denominations with several Aboriginal congregations include the Christian and Missionary Alliance, Free Methodist Church, and Mennonite Church Canada. For a substantial number of Aboriginal people, evangelical Protestantism in Canada is not just a 'white man's religion' (Careless 2002).

Pentecostalism among Aboriginal people is expressed through a variety of denominational forms. Many Inuit in the far north have embraced a charismatic version of Anglicanism.[12] In other regions, Full Gospel house churches, Foursquare Gospel Church congregations, and numerous independent Pentecostal churches have been established. The Pentecostal denomination with the most significant presence among Aboriginal groups is the Pentecostal Assemblies of Canada, with more than 100 Aboriginal congregations and numerous small Bible schools specifically focused on training Aboriginal leaders.

Aboriginal communities in Canada have faced monumental challenges during the past century. The loss of traditional lifestyles, widespread unemployment, poverty, and decades of government duplicity and inertia have precipitated an avalanche of despair that, in turn, has contributed to high levels of alcoholism, drug and sexual abuse, domestic violence, and suicide within Aboriginal communities. Despair and desperation have created a deep longing for meaning and hope, and have precipitated a widespread openness to spiritually oriented solutions. Since 1990, numerous communities in the North have witnessed unprecedented and well-publicized evangelical religious renewals that have often attracted large numbers of people, including many political leaders (Fieguth 2000, 2002; Parker 1999; *Christian Week* 2001; Stirk 2004). Some of the largest gatherings in this expansive region during the past two decades have been multi-denominational Bible conferences. For example, in April 2004 Iqaluit hosted the twentieth annual Arctic Bible Conference, which attracted more than 1,000 people. This was the largest gathering in the community since Nunavut became an independent territory in 1999, and included the active participation of prominent politicians such as Tagak Curley, the MLA for Rankin Inlet North, along with Patterk Netser, the MLA for Nanulik (Mathon 2005; Younger-Lewis 2004). These events have brought together people from denominations that have historically been suspicious of each other (for example, Pentecostals and Anglicans); this unprecedented collaboration has also generated ongoing debates within these denominations regarding, among other things, the question of which denomination best represents the authentic message of Christianity.

In some communities, religious renewal played a vital part in community revitalization. In isolated regions such as Canada's North it has been easier for the church to play a prominent role within community life. The urgent economic, social, and educational needs within First Nations communities prompted numerous Christian Aboriginal leaders to get involved in political leadership as advocates on behalf of their people (such as in land claim settlements and self-government negotiations). More than a few Pentecostal Aboriginal leaders have been at the forefront of political initiatives at local and national levels. Such political involvement has, however, sometimes complicated their relationship with their non-Aboriginal denominational counterparts. It would, for example, be hard to imagine two individuals with more widely divergent political views than former grand chief of Aboriginal First Nations Matthew Coon Come and Stockwell Day, former leader of the official opposition and leader of the Canadian Alliance Party (now Conservative Party), and yet both are Pentecostals.

While stories of native community transformation are still much too rare, Waskaganish, a Cree village with approximately 1,350 residents located on the edge of James Bay, Quebec, is one such exception. During the 1960s and 1970s, living conditions in the village were characterized by abject poverty, high levels of disease, suicide and infant mortality, almost 100 per cent unemployment, as well as rampant alcohol abuse. Since then, living conditions have changed dramatically and new economic opportunities have emerged. Native leaders are adamant that the remarkable social and economic transformation of the community was due both to a Pentecostal 'spiritual revival' precipitated by Johnny Whiskeychan during the 1970s, and the signing of the James Bay and Northern Quebec Agreement in 1975. The religious revival led to the establishment of a Pentecostal church in the village, and over time approximately 70 per cent of the residents became active Christians, including Billy Diamond, grand chief of the Council of the Crees of Quebec, who played a prominent political role in making sure the James Bay Agreement was implemented and in negotiating self-government for the Crees (*Christian Week* 1990; Dorsch 1991; Tarr 1987, 29, 31; Wallace 1986).

Although the number of Aboriginal leaders is still low, there has been a notable increase in the number of Aboriginals leading evangelical congregations in the past two decades. This has been due, in part, to the work of numerous small Bible schools that have been started to train Aboriginal pastors, making it possible to give voice to Aboriginal issues within denominations such as the Pentecostal Assemblies of Canada, and has helped to move Aboriginal congregations from dependency to a healthier interdependence (Fieguth 1994). Several associations designed to link Aboriginal evangelical leaders and to serve Aboriginal evangelical congregations have been formed; the most notable example is the Native Evangelical Fellowship, started in 1971 by Cree evangelists Tommy Francis, Stan Williams, and Bill Jackson (Cook 1995). It marks the first all-Aboriginal denomination in Canada, with more than thirty congregations in its network. Still others include Intertribal Christian Communications, founded in 1979, First Nations Fellowship, started in 1994, and My People International, started in 2000. During the 1990s, several large evangelical organizations, World Vision and Evangelical Fellowship of Canada, formed divisions within their organizations specifically focused on Aboriginal concerns.

All of these developments have increased awareness of Aboriginal issues among evangelical Protestants in Canada. During a decade when Aboriginal frustration led to blockades and armed confrontations, evangelical Aboriginal leaders were often at the forefront of organizing events to prompt greater understanding and reconciliation between Aboriginals and other Canadians (Fieguth 1996; Harvey 1997; Koop 1995a; Prayer Gathering to Focus on Healing 1999). Ross Maracle is a Pentecostal Mohawk clergyman, the past president of National Native Bible College, and host of *Spirit Alive*, a weekly television broadcast. He was a negotiator during the Oka Crisis in 1990 because of his ability to give eloquent expression of his people's distress and his ability to move between the lines occupied by Quebec provincial police and the Mohawk Warriors (Koop 1991; Maracle 1990).

Although historic denominational differences tend to be less meaningful to Aboriginal evangelicals than to some of their non-Aboriginal counterparts, Aboriginal evangelicals have their own divisions. One of the more notable internal debates is on questions concerning which traditional cultural practices to incorporate within Christian worship (Careless 2002; Cowan 1991). Robert Burkinshaw's work outlines the evolution among the Pentecostal Assemblies of Canada towards the indigenization of Aboriginal Pentecostalism. During the 1950s through to the 1970s, denominational leaders essentially ignored Aboriginal culture; during the 1980s and 1990s, many actively resisted the integration of aspects of Aboriginal culture. The recent influx of Asian and Latin American newcomers helped the denomination become more flexible in negotiating the margins of Aboriginal culture and Pentecostal expression (Burkinshaw in press). Contentious also are the debates over which specific strategies ought, or ought not, to be used by Aboriginal people for furthering their political objectives (Koop 1990). Similar to the pattern experienced by many immigrant groups, Aboriginal people struggle with generational conflicts between the young and old, gaps that have been widened by the general use of the English language, by the move of young people to urban areas (half of Aboriginal people now live in urban centres), and by education and use of technology.

Evangelical Protestants and Public Engagement

As the evangelical Protestant denominations began to emerge from their ethnic and religious enclaves during the 1960s, they began to take a deeper interest in exercising influence within Canadian culture in general and became more assertive within the political arena in particular. Becoming more politically active was necessary, they believed, because of the diminishing role of religious institutions within Canadian culture, the privatization of religious belief and behaviour, and the growing popularity of secularist ideologies (Egerton 2000, 107). In particular, the debates during the 1980s over the inclusion of a reference to God in the preamble to the *Canadian Charter of Rights and Freedoms* and the decriminalization of abortion galvanized a desire among evangelical Protestants to shape public policy at a national level.[13]

From 1960 onwards, candidates from evangelical denominations increasingly began to run for public office at municipal, provincial, and federal levels. A good example were the Mennonite Brethren, many of whom came to Canada during the late-nineteenth and early-twentieth century as part of a larger migration of Russian German Mennonites (see chapter 9 by Royden Loewen in this book). This denomination's Anabaptist tradition has historically discouraged participation in politics, but more than most other Mennonite denominations the Mennonite Brethren intentionally adopted a dual Anabaptist-Evangelical theological identity in North America. As is the case for most immigrant communities, it often takes several generations before members of such communities become engaged in politics in a new country. It was not until the latter half of the twentieth century that the number of Mennonite candidates – the majority being Mennonite Brethren – for public office showed a remarkable surge. The number running in provincial elections increased from thirty-six during the 1950s to ninety-five during the 1980s, and in federal elections from twenty-one during the 1950s to forty-six during the 1980s (Redekop 1995, 19–84). Similarly, evangelical Protestants who have arrived in Canada more recently are gradually becoming more politically active. This is especially true of Asian evangelicals, particularly the Chinese, many of whom have now been present in Canada for several decades or more. A notable example is Raymond Chan, who was first elected as a Liberal member of parliament for Richmond in 1993 and who was appointed as minister of state for multiculturalism in 2004.

There is not a clear consensus among evangelical Protestants on the best strategy for influencing public policy in a pluralistic, multicultural society. Some look back wistfully at the extensive influence of Christianity in Canadian history. This historical legacy, along with the increasing numerical strength of evangelical Protestants, has tempted some evangelicals to use the past to claim a kind of cultural entitlement for an agenda of re-Christianizing Canada. Others bemoan the marginalizing influence of secularism, while they simultaneously celebrate the generally peaceful character of Canadian multiculturalism. While seeking to have their own place recognized within Canadian pluralism, the majority of evangelical Protestants who are now involved in politics recognize the need to collaborate, introducing policy proposals on the basis of principles for the common good and using means that are persuasive rather than coercive (Evangelical Fellowship of Canada 1997; Posterski 1995; B. Stiller 1997; Vandezande 1999).

Despite general agreement among evangelical Protestants on basic principles such as the dignity of all persons as children of God, the sanctity of human life, the care and protection of vulnerable people, the sanctity of heterosexual marriage and family values, the universal right of religious freedom, and the value of cultural diversity, they continue to disagree on specific strategies to apply these principles. As a result, it is difficult to uniformly categorize evangelical Protestants within the traditional liberal–conservative or left–right division of partisan politics. The majority of evangelicals align themselves with social conservatives on issues they consider to be matters of morality such as abortion, gambling, and the traditional definition of marriage. While policies related to abortion and homosexuality are common flashpoints for evangelical Protestants, the top-ranked priorities within this constituency also include policies that support children living in poverty, prevent the exploitation of children in pornography and the sex trade, and reduce homelessness – issues that are often of greater concern to parties on the political left (Van Ginkel 2003, 8).

While evangelicals profess a united commitment to common princi-ples, their voting patterns do not reflect a parallel political unity. Contrary to media perceptions, research suggests that evangelical Prot-estant voting patterns generally mirror regional patterns in Canada, but with a slightly greater tilt towards right-of-centre parties, particularly in western Canada (Bowen 2004, 195–8; Clemenger 2005).[14] Important components of this pattern are the affinities between the evangelical Protestant emphasis on an individual's personal relationship with God on the one hand and the individual-oriented, laissez-faire economics that characterizes right-of-centre political parties on the other hand. An Ipsos-Reid survey reveals some variation in voting patterns between those who attend church regularly and those who do not. For example, during the 2004 federal election, Canadian Protestants who attended church weekly were 12 per cent more likely to vote Conservative than the average Canadian, and Roman Catholics who attended church weekly were 10 per cent more likely to vote Liberal (Grenville and Fled-derus 2004). The tilt to the right among churchgoers was more pronounced in the 2006 federal election as numerous churchgoing Catholics broke with a century-old tradition of voting Liberal (Gren-ville 2006). At present, all of the national political parties in Canada find support among evangelical Protestants. One estimate suggests that the 2004 election brought close to 100 'religious conservatives' to the 308-seat House of Commons. About half were in the Conservative Party caucus (O'Neil 2005). In the 2006 federal election, several evangelical Protestant candidates ran against each other: two notable examples were the riding of Richmond in which Raymond Chan, Liberal Party incumbent, defeated Darrel Reid, Conservative Party candidate and former president of Focus on the Family Canada, and the riding of North Vancouver in which two members of the same Christian and Missionary Alliance congregation, Liberal Party incumbent Don Bell and Conservative Party candidate Cindy Silver, squared off (Ward 2005b).

The growth of evangelical Protestants in Canada has generated fear that they may be intent on creating a Canadian version of the powerful 'religious right' lobby in the United States (McDonald 2006; Ward 2005a).[15] Canadian sociologist Sam Reimer identifies numerous simi-larities between evangelicals in the United States and Canada, but notes that one of the most prominent differences between evangelicals in the two countries is in their respective political attitudes (Reimer 2003).[16] It is unlikely, for a variety of reasons, that evangelical Protestants in Canada will form or dominate any political party (Clemenger, 2005; O'Toole 1996; Simpson and MacLeod 1985; Stackhouse 1994). Evangelical Protestants in Canada do not make up nearly as large a proportion of the population as in the United States, are not as concentrated in one geographical region (as, for example, evangelicals is in the American South), and therefore do not have the potential for exercising the same degree of influence. In addition, a much larger proportion of American evangelicals is both socially conservative as well as fiscally conservative. The same alignment is not the case among Canadian evangelicals, who show a greater interest in economic inequality and the government's role in society (Clemenger 2005, 94).[17]

In addition to running for public office, evangelical Protestants have become increasingly active in a range of special-purpose non-partisan organizations and ad hoc coalitions targeting specific government initiatives.[18] Despite the significant will of ordinary evangelicals to participate in society, few denominations have developed the necessary expertise or resources to launch effective national campaigns. Moreover, the absence of an evangelical consensus on strategy has made the support of trans-denominational organizations the most visible expression of social activism for evangelical Protestants. The more prominent groups include the moderate Evangelical Fellowship of Canada, the conservative Focus on the Family Canada, the social justice–oriented Citizens for Public Justice, and the international aid–oriented World Vision. These organizations generally 'enter the public policy conversation not only to defend their group's rights and privileges, but customarily, if not universally, to commend principles to govern the common life of all Canadians' (Stackhouse 2000, 122).[19]

By the end of the twentieth century, evangelical Protestants formed several ad hoc coalitions that included other religious groups, particularly Roman Catholics, with whom they share many common values (for example, the opposition to abortion and pornography). During the 1990s, several court cases in Ontario brought Muslims, Jews, Hindus, Sikhs, and Christians together to express their concern about government policies that required non-Catholic parents who wished to have their children educated in faith-based schools to pay tuition while still contributing to the fully funded public system through their property taxes (for example, *Bal v. Ontario* [1994], and *Adler v. Ontario* [1996]). The Ontario Multi-Faith Coalition for Equity in Education argued that distinctions between religious and secular education cannot be made because secularism is itself a value-laden orientation, and because it places a significant burden on parents for whom it is important that their children be educated from a particular faith perspective outside of the public educational system. They advocated an education system that fairly represents the religious plurality in Canadian society, will teach students about religion in general, and at the same time encourage them to explore the meaning and value of their own religious traditions (Evangelical Fellowship of Canada 2000). During the same period, leaders from these same religious groups joined to form the Interfaith Coalition for Marriage and Family, which tried to prevent the redefinition of marriage by intervening in court cases such as *Egan v. Canada* [1995], and *Halpern v. Canada* [2003] (Cere and Farrow 2004). This laid a foundation for the 'marriage movement' in Canada, which brought together a broad coalition of people from different political parties, professions, ethnicities, and religions who opposed the liberalization of the definition of marriage. Although this movement was unsuccessful, its emergence reflects the capacity of some religious communities in Canada to transcend ethnic and religious differences as they seek to influence public policy.

Conclusion

Two common theological convictions among evangelical Protestants reinforce the expectations created by Canada's official policy of multiculturalism, creating several points of compatibility between Canadian national interests and the efforts of evangelical Protestants to make their churches more diverse and inclusive.

The first of these theological affirmations is reflected in their commitment to promoting the message that Jesus Christ is the source of life and truth for all people; this remains the primary catalyst driving evangelical missionary efforts around the world. No other tradition within Christianity has been as aggressive in training and sending cross-cultural evangelists and missionaries around the world. Because of their sense of responsibility for engaging those who are not Christians, immigrants often find church communities to be more socially accessible and welcoming than other institutions (Chan 2003). The national and ethnic diversity of incoming immigrants is seen by many evangelical leaders as a unique ministry opportunity (Hilder 1988; van Kleist 1978). Not only has their activism helped diversify the evangelical movement, it has also helped connect evangelical Protestants in Canada with a burgeoning global evangelical community (Lewis 2002,

2004). The second affirmation, along with that of many other Christians, is a final optimistic vision of a restored world in which people of all races, nations, and cultures worship in unity and live together in peace. Many believe that this utopian vision ought to be at least partially realized in the church, as people bridge the divisions created by race, ethnicity, and gender. One can readily find evangelical Protestants who suggest that the increasing cultural diversity in Canadian congregations and denominations presages the culmination of this ultimate utopian vision (Adeney 1989; Seim 1999, 161). In the meantime, however, as the cultural diversity among evangelical Protestants increases, they wrestle with the challenge of building cross-cultural relationships and forming a common Canadian evangelical identity.

Canada's immigration policies have not only increased the number of religions in Canada, they have also added considerably to the ethnic diversity within Christian denominations. Few Christian traditions in Canada have benefited as much during the twentieth century from immigration and the intentional promotion of multiculturalism as have evangelical Protestants. The benefits included an increase in numbers as well as a considerable expansion of the ethnic and racial diversity within Canadian evangelical denominations. This ethnic variety has created a multiplicity of transnational points of contact with a larger global evangelical Protestant community.

The ethnic diversity among evangelical Protestants is only one dimension of the complexity within the movement. Inherent are several impulses that sometimes push in opposite directions. For example, the movement is simultaneously both conservative and remarkably flexible and innovative in adapting to cultural diversity (Burkinshaw 1995, 10–11, 15–17). Evangelical Protestants are conservative in that they are concerned about preserving, intact, theological emphases they consider to be essential. They are also conservative in their opposition to practices they consider to be immoral such as homosexuality, gambling, and abortion. These issues have united evangelicals across ethnic boundaries; opposition to same-sex marriage, for example, mobilized evangelicals from all ethnic groups. Many evangelical Protestant denominations also have conservative policies that exclude women from senior leadership responsibilities within their churches.[20] These positions have produced two sets of incongruities that have intensified debates among evangelicals over these policies. First, there is the incongruity between such exclusive policies and a virtual consensus on the equality of all persons among evangelical Protestants; second, there is incongruity between the roles assumed by some evangelical women outside of the church and those permitted inside. Positions on gender roles in the church do not consistently follow ethnic lines, but are generally determined by the theology of a particular denomination; such a situation is different from what one would encounter in the Anglican or United Church of Canada communities (see chapters 4 and 6 by Wendy Fletcher and Greer Anne Wenh-In Ng in this book) in which newer non-European members consistently tend to advocate conservative views on most gender-related issues. The flexibility and innovation of evangelical Protestants are most notable in their creative approach to evangelism, church-planting methods, use of technology, and ministry and worship styles. The mixing of ethnic and national groups has provided a forum within which to exchange ideas and practices.

Evident throughout this chapter is another discernible tension among evangelical Protestants created by varying responses to Canadian multiculturalism: some evangelicals use denominational and congregational environments as places to preserve and protect a particular cultural heritage and ethnicity, whereas others use these environments as places to promote a greater mixing and crossing of cultural boundaries. Evangelical Protestants claim to be committed to a common religious legacy and identity. This transcultural identity often, but not always, creates a unity that transcends the ethnic differences found in Canada.

Notes

1 Using data from the 2001 Census, Reginald Bibby claims that 8 per cent of Canadians identify themselves as 'conservative Protestants' (2002, 39). It is difficult, however, to use census data for calculating evangelical numbers: not all evangelical denominations are included as census categories; some census categories, such as Mennonite and Lutheran, encompass a range of denominations some of which are evangelical in orientation and others that are not; and it is impossible from census data to determine the proportion of those affiliated with the older, mainstream denominations in Canada who are evangelical in their theological orientation.

   An extensive survey done by Ipsos-Reid in 2003 claims 12 per cent of Canadians are Protestant evangelicals, and an additional 7 per cent are Catholic evangelicals (Van Ginkel 2003). The reported membership of evangelical Protestant denominations numbered approximately 1.3 million persons in 2001, or about 4.3 per cent of the Canadian population (see table 10.1). Several factors account for the variation between reported membership and the proportion of the population that identifies themselves as evangelical: some attend mainstream Protestant denominations, some attend house churches, and some continue to identify with the movement despite their lack of participation (the Ipsos-Reid survey reported that 34 per cent of those who claim to be evangelical Protestant do not attend church regularly).

2 Prior to 1961, more than 90 per cent of people born outside of Canada came from Europe. By 1991 this number had declined to 20 per cent, and the largest proportion (58 per cent) of Canadians born outside of Canada came from Asia, including the Middle East (*Canadian Social Trends* 2003).

3 The condescending and even xenophobic attitudes toward incoming immigrants on the part of the mainstream Protestant establishment during this era were disseminated through popular books such as *Strangers within Our Gates*, by James S. Woodsworth, champion of the social gospel movement (1909, 3–4, 11–12, 216–33).

4 The 2001 Census reported more than 369,000 Pentecostals, a decline of 15 per cent from the 436,000 reported in 1991, but this figure does not accurately reflect the numerical strength of the Pentecostal movement in Canada. It is likely that the census category 'Pentecostal' does not include all persons who identify themselves as part of 'apostolic' denominations, or who are part of a growing number of independent 'charismatic' congregations that have historical ties to the Pentecostal movement.

5 The Reform Party critique of multiculturalism, articulated by Preston Manning, was part of a larger concern that support for 'special interest' groups should not create an elite group of Canadians entitled to special favours and thereby undermine the Canadian value of equality.

6 At the outset of this rapid increase in the number of Chinese churches, some of the numerical growth came from the large number of Chinese students who were befriended by Chinese Christians while studying in Canada. Particularly influential were organizations such as Ambassadors for Christ and Chinese Christian Fellowship (Matthews 1997).

7 The number of English-speaking evangelical congregations in Quebec increased after 1960 as well, but not nearly at the same pace. From more than fifty congregations in 1950, the number of anglophone evangelical congregations increased to almost 100 congregations by the end of the 1990s (Smith 1988, 237).

8 Despite the political differences among French-speaking evangelical Protes-

tants, survey research reveals that the level of support among them for the cause of Quebec sovereignty lags behind that of the larger French-speaking population (Smith 1995).

9 See, for example, the La Danse tour, a theatrical celebration of a 'courtship' between anglophones and francophones (Buchanan 2003a).

10 One of the most prominent evangelical missionary organizations working in northern Canada is Northern Canada Evangelical Mission, which was started during the 1940s. Others include North America Indian Ministries and InterAct Ministries of Canada, started in 1959.

11 The numbers compiled by Robert Burkinshaw are considerably higher. He notes that 'just over 35,000 of all people in Canada who claimed some aboriginal origins also claimed to be Pentecostal' (Burkinshaw in press). Burkinshaw's calculation is similar to that of Graham Gibson, who suggests that approximately 41,300 Aboriginal Christians consider themselves to be evangelical Protestant, with the vast majority being Pentecostal (Gibson 1994, 10, 91, 161).

12 Studies show that the rate of regular church attendance among children under age twelve in the North is among the highest in Canada. Some 56 per cent attend services at least monthly and 34 per cent attend weekly. That compares to only 20 per cent of Canadians in general who attend church weekly. According to Inuit leaders, this difference is due to the impact of ongoing charismatic revivals (*ChristianWeek* 2001).

13 A compromise proposal (Bill C-43) intended to reduce the number of abortions in Canada was brought forward in 1991 by Conservative Health Minister Jake Epp, an evangelical Protestant. The defeat of this bill was a bitter pill to swallow for many evangelical Protestants, but it was a lesson on the importance of cooperation and compromise with other Canadians in order to be successful in influencing public policy (Stiller 1991, 114–23).

14 This finding is consistent with historic patterns between religious affiliation and partisanship in Canada, which has been one of the most consistent influences in federal elections (Guth and Fraser 2001; Johnson 1985).

15 Bruce Clemenger points out the general absence of commentary in Canada about the political aspirations of the religious left. He asks why is it that pronouncements by some Catholic bishops opposing same-sex marriage elicit vigorous demands that churches stay out of the debate over marriage, but the same demands are not articulated in response to the United Church of Canada's endorsement of civil marriage legislation (Clemenger 2005, 93).

16 Aside from short articles by John G. Stackhouse, Jr, and a recent book by

402   Bruce L. Guenther

sociologist Sam Reimer, comparative studies between evangelical Protestants in Canada and the United States are rare (Reimer 2003; Stackhouse
1995a).

17 Seymour Martin Lipset notes how different national ideologies have created variations in the way American and Canadian religious groups engage
in politics. In Canada, religious groups are expected to coexist and tend to
be more collaborative; in the United States, religious groups tend to be
more competitive and crusading (Lipset 1990, 74–89).

18 Social scientists such as Paul Reed have identified a 'civic core' of people
responsible for the majority of contributory effort in Canada. It is a relatively small number of people – approximately 12–15 per cent of Canadians
– who are the most active contributors within society. For example, 66 per
cent of all charitable giving is done by only 8 percent of the population
(Reed with Selbee 2000, 2001). This same research confirms that religious
commitment makes a significant difference in whether people will work for
the betterment of society; 'conservative Protestants' are identified as the
religious group most actively involved in volunteer activity and charitable
giving in Canada (Reed 2005).

19 Several organizations have set as their objective the 'restoration' of Canada's Christian heritage (for example, Ken Campbell's Renaissance Canada
movement, Charles McVety's Institute for Canadian Values, and the Christian Heritage Party), but they remain on the fringes of evangelical Protestantism (Stackhouse 1994, 394).

20 Integral to the debates among evangelicals on the leadership of women are
differences over how to interpret controversial biblical passages such as
Ephesians 5, Galatians 3, 1 Peter 3, 1 Corinthians 11, and 1 Timothy 2.

Works Cited

Adeney, Miriam. 1989. Color-blind or colorful? *Faith Today,* July/August, 30.
Airhart, Phyllis D. 1992. *Serving the present age: Revivalism, progressivism, and the
Methodist tradition in Canada.* Montreal and Kingston: McGill-Queen's Uni-
versity Press.
Anderson, Wendall B. 1995. *The Covenant Church in Canada, 1904–1994: A time to
remember.* Prince Albert: Evangelical Covenant Church of Canada.
Barlow, Maude. 2006. Election 2006: Maude Barlow. http://
forums.macleans.ca/advansis/?mod=for&act=dis&eid=8.
Baum, Gregory. 2000. Catholicism and secularization in Quebec. In Lyon and
Van Die 2000, 149–65.

Bebbington, David W. 1989. *Evangelicalism in modern Britain: A history from the 1730s to the 1980s*. London: Unwin Hyman.

Bibby, Reginald W. 1987. *Fragmented gods: The poverty and potential of religion in Canada*. Toronto: Irwin.

– 1993. *Unknown gods: The ongoing story of religion in Canada*. Toronto: Stoddart.

– 1995. *There's got to be more: Connecting churches & Canadians*. Winfield, BC: Wood Lake Books.

– 2002. *Restless gods: The renaissance of religion in Canada*. Toronto: Stoddart.

– 2004. *Restless churches: How Canada's churches can contribute to the emerging religious renaissance*. Montreal: Novalis.

Bowen, Kurt. 2004. *Christians in a secular world: The Canadian experience*. Montreal and Kingston: McGill-Queen's University Press.

Bramadat, Paul A. 2000. *The church on the world's turf: An evangelical Christian group at a secular university*. New York: Oxford University Press.

– 2005. Religion, social capital and the day that changed the world. *Journal of International Migration and Integration* 6 (2): 201–18.

Bramadat, Paul, and David Seljak, eds. 2005. *Religion and ethnicity in Canada*. Toronto: Pearson Education Canada.

Browne, Beverly. 2001. Churches revived by multiculturalism. *Faith Today*, July/August, 28.

Buchanan, Marg. 2003a. Cross-Canada courtship promotes cultural healing. *ChristianWeek*, 2 September, 4.

– 2003b. French evangelicals in Quebec: A searching church in a searching society. *Faith Today*, July/August, 27.

– 2004. Quebec Christians: The urban legend. *ChristianWeek*, 12 November, 2.

Burgess, Stanley M., and Gary McGee, eds. 2002. *The new international dictionary of Pentecostal and charismatic movements*. Grand Rapids: Zondervan.

Burkinshaw, Robert. 1995. *Pilgrims in lotus land: Conservative Protestantism in British Columbia, 1917–1981*. Montreal and Kingston: McGill-Queen's University Press.

– In press. Native Pentecostalism in British Columbia. In *Pentecostal Christianity in Canada*, ed. Michael Wilkinson.

Careless, Sue. 1998. Montreal's Haitian Community. *Faith Today*, March/April, 33.

– 2001. Christians at the forefront. *Faith Today*, March/April, 46.

– 2002. Not a white man's religion. *ChristianWeek*, 8 January, 1.

– 2003. Update on cultural diversity. *Canadian Social Trends* (Autumn): 19–23.

Carpenter, Joel A. 1997. *Revive us again: The reawakening of American fundamentalism*. New York: Oxford University Press.

Cere, Daniel, and Douglas Farrow, eds. 2004. *Divorcing marriage: Unveiling the dangers in Canada's new social experiment*. Montreal and Kingston: McGill-Queen's University Press.

Chan, Elic. 2003. Ethnic churches: A reservoir of social capital for Chinese immigrants. Paper presented at the Conference on Subethnicity in the Chinese Diaspora, University of Toronto, 12–13 September.

Chong, Laurie. 1997. Generation next. *Faith Today*, July/August, 33.

ChristianWeek. 1990. Christ is key to Indian future says Billy Diamond. *ChristianWeek*, 6 November, 2.

– 1999. Prayer gathering to focus on healing. *ChristianWeek*, 16 March, 3.

– 2001. Statistics reveal northern revival. *ChristianWeek*, 17 April, 1.

Chui, Tina, Kelly Tran, and John Flanders. 2005. Chinese Canadians: Enriching the cultural mosaic. *Canadian Social Trends* (Spring): 24–32.

Clark, Warren, and Grant Schellenberg. 2006. Who's religious? *Canadian Social Trends* (Summer): 2–9.

Clemenger, Bruce. 2005. Evangelicals and political engagement. *Canadian Issues* (Summer): 93–6.

Clements, Rob. 1997. The segregated church. *Faith Today*, July/August, 28.

Cook, Donna. 1995. NEFC celebrates 25th anniversary and makes history. *ChristianWeek*, 22 August, 9.

Couto, Joe. 2000. Ethnic Korean churches thrive in Canada. *Faith Today*, May/June, 18.

Cowan, Len. 1991. An indigenous church for indigenous people. *Faith Today*, July/August, 23.

Davenport, Mike. 2005. An insider's view of evangelicals. *Vancouver Sun*, 3 September.

Dorsch, Audrey. 1991. The Book of Acts on James Bay: A Native success story. *Faith Today*, July/August, 18.

Egerton, George. 2000. Trudeau, God, and the Canadian constitution: Religion, human rights and government authority in the making of the 1982 constitution. In *Rethinking church, state & modernity: Canada between Europe and America*, ed. David Lyon and Marguerite Van Die, 90–112. Toronto: University of Toronto Press.

Evangelical Fellowship of Canada. 1997. Being Christians in a pluralistic society: A discussion paper on pluralism in Canada. Toronto: Evangelical Fellowship of Canada.

– 2000. *Room for all: Religious freedom in education*. Toronto: Evangelical Fellowship of Canada.

Faith Today. 1988. Evangelical Opinion Poll Report: Readers support open doors. *Faith Today*, July/August, 25.

Fieguth, Debra. 1993. A strong, dynamic church. *ChristianWeek*, 13 July, 10.
– 1994. Native Pentecostals coming of age. *ChristianWeek*, 21 June, 2.
– 1996. A step towards reconciliation. *ChristianWeek*, 3 December, 2.
– 2000. Northern church grows and matures, and new spirit sweeps the Arctic. *ChristianWeek*, 16 May, 1.
– 2002. Arctic revival. *Faith Today*, January/February, 18.
– 2004. EFC holds true to its roots. *Faith Today*, September/October, 31.
Friesen, Carl. 1987. Toronto Chinese churches growing strongly. *ChristianWeek*, 5 May, 1.
Gauvreau, Michael. 1991. *The evangelical century: College and creed in English Canada from the great revival to the Great Depression*. Montreal and Kingston: McGill-Queen's University Press.
– 2006. *Catholic origins of Quebec's Quiet Revolution, 1931–1970*. Montreal and Kingston: McGill-Queen's University Press.
Ghosh, Sabitri. 2006. Every nation, tribe and people: How to become an intentionally intercultural church. *Faith Today*, September/October, 18.
Gibson, Graham. 1994. Native theological training within Canadian evangelicalism: Three case studies. MA thesis, Wilfrid Laurier University.
Grant, John Webster. 1984. *Moon of wintertime: Missionaries and the Indians of Canada in encounter since 1534*. Toronto: University of Toronto Press.
Grenville, Andrew. 2006. Church, conscience, corruption and the conservatives. *Faith Today*, March/April, 24.
Grenville, Andrew, and Bill Fledderus. 2004. How Canadian Christians voted. *Faith Today*, September/October, 28.
Guenther, Bruce L. 2001. Training for service: The Bible school movement in western Canada, 1909–1960. PhD diss., McGill University.
– 2004. Slithering down the plank of intellectualism? The Canadian Conference of Christian Educators and the impulse towards accreditation among Canadian Bible schools during the 1960s. *Historical Studies in Education* 16 (2): 197–228.
Guth, James L., and Cleveland R. Fraser. 2001. Religion and partisanship in Canada. *Journal for the Scientific Study of Religion* 40 (1): 51–63.
Hanson, Calvin B. 1984. *From hardship to harvest: The development of the Evangelical Free Church of Canada*. Edmonton: Evangelical Free Church of Canada.
Harvey, Bob. 1997. The role of churches in Native reconciliation. *Faith Today*, March/April, 18.
Haskell, David. 2005. Scary evangelicals: What's unsettling is the way our 'elite media' manipulate political coverage. *Hamilton Spectator*, 25 June.

Hilder, Monika B. 1988. Multiculturalism: Canadian tapestry. *Faith Today*, July/August, 22.

Hoyer, Ed. 1987. Evangelical growth in Quebec now in new stage. *Christian-Week*, 7 April, 16.

Jantz, Harold. 1991. Evangelicals in the Canada of the '90s. *Ecumenism* 101 (March): 13–16.

Johnson, Richard. 1985. The reproduction of the religious cleavage in Canadian elections. *Canadian Journal of Political Science* 18:99–113.

Johnstone, Meg. 2002. Chinese churches thrive. http://www.canadianchristianity.com/cgi-bin/na.cgi?nationalupdates/020409chinese.

Jones, Vernon Clement. 2000. Cracking the colour code. *Now*, 30 March–5 April. http://www.nowtoronto.com/issues/19/31/News/feature.html.

Ka-Lun, Leung, comp. 1998. *A centenary history of the Chinese C&MA*. Hong Kong: Christianity and Chinese Culture Research Centre.

Kleinsteuber, R. Wayne. 1984. *More than a memory: The renewal of Methodism in Canada*. Mississauga: Light and Life.

Koop, Doug. 1990. Listening to some evangelical Native voices. *ChristianWeek*, 9 October, 8.

– 1991. Believers invited to join Maracle in prayer. *ChristianWeek*, 5 February, 2.

– 1995a. Beyond bitterness: Reconciliation coming to Native concerns. *ChristianWeek*, 3 October, 1.

– 1995b. Quebec Christians wrestle with referendum questions. *ChristianWeek*, 3 October, 5.

Kwan, Joseph. 2001. We are in the same family: The growth of Chinese MB churches. *Mennonite Brethren Herald*, 9 November, 2–8.

Kylie, Tim. 1998. Bridging the Black/white divide. *Faith Today*, March/April, 22.

Larden, Robert A. 1971. *Our apostolic heritage*. Calgary: Apostolic Church of Pentecost.

Lewis, Donald M. 2002. Globalization, religion and evangelicalism. *Crux* 38 (2): 35–46.

– ed. 2004. *Christianity reborn: The global expansion of evangelicalism in the twentieth century.* Grand Rapids: Eerdmans.

Lipset, Seymour Martin. 1990. *Continental divide: The values and institutions of the United States and Canada.* New York: Routledge.

Lyon, David, and Marguerite Van Die, eds. 2000. *Rethinking church, state and modernity: Canada between Europe and America.* Toronto: University of Toronto Press.

Maclean's. 1993. God is alive: Canada is a nation of believers, 12 April, 32.

Mak, Chadwin. 1993. Chinese churches in Canada. *ChristianWeek*, 13 July, 9.

Maracle, Ross. 1990. I don't need tear gas to weep. *ChristianWeek*, 9 October, 8.

Marsden, George. 1980. *Fundamentalism and American culture: The shaping of twentieth-century evangelicalism, 1870–1925*. New York: Oxford University Press.

Mathon, Judy. 2005. Canada's North 'awakens' to God. *ChristianWeek*, 1 April, 6.

Matthews, Larry. 1995. What's in a name? *Faith Today*, May/June, 25.

– 1997. Poised for impact: Chinese Christians in Canada. *Faith Today*, July/August, 18.

McDonald, Marci. 2006. Stephen Harper and the theo-cons. *Walrus*, October, 44–61.

McLaurin, C.C. 1939. *Pioneering in western Canada: A story of the Baptists*. Calgary: McLaurin.

Miedema, Gary. 2005. *For Canada's sake: Public religion, centennial celebrations, and the re-making of Canada in the 1960s*. Montreal and Kingston: McGill-Queen's University Press.

Milan, Anne, and Kelly Tran. 2004. Blacks in Canada: A long history. *Canadian Social Trends* (Spring): 2–7.

Miller, Thomas William. 1994. *Canadian Pentecostals: A history of the Pentecostal Assemblies of Canada*. Mississauga: Full Gospel.

Motz, Arnell, ed. 1990. *Reclaiming a nation: The challenge of re-evangelizing Canada by the year 2000*. Richmond, BC: Church Leadership Library.

Moyles, R.G. 1977. *The blood and fire in Canada: A history of the Salvation Army in the dominion, 1882–1976*. Toronto: Martin.

Nagata, Judith. 2003. Chinese transnational Christianity: Religious versus (sub)ethnic affiliation. Paper presented to Conference on Subethnicity in the Chinese Diaspora, University of Toronto, 12–13 September.

Nelles, Wendy Elaine. 1989. A new wave of ethnic church growth. *Faith Today*, July/August, 20.

Noll, Mark A. 1992. *A history of Christianity in the United States and Canada*. Grand Rapids: Eerdmans.

– 1994. *The scandal of the evangelical mind*. Grand Rapids: Eerdmans.

– 1998. Religion in Canada and the United States: Comparisons from an important survey featuring the place of evangelical Christianity. *Crux* 34 (4): 13–25.

Oliver, Dennis. 1979. The new Canadian religious pluralism. Paper presented to the Canadian Society of Church History, Saskatoon, June.

O'Neil, Peter. 2005. Politics and prayer. *Vancouver Sun*, 23 July.

O'Toole, Roger. 1996. Religion in Canada: Its development and contemporary situation. *Social Compass* 43 (1): 119–34.

Parker, Fred J. 1971. *From east to western sea: A brief history of the Nazarene Church in Canada*. Kansas City: Nazarene.

Parker, Shafer. 1999. A call for prayer at the birth of a territory. *Faith Today,* March/April, 12–14.

Pinnock, Clark. 1990. Defining American fundamentalism: A response. In *The fundamentalist phenomenon: A view from within, a response from without,* ed. Norman J. Cohen, 38–55. Grand Rapids: Eerdmans.

Posterski, Donald C. 1995. *True to you: Living our faith in our multi-minded world.* Kelowna: Wood Lake Books.

Rawlyk, George A. 1984. *Ravished by the spirit: Religious revivals, Baptists, and Henry Alline.* Montreal and Kingston: McGill-Queen's University Press.

– 1996. *Is Jesus your personal saviour? In Search of Canadian evangelicalism in the 1990s.* Montreal and Kingston: McGill-Queen's University Press.

– ed. 1997. *Aspects of the Canadian evangelical experience.* Montreal: McGill-Queen's University Press.

Redekop, John. 1988. The church and Canada's Natives. *ChristianWeek,* 22 March, 3.

– 1995. Decades of transition: North American Mennonite Brethren in politics. In *Bridging troubled waters: Mennonite Brethren at mid-century,* ed. Paul Toews, 19–84. Winnipeg: Kindred Productions.

Reed, Paul. 2005. Active citizens: Who are they, how do they get that way, and why does it matter? Paper presented at Conference on Citizenship and the Common Good: Secularism or the Inclusive Society? Simon Fraser University, 19–20 May.

Reed, Paul, with Kevin Selbee. 2000. Distinguishing characteristics of active volunteers in Canada. *Nonprofit and Voluntary Sector Quarterly* 29 (4): 571–92.

– 2001. The civic core in Canada: Disproportionality in charitable giving, volunteering, and civic participation. *Nonprofit and Voluntary Sector Quarterly* 30 (4): 761–80.

Reimer, Sam. 2000. A generic evangelicalism? Comparing evangelical subcultures in Canada and the United States. In Lyon and Van Die 2000, 131–48.

– 2003. *Evangelicals and the continental divide: The conservative Protestant subculture in Canada and the United States.* Montreal and Kingston: McGill-Queen's University Press.

Rennie, Ian. 1994. Fundamentalism and the varieties of North American evangelicalism. In *Evangelicalism: Comparative studies of popular Protestantism in North America, the British Isles, and beyond (1700–1990),* ed. Mark A. Noll, David Bebbington, and George A. Rawlyk, 333–50. New York: Oxford University Press.

Reynolds, Lindsay. 1981. *Footprints: The beginnings of the Christian & Missionary Alliance in Canada.* Beaverlodge, AB: Buena Book Services.

– 1992. *Rebirth: The redevelopment of the Christian & Missionary Alliance*. Beaverlodge, AB: Evangelistic Enterprises.

Seim, Brian, ed. 1999. *Canada's new harvest: Helping churches touch newcomers*.
Scarborough: Serving in Mission Canada.

Seljak, David. 2000. The Catholic Church and public politics in Quebec. In
Lyon and Van Die 2000, 131–48.

Simmie, Scott. 2006. Is the religious right poised to set Harper's agenda? *Toronto Star*, 20 January.

Simpson, John H., and Henry MacLeod. 1985. The politics of morality in Canada. In *Religious movements: Genesis, exodus and numbers*, ed. Rodney Stark,
221–40. New York: Paragon House.

Smith, Glenn. 1988. The Québec Protestant church. In *Transforming our nation:
Empowering the Canadian church for a greater harvest*, ed. Murray Moerman,
203–66. Richmond, BC: Church Leadership Library.

– 1995. Francophone evangelicals say they will vote no. *ChristianWeek*, 17
October, 1.

Stackhouse, Jr, John G. 1991. The emergence of a fellowship: Canadian evangelicalism in the twentieth century. *Church History* 60 (2): 247–62.

– 1993. *Canadian evangelicalism in the twentieth century: An introduction to its
character*. Toronto: University of Toronto Press.

– 1994. Confronting Canada's secular slide. *Christianity Today*, 18 July, 38.

– 1995a. The National Association of Evangelicals, the Evangelical Fellowship
of Canada, and the limits of evangelical cooperation. *Christian Scholar's
Review* 25 (December): 157–79.

– 1995b. Three myths about evangelicals. *Faith Today*, May/June, 28.

– 2000. Bearing witness: Christian groups engage Canadian politics since the
1960s. In Lyon and Van Die 2000, 13–128.

Stiller, Brian C. 1991. *Critical options for evangelicals*. Markham: Faith Today
Publications.

– 1997. *From the Tower of Babel to Parliament Hill: How to be a Christian in Canada
today*. Toronto: HarperCollins.

Stiller, Karen. 2006. God, glory and gold. *Faith Today*, May/June, 18.

Stirk, Frank. 2004. Revival comes to the Arctic. *ChristianWeek*, 22 June, 1.

Swift, Allan. 1993. A nation of private Christians? *Faith Today*, July/August, 20.

Tarr, Leslie K. 1987. Canada's forgotten third world. *Faith Today*, May/June, 26.

Toews, John A. 1975. *A history of the Mennonite Brethren Church: Pilgrims
and pioneers*. Fresno, CA: General Conference of Mennonite Brethren
Churches.

Toews, Paul, and Kevin Enns-Rempel, eds. 2002. *For everything a season: Mennonite Brethren in North America, 1874–2002*. Fresno: Historical Commission.

Van Ginkel, Aileen. 2003. Evangelical beliefs and practices: A summary of the 2003 Ipsos-Reid Survey results. *Church and Faith Trends* (December): 1–9.

van Kleist, Dorothee. 1978. The world at our doorstep. *Faith Today,* April, 16.

Vandezande, Gerald. 1999. *Justice, not just us: Faith perspectives and national priorities.* Toronto: Public Justice Resource Centre.

Walker, James W. St G. 1980. *A history of Blacks in Canada.* Hull, QC: Minister of Supply and Services Canada.

Wallace, Bruce. 1986. Finding a future in the North. *Maclean's,* 14 July, 18.

Ward, Doug. 2005a. Politics and prayer: Social conservatives in Canada. *Vancouver Sun,* 23 July.

– 2005b. Religious right uses its clout. *Vancouver Sun,* 30 July.

Warner, R. Stephen. 2004. Coming to America: Immigrants and the faith they bring. *Christian Century,* 10 February, 20–4.

Whiteley, Marilyn. 1997. Sailing for the shore: The Canadian holiness tradition. In *Aspects of the Canadian evangelical experience,* ed. George A. Rawlyk, 257–70. Montreal and Kingston: McGill-Queen's University Press.

Whysall, Steve. 1988. Decade of rapid growth for Vancouver Chinese churches. *ChristianWeek,* 31 May, 4.

Wilkinson, Michael. 2000. The globalization of Pentecostalism: The role of Asian immigrant Pentecostals in Canada. *Asian Journal of Pentecostal Studies* 3 (2): 219–26.

– 2006. *The spirit said go: Pentecostal immigrants in Canada.* New York: Lang.

Wingender, Eric. 2005. Quebec Christians: The untold story. *ChristianWeek,* 15 April, 3.

Wink, Robin W. 2000. *The Blacks in Canada: A history.* 2nd ed. Montreal and Kingston: McGill-Queen's University Press.

Woodsworth, James S. 1909. *Strangers within our gates: Or, coming Canadians.* Toronto: Missionary Society of the Methodist Church.

Woyke, Frank H. 1976. *Heritage and ministry of the North American Baptist Conference.* Oakbrook Terrace, IL: North American Baptist Conference.

Wright, Robert A. 1990. The Canadian Protestant tradition. In *The Canadian Protestant experience, 1760–1990,* ed. George A. Rawlyk, 139–97. Burlington, ON: Welch.

Wuthnow, Robert. 1989. *The struggle for America's soul: Evangelicals, liberals and secularism.* Grand Rapids: Eerdmans.

Younger-Lewis, Greg. 2004. Bible conference brings big money to Iqaluit: Pastor. *Nunatsiaq News,* 23 April. http://www.nunatsiaq.com/archives/40423/news/nunavut/40423_02.html.

Appendix

Table 10.1 Evangelical Protestant Denominations in Canada

Name of Denomination	2001 Membership	2001 Attendance	Website
Baptist Denominations			
Association of Regular Baptist Churches	1,500	1,500	www.jsbc.org/arbc.htm
Atlantic Canada Association of Free Will Baptists	347	505	
Baptist General Conference	7,137	12,473	www.bgc.ca
Baptist Convention of Ontario & Quebec (member of Canadian Baptist Ministries)	31,010	30,432	www.baptist.ca and www.cbmin.org
Baptist Union of Western Canada (member of Canadian Baptist Ministries)	21,595	20,207	www.buwc.ca and www.cbmin.org
Convention of Atlantic Baptist Churches (member of Canadian Baptist Ministries)	62,276	26,812	www.baptist-atlantic.ca and www.cbmin.org
Union of French Baptist Churches of Canada (member of Canadian Baptist Ministries)	1,529	1,331	www.unionbaptiste.com and www.cbmin.org
Canadian Convention of Southern Baptists	10,189	9,606	www.ccsb.ca
Fellowship of Evangelical Baptist Churches	71,073	92,549	www.fellowship.ca
Gospel Missionary Association	800	800	
North American Baptist Church	17,460	21,668	www.nabconference.org
Sovereign Grace Fellowship	600	600	www.sgfcanada.com
Holiness Movement Denominations			
African Methodist Episcopal Church	600	600	www.ame-church.com
Associated Gospel Churches	10,293	20,477	www.agcofcanada.com
Bible Holiness Movement	954	954	www.bible-holiness-movement.com
Christian & Missionary Alliance in Canada	112,956	80,282	http://cmalliance.ca
Church of God in Christ, Inc.	500	800	www.cogic.org
Church of God of Prophecy in Canada	3,107	2,500	www.cogop.org
Church of God in Western Canada (Anderson)	3,751	3,830	www.chog.ca
Church of God – Canada (Cleveland)	11,206	10,577	www.cofg.net
Church of the Nazarene Canada	12,117	12,102	www.nazarene.ca
Evangelical Missionary Church of Canada	11,011	19,730	www.emcc.ca

Free Methodist Church in Canada	6,930	12,374	www.fmc-canada.org
Independent Holiness Churches	600	600	www.holiness.ca
Salvation Army in Canada	86,005	26,143	www.salvationarmy.ca
Wesleyan Church of Canada	5,600	10,050	www.wesleyan.org

Lutheran & Reformed Denominations

Association of Free Lutheran Churches	700	700	www.aflc.org
Christian Reformed Church	82,107	70,000	www.crcna.org
Church of the Lutheran Brethren	383	610	www.frcna.org
Free Reformed Churches	3,388	3,388	www.frcna.org
Lutheran Church - Canada	79,675	22,909	www.lutheranchurch-canada.ca
Lutheran Church - Missouri Synod	5,126	1,829	www.lcms.org

Mennonite Denominations

Bergthaler Mennonite Churches	1,326	1,326	
Brethren in Christ, Canadian Conference	3,278	4,599	www.canadianbic.ca
Canadian Conference of Mennonite Brethren Churches	34,288	45,528	www.mbconf.ca
Chortizer Mennonite Conference	2,000	1,300	
Christian Anishinabec Fellowship	100	100	
Church of God in Christ (Mennonite)	4,132	6,345	www.bibleviews.com/ holdeman.html (unofficial)
Conservative Mennonite Church of Ontario	450	450	
Conservative Mennonite Fellowship	100	100	
Eastern Pennsylvania Mennonite Church	194	194	
Evangelical Mennonite Conference	6,961	7,343	www.emconf.ca
Evangelical Mennonite Mission Conference	3,833	4,618	www.emmc.ca
Fellowship of Evangelical Bible Churches	1,506	2,133	www.febcministries.org
Markham-Waterloo Mennonite Conference	1,300	1,300	
Mennonite Church Alberta (affiliated with Mennonite Church Canada)	1,347	1,719	http://mennonitechurch.ab.ca and www .mennonitechurch.ca
Mennonite Church British Columbia (affiliated with Mennonite Church Canada)	3,698	4,532	www.mcbc.ca and www .mennonitechurch.ca
Mennonite Church Manitoba (affiliated with Mennonite Church Canada)	10,487	7,608	www.mennochurch.mb.ca and www.mennonitechurch.ca
Mennonite Church Saskatchewan (affiliated with Mennonite Church Canada)	4,547	3,597	http://mcsask.ca and www .mennonitechurch.ca
Mennonite Church Eastern Canada (affiliated with Mennonite Church Canada)	14,075	10,531	www.mcec.ca and www.mennonitechurch.ca

Northwest Mennonite Conference	1,317	889	http://www.nwc.mennonite.net
Mennonite Churches – Independent	2,268	2,268	
Midwest Mennonite Fellowship	2,001	2,000	
Nationwide Fellowship of Churches (Mennonite)	517	550	
Sommerfelder Mennonite Churches	4,590	3,300	
United Brethren in Christ (Ontario)	661	858	
Western Conservative Mennonite Fellowship	100	100	

Pentecostal/Charismatic Denominations

Apostolic Church in Canada	1,950	1,000	www.apostolic.ca
Apostolic Church of Pentecost	8,701	16,206	www.acop.ca
Apostolic Faith Church	1,000	1,000	www.apostolicfaith.org
Canadian Evangelical Christian Churches	5,000	2,835	www.cecconline.com
Canadian Fellowship of Churches and Ministers	43,500	45,000	www.cfcm.org
Church of Pentecost Canada, Inc.	2500	3,421	www.pentecost.ca
Elim Fellowship of Evangelical Churches and Ministers	1,300	1,755	www.elim.ca
Fellowship of Christian Assemblies	9,400	11,000	www.fcaoc.org
Foursquare Gospel Church of Canada	3,227	4,511	www.foursquare.ca
Independent Assemblies of God	24,000	32,400	www.iaogcan.com
Italian Pentecostal Church of Canada	2,000	2,200	
New Apostolic Church Canada	12,000	12,000	www.naccanada.org
Open Bible Faith Fellowship	10,000	5,680	www.obff.com
Partners in Harvest	3,000	4,050	www.partners-in-harvest.org
Pentecostal Assemblies of Canada	228,003	151,825	www.paoc.ca
Pentecostal Assemblies of Newfoundland	25,435	11,234	www.paonl.ca
Pentecostal Holiness Church of Canada	2,800	3,780	www.phcc.ca
Sovereign Grace Ministries	100	170	www.sovereigngraceministries.org
United Church of Jesus Christ (Apostolic)	100	100	
United Pentecostal Church in Canada	20,800	23,000	www.upci.org
Victory Churches International	5,000	6,750	www.victoryint.org
Association of Vineyard Churches Canada	7,100	2,297	www.vineyard.ca

Miscellaneous

Apostolic Christian Churches (Nazarean)	839	1,419	
Armenian Evangelical Church	500	500	www.aeuna.org
Calvary Chapels	740	740	

Canadian Sunday School Mission	1,700	2,295	www.cssm.ca
Christ Catholic Church			http://home.cogeco.ca/
International	2,200	2,200	~dmullan1/index2.htm
Christian (Plymouth) Brethren. See			
also Vision Ministries Canada	60,000	60,000	www.vision-ministries.org
Churches of Christ (A Cappella)	6,757	9,377	www.worldconvention.org
Churches of Christ (Independent)	8,800	8,800	www.worldconvention.org
Churches of Christ (Instrumental),			
or Disciples of Christ in Canada	4,066	4100	www.worldconvention.org
Congregational Christian			
Churches in Canada	7,500	14,000	www.cccc.ca
Dove Christian Fellowship	600	405	www.dcfi.org
Evangelical Covenant Church of			
Canada	1,384	2,543	www.canadacovenantchurch.org
Evangelical Free Church of			
Canada	8,153	18,718	www.efcc.ca
Every Nation Churches and			
Ministries	300	300	www.everynation.org
Fellowship of Grace Brethren			
Churches	200	90	www.fgbc.org
Life Links International Fellowship	2,500	3,375	www.lifelinks.org
Moravian Church in Canada	1,473	650	www.moravian.ca
Native Evangelical Fellowship of			
Canada	1,300	1,220	www.nef.ca
Salt and Light Ministries	1,800	1,800	www.saltlight.org
Seventh-Day Adventist Church	49,632	29,000	www.sdacc.org
United Church of God - Canada	2,000	2,000	www.ucg.ca
Village Missions	2,050	1,529	www.villagemissions.ca
Worldwide Church of God Canada	5,592	2,980	www.wcg.ca
Totals	**1,354,597**	**1,142,837**	

Compiled by Bruce L. Guenther and the Research Department of Outreach Canada

11 Conclusion: The Discourse of Loss and the Future of Christianity and Ethnicity in Canada

PAUL BRAMADAT AND DAVID SELJAK

Introduction

A visit to Marija Pomagaj, Toronto's Slovenian Canadian Roman Catholic Church featured in the introduction to this volume, reveals much about the development of the relationship between religion and ethnicity in Canada's Christian communities. Mass is still said in Slovenian, but there are fewer and fewer young people. Judging by the storefronts and restaurants, the surrounding neighbourhood – first populated by Italians and then by Portuguese – is now dominated by Koreans and other Asians. For some older Slovenian Canadians, these changes have led to a sense of sorrow. Their children now attend parish churches with no particular ethnic markers or have simply stopped going to church altogether. Demographic and social changes – including changes in immigration patterns, intermarriage, improved socio-economic mobility in the second generation, and secularization – have all worked to depopulate ethnic parishes such as Marija Pomagaj.

However, in other cases, these changes have had the opposite effects. During his years living in Montreal, David Seljak often passed one of Montreal's largely Irish Roman Catholic churches, St Kevin's, on Chemin-de-la-Côte-des-Neiges. St Kevin's had seen its traditional parishioners either move to more affluent suburbs or stay home on Sunday mornings. In the last ten years, however, it has witnessed an extraordinary growth in membership and attendance, and now the church is packed with recent immigrants – mostly young families – from the Philippines who significantly outnumber the traditional and increasingly elderly European-descent parishioners. One does not have to be a social scientist or historian to recognize what is happening.

Farther down the street in this same Montreal neighbourhood, one encounters Notre-Dame-des-Neiges, a comfortable francophone Roman Catholic Church, where Seljak's older two children were baptized, and where a more common process is being played out. Notre-Dame-des-Neiges serves a more established and better educated French Quebecois parish that includes residents who work at the neighbouring University of Montreal or one of the three nearby hospitals. While the church was once quite well used by its parishioners, these days the church is never full on Sundays – except for Christmas and Easter. Moreover, young families are almost completely absent from services, despite a very successful Scouts program run by the parish. In fact, on any given Sunday, the average age of parishioners is in the seventies, for whom the current situation must be discouraging. When Seljak attended Notre-Dame-des-Neiges, he spoke with elderly women over coffee in the church basement who recalled when the churches were filled with large French Quebecois families. One woman came from a pious family of fourteen children, another from a family of sixteen, and a third came from an astonishing family of twenty-one children. However, the children of these women – and their much smaller families – never come to Mass.

The three vignettes from Marija Pomagaj, St Kevin's, and Notre-Dame-des-Neiges speak volumes about the dynamic relationship between religion and ethnicity in the lives of Canadian Christians.

The Diversity of the Churches

The processes we can witness within these three churches remind us to be cautious about the accepted wisdom about the putatively static relationship between a particular ethnic group and a specific religious tradition. One of the surprises of this study has been the great diversity we have found in every denomination as well as the unstoppable dynamism within each community. A generation ago, most Canadians would have automatically equated the Presbyterians with Scots, Anglicans with the English, and the Lutherans with the Germans. Conversely, Canadians would also have identified ethnic groups with specific forms of Christianity; the Russians, Serbians, and Greeks were Orthodox Christians, and francophone Canadians were Roman Catholic, as were the Irish, Italians, and Poles. A generation ago these neat religious and ethnic assumptions – although never telling the whole story – at least made sense. This is less and less the case today. Just as denominations are becoming more diverse, members of ethnic groups are redefining themselves, especially their association with their traditional religion. As well, they are intermarrying, joining different churches, becoming religiously inactive, or consuming religious products 'à la carte,' as Canadian sociologist Reginald Bibby (1987) puts it.

The discourses that Roy Loewen elucidates in chapter 9 on Canadian Mennonites show that within any given denomination there is no single window through which one can glimpse the new dynamics of religion and ethnicity.[1] For example, some Mennonites now define themselves in uniquely ethnic terms, in the same way that some Jews indicate that they have no interest at all in Judaism as a religion but feel themselves still to be essentially Jewish. Evangelical Mennonites wish to keep some of the ethnic elements of the tradition, such as Low German and traditional cuisine, but denounce mainstream Mennonite piety as automatic or habitual and insufficiently true to their broader evangelical version of the faith. Others adopt a 'universalist' perspective that allows them to escape the particular ethnic trappings of the tradition and proclaim as universally valid the social activist ethos of the community. Then there are those Mennonites who wish to maintain the traditional symbiosis between Mennonite religious and ethnic identity. Their ethnic identity is instrumental in their understanding of their attachment to their faith, just as their religious identity reinforces their ethnic solidarity with other Mennonites. Finally, Loewen argues, there are some people – usually immigrants – who have adopted the Mennonite name but express neither a sense of Mennonite ethnicity nor a distinctively Mennonite religious affiliation. They are Mennonite, perhaps, because their sponsors were Mennonite or they have come to identify being Mennonite with being Canadian. On top of this, all Mennonites struggle with fidelity to older ethnic loyalties (Russlander, Swiss German, etc.) and the growing popularity in their communities of a wider Canadian ethnicity. Meanwhile, the Mennonite community struggles with the challenges raised by secularization and other social transformations, such as the loss of members and participants, the change in worship styles, changing attitudes to same-sex unions and the ordination of homosexuals, and the rise of a more pervasive individualism. Loewen's analysis of the identity discourses one finds within Mennonite tradition clarifies the ways Mennonites have responded to the social transformations of the last half century. Many of the explorations he discusses could be found in virtually every Christian community in Canada.

The Social Location of Ethnic and Religious Communities

To explain the new diversity and complexity, the scholars gathered in this book found that they had to situate the people they were depicting in a society that is itself undergoing dramatic transformations. In the decades since the dream of a Christian Canada reached its zenith just before the First World War, Canadians have witnessed remarkable changes. Throughout this book, authors have observed the forces that have worked together to undermine old dreams and assumptions. These include the following:

- dramatic growth and transformation in the Canadian economy;
- an exodus from farms to cities;
- new immigration policies that have dramatically increased the non-European population in Canada;
- the 'social disestablishment' of Christianity in the 1960s and 1970s;
- a related rise of the bureaucratic state that took over traditional functions of the churches in social welfare, education, and health care;
- dramatic cultural, economic, social, political, and legal changes in the status of women, and attitudes towards sexuality and sexual orientation;
- increased individual rights and freedoms associated with the *Charter of Rights and Freedoms*;
- the rise of multiculturalism as a formal policy and informal cultural tradition; and
- the often sharp numerical decline of Christian mainstream denominations traditionally associated with the ruling elite.

Of course, these forces affect Christian communities differently, depending on the 'social location' of the individuals and groups involved. However, a number of common themes surfaced in these chapters, and it is to these guiding themes that we now turn our attention.

Given the breadth of Canada, it came as no surprise that regionalism became a major concern in these studies. The Canadian sociologist S.D. Clark has shown that dissident religious groups were more likely to spring up and thrive 'in the margins' of society, where the established churches had the least influence.[2] Consequently, we found ourselves forced to ask how regionalism affected the project of building a Canadian Christianity and a Christian Canada – not to mention a politically unified Canada. The wealthy Anglican Montreal merchants described by Wendy Fletcher lived lives very different from those of the poor Lutheran farmers in Saskatchewan described by Bryan Hillis. The effect of regionalism on a single denomination is significant. Solange Lefebvre shows that the lives of Acadian Roman Catholics in eastern Canada were marked by exile and re-establishment and were therefore far removed from the more stable existence of their co-religionists in Quebec City or St Boniface, Manitoba.

Questions of social location, especially as they intersected with geographical territory and the unique experience of specific communities, became a special concern in the case of Quebec. We were constantly reminded of the fact that on almost every issue the situation of all Christian churches in Quebec was different from that of their counterparts in other areas of Canada. For example, almost all Anglicans, Presbyterians, and members of the United Church in Quebec were members of the anglophone community, a minority community that enjoyed, nevertheless, great privileges for much of Canadian history. However, anglophone Roman Catholics in Quebec had to find a place in a church dominated by their French-speaking co-religionists. Even though Quebec society was characterized until the 1960s by the awkward arrangement between its francophone majority and economically dominant anglophone minority, the francophone-dominated Roman Catholic Church exercised enormous social and cultural power long after the decline of the culture-defining power of Protestant churches in the rest of Canada. The unique situation in Quebec, Solange Lefebvre reminds us, led to the marriage of French Canadian national identity and Roman Catholicism, the latter of which is still understood by many French Quebecers to protect or symbolize the former.

The tensions between francophone and anglophone Catholics illustrate the fact that conflict, negotiation, and cooperation between ethnic groups are central features of Canadian Christianity and society. Ghanaian Presbyterians, as Stuart Macdonald illustrates, have to situate themselves in a church community that is itself defined by a strong sense of Canadian ethnicity that is nonetheless coloured by nostalgia for things Scottish. Ghanaian Presbyterians must therefore negotiate with their co-religionists for recognition and acceptance. In the anglophone Roman Catholic Church, the Irish, Scots, Germans, and Italians all vied for position among themselves, but they could unite when necessary against their Protestant neighbours and their francophone co-religionists. Along with Protestants, they discriminated against non-Christians and Aboriginal peoples. Meanwhile, they often found themselves the victims of Protestant discrimination and prejudice. Each denomination – and each group within denominations – has its unique story to tell of conflict, competition, cooperation, and consensus in its relations with others.

Finally, authors found that it was necessary to examine the communities' responses to the growing secularization of Canadian society as well as the new post-colonial context. As this book makes abundantly clear, the building of Canada was always imagined by most of the European colonialists as a Christian project. As such, the secularization of Canadian society has to be seen as a watershed both for society and the churches. Granted, the Christian roots of the Canadian project still help to define our society – and so some provinces still ban Sunday shopping and the major Christian feast days are statutory holidays. While the predictions of a decline in religious mentalities and a one-way privatization of religion have not come to pass, we do see other elements of secularization, including religious de-institutionalization and fragmentation, both symptoms of an increased individualism that is pervasive in Canada. All community ties (both horizontal and vertical) are challenged by the individualism promoted by Canada's political and economic structures as well as by its culture and social arrangements. Consequently, ethnic and religious identities – and the connections between the two – are more open to redefinition and renegotiation than they have ever been. Loewen's typology illustrates extremely well the way one of Canada's most cohesive communities has responded to the challenges associated with this fragmentation.

Secularization has blindsided the traditional Canadian Christian communities with the same force that the loss of empire hit Britons after the Second World War. Except for a number of evangelical communities, most churches are losing members. In the Presbyterian and Anglican churches, as Fletcher and Macdonald point out, the drop in membership and attendance has been especially precipitous (and Fletcher argues that the Statistics Canada figures are underestimations); in fact, some of these communities are being saved from extinction only because of the increased involvement of non-European Christians. Consequently, just as these communities are struggling with the new ethnic diversity in Canada and their denominations, they are also having to work with a shrinking and aging church population, declining financial resources, shortages of clergy, disaffected youth, and other symptoms of secularization. Wenh-In Ng's chapter outlines the United

Church of Canada's struggle to deal with newcomers from Asia as well as the secularization that has so dramatically diminished their denomination's size and place in the public arena. This struggle is unique, both because the United Church consciously defines itself as a 'national' church and because of the rather sophisticated social awareness and self-criticism that this community has developed. Ng observes that immigrant congregations (such as those affiliated with the Ethnic Ministries Unit) and the immigrant cohorts within other United Church congregations are frequently more vital and more conservative than their more established fellow adherents. Consequently, the mainstream congregations and more liberal church leadership find themselves forced to revisit questions they would have liked to have considered closed, such as the ordination of women, the moral status of homosexuality, the inerrancy of scripture, the exclusivity of salvation through Jesus, and attitudes to other religions.

In response to the declining numbers, resources, and social power of the Christian communities, several authors note what we came to call a 'discourse of loss' in the mainstream churches. Their members have come to understand that the Canada in which they grew up has changed and so have their churches. In his groundbreaking 1987 book *Fragmented Gods*, Reginald Bibby captures the sense of this loss when he nostalgically writes about how, when he was a child, almost everyone piled into their cars to get to church on Sunday morning (11). Such scenes are rarer and rarer in a post-colonial, post-Christian Canada. Furthermore, Christians have to deal with the lowered status of their denominations. They are no longer automatically called upon by civic leaders and government officials for their input on important public questions. Indeed, they sometimes find their contributions unwelcome. Christian churches and groups find that, like so many other pressure groups, they have to lobby for public attention.

The discourse of loss can be heard in almost all denominations in Canada, although it is articulated most urgently among mainstream Protestants, especially in those three denominations that formed a kind of shadow establishment: the Anglicans, Presbyterians, and the United Church. One also hears echoes of this discourse in the Roman Catholic and Lutheran communities. In Quebec, one hears it in conservative circles in the Roman Catholic Church and not infrequently from the church hierarchy. It is more common within older generations, among those who, like Bibby, remember the familial and communal solidarity produced by loyal Sunday church attendance. We also hear it from members of those ethnic parishes and congregations in decline.

However, we found that this discourse of loss is nearly non-existent within some Christian communities. Bruce Guenther notes that, in general, as a religious grouping conservative Christians seem to be avoiding the numerical declines plaguing the other churches.[3] As well, as Mark McGowan points out in his chapter, Roman Catholic churches in some cities have been rescued from decline by dynamic Asian immigrant communities, especially the Filipinos and Vietnamese. Finally, even within those mainstream Protestant denominations in numerical decline, there are dynamic groups of Christians from Asia and Africa that are growing in size.[4]

For scholars interested in the future of religion in Canada, what is significant about this discourse of loss is the possibility that we are witnessing the demise of traditional institutional religious structures that used to function as frameworks within which the Christian message and Christian culture were sustained and promulgated. In other words, perhaps Christianity is entering a post-church or post-institutional era. From the tone of lament one hears from some Christians, it seems as though a tectonic shift is occurring, which is not simply a religious change but a broad social transformation. That is, once a society ceases to be identified definitively with a religion that was once absolutely central to that society's existence – or its 'project,' as we have called it in this book – the society must find new pillars on which to rest its institutions and values. In this regard, it is important to note that secularization was not the only transformation that characterized post–Second World War Canadian society. Equally important to the religious development of Canadian society were socio-economic and political transformations that allowed and encouraged the state to take over education, health care, and social services – social functions that had until the Second World War been mostly the preserve of the churches. Moreover, after the war, and especially since 1960, Canadians have witnessed the rise (or acceleration) of a bewildering variety of cultural transformations such as consumerism, individualism, feminism, multiculturalism, environmentalism, sexual liberation, rapid changes in communications technologies, transnationalism, and globalization. Some 'liberal' Christians have welcomed these changes, while other 'conservative' Christians have lamented the losses that they inevitably entailed. Indeed, these transformations have led to a variety of new divisions, conflicts, and challenges.

Moral and Generational Tensions

This division between 'conservative' and 'liberal' Christians often follows the fault lines of ethnic communities and generations. For example, according to most of the authors in this book, Asian Christians are considerably more conservative on gender issues than others, but may find that their children share the more liberal values of their Canadian friends and neighbours. Moreover, as all of the authors in this book demonstrate, a cluster of patriarchal, communal, and what anthropologists sometimes call gerontocratic (i.e., relating to the privilege of elders) values continue to exert an enormous influence on Canadian Christians and communities of Asian, Arab, African, eastern European, and Latin American origins that constitute the majority of Canada's new Christian immigrants.

The more conservative form of Christianity that many immigrants from outside of Europe seek to reassemble when they come to Canada (Bramadat 2005) reminds us of the fact that many societies – e.g., Korea, Nigeria, India, the Philippines, Trinidad, Ghana, China/Hong Kong, etc. – were evangelized by European or North American missionaries whose particular form of Christianity was itself more conservative than the forms later developed by some of their Western co-religionists. There are many reasons for this, of course, but one main explanation is the power of the widespread assumption among early missionaries that new and prospective converts could not understand nuanced or liberal forms of the faith the missionaries wished to promote. As well, as a result of the often arduous nature of their work, missionaries tend to be ardent adherents of putatively more orthodox and exclusivist forms of their denomination's creed and moral convictions. This was especially true before discourses of human rights began to undermine this approach, and before safe and comfortable travel made missionary work less daunting. In any case, this earlier cohort of missionaries often promoted a conservative form of Christianity. Consequently, when Korean Presbyterians, African Anglicans, and Chinese Baptists immigrate to Canada, the denominations they find here are often far more liberal than the ones they left in their country of origin. As well, other factors that need to be considered when trying to understand the differences between the Christianity of many Asian and African newcomers and the dominant form they encounter in Canada are the moral and religious discourses that characterized the newcomer's previous country. For example, a Chinese Baptist who immigrates to Canada from

424 Paul Bramadat and David Seljak

Hong Kong in her thirties may have spent the first few decades of her life in a broader society in which traditional Chinese values of obedience and respect for her elders, parents, and authorities have become inextricably bound up with her personal and Christian sensibilities. She may well seek – and will find – within Christianity familiar touchstones on morality, respect, and so forth that reflect her broader Chinese moral sensibilities; she may do this in both Hong Kong and Canada, and throughout her religious development. In other words, since religion, culture, and ethnicity are so closely connected (Bramadat and Seljak 2005), it is not merely the case that her form of Christianity is more conservative than that of other non-Asians in her Canadian congregation, but also that the cultural matrix in which she was raised and in which she adopted this kind of Christianity is closely associated with more patriarchal, hierarchical, authoritarian, gerontocratic, and communal sensibilities.

There are other reasons why the cluster of values mentioned above is more evident among Christian newcomers from Asia, Africa, South America, and eastern Europe, than they are, generally speaking, among so-called mainstream Christians of European descent. However, this is not the place to discuss these questions. What we can do is to point out that the differences between the moral assumptions of many non-European newcomers and the largely European-origin culture into which they integrate when they arrive are being felt in two kinds of tensions in Canadian Christian communities.

First, these different approaches express themselves in tensions between generations. As even a cursory consideration of ancient tales, biblical stories, art, and literature reminds us, strains between generations are a fundamental feature of human life. However, the particular ways in which these tensions are expressed, and the issues at stake when they are expressed, depend entirely on the context in which people live. So, while it is common for many people to view their parents as standing on the other side of a generation gap, in Canadian Christian families in which the parents are newcomers and the children are raised in Canada, the size of this gap is often quite substantial. Obviously, common sense observation and the chapters in this book indicate that linguistic, economic, political, intellectual, cultural, and finally religious differences between generations can be greatly exacerbated by migration. Second, these different approaches to morality and authority sometimes result in tensions within churches between members of European and non-European origin. Although the generation gap mentioned above and the tensions between different communities within a congregation are philosophically distinct, in practice they are often intertwined. Readers will notice both issues at work – sometimes simultaneously – in the following discussion.

In his chapter on Presbyterians, Stuart Macdonald notes that the denomination is still actively imagined by both many outsiders and insiders as essentially Scottish. However, he also notes that this denomination – which the 2001 Census reveals has seen the single largest decline of any of the denominations or traditions we have considered – is now home to a growing number of Korean newcomers who might, in the end, help to save the denomination from extinction. However, this rescue itself introduces new challenges into the Presbyterian community and into families of Korean newcomers. After all, the new Korean members tend to be more active in the churches and tend to embrace a more theologically and morally conservative form of Presbyterianism than the dominant congregants of European origin. If we assume that the influx of more conservative Korean first-generation newcomers will, as it were, nudge the larger church toward more conservative stances, two issues arise: first, since the children of these newcomers will be raised by Korean parents but socialized in both the public education system and the perhaps more powerful classroom of North American popular culture, will these second-generation Korean Canadians be attracted to the fairly conservative Presbyterianism their parents embraced and promoted in Korea and more recently in Canada?[5] The answer is still unknown. The second associated question is more complicated: will future generations of European-origin members be able to identify with an emerging Presbyterianism that will likely become more conservative and multi-ethnic than it was as they remember it?

Of course, closely associated with the conservatism mentioned above are values related to authority and the respect for elders within the community. For example, in Bruce Guenther's and Wenh-In Ng's chapters, we see that respect for elders and ministers is a central value among many Asian newcomers. Of course, this can become problematic in three ways: first, it is difficult within families and within exclusive ethnic congregations (for example, entirely Chinese congregations) when the values of deference to the authority of elders and authority figures are challenged by the values of gender egalitarianism, individualism, and meritocracy that underlie most Canadian public schools. Second, this cluster of values can lead to conflicts within denominations when Asian and African newcomers are surprised and perhaps even offended by the latitude enjoyed by so many Canadian-born youth to oppose their parents' demands, not to mention the freedom congregants feel to criticize their ministers or priests. Third, these religious, cultural, and generational differences affect not only non-European newcomer families and their ethnically exclusive churches; established European-origin individuals and families must come to terms with the fact that their churches are now increasingly peopled with fellow worshippers whose views on authority and the relationship between clergy and lay people are quite different from their own.[6]

In contemporary Christian communities, the common concerns related to how to keep children interested in church life, and how to pass on Christian values to their children, are obviously quite common (and perhaps even ancient) concerns that are simply becoming more and more urgent and complex as privatization, differentiation, and secularization continue to redraw the social and religious maps of Canada. The relatively new concerns that have emerged out of the differences in values related to gender, parental and clerical authority, human rights, and individualism are becoming quite familiar to those in communities in which newcomers – especially those from non-European regions – make up a sizable minority, or in which these newcomers represent the only areas of growth.

Post-Colonial Renegotiations

Throughout this book, we have seen that tensions sometimes arise out of differences between the moral assumptions of the newcomer and those of established communities that have historically dominated particular denominations and traditions. These incidents can be considered to be expressions of the renegotiation of Christianity in a 'post-colonial' era– that is, in an era in which the moral supremacy of European societies is increasingly problematized. As we noted above, in some churches one can hear a discourse of loss about the changes affecting Christianity in Canada. Partly this is a function of deep concerns over the declines in membership, attendance, financial contributions, and identification that we are witnessing across the whole tradition (with a few notable exceptions). As well, partly this is a function of a growing awareness of the moral and theological conservatism of the increasingly non-European newcomers, many of whom interpret the meaning and purpose of their denominations in ways that are different from the interpretations of the dominant groups.

It might be tempting for some people to frame this difference in terms of a simple gulf between the conservative non-European 'other' and the well-balanced liberal democratic 'self.' This conclusion is problematic, since a much more complicated reality is unfolding in the churches we have considered. In particular, two caveats are in order: first, within the evangelical community in Canada (see Bruce Guenther's chapter), newcomers and more settled Canadians share relatively conservative values; in this community, ethnicity is not the crucial determinant of moral identity, nor do significant ethnic differences presage denomination schisms on moral grounds.[7] Second, while it might be the case that, in general, non-European newcomer Christians have more traditionally conservative views on sexuality, women's roles in the church, home and society, clergy, and parental authority, it is also the case that many members of these groups have many overseas 'transnational' connections and are more personally familiar with the plight of the world's poor and the vicissitudes of corporate globalization. As such, they might be somewhat more inclined than their co-religionists of European origin to adopt an active and putatively 'progressive' stance on issues related to politics and globalization. While we have heard anecdotal confirmation of this second possibility from several of our authors, it remains largely speculative.

Future Research

Although we set out in this book to address all of the most critical issues related to the intersection between ethnicity and the major forms of Christianity in Canada, naturally, certain issues fell just or well outside of the scope of our project. As we approach the end of this book, it is appropriate to discuss briefly some of the research topics that we hope others might explore.

Aboriginal Spiritualities

The first topic that the limitations of space did not allow us to explore to our satisfaction was Aboriginal religiosity. Originally, we had planned to include in this current study a chapter on Aboriginal Christians. However, it became clear fairly early in the planning that such a chapter did not fit well in an analysis in which ethnicity is the key variable. After all, peoples, nations, and nationalism are far more salient categories of analysis in contemporary Aboriginal discourse. For obvious reasons, many Aboriginals resent being considered as merely another Canadian ethnic minority group alongside Canadians of Latvian, Italian, and Bolivian descent. Their history and status are very different, of course. However, while we are witnessing across Canada a kind of renaissance of traditional Aboriginal spirituality, it is still the case that the vast majority of Aboriginals would say they are Christians of one denomination (or tradition) or another, even while some of them may also embrace traditional Aboriginal spiritual beliefs, values, and practices. In fact, there are no definitive studies to establish exactly how many Canadian Aboriginals consider themselves to be Christians. However, when we ask colleagues who specialize in Aboriginal religions and cultures to estimate the approximate percentage of Aboriginals who would likely identify themselves as Christian, the estimates range from 70 to 85 per cent.

Of course, as in the case of Christians in the non-Aboriginal world, sometimes this identity is merely nominal, but in other cases (for example, among Pentecostal Aboriginals in northern Canada), the Christian Aboriginal mode of identification speaks to a profound and life-altering commitment. Although there might be at least three major religious ways of being in the Aboriginal world – those who have returned to (or the few who have remained a part of) traditional spiritualities and who tend to see Christianity as the religion of the colonizer; those who remain loosely attached to some form of Christianity while perhaps also still practising some elements of traditional Aboriginal spirituality; and those who strongly identify themselves as Christians and formally reject all forms of Aboriginal spirituality – all three groups must grapple with the history of Christianity's complicity in the ethnocentricity that marked the vast majority of European relations with Aboriginals (including, of course, the disastrous legacy of residential schools). The communities involved are still struggling with the physical, economic, legal, social, and spiritual effects of that period of Canadian colonization, and it is impossible to separate religion from these challenges.

In light of what we now know about the ravages of the residential schools, precisely how one might simultaneously maintain one's ties with one's Aboriginal identity and, for example, one's Anglican identity, is by no means self-evident, and such questions now plague many churches and Aboriginal communities. For that matter, the effect of generations of exploitation and colonization on the development of a distinctive non- or at least post-Christian form of contemporary Aboriginal spirituality (which is often imagined in pristine terms) is also worthy of sustained analysis. Such discussions are urgently needed if we are to understand this vital and complex component of Canadian society; however, such an analysis is best reserved for a separate study.

Generations

In many of the chapters of this book, the authors have discussed the generational conflicts that can erupt during migration and integration. On one level, such tensions are, of course, probably a part of all ethnic communities, regardless of how recently they arrived in Canada. However, the authors have argued consistently that within their denominations and traditions it is slightly more common for these disagreements to become heated when relative newcomer families have to negotiate both the ways their form of Christianity can accommodate the dominant expression of that form of Canadian Christianity, and the way their ethnic or cultural habitus (Bourdieu 1977) can accommodate the features of the dominant Canadian ethos that are embedded in the denominations into which they wish to integrate. While the anecdotes, life histories, and ethnographies included in these chapters add a necessary phenomenological texture to our understanding of these issues, other scholars will need to analyse in greater depth the kinds of conflicts that are emerging between newcomers (especially more recent newcomers from Africa, South America, and Asia) and their children. Such explorations of the ways these tensions are affecting internal debates within these denominations – both within newcomer families and between these families and more settled families – will likely provide us with some insights into the futures of these denominations and ethnic communities. Several questions might guide these studies: If the children of newcomer parents continue to be active in these churches, will they align themselves with the moral, ideological, and religious sensibilities of their parents' migration cohort or with the established Euro-Canadians? What kinds of similarities and differences exist between the ways generational tensions manifest themselves in newcomer Christian communities and in more established Christian communities? How do these tensions affect these families and religious communities over the long term?

Sex and Gender

Throughout these chapters, it has become clear that in these ethnic and religious communities sexuality and gender are at the heart of some of the most pressing and controversial debates. Consider the following issues: the stance of denominations on the Canadian government's legalization of same-sex marriage; the moral and religious status of homosexuality; birth control and premarital sex; appropriate male and female gender roles in the family, the church, and society; the ordination of women and (more broadly) women's leadership in the churches. We witnessed an intensification of these debates in North America and Europe during and after the rise of the feminist movement, or, more generally, during and after the sexual liberation associated with the 1960s. In this volume, we have begun to explore whether there is a connection between ethnicity and the ways these pivotal debates have manifested themselves in Canada's Christian communities.

In Tatartyn's chapter on Eastern Christians, he demonstrates that many of the issues listed above are simply not on the proverbial radar of the denominations of which he writes. This is largely because these Eastern Christian churches tend to be tied quite closely to overseas ethnic and national communities that have not themselves been fundamentally challenged by the sexual revolution of the 1960s that so dramatically altered life and gender relations for so many people in North America and Europe. In the communities Tataryn examines, therefore, ethnicity and traditional Christian identities tend to function together as a relatively undifferentiated bulwark against the changes associated with gender and sexual liberation. It is always dangerous to presuppose that all communities (religious and ethnic) ineluctably move toward the values and beliefs of the surrounding mainstream society. Nonetheless, future researchers will need to examine what will happen to the ethno-religious communities Tataryn describes as more and more generations of their children are socialized within a Canadian society that appears to be moving more or less consistently toward liberal, progressive, and egalitarian stances on sexuality and gender.

Eastern Christians are in some ways exceptions to what is happening in the other communities profiled in this book. While the communities Tataryn discusses are unique and interesting because of their virtual silence on many of these matters, in most Canadian Christian communities sexuality and gender are central topics of often vociferous debates. In fact, in the three largest communities – the Anglican, United, and Roman Catholic churches – these broad debates have become profoundly divisive; in the first two denominations, the disagreements have split churches and alienated some members from the denomination; in the Canadian Anglican church, these controversies have even led some to question its role in the larger world communion of Anglicans; and in the Catholic tradition, the debates have widened the gap between the majority of the parishioners and an official church bureaucracy that is increasingly ignored by ordinary Catholics.

Again, in most Canadian Christian communities – with the possible exception of evangelicals, where one finds a general conservative consensus among most of its ethnic communities – ethnicity is an important variable that often determines the ways these issues manifest themselves. As Wenh-In Ng and Wendy Fletcher indicate, for example, there are often sharp differences of opinion on sexuality and gender among the relative newcomer communities that account for almost the only growth within their denominations on the one hand and the more settled (read: white, western European–origin) and numerically declining ethnic communities on the other hand. Since rapid and complex changes in sexuality and gender are still changing the surrounding Canadian society, we can assume that these issues will continue to be addressed in one way or another by the churches and the ethnic communities that are increasingly vocal constituents within these larger structures. Future studies will need to observe and analyse these changes over time and within these communities.

Social Class and Religion in Canada

Our discussion of these denominations, congregations, and religious communities as well as ethnic groups within them has convinced us that it is impossible to understand the current state of Christianity in Canada without some discussion of social class. Traditionally defined by sociologists as a combination of power, wealth, prestige, and education, social class unites and divides the Christian churches. For example, Kitchener, Ontario, is home to a Hmong Mennonite church filled with largely working-class immigrants.[8] The families are young and large; church members struggle with the English language and, therefore, are largely confined to lower-paying jobs. Down the road, another Mennonite church houses a wealthy, educated congregation that traces its ethnic roots to Europe. Here the families are small and the average age in the pews on Sundays is distinctly more advanced than in the Hmong congregation. Most of the congregants are well educated and some are university professors; almost all are professionals, and among them one finds a number of community leaders.

In this book, authors have explored some of the ways in which social status manifests itself in religious and ethnic communities. However, more work remains to be done on the pivotal influence of social class in the communities we have addressed.

Changes to a Christian Canada and a Canadian Christianity

If we were to bring a group of Canadians of European heritage from the early 1900s forward in time, they would marvel at the changes that have occurred within both Christianity and Canada. They would be surprised to see the increase in Muslims, Hindus, Jews, Sikhs, Buddhists, and other non-Christian religions. Perhaps they would be disturbed by the phenomenon of secularization as well as the number of people claiming to have no religion at all. However, they would be equally puzzled by some of the startling changes in Canadian Christianity: the dramatic declines in membership and participation in the bedrock Anglican, Presbyterian, and United churches; the popularity of evangelical Christianity within some First Nations communities; the Asian accents now echoing through some of Quebec's urban Roman Catholic churches; the exodus from other Roman Catholic churches in Canada by their historic European parishioners; the schisms that appear to be developing over waxing newcomer (African and Asian) and waning established (Euro-Canadian) interpretations of the 'same' denomination; the symbolic significance of debates over homosexuality; the arrival of Ukrainian-born priests who minister to communities that have been settled here for generations and in which Ukrainian is spoken mostly, if at all, by grandparents; or the rapid expansion in Toronto and Vancouver of suburban 'big box' churches catering to Asian evangelicals. In all likelihood, these scenes would have been unimaginable to a great many Canadians a century ago.

Two main forces are at work in the scenes depicted in this list and, for that matter, throughout this book. First, as we discussed in the first chapter, Canada has experienced its own form of secularization, which has resulted in a radical change in the way Christians identify themselves and the way Christianity is and can be framed in the public arena. We have already elaborated on the reasons for these changes, but the consequence has been that Christianity must compete with all other religions, world views, and ideologies for the attention of Canadians. The discourse of loss we have described has emerged among Christians who either lament the passing of the former era or who fear that the future does not look very promising for established Christian institutions.

The second force at work in the scenes depicted above is the beginning of the de-Europeanization of post-colonial Canadian Christianity. We are still in the very early decades of this sea change, so it is far too soon to determine or even speculate about its long-term consequences. At this moment, though, two things appear to be fairly certain. First, the increasing ethnic diversity of the Canadian – and thus Christian – community is dramatically transforming the tradition and the country. Second, many of the assumptions and theories that have hitherto guided the study of Christianity and ethnicity in Canada are no longer sufficient for understanding the processes that are evident to insiders and outsiders the moment they step into a church or talk at length with believers. We hope this book will play at least a small part in helping scholars and students to examine more rigorously and to elucidate more clearly the changes and challenges that are evident in contemporary Canadian Christianity.

Notes

1 See pages 347–57 of this book.
2 Clark (1948) established the importance of the study of history for the social scientific understanding of the social location of Christian churches. He demonstrated that the reason that dissident Protestant movements eventually won out over the established Church of England and other 'respectable' churches was that they offered people on the socio-economic margins and the geopolitical frontiers a religious community that spoke to them in an emotional and intellectual 'vernacular' and provided religious institutions and leaders better suited to their difficult conditions. In effect, they offered 'cheap religion' on Canada's 'frontiers,' both the literal frontier of westward and northward expansion and the urban frontier of the newly expanding industrial towns.
3 Actually, evangelical churches present us with a paradox in this discourse of loss. Given that their numbers are slowly rising or remaining stable and their resources increasing, they do not feel the same sadness about the empty pews other groups do. However, evangelical Christians have long lamented the declining social power of Christianity, especially Christianity's ability to define Canadian cultural values. They lament, for example, the legal sanction of same-sex marriages, the abandonment of Christian prayers before public meetings, and other symptoms of the privatization of religion. However, this lamentation over the loss of Christianity's social power has so long been a part of conservative evangelical culture in Canada (and more so in

the United States) that it has become a constitutive element of their religious culture rather than a sign of their decline.

4 There are many Christians – although a minority – in the large denominations who do not lament the decline in numbers. For example, Douglas John Hall (1997), Canada's most prominent Protestant theologian, argues that the end of the social establishment of Christianity allows the churches to be more faithful to their mission and to criticize governments and society. In Quebec, many female religious communities in the Roman Catholic Church that have seen dramatic declines in their number remain serene and hopeful. They have committed their resources to serving the poor and criticizing the Quebec state and society for being insufficiently egalitarian, open, and just (Laurin 2003).

5 For a consideration of the relationship between Korean ethnic and religious sensibilities in the context of migration to the United States, see Min and Kim (2005).

6 These are neither entirely new obstacles, nor insurmountable. Presumably, these generational tensions have always been a part of Canadian Christian communities. It is worth noting, however, that, especially among non-European Christian newcomers, in some cases the gaps between different generations within a given family are becoming nearly untraversable chasms. When grandparents, parents, and children do not share the same symbolic and actual languages, and when children are socialized into worlds that are almost totally foreign to the parents and grandparents, it is plausible to argue that we are witnessing something categorically different from the standard generation gaps that exist between, say, a third-generation European-origin parent and her fourth-generation European-origin child (both of whom are likely English-speaking, educated, life-long residents of a liberal democracy).

7 For a consideration of the power of inter-ethnic conservative Christian alliances might reshape churches and denominations, see Stevens (2004).

8 The Hmong are an ethnic group found in the mountains of North Vietnam.

Works Cited

Bibby, Reginald. 1987. *Fragmented gods: The poverty and potential of religion in Canada*. Toronto: Stoddart.

Bourdieu, Pierre. 1977. *Outline of a theory of practice*. Cambridge: Cambridge University Press.

Bramadat, Paul. 2005. Beyond Christian Canada: Religion and ethnicity in a multicultural society. In Bramadat and Seljak 2005, 1–29.

Bramadat, Paul, and David Seljak, eds. 2005. *Religion and ethnicity in Canada.* Toronto: Pearson Longman.

Clark, S.D. 1948. *Church and sect in Canada.* Toronto: University of Toronto Press.

Hall, Douglas John. 1997. *The end of Christendom and the future of Christianity.* Valley Forge, PA: Trinity.

Laurin, Nicole. 2003. Women's religious communities in Quebec. *Ecumenist* 40 (1): 1–4.

Min, P.G., and D.Y. Kim. 2005. Intergenerational transmission of religion and culture: Korean Protestants in the US. *Sociology of Religion* 66 (3): 263–82.

Stevens, W. David. 2004. Spreading the word: Religious beliefs and the evolution of immigrant congregations. *Sociology of Religion* 65 (2): 121–38.

Appendix: The Demographics of Christianity in Canada

COMPILED BY PETER BEYER

Table A.1. Christians in Canada, by gender, 2001

Type of Christian[1]	Canada total	Male	Female
Roman Catholic	12,793,125	6,200,855	6,592,270
United	2,839,125	1,318,535	1,520,590
Anglican	2,035,500	954,835	1,080,660
Evangelical[2]	1,676,005	783,265	892,785
Eastern Christian[3]	622,170	311,020	311,140
Lutheran	606,590	287,920	318,670
Presbyterian	409,830	189,270	220,560
Mennonite[4]	217,760	106,750	111,015
Other Christians not included above[5]	1,646,165	789,355	856,785

Source: Statistics Canada, 2003a, 2003b.

Notes: 1 Compiled according to Statistics Canada categorizations as Christian under the following broad headings: Catholic, Protestant, Christian Orthodox, and Other Christian.

2 Includes Apostolic Christian, Apostolic (not otherwise specified), Associated Gospel, Baptist, Brethren in Christ, Born Again Christian (not otherwise specified), Charismatic Renewal, Christian and Missionary Alliance, Christian Assembly, Christian or Plymouth Brethren, Christian Reformed Church, Church of Christ Disciples, Church of God (not otherwise specified), Church of the Nazarene, Congregational, Evangelical Free Church, Evangelical Missionary Church, Evangelical (not otherwise specified), Free Methodist, Methodist (not included elsewhere), Moravian, New Apostolic, Pentecostal, Salvation Army, Seventh-Day Adventist, Standard Church, Vineyard Christian Fellowship, Wesleyan, and Worldwide Church of God.

3 Includes Antiochan Orthodox, Armenian Apostolic, Armenian Catholic, Armenian Orthodox, Assyrian Catholic, Bulgarian Orthodox, Coptic Orthodox, Eastern Rite Catholic (other), Ethiopian Orthodox, Greek or Byzantine Catholic, Greek Orthodox, Macedonian Orthodox, Maronite, Melkite, Orthodox (not otherwise specified), Other Orthodox, Romanian Orthodox, Russian Orthodox, Serbian Orthodox, Syrian Catholic, Ukrainian Catholic, and Ukrainian Orthodox.

4 Includes Amish, Hutterite, and Mennonite.

5 Includes Canadian and American Reformed Church, Christadelphians, Church of Jesus Christ of Latter-day Saints, Doukhobors, non-denominational, interdenominational, Dutch Reformed Church, Iglesia Ni Cristo, Jehovah's Witnesses, Mission de l'Esprit Saint, Other Christian, Quakers, Reformed (not included elsewhere), Reorganized Church of Latter-day Saints, and Unitarians (very few of whom would describe themselves as Christians). It also includes Protestant (not included elsewhere), and Christian (not included elsewhere). The last two categories constitute about three-quarters of these numbers.

Table A.2. Christians in Canada, by province/territory of residence, 2001

	Roman Catholic	United	Anglican	Evangelical	Eastern Christian	Lutheran	Presbyterian	Mennonite	Other Christian
Newfoundland & Labrador	187,440	86,420	132,680	79,405	380	510	1,540	10	5,125
Prince Edward Island	63,270	26,570	6,525	10,025	270	165	7,885	10	9,135
Nova Scotia	328,695	142,525	120,315	117,775	4,345	11,075	22,450	790	33,260
New Brunswick	386,050	69,235	58,215	112,580	700	1,505	6,900	155	22,595
Quebec	5,939,715	52,945	85,475	85,760	109,550	9,640	8,770	425	149,115
Ontario	3,911,760	1,334,570	985,115	692,535	308,915	210,085	279,195	60,595	673,465
Manitoba	323,695	176,820	85,890	61,770	46,085	50,330	9,365	51,540	75,000
Saskatchewan	305,385	187,450	65,745	62,425	32,835	78,525	7,010	19,570	50,620
Alberta	786,365	396,060	172,430	213,215	74,750	142,530	29,200	22,785	279,565
British Columbia	675,320	361,840	298,375	235,090	43,960	101,145	37,120	35,490	343,150
Yukon	6,015	2,100	3,795	1,725	180	580	185	40	2,035
Northwest Territories	16,990	2,230	5,510	2,350	185	430	150	50	1,835
Nunavut	6,210	360	15,440	1,420	15	70	65	10	20

Source: Statistics Canada, 2003a.
Note: Included under each denominational heading are the same subgroups as in table A1.

Appendix   439

Table A.3. Christians in Canada, by metropolitan area, 2001

	Roman Catholic	United	Anglican	Evangelical	Eastern Christian	Lutheran	Presbyterian	Mennonite	Other Christian
Halifax	132,025	51,010	60,130	33,685	3,350	2,770	4,935	275	13,635
Quebec	617,460	780	960	3,395	1,070	185	150	0	6,400
Montréal	2,510,340	32,530	43,875	53,765	103,195	7,230	6,000	320	101,470
Ottawa-Gatineau	566,655	77,745	71,740	31,175	20,140	10,665	14,355	635	40,560
Kingston	43,760	27,920	19,165	7,830	1,300	1,290	2,885	50	9,890
Toronto	1,553,705	320,880	321,585	248,420	203,555	49,045	79,095	2,590	269,355
Hamilton	229,005	76,530	69,025	37,795	20,505	9,690	21,260	535	43,530
Kitchener-Waterloo	132,250	40,065	29,565	32,175	10,850	29,360	14,275	10,650	23,385
London	118,375	70,710	46,150	33,365	7,175	6,755	13,360	1,010	26,935
Windsor	158,840	18,180	21,375	13,905	12,500	4,110	4,985	280	18,640
Winnipeg	196,770	84,820	46,140	32,110	30,230	30,150	4,880	18,785	42,865
Regina	58,440	32,645	9,590	11,490	5,710	20,340	1,250	940	9,955
Saskatoon	63,170	38,595	12,195	14,155	9,260	13,090	1,885	8,780	13,715
Calgary	243,165	116,825	61,140	58,110	16,585	33,830	12,075	4,215	86,060
Edmonton	258,515	107,275	49,405	62,695	37,515	46,200	7,065	2,495	77,845
Vancouver	360,620	149,290	123,905	98,270	30,615	42,995	17,175	11,095	157,545
Victoria	47,555	32,175	43,155	16,200	2,155	6,185	4,605	475	24,610

Source: Statistics Canada, 2003a.
Note: Included under each denominational heading are the same subgroups as in table A1.

Table A.4. Christians in Canada, per cent immigrant and Canada-born, 2001

Type of Christian	Total adherents	Canada born (%)	Total immigrant (%)	Per cent of immigrants from before 1971	Per cent of immigrants from after 1971
Roman Catholic	12,793,125	85.85	13.74	38.40	61.60
United	2,839,125	94.62	5.38	62.85	37.14
Anglican	2,035,500	86.24	13.76	56.02	43.98
Evangelical	1,622,285	81.94	17.38	12.24	70.53
Eastern Christian	622,170	52.21	47.79	27.77	67.13
Lutheran	606,590	78.70	21.30	75.86	24.14
Presbyterian	409,830	82.15	17.85	54.62	45.38
Mennonite	217,760	86.18	13.82	39.34	60.65
Other Christians not included above	1,700,900	77.60	21.30	26.01	73.98

Source: Statistics Canada 2003c

Note: In light of the different source for this table, Evangelical includes most, but not all, of the groups as in the previous tables. Those not included have been absorbed into general 'other' categories and are therefore included under 'Other Christians' in the last line.

Contributors

Paul Bramadat is director of the Centre for Studies in Religion and Society and associate professor of history at the University of Victoria. He received his PhD from McMaster University in 1998. He teaches and publishes mainly in the area of contemporary post-colonial religion and public policy in Canada, but his interests also include fundamentalism, terrorism, and popular culture. He is the author of *The Church on the World's Turf: An Evangelical Christian Group at a Secular University* (2000), co-editor (with David Seljak) of *Religion and Ethnicity in Canada* (2005), co-editor (with John Biles) of a special issue of the *Journal of International Migration and Integration* (2005) devoted to the question of religious diversity and public policy, and co-editor (with Matthias Koenig) of a forthcoming book on the ways religion is governed in the international arena. He is author of a number of articles and commissioned policy papers on religion, public policy, and ethnic identity. He is working on a SSHRC-funded project on post-colonial religious identities in Canada.

Wendy Fletcher is professor and academic dean at Vancouver School of Theology. She serves as principal of that school and is the first woman to hold that position. She received her PhD from the University of St Michael's College. She is widely published in the history of Protestant women in the modern era, with particular attention to issues of gender, race, and social identity. Dr Fletcher is involved with the Christian church across the denominational spectrum at the national and international level, having served on many commissions and working groups, including the World Council of Churches and the Association of Theological Schools of the United States and Canada.

Bruce L. Guenther is associate professor of church history and Mennonite studies at Mennonite Brethren Biblical Seminary (Langley campus), which is one of six partners making up ACTS Seminaries (the Graduate School of Theological Studies at Trinity Western University) in Langley, BC. He received his PhD in Canadian religious history from McGill University in 2001. For more than two decades, he has worked with many different evangelical institutions and organizations in Canada, and has published numerous articles on Canadian evangelical Protestants, Mennonite history, and the history of theological education in Canada.

Bryan Hillis is professor of religious studies at Luther College at the University of Regina. He received his PhD from the University of Chicago in 1988. He works in the history of Christianity with emphasis on North American traditions, primarily Lutheranism. He is author of *Can Two Walk Together Unless They Be Agreed? American Religious Schism in the 1970s* (1991) and articles on Lutheran spirituality and Lutherans in Canada. He was also co-editor of the religion section of *The Encyclopedia of Saskatchewan* (2005).

Solange Lefebvre is director of the Centre d'étude des religions de l'Université de Montréal (CÉRUM), and holds the Religion, Culture and Society chair at the University of Montreal. She received her PhD in theology from the University of Montreal, and a master's degree in Social Anthropology from L'École des Hautes Études Sociales of Paris. She teaches in the areas of religious studies, religion in the public sphere, youth and religion, and practical theology. Her main research interests include Quebec Catholicism, religious education, pastoral ministries, socio-religious trends, and ethnicity and religion. She also serves on the Board of Directors of *Concilium: International Journal for Theology*. She is the author of *Cultures et spiritualités des jeunes* (2008), and has recently edited *La religion dans la sphère publique* (2005) and *Religion et identités dans l'école québécoise* (2000).

Royden Loewen is professor of history and holds the chair in Mennonite Studies at the University of Winnipeg. He teaches courses on Mennonite history and upper level courses in the history of North American immigration and ethnicity, which also comprise his main area of research. His most recent books include *Hidden Worlds: Revisiting the Mennonite Migrants of the 1870s* (2001) and *Diaspora in the Countryside:*

Two Mennonite Communities and Mid-20th Century Rural Disjunction (2006). His current projects include a history of immigrants in Canada's main prairie cities and the North American volume for the Global Mennonite History Project.

Stuart Macdonald is associate professor of church and society at Knox College at the University of Toronto. He received his PhD from the University of Guelph in 1998. He has researched and written in the field of the Scottish witch-hunt, including his book *The Witches of Fife* (2002). Since 2003, he has conducted research on religion in post–Second World War Canada. He is working on several articles on religion and the Canadian census with his colleague Dr Brian Clarke, Emmanuel College, and several projects related to the Presbyterian Church in Canada. An ordained minister, he served as basic degree director at Knox College for over nine years. He was recently seconded to be a researcher at the newly established Centre for Clergy Care and Congregational Health (a centre of Knox College and Emmanuel College in Toronto).

Mark G. McGowan is the principal of St Michael's College in the University of Toronto and professor in the Department of History and St Michael's Christianity and Culture Program. He teaches history of religion, immigration, and education in Canada, and has a particular interest in the development of the Catholic Church in North America. He is researching three books: 'The Great Irish Famine and Toronto,' 'Religion and Broadcasting in Canada, 1920–1968,' and 'A History of the Irish Catholic Canadian Responses to the Great War.' Among his publications he has written two award-winning books: *The Waning of the Green: Catholics, the Irish, and Identity in Toronto, 1887–1922* (1999) and *Michael Power: The Struggle to Build the Catholic Church on the Canadian Frontier* (2005).

Greer Anne Wenh-In Ng is associate professor emerita at Emmanuel College, Victoria University in the University of Toronto, and past coordinator of its Centre for Asian Theology. Previously, she taught at Vancouver School of Theology. Ordained in the United Church of Canada, Wenh-In has served in congregational, Conference, and national positions, most recently as interim General Council minister, Racial and Gender Justice, and as Toronto Conference minister for social justice and ethnic ministries, and as a consultant and resource person to the Ethnic Ministries Unit. A past president of the Association of Professors and Researchers in Religious Education, Wenh-In has published in the areas of feminist liberative pedagogies, Asian and Asian North American religious life and education, and post-colonial approaches to engaging the Judeo-Christian scriptures for anti-racism work.

David Seljak is associate professor of religious studies at St Jerome's University and chair of the Department of Religious Studies at the University of Waterloo. Until 2006, he served as the director of the St Jerome's Centre for Catholic Experience, a public education outreach program. He has published extensively in the field of religion and identity and has co-edited (with Paul Bramadat) *Religion and Ethnicity in Canada* (2005). He is also editor of the *Ecumenist: A Journal of Theology, Culture and Society,* which is published by St Paul University/Novalis. He has authored a series of reports on religion and multiculturalism for the Multiculturalism and Human Rights Program at the Department of Canadian Heritage.

Myroslaw Tataryn is professor of religious studies and vice-president and academic dean at St Jerome's University at the University of Waterloo. He received his ThD from the University of St Michael's College and the Toronto School of Theology in 1995. His primary interests lie in the contemporary theology of Eastern Christianity and the history of Eastern Christians in Canada. He has authored a number of books and numerous articles in English-language journals around the world and has lectured internationally.